ACCOUNTING

INFORMATION

SYSTEMS

ACCOUNTING INFORMATION SYSTEMS 9e

ULRIC J. GELINAS, JR.

Bentley University

RICHARD B. DULL

Clemson University

PATRICK R. WHEELER

University of Missouri

SOUTH-WESTERN
CENGAGE Learning™

Australia • Brazil • Japan • Korea • Mexico • Singapore • Spain • United Kingdom • United States

SOUTH-WESTERN
CENGAGE Learning

Accounting Information Systems, 9e
Ulric J. Gelinas, Jr., Richard B. Dull, and
Patrick R. Wheeler

VP of Editorial, Business: Jack W. Calhoun

VP/Editor-in-Chief: Rob Dewey

Team Assistant: Linda Chaffee

Acquisitions Editor: Matt Filimonov

Developmental Editor: Julie Warwick

Marketing Manager: Natalie Livingston

Marketing Comm. Manager: Libby Shipp

Marketing Coordinator: Nicki Parsons

Content Project Management:
PreMediaGlobal

Managing Media Editor: Matt McKinney

Sr. Manufacturing Buyer: Doug Wilke

Sr. Art Director: Stacy Shirley

Editorial Assistant: Ann Mazzaro

Production House: PreMediaGlobal

Cover Design: Lou Ann Thesing

Internal Design: PreMediaGlobal

Cover Image: ©Getty Images/
Photographer's Choice/Jan Cobb

For product information and technology assistance, contact us at
Cengage Learning Customer & Sales Support, 1-800-354-9706

For permission to use material from this text or product,
submit all requests online at **www.cengage.com/permissions**
Further permissions questions can be emailed to
permissionrequest@cengage.com

ExamView® is a registered trademark of eInstruction Corp. Windows is a registered trademark of the Microsoft Corporation used herein under license. Macintosh and Power Macintosh are registered trademarks of Apple Computer, Inc. used herein under license.

© 2012 Cengage Learning. All Rights Reserved.

Library of Congress Control Number: 2010936514

Student Edition

ISBN 13: 978-0-538-46931-9

ISBN 10: 0-538-46931-5

South-Western Cengage Learning
5191 Natorp Boulevard
Mason, OH 45040
USA

Cengage Learning is a leading provider of customized learning solutions with office locations around the globe, including Singapore, the United Kingdom, Australia, Mexico, Brazil, and Japan. Locate your local office at **www.cengage.com/global**.

Cengage Learning products are represented in Canada by Nelson Education, Ltd.

To learn more about **South-Western**, visit
www.cengage.com/South-Western

Purchase any of our products at your local college store or at our preferred online store **www.cengagebrain.com**

Printed in the United States of America
1 2 3 4 5 6 7 14 13 12 11 10

BRIEF CONTENTS

CONTENTS

PREFACE

Welcome to the beginning of a journey through the dynamic field of accounting information systems. We are very pleased that you have chosen to become another member of our international community of students, accounting professionals, and educators who make this book an integral part of their library as a text and reference tool. We are committed to making the journey through this complex, challenging, and exciting topic as straightforward and pleasant as possible. These challenging topics are tackled in a conversational and relaxed tone, rather than pretentious, technical language. At the same time, the text fully explores the integrated nature of the topic with its foundations in information technology, business processes, strategic management, security, and internal control. Thank you for the opportunity to serve as your guide on this journey.

Before beginning, let's discuss two key ideas that inspire the story in the text. First, the accountant is defined as an information management and business measurement professional. Second, information systems consist of integral parts working together to enable the organization to progress and move forward. These two philosophies are briefly described before addressing the most frequently asked questions (FAQs) by users of this book.

Accountant as an Information Management and Business Measurement Professional

There is no doubt that the long-standing image of the accountant as a conservative, green eye shaded, nonsocial employee who is tucked in the back room of an organization has been forever shattered. Today's accounting professional is relied on by owners and managers to identify and monitor enterprise risks (events that may cause an entity to fail to achieve its objectives); assure the reliability of information systems used to gather, store, and disseminate key information for decision making; and possess the essential general business knowledge, coupled with business process measurement and assessment skills, needed to evaluate the state of the business enterprise and its supporting operations. In a post-Enron/post-WorldCom era, a primary focus of organizations is on governance, both organizational and IT, and enterprise risk management (ERM). The accounting professional (as external auditor, internal auditor, corporate accountant, or manager) is increasingly expected to take the leadership role in enhancing organizational governance and identifying and mitigating enterprise risks.

Accordingly, the accounting professional must arrive on the job equipped with a solid understanding of (1) key information qualities, (2) critical information technologies that drive the information systems, (3) core business processes that allow an organization to operate effectively and efficiently, (4) common documentation tools used to diagram and assess business processes, and (5) vital organizational and IT governance and internal control concepts that can be applied to mitigate risks. Each of these fundamental knowledge requirements is addressed throughout this book.

Information Systems: Integrated Elements Moving the Organization Forward

In today's IT-centric world, organizations clearly can neither operate nor survive—much less thrive—without information systems. The quality of the information systems and the reliability of the information available through such systems dictate, to a large degree, the effectiveness of decision making within the organization. Without good information, managers cannot make sound decisions. It is imperative that all pieces of the information system be in sync and operating effectively if the enterprise as a whole is to operate effectively and efficiently and move forward in a positive direction. **Figure P.1** shows the integrated nature of information systems components. These elements must be sound across all dimensions for the organization to safely, yet quickly, move forward. Any weakness in these elements puts successful outcomes at risk. The enterprise depends on safe and secure information systems that allow the organization to move forward in a controlled, yet competitive, manner.

Following are the five integral components of the information system:

- *An enterprise database* stores data related to an enterprise's activities and resources. This includes views of the database for each business process that supports effective decision making and allows the processes to operate effectively.
- *Database controls* that safeguard data in an enterprise database from illicit access, destruction, and corruption.

FIGURE P.1 Information Systems—Integrated Elements

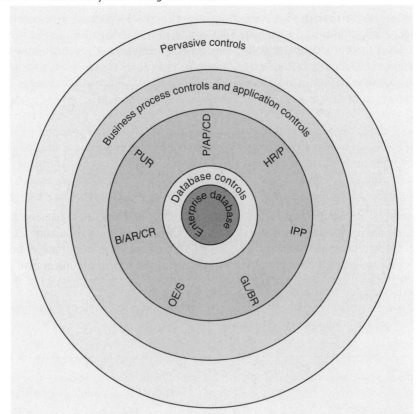

- *Business processes* (e.g., OE/S, B/AR/CR) that reflect the core activities undertaken by an organization in achieving its business objectives. These processes include such activities as selling goods or services, collecting payment, purchasing materials or inventory, paying for those items, hiring and retaining a quality set of employees, and producing goods or services for sale. All of the processes both use and generate data that is stored in the enterprise database.
- *Business process controls and application controls* are the procedures put in place within each business process to identify specific business risks, prevent identified risks from disrupting operations or corrupting data, detect failures that get past preventive measures, and correct detected errors and irregularities that slip past the control boundary.
- *Pervasive controls* represent the overall organizational governance structure and related control procedures that are designed to create a regulated organization that can face the challenges of the external business environment, keep the enterprise on track and moving forward in a controlled manner, as well as outperforming its competitors.

Each of these components is explored in detail throughout the book. After completing the study of the concepts presented in this text, you should have a strong grounding in the critical knowledge necessary to help an organization create and manage effective information systems that minimize related enterprise risks.

Frequently Asked Questions (FAQs)

When examining a book and considering how to most effectively acquire the information in which you are particularly interested, several questions may arise that need to be answered to help make this process more efficient. In the FAQ section of the preface, we will answer the questions most frequently asked by previous adopters and readers of this book. Hopefully, the answers to your most pressing questions can be found in the following paragraphs.

FAQ #1: What Are the Core Themes of This Book?

The book's focus is on providing the skills necessary for a foundation in enterprise risk management (ERM)—particularly as these risks pertain to business processes and their information systems components. Fundamental to an ERM orientation, from an information systems perspective, are the underlying enterprise systems, e-business systems, and controls for monitoring the operation of these systems. The emphasis on these core themes is apparent even by reviewing the table of contents. Chapters 2 and 3 immediately focus on enterprise systems and e-business in the introductory section of the text. Controls are the focus of Chapters 7, 8, and 9. More importantly, however, these themes are carried throughout the remainder of the text in the integrative fashion for which the previous eight editions have been written. Icons are included in the margins throughout the book to help emphasize the coverage of these core themes in their integrated state and to facilitate absorption of the material by the reader. Given the critical nature of these three themes, the following paragraphs provide brief explanations for each.

Enterprise Systems Enterprise systems integrate the business process functionality and information from all of an organization's functional areas, such as marketing and sales, cash receipts, purchasing, cash disbursements, human resources, production and logistics, and business reporting (including financial reporting). They enable the coordinated operation of these functions and provide a central information resource for the organization. The concept of enterprise systems can be realized in various ways. For instance, an organization might develop its own separate business process systems and tie them together in an integrated manner. Or an organization could purchase an enterprise system from a vendor. Such externally acquired systems are commonly called enterprise resource planning (ERP) systems—software packages that can be the core systems necessary to support enterprise systems. A number of ERP systems are commercially available, with SAP® and Oracle® dominating the large- and medium-sized enterprise markets. The Microsoft® Dynamics™ line of products is a major player in the small- and medium-sized enterprise markets. Many organizations use a combination of ERP systems, externally purchased subsystems, and internally developed subsystems to create an overall enterprise system that best fits their needs.

E-Business E-business (electronic business) is the application of electronic networks (including the Internet) to exchange information and link business processes among organizations and individuals. These processes include interaction between back-office (i.e., internal) processes, such as distribution, manufacturing, and accounting, and front-office (i.e., external) processes, such as those that connect an organization to its customers and suppliers. Traditionally, e-business has been driven in business-to-business (B2B) environments through electronic data interchange (EDI). The most familiar form of e-business is the business-to-consumer (B2C) model where interactions are largely driven by browser-based applications on the Internet. This communication medium has spilled over into the B2B arena, replacing EDI in some cases, while also providing opportunities for new B2B interaction in this rapidly changing environment.

Controls Internal control is a process—effected by an entity's board of directors, management, and other personnel—designed to provide reasonable assurance regarding the achievement of objectives in the following categories: effectiveness and efficiency of operations, reliability of reporting, and compliance with applicable laws and regulations. A strong system of internal controls is imperative for effective ERM and is of great interest to top management, auditors, and external stakeholders.

FAQ #2: How Does This Book Present Accounting Information Systems?

This book is organized into six parts. The following paragraphs discuss briefly each of the components of this book.

Part 1: **Understanding Information Systems** consists of three chapters. Chapter 1 provides an overview of basic information systems concepts and explores the critical characteristics of information that must be considered in systems design and evaluation. Chapter 2 introduces the concept of enterprise systems and the key role that these systems play in the successful and timely operation of contemporary enterprises. Chapter 3 addresses the extended enterprise environment, the e-business relationships that an organization forms when linking its organization with the individuals or other organizations that represent their customers and vendors, as well as other stakeholders.

Part 2: **Organizing and Managing Information** includes three chapters. Chapter 4 provides the basic tools necessary for diagrammatically documenting organizational data flows (data flow diagrams—DFDs) and business processes (systems flowcharts). This chapter is divided into sections focusing first on reading documentation and then on creating documentation to meet the varied needs of our readers. Chapter 5 provides a more comprehensive exploration of data storage methods, the role of databases in data management, and the various business intelligence tools that are available for making sense out of the vast enterprise databases to enhance strategic decision making. Chapter 5 also includes sections on reading and understanding entity relationship (E-R) diagrams (used to model database structures). Chapter 6 takes a deeper look at modeling information systems using the Resources-Events-Agents (REA) method, creating E-R diagrams, mapping these diagrams to relational databases, and using SQL to manipulate and retrieve data from relational databases.

Part 3: Enterprise Risk Management consists of three chapters exploring the various dimensions of organizational governance and associated effective internal control systems. Chapter 7 contains an overview of internal control frameworks, including the new framework *Enterprise Risk Management—Integrated Framework*; general organizational governance guidelines; and the changes effected by the Sarbanes-Oxley Act of 2002. Chapter 8 begins with a discussion of pervasive controls that apply to both manual and IT environments. This is followed by sections designed around COBIT, an internationally recognized framework for IT control that focuses on the controls that address risks emanating from information systems and can put an enterprise in a condition of acute risk if not properly monitored and controlled. Chapter 9 focuses on the control procedures applicable to minimize such risks and presents a methodology for comprehensively evaluating the risks and controls within a defined business process. This framework is subsequently demonstrated and applied across the business processes presented in Chapters 10 through 14.

Part 4: Business Processes examines the various processes that are necessary for an enterprise to successfully operate. These six chapters focus on applications supported by ERP system implementations (including exhibits of screens from SAP® and Microsoft Dynamics GP® software), the key controls for maintaining successful business processes, and the application of the methodology for evaluating risks and controls within a given business process. The order-to-cash (revenue) flows are captured in Chapter 10 and 11. The purchase-to-pay (expense) flows are captured in Chapter 12 and 13. We round out coverage of the core business processes with Chapter 14, "The Human Resources (HR) Management and Payroll Processes," and Chapter 15, "Integrated Production Processes (IPP)."

Part 5: Reporting includes Chapter 16, which deals with the reporting process, in which information from core business processes is developed into financial reports for internal and external usage. This chapter includes basics, such as information flows related to the process, as well current technologies, such as ERPs and XBRL.

Part 6: Acquiring an AIS consists of Chapter 17, which provides an overview of the selection of accounting information systems, including the choices related to the buy-versus-build decision. With extensive use of off-the-shelf software, including ERP software that can be modified to fit the business needs of an enterprise, Chapter 17 provides details that should be considered when selecting the appropriate software. The chapter also provides information to help interpret the proper use of internal and external sources. The chapter includes topics such as AIS acquisitions from third parties and the systems development life cycle (analysis, selection and design, implementation, and operation phases).

FAQ #3: Where Can I Find Information About the Sarbanes-Oxley (SOX) Act of 2002, Especially SOX Section 404?

To help you find information regarding the Sarbanes-Oxley Act of 2002, we have added SOX icons in the margins where the topic is covered. Chapter 1 provides an overview of Sections 404 and 409 of SOX, including the overall implications for the accountant as an information management and business measurement professional. Chapter 4 discusses preparing documentation of business processes, a first step in a SOX 404 review. Chapter 7 describes the effect of SOX Sections 210, 302, and 404 on organizational governance, IT governance, and ERM. Chapters 7 through 9 describe the requirements of SOX 404 and PCAOB Auditing Standard No. 5 regarding the "effectiveness of design of internal controls" (leaving the "effectiveness of operations of internal controls" for the auditing courses and texts). Chapters 7 through 14 also introduce and use the control matrix, a tool used by systems designers and auditors to assess the effectiveness of control design and by auditors to design tests for effectiveness of operations of internal control. Finally, Chapter 16 discusses the effect on internal control reporting and financial reporting as the requirements in SOX Sections 302, 401, 404, and 409.

FAQ #4: How Can This Book Be Adapted to Meet a User's Desired Content Coverage?

Learning from an enterprise risk management (ERM) approach,[1] a user should focus on three key components of the text: (1) documentation tools for diagramming and analyzing business processes, (2) ERM and component internal control concepts, and (3) core business processes enabling enterprises to successfully complete order-to-cash (revenue) and purchase-to-pay (expenditure) activities. An ERM focus also necessitates the consideration of enterprise systems and e-business concepts. But, given that these are fundamental threads running throughout the text, they should be covered with any approach. Coverage of ancillary topics related to database management systems and other key business processes is recommended (e.g., human resources management and payroll processes, integrated production processes, and the general ledger and business reporting process). Depending on a user's interests, exploring relational databases in detail or covering only the foundations of the systems development process may be necessary. Recommendations and options are depicted in **Figure P.2** to assist in the decision process.

Learning from a database or REA approach, a user would want to focus on two key components of the text: (1) documentation and modeling skills for relational databases and (2) core business processes that must be integrated in enterprise-level databases. Additionally, the user would want to confer with appropriate external support specifically focused on REA modeling techniques if extended coverage is desired. A database approach can be used with the text without these additional materials if REA models are not necessarily a preference. Again, a database approach also would necessitate the consideration of enterprise systems concepts, which are fundamental threads running throughout the text. A database approach may focus on only a limited core set of chapters combined with an outside database software text or may be supplemented with other key AIS topics, additional business processes, corporate governance, and IT controls. Our recommendations and options are depicted in Figure P.2 to assist in the decision process.

Learning from a systems development approach, a user would want to focus on three key components of the text: (1) documentation tools for diagramming and analyzing business processes, (2) structured systems analysis and design (Chapter 17), and (3) core business processes enabling enterprises to successfully complete order-to-cash

---

[1]This approach also might be called the *business process approach, the accounting applications approach,* or *the accounting cycles approach.*

FIGURE P.2   Selecting Chapters to Meet Selected Pedagogical Objectives

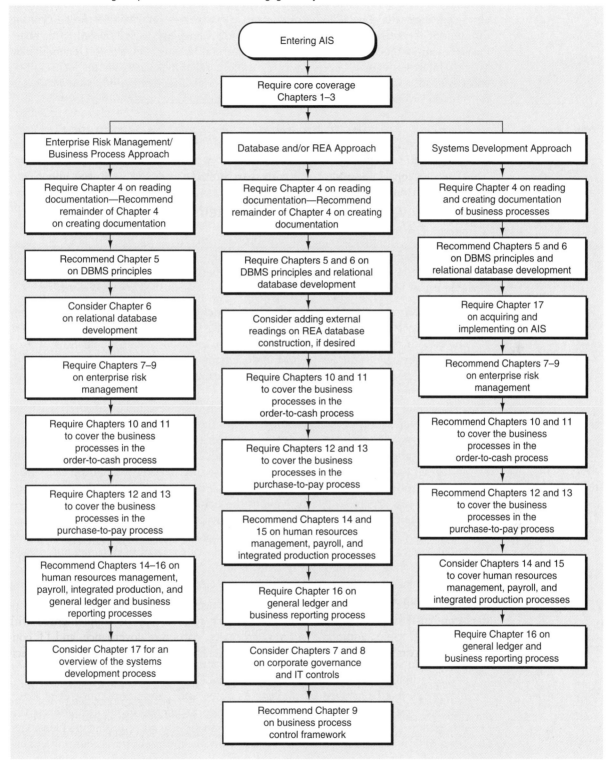

(revenue) and purchase-to-pay (expenditure) activities. A systems development approach also necessitates the consideration of enterprise systems—a fundamental thread running throughout the text. Coverage is recommended of ancillary topics related to database management systems, ERM, and general ledger and business reporting. Depending on a user's interests, it may be necessary to explore relational databases in detail and to cover human resources management and payroll and integrated production processes. Recommendations and options for this approach are also depicted in Figure P.2.

FAQ #5: Does the Book Fit the Core Competencies Guidelines of the AICPA Vision Project?

Several professional bodies across the globe have undertaken projects to better understand how the environment of professional accounting is changing and how these changes impact the required competencies for skilled professionals. Although responding to all of the reports around the globe is not possible in this preface, we will briefly review how the text facilitates the preparation of new professionals based on the results of one such report—the American Institute of Certified Public Accountants (AICPA) CPA Vision Project. Let's take a look at how this book supports the knowledge prerequisites for attaining each of the AICPA CPA Vision Project's five identified core competencies:

- *Communication and Leadership Skills:* Development of communication and leadership comes largely through practice. The study of AIS provides great opportunities for students to participate in written and oral presentations about the analysis of problems. Throughout the text, a host of documentation tools are covered and applied, including flowcharts, data flow diagrams, narratives, entity-relationship diagrams, and control matrices. Chapter 17 describes a variety of reports used in the systems analysis and design process. Mastery of these tools can facilitate effective synthesis and communication of complex information in an easily explained form.
- *Strategic and Critical Thinking Skills:* The documentation tools noted under the communication section further enhance a student's ability to link data, knowledge, and insight related to information technology, internal control, and business processes to solve complex problems. Numerous short and long cases along with concise problems are presented throughout the book to provide ample opportunity to practice the critical and strategic skills necessary to relate to business environments.
- *Focus on the Customer, Client, and Market:* The early segments of the book are oriented toward assembling a set of foundational skills related to documentation, systems environments, enterprise systems, e-business, and internal control assessment the later chapters bring all the information together to analyze the business processes of an entity. This analysis integrates the information for management decision making; the aggregation and processing of information, key controls, and business process objectives allows a student to better understand the full scope of an organization's business processes, not just the accounting aspects. This prepares students for entering different business environments, analyzing business activities, and identifying areas for strategic improvement.
- *Interpretation of Converging Information:* As noted under the prior competency statement on customers, clients, and markets, the core chapters of this text address the integration of financial and nonfinancial information to solve problems. Consideration of nonfinancial information is usually the weakest point for accounting graduates, and the strategies used in the text should help counteract this weakness.
- *Technologically Adept:* Throughout the text, emerging technologies that are reshaping the business environment are described and demonstrated within the context

of a business process. The focus on emerging technologies helps the student to understand how new technologies can be used to improve business efficiency and effectiveness, and to leverage competitive advantage.

FAQ #6: How Does the Text Help Prepare Students for the U.S. CPA Exam?

In the United States, the CPA Examination is of interest for those about to enter the accounting profession. Recent changes in the exam have not significantly affected this book because the philosophy has long been consistent with the exam's evolving content. Students need to have a broad understanding of the business environment, how information is used by business decision makers, and the organizational control structures that should be in place to minimize risk to the enterprise. Thus, this book continues to be an excellent source for helping students prepare for the testing methods and exam content. The exam testing methods require the use of certain software tools but also use a host of case studies, called "simulations," to provide information that must be critically examined and synthesized. The extensive use of small and large cases in this book should help students prepare for these simulation problems. The book's approach emphasizes several skills being tested by the current exam: communication, research, analysis, judgments, and comprehension.

As for content on the exam, this book is also well positioned to help. The auditing and attestation section of the exam requires examinees to have an understanding of enterprise-level controls and the technology-based environments in which auditing is conducted. This book emphasizes enterprise systems, e-business, database environments, control frameworks, IT controls, and business process environments—all of which will be helpful in the exam environment. Technology concepts are even more critical in preparing for the business environment and concepts portion of the exam. That section of the exam not only includes technology but also covers business structure (an item addressed within the context of each business process in the text), measurement (i.e., managerial), and general business environments and concepts. As to this latter section, the detailed business process chapters (Chapters 10 through 16) describe the overall business context and how information flows from the transaction side through to be used by key management decision makers. This presentation should aid in understanding how contemporary organizations operate. The focus in the book on enterprise systems and e-business should further aid in preparing for exam coverage of state-of-the-art technologically enabled business environments.

Instructors may also assign end-of-chapter questions and problems that are targeted to specific content standards of the CPA exam. See the *Instructional Supplements* section below, which describes the classification matrices in the *Test Bank* and *Solutions Manual*. These matrices identify where each end-of-chapter question/problem covers specific expectations of education, from the perspectives of the authors, based on the AICPA's content standards for the CPA Exam.

FAQ #7: Does the Book Provide a Foundation for ISACA's CISA Exam?

Another question that frequently arises is whether the foundation-level skills for the Information Systems Audit and Control Association's (ISACA) Certified Information Systems Auditor (CISA) Exam are covered. Foundation-level skills are also commonly required for several other global accounting organizations' certification processes for IT specialization.

Let's take a brief look at the six content areas covered by the CISA Exam (as of the June 2011 exam):

- *Content Area 1—IS Audit Process (10% of the exam):* Chapters 7 through 9 provide the foundation for understanding how to assess the risks that must be considered in contemporary risk-based audit approaches. Chapters 7 through 14 describe control objectives and controls related to information systems.
- *Content Area 2—IT Governance (15%):* Chapters 7 and 8 introduce organizational and IT governance frameworks and discuss related issues such as IT organizational structures, IT strategy, and risk management. Chapters 7 and 8 also give extensive coverage to the COSO, ERM, and COBIT control frameworks.
- *Content Area 3—Systems and Infrastructure Life Cycle (16%):* Chapters 8 and 17 describe best practices for project governance and systems development, including requirements analysis, systems acquisition, and change controls. Chapters 9 through 14 give extensive coverage to control objectives and techniques for IT systems applications/business processes. Finally, Chapters 2 and 3 describe enterprise architectures for data, applications, and technology, including enterprise systems, Web services, and Web-based applications. These are further discussed in the context of specific business processes in Chapters 10 through 14.
- *Content Area 4—IT Service Delivery and Support (14%):* Chapters 2 and 3 introduce IT infrastructures and discuss how these can support organization objectives. These issues are further discussed in the context of specific business processes in Chapters 10 through 14. Chapter 8 introduces best practices for the management of IT operations. Chapters 5 and 6 describe database management systems.
- *Content Area 5—Protection of Information Assets (31%):* Chapters 7 through 9 focus on the control structures that should be in place at the environmental, physical, and logical levels to provide both pervasive and specific controls over IT systems. These controls include logical and physical access to IT assets, encryption and public-key cryptography, and environmental protection.
- *Content Area 6—Business Continuity and Disaster Recovery (14%):* Chapter 8 provides an overview of the core concepts underlying disaster recovery and business continuity in business environments. Although the knowledge is at a foundational level, the concepts are easily extended because the business process environments are explored later in the text.

Instructors may also assign end-of-chapter questions and problems that are targeted to specific content areas of the CISA exam. See the *Instructional Supplements* section below, which describes the classification matrices in the *Test Bank* and *Solutions Manual.* These matrices identify where each end-of-chapter question/problem covers specific expectations of education from the perspectives of the authors, based on the AICPA's content standards for the CPA Exam.

Instructional Supplements

This book includes the following supplemental materials to assist the instructor:[2]

- The *Test Bank* presents a variety of questions, including true/false, multiple-choice, completion, problems, and essays. Included in the *Test Bank* is a matrix identifying

---

[2]Many text adopters use these materials for graded assignments and exams. In consideration of these adopters, we ask that you not post any of these materials to an open Web site.

where each question covers specific expectations of education, from the perspectives of the authors, based on the AACSB's content standards for the CPA exam. In the matrix, each question is coded to the specific CISA domains (from ISACA) and the AACSB's recommendations for undergraduate education (categories related to learning experiences in general knowledge and skill areas). Each question is also coded to the AICPA's content standards for the CPA exam's Auditing and Attestation, and Business Environment and Concepts segments. This matrix should provide guidance to instructors regarding the desired breadth of coverage of the questions and problems that they assign. The *Test Bank* can be easily used in two ways. Instructors can formulate custom quizzes and exams easily using the ExamView® testing software, which is included on the Instructor's Resource CD-ROM (IRCD). The *Test Bank* can also be found in a computerized Word® document on the IRCD.

- The *Solutions Manual* (available on the text Web site and on the IRCD), provides answers to Discussion Questions, Short Problems, and Problems in the text's end-of-chapter material. Included in the *Solutions Manual* is a matrix, similar to that included in the *Test Bank*, identifying where each question covers specific expectations of education, from the perspectives of ISACA, the AACSB, and the AICPA.

- *Note to Instructors:* The *Solutions Manual* provides instructors with ways to tailor how problems are assigned and how solutions are provided to students, for a more engaging learning experience. For example, instructors can provide a partially completed control matrix, asking students to complete the problem based on their studies. Alternatively, based on a completed flowchart, students can analyze the system to recommend improvements or generate a control matrix.

- PowerPoint® slides (available on the text Web site and on the IRCD) cover all major concepts and key terms and are presented in an appealing way designed to hold the student's interest and effectively communicate lecture material.

- The Bentley Term Project, (available on the text Web site and on the IRCD) is an updated version of a term project that has been used for more than 25 years with this text at Bentley University. The term project is designed to incorporate the concepts taught in the text into a comprehensive, cohesive project. The learning objectives of the project are to help the student examine an actual business process, document the process, analyze process controls, and recommend changes to improve operational and information process effectiveness.

- The IRCD includes the entire instructor resource package on one convenient disc. Included are the *Solutions Manual*, PowerPoint® slides, ExamView® testing software, a computerized version of the *Test Bank* and the Bentley Term Project. Materials provided on the IRCD will allow an AIS instructor using this text to incorporate this term project in their course with minimal development preparation.

- The instructor Web site for the text houses most of the resources that are also available on the IRCD, including the instructor PowerPoint® slides the Bentley Term Project and the *Solutions Manual*. Instructors can access online instructor resources at http://login.cengage.com. If you are a new instructor, you will need to register with Cengage Learning by creating a new instructor account. Instructors will be directed to the Cengage Learning dashboard after logging in. Here, you may add any Cengage Learning books to your 'bookshelf', including the 9th edition of *Accounting Information Systems* simply by searching by the author, title or ISBN (0538469315). After adding the book to your 'boookshelf' you will be able to access the links to the Instructor Companion Site and accompanying resources.

Student Supplements

This book includes the following supplemental materials to assist students:

- A student Web site is available for the 9th edition of *Accounting Information Systems* which houses ample study resources that are free to students. Visit www.cengagebrain.com. At the CengageBrain.com home page, search by author name (Gelinas), by title (*Accounting Information Systems*) or by ISBN (0538469315) using the search box at the top of the page. This will bring you for a link to the 9th edition of *Accounting Information Systems*. After clicking the link, you can access the student resources by clicking 'Access Now'. Here you will have access to all student resources, including chapter-by-chapter quizzes, flashcards, crossword puzzles and a list of key terms.
- Many chapters of the text now include *new* Microsoft Access® and/or Excel® exercises, enabling students to develop greater database and spreadsheet software skills. These exercises can be found in the Short Problems or Problems at the end of each chapter and are identified with Access® or Excel® icons.

New to this Edition

- New examples, such as cash receipt transactions in Chapter 11, provide support to help students understand current topics relating to accounting documentation.
- More technology applications related to GSS, audit teams, and brainstorming have been added to Chapter 5 and 17.
- Further coverage of "cloud computing" has been added to Chapters 3, 6, 8, and 10 to reflect the latest in business computing.
- Many chapter-opening vignettes have been rewritten to offer the most up-to-date examples when introducing chapter topics, providing important context from the very start of each chapter.
- Additional XBRL coverage has been added to Chapter 16.
- The Sarbanes-Oxley Act is highlighted with a new icon in the margins of the text every time the topic is covered.
- Many technology descriptions and references to companies have been updated to ensure current examples are reflected in the text.
- The Bentley University Term Project, now available on the IRCD and the text Web site, is designed to incorporate the concepts taught in the text and allow them to be applied in a cohesive project. The project can be assigned to students as part of their course with minimal development or preparation.
- All chapters now include Short Problems, providing instructors an alternative to the longer traditional problems. Students receive plenty of practice with a variety of questions covering multiple learning objectives and difficulty levels.
- Control framework is explained in one comprehensive example that begins with the introduction of an order entry/sales process in Chapter 4 to describe the preparation of data flow diagrams and systems flowcharts. This process example is carried into Chapters 7 and 9 where the control framework is introduced and explained.
- Each end-of-chapter question in the *Solutions Manual* is tagged to correspond with AACSB, AICPA, and CISA standards, allowing professors to more easily use the questions to focus on specific areas of interest. This may also help manage the task of reporting outcomes to accrediting bodies.

Acknowledgements

In closing, we must acknowledge that the pronoun "we" as used in this text extends far beyond the three authors. Over the years, there have been countless adopters, reviewers, students, and colleagues who have provided us with comments and suggestions that have cumulatively made a positive impact on this edition. We are most grateful to all of them for their dedication to the field of AIS and this text.

Thanks to the following reviewers and verifiers that worked on this edition:

Michael P. Martel
Ohio University

Theresa M. Phinney
Texas A&M University

Mary Hill
Kennesaw State University

Edward R. Walker
University of Central Oklahoma

Linda Bressler
University of Houston–Downtown

Jai Kang
San Francisco State University

Jeff Payne
University of Kentucky

Audrey Scarlata
East Carolina University

Fred Barbee
University of Alaska

Patricia Lopez
Valencia Community College

Lois Mahoney
Eastern Michigan University

We would also like to thank the editorial staff from Cengage Learning, including Rob Dewey, Publisher; Matt Filimonov, Acquisitions Editor; Julie Warwick, Developmental Editor; Jean Buttrom, Content Project Manager; Gowri Vasanthkumar, Project Manager; Natalie Livingston, Marketing Manager; and Ann Mazzaro, Editorial Assistant.

Finally, to our families, we thank you for your infinite patience throughout this project. Without your support and encouragement, this ninth edition would not have been possible.

Ulric J. Gelinas, Jr.
Richard B. Dull
Patrick R. Wheeler

Dedication

We dedicate this ninth edition to our wives, Roxanne, Susan, and Kay, with grateful appreciation for their patience and support throughout this project.

ABOUT THE AUTHORS

Ulric J. (Joe) Gelinas, Jr., Ph.D., is a Professor Emeritus at Bentley University, Waltham, Massachusetts. As a consultant to PricewaterhouseCoopers he developed and taught training programs for business processes, internal control, and IT audit. Dr. Gelinas was Senior Consultant for MIS Training Institute teaching courses in the IT Audit curriculum, and he teaches in the University of Maastricht's International Executive Master of Finance and Control Program. He received his A.B. in Economics from St. Michael's College, Winooski, Vermont, and his M.B.A. and Ph.D. from the University of Massachusetts, Amherst. Professor Gelinas has also taught at the University of Tennessee and at Vesalius College, Vrije Universtiteit Brussel, in Brussels, Belgium. As a captain in the U.S. Air Force, he was Officer-in-Charge of IT Operations. Professor Gelinas has published articles on interorganizational collaboration and coordination infrastructures, accounting information systems, using technology in business education, technical communications, and information privacy. These articles have appeared in academic and practitioner journals, including the *Journal of Information Systems, Issues in Accounting Education, IS Audit & Control Journal, Government Information Quarterly, Journal of Information Technology, International Journal of Technology Management, International Journal of IT Standards and Standardization Research, Journal of Information Systems Education, Technical Communications Quarterly,* and *IEEE Transactions on Professional Communication.* In 2003, Professor Gelinas received the Innovation in Auditing and Assurance Education Award from the American Accounting Association. In 2000, he received the John W. Beveridge Achievement Award from the New England Chapter of the Information Systems Audit and Control Association for outstanding contributions to the IS audit and control profession. He has made presentations and conducted workshops at the International Conference of the Information Systems Audit and Control Association (ISACA); ISACA's Computer Audit, Control, and Security (CACS) conferences; as well as other professional groups. He is a member of the American Accounting Association, the Information Systems Audit and Control Association, Beta Alpha Psi, and Beta Gamma Sigma. Professor Gelinas was a member of the U.S. expert panel that reviewed *Control Objectives for Information and Related Technology* (COBIT) and has conducted COBIT workshops throughout the world. In his spare time, Professor Gelinas is engaged in his favorite activities: sailing, hiking, and bird watching.

Richard (Rick) Dull, Ph.D., CPA/CFF, CISA, CFE, is an Associate Professor of Accountancy at Clemson University, Clemson, South Carolina. He received his B.B.A. (Accounting) and B.S. (Computer Applications) from Harding University, his M.B.A. from the University of North Carolina at Greensboro, and his Ph.D. (Business—Accounting/Information Systems) from Virginia Tech. Professor Dull has also taught at Indiana University–Indianapolis and High Point University. His professional experience includes application programming with a manufacturing firm as well as audit and information systems consulting experience with McGladrey, Hendrickson, and Pullen (and a premerger A.M. Pullen & Company). He was a founding partner of Weathersby, Dull, Bostian & Waynick CPAs and served as president of their successor consulting firm, Intelligent Technologies, Inc., until choosing to pursue a career in academia. His experience supports his teaching and research interest in accounting information systems, continuous assurance, forensic accounting, and technology in accounting education. His work on a project involving cross-departmental integration of enterprise systems earned a Microsoft Pinnacle Award for Excellence in Education as well as a Clemson University Board of Trustees Award for Faculty Excellence. Professor Dull has been published in academic and practitioner journals, including the *Journal of Information Systems*, *International Journal of Accounting Information Systems*, *Journal of Emerging Technologies in Accounting*, *Accounting Education: an International Journal*, *Issues in Accounting Education*, *CPA Journal*, and *Personal Financial Planning*. He has made frequent conference and continuing education presentations in local, national, and international venues on topics including continuous auditing and assurance, accounting information systems, and accounting education. Professor Dull is a member of the American Accounting Association, American Institute of CPAs, Association of Certified Fraud Examiners, and the Information Systems Audit and Control Association. His professional activities have included serving on the AICPA's Assurance Services Executive Committee and serving as the President of the AAA's Artificial Intelligence/Emerging Technologies Section. He recently served the AICPA as a member of BEC Subcommittee and currently serves as an Editorial Advisor for the *Journal of Accountancy*. Professor Dull was a recipient of a Fulbright Award in 2008, spending a semester lecturing and researching in Croatia. In addition to his work, he enjoys spending time with his family and church, as well as traveling and boating.

Patrick (Pat) Wheeler, Ph.D., CPA, CITP, is Associate Professor at the University of Missouri in Columbia, Missouri. He is the CBIZ MHM Scholar, teaches accounting information systems at the graduate and undergraduate levels, and has extensive training in databases and enterprise resource planning systems (SAP and Oracle Financials). Professor Wheeler received his Ph.D. in Accounting from Georgia State University in 1999 and a B.A. with honors from the University of Florida in 1979. Professor Wheeler is a CPA with the Louisiana Society of CPAs and a Certified Information Technology Professional (CITP) with the American Institute of CPAs. His research focuses on behavioral issues in information systems, especially in regard to the impact of computerized decision aids on business decision making. His articles, published worldwide in numerous academic journals and magazines, can be found in *The Accounting Review*, *Journal of Information Systems*, *Behavioral Research in Accounting*, *Advances in Accounting Behavioral Research*, *International Journal of Accounting Information Systems*, *International Journal of Disclosure and Governance*, *Studies in Managerial and Financial Accounting*, *Issues in Accounting Education*, and *Review of Accounting Information Systems*. He received the 2007 Outstanding Research Paper Award and the 2007 Finalist Research Paper Award from the Information Systems (IS) section of the AAA. He won the Outstanding IS Dissertation Award at the 2001 AAA Annual Meeting and currently serves on the editorial review boards of the *Journal of Information Systems* and *International Journal of Accounting Information Systems*. He received the 2006 Outstanding Service Award from the AAA IS Section. Professor Wheeler is active in the American Accounting Association (AAA) at both the national and regional levels, especially in the IS section, and is a member of Beta Gamma Sigma, the business honor society. He has made numerous local, regional, and national conference presentations on various IS and business decision-making topics, and recently spent a semester teaching accounting in the Republic of Georgia. He is a retired Navy officer, an active member of his church, and a devoted husband and father who enjoys biking, jogging, and reading.

Understanding Information Systems

CHAPTER 1

Introduction to Accounting Information Systems

Learning Objectives

After reading this chapter, you should be able to:

- Appreciate the complex, dynamic environment in which accounting is practiced.
- Know the relationship between the AIS and the organization's business processes.
- Know the attributes of information.
- Recognize how information is used for different types of decisions and at various levels in the organization.
- Recognize how the information system supports the management function.
- Recognize the accountant's role in relation to the current environment for the AIS.
- Understand how to use this textbook effectively to learn AIS.

At the beginning of your journey to acquire knowledge about accounting information systems (AIS), you should be aware of the importance of the topic to you personally, and to your long-term success as an accountant. To emphasize this importance, consider the following excerpts, relating to technology, from the Accountants and Auditors section of the *Occupational Outlook Handbook*:

> Because computer systems commonly automate transactions and make information readily available, internal auditors may also help management evaluate the effectiveness of their controls based on real-time data, rather than personal observation. They may recommend and review controls for their organization's computer systems, to ensure their reliability and integrity of the data.
>
> Technology is rapidly changing the nature of the work of most accountants and auditors. With the aid of special software packages, accountants summarize transactions in standard formats of financial records and organize data in special formats employed in financial analysis. These accounting packages greatly reduce the tedious work associated with data management and recordkeeping. Computers enable accountants and auditors to be more mobile and to use their clients' computer systems to extract information from databases and the Internet. As a result, a growing number of accountants and auditors with extensive computer skills specialize in correcting problems with software or in developing software to meet unique data management and analytical needs. Accountants also are beginning to perform more technical duties, such as implementing, controlling, and auditing computer systems and networks, and developing technology plans.

Accountants and auditors must be good at working with people, business systems, and computers. At a minimum, accountants and auditors should be familiar with basic accounting and computer software packages.[1]

In other words, technology is making information available to improve decisions for all decision makers—at the same time making the job of an accountant more interesting and challenging, as well as providing new opportunities for you. There is little doubt that the things you can learn from this book should help you increase your knowledge of information systems and take advantage of these new opportunities.

This chapter introduces the concept of technology applied to accounting. The material presented here, as well as throughout the text, is *essential* to your success as an accountant. Invariably, when we see students after they graduate and have been working for a few years, comments start flowing that reinforce the topics covered in this text. "I use the information from your class constantly in my job." "I actually draw data flow diagrams as part of our systems documentation." "I was in a meeting with my manager and was the only person who understood the technology concepts being discussed." Why do you think we repeatedly hear these and many similar comments? Technology and accounting cannot be separated in today's businesses. Read on to prepare for your successful accounting career.

Synopsis

In this chapter, we introduce you to the subject of accounting information systems (AIS), describe the importance of AIS to your future success, and lay out some important terms and concepts that we will use throughout the text. We begin by presenting a view of the practice of accounting. You will see that accountants today are shifting their focus from being business accountants and auditors to being information management and business measurement professionals providing value-added services to their organizations and clients. This view, rooted in changes in information technology and changes in a volatile business environment, reflects the practice of accounting for those on the leading edge of their profession. Next, we define and explain AIS and its relationship to the organization. Then, we describe the qualities that information must possess to drive the organization and enable the performance of key management functions. Finally, we summarize the role of the accountant in today's business environment.

Throughout the text, we will present three themes to connect our discussions to topics that are currently of great interest to accountants. These themes are *enterprise systems* and *enterprise resource planning (ERP) systems*—such as those sold by SAP®, Oracle®, Sage™, and Microsoft®; *e-business*, including retail e-businesses such as Amazon.com®, the online segments of traditional retailers, such as Walmart.com, and wholesale electronic marketplaces such as ECEurope.com and EC21.com; and *internal control*—those business practices that keep an organization out of trouble and heading toward achieving its objectives. We introduced these three themes in the Preface and will explore them further in this chapter.

---

[1]The *Occupational Outlook Handbook*, 2010–2011 Edition, was produced by the U.S. Department of Labor, Bureau of Labor Statistics, and is available at www.bls.gov/oco/ocos001.htm (accessed January 15, 2010). Many other countries produce documents indicating similar expectations.

Introduction

At the start of this chapter, we discussed the impact of technology and how it will affect your role as an accountant, but the impact extends well beyond accounting. The *Occupational Outlook Handbook* suggests that technology improves information available for decision making—this means that *all* decision makers within an organization benefit from accounting technology—it is not limited to accountants. For example, sales managers can make better decisions because computerized accounting systems should provide more timely sales and collections information than manual systems. The ability to automate controls means that the data should be more reliable, which is another benefit for the entire organization.

Accountants with technology skills are using computers to reduce the mundane part of their work, enabling them to be more efficient in their work. This efficiency increase means these accountants have time to do more interesting work and at the same time be more valuable to their employers. Now that you are aware of the importance of technology within accounting, let's begin exploring AIS.

This chapter provides you with some basics that are used throughout the text. Our introduction to AIS continues with some background material and definitions. We define and describe AIS, depict it as a major part of business processes of any organization, and describe the critical functions that AIS perform within an organization. Some of the terms in this chapter may not be familiar to you. Don't let that concern you at this point. We will define and illustrate these terms later in the book.

The Textbook's Three Themes

Enterprise Systems

Before digging into the material, you should understand the importance of the three themes of this book and how they will be included in the discussions throughout this text. The three themes—enterprise systems, e-business, and internal control—were introduced and defined in the Preface. *Enterprise systems* integrate the business processes and information from all of an organization's functional areas, such as marketing and sales, cash receipts, purchasing, cash disbursements, human resources, production and logistics, and business reporting (including financial reporting). *Enterprise resource planning (ERP) systems* are software packages that can be used for the core systems necessary to support enterprise systems. It is critical that accountants understand these systems because at some point in their careers, they will likely be members of teams that install and operate systems in their organizations. To install an enterprise system, the business processes of an organization must be understood and documented. If necessary, the business processes must be changed and then mapped to the enterprise system. A major part of the installation project is configuring the enterprise system to tailor it to the business processes. As consultants, business process owners, system users, or auditors, we must understand these systems and be able to install, use, and audit them. Enterprise systems are described more fully in Chapter 2 and are discussed throughout the remainder of the book.

E-Business

E-business is the application of electronic networks (including the Internet) to undertake business processes between individuals and organizations. These processes include interaction between back-office (i.e., internal) processes, such as distribution, manufacturing, and accounting, and front-office (i.e., external) processes, such as those that connect an organization to its customers and suppliers. E-business has created entirely new ways of working within and across organizations. For example, organizations are buying and selling goods and services at virtual marketplaces, which changes how organizations identify customers and select vendors. It should also change how they determine the costs of acquiring goods from a vendor and what price(s) they should charge their customers for their products. Obviously, accountants need to be aware of the opportunities and risks associated with this new way of doing business. E-business is explained more fully in Chapter 3 and is discussed throughout the remainder of the book.

Internal control is a process—effected by an entity's board of directors, management, and other personnel—designed to provide reasonable assurance regarding achieving objectives in the following categories: efficiency and effectiveness of operations, reliability of reporting, and compliance with applicable laws and regulations. For example, controls ensure that an organization's inventories (or other assets) are not stolen and that the organization does not have too much inventory (perhaps a waste of resources by incurring unnecessary storage costs) or too little inventory (leading, perhaps, to a lost opportunity to sell the product). Although top management is responsible for an organization's system of internal control, the accountant and other business process owners are given the authority to implement and operate the system of control. Therefore, it is incumbent on all managers and accountants to know how to use controls to ensure achievement of the organization's goals. In Chapter 7, we introduce internal control and then apply it throughout the remainder of the book.

Controls

Beyond Debits and Credits

Have your accounting studies to date convinced you that the most serious problem you may face in your career is that your trial balance doesn't balance? If so, here are a couple of examples that might persuade you otherwise. It wasn't too long ago that the procedures used to process credit card sales were completely manual. A sales clerk would prepare a paper credit card slip using a pen to write the amount by hand, run it through a device to imprint your name and account number, and—to reduce the possibility of credit card fraud—look up the credit card number in a book that listed stolen credit cards. But this book was printed only periodically and could never be up to date. As credit card usage increased, a procedure was developed where clerks would call the credit card companies for approval of a purchase. Although this took longer, the selling merchants were able to assure themselves that the credit card had not been reported stolen and that sufficient credit was available on the customer's account. The system has continued to evolve into what we have today: Approvals are obtained automatically by connecting directly (i.e., online) from the checkout to the credit card company. This method is used to ensure that the merchant and the credit card company get paid for the sale. And, as you will learn in Chapter 10, an accountant can't book a sale unless it is likely that they will get paid for the sale.

Controls

Many of you are familiar with a different control problem that exists today—the purchase of items using credit cards on the Internet. You can read the statistics about individuals who do not want to buy on the Internet because they fear that their private information, especially their credit card number, is not secure. Controls have been put in place to protect the consumer, merchant, and credit card company (you'll read about these controls in Chapters 3, 8, and 9). Still, fraudulent transactions occur and millions of dollars are lost every year. Again, controls are used to protect the assets of the organization and ensure the effectiveness of operations. After all, if customers are not confident in the security of a merchant's Web site they will go elsewhere with their purchases.

E-Business

Enterprise Systems

Another example comes from a large multinational company in the health care industry. The company acquired a new, large division after having just installed an ERP system in all of its worldwide operations. After installing the ERP system in the new division, the data related to the previous year's purchases and sales for the entire company, including the new division, were exported from the ERP system into a separate database (i.e., a data warehouse, as will be explained in Chapter 5). The cost accountants were then asked to analyze the costs and selling prices for a line of products and to suggest a new pricing structure that would make sense in light of the incorporation of the products from the new division. To accomplish this task, the cost accountants needed to know how the data was defined and stored in the ERP systems, how it had been exported, and finally how to get it out of the data warehouse in a form that they could use. What seemed like a simple analysis, one that would be performed all the time by a staff accountant, became something quite different!

These examples demonstrate that knowledge of traditional accounting concepts is not enough to succeed in today's business environment; the underlying technology is a critical part of any accountant's job. These examples indicate challenges for you, while offering opportunities to those who learn in this course to be effective information management and business measurement professionals.

Legal Issues Impacting Accountants

Inherent in the work of accountants, and therefore in the study of accounting and information systems, is compliance with laws and regulations. One such law, the Sarbanes-Oxley Act of 2002 (SOX), has dramatically changed the daily work of financial accountants, auditors, and many others as well.

The Sarbanes-Oxley Act of 2002

SOX

At this point in your academic career, you have probably studied the Sarbanes-Oxley Act (SOX) and the impact that it has had on publicly traded companies.[2] Because of your prior knowledge, the discussion at this point is limited to Sections 404 and 409 and their applicability to the study of AIS.

Section 404 of SOX, and PCAOB Auditing Standard No. 5,[3] has meant changes for both auditors and the companies that they audit. To comply with SOX, management must identify, document, and evaluate significant internal controls. Auditors must, as part of an integrated audit of financial statements, report on the effectiveness of the organization's system of internal control. These requirements represent significant expansions of the internal control–related roles of management and auditors. These responsibilities are increasing at the same time that computer-based systems are becoming more sophisticated, thus adding to the complexity of the systems of internal control. It is important that you understand the systems in order to comply with SOX.

Section 409 of SOX requires disclosure to the public on a "rapid and current basis" of material changes in an organization's financial condition. Compliance with this section requires the application of legal, financial, and technical expertise to ensure that the organization's AIS are able to produce financial data in a timely and accurate manner. Who else but the accountant, armed with the latest knowledge of accounting and information technology, can ensure compliance with these provisions of SOX?

---

[2]For the full text of the Sarbanes-Oxley Act of 2002, see www.sec.gov/about/laws/soa2002.pdf (accessed January 15, 2010).

[3]Auditing Standard No. 5, "An Audit of Internal Control Over Financial Reporting That Is Integrated with an Audit of Financial Statements," PCAOB, July 12, 2007.

Challenges and Opportunities for the Accountant. Are you preparing yourself to be effective in the future? Will you be able to adapt to advances in technology, and will you look ahead and prepare yourself to take advantage of technology advancements? Could you perform an analysis of the cost and price data by extracting and evaluating information from an information system? Could you help assess the risks and benefits related to an organization's e-business and develop the controls necessary to ensure a secure and reliable Web presence? Could you consult with management to help them comply with SOX Section 404 or evaluate management's internal control system? What do your technology abilities mean to you personally? Those abilities may mean more job opportunities and money. We intend to help you prepare to use available technology and plan for the future by helping you grow with emerging technologies.

Management accountants and internal auditors find themselves buying, using, and evaluating complex computer-based information systems. Financial accountants must be sure that their AIS can produce financial statements to comply with SOX Section 409. The management accountant must be sure that a new information system has the necessary features, such as controls and the ability to access data and to trace data from input to output. Also, these information systems must be protected from fraud and other abuses. How effectively you use technology to perform these functions will determine how well you can do your job, which may determine the very survival of your company in a competitive, international marketplace.

Technology is also influencing public accounting firms. The business-consulting or advisory services units of the Big Four public accounting firms have accounted for a significant percentage of the firms' business and were growing faster than the accounting, auditing, and tax portions of their businesses. The consulting units of three of these firms have been split off from the "accounting" portions of the firms (Ernst & Young Consulting was acquired by Capgemini™, KPMG Consulting became BearingPoint™, and the consulting division of PricewaterhouseCoopers was sold to IBM®). Still, the growth portion of the remaining "accounting" firms will remain in their value-added, business advising lines. For example, a major line of business for these firms has been to assist their clients in complying with SOX Section 404.[4] You should not be surprised to find the need for strong technology skills continuing in these firms. The consulting firms also actively recruit personnel with both accounting and technology skills. If you aspire to a career in public accounting, your success in the consulting segment of public practice will depend on your knowledge and experience in relatively technical areas that, at first glance, are far from the practice of accounting.

Independent auditors are faced with deciding on the "reasonableness" of financial statements produced from data contained in the information system. As an auditor, you will be asked to execute your audit tasks and to provide additional "value-added" service to the client. You will, for example, provide your client with advice on improving operations and reducing risks. Successful public accounting firms provide cost-effective audits along with broader, high-quality service to the client.

These conclusions were confirmed by the report of a project sponsored by the American Accounting Association (AAA), the American Institute of Certified Public Accountants (AICPA), the Institute of Management Accountants (IMA), and the Big Five (there were five at the time) public accounting firms. Practitioners surveyed

---

[4]The type of service that can be performed depends on whether the work is performed for an audit client.

reported that accounting graduates would need to be able to provide services in the areas of financial analysis, financial planning, financial reporting, strategic consulting, and systems consulting.[5]

Historically, the accountant has performed an attest function to determine the reliability of financial information presented in printed financial statements. This role is expanding to include the following:

- Nonfinancial information (that is, information not measured in monetary units; e.g., accountants might help determine occupancy rates for hotels or apartment complexes)
- Use of information technology to create or summarize information from databases
- Information interpretation to determine the quality and relevance of information to be used for decision making (e.g., evaluating information for the assessment of risk)

The Assurance Services Executive Committee (ASEC) of the AICPA identifies, develops, and promotes nonaudit assurance services that can be offered by accountants.[6] The technology-related services include the following:

- Information systems reliability (SysTrust; Chapters 3 and 8)
- Electronic commerce (WebTrust; Chapter 8)

Historically, the development of these services has been a joint effort between the AICPA and the Canadian Institute of Chartered Accountants (CICA). The ASEC currently has task forces in place to consider assurance issues related to XBRL (eXtensible Business Reporting Language) (see Chapter 16 for a discussion of XBRL) and Trust Services/Data Integrity. In addition to the development of assurance services, the AICPA has, in cooperation with CPAs across the United States and other professional organizations, proposed a vision of the profession's future called the CPA Vision Project.[7] Three of the five core services proposed in the project involve information technology. They include "assurance and information integrity," "management consulting and performance measurement," and "technology services." Among the core competencies that will be required of those performing these services are "interpretation of converging information" (able to interpret and provide a broader context using financial and nonfinancial information) and "technology adept" (able to use and leverage technology in ways that add value to clients, customers, and employers).

Finally, the AICPA has created a credential, the certified information technology professional (CITP), to recognize CPAs who can provide skilled advice on using IT to implement business strategy.[8] Skills necessary to obtain this accreditation include (chapter coverage in this text is shown in parentheses) the following:

- An understanding of project management (Chapter 17)
- Familiarity with IT and business processes (IT throughout the text, business processes in Chapters 10 through 16)
- Competence in technology (throughout the text)

---

[5] W. Steve Albrecht and Robert J. Sack, *Accounting Education: Charting the Course Through a Perilous Future* (Sarasota, FL: American Accounting Association, 2000): 15.

[6] See www.aicpa.org/ for a description of the assurance services and other services being defined by the AICPA. See www.cica.ca/ for those services being defined by the Canadian Institute of Chartered Accountants (CICA).

[7] See www.aicpa.org/vision/index.htm for a description of the CPA Vision Project.

[8] See http://infotech.aicpa.org/ for a description of the CITP designation.

Components of the Study of AIS

Figure 1.1 depicts the elements central to our study of AIS. Many are probably familiar to you, and many have been introduced earlier in this chapter. We will briefly discuss each element, with special emphasis on how the accountant is affected. Before beginning, you should understand two things. First, the study of AIS is our broad view, and the accounting information system itself is our narrow view. Second, you shouldn't assign any meaning to the placement of the elements in Figure 1.1. The figure just tells you that there are 10 elements.

- **Technology.** Your ability to plan and manage business operations depends partly on your knowledge of the technology available. For instance, can we manage production without knowledge of robotics? Obviously, technological developments have a profound effect on information systems; enterprise systems, ERP systems, e-business, databases, and intelligent systems are but a few examples. Technology provides the foundation on which AIS and business operations rest, and knowledge of technology is critically important to your understanding of the AIS discipline. **Exhibit 1.1** (pp. 10–11) describes the 10 primary technological challenges and opportunities facing chartered accountants (CAs) at the close of 2009. These technologies were selected by a group of CAs, who are members of the Canadian Institute of Chartered Accountants (CICA). The CICA's Information Technology Advisory Committee sponsored this survey and published the results.[9] The exhibit indicates where these technologies are discussed in this text.

- **Databases.** Your other accounting courses have emphasized accounting as a reporting function. The full accounting cycle, however, includes data collection and

FIGURE 1.1 Elements in the Study of Accounting Information Systems

---

[9]The top ten IT issues, *CA Magazine*, September, 2009 (available at www.camagazine.com/archives/print-edition/2009/sep/features/camagazine29323.aspx, accessed, May 6, 2010)

EXHIBIT 1.1 CICA's 2009 Top Ten IT Issues

1. **Maintaining adequate controls during the recession.** Maintaining an adequate and effective control framework in times of economic constraint is a challenge for companies when they are downsizing. They have fewer employees to execute controls properly and support an adequate segregation of duties. (Necessary segregation of duties are discussed in Chapter 8, as well as in the application context of Chapters 10–14.)

2. **Maintaining security over moving data.** The number of small portable devices such as laptops, smart- phones and BlackBerrys continues to grow within organizations, making it difficult to maintain proper security over data on the move. In addition there are USB memory sticks or integrated wireless device media cards that are not encrypted or even password protected. Now, USB sticks can contain executable programs, becoming essentially a computer on a stick. These devices lead to an easy movability of data that quickly passes through various control environments. Also, it raises the risks associated with the same data residing in several locations, perhaps even inappropriate ones. Some organizations, for example, hold private personal data, with multiple copies kept in various parts of the system, complicating compliance with privacy laws. The press is rife with reports of lost laptops, netbooks, and BlackBerrys containing private customer data. (Discussed in Chapter 8.)

3. **Lack of effective IT governance.** The concerns stated this year include: lack of effective IT governance activities; poor alignment of IT with organizational strategy; and limited awareness of IT issues at the board level. All these concerns indicate a need for an IT committee of the board of directors, which some companies have but most do not. Boards are aware of the importance of IT to business. They know that an IT failure can seriously damage the business, its reputation and even earnings. But, according to respondents, they are not aware of the IT issues that need to be addressed, including those that bear on the organization's ability to meet its overall governance responsibilities. (Discussed in Chapters 7 and 8.)

4. **Coping with information overload.** Sorting and filtering all of the currently available information takes time and reduces employee productivity. In addition, much of the information coming through channels such as smartphones, email, and netbooks is not needed to run the business. Information overload results in distractions that prevent people from focusing on the tasks at hand. Time is wasted as people are forced to refocus their concentration after being distracted by another piece of information. In some cases, it results in people becoming selective about the sources they pay attention to, simply ignoring others. (Discussed in Chapters 5 and 16.)

5. **Impact of IFRS on information systems.** IFRS convergence is not generally thought of as an IT issue. However, it is because IFRS requires companies to obtain and track information that has not been in their accounts before. This would include, for example, information on market values for property, plant and equipment; sufficient information to track asset revaluations under IFRS; information to track discount rates; information to support different methods of income recognition, etc. The IT implications include capturing and processing the additional information, changes in business processes to implement and execute the new information requirements and consequent changes in the control environment for the data and business processes. (Discussed in Chapter 16.)

6. **Green computing.** Green computing encompasses not only basic awareness of green IT, but more specifically energy consumption, disposal of equipment and printing policies. "Companies are keen to catch up with the green trend," says one survey respondent, "especially as new recruits [and the next generations] have green thinking as a core value, and will consider that when evaluating a company." That means companies must work green values into their daily activities, including IT purchases and disposals, printing policies and power usage. A significant problem with green computing is that while many companies are aware of the issues, many do not know what to do about them. (Discussed in Chapter 16. Risk management is also discussed in Chapter 7.)

7. **Security requirements of the Payment Card Industry (PCI)** A new issue arose this year when PCI mandated increased security requirements for merchants, card issuers and card acquirers requiring self-assessments for handling credit and debit cards. There are significant compliance costs involved with these rules and not all merchants have the budget to comply. Moreover, the implications of the PCI requirements are not well understood by organizations. Their willingness to accept credit cards is driven by business needs and they normally do not perform a comprehensive risk and control analysis. (Discussed in Chapter 11.)

8. **Malicious activity by laid-off employees.** An issue as old as time but one bound to pop up in a recession is that of increased malicious activity by disgruntled or recently laid-off employees. The long-established approach is to lay off employees at the end of the day, disconnect their system access privileges when they are in their exit interview and then escort them from the building. It is a somewhat humiliating approach for the employees, but one that many companies have discovered from experience to be necessary, especially in higher risk situations involving personnel with powerful system privileges and intricate system knowledge. (Discussed in Chapter 8.)

9. **The role of Web 2.0 applications in organizational information systems.** Web 2.0 focuses on the Internet as a means

of human interaction. It includes social networking, wikis, blogs, etc. Social networking, in particular, has raised a set of perplexing issues. Some companies see the benefits of social networking for improving communications within the company, and essentially forming communities to deal with particular business areas, needs and projects. The issue is whether and how social networking fits into an organization's information systems and culture. (Discussed in Chapter 10.)

10. **The shortage of IT skills.** The recession has exacerbated the IT skills shortage that has been an issue for the past few years. Some boomers have re-tired (forced or voluntary) or have been laid off, and some respondents mention watching important IT skills go out the door with them. Although the generation coming in has significant Internet skills, it generally does not have an appreciation of IT issues in an organizational and managerial context. As a result, companies are losing IT skills and having difficulty replacing them. The importance of this issue will grow over the next decade as more retirements take place. Even an economic rebound will not necessarily be the salvation, because then there is a risk that companies will lose their most talented professionals on the upswing of the economy. (Throughout the text, we emphasize the IT skills required for successful accountants.)

Source: The top ten IT issues, *CA Magazine,* September, 2009 (available at www.camagazine.com/archives/print-edition/2009/sep/features/camagazine29323.aspx, accessed, May 6, 2010).

storage, and these aspects must become part of your knowledge base. In addition, important to a complete understanding of AIS are the variety of databases, both private and public; the quantity and type of data available in these databases; and methods of retrieving those data. To perform analysis, to prepare information for management decision making, and to audit a firm's financial records, an accountant must be able to access and use data from public and private databases. Chapters 5 and 6 explore the design and use of an organization's own databases.

- **Reporting.** To design reports generated by an information system, the accountant must know what outputs are required or are desirable. Often, the user will prepare a report on an ad hoc basis using powerful report-generating tools or a database query language (discussed in Chapters 5 and 6). These reports often support management decisions as well as fulfill certain reporting obligations. GAAP-based financial statements are but one example of reporting that will be considered in our study of AIS.

- **Control.** Traditionally, accountants have been experts on controlling business processes. As a practicing accountant, you will probably spend much of your time providing such expertise. Consider how much more difficult it will be to control modern, complex business processes. You must develop an understanding of control that is specific to the situation at hand, yet is adaptable for the future. Control—the means by which we make sure the intended actually happens—will be introduced in Chapter 7 and explored in detail in Chapters 8 and 9 and in the business process chapters, Chapters 10 through 16.

The next three elements—business operations, events processing, and management decision making—comprise a major focus of this text, *business processes*. The logical components of business processes are described later in this chapter. Knowledge of these processes is essential for success as an accountant, consultant, business process owner, or IT specialist.

- **Business operations.** Organizations engage in activities or operations, such as hiring employees, purchasing inventory, and collecting cash from customers. An AIS operates in concert with these business operations. Many AIS inputs are prepared by operating departments—the *action* or *work* centers of the organization—and many AIS outputs are used to manage these operations. Therefore, we must analyze and manage an AIS in light of the work being performed by the organization. For example, to advise management and to prepare reports for management decision making, a management accountant must understand the organization's business.

- **Events processing.** As organizations undertake their business operations, events, such as sales and purchases, occur. Data about these events must be captured and recorded to mirror and monitor the business operations. The events have operational and AIS aspects (i.e., some do not have a direct accounting impact, and some are accounting "transactions" that result in entries in the general ledger). To design and use the AIS, an accountant must know what event data are processed and how they are processed.

- **Management decision making.** The information used for a decision must be tailored to the type of decision under consideration. Furthermore, the information is more useful if it recognizes the personal management styles and preferences of the decision maker. For instance, the manager of department A prefers to receive a monthly cash flow statement that groups receipts and payments into broad categories. The manager of department B, on the other hand, wants to see more detailed information in the form of an analysis of payments by vendors. Beyond the information available to managers, many decision makers now use *intelligent systems* to help them make decisions. Later in this chapter, we introduce management decision making and then discuss management's use of the data collected by each business process (Chapters 10 through 16). In Chapter 5, we examine intelligent systems.

- **Systems development and operation.** The information systems that process business events and provide information for management decision making must be designed, implemented, and effectively operated. An accountant often participates in systems development projects as a user or business process owner contributing requests for certain functions, or as an auditor advancing controls for the new system. Choosing the data for a report, designing that report, and configuring an enterprise system are examples of systems development tasks that can be accomplished by an accountant. In Chapter 8, we describe the controls related to the systems development process, and in Chapter 17, we examine systems development and operation and the accountant's role in those processes.

- **Communications.** To present the results of their endeavors effectively, accountants must possess strong oral and written communication skills. Have your professors been drumming this message into you? If not, you'll become acutely aware of its importance when you enter the job market. Unlike in other accounting courses, there are few right or wrong answers in the study of AIS. Throughout this course, you will be required to evaluate alternatives, to choose a solution, and to defend your choice. Technical knowledge alone won't be enough for the last task.

- **Accounting and auditing principles.** To design and operate the accounting system, an accountant must know the proper accounting procedures and must understand the audits to which the accounting information will be subjected. As an illustration, suppose you were designing an AIS for the billing function at XYZ, Inc. Would you invoice a customer at the time the customer's purchase order was received, or would you wait until XYZ's shipping department notified you that the goods had been shipped? The answer is, it depends, and we must have knowledge of business operations and the related accounting process to properly synchronize the two.

What Is an Accounting Information System?

In this section, we suggest a definition for AIS (this is our *narrow view* of AIS) and discuss related terms to help you understand the subject matter of this textbook. Because these definitions establish a background for later study, you should read this section carefully. The section begins with a definition of a system and then a discussion of an AIS. The section concludes with an explanation of how the accountant interacts with the AIS and with the current business environment.

Systems and Subsystems

A **system** is a set of interdependent elements that together accomplish specific objectives. A system must have organization, interrelationships, integration, and central objectives. **Figure 1.2(a)** depicts a system consisting of four *interrelated* parts that have come together, or have been *integrated*, as a single system, which we have named System 1.0. Each part of a system—in this case, parts 1.1, 1.2, 1.3, and 1.4—is known as a **subsystem**. Within limits, any subsystem can be further divided into its component parts or subsystems. Figure 1.2(b) depicts subsystem 1.2 as a system consisting of three subsystems. Notice that we use the term *system* (versus *subsystem*) to describe the area of current interest. For example, in a typical university, the College of Business and the College of Engineering are subsystems of the university system, whereas the School/Department of Accountancy and the Marketing Department are subsystems of the College of Business system.

In Figure 1.2, parts (a) and (b) depict the *interrelationships* (A through H) in a system; part (c) depicts the hierarchical *organization* structure inherent in any system. Again, picture System 1.0 as a university and System 1.2 as the College of Business. Interrelationship F might be a finance student being sent by the Finance Department (1.2.1) to the School/Department of Accountancy (1.2.2) for a minor in accounting.

A system's *central objectives* depend on its type—natural, biological, or man-made—and on the particular system. For example, the human circulatory system is a biological system (a subsystem of the human body) whose purpose is to carry blood containing oxygen and carbon dioxide to and from the organs and extremities of the body.

Determining the purpose of man-made systems—such as governments, schools, and business organizations—is a matter we must discuss and understand. Disagreement over the basic functions of the government of the United States has always led to spirited debate among political parties. For example, is the U.S. government the "employer of last resort" and therefore responsible for providing jobs for every citizen? Even when

FIGURE 1.2 Systems and Subsystems

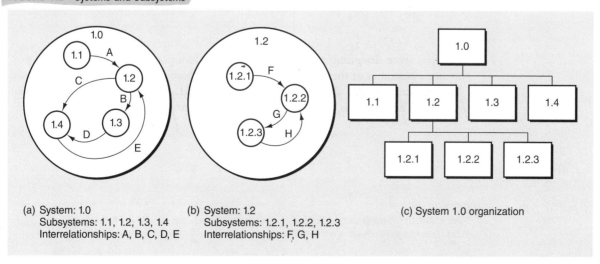

(a) System: 1.0
   Subsystems: 1.1, 1.2, 1.3, 1.4
   Interrelationships: A, B, C, D, E

(b) System: 1.2
   Subsystems: 1.2.1, 1.2.2, 1.2.3
   Interrelationships: F, G, H

(c) System 1.0 organization

we agree on what the objectives should be, we may disagree on how they should be attained. For example, we might all agree that the objective of a municipal school system is to "educate the young citizens of the city." However, if you attend a meeting of a local school board, you probably won't discover consensus over how to meet that objective.

Business organizations usually have more straightforward purposes that are normally related to the "bottom line"—profitability. However, many businesses establish goals other than financial return to the owners. For example, a business might strive to improve the quality of life of its employees or to use its natural resources responsibly. Here is the ultimate "bottom line": You must know a business organization's objectives to understand that business as a system and to understand the actions and interactions of that business's components or subsystems. This is a central theme of this study of AIS.

The Information System (IS)

An **information system (IS)** (or **management information system [MIS]**) is a man-made system that generally consists of an integrated set of computer-based components and manual components established to collect, store, and manage data and to provide output information to users. **Figure 1.3** depicts the functional components of an IS. Imagine a simple IS used to maintain inventory balances for a shoe store. The inputs for such a system might be receipts of new shoes or sales of shoes; the processing might be to update (in storage) the inventory records for the particular shoe; and the output might be a listing of all the kinds and sizes of shoes and their respective recorded balances. That is, a simple information system is directed at the processing of business events.

The IS facilitates these operational functions and supports management decision making by providing information that managers can use to plan and control the activities of the firm. The IS may have advanced elements, such as a database for storage, and can use decision models to present output information for decision making. For example, assume that, while entering data about shoe sales, you also enter data about who purchased the shoes, how they paid for the shoes, and why they decided to buy their shoes at your store. You might store those data and periodically print reports useful in

FIGURE 1.3   Functional Model of an Information System

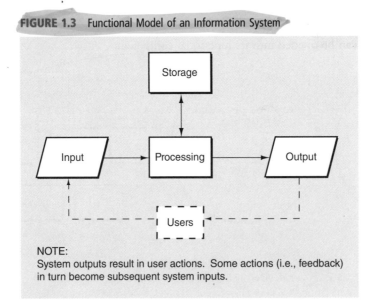

NOTE:
System outputs result in user actions. Some actions (i.e., feedback) in turn become subsequent system inputs.

making decisions about advertising effectiveness. Or you might decide, on the basis of analysis of the sales data, to engage in joint advertising campaigns with a credit card company whose cards are often used in the store.

The Accounting Information System (AIS)

The IS used in the shoe store might have components designed specifically for the organizational function being supported. For example, the IS in the shoe store supports inventory control (a logistics function) by maintaining records for each shoe stocked in the store. The shoe store IS also supports a sales and marketing function by analyzing sales in a variety of ways. Other typical IS components include personnel, production, finance, and accounting. However, integrated IS processing, such as that in an *enterprise system*, has allowed the distinctions among these separate systems to become blurred.[10]

So, historically, an IS incorporated a separate accounting information system (AIS), which is a specialized subsystem of the IS. The purpose of this separate AIS was to collect, process, and report information related to the financial aspects of business events. For example, the input to your AIS might be a sale, such as the shoe sale in the earlier example. You process the sale by recording the sales data in the sales journal, classifying the data using a chart of accounts, and posting the data to the general ledger. Periodically, the AIS will output trial balances and financial statements. However, given the integrated nature of information systems today, seldom is an AIS distinguished separately from the IS.

This textbook studies the discipline of AIS and takes the view that the AIS often cannot be distinguished from the IS. This view is consistent with our assertion that contemporary accountants are information management and business measurement professionals. Our coverage of AIS is based on the 10 elements of Figure 1.1 (pg. 9). We cover these elements because, as an accountant, your skills must go beyond the processing of financial data. You must understand the technology and the operating goals of the organizational functions for which the financial data are processed. For example, supermarket checkout scanners simultaneously collect accounting and operational sales data. Therefore, you must understand sales and marketing goals and the technology used in operations if you are to effectively operate, analyze, or audit a supermarket's AIS. These skills become even more critical as organizations evolve toward highly integrated information systems, such as *enterprise systems*. In summary, a comprehensive study of the AIS should consider all 10 elements of Figure 1.1.

Finally, just as an IS can be divided into its functional components, the AIS may be divided into components based on the operational functions supported. In the sales example, the sales data might originate in the billing/accounts receivable/cash receipts subsystem. We call these AIS components the AIS *business processes* or AIS *subsystems*. In this text, we subdivide the AIS into these processes to facilitate discussion and your understanding of the elements of the AIS. These business processes are described in Chapters 10 through 16.

Logical Components of a Business Process

Figure 1.4 (pg. 16) depicts the three logical components of a business process; the information process is that portion of the overall IS (introduced earlier and depicted in Figure 1.3,

Enterprise Systems

---

[10]These separate IS components and their related business processes are often referred to as "stovepipes."

pg. 14) related to a particular business process.[11] In this section, we define the other two processes, describe how the three processes work together, and emphasize the critical role that the management information process plays.

The **operations process** is a man-made system consisting of the people, equipment, organization, policies, and procedures whose objective is to accomplish the work of the organization. Operations processes typically include production, personnel, marketing and sales, accounting, finance, warehousing, and distribution.

The **management process** is a man-made system consisting of the people, authority, organization, policies, and procedures whose objective is to plan and control the operations of the organization. The three most prominent management activities are planning, controlling, and decision making, which are discussed in the next section of this chapter.

FIGURE 1.4   A Logical Model of a Business Process

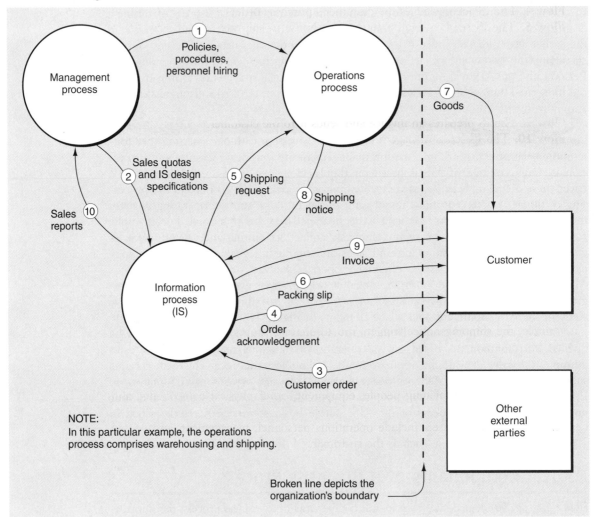

---

[11]Many would use the terms information *process* and information *system* interchangeably. However, we ask you to think of an information process as the portion of the information system that is related to a particular business process.

If you follow the flows connecting the three processes of Figure 1.4, you can understand how these processes work together to accomplish the business process's—and therefore the organization's—objectives. To focus the discussion, we chose a customer order/sales event to illustrate Figure 1.4 on page 16. We will discuss each of the numbered flows in the figure.

- **Flow 1.** Management hires personnel and establishes the means for accomplishing the work of the organization. For example, management would design the procedures used to store inventory and to ship those goods to customers.
- **Flow 2.** Management establishes broad marketing objectives and assigns specific sales quotas by which progress toward the long-run objectives can be measured. In addition, management designs the IS's procedures for facilitating operations, such as the procedures used to pick and ship goods to customers.
- **Flow 3.** Normal operations begin with the IS receiving a customer's order to purchase goods.
- **Flow 4.** The IS acknowledges the customer's purchase order.
- **Flow 5.** The IS sends a request to the warehouse to ship goods to the customer. This request identifies the goods and their location in the warehouse.
- **Flow 6.** A document (i.e., a packing slip) identifying the customer and the goods is attached to the goods.
- **Flow 7.** The goods are shipped to the customer.[12]
- **Flow 8.** The shipping department reports to the IS that the goods have been shipped.
- **Flow 9.** The IS prepares an invoice and sends it to the customer.
- **Flow 10.** The IS sends management a report comparing actual sales to previously established sales quotas.

These 10 flows highlight several important concepts:

- The information process facilitates operations by maintaining inventory and customer data and by providing electronic signals (such as those used in automated warehouses) and paper documents with which to execute business events, such as shipments to customers.
- The information process provides the means by which management monitors the operations process. For example, management "learns" sales results only from the sales report.
- Operations-related processes and accounting-related processes are integrated. For example, the shipping notice triggers the accounting process of updating the sales and accounts receivable data in conjunction with preparing the invoice, which is an operational activity.
- Management designs the operations and information processes and implements these processes by providing people, equipment, other physical components, and policies.
- Information process users include operations personnel, management, and people outside the organization, such as the customer.

Our discussion of Figure 1.4 should make it clear that the IS can be crucial to an organization's success by facilitating the day-to-day operations processes and by providing useful information for the organization's management. Let's examine the attributes

---

[12]Note that flow 6 is shown as coming from the IS, whereas flow 7 comes from the operations process. Physically, the two flows are really inseparable; logically, however, they are separate. In later chapters, we will have more to say about the difference between logical and physical system features.

that make information useful to a decision maker and how management can make use of that information to drive the organization toward achieving its strategic objectives.

Management Uses of Information

An IS serves two important functions within an organization. First, the IS assists daily operations. It can be used as "leverage" to improve operational effectiveness and efficiency. For example, by computerizing the exact warehouse locations of inventory, items to be sent to customers can be retrieved more quickly, making the shipping process more efficient. The IS also mirrors and monitors actions in the operations system by processing, recording, and reporting business events. For example, the IS processes customer orders; records sales to customers by updating sales, accounts receivable, and inventory data; and produces invoices and sales summaries.

The second major function of the information system is to support managerial activities, including management decision making. How do managers use this information? First, they monitor current operations to keep their "ship" on course. For example, managers need to know that enough inventory is being produced or acquired each day to meet expected demand. Managers' second use of information is to help measure and report results for their stakeholders (e.g., customers, stockholders). For example, information can measure attainment of goals regarding product quality, timely deliveries, cash flow, and operating income. Finally, managers use the IS to recognize and adapt in a timely manner to trends in the organization's environment. For example, managers need answers to such questions as: "How does the time it takes us to introduce a new product compare to that of our competitors?" and "Does our unit cost to manufacture compare favorably to those of our competitors?" Because information systems provide critical support to such management activities, we must understand these activities, including decision making, to understand the required design features of good information systems. In this section, we discuss, in general terms, management uses of information.

Data versus Information

Our definitions of *data* and *information* are a bit circular. **Information** is data presented in a form that is useful in a decision-making activity. The information has value to the decision maker because it reduces uncertainty and increases knowledge about a particular area of concern. **Data** are facts or figures in raw form. Data represent the measurements or observations of objects and events. To become useful to a decision maker, data must be transformed into information. **Figure 1.5** illustrates the transformation process. Notice that part (a) repeats the functional model of an IS that we saw in Figure 1.3 (pg. 14), whereas part (b) uses the same symbols with different labels. Might you conclude, then, that the function of the information system is to capture and transform data into information? Absolutely!

We said, however, that *information* must be *useful* in decision making. What attributes give information its utility value? Let's answer this question next.

Qualities of Information

To provide output useful for assisting managers and other users of information, an IS must collect data and convert them into information that possesses important qualities. In this section, we examine some of the elements of information quality that allow you to design and control the collection and processing of data. **Exhibit 1.2** describes qualities of information that, if attained, will help an organization achieve its business objectives.

FIGURE 1.5   Transforming Data into Information

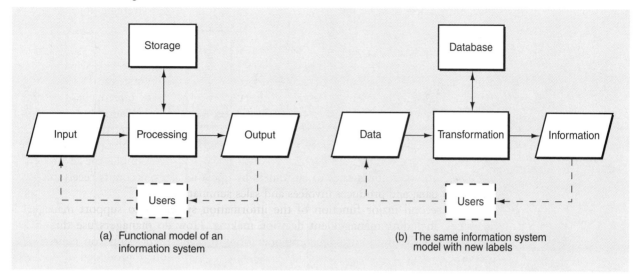

(a) Functional model of an
information system

(b) The same information system
model with new labels

Figure 1.6 (pg. 20) presents an overview of information qualities depicted as a hierarchy. In the following paragraphs, we discuss and expand upon these various information qualities.

You can see from the exhibit that the *effectiveness* quality overlaps with other qualities because it includes such measures as "timely" (i.e., available) and "correct" (i.e., with integrity). The effectiveness of information must be evaluated in relation to the purpose to be served—decision making. Effective information is information that is useful for the decision to be made. Effectiveness, then, is a function of the decisions to be made, the method of decision making to be used, the information already possessed by the decision maker, and the decision maker's capacity to process information. The superior factors in Figure 1.6, such as "users of information" and "overall quality (decision usefulness)," provide additional emphasis for these points. The examples should make these points clear.[13]

EXHIBIT 1.2   Qualities of Information

Effectiveness: Deals with information being relevant and pertinent to the business process as well as being delivered in a timely, correct, consistent, and usable manner.

Efficiency: Concerns the provision of information through the optimal (most productive and economical) use of resources.

Confidentiality: Concerns the protection of sensitive information from unauthorized disclosure.

Integrity: Relates to the accuracy and completeness of information as well as to its validity in accordance with business values and expectations.

Availability: Relates to information being available when required by the business process now and in the future. It also concerns the safeguarding of necessary resources and associated capabilities.

Compliance: Deals with complying with the laws, regulations, and contractual arrangements to which the business process is subject—that is, externally imposed business criteria, as well as internal policies.

Reliability: Relates to the provision of appropriate information for management to operate the entity and exercise its fiduciary and governance responsibilities.

Source: COBIT 4.1 © 2007 IT Governance Institute.

---

[13] The descriptions of many of these terms are adapted from *Statement of Financial Accounting Concepts No. 2: Qualitative Characteristics of Accounting Information*, Financial Accounting Standards Board (FASB), May 1980.

FIGURE 1.6   A Hierarchy of Information Qualities

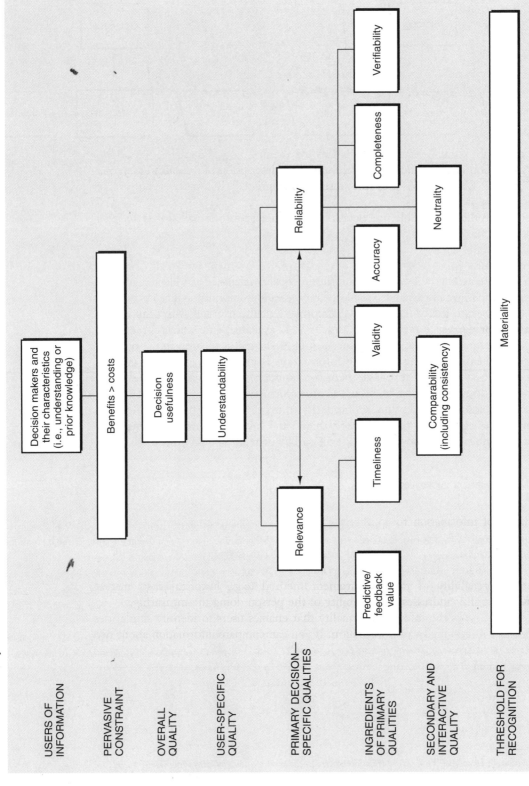

Source: Adapted from Statement of Financial Accounting Concepts No. 2: Qualitative Characteristics of Accounting Information. Financial Accounting Standards Board (FASB). May 1980, p. 15. Copyright by Financial Accounting Standards Board, 401 Merritt 7, P.O. Box 5116, Norwalk, CT 06856-5116. Reprinted with permission. Copies of complete documentation are available from the FASB.

Understandability enables users to perceive the information's significance. Valued from the user's point of view, understandable information is presented in a form that permits its application by the user in the decision-making situation at hand. For example, information must be in a language understood by the decision maker. By language, we mean spoken/written language, such as English or French, as well as technical language, such as those used in physics or computer science. Also, information that makes excessive use of codes and acronyms may not be understandable to some decision makers.

Information has **relevance** when it is capable of making a difference in a decision-making situation by reducing uncertainty or increasing knowledge for that particular decision. For example, a credit manager making a decision about whether to grant credit to a customer might use the customer's financial statements and credit history because that information could be relevant to the credit-granting decision. The customer's organization chart would not be relevant. The description of *reliability of information* in Exhibit 1.2 (pg. 19) uses the term "appropriate." Relevance is a primary component of appropriateness.

Information that is available to a decision maker before it loses its capacity to influence a decision has **timeliness**. Lack of timeliness can make information irrelevant. For example, the credit manager must receive the customer's credit history before making the credit-granting decision. If the decision must be made without the information, the credit history becomes irrelevant. Exhibit 1.2 describes *availability* as "being available when required." Thus, availability can increase timeliness.

Predictive value and **feedback value** improve a decision maker's capacity to predict, confirm, or correct earlier expectations. Information can have both types of value because knowledge of the outcomes of actions already taken will generally improve a decision maker's abilities to predict the results of similar future actions. A buyer for a retail store might use a sales forecast—a prediction—to establish inventory levels. The buyer continues to use these sales forecasts and reviews past inventory shortages and overages—feedback—to refine decision making concerning inventory.

If there is a high degree of consensus about the information among independent measurers using the same measurement methods, the information has **verifiability**. In accounting, we initially record assets at their historical cost because evidence of the assets' cost will permit independent people to arrive at a similar estimate of the book value of the asset.

Neutrality or **freedom from bias** means that the information is objective. Bias is the tendency of information to appear more often on one side than on the other of the object or event that it represents. That is, information about the object or event is systematically overstated or understated. For example, an accounts receivable balance that is usually higher than what can be collected is biased. Notice that verifiability addresses the reliability of the measurement method (e.g., historical cost, market value), and neutrality addresses the reliability of the person doing the measuring.

Comparability is the information quality that enables users to identify similarities and differences in two pieces of information. If you can compare information about two similar objects or events, the information is comparable. For example, in either your financial or managerial accounting course, you probably studied ratio analysis of financial statements. You also learned that one of the "benchmarks" against which you might evaluate the ratios of company A would be similar ratios for competitor company B or for the industry as a whole. But how good is your comparison of two companies if one uses FIFO (first in, first out) inventory costing and the other uses average costing? Generally accepted accounting principles strive to make accounting information as comparable as possible across firms by establishing common practices for accounting for inventory, fixed assets, leases, and so on.

If, on the other hand, you can compare information about the same object or event collected at two points in time, the information is **consistent**. Again, in doing ratio analysis, you probably performed horizontal or trend analysis for two or more years for one company.

As noted in Exhibit 1.2 (pg. 19), *integrity* is an information quality that can be expanded into three very important qualities: validity, accuracy, and completeness. In Figure 1.6, these are components of reliability. Information about actual authorized events and objects has **validity**. For example, suppose that the IS records a sale and an account receivable for a shipment that wasn't authorized or didn't occur. The *recorded* information describes a fictitious, unauthorized event; therefore, the information lacks validity.

Accuracy is the correspondence or agreement between the information and the actual events or objects that the information represents. For example, you would have inaccurate information if the quantity on hand in an inventory report was reported as 51 units, when the actual physical quantity on hand was 15 units (note the transposition). Inaccurate information also would result if, for instance, 15 units were actually on hand, yet the inventory report indicated only 10 units.

Completeness is the degree to which information includes data about every relevant object or event necessary to make a decision and includes that information only once. We use *relevant* in the sense of all objects or events that we *intended* to include. For example, in Chapter 7, you will learn that an accountant must ensure that an accounting system captures and records all *valid* accounting event data once and only once; otherwise, the accounting database is not complete. For instance, suppose the shipping department prepared 50 shipping notices for 50 actual shipments made for the day. Two of the notices were accidentally blown to the floor and were discarded with the trash. As a result, the billing department prepared customer invoices for only 48 shipments, not 50. On the other hand, if we recorded any or all of those shipments more than once, we would also fail to achieve the completeness quality.

In summary, the *effectiveness* of information can be measured in many ways. Those previously discussed and included in Exhibit 1.2 and Figure 1.6 (pg. 20) include *understandability*, *relevance* (or *reliability*), *timeliness* (or *availability*), *predictive value*, *feedback value*, *verifiability*, *neutrality* (or *freedom from bias*), *comparability*, *consistency*, and *integrity* (or *validity*, *accuracy*, and *completeness*). You will see these qualities again, in addition to those not discussed here (*efficiency*, *confidentiality*, and *compliance*), in subsequent chapters.

Documenting Information Qualities

One of the challenges when working with an information system is ensuring that desired information qualities exist within that system. Processes and controls are required to make sure the information qualities are present; ideally, those processes and controls are embedded in the system to keep you from constantly having to manually verify the information. The technique used to document which processes are associated with which information quality is a matrix. Generally, a **matrix** is a tool designed to help you analyze a situation and relate processes to desired results. **Figure 1.7** shows how you can use a matrix to match processes with qualities of information to provide reasonable assurance that, if the processes are effective, your goals for the information qualities will be achieved.

Conflicts Among the Information Qualities

Controls

Simultaneously achieving a *maximum* level for all the qualities of information is virtually impossible. In fact, for some of the qualities, an increased level of one generally requires a reduced level of another. In one instance, obtaining *complete* information for a decision may require delaying use of the information until all events related to the decision have

FIGURE 1.7 Information Qualities Matrix

Processes (with controls)	Information qualities			
	Effectiveness (timeliness)	Validity	Completeness	Accuracy
Process 1	✓	✓		
Process 2			✓	✓
Process 3		✓		
Process n	✓			✓

taken place. That delay may sacrifice the *timeliness* of the information. For example, to determine all the merchandise shipments made in November, an organization may have to wait until several days into December to make sure that all shipments get posted.

Let's look at another example. To obtain *accurate* information, you may carefully and methodically prepare the information, thus sacrificing the *timeliness* of the information. For example, to ensure the accuracy of a customer invoice, billing clerks might check the invoice for accuracy several times and then get their supervisor to initial the invoice, indicating that the supervisor also has checked the invoice for accuracy. These procedures certainly delay the mailing of the invoice.

Controls

Management Decision Making

We have asserted that the purpose of an information system is to facilitate an organization's business processes and to support management *decision making* by providing information that managers can use to plan and control the activities of the firm. Let's pursue the meaning and importance of decision making. Very simply, **decision making** is the process of making choices, which is the central activity of all management. Managers make decisions or choices that include what products to sell, in which markets to sell those products, what organizational structure to use, and how to direct and motivate employees. Herbert A. Simon, a Nobel Prize–winning economist, described decision making as a three-step process:

1. **Intelligence.** Searching the environment for conditions calling for a decision.
2. **Design.** Inventing, developing, and analyzing possible courses of action.
3. **Choice.** Selecting a course of action.[14]

Figure 1.8 (pg. 24) depicts these three steps. Analyze the figure to see what information is required for each step. Information from and about the environment and the organization is needed to recognize situations or problems requiring decisions. For example, information about economic trends, marketing intelligence, and likely competitor actions should help management recognize opportunities for new markets and products. Information about inefficient or overworked processes in the organization should focus management's attention on problems in the organization. Managers use information from inside and outside the organization to design courses of action. For example, information about personnel resources, production capacity, and available distribution channels should help management develop

---

[14]Herbert A. Simon, *The New Science of Management Decision* (New York: Harper & Row, 1960): 2.

FIGURE 1.8 Steps in Decision Making

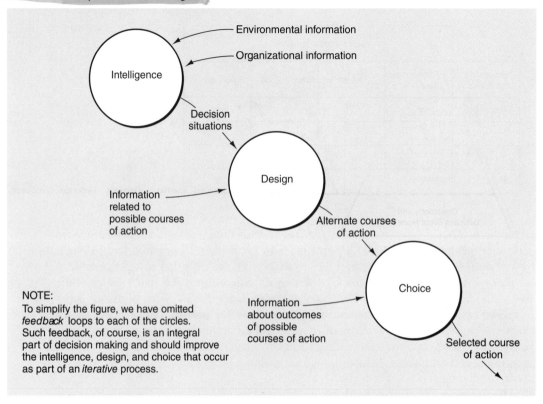

NOTE:
To simplify the figure, we have omitted *feedback* loops to each of the circles. Such feedback, of course, is an integral part of decision making and should improve the intelligence, design, and choice that occur as part of an *iterative* process.

alternative methods for producing and distributing a new product. Finally, a manager requires information about the possible outcomes from alternative courses of action. For example, to choose among alternative production options, a manager needs information about the costs and benefits of the alternatives or about the probability of success of each option.

The pyramid in **Figure 1.9** represents data flows related to the processing of business events. It emphasizes that operations and information flows are both horizontal and vertical and that there are several levels of management[15]. At the level of operations and business events processing, the flows are horizontal, as the information moves through operational units such as sales, the warehouse, and accounting. In the sales example of Figure 1.4 (pg. 16), the operational documents and records are the outputs of these horizontal flows.

Horizontal flows relate to specific business events, such as one shipment, or to individual inventory items. This information is narrow in scope, detailed, accurate, and comes largely from within the organization. The data captured at the operations and business event–processing level constitute the foundation for the vertical information flows that service a multilevel management function.

On the other hand, information useful to operations management personnel is often an aggregate of data related to several business events. For example, a report summarizing shipments made each day might be useful to the shipping manager. At the operations management level, supervisors use this type of information to monitor the daily functioning of their operating units. The vertical information useful to operations management is a summarized and tailored version of the information that flows horizontally.

---

[15]Because Figure 1.9 depicts data from business events, the vertical information flows upward. Other data, such as budgets, would flow downward.

FIGURE 1.9   Management Problem Structure and Information Requirements

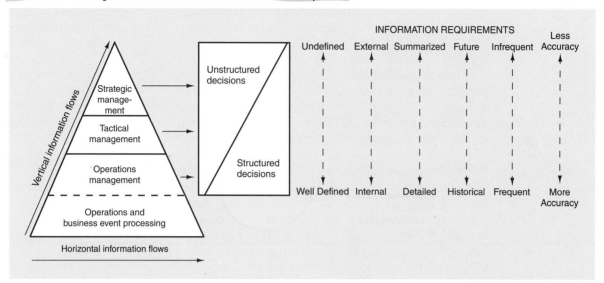

Tactical management requires information that focuses on relevant operational units and is more summarized, broader in scope, and need not be as accurate as the information used by operations management. Some external information may be required. For example, a warehousing and distribution manager might want information about the timeliness of shipments each month.

Finally, strategic management requires information to assess the environment and to project future events and conditions. Such information is even more summarized, broader in scope, and comes from outside the organization more than does the information used by tactical management. To be useful to division managers, chief financial officers (CFOs), and chief executive officers (CEOs), information must relate to longer time periods, be sufficiently broad in scope, and be summarized to provide a means for judging the long-term effectiveness of management policies. External financial statements, annual sales reports, and division income statements are but a few examples of strategic-level information. We should note, however, that current computer technology facilitates access to detailed data at all management levels.

The decision's structure, or lack thereof, also heavily influences the kind of information required to make a decision. *Structure* is the degree of repetition and routine in the decision. Structure implies that you have seen this very decision before and have developed procedures for making the decision. You can use the degree of structure inherent in each decision-making step to categorize the decisions as structured or unstructured. **Structured decisions** are those for which all three decision phases (intelligence, design, and choice) are relatively routine or repetitive. In fact, some decisions are so routine that a computer can be programmed to make them. For example, many organizations have automated the decision of when and how much credit to grant a customer when an order is received. At the time the customer's order is entered, the computer compares the amount of the order to the customer's credit limit, credit history, and outstanding balances. Using this information, the computer may grant credit, deny credit, or suggest a review by the credit department. These procedures are described in more detail in Chapter 10.

Consider, on the other hand, a manager's decision-making process when choosing what research and development projects to undertake in the next year. This is only one

Controls

example of an **unstructured decision**, one for which none of the decision phases (intelligence, design, or choice) are routine or repetitive. Of course, many—probably most—management decisions fall between the extreme examples of structured and unstructured decisions presented above. The three decision phases will vary in their degrees of routineness or repetitiveness.

Look again at Figure 1.9 (pg. 25) and see that it summarizes several concepts introduced in this section and also helps explain the nature of the characteristics associated with information used by the three levels of management for decision making. Further, this figure indicates the proportion of structured and unstructured decisions handled by the three management levels.

Information Qualities and Decision-Making Level

The level of the decision maker and the type of decision to be made determine the preeminence of certain information qualities. For example, strategic management may require information that is high in predictive value. Information used for strategic planning should help managers "see" the future and thereby assist them in formulating long-term plans. The strategic manager may be more concerned with accuracy than with timeliness and would therefore prefer an accurate but later quarterly sales report to a daily report with a higher degree of error. Operations management must make frequent decisions, with shorter lead times, and may therefore require the daily sales report to be able to react in a timely manner to changes in sales patterns. Operations management may require both timely and accurate information and may not be concerned about the predictive value of the information.

Conclusions About Management Decision Making

From Figures 1.8 and 1.9 (pp. 24, 25) and their related discussions, you can see that information needed for decision making can differ in degree of aggregation and detail, in source, and in fundamental character. You have also seen that the required qualities of information differ by decision type and level of management.

Within the organization, managers can secure inputs to their decisions directly from the environment or from direct observation of business processes. Managers can also receive information indirectly through the IS, which retrieves and presents operational and environmental information. As you understand more about the decisions to be made and can better anticipate the data needed to make those decisions, the IS can be designed to provide more of the required information. For example, in ever-increasing numbers, organizations' information systems are obtaining information about economic trends and indicators that is available in public databases. Because data requirements for structured decisions are well defined, we strive to improve our understanding of decisions so that we can make more structured decisions, anticipate the data needed for those decisions, and regularly provide those data through the IS.

Enterprise Systems

Let's conclude this section by asking the following question: How does the IS support the multiple information uses suggested by the preceding discussions? For example, how does the IS support such users as the organization's operations units, the organization's management, and people outside the organization? How does the IS supply the information needed by three levels of management? While all of the above are "business information users," they require radically different types or combinations of business information. One key component enabling the IS to meet the needs of this diverse constituency is the enterprise database. As noted in the Preface, the **enterprise database** is the central repository for all the data related to the enterprise's business activities and resources. IS processes—such as order entry, billing, and inventory—update the database. Output can be obtained by other IS processes and by other users, such as management. When processes or other users access the enterprise database, they are given a view of the database appropriate for their needs. For example, when entering the customer order in Figure 1.4 (pg. 16), the IS was given access to the *portion* of the database that was required, such as the applicable customer and inventory data.

The Accountant's Role in the Current Business Environment

Let's return to a discussion of the accountant as an information management and business measurement specialist that we began in the Preface, and examine the accountant's role in and for the modern business and the AIS. Regarding the AIS, the accountant can assume three roles: designer, user, and auditor.

As a *designer* of an AIS, the accountant brings knowledge of accounting principles, auditing principles, IS techniques, and systems development methods. In designing the AIS, the accountant might answer such questions as the following:

- What will be recorded (i.e., what is a recordable business event)?
- How will the event be recorded (i.e., what data elements will be captured and where will they be stored? For example, what ledger accounts will be used)?
- When will the event be recorded (i.e., before or after occurrence)?
- What controls will be necessary to provide valid, accurate, and complete records; to protect assets; and to ensure that the AIS can be audited?
- What reports will be produced, and when will they be produced?
- How much detail will the reports include?

It might be helpful to broaden our notion of the designer of an AIS. The designer role can also be thought of in terms of the consulting and advisory services in many accounting firms. But, regardless of the terminology, accountants often participate in designing and implementing the AIS. Today, these consulting firms also recruit accountants straight out of college—soon, perhaps you!

Accountants perform a number of functions within organizations, including those of controller, treasurer, tax specialist, financial analyst, cost accountant, general accountant, and IS and budgeting specialist. In all cases, accountants *use* the AIS to perform their functions. Their effectiveness depends on how well they know the AIS and the technology used to implement it. For instance, to analyze financial information (e.g., to function as a financial analyst or managerial accountant), an accountant must know what data are stored in the AIS, how to access those data, what analysis tools exist and how to use them, and how to present the information using available report-writing facilities.

As a *user*, the accountant may also be called on to participate in the AIS design process. In fact, an IS user should insist on being involved to make sure that a new system contains required features. To be effective in the design process, the user must know how systems are developed, the techniques used to develop a system, and the technology that will be used in a new system.

As internal and external auditors, accountants *audit* the AIS or provide the assurance *services* mentioned earlier in this chapter. Auditors are interested in the reliability of the accounting data and of the reports produced by the system. They may test the system's controls, assess the system's efficiency and effectiveness, and participate in the system design process. To be effective, the auditor must possess knowledge of systems development techniques, of controls, of the technology used in the IS, and of the design and operation of the AIS.

Summary

Over the years, the International Federation of Accountants has published many documents emphasizing the importance of technology in accounting. In October 2007, they published the International Education Practice Statement (IEPS) 2, *Information Technology for Professional Accountants*,[16] "to assist IFAC member bodies in the implementation of generally accepted good practice in the education and development of professional accountants" (pg. 4). IEPS 2 describes in detail the technology competencies required by audit professionals, systems designers, systems evaluators, and managers of information systems. If there is still doubt on your part as to the importance of the topic, in response to an earlier IFAC document (Education Guideline 11), in 1996, the largest member body of IFAC, the American Institute of Certified Public Accountants (AICPA), published the report, *Information Technology Competencies in the Accounting Profession: AICPA Implementation Strategies for IFAC International Education Guideline No. 11*,[17] to encourage implementation of the guideline in the United States. Although 15 years old, the words of this document still ring true. Several passages in the AICPA report serve to emphasize the importance of the AIS course in your studies, as well as to validate the approach that we take in presenting the AIS material to you.

Regarding the importance of information technology to an accounting career, the AICPA concludes, "... professional accounting has merged and developed with IT to such an extent that one can hardly conceive of accounting independent from IT" (pg. 5). The AICPA goes on to describe three important challenges currently facing the accounting profession. Information technologies are:

- affecting the way in which organizations operate;
- changing the nature and economies of accounting activity;
- changing the competitive environment in which accountants operate (pg. 6).

In discussing the teaching of technology concepts, the AICPA report reads, "... it is important to emphasize the need for strategic, conceptual understanding of information technology as a resource to enable achievement of business objectives. A *strategic, conceptual understanding* of information technology focuses on the functions of each information component, the objectives of technology achievements for each information technology component, the potential business impact of new technology ... understanding the concepts behind the technology helps students to learn to use, evaluate, and

---

[16]Available online as part of the *Handbook of International Education Pronouncements, International Education Practice Statement 2: Information Technologies for Professional Accountants*, International Federation of Accountants (IFAC) (www.ifac.org, accessed January 15, 2010).

[17]IFAC International Education Guideline 11 is a predecessor to the IFAC's current International Education Statement series. The material in the remainder of this section is taken from *Information Technology Competencies in the Accounting Profession: AICPA Implementation Strategies for IFAC International Education Guideline No. 11* (New York: AICPA, 1996). Page numbers in parentheses in this section refer to that report.

control technology more effectively … encourages students and professionals to concentrate on applying and using technology to achieve business purposes" (pg. 7).

When you have completed your journey through AIS, we hope that you will confirm that we have followed that philosophy in this text. Further, we firmly believe that, years from now, you will conclude that the knowledge and skills developed in the AIS course were central to your career success.

Key Terms

system, 13

subsystem, 13

information system
(IS), 14

management information
system [MIS], 14

accounting information
system (AIS), 15

operations process, 16

management process, 16

information, 18

data, 18

effectiveness, 19

efficiency, 19

confidentiality, 19

integrity, 19

availability, 19

compliance, 19

reliability, 19

understandability, 21

relevance, 21

timeliness, 21

predictive value, 21

feedback value, 21

verifiability, 21

neutrality, 21

freedom from bias, 21

comparability, 21

consistent, 22

validity, 22

accuracy, 22

completeness, 22

matrix, 22

decision making, 23

structured decisions, 25

unstructured decision, 26

enterprise database, 26

Review Questions

RQ 1-1 Describe this textbook's three themes.

RQ 1-2 What 10 elements are included in the study of AIS?

RQ 1-3 A system must have organization, interrelationships, integration, and central objectives. Why must each of these four components be present in a system?

RQ 1-4 Are the terms *system* and *subsystem* synonymous? Explain your answer.

RQ 1-5 What is the relationship between an AIS and an IS?

RQ 1-6 What are three logical components of a business process? Define the functions of each. How do the components interact with one another?

RQ 1-7 Why is the information system important to the organization?

RQ 1-8 What are the two major functions of an information system?

RQ 1-9 What factors distinguish *data* from *information*?

RQ 1-10 What are the qualities of information presented in this chapter? Explain each quality in your own words and give an example of each.

RQ 1-11 What are the three steps in decision making?

RQ 1-12 Refer to Figure 1.9 (pg. 25). Characterize the horizontal information flows and the vertical information flows.

RQ 1-13   What factors distinguish the types of information required by strategic managers, by tactical managers, and by operational managers?

RQ 1-14   In your own words, explain *structure* as it relates to decisions.

RQ 1-15   What three roles can an accountant fill in relation to the AIS? Describe them.

Discussion Questions

DQ 1-1   "I just want to be a good accountant; technology does not interest me." Comment on this statement, considering today's technology environment.

DQ 1-2   Examine Figure 1.1 (pg. 9). Based on any work experience you have had, with which elements are you least comfortable? With which are you most comfortable? Discuss your answers.

DQ 1-3   Examine Figure 1.1. Based on your college education to date, with which elements are you most comfortable? With which are you least comfortable? Discuss your answers.

DQ 1-4   Why might you have more trouble assessing the success of a not-for-profit organization or federal government entitlement program than you would have judging the success of a business organization?

DQ 1-5   Why must you have knowledge of a system's objectives to study that system?

DQ 1-6   Do you think your accounting education is preparing you effectively to practice accounting? Why or why not? Discuss, from both a short-term (i.e., immediately upon graduation) and a long-term (i.e., 5 to 10 years after beginning your career) standpoint.

DQ 1-7   Examine Figure 1.9 (pg. 25). Discuss the importance of horizontal information flows to the daily operations of a manufacturing entity.

DQ 1-8   Examine Figure 1.9. Discuss how vertical information flows may be important to the executive director of an organization that is a public charity.

DQ 1-9   Give several examples not mentioned in the chapter of potential conflicts between pairs of information qualities.

DQ 1-10   Regarding financial reporting, which quality of information do you think should be superior to all other qualities? Discuss your answer.

DQ 1-11   Between relevance and reliability, which information quality is most important? Support your answer with examples.

DQ 1-12   Describe two structured decisions and two unstructured decisions. Discuss the relative amount of structure in each decision.

DQ 1-13   "To be of any value, a modern information system must assist all levels of management." Discuss.

Short Problems

SP 1-1   Match the items in the following two lists by matching the letter (or letters) of the information quality (qualities) that best describes the information quality violation presented in the second column. Some letters may not be used at all and some may be used more than once.

A. Accuracy	___1. Clerks at Easley Corp. enter customer orders into PCs connected to the accounting system. The clerks are supposed to enter a code into a field to indicate if the order was mailed, faxed, or phoned in. But they do not always enter this code. Consequently, data on the recorded orders regarding the type of order is not reliable.
B. Completeness	___2. Allan in the shipping department has been given the job of monitoring shipments to make sure that they are shipped in a timely manner. To do this, he uses a monthly report of items ordered but not shipped in the past month.
C. Relevance	___3. At Fenwick, Inc., warehouse personnel write the picked quantity on the picking ticket as the goods are picked from the shelf. These clerks are not very careful, and the recorded picked quantities are often wrong.
D. Timeliness	___4. Barth Company has been recording shipments of goods that were never ordered by their customers.
E. Validity	___5. Shipments at Southwick Company are entered into PCs in the shipping department office. The paperwork often gets lost between the shipping dock and the office, and some shipments do not get entered.

SP 1-2   Consider the inventory of a retailer. How can the qualities of information, as described in this chapter, help enable the efficiency and effectiveness of the organization?

Problems

P 1-1   In his first address as Chairman of the Board of the American Institute of Certified Public Accountants (AICPA), Robert K. Elliott said:

> "Knowledge leveraging will shape a wide range of CPA services. CPAs will be able to identify relevant information and its sources, perform modeling, devise and apply performance measures of all kinds, design systems to obtain needed information, advise on controls and security, and otherwise ensure relevance and reliability. CPAs will identify and deploy knowledge needed for strategic planning and investments, for marketing decisions, for monitoring internal and external conditions, for conducting daily operations, for maximizing the productivity of employee behavior, and for measuring the effectiveness of operations, personnel and processes. All this and more."[18]

---

[18]Robert K. Elliott, "Who Are We as a Profession—and What Must We Become?" *Journal of Accountancy* (February 2000): 84.

Write a paper (your professor will tell you how long the paper should be) to discuss ways in which this chapter agrees with this quote. Discuss any disagreements. Do you think that the CPA should be performing these services? Why or why not?

P 1-2   Conduct research on the expansion of the role of the accountant into areas such as nonfinancial information, assurance services, and similar functions. Write a paper (your professor will tell you how long the paper should be) to discuss the positives and negatives of this expansion.

P 1-3   Conduct research on the implementation of Section 404 of the Sarbanes-Oxley Act of 2002. Write a paper (your professor will tell you how long the paper should be) to discuss how accountants within an organization are involved in helping their organizations comply with this section. Describe also how accountants in public accounting and consulting are affected by this section of SOX.

P 1-4   Assume that a manager can obtain information from the organization's database in three ways: by direct inquiry using a computer, by a daily printout, and by a monthly report. Using the qualities of information discussed in this chapter (*understandability, relevance, timeliness, predictive value/feedback value, neutrality/freedom from bias, comparability, consistency, validity, accuracy,* and *completeness*), compare and contrast these three sources of information.

P 1-5   Using Internet resources, locate openings for at least three jobs, other than traditional public accounting positions, which require strong accounting and technology skills. Select one of these jobs, and develop a plan to get you from your current level of knowledge to a point where you will qualify for the job.

P 1-6   Contact a CPA or CA firm to find out about their current expectations regarding your technical knowledge as an entry-level accountant. Write a brief memo (your professor will tell you how long) summarizing what you learned.

P 1-7   Find the most current listing of the CICA's Top Ten IT Issues. Research and write a paper on the accounting and business implications for the number 1 item on the list. Include any external pressures that may impact the inclusion of this item on the list. Your professor will tell you how long your paper should be.

P 1-8   Find the most current listing of the CICA's Top Ten IT Issues Compare the listing to prior years' listings. Identify and discuss trends among the years. Your professor will tell you how long your paper should be.

CHAPTER 2

Enterprise Systems

Learning Objectives

After reading this chapter, you should be able to:

- Describe enterprise systems and enterprise resource planning systems.
- Illustrate the organization value chain.
- Describe the relationship of the organization value chain and an enterprise system.
- Demonstrate the value of systems integration.
- Describe how an enterprise system supports major business event processes.
- Enumerate the pros and cons of implementing enterprise systems.

At any time, but especially in difficult economic times, it is important for decision makers to be able to access and use enterprise-wide information. When the global economy experienced a downturn, Hubbell Lighting Inc. was able to take advantage of its prior technology investments to align the company's supply with customer demand.

Hubbell Lighting provides lighting for commercial and residential applications. The company's global supply chain is diversified and complex because of the variety of products provided and markets served. The supply chain includes diversity in product life cycles, sales channels, and supply models. It also includes multinational manufacturing operations and outsourcing. It would be difficult for a company like this to make management decisions without an excellent information system.

During good economic times, Hubbell chose an SAP ERP system to standardize technology across 18 business systems the company inherited through acquisitions. The company also implemented SAP's NetWeaver platform to enable communication between the ERP system and other systems within and outside the corporate boundaries. NetWeaver allows Hubbell's sales agents to use specialized software to retrieve information such as stock availability and order status.

Because of Hubbell's state-of-the art attitude and information system, during a recent period of economic volatility it was able to implement Kinaxis's RapidResponse software to help identify and respond to unexpected changes in the supply chain. Being able to use a corporate-wide ERP and having the ability to deal with unexpected events helps provide Hubbell with a competitive advantage during good or bad economic times.[1]

Hubbell Lighting undertook its SAP project to take advantage of various benefits, including the competitive advantage that can accrue to organizations that integrate business processes and implement ERP systems. As Hubbell learned, however, having such a system in place can lead to significant additional benefits when management needs information to make decisions in difficult economic times. To function effectively in any modern organization, you need to understand that the enterprise-wide integration of information systems and ERP software, when effectively implemented, can provide management information to support critical decisions.

In this chapter, we explore the enterprise systems that assist in the operation of an organization's business processes and integrate, in the enterprise database, all of the data related to those business processes. We describe these systems and the functionality they provide. We broadly introduce the business processes that ERP systems support. What you learn here, although important in its own right, will provide important background for your study in later chapters of the text.

Introduction

The Enterprise Systems icon appears here to indicate that this entire chapter is about enterprise systems. The other two icons, Controls and e-Business, will be placed at appropriate places throughout the remainder of the chapter.

Enterprise Systems

As defined in the Preface and Chapter 1, **enterprise systems** (also known as **enterprise-wide information systems** and **enterprise information systems**) integrate the business process functionality and information from all of an organization's functional areas, such as marketing and sales, cash receipts, purchasing, cash disbursements, human resources, production and logistics, and business reporting (including financial reporting). They make possible the coordinated operation of these functions and provide a central information resource for the organization. For example, the enterprise system might facilitate the purchase of some office equipment by:

- Providing an electronic order form (a purchase requisition).
- Applying business rules to ensure that complete information and proper approvals have been obtained. For instance, the system might need to connect to accounting processes and data to determine that the purchase is within the requester's budget.
- Routing the order to the appropriate authorities for specific approvals. The system may need to connect to human resource processes and data to determine appropriate approvers.

---

[1]The sources of this vignette are the following: "Supply Chain Management amid Dim Economic Conditions: A Look at How Hubbell Lighting Mitigates Its Risks," *IndustryWeek.com*, August 14, 2009; "Lighten Up: Recessionary Times Call for Business Intelligence-Based Insight to Lean Supply Chain Performance," *Manufacturing Business Technology* (www.mbtmag.com), March 1, 2009; "SAP Customer Success Story: Hubbell Lighting," www.sap.com (accessed January 18, 2010).

- Sending the order to a buyer in purchasing for preparation of a purchase order to be sent to a vendor. The system may assist the buyer with selecting an appropriate vendor, perhaps by consulting a list of pre-approved vendors.
- Connecting directly to the enterprise systems of business partners, such as the vendor that will sell you office equipment.

E-Business

- Completing the business process by making data available for ongoing management and analysis of the purchase and subsequent related events. For example, data would be available for (1) receiving equipment and enabling routing of the equipment to the purchasing party; (2) projecting funding requirements to pay for purchases; (3) analyzing the vendor's performance (e.g., timeliness, quality, and price); and (4) comparing the purchasing party's budget and actual expenditures.

Notice that there are several points during this purchase process where controls might be implemented by the enterprise system. For example, by ensuring that proper approvals are obtained and that the purchase is within the purchaser's budget, the enterprise system reduces the risk that unauthorized purchases will be made. Similarly, by using only vendors on a pre-approved list for purchase orders, the chances of a purchasing agent engaging in fraudulent purchases with a bogus vendor are reduced, if not eliminated.

Controls

The purchase of goods or services is just one example of a **business event**. Business events include any meaningful change in the state of an enterprise, such as creating a new employee record, submitting a purchase order to a vendor, receiving a payment from a customer, picking goods from a warehouse and delivering them to the shipping department, and revaluing inventory. Even customer queries about inventory availability can be business events, should the company decide it is important for operations or decision making. Enterprise systems are used to capture events and implement controls related to the events.

Organizations install enterprise systems to differentiate themselves from their competitors. For example, with an enterprise system, an organization should be able to conduct business in a timelier and less costly manner and provide services to its customers that would otherwise not be possible. Also, as previously noted, the enterprise system collects data about each business event, as well as data about an organization's business partners and other aspects of the business, such as inventory, manufacturing, and human resources. This data contains nuggets of gold that management can mine and use to monitor the organization's operations, improve performance, and create additional business opportunities. We'll tell you more about the advantages and disadvantages of enterprise systems as our discussion continues.

Enterprise Resource Planning (ERP) Systems

Enterprise resource planning (ERP) systems are software packages that can be used for the core systems necessary to support enterprise systems. Think of the relationship between enterprise systems and ERP this way: An organization's enterprise system might comprise customer relationship management (CRM) software from one vendor, warehouse and shipping software that was developed internally by the company's IT personnel, and an ERP system from a second vendor. Any combinations like this are possible.

The point is that a company might adopt all modules offered by an ERP vendor. In that particular case, the ERP system and the enterprise system are, for all practical matters, one and the same. Or the ERP system might be one of many software solutions that comprise the enterprise system. You might find it helpful to think about enterprise systems as the general phenomenon and ERP systems as a specific instance of the

Enterprise Systems

phenomenon. A number of ERP systems are commercially available. At present, the dominant player in the large system arena is SAP, whose ERP product commands the largest percentage of the Fortune 500 market. **Table 2.1** lists some of the major ERP vendors and the type of customer they serve. Note, however, that because of consolidation of companies, any list of ERP software is subject to frequent changes.

ERP products are designed to offer integration of virtually all of an organization's major business functions. **Figure 2.1**, depicts this integration in the SAP Business Suite. The square in the center depicts the core of the suite, including Financials (e.g., financial and managerial accounting, treasury and risk management), Human Resources (HR), Corporate Services (e.g., real estate management, project and portfolio management), and Operations (e.g., procurement and logistics, product development and manufacturing). Above and around this core, you see four modules—SRM, PLM, SCM, and CRM—that an organization might adopt to extend the core system's functionality. The SAP NetWeaver® portion of the figure is explained in Technology Summary 2.2 later in this chapter.

The SRM, PLM, SCM, and CRM modules that you see in Figure 2.1 are examples of modules that complement the core elements of an ERP system to provide the full range of functionality required of an enterprise system. Some of these modules, such as Web interfaces for customers and business partners, may be required to engage in e-business (discussed in Chapter 3). You might choose to acquire the modules provided by the ERP vendor, such as those shown in Figure 2.1, or you might choose to acquire them from a third party. The most common add-on modules include the following:

- **Customer relationship management (CRM) software**, such as Microsoft Dynamics CRM, Oracle's Siebel CRM, and Salesforce.com's CRM, builds and maintains an organization's customer-related database. This data is collected from multiple customer interactions, such as the Web, call centers, field sales, service calls, and dealer and partner networks. The data are aggregated, managed, and coordinated across the entire organization (e.g., channels, departments, lines of business, worldwide) to support identification, acquisition, and retention of customers and to maximize the benefits of those relationships. CRM can help make it easy for a customer to do business with an organization and to make customers feel that they are dealing with one unified organization. You have experienced the

TABLE 2.1   Selected ERP Vendors[a]

Company Name	Market[b]
Oracle[c]	Large
SAP	Large
Lawson	Large, SME
Infor™ ®	Large, SME, Small
Microsoft Dynamics™ [d]	SME, Small
Sage Group	SME, Small

Notes:
[a] Table contains several companies, listed in order of market segments and alphabetically within market, that are generally considered to be leaders in providing ERP solutions.
[b] Large: Sells mostly to large enterprises (>$1b revenues). SME: Sells mostly to small and medium-sized enterprises ($30m–$1b revenues). Small: Sells mostly to enterprises with <$30m in revenues. It should be noted that most of the organizations listed are currently expanding outside of their traditional markets.
[c] Includes PeopleSoft, Inc. and JD Edwards & Company.
[d] Microsoft Dynamics includes AX (Axapta), GP (Great Plains), NAV (Navision), and SL (Solomon).

FIGURE 2.1 SAP Business Suite

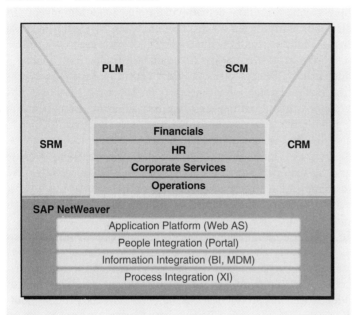

Source: Copyright by SAP AG. Reprinted with permission from SAP.

functionality of a CRM system if you have set up an account with Amazon.com or other Web vendors. These vendors keep track of such things as your name, address, and purchases. In this way, they can personalize your shopping experience and increase their business by making the experience pleasant and more efficient for you and by offering to sell you products that are consistent with your buying habits. For example, Amazon.com also looks across its customer base and suggests items to you that other people with your purchasing habits have bought.

- **Customer self-service (CSS) software**, often an extension of CRM software, allows an organization's customers to complete an inquiry, perform a task (including sales), or troubleshoot problems without the aid of the organization's employees. These solutions integrate with ERP systems to allow customers to check the status of their orders, review inventory availability, and even check production plans. Vendors such as Broad Daylight offer self-service solutions as well as agent-assisted solutions to assist call center employees in much the same way that self-service solutions assist customers directly. Again, you have experienced such software when making purchases on the Internet. In addition to Internet purchases, retail outlets such as grocery stores are installing "self-service" options for customers. These options range from check-out queues dedicated to customers who do not want to wait in lines, to hand-held scanners that customers use to scan their items at the point of selection, thus eliminating the need for handling items again when paying.
- **Sales force automation (SFA) software**, such as that from Salesforce.com, automates sales tasks such as order processing, contact management, inventory monitoring, order tracking, and employee performance evaluation. Even though SFA automates sales tasks, which CRM does not, the two terms are often used interchangeably.

- **Supply chain management (SCM) software** helps plan and execute the steps in an organization's supply chain, including demand planning; acquiring inventory; and manufacturing, distributing, and selling the product. Kinaxis's RapidResponse software, used by Hubbell Lighting, fits into this category of software.
- **Product life-cycle management (PLM) software** manages product data during a product's life, beginning with the design of the product, continuing through manufacture, and culminating in the disposal of the product at the end of its life. PLM software integrates data across many units of an organization, such as engineering, logistics, and marketing, and data from partner organizations, such as vendors, contract manufacturers, and distributors. For example, Staples, Inc.'s internal designers, buyers, and financial experts use PLM software to collaborate with business partners, including designers, manufacturers, and quality-test houses, around the world to design and develop Staples-branded products.[2] PLM software is offered by vendors of engineering software, ERP vendors, and specialized providers such as Siemens, Arena Solutions, and Oracle.
- **Supplier relationship management (SRM) software** manages the interactions with the organizations that supply the goods and services to an enterprise just as CRM software streamlines the processes between the enterprise and its customers. SRM functionality includes procurement and contract management. The goal of SRM is to reduce product costs and production costs and to enhance product quality. SAP's SRM module, for example, can automate requisitioning new inventory and the paying of vendors once orders are received into the system, making the procurement process more efficient and building goodwill with vendors.
- Other third-party modules extract data from ERP systems and from legacy systems that may still exist within an organization (or subsidiary of the organization). For instance, Oracle's Hyperion Software focuses on financial and accounting applications but is very effective at executing consolidations of financial information for multinationals.

E-Business

SAP and other similar products reflect large ERP systems made up of a number of modules that can be selected for implementation, based on specific needs. However, the ERP system modules may not be the best software for every organization. The **best-of-breed approach** combines modules from various vendors to create an information system that better meets an organization's needs than a standard ERP system. Typically, third-party add-ons are selected by organizations to obtain *best-of-breed* functionality for CRM, CSS, SFA, or other software solutions. There are potential problems related to a best-of-breed approach. The approach may sacrifice the tight integration offered by ERP systems because the third-party modules must be connected together and to the ERP system. Errors may occur during the translation and transmission between modules. The organization may also experience higher total licensing, implementation, and maintenance costs than with an ERP system from a single ERP provider. However, these problems are being solved by a number of integration approaches and products, as described next.

Third-party modules are connected to the ERP system using **middleware**, a software product that connects two or more separate applications or software modules. Middleware might be used to stitch together a number of legacy systems, an ERP system, best-of-breed applications, and Web-based applications. This middleware might be an **application programming interface (API)**, which is a means for connecting to a

---

[2]L. Sullivan, "Retailers Ply Their Own Brands," *InformationWeek*, April 18, 2005, pp. 61–62, 66–67.

Technology Summary 2.1

EVENT-DRIVEN ARCHITECTURE (EDA)

Event-driven architecture (EDA) is an approach to designing and building enterprise systems in which business events trigger messages to be sent by middleware between independent software modules that are completely unaware of each other. This differs from the traditional, internally driven, enterprise architectures. Event-driven processes operate in the following manner:

1. Each business event is handled individually as it appears, rather than waiting for a batch of events to accumulate. Business events are then processed in a timely manner.

2. The business unit that experiences a business event "pushes" the event to the recipient rather than waiting for the recipient to request, or "pull," the event. Recipients learn immediately about relevant business events.

3. Business events are pushed immediately and simultaneously to all interested parties. For example, when a vendor sends a notice that a shipment will be delayed, interested parties such as purchasing, receiving, manufacturing, sales, and the customer are notified.

4. The meaning and attributes of each business event are documented—as a process is developed—and are shared across multiple processes within the system.

5. Event notifications are managed in a systematic way to ensure that event data are sent to the correct recipient at the right time and that there is appropriate follow-up.

These technical-level design aspects of an EDA generate two business-level opportunities that enable the enterprise to operate in real time and to choose the best available modules for the enterprise system—the best-of-breed approach to software selection. A "real-time enterprise" driven by an EDA experiences reduced delays and business processing overhead, resulting in more responsive and flexible business units. For example, senders and receivers can operate asynchronously, and the sender is not tied up waiting for the receiver to respond or to process the event. And, not being restricted to software modules provided by the ERP vendor or those that can be connected to existing ERP and legacy systems, the organization can put together an enterprise system that is more closely tailored to the needs of each business unit and business process. These modules need not know about the existence or location of any other modules. When a business event occurs, they send an event notification to the middleware (also known as a "publish" or "send"), and the middleware notifies those modules that have asked to receive this type of event (also known as "subscribe").

Source: Carol Sliwa, "Event-Driven Architecture Poised for Wide Adoption," *Computerworld*, May 12, 2003, p. 8; Roy Schulte, "A Real-Time Enterprise Is Event-Driven," Gartner, Inc. Research Note T-18-2037, September 26, 2002.

system or application provided by the developer of that application. For example, the Process Integration (XI) portion of SAP NetWeaver (refer to Figure 2.1 on pg. 37) would provide an API for connecting SAP to a piece of legacy software or to a third-party module such as CRM. As another example, the Microsoft Dynamics Snap line of tools connects Dynamics ERP software (e.g., Dynamics GP, Dynamics SL, and Dynamics AX) to the Microsoft Office productivity suite.

Enterprise application integration (EAI) is an approach that combines processes, software, standards, and hardware to link two or more systems together, allowing them to act as one system. *EAI* can be used to connect pieces of an enterprise system to legacy systems, or to add-on modules such as CRM software. EAI is also an approach to connecting the enterprise systems of different organizations, such as would be needed for B2B integrations.

Technology Summary 2.1 describes event-driven architecture, which is an alternative approach to integration whereby loosely coupled applications react intelligently to changes in conditions and launch several responses rather than waiting to be called into action. Communications-broker software called **Enterprise Services Bus (ESB)** uses standardized protocols to let event-driven applications communicate in a less expensive manner than can the tightly coupled, synchronous EAI platforms. ESBs may be the means by which *Web Services*, another method used for systems integration, will be implemented. We describe the Web Services approach in Chapter 3.

Technology Summary 2.2 describes NetWeaver, a Web Services platform from SAP (refer to Figure 2.1 on pg. 37) used to build applications that integrate business processes and databases from a number of sources within and between organizations.

Technology Summary 2.3 describes business process management (BPM), a concept much larger than systems integration that provides a comprehensive method for

---

Technology Summary 2.2

SAP NETWEAVER

SAP NetWeaver is a platform or collection of capabilities constructed from a number of SAP products that work with each other to make applications work together. NetWeaver is the technology upon which SAP's Business Suite is built, a Web-based bundle of business applications and an alternative to SAP's module-based ERP system. The following figure depicts the core capabilities of SAP NetWeaver: the integration of people, information, and processes.

We'll describe here a few of the SAP NetWeaver integration components that are related to the discussion of systems and applications integration. The Enterprise Portal (Portal, Collaboration, and Knowledge Management) gives users access on a single screen/

consistent user interface to software and data that they need for their job, using links to, for example, SAP, e-mail, calendar, an intranet, and the Internet. Business Intelligence integrates information from various sources and processes inside and outside the organization. Master Data Management provides consistency of data (e.g., formats) within and across applications and systems. The Exchange Infrastructure (Integration Broker and Business Process Management) allows different applications within and between organizations (i.e., B2B) to communicate by, for example, sending, receiving, and translating messages. The Business Process management component allows systems to monitor a complex series of events and react to them automatically.

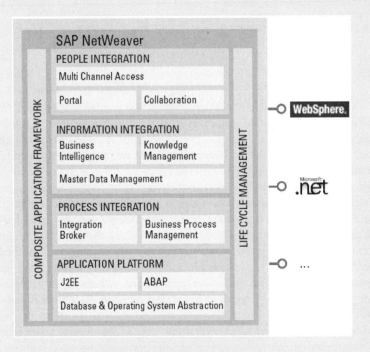

Source: Ellen Monk and Bret Wagner, *Concepts in Enterprise Resource Planning*, 2nd edition (Thomson Course Technology, 2006); Dan Woods and Jeffrey Word, *SAP NetWeaver® for Dummies* (John Wiley and Sons, Inc., 2004). Figure reprinted with permission from John Wiley and Sons, Inc.

Technology Summary 2.3

BUSINESS PROCESS MANAGEMENT (BPM)

Business process management (BPM), a term often used interchangeably with business process management systems, includes modeling, automating, managing, and optimizing business processes. BPM usually includes the following:

- A design environment for modeling and documenting business processes. This is often integrated with the process engine to support iterative design and implementation efforts for maximum process agility.
- Conversion, wherever possible, of manual processes to electronic processes.

- A BPM engine to execute processes, including calls for manual execution of tasks (i.e., workflow), automated tasks, and calls to other applications (e.g., an ERP, legacy applications), to services (e.g., Web Services), or to external partners (i.e., e-business).
- Flexible interfaces for developers, users, and linking to other applications.
- The BPM engine that is separated from data and business rules on which the engine operates, thus facilitating changes to facts, rules, and process flows.
- An audit trail of all process activity to provide visibility about the status of processes and to enable process improvement and optimization.

Source: "A Closer Look at BPM," Ultimus, Inc., January 2005 (www.ultimus.com, accessed January 18, 2010); Setrag Khoshafian, "Web Services and Virtual Enterprises," © Tect, 2002, accessed on January 18, 2010 at www.webservicesarchitect.com/downloads.asp.

integrating manual and automated internal processes, applications, and systems, as well as integration to external partners and services.

Originally, the implementation of ERP systems was targeted to large multinational manufacturers such as General Motors, Goodyear, and General Mills. Such early adoptions made sense because companies like these expected to see the greatest benefits from ERP systems; large multilocation and multidivision companies often present the greatest challenges to managers who want to coordinate worldwide activities and mine data from corporate databases to improve overall organizational decision making. In addition, ERP systems arose from early manufacturing requirement planning (MRP) applications, which were specifically designed for manufacturing companies; hence, it is no surprise that the early adopters were in the business of making products.

ERP systems have seen many improvements over time. Most ERP system vendors now offer solutions for a wide variety of industries, such as retail, banking, financial, entertainment, construction, and so on. As most large organizations have implemented ERP solutions, to look for new growth areas, ERP vendors are adding products targeted at smaller organizations. ERP systems allow companies to standardize systems across multiple locations and multiple divisions to link business processes and data in a consistent fashion and provide organization-wide data accessibility. To provide the flexibility to address a multilocation or international organization, an ERP package must have the ability to add capacity as needed.

Not only were early adopters primarily involved with manufacturing, but also they were very large enterprises, primarily because implementation costs were so enormous that smaller companies simply could not withstand the economic burden. These systems typically took a year or more to implement, at a cost of up to hundreds of millions of dollars, which necessitated a similarly significant return in benefits. As advances in the technology underlying these systems have evolved, small and medium-sized enterprises (SMEs) have driven the new implementation base. You can see in Table 2.1 (pg. 36) that there are some major players in the market for ERP systems for SMEs. For instance, Microsoft's acquisition of Great Plains and Navision and formation of the Dynamics line of products speaks to the importance of this market segment.

Enterprise Systems Value Chain

To examine the role that enterprise systems play in the success of an organization, you can look at the activities performed by the organization as a **value chain**, a chain of activities performed by the organization to transform inputs into outputs valued by the customer. An organization creates a competitive advantage by creating more value for its customers than does its competition. Organizations create value by performing the activities at lower cost or by enhancing differentiation of their products or services.[3] Differentiation is created through production of superior quality with innovative products and services, by responsiveness to customer requirements for such features as product design and customization, and through quality of service during and after the completion of a sale.

You may be familiar with Dell[TM], Inc. (www.dell.com), the online seller of computers, printers, TVs, MP3 players, and related goods and services. The company has a reputation as an extremely efficient manufacturer and distributor. Dell's value chain is, in fact, one of the best in the world. Dell takes raw materials, manufactures computers and other products, and delivers them to customers in a timely manner at an attractive price. One key to Dell's success is its business processes and the application of IT to drive those processes and to integrate its suppliers, customers, manufacturing, shipping, and after-sales support (i.e., the value chain). Dell holds nearly 2,000 patents on processes and products, including processes such as "order preparation and shipping" (U.S. Patent 6560509). In this section, we describe some ways that enterprise systems play a key role in creating the value customers seek.

Figure 2.2 depicts a generic organization value chain and value system. The activities in the value chain, the value activities, are *business processes* that convert inputs to valued outputs. For example, the "move raw materials" activity converts cash into raw materials for the production activity. These activities may be divided into two categories: primary and support activities.[4] The primary activities are depicted in the figure and are those directly involved in marketing, selling, producing, and delivering the good or service to the customer, including functions such as moving raw materials into and around the organization, producing and delivering goods to the customer, and performing services such as installation and after-sales support. The supporting activities provide the supporting infrastructure to enable the primary activities and include functions such as procurement, information technology (IT), human resources, and accounting. Note that we depict the value chain as overlaying the functional activities of an organization. To efficiently and effectively serve the customer, the value chain must traverse these traditionally independent activities, often referred to as "silos,"[5] and join these activities together into an end-to-end business process (often called *cross-functional integration*).

IT has been able to assist in creating additional value by reducing the cost or improving quality in the performance of these activities. For example, IT has been successfully applied to optimize the cost and quality of raw materials by providing information to help select the right material at the right cost from the right vendor. Also,

[3]M. E. Porter and V. E. Millar, "How Information Gives You Competitive Advantage," *Harvard Business Review*, July–August 1985, pp. 149–160.

[4]M. E. Porter and V. E. Millar, "How Information Gives You Competitive Advantage," *Harvard Business Review*, July–August 1985, pp. 149–160.

[5]The term *silo* is used to refer to organization functions—such as product development, marketing, and manufacturing—that stand alone, disconnected and often unaware of activities taking place in the other functions.

FIGURE 2.2   Value Chain and Value System

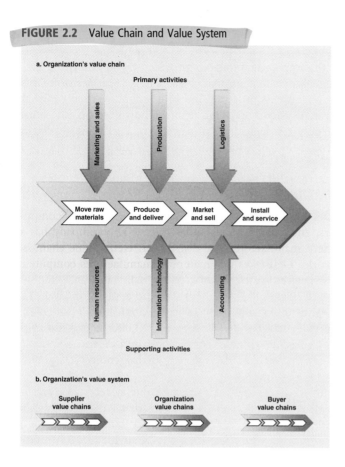

IT has been applied to the production-scheduling process to balance the cost and timeliness of manufacturing. Notice that in both of these examples, IT assisted in creating value by lowering costs and differentiating the product. In the first case, quality differentiates the product in that we obtain the materials that allow us to manufacture a product that is consistent with our quality objectives. In the second case, the timeline of product availability was the differentiating factor.

In these two examples, IT assisted in value creation within individual activities. However, value activities are interdependent and need to be closely coordinated to be most effective in creating value for the customer. As described in the next section, enterprise systems are required to provide the necessary interactivity (and interbusiness processes), communication, and coordination. For example, to really optimize value to the customer (e.g., Dell), the activities related to marketing the product, receiving the customer order, scheduling the order into production, delivering and installing the product, and providing after-sales support must all be coordinated to ensure the delivery of the product at the cost and with the quality that the customer expects.

Finally, an organization's value chain is but one component in a value system that extends back (upstream) to the organization's suppliers—each with its own value chain and value system—and forward (downstream) to the customers—each with its own value chain and value system. Value optimization in the value system requires interorganizational information sharing and coordination in the supply chain, which is discussed in Chapter 10.

The Value of Systems Integration

As previously discussed, one of the important functions provided by an enterprise system is the coordination of value activities in the value chain. The system performs this coordination by sharing data across business processes. In this section, we describe what life would be like without integrated systems and then describe how enterprise systems solve some of those problems. **Figure 2.3** depicts the processing of a customer order in the Customer Service Department at Sudbury, Inc., a hypothetical company that manufactures and sells electronic subassemblies. As you can see in the figure, Sophia the Sudbury customer service representative (CSR) needs to have access to information from a variety of sources to tell customers when and if they can expect to receive their order and how much that order will cost.

The Problem

Imagine, first, that Sudbury's information processes are completely disaggregated, and follow along as we describe the problems that this causes for Sophia. First (flow 1), Sophia needs to know if this is an existing customer in good standing (i.e., that the customer has good credit). Let's assume that Sophia can key in the customer's name and obtain this data.

FIGURE 2.3   Sudbury Customer Service Process

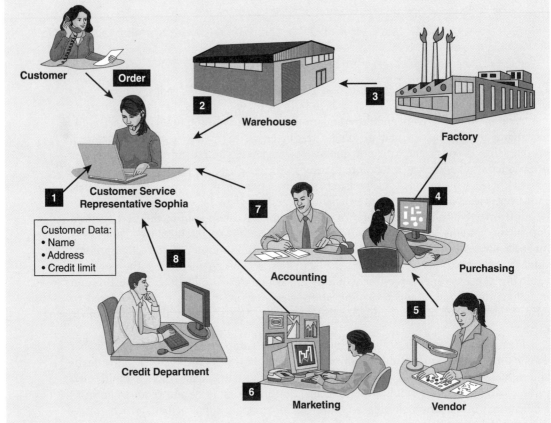

Second (flow 2), Sophia needs to be able to tell the customer when she will receive the item. This date, known as available to promise (ATP), may be a function of several elements of data:

- If the item is on the shelf in one of Sudbury's warehouses and is not committed to another customer, the item will be available after it has been picked from the shelf, packed for shipment, and delivered to the customer. With no automated link to current inventory data, Sophia needs to examine computer printouts of inventory balances or call the warehouses to ask someone to look on the shelf.

- If the item is not on the shelf (flow 3), the item will be available when released from manufacturing, unless that quantity has been committed to another customer. Sophia reviews production schedules to determine when the item will be available and adds to that the time normally required to pick, pack, and ship the item to this customer. This does not, however, tell her if the item has already been allocated to another customer.

- In the event that the item is not available and must be scheduled for manufacturing, Sophia needs to know when it can be scheduled and how long the manufacturing process will take. This depends on the availability of the production line and personnel, as well as the required raw materials (flow 4). This latter piece of information may require contacting the vendors that supply these materials to determine when they can promise delivery (flow 5). This is the ATP from Sudbury's vendors.

- Let's assume that Sophia has determined when the item will be available to ship to the customer. What price will be charged to this customer for this order? This price may be found on a static price list that Sophia keeps near the phone. However, the marketing department may determine prices dynamically (flow 6) based on customer status, market conditions, quantity being purchased, and current manufacturing costs. This implies multiple flows to and from marketing that are not depicted in Figure 2.3.

- After pricing has been determined, Sophia needs to know if the total price charged for the order falls within this customer's credit limit. Now, we assume that Sophia has obtained the credit limit from the customer data that she has (flow 1); however, let's assume that the amount of money that the customer already owes Sudbury must be considered (flow 7). Without direct access to the open accounts receivable data, Sophia needs to call accounting to approve this order.

- Finally, let's assume that it is Sudbury policy not to turn down an order for insufficient credit without first checking with the credit department (flow 8). Without an integrated system, this requires that Sophia call the credit department.

Controls

Is it feasible for Sophia to keep the customer on the phone throughout this process? Not likely. Do you consider this to be good customer service? We hope not. What does Sudbury need to do?

The Solution

The solution, as we are sure you have surmised, is to integrate the disaggregated processes of Figure 2.3 into an enterprise system. Look again at Figure 2.3, and let's see how the process changes if the pieces of the customer service process were integrated:

- As before, input of the customer name or number gives Sophia access to the customer data (flow 1).

- Upon entering the number of the requested item, the enterprise system establishes the ATP date by determining whether the item is available in any of Sudbury's worldwide warehouses (flow 2), is scheduled to be manufactured (flow 3), and if scheduled for manufacture, when it will be available (flows 4 and 5).
- After the source of the item is known, the system automatically determines the price (flow 6) and the customer's creditworthiness (flows 7 and 8).

So Sophia does not need to keep the customer on the phone forever! With an integrated system, all of the previous steps are determined in a matter of seconds. If the item will not be available in a time consistent with the customer's request, the system can provide data with which management can make decisions to allocate available items from other customers; plan increased production; streamline warehouse and factory logistics to reduce manufacturing, picking, packing, and shipping time; and other such decisions. This process, called capable to promise (CTP), and ATP will be discussed further in Chapter 12.

Additional Value

In addition to support for Sophia and the Sudbury supply chain activities, the integration provided by an enterprise system provides additional value. For example, data stored in various systems must be manually shared, checked, or entered into multiple systems. Data entered multiple times may lack *consistency*, *completeness*, and *accuracy*. Multiple versions of data must, therefore, be reconciled, consuming valuable time. Inadequate integration of financial systems with logistics, fixed assets, and other systems can cause delayed and inaccurate financial reporting, analysis, and monitoring of operations. For example, integration of marketing, sales, and financial systems is required to obtain timely assessment of sales, margins obtained on sales, impact of marketing campaigns, and so on. The bottom line is that without integrated information systems, organizations have difficulty managing on a day-to-day basis and being successful in the long run.

Enterprise Systems Support for Organizational Processes

An information system supports the functioning of an organization in several ways. First, it facilitates the functioning of the organization's operations as business events occur by, for example, providing data as required to complete the event, applying business rules to ensure that the event is handled properly, and communicating the need for action to business units. Second, the information system retains records about business events that have occurred. Third, the information system stores data that is useful for decision making. In the following sections, we describe how the information system provides this support and how that support is more robust when an enterprise system provides the support. First, however, we provide an overview of capturing data during the execution of business processes.

Capturing Data During Business Processes

The data captured as business processes unfold should be sufficient for someone who was not a party to the business event to reconstruct every relevant aspect of what happened—whether in accounting, marketing, human resources, financial management, manufacturing, or any other part of the organization. There are, of course, judgment calls as to whether or not data are relevant enough to be worth the cost of capturing, but, as a rule of thumb, data to be collected and stored should be related to the four Ws:

- The *who* relates to all individuals and/or organizations that are involved in the event (sometimes called *agents* to the event).
- The *what* relates to all resources that are exchanged as a result of the event.
- The *where* relates to the locations in which (1) the event takes place, (2) exchanged resources reside before and after the event, and (3) the agents are located during the event.
- The *when* relates to the time periods involved in completion of the event, including future exchanges of resources (e.g., payment of cash for an account receivable) arising from the event.
- After the details of the four Ws (i.e., the event data) are collected and recorded, the data can be aggregated and summarized in any manner that a given user chooses. Aggregations and summarizations are temporary and for the user's application or report only, but the event data remain available to other users in their original form. For routine applications such as the generation of accounting reports, programmed procedures can be developed to generate such reports automatically.

Enterprise Systems Facilitate Functioning of the Organization's Operations

Within enterprise systems, there are two basic types of data: master data (entity-type data) and business event data (event-type data). Normally, a business event processing system operates with one or more data tables (often called "files"). Some of these tables are used to obtain reference information, such as the warehouse location of an item of merchandise. Other tables are used to organize and store the data that are being collected, such as sales order or inventory data. We hope that the hierarchy of data pictured in the table on the right side of **Figure 2.4** (pg. 48) is familiar to you from your computer science or management information systems courses. Let's quickly review.

- A *character* is a basic unit of data such as a letter, number, or special character.
- A *field* (a single cell in a table) is a collection of related characters that comprise an attribute, such as a customer number or a customer name.
- A *record* (a row in a table) is a collection of related data fields (attributes) pertaining to a particular entity (person, place, or thing, such as a customer record) or event (sale, hiring of a new employee, etc.).
- A *table* (or file) is a collection of related records (sometimes called entity/event instances), such as a customer table or a sales order table.

Figure 2.4 depicts a typical data maintenance activity—the addition of a new customer record to the customer table—and provides an example of how an information system can facilitate the functioning of the organization's business processes. For example, the name and the address fields will be used to prepare monthly invoices. **Figure 2.5** (pg. 49) depicts how the existence of the customer record—including the credit limit—provides the basic authorization required to accept and record the customer's order. Without the customer record, the computer should reject the customer order and require that the credit department (or some entity *other than* the sales department) create the customer record before proceeding with entering

Controls

FIGURE 2.4   Data Maintenance: Create Customer Record

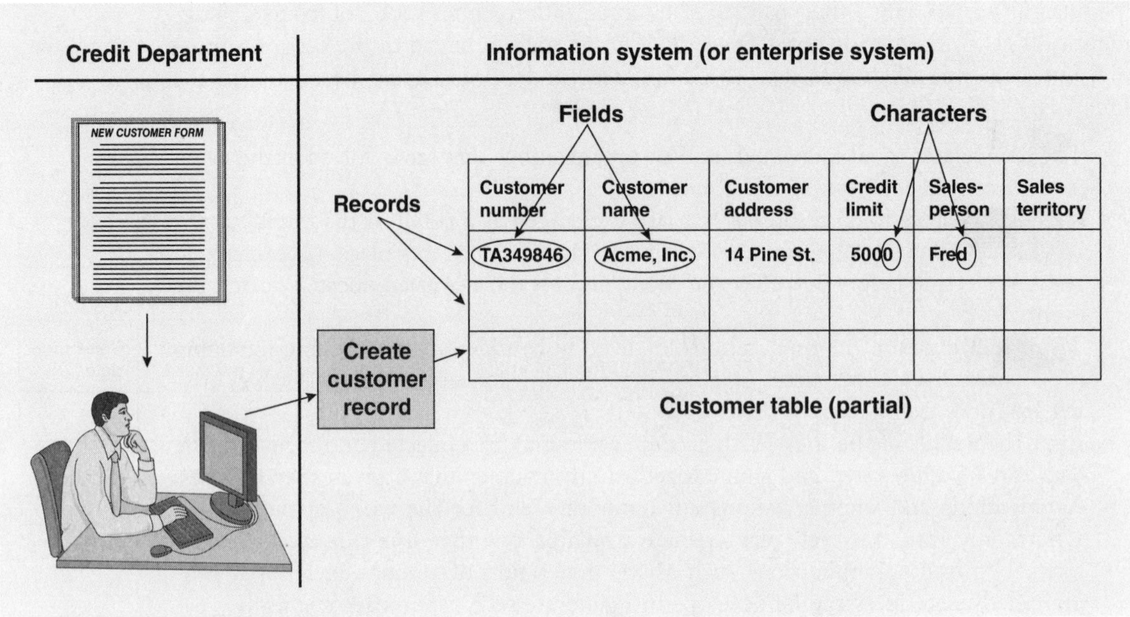

the customer's order. Thus, it is important to separate authorizations for data-maintenance activities from authorizations for business event–processing activities. This separation between, for example, the credit department in Figure 2.4 and the sales department in Figure 2.5 provides an important control, *segregation of duties*, which is explored in greater detail in Chapters 8 and 9.

Figure 2.5 depicts a typical business event–processing activity—entering a customer's order. Let's examine a series of events that might take place during the course of capturing a customer's order and delivering the goods to the customer. First, as noted previously, the customer table provides the credit and other customer data required to authorize the order. Next, data regarding the quantity and selling price of the inventory is obtained from the inventory table. Finally, an order to pick, pack, and ship the ordered goods (including the inventory location obtained from the inventory table) is sent to the warehouse.[6]

Enterprise Systems

In enterprise systems, there should be only one version of each of the tables depicted in Figure 2.5, and that central database is used by all functions in the organization, such as marketing, accounting, and logistics. For example, there is only one record for each customer and one credit limit, worldwide. All of the inventory data worldwide is available (often called "visible") during the processing of customer orders. The centralization of the data permits an organization to have accurate and reliable data and to operate its business processes in a consistent manner throughout the organization.

In addition, communicating across functions is enhanced in enterprise systems. For example, in Figure 2.5, data related to the inventory is readily available during entry of the customer order, and a request for shipment is sent directly to the warehouse. (We don't see any document here because the transmission to the warehouse is

---

[6]Notice the direction of the flows into and out of the tables. We obtain data *from* the customer and inventory tables and send data *to* the sales order (e.g., to record a new sales order) and inventory (e.g., to change the quantity on hand) tables.

FIGURE 2.5 Business Event Data Processing: Enter Customer Order

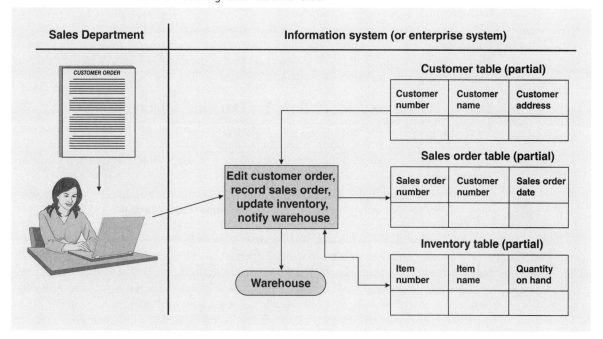

electronic.) Finally, although not shown in the diagram, the purchasing function could be informed immediately that merchandise has been sold and may need to be replenished. Thus, the enterprise system with a centralized database and communication among the organization business functions provides a higher level of support for the functioning of the business than is possible by less integrated approaches to the information system.

Enterprise Systems Record That Business Events Have Occurred

As the business event progresses, the information system must capture the multifaceted data to track the progression of the process. To capture the sales event, we need to record data related to the customer and the salesperson (the who), the goods ordered (the what), the delivery location (the where), and the date of sale and promised delivery (the when). This information is then linked with information already stored that relates to, for example, the supplier of goods that might not have been available. Based on the combined information, a purchase order might be sent to the supplier. For the purchase order, we record the supplier (the who), the goods (the what), the location to which the goods will be delivered (the where), and the delivery date from the supplier to our company (the when), and then link the purchase order to the order from our customer.

All of the data in our example that are required for the sales, billing, purchasing, and general ledger functions are captured and available in a typical information system; however, with an enterprise system, the data are linked together. Thus, if the supplier changes the delivery date, the salesperson has immediate access to the change and can notify the customer. To accomplish this, the salesperson pulls together the necessary data by using links between the changed order information, the sales order, and the customer, and narrows the search to only the sales that salesperson is handling. Very quickly, the salesperson has the information needed to notify the customer of any delay in shipment.

Notice how this discussion relates to the event-driven architecture in Technology Summary 2.1 (pg. 39). If there was an event-driven architecture, the notice from the supplier about a changed delivery date would cause the "pushing" of notices to the salesperson, the customer, and other interested parties.

Enterprise Systems Store Data for Decision Making

Figure 2.6 depicts a manager using the data collected and stored by the organization's information system. We show only those data tables that we had in Figure 2.5 (pg. 49). Hundreds, indeed thousands, of tables of data are available in a typical information system.

Some simple examples follow of how our manager might use the data to make decisions. A warehouse manager might look at sales orders that have not yet been shipped to follow up and find out why. An inventory manager might look at the inventory data to follow up on those items with low balances on hand.

With an enterprise system, potential queries can be complex and may yield results that are more significant. For example, a marketing manager might want to have a list of those customers who have not made a purchase in a month. To obtain this information, the manager would need to combine the customer and sales tables. Or the credit manager might want to compare customer credit limits, sales, billing, and payment data to determine whether credit limits need to be adjusted for customers with high sales or late payments. Finally, a logistics manager might want to examine the time of day that orders are received and delays in shipping those orders to determine whether staffing in the warehouse needs to be scheduled at different times. All of these queries assume that data can be shared across multiple functional areas, which is a common situation with enterprise systems.

Enterprise Systems

FIGURE 2.6 Using Stored Data for Decision Making

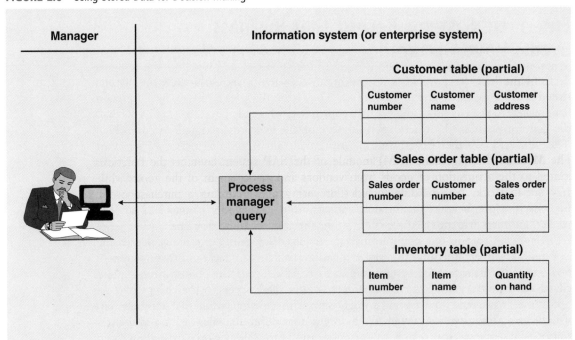

Major ERP Modules

To give you an appreciation for the typical core modules in an ERP system, we will describe five modules in the SAP system: (1) Sales and Distribution (SD), (2) Materials Management (MM), (3) Financial Accounting (FI), (4) Controlling and Profitability Analysis (CO/PA), and (5) Human Resources (HR). These modules are part of the SAP Business Suite, shown in Figure 2.1 (pg. 37). Most ERP systems have modules with comparable functionality.

Sales and Distribution

The Sales and Distribution Module (SD) of the SAP system contains the functions related to the sale of goods to customers and includes recording a customer order, shipping goods to the customer, and billing the customer. There are connections to the Materials Management (MM) module to check the availability of inventory and to record the issue of the goods, to the Financial Accounting (FI) module to post the sale, and to the Controlling (CO) module for profitability analysis related to the sale. The three major steps in the SD process (order entry, shipment, and billing) are briefly outlined here.

The SD order entry process might start with receiving and recording an inquiry from a customer and preparing and recording a sales quotation. Should the customer choose to place an order, the process continues with the receipt and entry of a customer order. Upon entering the order, the SAP system checks the customer's credit, determines availability of the goods ordered, and records the customer's order (after the order is entered, it is called a *sales order*). If this is a new customer, the customer data is added to the database using a data-maintenance activity similar to that shown earlier in Figure 2.4 (pg. 48) *before* the customer order can be entered.

The SD shipment process includes scheduling the shipment, picking the goods from the shelf, packing the goods for shipment, and recording the shipment. Organizations often choose to record each of these steps as they occur to keep a complete record of the sale as it progresses. After the shipment has been recorded, the inventory quantity-on-hand is reduced, and the sale is scheduled for billing.

The SD billing process creates invoices for all shipments. The billing process may be automatically triggered by each shipment or may be executed periodically by a billing clerk. In the latter case, multiple shipments to a customer might be consolidated and placed on a single invoice.

Materials Management

The Materials Management (MM) module of the SAP system contains the functions related to the acquisition of goods from vendors and management of the goods while they are in stock. The module includes preparing and recording a purchase order, receiving the goods from the vendor, and recording the vendor's invoice. The MM module interacts with the SD module during the processing of customer orders, with the FI module to post the receipt of the goods and the vendor invoice, and with the CO module for analysis of the costs associated with the purchases. The three major steps in the MM process (creating a purchase order, receiving the goods, and recording the vendor invoice) are briefly outlined here.

The MM purchase order process might start with the preparation of a purchase requisition by a person or function within the organization and sending a request for quotation (RFQ) to one or more vendors. After responses to the RFQ have been processed and a vendor selected, the purchase process continues with the creation and recording of a purchase order and communication of that purchase order to the vendor. If this is a new vendor, the vendor data is added to the database using a data-maintenance activity similar to that in Figure 2.4 (pg. 48) *before* the purchase order can be entered.

The MM goods receipt process includes comparing the received and ordered quantities, recording the receipt, and increasing the quantity-on-hand. When the vendor invoice is received and entered, the system performs a three-way match among the purchase order, the receipt, and the invoice. If these agree, the invoice is recorded.

Financial Accounting

The Financial Accounting (FI) module plays a central role in the SAP system. Business events from other modules, such as SD and MM, are incorporated by the FI module into the general ledger accounts and included in the external statements, balance sheet, profit and loss statement, and statement of cash flows. The FI module also includes accounts receivable and accounts payable functions to record and manage that data directly and to complete events begun in the SD and MM modules. Some specific examples follow.

After a customer is billed in the SD module, the accounts receivable portion of the FI module manages that receivable until paid (e.g., aging of open receivables, dunning for late payments) and records the customer payment. Also, in the absence of the SD module and for special circumstances, such as one-time sales of nonmerchandise items, invoices may be directly entered in the FI module.

After a vendor invoice has been entered in the MM module, the accounts payable portion of the FI module schedules the invoice for payment and executes that payment at the appropriate time.

Controlling and Profitability Analysis

The Controlling (CO) module of the SAP system, often called Controlling and Profitability Analysis (CO/PA), handles internal accounting, including cost center accounting, profitability analysis for sales, activity-based accounting, and budgeting. For example, the CO module can produce internal profit and loss statements for portions of an organization's business.

Human Resources

The Human Resources (HR) module of SAP includes functions related to the recruitment, management, and administration of personnel, payroll processing, and personnel training and travel. For example, when a new employee is hired, it is from within the HR module that the human resources department adds the personnel data to the database using a data-maintenance activity similar to that in Figure 2.4. The HR module is also used to maintain data related to benefits, training, and work shifts. Finally, the payroll function facilitates the processing of payroll for countries throughout the world and the preparation of payroll reports in accordance with the jurisdictions of those countries.

Enterprise Systems Support for Major Business Event Processes

Most organizations group their major business events into two processes: the order-to-cash (or revenue) process and the purchase-to-pay (or expenditure) process. For ease of presentation, this book divides these further into processes comprised of a few closely related events. For example, we describe the process employed to enter a customer's order and to ship the goods to the customer as the order entry/sales process, whereas billing the customers, managing the accounts receivable, and recording customer payments are included in the billing/accounts receivable/cash receipts process. In the sections that follow, we describe the two major processes, order-to-cash and purchase-to-pay; describe how an enterprise system supports those business processes; and map those processes into the chapters where they are covered in this book. Our discussion is limited to the purchase of goods, not services, and to goods acquired for resale, not goods acquired as raw material inputs to a manufacturing process.

Order-to-Cash

Figure 2.7 depicts the **order-to-cash process**, which includes the events surrounding the sale of goods to a customer, the recognition of the revenue, and the collection of the customer payment. The order-to-cash process comprises all activities in the *order entry/sales process* (Chapter 10), the *billing/accounts receivable/cash receipts process* (Chapter 11), and the applicable parts of the *general ledger process* (Chapter 16). Follow along as we describe the numbered steps in Figure 2.7 and how an enterprise system supports the business activities in those steps. The order-to-cash process includes the following:

- Step 1, presales activities, includes responding to customer inquiries and RFQs. Organizations may choose to collect and retain a rich assortment of customer-related data about prospective and active customers. This data are recorded in an ERP system and can be analyzed to determine the goods being requested by customers and the RFQs that do, and do not, result in customer orders. Some organizations purchase separate CRM packages to supplement the customer-related features in standard ERP systems.
- Step 2, sales order processing, includes capturing and recording customer orders. At this point in the process, an enterprise system links together customer, inventory,

FIGURE 2.7 Order-to-Cash Process

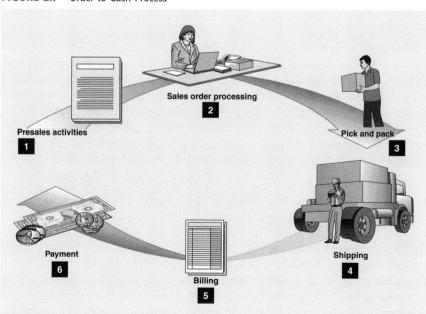

purchasing, and vendor data to determine whether the customer is in good standing and likely to pay the bill (e.g., using customer credit and inventory pricing data) and where and when inventory will be available to send to the customer (i.e., ATP using worldwide inventory quantity-on-hand, on-order, and vendor data). At the conclusion of step 2, the enterprise system schedules the order for delivery and sends a picking request to the appropriate warehouse. If goods are not available within the organization, a purchase order is sent to a vendor.

- Step 3, pick and pack, includes picking the goods from the shelf in the warehouse and packing the goods for shipment. Each of these events may be recorded in the enterprise system to maintain a record of the progress and to retain control over the location of the goods.
- Step 4, shipping, includes transferring the goods to the organization's transportation function, or to a third-party carrier, for shipment to the customer. The enterprise system chooses the appropriate routing and carrier, records the reduction in the inventory quantity-on-hand, calculates and records the cost of goods sold and inventory reduction in the general ledger, and records data to be used in the billing process. Some enterprise systems are configured to immediately trigger the billing process when a shipment takes place.
- Step 5, billing, includes preparing the customer invoice and recording sales and accounts receivable data in the general ledger. The enterprise system links together sales, customer, and inventory data to ensure that the invoice contains correct quantities, prices, terms, addresses, and so on. At this point, the enterprise system can be used to analyze sales profitability by comparing product costs to selling price.
- Step 6, payment, includes capturing and recording cash receipts and updating cash and accounts receivable amounts in the general ledger. Data in the enterprise system are used to manage customer credit and invest available cash.

Figure 2.8 depicts the Sales and Distribution (SD) menu from the SAP system and points to the SD options described previously. **Figure 2.9** shows the audit trail that the system retains to document the completion of the steps in the sales process. The accounting document includes the entry to the general ledger associated with the invoice.

Purchase-to-Pay

Figure 2.10 on page 56 depicts the **purchase-to-pay process**, which includes the events surrounding the purchase of goods from a vendor, the recognition of the cost of those goods, and the payment to the vendor. The purchase-to-pay process comprises all of the activities in the *purchasing process* (Chapter 12), the *accounts payable/cash disbursements process* (Chapter 13), and the applicable parts of the *general ledger process* (Chapter 16). Follow along as we describe the numbered steps in Figure 2.10 and how an enterprise system supports the business activities in those steps. The purchase-to-pay process includes the following:

- Step 1, requirements determination, includes preparing a purchase requisition to request the purchase of goods from a vendor. An enterprise system may automatically generate the purchase requisition on the basis of data such as quantity-on-hand, quantity-on-order, and expected demand. Authorized individuals within the organization may enter ad-hoc requests. An enterprise system reviews purchase requests to determine that they are authorized and within budget.
- Step 2, purchase order processing, includes preparing and recording purchase orders. An enterprise system assists the buyer in identifying sources of supply for the requested item, preparing RFQs to be sent to vendors, analyzing vendor quota-

FIGURE 2.8 SD Menu Options in the SAP System

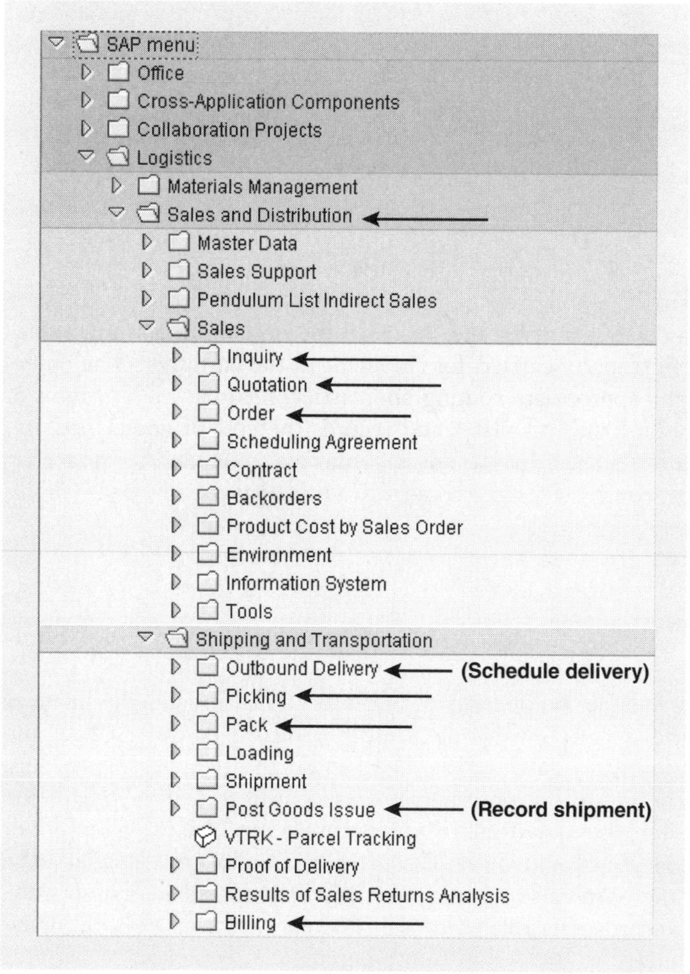

```
▽ 🗂 SAP menu
   ▷ 🗀 Office
   ▷ 🗀 Cross-Application Components
   ▷ 🗀 Collaboration Projects
   ▽ 🗂 Logistics
      ▷ 🗀 Materials Management
      ▽ 🗂 Sales and Distribution  ←—————
         ▷ 🗀 Master Data
         ▷ 🗀 Sales Support
         ▷ 🗀 Pendulum List Indirect Sales
         ▽ 🗂 Sales
            ▷ 🗀 Inquiry  ←—————
            ▷ 🗀 Quotation  ←—————
            ▷ 🗀 Order  ←—————
            ▷ 🗀 Scheduling Agreement
            ▷ 🗀 Contract
            ▷ 🗀 Backorders
            ▷ 🗀 Product Cost by Sales Order
            ▷ 🗀 Environment
            ▷ 🗀 Information System
            ▷ 🗀 Tools
         ▽ 🗂 Shipping and Transportation
            ▷ 🗀 Outbound Delivery  ←—— (Schedule delivery)
            ▷ 🗀 Picking  ←—————
            ▷ 🗀 Pack  ←—————
            ▷ 🗀 Loading
            ▷ 🗀 Shipment
            ▷ 🗀 Post Goods Issue  ←—— (Record shipment)
              📦 VTRK - Parcel Tracking
            ▷ 🗀 Proof of Delivery
            ▷ 🗀 Results of Sales Returns Analysis
            ▷ 🗀 Billing  ←—————
```

Source: Copyright by SAP AG. Reprinted with permission from SAP.

FIGURE 2.9 SD Audit Trail for Completion of Steps in the SAP Sales Process

Document	On	Status
▽ 📄 Quotation 0020000019	10/16/2007	Completed
▽ 📄 ➡ Standard Order 0000012071	10/22/2007	Completed
▽ 📄 Delivery 0080015185 **(Schedule delivery)**	10/22/2007	Completed
📄 WMS transfer order 0000001511 **(Picking ticket)**	10/22/2007	Completed
📄 GD goods issue:delvy 4900035532 **(Shipment)**	10/22/2007	complete
▽ 📄 Invoice (F2) 0090036264	10/23/2007	
📄 Accounting document 1400000000	10/23/2007	Cleared

Source: Copyright by SAP AG. Reprinted with permission from SAP.

FIGURE 2.10 Purchase-to-Pay Process

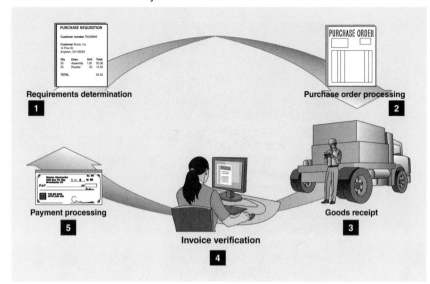

tions, and selecting vendors by comparing vendor prices, terms, and past performance (e.g., timely, accurate deliveries).

- Step 3, goods receipt, includes comparing the on-order quantity and the quantity received, increasing the quantity-on-hand, creating a record of the receipt, and recording the cost of inventory in the general ledger. If the two-way match fails, the enterprise system notifies the proper personnel to ensure timely reconciliation of differences. The enterprise system also ensures timely availability of the goods by routing them to the function that requested them or directing that they be placed on the shelf in the warehouse and made available for immediate sale. Finally, the enterprise system records data related to the vendor's performance (e.g., delivery accuracy and timeliness) to be used in future purchasing decisions.
- Step 4, invoice verification, includes receiving vendor invoices; three-way matching of the purchase order, receipt, and vendor invoice; and recording accounts payable in the general ledger. An enterprise system links this data together to make the three-way match possible and provides the interface to the general ledger. If the three-way match fails, the enterprise system notifies the proper personnel to ensure timely reconciliation of differences.
- Step 5, payment processing, includes preparing and recording cash disbursements and updating cash and accounts payable amounts in the general ledger. An enterprise system facilitates this process by using vendor and accounts payable data to schedule payments in accordance with vendor terms and to receive discounts, as appropriate.

Figure 2.11 depicts the Materials Management (MM) menu from the SAP system and points to the options described previously. **Figure 2.12** shows the audit trail that the SAP system retains to document the completion of the steps in the purchase process.

FIGURE 2.11   Materials Management Menu Options in the SAP System

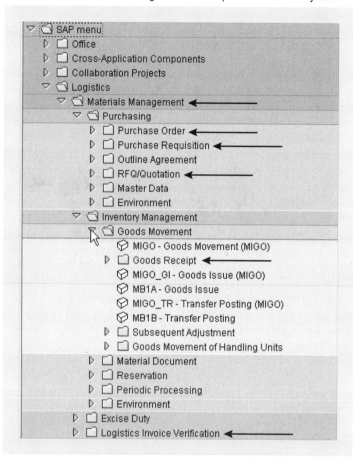

Source: Copyright by SAP AG. Reprinted with permission from SAP.

FIGURE 2.12   Audit Trail for Completion of Steps in the SAP Purchase Process

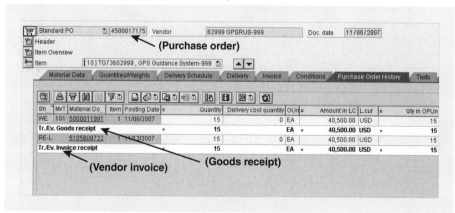

Source: Copyright by SAP AG. Reprinted with permission from SAP.

Summary

Enterprise systems achieve quality of information goals (Figure 1.6, pg. 21 and Exhibit 1.2, pg. 20) in the following manner:

- Enterprise systems can collect a wide variety of data about business events and make that data available for use by all interested and authorized parties inside and outside the organization. The data should help all users (i.e., *relevance, understandability*) make decisions (i.e., *decision usefulness*) and analyze past events to make predictions about future events (i.e., *predictive/feedback value*).
- An enterprise system's central database retains one version of data elements, uses that data to verify the accuracy of new data elements entered into the database, and applies business rules to permit only authorized changes to the database. Combined, these improve the *reliability, validity,* and *accuracy* of the database.
- Organization-wide enforcement of data standards and business rules means that business events will be handled *consistently* across the organization, that all relevant data will be collected (i.e., *completeness*), and that the collected data will be *verifiable* and *neutral.*
- The integrated nature of the enterprise system makes all data available in a *timely* manner.
- The system facilitates the sharing of services for *efficiency* and *consistency*. For example, an organization can ship products to customers from multiple shipping points while billing its customers from one central location.

Table 2.2 summarizes some of the advantages and disadvantages of enterprise systems for an organization. Notice that some of the advantages and disadvantages relate to the ERP systems that are used to support the core systems of the enterprise system.

TABLE 2.2 Pros/Benefits and Cons/Disadvantages of Enterprise Systems

Pros of Enterprise Systems
• Single database
• Integrated system (e.g., capability to determine ATP)
• Process orientation (versus function orientation)
• Standardization of business processes and data, easier to understand across the organization
• Faster business processes (e.g., customer fulfillment, product development)
• Timely information
• Better financial management (partly due to integration)
• One face to the customer
• Optimal inventory levels
• Improved cash management
• Productivity improvements, reduced personnel expense
• Improved financial disclosures
• Improved budgeting, forecasting, and decision support
• Seamless integration and accessibility of information across the organization
• Catalyst for reengineering old, inefficient business processes
Pros of ERP Packages
• One package across many functions (if one ERP)
• "Best practices"
• Modular structure (buy what you need)
• No development needed (unless modifications are required)
• Configurable
• Reduced errors (e.g., business rules, enter data once)

TABLE 2.2   (continued)

Cons of Enterprise Systems
• Centralized control versus decentralized empowerment
• Inability to support traditional business processes that may be best practices for that organization
• Loss of flexibility in rapidly adapting to desired new business processes in the post-implementation period
• Increased complexity of maintaining security, control, and access permissions for specific information embedded in central database
• The rigidity of "standardization" can impede creative thinking related to ongoing business process improvements

Cons of ERP Packages
• Complex and inflexible
• Best practices are shared by all who buy
• Difficult to configure
• Long implementation
• Best of breed might be better (than single ERP package)
• Can't meet all needs (i.e., developed for many user types)

Key Terms

enterprise systems, 34

enterprise-wide information systems, 34

enterprise information systems, 34

business event, 35

enterprise resource planning (ERP) systems, 35

customer relationship management (CRM) software, 36

customer self-service (CSS) software, 37

sales force automation (SFA) software, 37

supply chain management (SCM) software, 38

product life-cycle management (PLM) software, 38

supplier relationship management (SRM) software, 38

best-of-breed approach, 38

middleware, 38

application program interface (API), 38

event-driven architecture (EDA), 39

enterprise application integration (EAI), 39

enterprise Services Bus (ESB), 39

Business process management (BPM), 41

business process management systems, 41

value chain, 42

order-to-cash process, 53

purchase-to-pay process, 54

Review Questions

RQ 2-1   Describe the key features/characteristics of an enterprise system.

RQ 2-2   Describe the key features/characteristics of an enterprise resource planning (ERP) system.

RQ 2-3   Describe the add-on modules that may be used to complement the core functionality of an ERP system.

RQ 2-4   Describe the methods used to integrate ERP systems with third-party modules, back-end or legacy systems, the Web, and business partners.

RQ 2-5   What is a value chain?

RQ 2-6   What is the relationship of the organizational value chain and an enterprise system?

RQ 2-7   Describe the problems caused by lack of information systems integration.

RQ 2-8   Explain why it is important to capture the who, what, where, and when in describing business events.

RQ 2-9   Describe the three ways that an enterprise system supports the functioning of an organization's processes.

RQ 2-10   Describe the activities performed by the five modules of the SAP system.

RQ 2-11   Describe the six steps in the order-to-cash process.

RQ 2-12   How does an enterprise system support the order-to-cash process?

RQ 2-13   Describe the six steps in the purchase-to-pay process.

RQ 2-14   How does an enterprise system support the purchase-to-pay process?

RQ 2-15   List the advantages and disadvantages of an enterprise system.

Discussion Questions

DQ 2-1   After the core of an ERP system has been implemented, any of the modules may then be implemented separately. What is the implication of being able to implement an ERP system on a piece-by-piece basis?

DQ 2-2   The Bluffs Company is considering taking customers' orders on its Web site.

    a.   What information would Bluffs collect from the customer during this process?

    b.   What information would need to come from Bluffs' Web site and back-end systems to complete the order?

    c.   How would an enterprise system facilitate this exchange of information?

DQ 2-3   Periodically, you will read in the news about one company in the ERP industry acquiring another company in that industry. Discuss the pros and cons of the consolidation of the ERP software industry.

DQ 2-4   Describe how an enterprise system can assist an organization in optimizing its value system.

DQ 2-5   Consider a business process that you have experienced at work, as a customer, or as a student. Examples might include any process in a work setting, such as payroll and purchasing, or any process with which you have interacted, such as ordering from a Web site, obtaining a loan, eating at a restaurant, or registering for classes at your college or university. Describe the degree to which the steps in the process are integrated. What is/was the impact of that integration on you and on the organization?

DQ 2-6   Describe a situation in which information would be shared between two of the "silos" in Figure 2.2 (pg. 43). What data would be shared? Why would the data be shared? (*Hint:* You might refer to Figure 2.3 [pg. 44], Figure 2.7 [pg. 53], or Figure 2.10 [pg. 56].)

DQ 2-7   Why might a firm decide to implement only certain modules in an ERP system rather than a complete implementation?

DQ 2-8   In what circumstances would a company choose a best-of-breed approach over a traditional ERP system?

DQ 2-9   Describe the primary and supporting activities involved in an organization's value chain. Explain the importance of having an effective value chain.

Short Problems

SP 2-1   Consider the business event–processing activity, entering a customer's order. Identify the key business event data (who, what, where, and when) you would want to capture. (For an example of the event you may refer to Figure 2.5, pg. 49.)

SP 2-2   Enterprise systems may provide better information than non-integrated systems for management decisions. Provide specific examples that support (or refute) this claim.

SP 2-3   Provide an example of a business event. Explain how an enterprise system can provide the ability to share information and make the execution of the event efficient.

Problems

P 2-1   Conduct research on the Web sites of either *CIO Magazine* or *CFO Magazine* (or another that your instructor suggests) for stories about ERP implementation successes and failures. Using specific examples, describe the reasons for the successes and failures. What conclusions can be reached?

P 2-2   Conduct research on an ERP package other than SAP that would be suitable for a large organization (>$1b in revenues) and compare the modules that it has to those described within this chapter for the SAP system.

P 2-3   Conduct research on an ERP package, such as Microsoft Dynamics GP or Microsoft Dynamics NAV, for small to medium-sized (SME) organizations (between $30m and $1b in revenues). Compare that package to the SAP system in terms of available modules, functionality, and so on.

P 2-4   Choose a familiar Web site, such as Dell, Amazon.com, or Walmart. Describe the order-to-cash process from the customer's perspective as illustrated by that site.

P 2-5   Imagine that you are conducting a field-based research project for your AIS class in a small local business. Assume that the business is a custom furniture manufacturer. In the course of your project, you tell the owner that you are using SAP in your AIS class. The owner asks if he should be using SAP or some other ERP system in his business. What would be your response? What questions would you ask or what information would you need in order to answer that question?

P 2-6   Interview an accountant at an organization in your area. Write a summary of what accounting information system is used in the organization, why the software was chosen, and the overall satisfaction of the organization with the software. (Your instructor will provide you with the expected length of the summary.)

CHAPTER 3

Electronic Business (E-Business) Systems

Pg. 62-80, 88-95,
Technology summary 3.2 (pg 84-85)
Figure 3.6

Learning Objectives

After reading this chapter, you should be able to:

- Appreciate the possible changes to organizational processes that occur when e-business is introduced.

- Understand the major approaches used to transfer electronic data during business events processing.

- Understand the complexities surrounding electronic data interchange (EDI) that are introduced when linking two different organizations' computer systems for joint business event data processing.

- Relate to the challenges faced by organizations when they pursue direct business links with customers via the Internet or other networks.

- Appreciate the business advantages gained through effective use of e-business.

For the quarter ending March 31, 1996, Amazon.com reported sales of $875,000.[1] Fast-forward 13 years ... for the quarter ending December 31, 2009, Amazon.com reported sales of more than $9.5 billion![2] The amazing part of the story is that in 1996, very little retail business was taking place on the Internet. Amazon.com began business with only a few workstations and no physical sales locations (i.e., no "bricks and mortar"). Because it began early in the era of business-to-consumer (B2C) e-business, many customers were skeptical of providing credit card information online. To provide comfort to these customers, Amazon.com processed credit card orders by receiving orders on one computer, writing the information to a floppy disk, and physically walking the order to a separate computer. Amazon.com could not have grown to nearly $25 billion in annual sales on such primitive systems. Instead, Amazon.com grew by developing and implementing secure transaction software, online shopping carts, and sophisticated data-analysis programs.

Amazon.com's e-business model would not be feasible without this software. The model is based on Amazon.com's "almost-in-time" inventory concept, which supplements

---

[1] From Amazon.com's Form S-1, filed with the SEC on March 21, 1997, available at www.amazom.com, accessed January 29, 2010.

[2] From Amazon.com's Form 10-K, filed with the SEC on January 29, 2010, available at www.amazon.com, accessed January 29, 2010.

the B2C interface that you see as a customer with an innovative business-to-business (B2B) interface for quick acquisition and shipment of non-stocked items. That is, if the item that you order is not in stock, the company gets it from its supplier for shipment to you, the customer. It is interesting that over time, the use of technology has allowed Amazon.com to grow from a company known as a "bookseller"[3] to an organization with a vision "to be earth's most customer centric company; to build a place where people can come to find and discover anything they might want to buy online."[4]

Through the development of technology, Amazon.com has been able to develop its e-business model as well as use its technology to provide similar services to a wide variety of companies, including some which traditionally would have been its competitors. Additionally, Amazon.com is promoting Web Services, which will allow access to many of the company's internal functions and methods.[5] Amazon.com's future may revolve around marketing its B2C and B2B technology capabilities, rather than simply its capability to sell books, CDs, DVDs, and other products.

Synopsis

This chapter introduces the concept of **electronic business (e-business)**, which was defined in the Preface and Chapter 1 as the application of electronic networks (including the Internet) to exchange information and link business processes among organizations and individuals. These processes include interaction between back-office (i.e., internal) processes, such as distribution, manufacturing, and accounting, and front-office (i.e., external) processes, such as those that connect an organization to its customers and suppliers.[6] We also explore how communications technology is revolutionizing the way individuals and organizations conduct business.

E-Business

As organizations venture down the trail to electronic communications–driven business processes, the paper trail, including invoices, check payments, and so forth, quickly disappears when capturing business event data at the e-business connection with a customer or supplier and when using *enterprise systems* to store data and make it accessible. The evolution to e-business has been slow in the past, but advances in Internet communication have switched the evolution into high gear. As you read and study this chapter, you will learn about underlying technologies and processes that facilitate e-business, the complexities of displacing paper records with electronic ones, the challenges faced in overcoming differences in technology and accounting systems design to link two companies' computer systems, and finally the barriers that must be overcome for successful execution of secure business events over the Internet. All these technologies, along with

Enterprise Systems

Controls

---

[3]Amazon.com's, October 4, 1995, news release, "World's Largest Bookseller Opens on the Web."

[4]From the FAQ section of Amazon.com's investor relations site, http://phx.corporate-ir.net/phoenix.zhtml?p=irol-irhome&c=97664. Accessed January 30, 2010.

[5]Web Services will be discussed later in this chapter. See http://aws.amazon.com/ for Amazon.com's current offerings.

[6]Some would distinguish the terms e-business, the comprehensive concept we have defined, and e-commerce, the external e-business processes (i.e., the buying and selling of products and services electronically, typically on the Internet). For simplicity, we do not distinguish the terms e-business and e-commerce in this text.

the flexible processes they allow to exist, are fundamental to providing traditional companies with the capability to implement new streamlined processes and new services for their customers. These new technologies also have enabled e-businesses such as Amazon.com to exist and prosper. Amazon.com's business processes are dependent on technology to provide efficient processing and the analysis of information to support product sales, product delivery, and replacement product acquisitions—virtually all of the company's *value chain*.

Introduction

The power of computers in transforming society is perhaps most obvious today in the way communications have changed. Our society has evolved from one that relied on face-to-face communication, to one in which phones became the primary medium, to a contemporary society that is dependent on electronic messages (e.g., e-mail, messaging, Twitter, and Facebook). In essence, the richness of the media has been sacrificed for efficiency and effectiveness. In other words, the phone took away the ability to detect emotions through an individual's appearance, including smiles, frowns, or other facial expressions. E-mail went a step beyond the phone and also took away the ability to detect emotions through voice inflection and context sounds such as a chuckle. For example, you may have chosen in the past to send a family member or friend a voice mail, e-mail, or fax when you wanted to get them a message quickly but didn't really have time to talk beyond what you could deliver in the message. In effect, you used technology to make the delivery of the message more efficient. Through these actions, you made the completion of the necessary activities a more efficient process—much like the objectives of most business organizations in today's heavily competitive business environment.

E-Business

Enterprise
Systems

Controls

From a business perspective, the shift toward increasingly automated business processes and communications based on the transfer of electronic data is designed to achieve greater efficiencies in business processing. When an organization engages in *e-business*, it completes electronic-based business events (i.e., the partial or complete elimination of paper documentation during business processes in favor of more efficient electronic-based communication). These electronic-based business events entail the interconnection of the underlying back-office processes of both organizations, effectively eliminating the errors associated with a paper-driven process. A by-product of e-business is often the elimination of the sales staff that would normally serve as the intermediary between the two parties to the business event. Bypassing the sales staff speeds up the business event by eliminating the interaction with a salesperson, establishing a direct and therefore immediate linkage to the vendor's computerized information system (which for many organizations participating in e-business today will be their *enterprise systems*) for faster communication of an order, and facilitating the electronic transfer of funds for immediate payment. The business event is completed more rapidly than in a traditional manual business model. Additionally, the purchaser normally electronically solicits pricing and quickly determines the best price, which increases price efficiency as well. The computer can even check prices automatically, which eliminates the waste of the purchaser's time on such activities.

Amazon.com's success is not solely driven by its B2C sales systems. As we mentioned earlier, sophisticated B2B systems that are integrated with Amazon.com's suppliers' systems must exist to support acquiring products that consumers want. When

Amazon.com needs to obtain a book or other item, it electronically sends a purchase order (PO) to the manufacturer or distributor of the item. The vendor provides Amazon.com with the product (a physical flow) and also the expected warehouse delivery time—information that is ultimately used to provide the expected shipping and delivery dates to its customer.

B2B systems are not limited to companies that sell predominantly over the Internet. Using processes similar to Amazon.com, companies such as Wal-Mart, which sell most of their merchandise in retail stores, also rely heavily on B2B. When the cashier at Wal-Mart scans an item, not only are sales recorded, but the warehouse inventory balance is also updated. Wal-Mart's vendors read that data, and, if the warehouse quantities fall below the reorder point for the item, the vendor ships replenishment stock to the Wal-Mart warehouse automatically.[7] Today, the majority of e-business volume is conducted between business trading partners rather than consumers and businesses. That is, B2B is much bigger than B2C.

Big organizations aren't the only ones using such technologies to quicken the process. For instance, your favorite pizza joint or sandwich shop may accept e-mail or online ordering—allowing you to avoid being put on hold when you phone in your order and avoid the risk of having the employee who is taking your order recording the wrong ingredients for your pizza or sandwich. You simply create the order yourself and send it off, reducing the need for people to answer the phones and take orders.

With the Internet, many organizations have the opportunity to directly reach customers through electronic communication. The potential in this market has led to the explosion of e-business over the Internet. Airlines had such success with ticket sales over the Internet that they discontinued paying commissions to travel agents for domestic airline tickets. In this chapter, we will explore a variety of technologies that enable e-business. You also will learn about the various forms of e-business that are used by organizations in today's business environment.

Throughout this book, the discussion of e-business is highlighted as it relates to various business processes, controls, and systems-development issues. Because this chapter specifically discusses e-business, we will reserve use of the e-business icon to those places in the chapter where a particularly critical e-business technology or concept is discussed.

Applying E-Business to the Value Chain

Amazon.com has grown because it uses technology to enhance the company's *value chain* and to satisfy customer needs. The basic function of providing a product to a customer is not new; merchants have been in existence for thousands of years. Historically, booksellers, for example, have stocked books that are consistent with their target customers. The customers personally visited the store for their selection, or perhaps in the case of a specialty store, corresponded by mail. Amazon.com's primary innovation was to offer a vast selection of books and other items that were not necessarily in stock and to have the systems in place to acquire the non-stocked items quickly and relatively inexpensively. This concept allows a customer to shop at one "location" (although it is not a physical location) for many different items without burdening Amazon.com with the inventory-carrying expenses of traditional retailers.

---

[7]This process, called Vendor Managed Inventory (VMI), is described in Chapter 12.

A second major innovation from Amazon.com is the collection and analysis of customer purchase data. The analysis process uses sophisticated software to identify patterns and trends in customer preferences. When such information is identified, Amazon.com suggests items that customers with similar buying patterns have purchased, in other words, items that the customer has not purchased but might want.[8] This process can obviously benefit Amazon.com through increased sales but may also increase customers' satisfaction by offering additional products they may enjoy.

Amazon.com has used each of these technological innovations to enhance its value chain and value system. By offering a wide variety of books (and ultimately other products) online and having the procurement and delivery systems in place to satisfy orders in a timely manner, Amazon.com has been able to grow substantially. This growth has come without having a physical retail presence or vast numbers of items in inventory. Another major component of Amazon.com's value chain is the capability to market and sell items to customers based on customer interest. Today, Amazon.com is also a "storefront" where purchasers have access to a variety of vendors in addition to products that are sold by Amazon.com Each of these items has provided Amazon.com a competitive advantage in the online retailers' marketplace.

Extending the storefront into the mobile arena, many companies and consumers have included social networking applications such as Twitter and Facebook as part of their value chain. These relatively new technologies are being used to get recommendations and information from friends, other shoppers, retailers, and manufacturers. Because of the real-time nature of the information exchange, these applications can also be used to share the latest information regarding availability and location of scarce products, as well as pricing and discount updates. Technology not only helps create efficient operations but can also enable organizations to become part of new value chains that were previously not available to them.

The Changing World of Business Processing

For centuries, the basic manner in which commerce transpired changed very little. In the past, a merchant would meet with a customer or another merchant and form an agreement to provide goods to customers in exchange for cash or other goods and services. The merchant would then record these exchanges in books of accounts and periodically consolidate the entries recorded in the books to determine how much various individuals owed the merchant, how much the merchant owed other people, and the excess cash and assets that the merchant owned.

Enterprise
Systems

Over the past three decades, the relative change in commercial practices has been exponential. At the leading edge of technological advance, cottage industries now are springing up on the Internet where personal contacts and face-to-face negotiations do not occur. Online catalogs can be viewed through an Internet browser, and orders can immediately be placed and paid for over the Internet. Of course, the bookkeeping functions may be done in much the same way as the historical merchant did them, but in many cases, the system automatically triggers collection from the credit card company, automatically records the business event in the electronic database, and concurrently updates all of the related accounts. Many companies are using Web development tools

---

[8]Innovations by companies such as Amazon.com, have become central to CRM modules (Chapter 2) available for enterprise systems.

from their ERP vendors to build Web sites that are linked to the ERP system's processing and central database.

Although it may appear that companies have switched from an old way of doing commerce to a brand new way, many organizations actually use both methods. The evolution of information technology has simply provided for alternative forms of business processes and business event data processing that enable some organizations to become more efficient and effective by altering the traditional means by which they have done business. To fully understand how technology can enable an organization to reengineer its business processes and more effectively enter into commerce activities, you first must have a solid understanding of how business event data processing can be completed. After you understand how processing is done, then the exploration of the technologies that enable improved efficiencies in business event data processing will be more meaningful to you.

In this chapter, the evolution of business event data processing is examined to help you understand and appreciate the evolution of business processes, including the different stages of e-business.

A Comparison of Manual and Automated Accounting Information Systems

Over the past several decades, there has been a major shift from manual to automated accounting information systems (AIS). In your work-life, you may never have to make a pencil entry into a sales journal, but it is very important to understand the flow of data through a manual system and how those manual steps have become automated. Although many similarities exist, there are differences in terminology between manual and automated AIS. In this section, we compare portions of a manual AIS with an automated AIS. We describe the terminology used in these processes and show that computerizing an AIS merely changes *how* the data are processed, not what tasks are performed. **Figure 3.1** (pg. 68) depicts the journal, ledgers, and trial balance for Waltham Company for the month of June 20X1, the first month of operations. As we describe the activities depicted in the figure, assume that prior to these activities, we prepared two sales invoices:

* Number 601, dated June 5, 20X1, to Stan Smith for $75.00
* Number 602, dated June 16, 20X1, to Julie Jones for $50.00

1. The first activity in the manual accounting process is to **journalize** the business event (i.e., accounting transaction) in a book of original entry (i.e., a special or general journal). Books of original entry contain events listed in chronological order. In Figure 3.1, two entries are made in the sales journal, one for the Smith sale and one for the Jones sale.
2. The second activity is to **post** the business event from the journal to a subsidiary ledger. Ledgers and subsidiary ledgers are organized by accounts, not chronologically. In this case, we post the sales to the AR subsidiary ledgers by increasing Smith's AR balance by $75.00 and Jones' AR balance by $50.00. Notice the posting reference in the sales journal to the subsidiary ledger numbers 10 and 4 and in the AR subsidiary ledger to the relevant page (page 1) in the sales journal (SJ). (If there is no subsidiary ledger for the event, this step is skipped.)
3. The third activity is to post the total from the journal to the general ledger. In Figure 3.1, the general ledger sales and AR accounts are each increased by $125.00.

FIGURE 3.1   Journalizing, Posting, and Summarizing in a Manual Accounting System

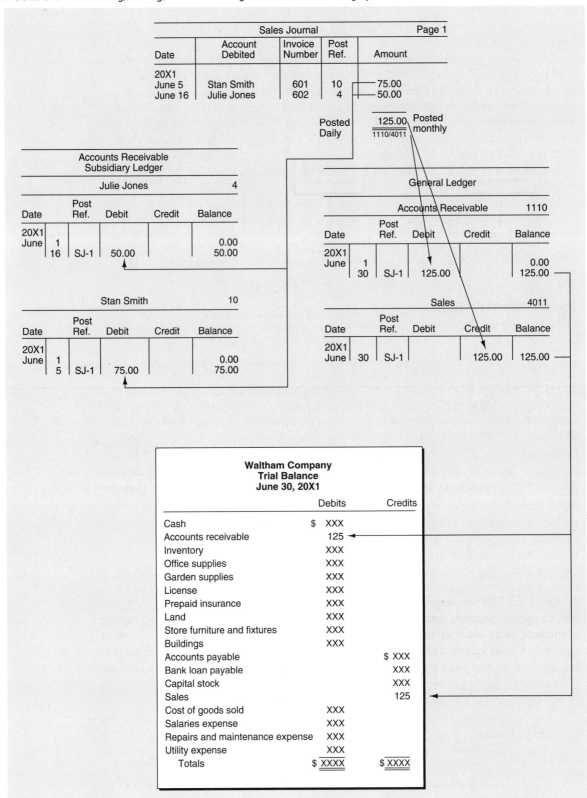

FIGURE 3.2 Automated Accounting System

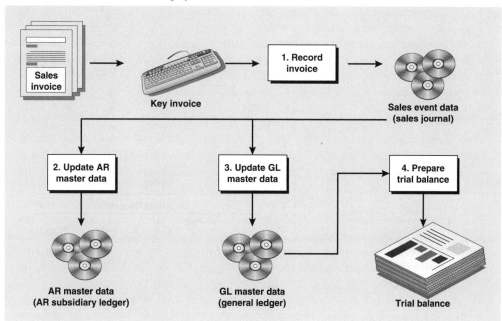

4. The fourth activity is to **summarize** the business events by preparing a trial balance. As you can see in Figure 3.1, the debit and credit balances in the only two general ledger accounts considered in our example are listed in the trial balance. (Additional steps in the manual accounting process usually include adjusting entries, preparing financial statements, and closing entries.)

Figure 3.2 depicts the automated equivalent of the Waltham Company's manual accounting system. Let's compare the activities and related terminology used in Figures 3.1 and 3.2. We also repeat the terms introduced in Chapter 1 with Figure 1.3 (pg. 14), *input*, *processing*, *storage*, and *output*. The four numbered boxes in Figure 3.2 are equivalent to the four activities in the manual accounting process.

The first process, *record invoice*, is equivalent to the *journalizing* activity in the manual system (Figure 3.1) and to the *input* stage in Figure 1.3. This stage includes capturing data (e.g., completing a source document such as the sales invoice) and, if necessary, converting the data to machine-readable form, such as the keying depicted in Figure 3.2.[9] In the same manner that accounting transactions are recorded in a general or special journal, data input to a computer are normally recorded in a business event data store such as the sales event data store in Figure 3.2. A **business event data store** (also known as a *transaction file*) is a book of original entry used for recording business events. These business events comprise the activities of the organization, such as purchasing goods from vendors and collecting cash from customers. The general and special journals used in manual accounting systems are automated as

---

[9]When inputs are keyed into a computer directly without the use of a source document, the capture and conversion steps are combined. For instance, order entry clerks might key in a customer's telephone order without first transcribing it onto an order form. When inputs are received electronically, such as when an order is sent from a customer via the Internet, the capture and conversion steps do not involve any keying within the capturing organization.

specialized views of the business event data store. Note that some events do not automatically generate traditional accounting journal entries. For example, issuing a PO is a business event, but generally, until title of the goods passes, no debit or credit is recorded. Business event data reflect the business events for a certain time period, such as one day. When automated, this data store can include more data than we see in the sales journal in Figure 3.1. (pg. 68) For example, we could include salesperson, customer PO number, order date, terms, and description, price, and quantities of the items sold.

The second process, *update AR master data*, is equivalent to the *post* of business event data to the subsidiary ledger activity in Figure 3.1 and to the *processing (update of storage)* stage of Figure 1.3. (pg. 14) This process can be performed for each invoice as it is recorded on the sale event data store or periodically for a group (or batch) of invoices. When automated, this data store can include more data than you see in the AR subsidiary ledger in Figure 3.1. Such additional data could include salesperson, customer PO number, order date, terms, amounts paid, discounts taken, and description, price, and quantities of the items sold.

The third process, *update GL master data*, is equivalent to the *post* of the total from the journal to the general ledger activity in Figure 3.1 and to the *processing (update of storage)* stage in Figure 1.3. (pg. 14) As with process 2, this process can be performed for each invoice as it is recorded on the sales event data store or periodically for a group (or batch) of invoices. When recorded on an individual basis, the general ledger data may include a summary of *each* sale rather than totals from a journal.

Business event data are used often as a key source to update various master data. These master data updates incorporate new master data into existing master data by adding, deleting, and replacing master data or records. In this case, the sales event data are used to update the accounts receivable master data by adding new accounts receivable records.

Master data are repositories of relatively permanent data maintained over an extended period of time.[10] Master data contain data related to *entities*—persons and organizations (e.g., employees, customers), places (e.g., buildings), and things (e.g., accounts receivable, inventory). Master data include such data as the accounts receivable master data (i.e., the accounts receivable subsidiary ledger), the customer master data, and the general ledger master data (i.e., the general ledger).

Two types of updates can be made to master data: information processing and data maintenance. **Information processing** includes data processing functions related to economic events such as accounting events, internal operations such as manufacturing, and financial statement preparation such as adjusting entries. The updates in Figure 3.2 (pg. 69) are information processing updates related to a sales event. **Data maintenance**, on the other hand, includes activities related to adding, deleting, or replacing the standing data portions of master data. **Standing data** include relatively permanent portions of master data, such as the credit limit on customer master data and the selling price and warehouse location on inventory master data. In this textbook, we emphasize information processing, and our analysis of the internal controls related to master data updates is restricted to master data updates from information processing. However, at appropriate points in the text, we refer to controls related to data maintenance.

The fourth process, *prepare trial balance*, is equivalent to *summarizing* the business events by preparing a trial balance activity in Figure 3.1 and to the *process* (of preparing

---

[10]As we will discuss later in this chapter, business event data and master data represent the relevant portions (or views) of the enterprise database being used for a particular application/business process.

output) in Figure 1.3. To do so, this process retrieves general ledger master data from storage and prints the trial balance.

To summarize, a computerized AIS automates the manual accounting process, with which you are already familiar, to make the automated process roughly equivalent to the manual process. That is, when an AIS is computerized, we change *how* the data are processed, but we do not usually change *what* tasks are performed.

Automating an Accounting Information System

Since the earliest days of manual AIS, accountants recognized that the cheapest and most efficient way to do data processing on large volumes of similar business event data was to aggregate (i.e., batch) several events together and then periodically complete the processing on all the event data at once. **Batch processing** is the aggregation of several business events over some period of time with the subsequent processing of these data as a group by the information system. The **periodic mode** is the processing mode in which a delay exists between the various data processing steps. The periodic mode is heavily dependent on the use of batch processing, and although technically not the same, the two terms are often used interchangeably. Periodic mode can be contrasted with **immediate mode**, the data processing mode in which little or no delay occurs between any two data processing steps. Under periodic mode, a significant delay occurs between two or more data processing steps, while under immediate mode, master files are updated immediately, each time an event is recorded. Immediate mode processing is often used interchangeably with real-time processing. **Figure 3.3** Depicts the automation of our manual accounting system using the batch/periodic mode of processing. The batch mode was originally chosen as the automation technique because it so closely resembled the steps in the manual process.

FIGURE 3.3   Batch Processing of Accounting Data

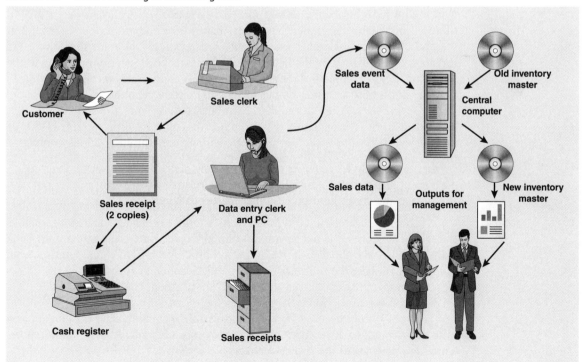

The manual accounting system that we described previously and many automated systems use the *periodic mode*. We start by recording a set of journal entries that represent the business activities that have occurred. These journal entries are then transferred as a group (posted) to the general ledger and then to the trial balance. Executing the journal entry transfers as a *batch* is a more efficient way of maintaining the financial statements than transferring each business event individually to create a complete set of financial statements after each event was recorded (i.e., after each journal entry, you would have to post to the general ledger and recreate the trial balance). In a computerized environment, the easiest approach to automating the accounting process is to simply mirror these manual batch processing systems, which are relatively simple to develop and provide for the most efficient use of employees and computer hardware.

Batch processing systems typically require four basic subprocesses to be completed before an event is converted into information reports that can be used by decision makers. Follow along with Figure 3.3 (pg. 71) to see how each of these four subprocesses is typically completed.

1. *Business event occurs.* At the point of occurrence for the business event, the information for the event is recorded on a source document (by the sales clerk in Figure 3.3). For example, if you think of one of the small businesses you might frequent, such as a used book store, they often have you bring the books you want to purchase to a clerk at the front of the store. The clerk then writes a description of the items purchased on a sales slip (prepared in duplicate) and totals the sale. The clerk returns one copy to you and stuffs the other copy into the cash register drawer.

2. *Record business event data.* A batch of source documents is transferred (taken out of the cash register and sent) to a data entry operator, who takes the information from the source documents and enters the data in a computerized format. The business event data are usually entered using an **offline** device (i.e., one, such as the PC in Figure 3.3, which is not directly connected to a central computer or network). The resulting computerized format becomes the sales event data store. In the used book store example, the owner–manager or the employee closing up at the end of the day may take responsibility for keying all the sales slips into a PC for storage on a disk. The PC becomes simply a data entry device for keying in the sales data. Upon completing the entry, the copies of the sales receipts are clipped together and stored in a file cabinet for possible future reference.

3. *Update master data.* After all the data have been entered into the system, the sales event data store is brought to the computer (possibly by using a CD, DVD, or flash drive) to be processed and any calculations and summarizations completed (represented by the central computer symbol in Figure 3.3). This information is used to update the master data. In the sales example, this might include taking prior inventory totals and subtracting the items sold to derive the new inventory levels. The new inventory levels are accordingly written to an updated master data store. The sales event data also is stored in a more permanent data store, such as the sales data store. It is not uncommon for the owner–manager of the used book store to either take the data stores home and process them on a computer or, even more likely, to take the information to a public accountant for processing.

4. *Generate outputs.* After all the calculations have been completed and the data updated, the system periodically generates the outputs for management (as shown in Figure 3.3). For the used book store, this might include such documents as a sales report and an inventory update report. For this small store, both reports would probably go to the owner–manager.

Note that after each step there is a time delay before the next step occurs. We might think of this form of automated system as a *pure* periodic system in that the entire process uses a periodic mode for processing. For instance, in the used book store example, the day's sales documents are collected before being passed on for keying. After keying, the sales data are held until the data can be transferred to the location and person where the data can be used to update the master data. After the data are updated each day, the reports still may not be generated until later—perhaps on a weekly or monthly basis.

A disadvantage of periodic mode systems is that the only time the master data are up to date is right after the processing has been completed. As soon as the next business event occurs, the master data are again no longer up to date. As a result, little reason exists to provide a query capability (discussed in Chapters 5 and 6) for data that are used in a periodic mode system. Usually, systems users will simply get a copy of the reports generated at the end of a processing run and use this information to make their decisions until the next processing run, and a new set of reports is available. Only in rare situations is a query capability provided, and then only to eliminate the needless printing of reports for occasional users of the information generated by the system.

Technology has also provided other choices for accounting system internal processes. Independent of how a system is implemented (manually or automated), you need to consider how information is aggregated within the system, as well as how that information is reported. The last comparison of manual and automated systems includes reporting. In a manual system, periodically, accounts are summarized, a trial balance is prepared, and financial statements are produced. In contrast, an automated system allows a user to retrieve the trial balance and financial statements with all data that have been processed at the time the report is desired. Technology enables more frequent reporting concurrently with the elimination of many of the compilation tasks.

Online Transaction Entry (OLTE)

Information technology improvements in recent years have provided a low-cost means for improving the efficiency of these traditional automated equivalents to manual accounting systems. The most prevalent change has been the increasing use of online transaction entry to reduce redundancies in pure periodic mode processing (as shown in **Figure 3.4** (pg. 74)). In an **online transaction entry (OLTE)** system, use of data entry devices allows business event data to be entered directly into the information system at the time and place that the business event occurs. These systems merge the traditional subprocesses of business event occurrences (including completion of the source document) and record business event data into a single operation. At the point of the business event, a computer input device or PC is used to enter the event data into the data entry system rather than onto a source document. Generally, prices are automatically generated by the system as the computer retrieves the data from the system data stores. Such a system is considered **online** because the data entry device is connected to the computer. The input system will print documents when source documents are required. As business events occur, they are accumulated on electronic media, such as disk drives.

If we go back to our used book store scenario, it may be that you prefer to buy your books at one of the chain stores such as Barnes & Noble and Borders. When you take your books to the clerk at the counter in these stores, the clerk generally keys or scans the purchase straight into the cash register. As noted in Figure 3.4, at this point, the sales items are being entered into a terminal that is creating (recording) a log of the sales event (the sales event data store), retrieving price list information, and generating duplicate copies of the sales receipt. One copy of the sales receipt is given to you (the customer), and a second copy may be placed in the cash register drawer (for filing in the

FIGURE 3.4   Online Transaction Entry (Batch Processing Environment)

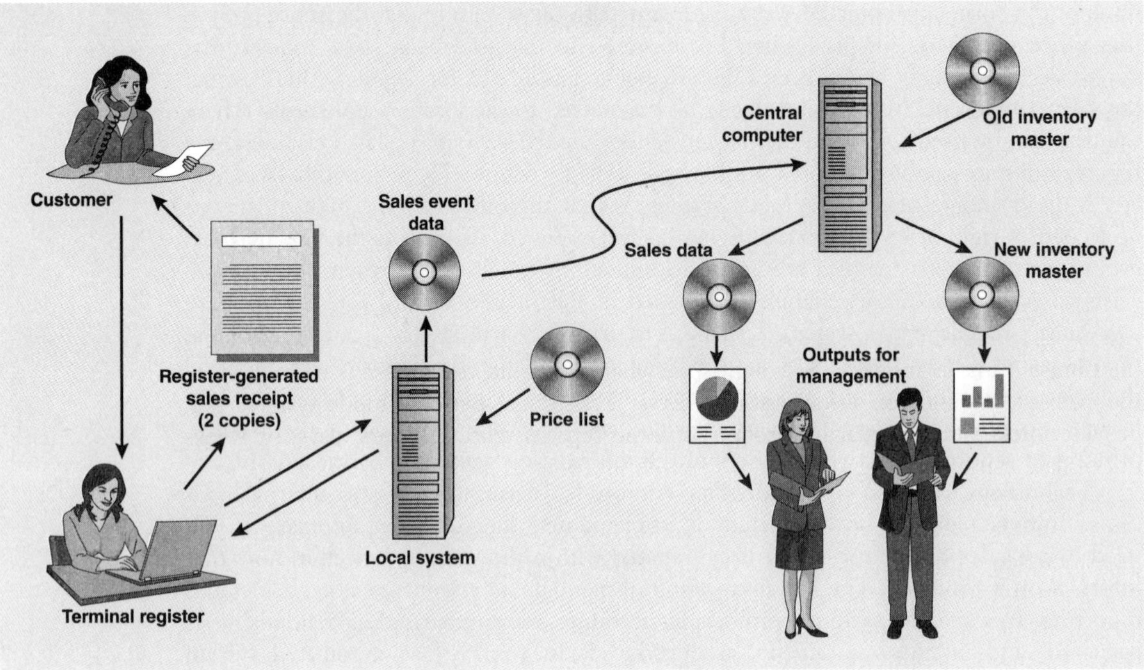

audit file). Note the differences between Figures 3.3 (pg. 71) and 3.4. The manual preparation of the sales receipt and entry into the cash register by the sales clerk in Figure 3.3 becomes one process (keying or scanning at the terminal register) in Figure 3.4. After that, the two processes are the same.

The use of OLTE eliminates the need to have one person enter business event data on a source document and then have a second person perform the data entry to convert the business event data to a computer-ready form. In an OLTE system, one person performs both operations. In many contemporary systems, this data entry is completed using *bar code readers*, *scanners* (Chapter 10), or *RFID (Radio-Frequency Identification) readers* (Chapter 12). The use of such technologies eliminates the human error that can result from entering the data manually. Thus, in many OLTE systems, the only human impact on the accuracy of the input data is the necessity to properly scan items into the system. Various control procedures that are used to ensure data accuracy are discussed in detail in Chapter 9.

Note that the processing of the data in Figure 3.4 is still completed on a batch of event data at a later time. For many sophisticated systems in use by businesses today, sales event data are aggregated by cash register terminals or PCs for the entire day; after the store has closed, the data is electronically transferred over phone lines or a network to a central computer system where the business event data are processed. This is reflected in Figure 3.4 by the communications line connecting the sales event data in the local system to the central computer. The processing is typically completed overnight while all stores in a region are closed, and updated reports are periodically generated to reflect the sales event updates to the master data.

Also note that the use of electronic communication technology does not change the traditional periodic approach but rather makes the approach more efficient. Hence, we encounter one of the first steps in the evolution toward advanced-level e-business systems.

Periodic mode systems traditionally have been the most common method for completing business event data processing. Nonetheless, with AIS being transferred almost exclusively to computerized systems, and given the rapid improvements in information technologies, periodic mode systems are becoming less common for most activities. However, for some applications, periodic mode processing is the preferred approach. For instance, payroll systems are a natural match with the batching of business event data because all employees are generally paid on a periodic basis and at the same time. It is unlikely that payroll will be processed using systems other than periodic mode.

Online Real-Time (OLRT) Processing

Among the many clichés that you hear in today's rather harried business environment is the phrase "time is money." Although somewhat worn out, the phrase is descriptive of the current demands on information systems. Traditional periodic mode systems that provide information primarily through periodic reports that are hours, days, or weeks out of date can put an organization's decision makers at a disadvantage if its competitors are using up-to-date information to make the same decisions (e.g., recall the importance placed on *timeliness* and *relevance* in Chapter 1). The pressures for timely information flows coupled with significant advances in information technologies have led to a rapid migration toward online real-time systems. **Online real-time (OLRT) systems** gather business event data at the time of occurrence, update the master data essentially instantaneously, and provide the results arising from the business event within a very short amount of time—that is, in *real time*. OLRT systems complete all stages of business event data processing in *immediate mode*.

OLRT systems typically require three basic subprocesses to be completed before an event is converted into information that can be used by decision makers. Follow along with **Figure 3.5** as we discuss each of these subprocesses.

FIGURE 3.5   Online Real-Time Processing (OLRT)

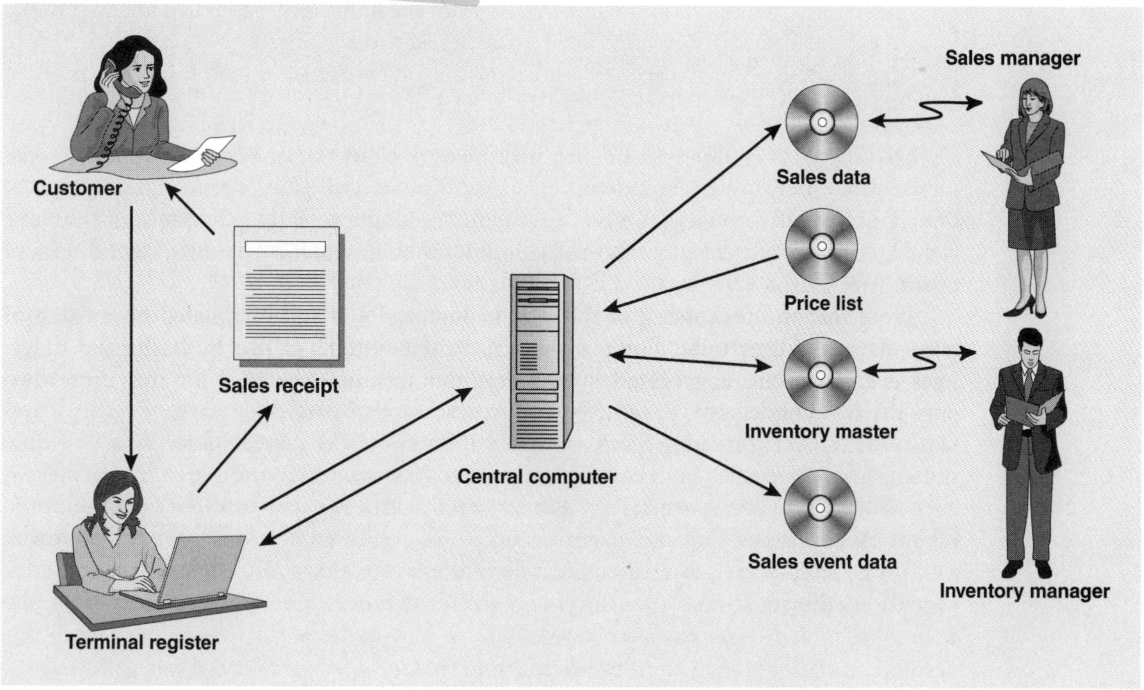

1. *Business event occurs and record business event data.* At the time of the business event, the related data are entered directly into the system. Source documents are almost never used because they significantly slow the process and remove some of the advantages of nonredundant data entry. Notice that the data entry process where the sale is entered into the system is the same as in Figure 3.4 (pg. 74) (other than the absence of the filed copy of the sales receipt). This is consistent with the use of OLTE for OLRT systems.

2. *Update master data.* Each business event that has been entered into the system is processed individually and any calculations and summarizations completed. This information is then used to update the master data. Note in Figure 3.5 (pg. 75) that the processing is now being done at the point-of-sale when the sales event data are entered. Because each business event is processed independently and immediately, the master data at any given point in time will be within minutes or seconds of being up to date. When your bookstore is entering your information into the terminal, it may actually be using an OLRT system if it is important to the store to know whether a given book title is in stock at a given point in time—perhaps to answer a customer's question.

3. *Generate reports (and support queries).* It is neither practical nor desirable that reports and other types of output be generated after each business event is recorded and master data have been updated. Typically, applicable reports and output will still be generated by the system on a periodic basis. At the same time, however, these reports and output will usually be instantaneously available through access to the system on an as-needed basis, as demonstrated in Figure 3.5 with the communications links to the sales and inventory managers. One of the main advantages provided by many OLRT systems is an ability to check the current status of master data items at any point in time. In the bookstore, it allows the sales staff to quickly check whether a certain book is in stock. In many cases, rather than using prespecified reports that may not necessarily provide the information that decision makers need, these information systems users will use a query language (as discussed in Chapters 5 and 6) to dynamically create unique reports that provide the one-time information they need to make key decisions. For instance, the store manager may want to run a report on the inventory stock for the 10 top-selling books.

OLRT systems allow users to nearly eliminate the delay in accessing up-to-date information. However, the primary disadvantage of real-time systems is clearly the cost. To efficiently operate an OLRT system, it is imperative that the point of the business event be linked directly with the computer system—that is, online. Accordingly, to operate an OLRT system, OLTE methods must also be used.

It was noted previously that OLTE systems are increasingly being used with systems that use the periodic mode. Although the data entry performed in all OLTE systems is essentially the same, the mode of subsequent processing may vary. Whereas a pure periodic mode system still processes business event data in batches, an OLRT system using OLTE processes each recorded business event in real time. In a real-time system, business event data cannot be aggregated on a local computer to be transferred later to the data processing center. Rather, each business event must be communicated for processing at the time the event occurs. This results in a more expensive approach to OLTE. In essence, rather than creating a temporary electronic communications connection to download the data to the central computer, an OLRT system generally

Technology Summary 3.1

COMMUNICATION NETWORKS

The key component for electronic communication systems is the network that provides the pathways for transfer of the electronic data. Communication networks range from those designed to link a few computers together to the Internet, where the goal is to link most of the computers in the world together.

Within organizations, a major focus of network computing has been on client/server technology. Client/server technology is the physical and logical division between user-oriented application programs that are run at the client level (i.e., user level) and the shared data that must be available through the server (i.e., a separate computer that handles centrally shared activities—such as databases and printing queues—between multiple users). The enabling networks underlying client/server technologies are local area networks (LANs) and wide area networks (WANs). LANs are communication networks that link several different local user machines with printers, databases, and other shared devices. WANs are communication networks that link distributed users and local networks into an integrated communications network. Such systems have traditionally been the backbone of enterprise systems technology, but recent advances in communications technology are rapidly changing the underlying infrastructure models.

These network technologies are driving the future of e-business. These technologies allow for more simplified user interaction with networks and empower users to access broad arrays of data for supplementing management decision making as well as opening new avenues for direct commerce linkages. The leading technology in this arena is the Internet. As you likely know, the Internet is a massive interconnection of computer networks worldwide that enables communication between dissimilar technology platforms. The Internet is the network that connects all the WANs to which organizations choose to allow access. With the expansion of the Internet has also come increased accessibility to public databases that provide rich information sources that are searchable either for free or on a for-fee basis.

Web browsers are software programs designed specifically to allow users to easily view various documents and data sources available on the Internet. The advent of this easy-to-use software has rippled through organizations and caused a rethinking of how companies can set up their own internal networks to be more accessible to decision makers. The result has been the growing development of intranet, which are essentially mini-internal equivalents to the Internet that link an organization's internal documents and databases into a system that is accessible only to members of the organization, through Web browsers or, increasingly, through internally developed software designed to maximize the benefits of using organizational information resources.

By combining the benefits of the Internet and intranets, many organizations have begun to allow customers, vendors, and other members of their value system access to the company's intranet. This type of network, which has been extended to limited external access, is referred to as an extranet.

The by-product of the expansion in intranets, extranets, and the Internet is a rich medium for e-business. These networks provide the foundation for what likely will be exponential growth in e-business—both at the resale level and in supplier–buyer relationships.

requires a continuous electronic communication connection that will usually necessitate the use of some form of network (covered later in this chapter).

Automated systems that model manual systems and OLRT systems are the two extremes in business event data processing. The systems that mimic manual systems are what we might term pure periodic mode systems in that a delay occurs after every step of the processing. On the other hand, OLRT systems represent pure immediate mode systems in that little or no delay occurs between any steps in the processing. We note these as the extremes because many systems lie somewhere between these two extremes, exhibiting a mix of periodic and immediate mode processes at various stages. For example, OLTE used with batch processing results in an immediate mode approach for combining the *business event occurrence* and *record event data* steps, whereas periodic mode processing might be used for the remainder of the steps.

Each of the described processing methods requires data communications pathways among PCs, terminals, or other systems. **Technology Summary 3.1** describes the interconnectivity of such systems.

Methods for Conducting E-Business

To this point, the discussion has focused on the modes of business event data processing and related communication technologies that underlie the capability of organizations to enter into e-business. In this section, we redirect the discussion to specific methods for conducting e-business and how these methods use alternative modes of business event data processing and available electronic communication technologies.

The four methods of e-business that we will discuss are fairly diverse. First, we provide an overview of the role of *electronic mail* (e-mail) in e-business—a lesser used but more directed approach. Second, we discuss *electronic document management* (EDM). Many would not include EDM as part of e-business because the majority of such applications support events that are not e-business related. We chose to include it in this section because of the integral role it plays on its own and in supporting the other methods. *Electronic data interchange* (EDI) is the third area, which currently represents the predominant form of e-business—the B2B segment discussed above. The fourth method is *Internet commerce*, which represents the fastest-growing segment of e-business. Concurrent with the development of Internet businesses that sell physical products, new organizations have surfaced existing solely to provide data, software, data storage, and so on through the Internet.

Commerce Through E-Mail

Electronic mail (e-mail) is the electronic transmission of nonstandardized messages between two individuals who are linked via a communications network (usually an intranet or the Internet). E-mail represents a weak form for e-business because of the nonstandardized format by which messages are transmitted. Before exploring the use of e-mail as a mode for e-business, let's briefly examine the limitations of using a nonstandardized format.

If you think back to our earlier discussions in this chapter related to various technologies that can be used to automate the data entry process, all the technologies relied on a standardized format for the data (e.g., a bar code or a printed response such as *amount paid* on the sales receipt). This is almost the antithesis of e-mail. E-mail tends to be a very free-form mode of expression and, for the most part, a fairly casual and informal mode of communication. This unstructured nature of the communication mode makes data capture more difficult and generally requires human translation and entry of the data. This increases the likelihood of error and requires more stringent data control procedures to be in place. The e-mail essentially becomes a source document for use in the business event data processing. Generally, e-mail will be used only for low-volume solicitations. Organizations using e-mail as a method of conducting e-commerce must also have a mechanism in place to deal with unsolicited, nondocument mail (spam). As cell phones become an increasingly important part of business operations, text messaging becomes more common in and important to businesses. Accordingly, the nonstructured format and limitations of e-mail also apply to texting. In text messaging there is frequently even less structure than in traditional e-mail.

Despite the limitations, e-mail (and texting) does have several characteristics that make it tolerable for some e-business events. From a sales standpoint, a targeted market can often be identified by locating an appropriate e-mail list. Much like their mailing list counterparts that are used for postal delivery, lists of e-mail addresses for individuals that are likely to be interested in a given product can be useful. Generally, if the marketing medium is e-mail, then the purchase request sometimes will be transmitted in this manner.

Technology Application 3.1

GENERAL USES OF ELECTRONIC DOCUMENT MANAGEMENT SYSTEMS

Case 1

The need to organize client files for quick access and processing leads many accounting firms to adopt document management systems. Firms can increase productivity by adding tools to those document management systems. One such tool, eRoom Enterprise from EMC2®, helps manage content across the life of a project. It also allows cross organization (and cross time-zone) participation in the project, allowing employees to operate with flexibility while complying with regulatory requirements. From an accounting firm perspective, the tool could be used by audit teams working on an engagement in multiple locations, each team member having access to the appropriate part of the working papers. Alternatively, when preparing tax returns, eRoom can be used to enable a client to

review and comment on tax return drafts without giving clients access to internal firm information systems.

Case 2

The Check Clearing for the 21st Century Act (Check 21) became effective on October 28, 2004. The Check 21 Act allows (but does not require) banks to substitute electronic images for paper checks in the check clearing and settlement process. The legislation is expected to save the banking industry billions of dollars. The law allows for "electronic replacement documents" or "substitute checks" to be used in the clearing process. From a different perspective, because of decline of using paper checks, the UK's Payment Council[a] has agreed to close the UK's central check clearing service as of October 31, 2018. Currently there is a study underway to identify easy-to-use alternatives for small transactions where checks are considered most important.

[a]The Payments Council is the organization that sets strategy for UK payments.

Sources: "EMC Documentum eRoom Enterprise," www.emc.com/collateral/software/data-sheet/h3100_eroom_enterprise_ds.pdf, accessed January 30, 2010; Federal Reserve Board, "Consumer Guide to Check 21 and Substitute Checks," www.federalreserve.gov/pubs/check21/consumer_guide.htm, accessed January 30, 2010.

As a means of getting around the unstructured nature of e-mail transmissions, marketers frequently provide an electronic order form that adds structure to the information content of the message. However, even with the electronic order form, entry of the data into the system generally requires some keying by data entry personnel. Thus, the general objectives of e-business—to avoid the need for a salesperson to make the contact and to avoid the business event recording activities during business event data processing—are not achieved.

Electronic Document Management (EDM)

Electronic document management (EDM) is the capturing, storage, management, and control of electronic document images for the purpose of supporting management decision making and facilitating business event data processing. The capturing and storage of document images typically relies on *digital image processing systems* (Chapter 10). The added dimensions of management and control are critical to maintaining the physical security of the documents while at the same time assuring timely distribution to users requiring the information. **Technology Application 3.1** discusses some general uses of EDM.

In general, business applications of EDM fall into two categories:

- *Document storage and retrieval:* For example, mortgages, deeds, and liens are archived and made available to the public for such uses as title searches. Other documents in this category include birth certificates, death certificates, marriage licenses, banking-account signature cards, user manuals, price lists, and catalogs. An EDM system stores the images (e.g., PDF files) of these items and displays or prints a copy of them upon request. Document storage and retrieval also could be implemented using micrographic-based image processing systems (i.e., microfilm).

- *Business event data processing:* For example, loan and insurance applications must pass through several stages, such as origination, underwriting, and closing. The EDM system can manage the workflow and route the documents to the appropriate people—even if these people are geographically dispersed. *Digital image processing systems* must be used for this type of application. An organization's communications networks also must be interconnected in a manner that facilitates access and transmission of document images.

EDM systems provide a relatively inexpensive alternative to paper documentation. Although computer storage and processing requirements are much greater than for key-entered documents, the ability to access and manipulate real images of business documents offers great opportunities for improving the efficiency and effectiveness of many business applications and can create significant competitive advantages for an organization. For instance, fast access to imaged documents often translates into faster, better customer service and results in increased customer loyalty. Because they can be used to digitally store and organize a company's policy and procedure documents, EDM systems often serve as a prerequisite technology for implementing knowledge management systems (discussed in Chapter 5). The typical benefits of EDM systems include the following:

- Reduced cost of handling and storing paper
- Improved staff productivity
- Superior customer service
- Enhanced management of operational workflow
- Faster processing

However, as with any technology, the applications selected for EDM should be chosen wisely. Applications with a high chance of success might be those in which the following is true:

- A large amount of paper is produced and stored. We know of an organization that adopted EDM because it had no more room to store paper within its existing office space. In fact, the engineers said the floor could not support another file cabinet! Imaging systems also can produce economies in situations where paper documents are not abandoned altogether but are moved from storage in expensive office locations to cheaper off-site warehouse storage.
- Data, such as signatures, must be scanned. For example, banks use image processing for signature verification cards.
- Frequent access to the stored data from geographically dispersed locations is needed. For example, clerks at every branch of a bank must be able to view signature verification cards.
- Processing of the stored data are extensive and complex and takes place from multiple locations, as in the case of loan and insurance applications that must be processed, reviewed, and approved by many people.

Electronic Data Interchange (EDI)

EDM also is becoming an increasingly important component of **electronic data interchange (EDI)**, the computer-to-computer exchange of business data (i.e., documents) in structured formats that allow direct processing of those electronic documents by the receiving computer system. EDI has had a significant impact on streamlining data communication among organizations. In many cases, organizations are requiring document and image support for EDI data. Most notable are manufacturing- and engineering-related event data where specifications may need to be more clearly defined with computer-aided design/computer-aided manufacturing drawings. Computer and communications technologies have been successfully applied by organizations to improve accuracy and control and to eliminate paper *within* their information systems applications. However, direct, paperless, business communication *between* organizations has been slowed by the lack of transmission and presentation standards. What this often means is that an organization uses its computer technology to prepare a PO, for example, completely without paper and human intervention—an efficient, fast, and accurate process. But the PO must then be printed and mailed to the vendor. Then, at the vendor, the PO must be sorted from other mail in the mailroom, routed to the appropriate clerk, and entered in the vendor's computer. The efficiency, timeliness, and accuracy gained by the automated purchasing process at the originating organization are lost through the mailing and reentry of the data at the vendor. This is where EDI becomes important by providing standardization of transactions, which in turn has significant control implications and advantages.

Figure 3.6 (pg. 82) depicts the typical EDI components. Follow along as we describe those components; the numbers in circles are cross-references to corresponding locations in the narrative description.

Application Software (circles 1 and 7)

An originating application prepares an electronic business document, such as a PO. At the destination organization, an application processes the business data. For example, the originating application's PO is processed as a customer order by the destination organization's order entry/sales (OE/S) process.

Translation Software (circles 2 and 6)

An application's electronic business document must be translated to the structured EDI format that will be recognized by the receiving computer. Presently, two major, non-proprietary public translation standards exist:

- In the United States and Canada, the American National Standards Institute (ANSI) X12 standard has been used.
- EDIFACT (EDI for Administration, Commerce, and Transport) is the predominant standard for international EDI transactions. Actively promoted by the United Nations for member nations, this standard includes some aspects of ANSI X12 and permits global communication between trading partners.

In addition, several standards are specific to particular industries, such as the Automotive Industry Action Group (AIAG), Transportation Data Coordinating Committee (TDCC), and Chemical Industry Data eXchange (CIDX). Some of these industry standards are compatible with the public, inter-industry standards (e.g., ANSI X12); some are not compatible.

Translation standards include formats and codes for each transmission type, called a *transaction set*, as well as standards for combining several transaction sets for transmission. For example, under the ANSI X12 standard, a PO is a transaction set "850," a shipping notice is a transaction set "856," an invoice is a transaction set "810," and so forth. The ANSI *data dictionary* for transaction set 850 defines the length, type, and acceptable coding for each data element in an EDI purchase order. For example, ANSI X12 describes the format and location within the message of the customer name and address, the part numbers and quantities ordered, the unit of measure of the items ordered (e.g., each, dozen, ton), and so on. **Figure 3.7** depicts the translation process and includes an example of the PO transaction set. The figure shows a sample PO as it might appear as a conventional paper document and then illustrates how the PO is transformed into EDI transaction set 850.

Controls

For a PO example, the translation software translates an outgoing PO to a standard message format (e.g., ANSI X12) and translates the standard formatted message incoming to the receiver of the PO into the form understood by the receiver's application system. This intermediate translation to/from the EDI format prevents the need for an organization to reprogram its application so that it can communicate with *each* trading partner's application.

FIGURE 3.6   Electronic Data Interchange Components

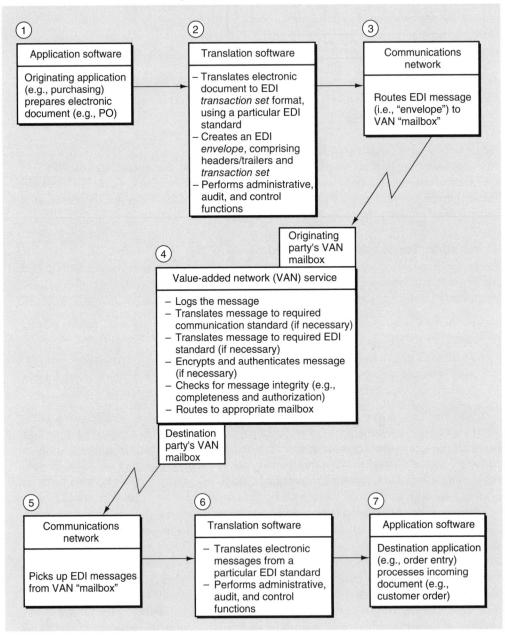

FIGURE 3.7   Electronic Data Interchange Transaction Set

PURCHASE ORDER DOCUMENT	EDI TRANSACTION SET	**850 Purchase Order Transaction Set**	**Explanation**

Heading Area

	Explanation
ST*850*73561 N/L	Start transaction set (ST), identify purchase order (850), and provide sender-assigned control number (73561)
BEG*00*SA*BL2-1563 ***950901 N/L	Begin (BEG) transaction set for a new (00) stand-alone (SA) PO, number (BL2-1563) of September 1, 2007 (950901)
N1*SE*Compu Supply**82645 N/L	Identify (N1) the seller (SE), Compu Supply, vendor number (82645)
N1*BY*Delta Fabricating**29327 N/L	Identify (N1) the buyer (BY), Delta Fabricating, whose customer number to Compu Supply is (29327)
ITD*01*03*2**10*N30 N/L	Specify terms of sale (ITD): basic sale (01), 2% (2) discount if paid within 10 days (10) of invoice date (03), net invoice due in 30 days (N30)
SHH*SD*010*950904 N/L	Specify (SHH) ship date (SD) requested (010) of September 4, 2007 (950904)
SHH*DD*002*950907 N/L	Specify (SHH) delivery date (DD) requested (002) of September 7, 2007 (950907)
FOB*PP N/L	FOB information (FOB): freight prepaid (PP)

Detail Area

PO1*01*140*CA*29.6*QT*IN*A235* *VN*86240 N/L	Order line item data (PO1): line no. (01), 140 (140) cases (CA) ordered, quoted (QT) unit selling price of $29.60 (29.6), with buyer's ID (IN) number of (A235) and seller's ID (VN) of (86240)
PO1*02*25*EA*269.95*QT*IN*1936* *VN*15965 N/L	Order line item data (PO1): line no. (02), 25 (25) units (each) (EA) ordered, quoted (QT) unit price of $269.95 (269.95), with buyer's ID (IN) number (1936) and seller's ID (VN) of (15965)

Summary Area

CTT*2*165 N/L	Control totals (CTT): number of PO lines (2) and total of the number of units ordered (140 + 25) = (165)
SE*12*73561 N/L	End the transaction set (SE), give the number of segments included (12) and the control number from the header (73561)

NOTES: The asterisk (*) character designates a field separator. Consecutive field separators (***) signify omitted data. N/L denotes a new line (e.g., a carriage return).

Purchase Order

To:	Compu Supply 82645	Date: 09/01/07
	986 Silicon Drive	Order No.: BL2-1563
	Napa Valley, CA 97624	
From:	Delta Fabricating 29327	
	2901 Second Ave.	
	Van Nuys, CA 95862	

Freight	Terms	Ship Date	Due Date
Prepaid	2/10; n/30	09/04/07	09/07/07

Line No.	Your Item No.	Our Item No.	Item Description	Unit Price	Quantity	Unit of Meas.
1	86240	A235	4-meg DRAM 50 mhz	29.60	140	CA
2	15965	1936	486 CPU 32 bit	269.95	25	EA

Source: Adapted with permission from A. Faye Borthick and Harold P. Roth, "EDI for Reengineering Business Processes," *Management Accounting* (October 1993): 35–36.

Communications Network (circles 3 and 5)

The two trading partners must have a method of communicating the electronic messages to each other. One method is to establish a direct computer-to-computer link between the origination computer and one or more destination computers. However, communications system incompatibilities may require that one partner or the other purchase communications hardware or software, which makes this a costly option. Further, agreeing on such details as what time of day to send and receive data from trading partners makes this option difficult to manage.

To overcome some of the shortcomings of direct connections, organizations may use either EDI service bureaus or the Internet. The EDI *service bureau* is an organization that acts as an intermediary between trading partners, providing some or all of the services in circles 2–6. The EDI service bureau generally works with smaller suppliers that are reluctant to acquire in-house translation and communications software. In such a case, the translation software (circles 2 and 6) and communications software (circles 3 and 5) reside on the service bureau's computer system. For a fee, the service bureau takes EDI messages—such as POs—from the company (i.e., circle 1), translates the messages into formats that are usable by the suppliers' computer applications, and forwards them to the suppliers (i.e., circle 7). In the other direction, the bureau translates suppliers' documents—such as shipping notices or invoices—into a standard EDI format and sends the electronic documents to the company. The Internet provides organizations with a modern network infrastructure to accomplish direct communications and has increasingly become the communication method of choice for EDI transmissions. (We discuss Internet connections later in this chapter.)

Value-Added Network (VAN) Service (circle 4)

Rather than connecting to *each* trading partner, an organization can connect to a **value-added network (VAN)** service. A VAN service acts as the EDI "post office." An organization can connect to the VAN when it wants, leave its outgoing messages, and, at the same time, pick up incoming messages from its "mailbox." A VAN generally operates as a hub by linking many business partners together. Like an EDI service bureau, the VAN can perform translation service (circles 2 and 6) and communications services (circles 3 and 5) as well as the other services noted at Circle 4 in Figure 3.6 (pg. 82). When the Internet, with or without an EDI service bureau, is employed for communication, the VAN mailboxes are often replaced by secure FTP sites hosted by EDI service bureaus or one of the trading partners. **Technology Summary 3.2** presents some management, operational, and control issues associated with EDI.

Technology Summary 3.2

EDI MANAGEMENT, OPERATIONS, AND CONTROL CONSIDERATIONS

Benefits of EDI include the following:

- Many organizations have survived (and thrived) by being "forced" to implement EDI if they wanted to continue doing business with certain customers. For instance, Wal-Mart Stores and Kmart Corporation require EDI capabilities of all their vendors.
- Responsiveness to customers' needs has improved. In many cases, trading partners have discovered that the cooperation engendered by EDI has reduced conflicts between them, improved communication, and fostered trust. In some cases, customers give suppliers access (through EDI communication links) to real-time, point-of-sale (POS) information about what is and is not selling at its various retail outlets. With that information available, the suppliers can forecast customer demand more accurately, fine-tune their production schedules accordingly, and meet that demand in a highly responsive manner. This is discussed further in Chapter 12.
- By not reentering data at the receiving organization, processing costs are reduced and accuracy is improved. To better

appreciate the potential impact of this benefit, consider that, according to one estimate, 70 percent of the data processed by a typical company's computer had been output by another computer system.

- Mailroom and other document preparation and handling costs are eliminated. For example, in the automobile industry, it is estimated that $200 of the cost of each car is incurred because of the amount of paper shuffling that has to be done.
- By providing timely and accurate data, forecasting, analysis, and cash flow are improved, and the occurrence of stock-outs is reduced.
- In the course of implementing EDI, an organization has the chance to rethink and redesign existing processes and controls.

Costs of EDI include the following:

- Modifying trading relationships and negotiating contracts
- Buying or leasing hardware and software
- Establishing relationships with VANs and negotiating contracts
- Training employees
- Reengineering affected applications
- Implementing security, audit, and control procedures

(Continued)

Technology Summary 3.2 (continued)

Control considerations include the following:

- Because physical signatures will no longer evidence authorizations, controls must ensure proper authorization. At some point during the process, we must authenticate that the message is sent to—and received from—the party intended and is authorized by someone with the proper authority.
- Without external, visual review, some business event data can be significantly in error. For example, a payment could be off by one decimal point! Therefore, controls must *prevent* rather than *detect* such errors.
- Given that the computer initiates and authenticates messages, controls over the computer programs and data—*program change controls* and *physical security* (see Chapter 8)—become even more important than in non-EDI systems.
- If a VAN is used for communicating between partners, security procedures must prevent compromise of sensitive data, and controls must ensure correct translation and routing of messages.

Therefore, controls must be in place to ensure the following:

- All transaction sets are delivered to/received from authorized trading partners.
- All recorded business event data are recorded once and only once.
- Data are accurately received (sent). Data are accurately translated.
- Data are accurately translated in the application interface.
- Senders are authorized to send the transaction type.
- Messages are not intercepted or altered during transmission.
- The log of business event data is protected.
- Unauthorized messages are prevented from being sent.

To attain these control goals, organizations have implemented the following control plans, among others:

- Some control plans are inherent in the very nature of the way EDI is implemented. As we noted, the EDI headers and trailers accompanying transaction sets contain important control data. For example, the next to last line in Figure 3.7 (pg. 86) contains an item/line count and a hash total of the number of units ordered. The last line includes a control total of the number of segments comprising the transaction set (12) and a control number (73561) that should agree with the corresponding number from the header on line one of the table. Functional acknowledgements (FAs) also

help to ensure the integrity of EDI messages (i.e., that data have not been lost or garbled in transmission).

- Expert systems (see Chapter 5) may be used to determine that incoming messages are reasonable—consistent with normal message patterns—to authenticate the source and authorization for the message.
- Access to EDI applications may require a *biometric security system*, a *smartcard*, or a physical key as well as a *password* (see Chapter 8).
- *Data encryption* (see Chapters 8 and 9) may be employed to protect data during transmission.
- *Digital signatures* (see Chapter 9) may be used. Much like a password or other access code, the digital signature uniquely identifies who approved a business event and also helps to ensure that the EDI message was not altered during transmission.
- "Continuous auditing" may be implemented through the use of *integrated test facilities (ITF)* or *imbedded audit modules*. An ITF creates dummy corporations or branches in the system data and processes test data for these dummy entities at the same time that live data are being processed for real entities. An imbedded audit module acts like an audit "alarm" that is programmed to alert the auditor—by printing an audit log—to suspect data (e.g., business event data of an unusually high dollar amount) or unauthorized attempts to access the system.

Finally, contracts between trading partners and with the VANs must specify responsibility for controls and for erroneous transmissions. For example, who is responsible for authenticating the source and destination of messages? If a message is garbled by the VAN, who is responsible for any resulting financial loss—the sender, the receiver, or the VAN? Contracts might address the following issues:

- When is a message considered received? When it is sent, when it is transmitted, when it gets to the mailbox, or when it is picked up? The answers to such questions are important in establishing the point at which an agreement, such as a purchase, legally exists between trading partners. Resolving such questions also is critical in situations where the message is a bid with a time deadline.
- Who is responsible for data integrity, audit trails, security, and so on?
- What are the penalties for failing to perform as required?

EDI and Business Event Data Processing

If we consider the implications of EDI to business event data processing, one of the main advantages is the significant reduction in the need for interaction between purchasers and salespeople, coupled with the standard implementation of OLTE. You should recall from our earlier discussion in this chapter that OLTE eliminates the redundancy between source document capture of business event data and subsequent keying in of the source document. With EDI, both activities are eliminated for the selling organization because OLTE activities are initiated and completed by the linking purchaser. This eliminates any risk of erroneous data entry from within the selling organization. As we go forward, keep in mind that EDI may be completed through traditional modes using dedicated communications lines, but EDI is increasingly moving to the Internet, allowing companies to save the cost of the VANs. Recent evidence of this move suggests that Internet EDI is the source of EDI growth, whereas traditional EDI modes are relatively flat.[11] By eliminating VANs through switching from traditional to Internet EDI, it is possible for a company to have a significant reduction in costs. In the future, we should expect Internet EDI to dominate B2B e-commerce.

Be careful, however, not to make any assumptions as to the mode of business event data processing. You will recall from our earlier discussion that OLTE can be used with both periodic and immediate modes of processing. The same holds true for the core business processing activities in an EDI environment.

When trading partners communicate with each other electronically, they also discover that they have to communicate *internally* in new ways to achieve the full benefit of EDI. That is, EDI forces an organization to assume that all information flows—both internally and externally—are instantaneous. Accordingly, for many, EDI—along with other enabling technologies such as electronic document management (EDM)—has been the catalyst for change in a firm's basic business processes. In other words, EDI has been the forerunner to significant technology innovations for those companies.

To date, EDI has clearly been the dominant domain in e-business. In fact, a mere decade or so ago, e-business was basically EDI. The Internet is radically changing the nature of e-business, to the point that in the not-too-distant future, the Internet will become the dominant platform for not only e-business but EDI as well. Does this mean EDI is dying? Well, not exactly. Many experts believe EDI is here to stay, and currently EDI volume, while not growing substantially, is still heavy in many industries. Still, the Internet shows far more potential growth—primarily from the potential seen in the emerging replacement language for HTML on the Web: XML. *XML (eXtensible Markup Language)* is an environment using tags to describe data for the purpose of easy transmission over networks. XML is currently being used to develop technologies known as Web Services and service-oriented architecture (SOA) applications.

Web Services and Service-Oriented Architectures

What exactly is meant by the term *Web Services*? When talking about Web Services, most people are referring to a set of technologies used for connecting two systems and allowing the implementation of an SOA. The technologies normally included are WSDL (Web Service Definition Language), UDDI (Universal Description, Discovery and Integration), and SOAP (Simple Object Access Protocol).[12] Our working definition of **Web Services** is a software application that supports direct interactions with software

---

[11]Ann Bednarz, "Internet EDI: Blending Old and New," *Network World*, 21(8) (February 23, 2004): 29–30.

[12]A good source of information on Web Services is www.service-architecture.com.

FIGURE 3.8   A Web Service Implementation of an SOA Application

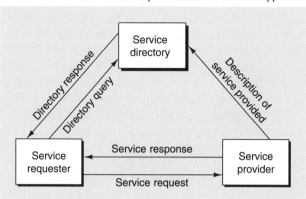

objects over an intranet or the Internet. In this section, we describe SOAs from the perspective of Web Services.

Service-oriented architecture (SOAs) refer to well-defined, independent functions (or applications) that can be distributed over a network via Web Services. The SOA applications are essentially plug-and-play components that are available over the Internet. To be plug-and-play, they must be for a well-defined process, as well as self-contained and independent of other processes.

An SOA application may be implemented as a Web Service with existing technology. Consider the system displayed in **Figure 3.8**. A Service Directory lists available services and the provider of each service. A Service Provider must register with the directory and provide the description of the service provided. When a Service Requester needs a service, the requester queries the Service Directory. The Service Directory then responds with information on a Service Provider that meets the need. That response will include how to contact the provider and in what form the information must be requested. The next step is for the Service Requester to contact the Service Provider with the request. The Service Provider responds to meet the requester's needs.

Next, consider a simple example of an SOA application, implemented as a Web Service. Suppose you are planning a trip to the XXII Winter Olympic Games in Sochi, Russia. Your first concern is the weather. What are your options for accessing the weather? You can use a computer with Internet access. You can use your mobile phone. You may be able to use your cable or satellite television connection. Think of the Hydrometeorological Centre of Russia's (HCR) forecast system operating as an SOA. You can request the weather (from the HCR) at any point during your trip via mobile phone, computer, television, or practically any other device, and receive an updated weather forecast. Separate applications are not required for each device used. This trivial example should show you the potential of SOAs to help reach many users of a service at a much lower cost than building application interfaces for every device. At the same time, you can see how easy it would be to switch to another service if a different service provider has a preferable product (one that is more accurate, faster, or an improvement in any dimension that is important to you).

Web Services, combined with SOA, are growing rapidly. Currently, many applications are under development and using Web Services to connect dissimilar technologies. This application growth has the potential for a major impact on e-business. As the numbers of these applications increase, so will the business potential. As applications become modular and generic, there is the possibility of reduced cost and better integration within and among organizations. Improved integration among organizations may someday replace many of the EDI applications that are required for e-business in today's environment.

Internet Commerce

Internet commerce is the computer-to-computer exchange of business event data in structured or semistructured formats via Internet communication that allows the initiation and consummation of business events. In many cases, the goods or services that are contracted for through the Internet are immediately (or soon thereafter) forwarded back to the consumer via the Internet as well (i.e., when the goods or services can be provided in electronic format, such as with software, movies, and music). Internet commerce radically simplifies e-business by allowing the organization that is receiving and processing business event data to project template formats across the Internet to business partners for easy data entry and data transmission. For instance, if you connect across the Internet with Lands' End (a direct merchandiser of clothing), it has the "catalog quick order" form. With this form, you are provided an entry box to key the product number for the item you want to order. The Web page automatically takes the number and identifies what additional information is needed (e.g., for most clothing, it will be size, color, and quantity). The additional information is presented in menu form for you to select from the options that are available (e.g., for color, the menu might show red, navy, black, white, and green). As you enter the responses on your computer, the data are automatically captured and recorded on the Lands' End computer. **Technology Summary 3.3** provides some management, operational, and control issues associated with Internet commerce.

Two primary categories of e-business exist over the Web: business-to-consumer (B2C) (e.g., Lands' End), and business-to-business (B2B). **Figure 3.9** (pg. 90) depicts a typical secure Internet commerce arrangement. Follow along as we describe the components in the commerce relationship. Note that the numbers in the circles are cross-references to corresponding locations in the narrative description.

Client/Server Relationship (circles 1 and 7)

The connection created between the customer and the vendor is an extended form of client/server applications. The customer (circle 1) is the client node—dictating that during connection, the customer computer environment should be secure and essentially nonaccessible via the network. The vendor (circle 7) is the server node and therefore must have the capability to receive the customer's transmission and translate that transmission into processable data for use in the vendor's application programs. This translation is made through *common gateway interface (CGI)* software. The vendor, acting as the server part of the relationship, then provides the necessary correspondence back to the customer (client) in an understandable format (i.e., Internet-based language). To use the Lands' End example again, this means that when you place your order, your computer should be nonaccessible (i.e., secure) over the Internet, and the type of computer and software you are using will be unknown on the system. The Lands' End computer will receive your order and use CGI to translate your message into a form its program can understand and process. Similar to EDI environments, after the vendor collects the business event data, the applications can be completed through any of the modes of business event data processing. For instance, Lands' End uses an immediate mode approach to process sales events upon receipt.[13]

---

[13]Lands' End, www.landsend.com/customerservice/services_policies/PS_security.html, accessed January 28, 2010.

Network Providers (circles 2 and 5)

Much like the examples discussed with EDI, to participate in Internet commerce, both parties to the business event must have the capability to communicate. For Internet commerce, this means being connected to the Internet. For many companies and organizations (as well as some individuals), this access will be obtained through a direct connection between the entity's computer networks (or a single server) and the Internet. For other companies and organizations, as well as the vast majority of individuals, it will be more desirable to gain access through a network provider.

Network providers are companies that provide a link to the Internet by making their directly connected networks available for access by fee-paying customers. From the customer side, this physical connection is made in Figure 3.9 using one of many options, such as a cable (TV), DSL, direct Ethernet, satellite dish, or the traditional telephone line, to connect with the network provider's network. Companies and

---

Technology Summary 3.3

INTERNET COMMERCE MANAGEMENT AND OPERATIONS CONSIDERATIONS

Benefits of Internet commerce include the following:

- Many organizations have survived by being "forced" to implement Internet commerce to compete in the changing nature of their industry. If they want to remain competitive with other industry companies that may be taking advantage of the cost savings accruing from use of the Internet for commerce, they may need to venture to the Web.
- Responsiveness to customers' needs has improved. Increasingly, customers are expecting immediate feedback and easy availability of information and help (e.g., *customer self-service* systems). The Internet can be a useful tool for servicing customer and client needs—forming the communications medium for distributing information and support services.
- Many organizations have achieved global penetration. The Internet is generally the easiest and least expensive way to reach global customers that an organization may never have been able to reach before. The Internet commerce marketplace is truly global.
- By not reentering data at the organization receiving the electronic transmission, processing costs are reduced, and accuracy is improved. Customers now provide most of the data entry themselves, removing the need for the selling organization to key most of the business event data.
- Mailroom and other document preparation and handling costs are eliminated. The business event data processing side of a business can operate with virtually no human intervention until it is time to prepare and deliver goods.
- In the course of implementing Internet commerce, an organization has the opportunity to rethink and redesign existing business processes and controls.

Costs of Internet commerce include the following:

- Organizational change to a completely different way of doing business.
- Buying equipment and maintaining connection to the Internet (or leasing through a network provider).
- Establishing connections with a new set of customers.
- Staffing and training employees to work in a technology-driven environment.
- Reengineering application systems to process data acquired through the Internet.
- Maintaining security of the Internet site.

Risks of Internet commerce include the following:

- Hackers attempting to access sensitive information such as customer lists or customer credit card information.
- Denial-of-service attacks (see Chapter 7) are expected to escalate over the next few years as individuals or organizations attempt to knock out Web sites by overloading them with site visits and preventing customers or other users from gaining access. These attacks may occur simply for the challenge or frequently due to a political or other difference with the organization that hosts the site.
- Increasingly, the success of B2B Internet commerce relationships necessitates the identification of business partners that are allowed to gain access to sensitive internal information. Trust must be placed with these business partners, but certainly a breakdown of that trust can have grave consequences to the organization making its information available.

FIGURE 3.9 Typical Electronic Communications Connection for Internet Commerce

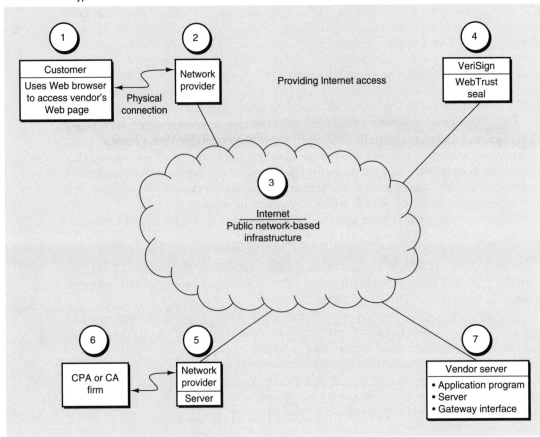

other organizations are also using high-speed direct "Trunk Level" lines (referred to as T1/T2/T3/T4 lines, depending on the speed of the line) to maintain continuous broadband access.

Most network providers bring a host of other benefits along with Internet access. Common benefits include e-mail access, e-mail boxes, space allocation for personal Web pages, and remote connection to other computer sites (e.g., telnet and FTP connection). Many organizations also use network providers to run their Internet servers for them, thus hosting their Web presence. In Figure 3.9 (pg. 90), circle 5 denotes a network provider that is providing server management services for the CPA or CA firm denoted by circle 6. Hence, when the business event is being completed between the customer and the vendor, information from the accounting firm is acquired from a server operated by the firm's network provider.

Assurance Providers (circles 4 and 6)

A major concern with participating in Internet commerce for most organizations and individuals has been Internet security. This is the single most critical factor that has hampered the growth of Internet commerce to date. As security technology has increased, so has the public's willingness to participate in Internet commerce, although concerns of privacy and identity theft are significant. A recent survey indicates 79 percent of Internet users are concerned that their personal information will be sold, whereas 74 percent of users are concerned with identity theft.[14] Many stories exist about credit card misuse and identity theft. The U.S. Federal Trade Commission estimates that 9 million Americans have their identities stolen each year. In 2005, 3.7 percent of U.S. households were exposed to some type of identity theft (including credit card misuse). The total annualized losses for the year were more than $15.6 billion![15] The Internet has spawned a whole array of cottage industries that have no physical storefronts but rather are operated completely from Internet server-supported Web pages. Many Internet users are rightfully concerned about the possibility that a company may be fictitious, with the electronic storefront merely being a means by which to gather credit card and debit card information for illicit use. In Chapters 8 and 9, you will be introduced to technologies such as encryption that provide organizations and their customers a protected environment in which to transact business.

Concerns over security have spurred the development of a new line of business—Internet assurance services. **Internet assurance is a service provided for a fee to vendors to provide limited assurance to users of the vendor's Web site that the site is in fact reliable and event data security is reasonable.** Technology Application 3.2 (pg. 92) provides a more detailed discussion of Internet certification programs and assurance services.

In Figure 3.9 (pg. 90), we demonstrate how one common type of assurance provider operates using the WebTrust® program as discussed in Technology Application 3.2. The vendor (circle 7) displays the WebTrust certification seal and a reference to the assurance provider on its server Web page. When accessing the vendor's Web page, the customer can click on the WebTrust symbol to determine that it continues to be applicable. Clicking on the WebTrust symbol executes a link to the VeriSign® server (circle 4) for verification of the authorized use of the symbol. VeriSign, which simply operates as a verification company, verifies the symbol's appropriate use by sending a message to the customer (circle 1). The customer also can get a report on the level of assurance provided with the certification by clicking on the Web link (contained on the vendor's Web page) for the accounting firm. Clicking on this link connects the customer with the accounting firm's (circle 6) server—operated by its network provider (circle 5)—and the auditor's Internet assurance report for the vendor is displayed on the customer's computer (circle 1).

In addition to concerns regarding event data, many customers have apprehensions over the protection and use of their personal information. To address this issue, the AICPA/CICA Privacy Framework was developed.[16] The framework includes the AICPA/CICA Trust Services Privacy Principle and Criteria to be used in all assurance engagements.

Internet Connection (circle 3)

We briefly note here how the Internet connection is provided between two or more entities. The network diagram of a cloud, displayed at circle 3, pictorially represents how the Internet operates. The choice of a cloud for this diagram is no coincidence.

---

[14]"Security Concerns Dog U.S. Online Shoppers, Says Survey," www.computerworld.com, November 22, 2005.

[15]"Federal Trade Commission—2006 Identity Theft Survey Report," November 2007, www.ftc.gov/os/2007/11/SynovateFinalReportIDTheft2006.pdf, accessed January 29, 2010.

[16]Available, as of June 3, 2008, for download at www.aicpa.org.

Cloud computing, the use of the Internet to provide scalable services, such as software, and resources, such as data storage, to users, is increasing in popularity. An example with which you may be familiar is an e-mail service such as Gmail. Using a browser, you do not need another e-mail program or storage to house your e-mail messages. It is accessible anywhere you have an Internet connection, but you do not know physically where the programs are, nor where your messages are stored. It is as if the service exists somewhere in a "cloud." Typically, users can purchase as much of these services and resources as they need at the time, thus eliminating the up-front, fixed costs normally associated with acquiring such resources. However, as we will see in Chapter 8, cloud computing's nebulous, unstructured nature raises some significant control issues.

With our Internet commerce example, you must have a link to one of the network providers that are connected to the Internet (as discussed earlier), represented by the cloud. The client machine provides an Internet address indicating the Internet site with which the client wants to connect. A connection is then made between the client and the desired site—the server. This connection is made by working a path between the network provider (circle 2) and the server connection (circle 7). The path chosen will differ from one time to the next based on what links in the Internet may not be working at a given time and based on how busy the traffic is on various network connections between the client and the server. The amount of traffic also influences the

---

Technology Application 3.2

INTERNET SECURITY CERTIFICATION

CPA WebTrust

How do you know that an Internet merchant can be trusted? One source of confidence is a brand name—a vendor that has a good reputation for service and quality. Typically, large vendors such as Amazon.com or Wal-mart.com have a reputation for dealing honestly with their customers. In an attempt to provide small vendors with a reputation, eBay® uses the feedback from each vendor's trading partners. For each vendor, you are allowed to see the feedback before you purchase. You would obviously be cautious if frequent posts indicate that the vendor did not ship items in a timely manner or of an advertised quality. Besides eBay, there are services that provide assurance (in varying degrees) to give you confidence in Web sites. Some of these services are VeriSign, TRUSTe®, and CPA WebTrust. Our discussion will focus on the CPA WebTrust Seal of Assurance because it was developed by accountants under a joint venture between the American Institute of Certified Public Accountants (AICPA) and the Canadian Institute of Chartered Accountants (CICA). CPA WebTrust is designed to provide comfort and assurance that a Web site is reasonably safe for users participating in B2C Internet commerce. Upon receiving an unqualified opinion from an accounting practitioner, a seal is placed on the

client's Web page. A user of the Web page can click on the seal to receive verification of the rights for the symbol to be displayed on the given Web page. By selecting the link provided with the seal, the user can view the practitioners' actual report on the client's Web site. The Web Trust seal provides assurances that a CA or CPA has evaluated the business practices and controls of the given client to determine whether its Web page is in accordance with WebTrust criteria. After a site receives WebTrust certification, the practitioner should review the site periodically to ensure that adequate standards have remained in place and the site remains reasonably secure. Basically, a Web site must meet the following principles:

- *Security:* The system is protected against unauthorized access (both physical and logical).
- *Availability:* The system is available for operation and use as committed or agreed.
- *Processing integrity:* System processing is complete, accurate, timely, and authorized.
- *Online privacy:* Personal information obtained as a result of e-business is collected, used, disclosed, and retained as committed or agreed.
- *Confidentiality:* Information designated as confidential is protected as committed or agreed.

Sources: AICPA/CICA, "CPA/CA WebTrust® Version 2.0," www.cica.ca, August 2000; AICPA/CICA, "Suitable Trust Services Criteria and Illustrations for Security, Availability, Processing Integrity, Online Privacy, and Confidentiality (Including WebTrust® and SysTrust®)," www.aicpa.org/download/trust_services/final-Trust-Services.pdf, accessed January 28, 2010.

Technology Summary 3.4

INTERNET AUCTION MARKETS

Internet auction markets provide an Internet base for companies to put products up for bid or for buyers to put proposed purchases up for bid. In the first case, a scenario common to the eBay exchange, a market participant puts an item up for bid, sets a minimum bid price, and awaits completion of the bidding process. While this market is fairly successful for B2C Internet commerce, it is not so effective for B2B Internet commerce. For B2B Internet commerce, a company may put specifications for a product out on the marketplace as a request for proposals (RFPs). Participating organizations in the market can then bid on the sales by providing a proposal that includes details on product specifications, costs, availability (i.e., timing of delivery), and logistics. The buying organization can then select the proposal that seems most desirable for meeting the organization's needs at a minimal cost and risk.

---

speed of connection and is the reason why the Internet is slower at some times than at others.

A couple of other issues related to the organization of the Internet and its impact on such commerce should be noted. First, by the nature of the Internet being a "public network-based infrastructure," it has greatly leveled the field in e-business. With traditional EDI, only fairly large businesses could afford the communications hardware and software to effectively use e-business as a competitive weapon. The creation of a public network and the subsequent creation of relatively inexpensive (or even free) software for using the network have brought the costs of e-business within the threshold of economic feasibility for most small and medium-sized enterprises (SMEs). These changes in cost structure and ease of use are the two forces driving the strong growth in Internet commerce.

The other phenomenon that has arisen from the new economic feasibility of e-business is an explosion in cottage industries and electronic storefronts. These cottage industries that have sprung up to support Internet commerce include companies that provide one or more of the following: Internet access, Web page development, interface software for linking between Web pages and application programs, e-mail, and related goods and services. **Electronic storefronts** represent the creation of Internet-located resources for displaying goods and services for sale and for conducting related sales events. For many emerging small companies, these electronic storefronts are the only storefronts, and no sales staff or physical storefronts need to be maintained. Even better, you can run your operation from that ski chalet in Vermont or the beach condominium in Florida, regardless of where your potential customers live. Further, the world is now your marketplace!

Other Internet Uses for E-Business

Before leaving this chapter on e-business, we should discuss other ways in which the Internet is being used to support commerce. Although we have focused in this chapter on the most common forms of Internet commerce and the direct linkages between customer and vendor, a number of intermediaries are evolving that promise to reduce costs for organizations. The two forms that seem most likely to have long-term success are *auction markets* and *market exchanges*. These are explained in greater detail in **Technology Summary 3.4** and **Technology Summary 3.5** (pg. 94).

The Internet is not only a place for completing sales but is also an environment for improving customer support for non–Internet-based commerce. Probably the biggest use for the Internet at this point in time is to support the delivery of goods and services

Enterprise Systems

Technology Summary 3.5

INTERNET MARKET EXCHANGES

Internet market exchanges bring together a variety of suppliers in a given industry with one or more buyers in the same industry to provide Internet commerce through organized markets. Suppliers can put their products online, generally feeding into electronic catalogs that allow the buyer(s) to sort through alternatives from different suppliers and electronically place an order. Often, only one supplier will carry a certain item, but efficiencies are still gained by avoiding the PO process (described in detail in Chapter 12) and executing an order through selection from a Web catalog. In some cases, buyers make their needs known on the marketplace, and suppliers review the needs and determine whether to fill the orders. The key is to make sure the market is efficient enough to ensure that the buyer will get the product purchased on a timely basis for when it is needed—often meaning that the purchased goods arrive at an assembly line within an hour of when the goods will be needed for production. This part can be tricky, and the exchange must be set up carefully.

Internet market exchanges can be either private or public. Private exchanges restrict the buyers and suppliers that can participate in the market. Public exchanges bring together suppliers and buyers and allow essentially any organization to participate, subject sometimes to credit approval and background checks. Because of their exclusive nature, private exchanges have drawn the watchful eye of the Federal Trade Commission (FTC), which maintains concerns over fair trade practices and potential anticompetitive practices that evolve from restricting participation in the market exchange.

for customers. In its simplest form, a Web page may simply be one more venue in which to advertise and market an organization's goods and services. At the next level, it may be an arena for providing ongoing customer support. For instance, Symantec® is one of many companies that provide software upgrades over the Internet—in this case, providing multiple daily updates for its anti-virus software. For many courier companies (such as Federal Express®), the Internet has become a means for allowing customers to instantly access information to track their packages at any given point and to know when they have reached their destination. These latter examples of customer support have become a huge new market for major software vendors. These systems fall under the broader category of *customer relationship management (CRM)* and *customer self-service (CSS)* systems, both introduced in Chapter 2. These systems provide CSS capabilities (i.e., let the customers inspect their accounts or get product help through a Web interface rather than through interaction with a support person), electronic catalogs, and shipment update information. They aid the salesperson by storing an analyzable history of the customer and the customer's past business interactions. One of the bigger challenges has been to get the CRM systems to interact with the ERP system to share data between the two systems and enhance their power and capability. In an effort to improve the integration, all the major software firms are involved in initiatives to further empower CRM extensions to their ERP systems.

Summary

The future of e-business will see an increased merging of technologies as the lines between EDI and Internet commerce become less defined. The major impediment to most organizations (and individuals) conducting business over the Internet is the concern about security. However, advances in Internet security have been significant in the past few years, with the potential major benefactors of Internet commerce pushing the charge. For instance, software companies such as Microsoft and Mozilla®, along with financial providers MasterCard® and Visa®, have been at the forefront of development efforts to assure safe use of the Internet in commerce.

The evolution of EDI practices toward the Internet will be greatly facilitated by increased use of corporate extranets. Moving EDI applications to an extranet environment can help simplify the processing while maintaining higher levels of control and security. These extranets will be open to business partners using programs that limit access to selected business partners—hence the corporate networks will not be accessible by unintended Internet users. As Internet security increases, extranets will lose their appeal, and the Internet will increasingly become a viable alternative as the communication infrastructure of choice.

These same increases in security will help fuel the growth of Internet commerce. As Internet commerce becomes an increasingly acceptable way of doing business, technologies such as Web Services and service-oriented architectures will continue to move forward and allow companies to experience newfound opportunities for reaching customers; for many companies, a new globalization of their customer base will occur. On the other hand, new competition also will arise from distant companies that now have access to the same customers.

Entering the e-business domain is not simply a matter of switching on the connection. E-business is nothing less than a fundamental change in the way organizations do business and, as such, is a driver of organizational change. To succeed in an e-business environment, an organization must recognize the need to embrace change and must effectively plan and manage change. Management must take a proactive stance and lead the charge.

Success in your own career will depend heavily on your understanding of how to manage and control change. As a crucial step in this direction, in Chapters 7 through 9, you will learn how to implement and maintain effective organizational and information systems control structures.

Key Terms

electronic business (e-business), 63

journalize, 67

post, 67

summarize, 69

business event data store, 69

master data, 70

information processing, 70

data maintenance, 70

standing data, 70

batch processing, 71

periodic mode, 71

immediate mode, 71

offline, 72

online transaction entry (OLTE), 73

online, 73

online real-time (OLRT) systems, 75

client/server technology, 77

local area networks (LANs), 77

wide area networks (WANs), 77

Internet, 77

Web browsers, 77

intranet, 77

extranet, 77

electronic mail (e-mail), 78

electronic document management (EDM), 79

electronic data interchange (EDI), 80

value-added network (VAN), 84

Web Services, 86

service-oriented architecture (SOAs), 87

Internet commerce, 88

network providers, 89

Internet assurance, 91

cloud computing, 92

electronic storefronts, 93

Internet auction markets, 93

Internet market exchanges, 94

Review Questions

RQ 3-1   Define e-business.

RQ 3-2   Describe how technology has supported Amazon.com's growth.

RQ 3-3   Describe the activities associated with a manual accounting process.

RQ 3-4   Describe the stages of an automated accounting process.

RQ 3-5   Regarding data stores, compare/contrast business event data and master data.

RQ 3-6   Explain the relationship between the periodic mode and batch processing.

RQ 3-7   List and describe the four basic subprocesses completed in processing business event data using batch processing.

RQ 3-8   Explain how the use of online transaction entry (OLTE) can increase efficiency when using batch processing.

RQ 3-9   Explain the relationship between online real-time (OLRT) and immediate mode processing.

RQ 3-10   List and describe the three basic subprocesses completed in processing business event data using OLRT processing.

RQ 3-11   Explain the difference between wide area networks (WANs) and local area networks (LANs).

RQ 3-12   What are the four methods of conducting e-business?

RQ 3-13   How can e-mail be adapted to a more structured form to aid in capturing business event data?

RQ 3-14   Explain the advantages of using electronic document management (EDM) rather than traditional paper-based document systems.

RQ 3-15   Explain how electronic data interchange (EDI) is used to link two companies' business processes together.

RQ 3-16   What is the main advantage of using EDI to capture and process business events?

RQ 3-17   Explain how value-added networks (VANs) are used to simplify EDI between two or more companies.

RQ 3-18   Define *Web Services*.

RQ 3-19   Describe *service-oriented architecture (SOA)*.

RQ 3-20   How does Internet commerce simplify the world of e-business?

RQ 3-21   What role do network providers play in the Internet commerce environment?

RQ 3-22   Explain the concept of Internet assurance services. What types of assurance are provided?

RQ 3-23   Describe CPA WebTrust.

RQ 3-24   Describe uses of the Internet, other than completing sales, which help improve the success of businesses and other organizations.

Discussion Questions

DQ 3-1   The business environment is increasingly demanding the use of OLRT systems for more up-to-date information. Identify one business process and the environment in which it would be used as an example of why immediate mode processing is so critical. Be prepared to explain your answer to the class.

DQ 3-2   Consider a business that you patronize. Could it operate without automated information systems? Why or why not?

DQ 3-3   Consider your favorite fast food chain restaurant. How do you think this restaurant might use OLTE to improve its business event data-processing activities? Explain.

DQ 3-4   How could (or does) your university bookstore use technology to improve customer interactions with students, faculty, and staff?

DQ 3-5   What do you perceive to be the advantages and disadvantages of conducting business on the Internet? Be prepared to explain your answer.

DQ 3-6   Why is it important to have standards, such as X12 and EDIFACT, when conducting EDI transactions and other forms of e-business? Is there a down side to using standards?

DQ 3-7   Discuss the benefits of SOAs to the growth of e-business.

DQ 3-8   Why has the Internet caused such an explosion in e-business when EDI has been available for decades?

DQ 3-9   One of Amazon.com's marketing strengths is the capability to collect and analyze customer purchase data. How does this add value to the company? From the customer's perspective, is value added?

DQ 3-10   Some potential e-business customers have security concerns regarding online purchases. How do Internet security certifications attempt to address these concerns?

Short Problems

SP 3-1   Some people believe that an automated accounting system is always better than a manual system. Describe circumstances where you would recommend a manual system rather than automation. Provide an example of such an organization.

SP 3-2   Provide an example of a business where the evolution of communication (i.e., face-to-face, phone, e-mail, etc.) has altered its business activities. What are the advantages and disadvantages associated with these changes?

SP 3-3   E-business has allowed companies to reduce inventory while simultaneously offering a wide variety of items. Amazon.com is an example of such a company. Identify another organization that has expanded or improved (or could potentially expand or improve) by developing its value chain. Provide examples and explain your reasoning.

SP 3-4   Identify a specific situation in which periodic processing is sufficient to support the business process, and a second situation where immediate processing is necessary to adequately support the process.

Problems

P 3-1   Find a merchandising business on the Internet (other than the Lands' End or Amazon.com examples used in this chapter). Explore its Web page and how the order processing system works.

a.   Is there any information provided on how secure the Web page is? What level of comfort do you feel with its security? Explain.

b.   Does the business provide information regarding delivery time/stock-outs on purchases?

c.   What methods of payment does it accept?

d.   Analyze the design of the Web page in terms of usability and completeness of information content. Write a brief critique of the company's page.

P 3-2   Consider a business you might want to start on the Internet using e-mail to communicate with customers and capture business data. Explain why e-mail would be a good approach for your business. Draft a brief business plan evaluating the advantages and disadvantages of e-mail-based commerce in your business, and how you plan to get your business rolling (your professor will tell you how long the report should be).

P 3-3   Identify a business venture that you believe could be successful using only Internet commerce. Explain how you would design your Web page, how you would capture business event data, and the mode of processing you would use. Provide a report detailing support for your design decisions (your professor will tell you how long the report should be).

P 3-4   Develop a research paper on the use of the Internet to support EDI between companies. Your paper should consider how companies set up communications over the Internet to maintain the same security and standardization that are achieved using VANs for non-Internet EDI (your professor will tell you how long the paper should be).

P 3-5   Explain how EDM could be used in your AIS class to eliminate all paper flow between the students and professor. Include in your explanation what technologies would be necessary to facilitate your plan (your professor will tell you how long the paper should be).

P 3-6   Using the Internet, find and describe an Internet market exchange or Internet auction market. Your discussion should include the products and services available and the type of buyers and sellers you expect to participate. If you choose a private market, also identify the owner/sponsor of the exchange and the requirements for participation.

P 3-7   Use the Internet to locate www.cia.gov and www.Amazon.com. Find the privacy and security policies for each. Compare and contrast the use of privacy statements, encryption, SSL, and cookie policies.

P 3-8   The chapter describes how a batch processing system works with a used book shop as an example. Looking at Figure 3.2 (pg. 69) and its description of how the system works, identify another type of business that might use a similar batch processing system, and describe each of the steps in detail.

P 3-9   Using the four methods of conducting e-business (e-mail, EDM, EDI, and Internet commerce), select a business of your choice and describe how each method is currently integrated into their business or how each method could be incorporated into their business in the future.

P 3-10   Although CPA WebTrust has been in existence for several years, it has met limited acceptance by business. If Internet assurance is truly important, why do you think that WebTrust has a limited share of the market? (Include in your discussion the criteria that an organization might use when choosing an assurance service.)

Organizing and Managing Information

CHAPTER 4

Documenting Information Systems

Learning Objectives

After reading this chapter, you should be able to:

- Read and evaluate data flow diagrams.
- Read and evaluate systems flowcharts.
- Prepare data flow diagrams from a narrative.
- Prepare systems flowcharts from a narrative.

SOX To understand the importance of business process flowcharts and how organizations leverage them in relation to internal controls and in support of various other engagements, we spoke with a principal at PricewaterhouseCoopers LLP and asked her how she was using flowcharting in her work. Her response follows:

> We use business process flowcharts[1] in support of numerous types of engagements, for example, as part of a new system implementation, as part of a business process reengineering engagement, as part of a transformation of the finance function, or as part of the assessment of internal controls. Various people may be involved in preparing this documentation, including financial managers, business process owners, internal auditors, external auditors, and others.
>
> Compliance with the Sarbanes-Oxley Act of 2002 (SOX) reemphasized the importance of understanding how internal controls are integrated into business processes. SOX Section 404 requires that publicly listed companies have internal controls that support the prevention or detection of material misstatements in the financial reports. Business process flowcharts assist the company and the audit or engagements teams in understanding the flow of transactions through the process, identifying where controls have been implemented, identifying where gaps may exist in the control structure, and defining or improving controls to close any gaps. Auditing Standard 5 (AS5) directed organizations toward a risk based approach and a greater emphasis on those controls that detect or prevent material misstatement versus all controls within a process. Good process documentation makes it significantly easier to clearly understand where material misstatement risks may occur and to focus on those elements of the process where controls can be most effective.[2]

---

[1]While not exactly the same, we use the terms business process flowchart and systems flowchart interchangeably.

[2]Sally Bernstein, Principal, PricewaterhouseCoopers LLP, assisted us in the preparation of this narrative.

Synopsis

In this chapter, you will learn to read and prepare documentation that depicts business processes and the controls within those processes. You will learn that data flow diagrams portray business process activities, stores of data,[3] and flows of data among those elements. Systems flowcharts, on the other hand, present a comprehensive picture of the management, operations, information systems, and process controls embodied in business processes. In Chapters 5 and 6, we show you how to read and prepare entity-relationship diagrams. Proficiency with these tools will help you understand and evaluate business processes, information systems, and internal controls.

Auditors, systems analysts, students, and others use documentation to understand, explain, evaluate, and improve complex business processes, information systems, and internal controls. Let's consider, for example, the order-to-cash process described in Chapter 2. Recall that this process includes all of the activities associated with receiving a customer order, picking the goods off of a warehouse shelf, packing and shipping the goods, billing the customer, and receiving and depositing the customer's payment. Further, the information system supporting this business process is likely an enterprise system, has a number of PCs connected to it via telecommunications links, is used by dozens of people within and outside the organization, has one or more ERP systems with many modules and perhaps hundreds of programs, and performs functions for virtually every department in the organization. This system processes thousands of business events and hundreds of requests for management information and has people throughout the organization preparing inputs and receiving system outputs. In an e-business environment, this system might be accessed directly, perhaps automatically, by systems and individuals in the organization's supply chain.

For such a system, we often require "pictures," rather than a narrative description, to "see" and analyze all the activities, inputs, and outputs. Being able to draw these diagrams demonstrates that we understand the system and can explain the system to someone else. For example, with a systems flowchart, we can understand and analyze document flows (electronic and paper) through the operations, management, and information processes. Perhaps our analysis will lead to system improvements.[4] We are convinced that, after preparing and using systems documentation, you will agree that data flow diagrams, systems flowcharts, and entity-relationship diagrams are much more efficient (and effective) than narratives for working with complex systems. The application of these tools, even to the relatively simple systems depicted in this textbook, should convince you of this.

An organization can use documentation for other important purposes besides understanding and improving systems. For example, documentation is used to explain systems and to train personnel. Also, management and auditors use documentation to understand systems and to evaluate systems controls. Management, internal auditors, consultants, and independent auditors have recently become more engaged in this latter activity to comply with Section 404 of the Sarbanes-Oxley Act of 2002. AS5 (and by reference, Auditing Standards Section AU 319, paragraph 75) suggests that auditors consider using flowcharts and other documentation techniques to understand the flow of transactions and to identify and analyze the effectiveness of the design of internal controls.

Enterprise Systems

E-Business

Controls

Controls

SOX

---

[3] Depending on the specific context, we refer to stored data as a file, store of data, table of data, or database.

[4] See Michael H. Hugos, "Five Diagrams Beat a Victorian Novel," *Computerworld*, September 24, 2007, p. 23, for a description of five different types of diagrams, including data flow diagrams and flowcharts, that improve the effectiveness of systems development projects.

Introduction

We will begin by showing you how to read data flow diagrams and flowcharts. Next, we will show you how to prepare those diagrams and flowcharts. These documentation tools will be used throughout the remainder of the textbook. If you invest time now to study and practice using these tools, your improved understanding of the following chapters will reward your effort. You cannot achieve this chapter's learning objectives with traditional study methods; you cannot be a passive observer in these proceedings. You must work along with us as we demonstrate these tools. Further, you must practice these tools to develop your skills.

Reading Systems Documentation

The two types of systems documentation considered in this chapter are data flow diagrams and systems flowcharts. In the following section, you will learn how to read and interpret this documentation.

FIGURE 4.1 Data Flow Diagram (DFD) Symbols

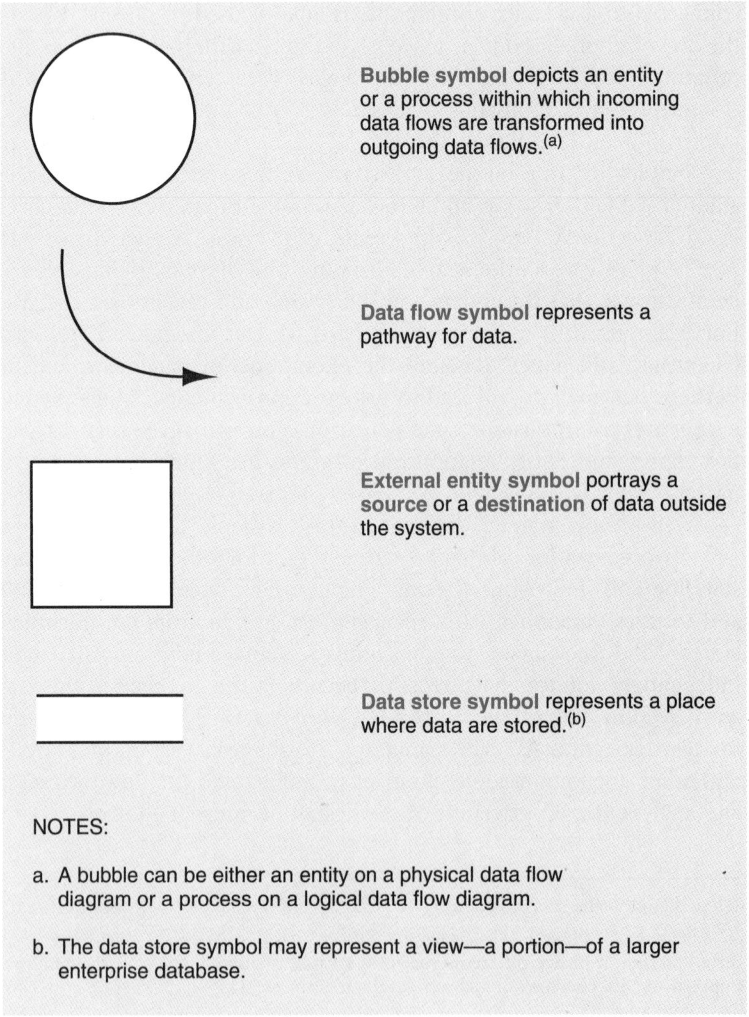

Bubble symbol depicts an entity or a process within which incoming data flows are transformed into outgoing data flows.[a]

Data flow symbol represents a pathway for data.

External entity symbol portrays a **source** or a **destination** of data outside the system.

Data store symbol represents a place where data are stored.[b]

NOTES:

a. A bubble can be either an entity on a physical data flow diagram or a process on a logical data flow diagram.

b. The data store symbol may represent a view—a portion—of a larger enterprise database.

Reading Data Flow Diagrams

A **data flow diagram (DFD)** is a graphical representation of a system.[5] A DFD depicts a system's components; the data flows among the components; and the sources, destinations, and storage of data. **Figure 4.1** shows the four symbols used in a DFD. Study these symbols and their definitions before reading on.

Context Diagram

Figure 4.2 is an example of our first type of DFD, the **context diagram**. A context diagram is a top-level, or least a detailed, diagram of a system depicting the system and all its activities as a single bubble and showing the data flows into and out of the system and into and out of the external entities. **External entities** are those entities (i.e., persons, places, or things) outside the system that send data to, or receive data from, the system.[6]

Physical Data Flow Diagram

A **physical data flow diagram** is a graphical representation of a system showing the system's internal and external entities and the flows of data into and out of these entities. An **internal entity** is an entity within the system that transforms data.[7] Internal entities include, for example, accounting clerks (persons), departments (places), and computers (things). Therefore, physical DFDs specify *where*, *how*, and *by whom* a system's activities are accomplished. A physical DFD does not tell us *what* activities are being accomplished. For example, in **Figure 4.3** (pg. 106), a physical DFD, you see that the sales clerk receives cash from the customer and sends cash, along with a register tape, to the cashier. So you see *where* the cash goes and how the cash receipts data are captured (that is, on the register tape), but you don't know exactly *what* the sales clerk did.

Note that the physical DFD's bubbles are labeled with nouns and that the data flows are labeled to indicate *how* data are transmitted between bubbles. For example,

FIGURE 4.2   A Context Diagram

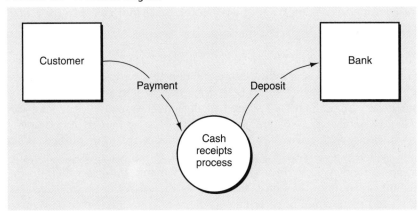

---

[5]Again, we often use the terms system, process, and business process interchangeably.

[6]Used in this manner, entities is a narrower concept than that used in Chapter 1, where they were all persons, places, and things.

[7]As with external entities, internal entities here is a narrower concept than entities as described in Chapter 1.

FIGURE 4.3   A Physical Data Flow Diagram

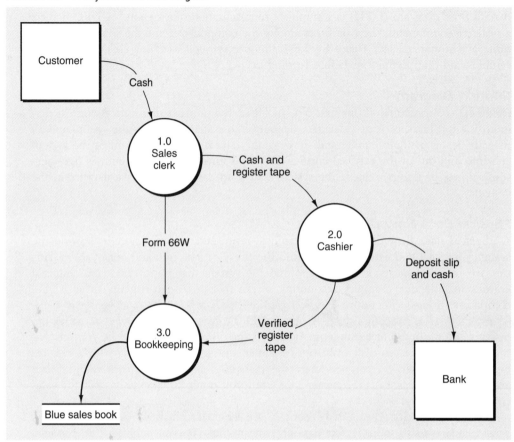

the sales clerk sends Form 66W to bookkeeping. Note that a data store's location indicates exactly *where* (in bookkeeping), and a data store's label indicates *how* (in a blue sales book), a system maintains sales records.

Logical Data Flow Diagram

A **logical data flow diagram** is a graphical representation of a system showing the system's processes (as bubbles), data stores, and the flows of data into and out of the processes and data stores. Logical DFDs are used to document systems because we can represent the logical nature of a system—what activities the system is performing—without having to specify *how*, *where*, or *by whom* the activities are accomplished. *What* a system is doing will change less over time than *how* the system is doing it. For example, a cash receipts system typically receives customer payments and posts them to the customer's account. Over time, however, the form of the payment—cash, check, or electronic funds—and the method of recording—manual or computer—may change.

The advantage of a *logical* DFD (versus a *physical* DFD) is that we can concentrate on the activities that a system performs. See, for example, **Figure 4.4**, where the labels on the data flows describe the nature of the data, rather than *how* the data are transmitted. Is the payment in the form of a check, cash, credit card, or debit card? We don't know. Is the sales journal a book, card, or electronic file? Again, we don't know. We do know that customer payments are received, verified for accuracy, recorded in a sales journal, and deposited in the bank. So a logical DFD portrays a system's activities, whereas a physical DFD depicts a system's infrastructure. We need both pictures to understand a system completely.

Finally, note that the processes in Figure 4.4 are labeled with verbs that describe the activities being performed, rather than with nouns, as we saw in the physical DFD.

Figure 4.4 is a top-level view of the single bubble in Figure 4.2, the context diagram. Because all of the bubbles in Figure 4.4 contain numbers followed by a decimal point and a zero, this diagram is often called a "level 0" diagram.[8] Notice that each of the data flows into and out of the context bubble in Figure 4.2 (pg. 105) also flows into

FIGURE 4.4   A Logical Data Flow Diagram (Level 0 Diagram)

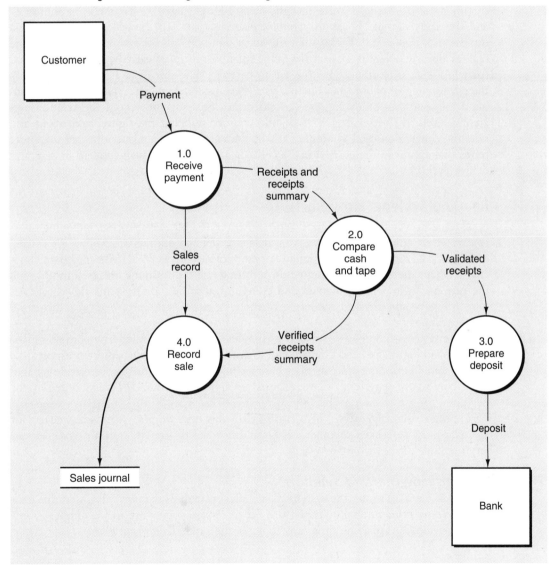

---

[8]Even though physical DFDs are similarly numbered, we do not use the term "level 0" when referring to a physical DFD because there are no lower-level physical DFDs.

and out of the bubbles in Figure 4.4 on page 107 (except for the flows between bubbles, such as "Sales record," which were contained *within* the bubble in Figure 4.2). When two DFDs—in this case, the context and the level 0—have equivalent external data flows, we say that the DFDs are **balanced**. Only balanced sets of DFDs (that is, a context diagram, a logical DFD, and a physical DFD) are correct.[9]

To derive Figure 4.4 (pg. 107), we have "exploded" the context diagram in Figure 4.2 (pg. 105) into its top-level components. We have looked inside the context diagram bubble to see the major subdivisions of the cash receipts process. The successive subdividing, or "exploding," of logical DFDs is called **top-down partitioning**, and when properly performed, it leads to a set of balanced DFDs.

We will use **Figure 4.5**, which depicts a generic set of balanced DFDs, to study partitioning and balancing. Notice that the level 0 DFD (part [b]) has the same input "A" and the same output "B" as the context diagram (part [a]). Now look at part (c), an explosion of bubble 1.0. Part (c) has the same input "A" and the same outputs "C" and "D" as does bubble 1.0 in part (b). This relationship must exist because diagram 1.0 (part [c]) is an explosion of bubble 1.0 in part (b). The same can be said for part (d), the partitioning of bubble 3.0. Finally, part (e) shows diagram 3.1, a partitioning of bubble 3.1 in part (d). Study Figure 4.5 and make sure you understand the relationships among levels in this set of DFDs. While you are studying the figure, you might also note the convention used to number the bubbles at each level. Also, note that the entity boxes that appear in the context and level 0 diagrams do not usually appear in diagrams below level 0.

Reading Systems Flowcharts

A **systems flowchart** is a graphical representation of a business process, including *information processes* (inputs, data processing, data storage, and outputs), as well as the related *operations processes* (people, equipment, organization, and work activities). These flowcharts depict the sequence of activities performed as the business events flow through the process.[10] Containing manual and computer activities, the systems flowchart presents a logical and physical rendering of the *who*, *what*, *how*, and *where* of information and operations processes.

Controls

SOX

The systems flowchart gives you a complete picture of a system by combining the physical and logical aspects. Physical and logical DFDs each depict different aspects of a system. In addition, the systems flowchart includes the operations process and management context for a system. These aspects are ignored in the DFDs. As noted at the beginning of the chapter, auditors and managers use systems flowcharts to understand a system and to analyze a system's controls. In this text, we use systems flowcharts for a similar purpose. Taken together, DFDs and flowcharts provide multiple, complementary methods for describing a system.

Systems Flowcharting Symbols

Figure 4.6 (pg. 110) shows the systems flowcharting symbols that we will use in this textbook. We have intentionally limited this set to reduce your work in learning the symbols. You should take some time now to study the symbols in Figure 4.6.

---

[9]A balanced set of DFDs is also known as a leveled set of DFDs.

[10]Because the systems flowcharts in this text depict information and operations processes, they are often referred to as "process flowcharts" or "business process flowcharts."

Common Systems Flowcharting Routines

Figure 4.7 (pp. 111–114) contains routines often found on systems flowcharts. Follow along as we describe each of these routines.

Figure 4.7, part (a), depicts a typical two-step data entry process that might be described as follows:

> The data entry clerk keys an input document into a computer. The computer accesses data in data store 1 (perhaps a table of valid codes, such as customer codes) and in data store 2 (perhaps a table of open sales orders) to edit/validate the input. The computer displays the input, including any errors. The clerk compares the input document to the

FIGURE 4.5   A Set of Balanced DFDs

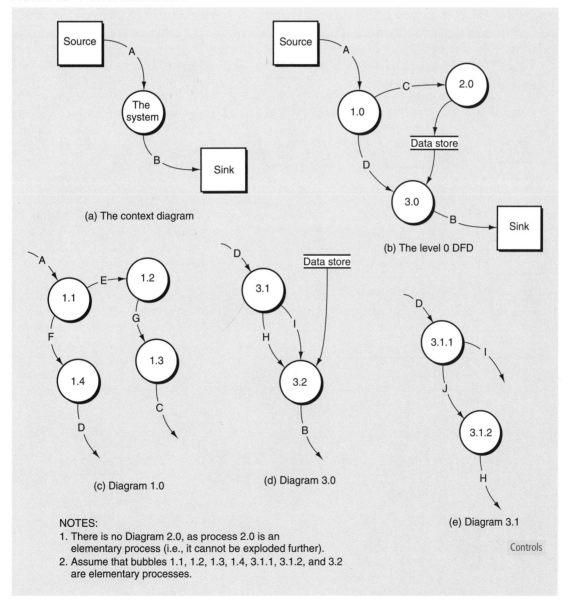

(a) The context diagram

(b) The level 0 DFD

(c) Diagram 1.0

(d) Diagram 3.0

(e) Diagram 3.1

NOTES:
1. There is no Diagram 2.0, as process 2.0 is an elementary process (i.e., it cannot be exploded further).
2. Assume that bubbles 1.1, 1.2, 1.3, 1.4, 3.1.1, 3.1.2, and 3.2 are elementary processes.

Controls

display, keys corrections as necessary, and accepts the input. The computer updates the table of data in data store 2 and notifies the clerk that the input has been recorded.

Notice the following about Figure 4.7 (pp. 111-112), part (a):

- The edit or validate step may be performed with one or more data stores.
- The display is implied with most, if not all, data entry processes.
- By combining the "Edit/validate input" rectangle with the "Record input" rectangle, we could depict this input process in one step without losing much detail about the activities being performed.

FIGURE 4.6 Systems Flowcharting Symbols

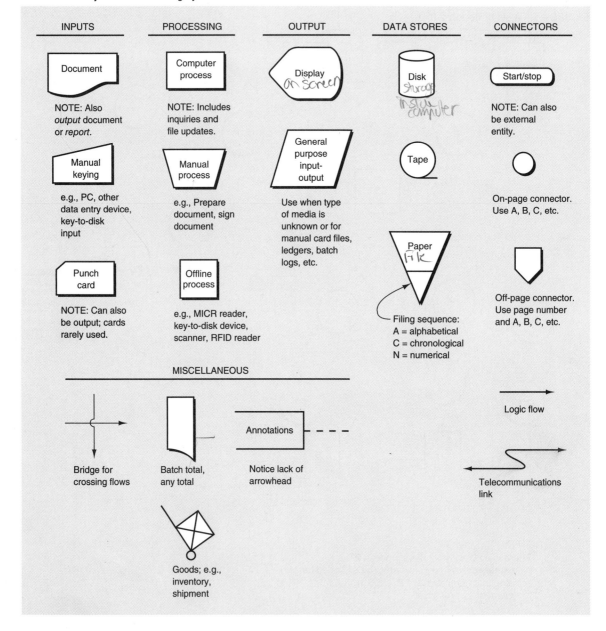

FIGURE 4.7   Common Systems Flowcharting Routines

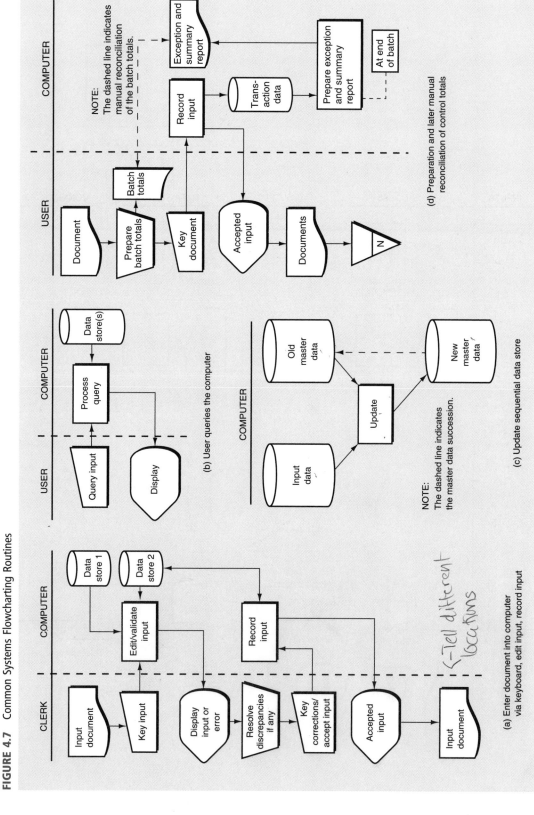

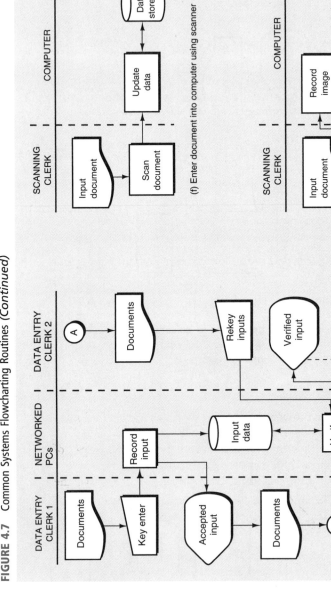

FIGURE 4.7 Common Systems Flowcharting Routines *(Continued)*

(e) Key and key verify inputs

(f) Enter document into computer using scanner

(g) Enter document into computer using scanner and manual keying

- The manual processes undertaken by the clerk are isolated in a separate column to distinguish them from the automated processes undertaken by the computer.
- We show the input document at the bottom of the column to indicate that the document "flows" through the input process. Although not shown, this document might be filed at the end of this process (such as shown in Figure 4.7, part [d]).

Figure 4.7, part (b), depicts a typical computer query, which might be described as follows:

> A user keys a query request into a computer. The computer accesses data in the table(s) in one or more data stores and presents a response to the user.

Notice the following about Figure 4.7, part (b):

- The user and computer activities are again isolated in separate columns.
- The display is an implied element of the query request.

Figure 4.7, part (c), depicts the update of master data stored in a sequential data store and might be described as follows:

> Inputs (e.g., cash receipts) that had previously been recorded on a magnetic disk are input to the computer, along with the existing (old) master data (e.g., accounts receivable master data). The computer updates the existing master data and creates a new version of the master data.

Notice the following about Figure 4.7, part (c):

- When sequential master data are updated, we show two data store symbols on a flowchart. One symbol represents the existing (old) version, and the other represents the new version.
- A dashed line connects the new with the old master data version to show that the new becomes the old version during the next update process.

Figure 4.7, part (d), depicts the input and reconciliation of computer inputs and might be described as follows:

> The user batches the input documents, prepares batch totals, and keys the documents into the computer. The computer records the inputs on a disk and notifies the user as each input is accepted. The user files the input documents in numerical sequence. At the end of the batch, the computer prepares an exception and summary report that includes batch totals. The user compares the computer batch totals to those prepared prior to entry of the documents.[11]

Controls

Notice the following about Figure 4.7, part (d):

- The annotation makes it clear that the computer prepares the exception and summary report after the user has completed entry of the batch.
- The user's comparison of the batch totals is depicted with a dashed line instead of the manual process symbol. Either method correctly depicts the comparison.
- If the batch totals had been input with the batch, the computer—rather than the user—could compare the batch totals.

Figure 4.7, part (e), depicts the entry and key verification of inputs into a system of networked PCs; it might be described as follows:

> A data entry clerk (perhaps clerk 1) enters documents into a system of networked PCs. The system records the inputs on a disk and notifies the user of the acceptance of each

Controls

---

[11]Batch totals are discussed in Chapter 9.

input. The documents are then forwarded to a different clerk (say clerk 2), who keys the documents again.[12] Differences are resolved, and the event data are updated to reflect the verifications and corrections.

Notice the following about Figure 4.7 (pp. 111-112), part (e):

- The networked PCs are offline devices and should be depicted with a square— rather than a rectangle—and in a column separate from the computer.
- We show the data entry clerks in two columns to emphasize that the keying and verification are performed by two different clerks. An annotation, rather than separate columns, could be used for this purpose.
- Clerk 2 probably follows an established procedure to reconcile differences found during the verification step. We use an annotation ("Error routine not shown") to suggest the existence of these procedures.

Figure 4.7, part (f), depicts the entry and recording of an input using a scanner and might be described as follows:

A clerk scans a document into the computer. Using the data from the scanned document, the computer updates the data located on one or more data stores.

Notice the following about Figure 4.7, part (f):

- We represent the scanner with the offline process symbol.
- We could include a display coming from the scanner, showing the clerk the document that had just been scanned.
- To be able to read data from the document, the scanner must have optical character recognition (OCR) capabilities.[13]

Figure 4.7, part (g), depicts the entry and recording of an input using a scanner and a keyboard; it might be described as follows:

A clerk scans a document into the computer. The computer routes an image of the scanned input to a data entry clerk, who keys data from the document's image into the computer. The computer records the keyed data with the scanned document.

You should quickly become reasonably proficient in reading flowcharts if you learn these routines. You may encounter many different flowcharting methods during your career, but the principles you learn here will carry over to those techniques.

Preparing Systems Documentation

In this section, we show you how to prepare data flow diagrams and systems flowcharts. We also give you our own tried and true guidelines for creating DFDs and systems flowcharts. As mentioned earlier in this chapter, you will learn these concepts best by studying and practicing these steps as you go along.

Preparing Data Flow Diagrams

We use DFDs in two main ways. They are drawn to document an existing system or created from scratch when developing a new system. In this section, we explain a process for deriving a set of DFDs from a narrative that describes an existing system.

---

[12]The majority of data processing errors occur at the data entry stage, and the majority of these errors can be attributed to misreading or miskeying the input. Because it is unlikely that two different clerks will make the same reading or keying mistake, the rekeying by a different clerk will discover the majority of these errors.

[13]Document scanning and OCR are discussed in Chapter 10.

The Narrative

Figure 4.8 contains a narrative describing the order entry system for Suprina Athletic Supply Company.[14] The first column indicates the paragraph number; the second column contains the line number for the text of the narrative.[15] We describe here an orderly method for drawing the DFDs for the Suprina system. You will get the most benefit from this section if you follow the instructions carefully, perform each step as directed, and don't read ahead. As you follow along, you may want to draw your diagrams by hand or use the software package of your choice.

FIGURE 4.8   Narrative for the Suprina Order Entry Process

Para	Line	Text
1	1	Suprina Athletic Supply Company specializes in selling
	2	sporting goods, gymnasium equipment and other athletic
	3	supplies to high schools, colleges, and universities. Customers
	4	give their orders to the company's sales representatives at
	5	customer locations using the following procedures.
2	6	At the customer locations Suprina's sales representatives
	7	enter customer orders on their laptop computers where they
	8	are added to the daily orders file. Once entered, two copies
	9	of the order are printed and the sales rep gives copy 1 to the
	10	customer and retains copy 2 for his files.
3	11	At the end of each day the laptop retrieves the day's orders
	12	and sends them to the computer at Suprina headquarters.
	13	The computer calculates various totals, such as number of
	14	orders and number of line items on those orders, and records
	15	those totals with the orders in the customer order file.
4	16	Each morning, the computer at Suprina headquarters displays
	17	the customer order file (with totals) to the order entry clerk
	18	(also at Suprina headquarters). The clerk reviews the orders
	19	and compares the totals for each sales rep's orders with the
	20	overall totals that the computer has provided. After being
	21	notified by the clerk, the computer begins processing the
	22	customer orders by performing a series of programmed edits
	23	as follows. Data from the customer master file is accessed to
	24	validate customer name and address. The inventory master
	25	file is accessed to check for inventory availability and pricing.
	26	The customer's credit limit (from the customer master file) is
	27	then compared to the amount of the order, outstanding sales
	28	orders (sales order master file), and accounts receivable
	29	balances. If any orders fail these edits, the clerk is notified.
5	30	Customer orders that pass these tests are then recorded on
	31	the sales order master file and the inventory balances are
	32	reduced. Two copies of the sales order are printed and sent
	33	to the customer (copy 1, an order acknowledgement) and to
	34	the warehouse (copy 2, a picking ticket).

---

[14]For the examples here and for the problems at the end of chapters in this text, you are given the relevant process narrative. In practice, this narrative would be prepared by making inquiries of appropriate personnel, inspecting documentation, and observing the process (see, for example, AS5 paragraph 37 and AU 319.75).

[15]We add paragraph and line numbers to our narrative here only to help with our discussion. Normally you would not include these numbers.

Table of Entities and Activities

Our first step is to create a table of entities and activities. In the long run, this list will lead to quicker and more accurate preparation of DFDs and systems flowcharts because it clarifies the information contained in a narrative and helps document the system correctly.

To begin your table, go through the narrative line by line and circle each activity being performed. An **activity** is any action being performed by an internal or external entity. Activities can include actions related to data (send data, transform data, file or store data, retrieve data from storage, or receive data) or to an operations process. Operations process activities might include picking goods in a warehouse, inspecting goods at a receiving dock, or counting cash. For each activity, there must be an entity that performs the activity. As you circle each activity, put a box around the entity that performs the activity.

Now you are ready to prepare your table. List each activity in the *order* that it is performed, regardless of the sequence in which it appears in the narrative. List the activity, along with the name of the entity that performs the activity and the paragraph number indicating the location of the activity in the narrative. After you have listed all activities, consecutively number each activity.

Compare your table to **Table 4.1**. Notice that the narrative refers to some entities in more than one way. For example, we have "order entry clerk" on line 17 and "the clerk" on line 18. Notice that we listed activity 15 and activities 16–18. It might be that activity 15 describes activities 16–18 and does not need to be listed. However, it is better to list doubtful activities than to miss an activity. See how we listed activity 4, found on lines 8 and 9. We changed to the active form of the verb "print" so that we could show the activity next to the entity that performs the action (i.e., the laptop prints the customer order). Also, in lines 21 and 22 we find that the computer begins a process "after being notified by the clerk." We added activity 14 to the table for this step. Before reading on, resolve any differences between your list of entities and activities and those in Table 4.1.

Drawing the Context Diagram

We are now ready to draw the context diagram. Because a context diagram consists of only one circle, begin the context diagram by drawing one circle in the center of your page (paper or computer). Next, you must draw the external entity boxes. To do this, you need to decide which of the entities in Table 4.1 are external and which are internal.

> **DFD guideline 1:** Include *within* the system context (bubble) any entity that performs one or more information processing activities.

Information processing activities retrieve data from storage, transform data, or file data. Information processing activities include document preparation, data entry, verification, classification, arrangement or sorting, calculation, summarization, and filing data—both manual and automated. The sending and receiving of data between entities is not an information processing activity because it does not transform data. If you send data to another entity, you do not process data. If, however, you file data, you do perform an information processing activity. Likewise, if you receive data from another entity, you do not perform an information processing activity. However, if you retrieve data from a computer file or table, you do perform an information processing activity. Operations process activities, such as picking goods in a warehouse, are not information processing activities.

To discover which entities perform no information processing activities, you must inspect the table of entities and activities and mark those activities that are not information processing activities. Review your table of entities and activities, and mark all activities that do not perform information processing activities. Many of these marked activities are sends and receives. These indicate your data flows.

TABLE 4.1 Table of Entities and Activities for Suprina Order Entry Process *Chronological*

Entities	Para	Activities
Customer	1	1. Give order to sales rep. *who*
Sales rep	2	2. Enter customer order data. *Sales Rep Activity*
Sales rep laptop	2	3. Add order to daily orders file. *Laptop Activity*
	2	4. Print customer order (2 copies).
Sales rep	2	5. Give copy 1 of the order to customer. *Sales Rep Activity*
	2	6. File copy 2 of the order.
Sales rep laptop	3	7. Retrieve day's orders from the daily orders file. *Laptop Activity*
	3	8. Send orders to headquarters. *Entity*
Computer (Headquarters)	3	9. Calculate totals.
	3	10. Record orders (and totals) in customer orders file.
	3	11. Display customer orders (with totals) to order entry clerk.
Order entry clerk	4	12. Review orders.
	4	13. Compare totals.
	4	14. Initiate computer process.
Computer	4	15. Perform a series of programmed edits.
	4	16. Validate customer name and address.
	4	17. Check inventory availability and pricing.
	5	18. Compare credit limit to order, sales orders, and accounts receivable.
	5	19. Notify clerk of errors.
	5	20. Record customer orders on sales order master file.
	5	21. Reduce inventory balances.
	5	22. Print acknowledgement (sales order copy 1) and picking ticket (sales order copy 2).
	5	23. Send acknowledgement and picking ticket.
Warehouse	5	

Identifying who or where. Activity: what their doing

External Customer

External Warehouse

You should have indicated activities 1, 5, 8, and 23 because these activities only send or receive data. As mentioned earlier, activity 15 only describes activities 16–18 and can also be marked.

Finally, activity 19 can be marked because of the following guideline:

DFD guideline 2: For now, include only *normal* processing routines, not exception routines or error routines, on context diagrams, physical DFDs, and level 0 logical DFDs.

Because activity 19 occurs only when an order contains an error, we will not consider this activity *for now*.

Any entities that do not perform *any* information processing activities are external entities; the remaining entities are internal. Your table of entities and activities, with certain non–information processing activities marked, should indicate that the sales rep, sales rep's laptop, computer, and order entry clerk perform information processing activities and will be included in our diagrams as internal entities. The customer, on the other hand, does not perform any such activities and will be an external entity.

Are there other external entities to be included in our diagrams? To answer this question, you must go through the narrative one more time and put a box around those entities not yet marked. You should find that the warehouse (line 34), in this system, does not perform information processing activities. This entity, as well as the customer, are external entities and are included in the context diagram as sources or destinations of data. We now have two external entities, four internal entities, and 23 activities. No other entities or activities are to be added because of the following guideline.

DFD guideline 3: Include in the process documentation all (and only) activities and entities described in the process narrative—no more, no less.

When we say "narrative," we are talking about the narratives that you will find as problem material in this book. You are to assume, in those cases, that the narrative is complete and accurate. However, when you prepare a narrative to document a real-world case, you cannot assume that your narrative is perfect. When you have verified that your narrative is complete and that it accurately reflects reality, you must then follow DFD guideline 3.

Because there are two entities external to the Suprina order entry system—the customer and the warehouse—you must draw on your page two boxes surrounding the one context bubble. Next, draw and label the data flows that connect the external entities with the bubble. Because logical (versus physical) labels are normally used on a context diagram, you should do your best to derive logical labels for the flows. The final step is to label the context bubble. Write a descriptive label that encompasses the processing taking place within the system. Our label in **Figure 4.9** indicates the scope of the Suprina system—namely, an order entry process.

Figure 4.9 is the completed Suprina context diagram. Compare it to your context diagram, and resolve any differences. Notice that we include a single square for many customers. The following guideline applies.

DFD guideline 4: When multiple entities operate identically, depict only one to represent all.

FIGURE 4.9 Suprina Context Diagram

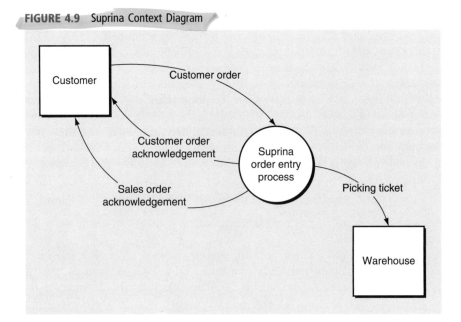

Drawing the Current Physical Data Flow Diagram

To keep the current physical DFD balanced with the context diagram, start your current physical DFD by drawing the two external entities from the context diagram near the edges of a page. Next, draw and label data flows going into and out of those external entities. Leave the center of the page, where you will sketch the rest of the diagram, blank. Because this is a physical DFD, the data flows should have labels that describe the means by which the flow is accomplished. For example, the "Customer order acknowledgement" is now labeled "Customer order copy 1," and the "Sales order acknowledgement" is now labeled "Sales order copy 1."

Because each internal entity listed in Table 4.1 (pg. 117) becomes a bubble in the physical DFD, we know that our current physical DFD will contain four bubbles: one each for the sales rep, sales rep laptop, computer, and order entry clerk. You will add these four bubbles by first drawing the bubbles that are connected to the external entities (i.e., the sales rep and the computer). During this process, you must consider all send and receive activities and the implied reciprocal activities. (Many of these were marked earlier to indicate that they were not data processing activities.) For example, activity 1 indicates that the customer gives customer order data to the sales rep. Draw and label a sales rep bubble (let's label it "1.0" because it is at the start of the process) and a computer bubble (let's label it "3.0"; you'll see why in a minute). Use a data flow symbol (i.e., a curved line with an arrowhead) to connect these bubbles to their related external entities. You should now have the customer square connected to the sales rep bubble with two flows, one labeled "Customer order data" and another labeled "Customer order copy 1." The computer bubble should be connected to the warehouse square with a flow labeled "Sales order copy 2" and to the customer bubble with a flow labeled "Sales order copy 1."

To complete the physical DFD, we must go through the table of entities and activities again and draw all the remaining entities and flows. Follow along with us as we complete the diagram. For activity 2, add a sales rep laptop bubble (let's label it "2.0") and draw and label a flow from the sales rep bubble to the sales rep laptop bubble. For activity 3, we must add a data store for the daily orders file. Notice that the label on the data store shows that the physical storage medium is a disk. Draw a flow into that data store to complete activity 3. We don't need to label flows into and out of data stores because those flows are records/rows in a relational table (e.g., a customer record from a customer master file) and need not be specifically identified. Activity 4 is a flow from the sales rep laptop to the sales rep. Draw and label this flow. We previously drew the flow for activity 5; it is the flow "Customer order copy 1." To show activity 6, we need to create a data store, labeled "sales rep customer orders file" (a paper file), with a flow from the sales rep to that data store. To show activity 7, draw a flow from the daily orders file to the sales rep laptop bubble. We draw a flow only from the data store because a data request is not a flow of data. Therefore, we do not show the request for the daily orders records. The movement of the records out of the data store in response to this request is a flow of data and is shown. To show activity 8, we need to add a flow from the sales rep laptop to the computer bubble. Now we see why the computer is number 3.0; it is the next entity encountered in the process flow. Activity 9 is performed *within* the computer bubble. To show activity 10, we need to add a customer orders file (a disk file) and a flow from the computer into that file. Activity 11 is a flow from the computer to our last entity, the order entry clerk (bubble "4.0"). Draw and label a flow from the computer to the order entry clerk bubble. Activities 12 and 13 are performed *within* the order entry clerk bubble. Draw and label a flow from the order entry clerk to the computer to show activity 14. Activities 16 through 18 and 20 through 22 are performed *within* the computer bubble. However, we must show many data flows into and out of that bubble as each activity is performed. To obtain the data necessary to perform activity 16 we need to add a customer master data file (disk) and a flow from that data store into the computer bubble. To obtain the data necessary to perform activity 17, we need to add an inventory master data file (disk) and a flow from that data store into the computer bubble. To obtain the data necessary to perform activity 18, we need to add a sales order master data file (disk) and an accounts receivable master file (disk) and flows from those data stores into the computer bubble. The credit limit data is obtained from the flow from the customer master file shown for activity 16. Activity 19, an error routine, is not included in the physical DFD. For activity 20, we need to show a flow from the computer into the sales order master file. To perform activity 21, the inventory master record must be read into the computer, updated, and then written back to the inventory master file. This requires a data flow *from* and a data flow *to* the inventory data store. Because we already drew a flow from that data store for activity 17, however, we need only draw a flow back to the data store. Because the customer, inventory, sales order, and accounts receivable master files are on a computer disk, only the computer can read from or write to them. This also excludes any direct connection between computerized data stores. To update the data on one computerized data store from another, you must go through a computer bubble. In case you think that all these flows into and out of the data stores aren't necessary, consider the following guideline.

DFD guideline 5: For clarity, draw a data flow for each flow into and out of a data store. You may also, for clarity and to help you determine that you have included all necessary flows, label each flow with the activity number that gives rise to the flow or with a description of the flow (e.g., "retrieve accounts receivable master data"). NOTE: These activity numbers and descriptions may be removed after you are certain that the diagram is complete and correct.

Figure 4.10 is the completed Suprina current physical DFD. Previously, we documented activities 22 and 23 with flows to the customer and warehouse. Compare it to your diagram and resolve any differences before reading on. All of the data stores in this diagram were explicitly mentioned in the narrative. In some cases, the narrative may not be so explicit. For example, lines 24 and 25 in the narrative might have said "the computer checks for inventory availability and pricing." In this case we would need to include a source for the inventory date, and that, typically, is the inventory master file. We offer the following guideline.

DFD guideline 6: If a data store is logically necessary (that is, because of a delay between processes or to provide data to complete an activity), include a data store in the diagram, even if it is not mentioned in the narrative.

You must use DFD guideline 6 carefully, however, so that you don't draw DFDs that are cluttered with data stores and are therefore difficult to read. You need to use your judgment. Does this guideline contradict DFD guideline 3? No. DFD guideline 3 tells you to include in your diagrams only those activities included in your narrative, whereas DFD guideline 6 tells you to completely describe those activities. So, if the narrative implies an activity or data store, include it in the diagrams. How about an example that would violate DFD guideline 6? Activities *outside the context* of a system (not described in the system narrative) should not be included in the diagrams. For example, the following activities are not in the narrative in Figure 4.8 (pg. 115) and should not be included:

- Update of the general ledger data to reflect the reduction of the inventory
- Payments that may have been collected by the sales rep
- Customer billing

FIGURE 4.10 Suprina Current Physical DFD

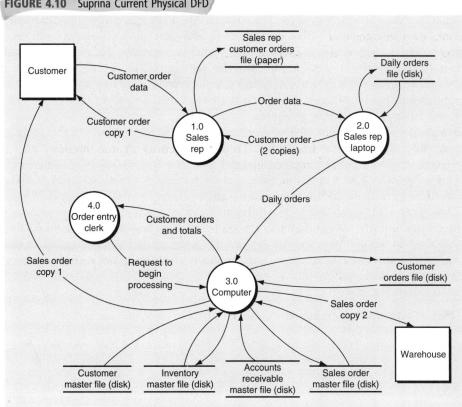

Drawing the Current Logical Data Flow Diagram

The current logical DFD portrays the logical activities performed within the system. Level 0 DFDs depict a particular grouping of the logical activities, so we start the level 0 DFD by enumerating the activities in the system and then we group those activities. If you have been following along with us, you already have a list of the activities to be included in the level 0 DFD. These are the *unmarked* activities on the table of entities and activities, Table 4.1 (pg. 117). Our list includes activities 2–4, 6, 7, 9–14, 16–18, and 20–22. Recall that, at this time, we don't consider any other activities because the other activities either are actions performed in other-than-normal situations and therefore not included on a level 0 DFD, are actions that merely send or receive data rather than transform data, or are activities performed by the operations process, such as picking goods. Several guidelines will help you group the activities remaining in the list.

> **DFD guideline 7:** Group activities if they occur in the same place and at the same time. For example, activities 2 and 3 are performed as each order is entered.

> **DFD guideline 8:** Group activities if they occur at the same time but in different places. For example, the order entry clerk performs activities 12 and 13 right after the computer displays the orders in activity 11.

> **DFD guideline 9:** Group activities that seem to be logically related. For example, activities 2, 3, 4, and 6 are related to securing the customer order.

> **DFD guideline 10:** To make the DFD readable, use between five and seven bubbles.[16]

---

[16]For very simple systems, such as those described in the narratives in this textbook, your solutions may have fewer than five bubbles.

To start preparing your logical DFD, try bracketing the activities in Table 4.1 as you think they should be grouped (do not consider the marked activities). For example, if we apply DFD guideline 7 (that is, same time and same place), we could combine activities 2 and 3; activities 4 and 6; activities 9 and 10; activities 12, 13, and 14; and activities 16, 17, 18, 20, 21, and 22. Although this would provide a satisfactory solution, there would be seven bubbles, and two bubbles would contain only one activity. Because we prefer not to have too many single-activity bubbles until we get to the lowest-level DFDs, we proceed with further groupings.

If we apply DFD guideline 8 (that is, same time but different place) to the preceding grouping, we could combine activity 7 with 9 and 10; 11 with 12 and 13; and 14 with 16, 17, 18, 20, 21 and 22.

This solution is better than our first solution because we now have five bubbles (activities 2 and 3 and activities 4 and 6 remain grouped) and no single-activity bubbles.

If we apply DFD guideline 9 (that is, logically related activities), we can combine activities 2 and 3 with 4 and 6. This is a good solution and we could stop there. But let's suggest that we combine the last two groups together. This combines all of the activities related to validating the order and producing the picking ticket (and necessary file updates and acknowledgements).

In summary, our groups are:

* *Group 1:* activities 2, 3, 4, and 6
* *Group 2:* activities 7, 9, and 10
* *Group 3:* activities 11–14, 16–18, and 20–22

After we choose our groupings, we must give each group a name that describes the logical activities within the group. For Suprina, we chose the following labels:

* Group 1 (activities 2, 3, 4, and 6) is bubble 1.0 and is labeled "Capture customer order" because that bubble comprises all the activities after the order data is given by the customer until the customer order documents are prepared and filed.
* Group 2 (activities 7, 9, and 10) is bubble 2.0 and is labeled "Record customer order" because the activities in bubble 2.0 record the order in the customer order file in the computer at headquarters.
* Group 3 (activities 11–14, 16–18, and 20–22) is bubble 3.0 and is labeled "Record sales order" because the activities generate a picking ticket, send the acknowledgement to the customer, and record the sales order to reflect these activities.

Mark these groups and labels on Table 4.1 (pg. 117). **Table 4.2** demonstrates how you should annotate your table of entities and activities. (Notice that we have not carried forward the marked activities from Table 4.1.)

Follow along now as we draw the current logical DFD for Suprina. You'll need paper and pencil (or your computer), the Suprina context diagram (Figure 4.9, pg. 118), the Suprina current physical DFD (Figure 4.10, pg. 121), your annotated table of entities and activities (Table 4.2), and your original table of entities and activities (Table 4.1, pg. 117). To draw the logical DFD, you should begin in the same manner as you began to draw the current physical DFD. Draw the external entities near the edges of a page. Draw and label flows to and from the external entities while leaving the center of the page blank to receive the remainder of the diagram. Because this is a logical DFD, the data flows to and from the entities must have logical descriptions (e.g., the descriptions used on the context diagram).

After we have completed the external flows, we can begin to draw the internal bubbles and flows. The "Customer order" from the "Customer" is the input to bubble 1.0.

TABLE 4.2 Table of Entities and Activities for Suprina Order Entry Process (Annotated)

Entities	Para	Activities	
Sales rep	2	2. Enter customer order data.	*1.0 Capture customer order.*
Sales rep laptop	2	3. Add order to daily orders file.	
	2	4. Print customer order (2 copies).	
Sales rep	2	6. File copy 2 of the order.	*These became our bubbles*
Sales rep laptop	3	7. Retrieve day's orders from the daily orders file.	*2.0 Record customer order.*
Computer	3	9. Calculate totals.	
	3	10. Record orders (and totals) in customer orders file.	
Computer	3	11. Display customer orders (with totals) to order entry clerk.	
Order entry clerk	4	12. Review orders.	
	4	13. Compare totals.	
	4	14. Initiate computer process.	*3.0 Record sales order.*
Computer	4	16. Validate customer name and address.	
	4	17. Check inventory availability and pricing.	
	4	18. Compare credit limit to order, sales orders, and accounts receivable.	
	5	20. Record customer orders on sales order master file.	
	5	21. Reduce inventory balances.	
	5	22. Print acknowledgement (sales order copy 1) and picking ticket (sales order copy 2).	

Activities 2, 3, 4, and 6 happen within the bubble. What are the outputs? There is a flow to the "Daily orders file" (activity 3) and to the "Sales rep customer orders file" (activity 6). The "Customer order acknowledgement" flows to the customer. Before moving on, compare your drawing to bubble 1.0 in **Figure 4.11** (pg. 124).

The flow from the Daily orders file (activity 7) is the input to bubble 2.0, and activity 9 is performed within the bubble. The only output is to the Customer orders file. Before moving on, compare your drawing to bubble 2.0, Figure 4.11.

Finally, let's draw bubble 3.0. To display the customer orders and totals (activity 11), bubble 3.0 must obtain the records stored on the Customer orders file. Draw a flow from that file's data store into bubble 3.0. Activities 12, 13, and 14 are performed within bubble 3.0. To validate the customer name and address (activity 16), bubble 3.0 must obtain the data contained in the Customer master file. Draw a flow from that file's data store into bubble 3.0. To check inventory availability and pricing (activity 17), bubble 3.0 must obtain the data contained in the Inventory master file. Draw a flow from that file's data store into bubble 3.0. In addition to the data already obtained from the Customer and Inventory master files, bubble 3.0 must obtain the data contained in the Sales order and Accounts receivable master files to perform activity 18. Draw flows from the data stores for those files into bubble 3.0. To complete activities 20 and 21, there must be flows into the Sales order and Inventory master files. Draw flows from bubble 3.0 into those files. The final outputs from bubble 3.0 are the Sales order acknowledgement (a flow to the customer) and the Picking ticket (a flow to the Warehouse) that we drew when we started the diagram.

We have finished drawing the Suprina current logical DFD. Compare your diagram to the solution in Figure 4.11. Resolve any discrepancies. Your diagram should look like that in Figure 4.11 *if you use the groupings we described*. Many other groupings are possible within the guidelines. Each different grouping should lead to a different logical DFD. Problem 4.9 at the end of this chapter provides an alternative grouping and asks you to prepare a logical DFD for that grouping. The solution to that problem is just as correct as is Figure 4.11.

Summary of Drawing Data Flow Diagrams

First and foremost, don't let the rigor of the documentation get in the way of using the diagrams to understand the system. We have presented many guidelines, hints, and instructions to help you draw DFDs. Use your judgment in applying this information.

Sometimes, an operations process function performs information processing activities. Here are a few new DFD guidelines and examples that didn't come up when we

FIGURE 4.11   Suprina Current Logical DFD (Level 0)

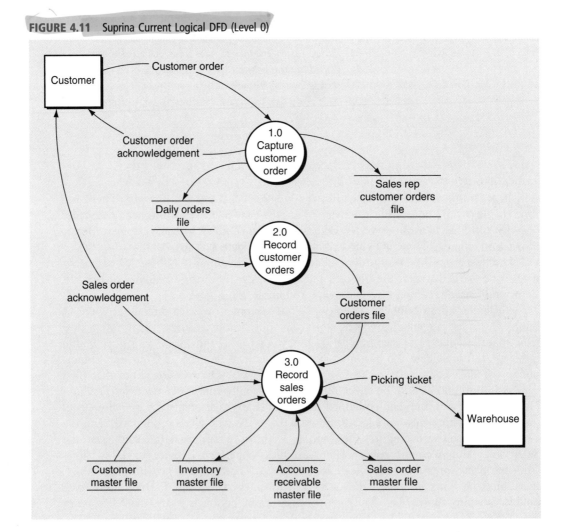

drew the Suprina DFDs. For example, when the receiving department (primarily an operations process unit) prepares a document indicating how many widgets have been received, it is performing an information processing activity. The warehouse and the shipping department are other operations process units that often perform information processing activities. The following guidelines apply:

DFD guideline 11: A data flow should go to an operations process entity *square* when only operations process functions (that is, work-related functions such as storing goods, picking goods from the shelves, packaging the customer's order, and so on) are to be performed by that entity. A data flow should enter an entity *bubble* if the operations process entity is to perform an information processing activity. For example, when an operations process entity is receiving goods, a physical DFD could show either a "receiving" square or a "receiving" bubble, whereas the logical DFD might show either a receiving department square or a "Complete receiving report" bubble.

DFD guideline 12: On a physical DFD, reading computer data stores and writing to computer data stores must go through a computer bubble.

DFD guideline 13: On a logical DFD, data flows cannot go from higher- to lower-numbered bubbles.

If on a logical DFD you have a data flow going back to a previous processing point (that is, to a lower-numbered bubble), you have a physical representation of the flow or process. Flows may, however, flow backwards to a data store. For example, what if the Sales order acknowledgement (Sales order copy 1) in the Suprina process was printed by the computer and sent to the sales rep to be given to the customer? Would that flow go to bubble 1.0? The answer is no! It would be depicted exactly as we have shown it in Figure 4.11. Bubble 1.0 in the logical DFD is not the sales rep or the sales rep's laptop; it is a process containing logical activities.

At times, processing can't proceed as planned. In such cases, processes called **exception routines** or **error routines** handle the required actions. These are processes for out-of-the-ordinary (exceptional) or erroneous events data. Processing performed in other-than-normal situations should be documented below the level 0 DFD with reject stubs that indicate that exceptional processing must be performed. A **reject stub** is a data flow assigned the label "Reject" that leaves a bubble but does not go to any other bubble or data store. These reject stubs, which are shown only in lower-level diagrams, may be added without bringing the set of diagrams out of balance. As we will see in the next section, these exception or error routines will be shown on the systems flowcharts.

Preparing Systems Flowcharts

In this section, we describe the steps for preparing a systems flowchart. The following guidelines outline our basic flowcharting technique. Study each guideline before proceeding.

Systems flowcharting guideline 1: Divide the flowchart into columns: one column for each internal entity and, optionally, one for each external entity. Label each column.[17]

Systems flowcharting guideline 2: Flowchart columns should be laid out so that the flowchart activities flow from left to right, but you should locate columns to minimize crossed lines and connectors.

---

[17]In business process flowcharts, these columns may be shown horizontally and be called "swimlanes."

Systems flowcharting guideline 3: Flowchart logic should flow from top to bottom and from left to right. For clarity, put arrows on all flow lines.

Systems flowcharting guideline 4: Keep the flowchart on one page. If you can't, use multiple pages and connect the pages with off-page connectors.

To use an off-page connector, draw the symbol shown in Figure 4.6 (pg. 110) at the point where you leave one page and at the corresponding point where you begin again on the next page. If you leave page 1 for the first time, and you are going to page 2, then the code inside the symbol on page 1 should be "P. 2, A"; on page 2, the code inside the symbol should be "P. 1, A." That is, you point to page 2 from page 1, and you point back to page 1 from page 2. Disciplining yourself to draw flowcharts on pages of limited size is essential when you must draw flowcharts on standardized forms for work papers and systems documentation. Also, as you might expect, computerized flowcharting packages will print your flowcharts only on paper that will fit in your printer!

Systems flowcharting guideline 5: Within each column, there must be at least one manual process, keying operation, or data store between documents. That is, do not directly connect documents within the same column.

This guideline suggests that you show all the processing that is taking place. For example, if two documents are being attached, include a manual process to show the matching and attaching activities.

Systems flowcharting guideline 6: When crossing organizational lines (i.e., moving from one column to another), show a document at both ends of the flow line unless the connection is so short that the intent is unambiguous.

Systems flowcharting guideline 7: Documents or reports printed in a computer facility should be shown in that facility's column first. You can then show the document or report going to the destination unit.

Systems flowcharting guideline 8: Documents or reports printed by a centralized computer facility on equipment located in another organizational unit (e.g., a warehouse or a shipping department) should not be shown within the computer facility.

Systems flowcharting guideline 9: Processing within an organizational unit on devices such as a PC, laptop, or computerized cash register should be shown within the unit or as a separate column next to that unit but not in the central computer facility column.

Systems flowcharting guideline 10: Sequential processing steps (either computerized or manual) with no delay between them (and resulting from the same input) can be shown as one process or as a sequence of processes.

Systems flowcharting guideline 11: The only way to get data into or out of a computer data storage unit is through a computer process rectangle or offline process square.

For example, if you key data from a source document, you must show a manual keying symbol, a rectangle or square, and then a computer storage unit (see, for example, Figure 4.7, part [a], pg. 112).

Systems flowcharting guideline 12: A manual process is not needed to show the sending of a document. The sending should be apparent from the movement of the document itself.

Systems flowcharting guideline 13: Do not use a manual process to file a document. Just show the document going into the file.

Drawing Systems Flowcharts

We are now ready to draw the Suprina flowchart. Get some paper (or your computer) and follow along with us. The entities in our current physical DFD (Figure 4.10, pg. 121) should help us set up and label our columns. Although we set up columns for each entity, we do not have to include columns for the customer or warehouse because these entities do not perform any information processing activities (systems flowcharting guideline 1). Columns for entities are typically located from left to right to match the processing flow. However, when two entities interact with the computer, you might locate them on either side of the "Computer" column (see systems flowcharting guideline 2). For the Suprina process, the flows are not complicated and so the columns from left to right should be "Sales rep," "Sales rep laptop," "Computer," and "Order entry clerk." Including a column for both the sales rep and for the sales rep laptop may not seem necessary, but we include both because the laptop is an internal entity that is performing information processing activities and because of systems flowcharting guideline 9. Notice the "Headquarters" heading over the "Computer" and "Order entry clerk" columns. We use superior headings to emphasize physical locations and reporting relationships.

We usually start a flowchart in the top-left corner (systems flowcharting guideline 3) with a start symbol. Because we have eliminated the Customer column, we must start the flowchart with a start symbol labeled "Customer" in the sales rep column to represent the customers giving their orders to the sales reps, as described on lines 3, 4, and 5 of the narrative. This is followed by the sales reps entering the orders on their laptops (narrative lines 6 and 7). Figure 4.7 (pg. 112) depicts the process of entering data on a computer (part [a]) and on an offline device such as a laptop (part [e]). Notice the use of the keying symbol, the process symbols (a rectangle for a computer and a square for an offline device), a data store (typically a disk), and the display symbol. Notice also that the keying and display symbols are located in the clerk columns and the process and data store symbols are located in the computer and offline device columns. We will model the sales rep data entry (narrative lines 6 and 7) and recording on the daily orders file by the laptop (line 8), after Figure 4.7, part (e), but we will not use the document symbol because we do not know how the order is communicated to the sales rep. Let's just connect the "Customer" start symbol directly to a manual keying symbol in the sales rep column. This is followed by the offline process and disk symbol in the laptop column and then back to the sales rep column to a display symbol. Draw this portion of your flowchart and then compare your drawing to that portion of the flowchart in **Figure 4.12**. (pg. 128) Notice how we have labeled each symbol and linked them together with flow lines and arrows (see systems flowcharting guideline 3). Resolve any differences before reading on.

To document narrative lines 8 through 10 we need to show the laptop printing the orders (a process) and giving them to the sales rep (a flow). The printed orders could flow directly from the process symbol that recorded the order or from a separate process symbol (see systems flowcharting guideline 7). Let's use a separate process symbol (again, a square symbol for the offline process), followed by the printed order. To show two copies of the order we use two document symbols on top of each other, with the back document a little above and to the right of the front document. Systems flowcharting guideline 7 tells us to show the documents in the sales rep laptop column, and systems flowcharting guideline 6 tells us that we may show the documents again in the sales rep column. Let's show the documents in both columns to make it easier to show the next actions taken by the sales rep. Because we have no customer column, we show the sales rep sending copy 1 of the printed order to a stop symbol labeled "Customer." To keep the flow moving down as much as possible, don't use the Customer start symbol at the top of the sales rep column. Systems flowcharting guideline 12 tells us that we don't need to use a manual process to send the order copy to the customer. To

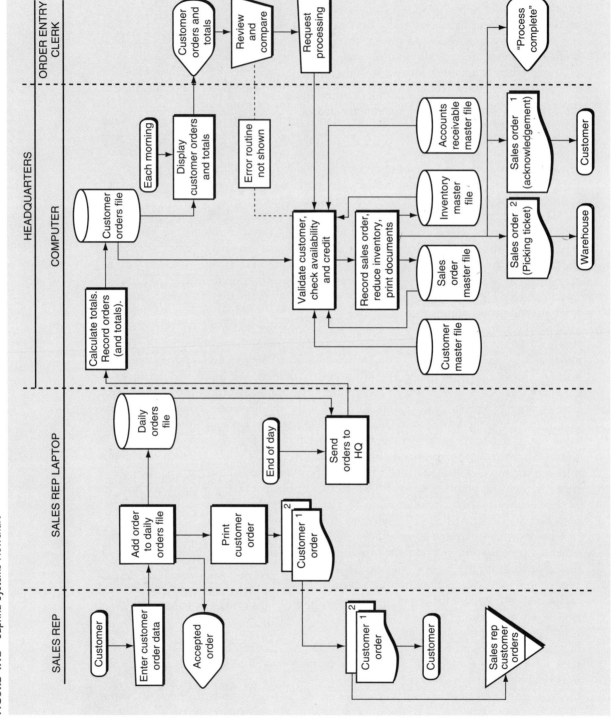

FIGURE 4.12 Suprina Systems Flowchart

complete narrative line 10 we need to show the sales rep filing copy 2 of the order. We don't need a manual process (see systems flowcharting guideline 13); we just need to show a flow into a paper data store. Draw this portion of your flowchart and then compare your drawing to that portion of the flowchart in Figure 4.12. Notice how we have labeled copies 1 and 2 of the customer order. Resolve any differences before reading on.

Narrative line 11 indicates that the process continues at the end of each day. We could indicate this timing by using an annotation or a start symbol labeled "End of day." Let's use this latter method to restart the process in the sales rep laptop column. The start symbol should be followed by a process symbol (a square) to extract and send the order data to the computer at Suprina headquarters (the "Computer" column). In the computer column we need a computer process (rectangle) to receive the data and to calculate and store the totals and orders on the "customer orders file" (a disk symbol). Draw this portion of the process to complete narrative paragraph 3 and review Figure 4.12 to correct any discrepancies that you may have.

In line 16, the process continues each morning. Let's show this process with a start symbol labeled "Each morning," a computer process to extract and display the orders and totals, and a display symbol in the order entry clerk column. Remember, as required by systems flowcharting guideline 11, you must show a flow from the customer orders file to the computer process that extracts and displays the orders and totals. Lines 18–20 describe a manual process performed by the clerk using data from the display. Draw the manual process symbol and connect it to a flow from the display screen. Narratives lines 20 and 21 (see also activity 13 in Tables 4.1 and 4.2, pp. 117 and 123) indicate that the clerk initiates the next computer process. We can use the manual keying symbol for this activity. What if the clerk finds some errors when she reviews the orders and totals? We assume that some corrections would be made. To show this, connect—with a dashed line and no arrow—an annotation symbol to the manual process symbol. Include the phrase "Error routine not shown" within the annotation symbol.

A computer process will perform the actions in narrative lines 21 through 29 (activities 16–18 in Tables 4.1 and 4.2). We could show three processes here (one for each activity), but systems flowcharting guideline 10 allows us to use one process symbol. Connect the manual keying symbol to this process. What data are needed to perform this process? First we need the customer orders. Draw a connection from that file to the process. Line 23 tells us that we need data from the customer master file; lines 24 and 25 tell us that we need data from the inventory master file; lines 27 and 28 tell us that we need data from the sales order master file; and lines 28 and 29 tell us that we need data from the accounts receivable master file. Draw these four files (computer disk symbols) and connect them with flows to the computer process. As discussed above, activity 19 is an *exception routine* and is often not documented in the main process flow. To show that there would be an exception routine, we can connect an "Error routine not shown" annotation symbol to the computer process. After you have drawn these activities, review Figure 4.12 and resolve any discrepancies you may have.

To show the activities in narrative paragraph 5 we need to add another computer process symbol flowing directly from the process symbol that performed the programmed edits in paragraph 4. Then, add a flow from this new process *to* the sales order master file to show lines 30 and 31 (activity 20). To show line 30 and 31 (activity 21), add a flow *to* the inventory master file from the process. Next, draw two documents, one for the picking ticket and the other for the sales order acknowledgement. Connect these to the computer process. You can either draw this as one document on top of another, as we did with the customer order printed by the sales rep laptop, or as two documents. In either case, indicate copy 1 and copy 2. Following systems flowcharting guideline 7, we print these documents in the computer column and then send them to their destinations. Because we do not have customer or warehouse columns, we can send these documents to stop symbols labeled for these entities. Have we completed the flowchart? Not quite. Review the examples in Figure 4.7 (pg. 112) and see that the user is notified by the computer when a process has been completed. Add a display screen (labeled "Process complete") to the order entry clerk column and connect it to the last computer process.

We have now completed the flowchart. Verify your work by checking the table of entities and activities (Table 4.1, pg. 117) to make sure that each activity has been diagrammed. Compare your flowchart to the narrative (Figure 4.8, pg. 115) to see that the system has been accurately documented, and compare your flowchart to the DFDs to see whether the flowchart and DFDs are consistent. Finally, compare your flowchart to the solution in Figure 4.12 (pg. 128). Resolve any discrepancies.

Summary of Systems Flowcharting

Drawing flowcharts requires judgment, which you can develop through practice. We have provided you with a number of guidelines that will help you as you learn to draw flowcharts. Before you get locked into the guidelines and the details of flowcharting, or of drawing DFDs, remember that the purpose of creating this documentation is to simplify and clarify a narrative. We draw these diagrams so that we can better analyze and understand a system. Because we want to portray a system's logic and implementation accurately, there can be many correct solutions. With practice, you can learn to use these techniques to create many correct solutions.

We leave you with the following flowcharting hints, which should help you develop your flowcharting skills:

- Strike a balance between clarity and clutter by using annotation judiciously and by using on-page connectors whenever flow lines might create clutter.
- Avoid crossing lines wherever possible. If you must cross lines, use a "bridge."
- Flowchart normal routines, and leave exception routines for another page of the flowchart.

Documenting Enterprise Systems

In Chapter 2, we described *enterprise systems* and how they integrate the business processes from all of an organization's functional areas and have a central enterprise database. How else will an enterprise system manifest itself? The answer is "it depends." It depends, for example, on how the organization chooses to reengineer the business processes when it installs the enterprise system and how many *ERPs* and other software packages comprise the enterprise system. Let's look at Figure 4.12 (pg. 128), the Suprina systems flowchart, and see what would definitely change if the order entry process was part of an enterprise system. First, the central computer would have one data store/disk symbol that would be labeled "Enterprise database," not the five computer data stores that are in Figure 4.12.

What else *might* change if we had an enterprise system? In general, an enterprise system facilitates the streamlining of business processes, the replacement of paper reports with online "electronic reports," and the automation of manual processes. How will this affect our systems documentation, the DFDs and flowcharts? **Figure 4.13** depicts the Suprina system with the only change that *must* be made if Suprina employed an enterprise system—the central computer's data stores have been replaced by an enterprise database. Other changes could be made if we knew how else the business processes would be changed if Suprina installed an enterprise system.

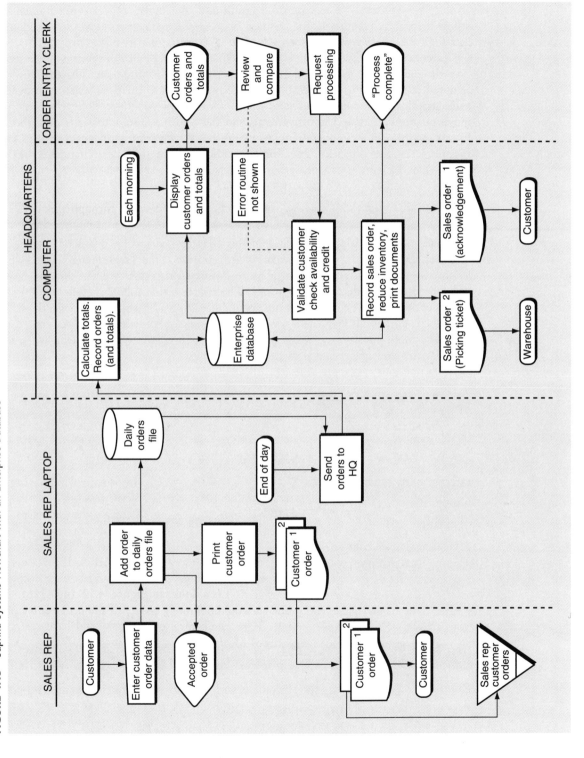

FIGURE 4.13   Suprina Systems Flowchart with an Enterprise Database

How would the DFDs change? The data stores connected to the computer in the physical DFD (Figure 4.10, pg. 121) would be replaced by one data store labeled "Enterprise database." The context diagram and the logical DFD would not change unless there were changes to the business processes. The data stores would not change. In a logical DFD, we want to see each table of data that is part of the process.

In conclusion, let us repeat DFD guideline 3: "Include in the systems documentation all (and only) activities and entities described in the systems narrative." Don't be tempted to depict improvements to a system as you document its existing processes and data flows. Document what is there! Only after you have done that can you move on to analysis and improvements. So the Suprina system, as it is described in Figure 4.8 (pg. 115), is documented in Figure 4.9 (the context diagram on pg. 118), Figure 4.10 (the physical DFD on pg. 121), Figure 4.11 (the logical DFD on pg. 124), and Figure 4.12 (the systems flowchart on pg. 128).

Summary

The documentation tools introduced in this chapter—narratives, tables of entities and activities, DFDs, and systems flowcharts—illustrate common techniques business professionals employ to describe and analyze business processes. Each technique has its own purpose, strengths, and weaknesses. The chapters that follow include many examples of each technique to help you understand how to read them, when to use them, and how to create them. If ever there was a good example of "practice makes perfect," this is one. The more you use the techniques, the better prepared you will be to work with them later in your professional career.

Key Terms

bubble symbol, 104

data flow symbol, 104

external entity symbol, 104

source, 104

destination, 104

data store symbol, 104

data flow diagram (DFD), 105

context diagram, 105

external entities, 105

physical data flow diagram, 105

internal entity, 105

logical data flow diagram, 106

balanced, 108

top-down partitioning, 108

systems flowchart, 108

activity, 116

information processing activities, 116

exception routines, 125

error routines, 125

reject stub, 125

Review Questions

RQ 4-1   Why do we need to document an information system (or business process)?

RQ 4-2   What is a data flow diagram (DFD)?

RQ 4-3   Describe each symbol used in constructing DFDs.

RQ 4-4   What is a context diagram?

RQ 4-5   What is a physical data flow diagram (DFD)?

RQ 4- 6   Distinguish internal and external entities.

RQ 4- 7   What is a logical DFD?

RQ 4- 8   What are the differences among a context diagram, a logical DFD, and a physical DFD?

RQ 4- 9   When is a set of DFDs balanced (i.e., leveled)?

RQ 4- 10   What is a systems flowchart?

RQ 4- 11   What is a table of entities and activities? What uses does it serve?

RQ 4- 12   What are information processing activities?

RQ 4- 13   Why are some entities found in a narrative included in the context diagram as external entities, whereas others are included as internal entities?

RQ 4- 14   What are the guidelines for grouping logical activities for a logical DFD?

RQ 4- 15   Where are error and exception routines shown on DFDs?

RQ 4- 16   Where are error and exception routines shown on systems flowcharts?

RQ 4- 17   How will systems documentation differ between business processes that employ an enterprise system and those that do not?

Discussion Questions

DQ 4-1   "Data flow diagrams and systems flowcharts provide redundant pictures of an information system (or business process). We don't need both." Discuss fully.

DQ 4-2   "It is easier to learn to prepare data flow diagrams, which use only a few symbols, than it is to learn to prepare systems flowcharts, which use a number of different symbols." Discuss fully.

DQ 4-3   Describe the *who, what, where,* and *how* of the following scenario: A customer gives his purchase to a sales clerk, who enters the sale in a cash register and puts the money in the register drawer. At the end of the day, the sales clerk gives the cash and the register tape to the cashier.

DQ 4-4   Why are *many* correct logical DFD solutions possible? Why is only one correct physical DFD solution possible?

DQ 4-5   Explain why a flow from a higher- to a lower-numbered bubble on a logical DFD is a physical manifestation of the system. Give an example.

DQ 4-6   Compare and contrast the purpose of and techniques used in drawing physical DFDs and logical DFDs.

DQ 4-7   "If we document a system with a systems flowchart and data flow diagrams, we have overdocumented the system." Discuss fully.

DQ 4-8   "Preparing a table of entities and activities as the first step in documenting systems seems to be unnecessary and unduly cumbersome. It would be a lot easier to bypass this step and get right to the necessary business of actually drawing the diagrams." Do you agree? Discuss fully.

DQ 4-9   "PCAOB Audit Standard No. 5 (AS5) paragraph 37 and Statement on Auditing Standard Section 319 (AU 319) paragraph 75 suggest that management, business process owners, and auditors prepare and analyze systems documentation to understand the flow of transactions through a process and to identify and assess the effectiveness of the design of internal controls. However, organizations, internal audit departments, and public accounting firms have developed their own methods for documenting systems. Therefore, I am not going to learn to prepare systems documentation until I know exactly what technique I will need to use in my job." Do you agree? Discuss fully.

DQ 4-10 "Because there are computer-based documentation products that can draw data flow diagrams and systems flowcharts, learning to draw them manually is a waste of time." Do you agree? Discuss fully.

Short Problems

SP 4-1   a.   Prepare a table of entities and activities for the Webster, Inc. process described below.

Webster, Inc.

Webster, Inc. sells plumbing supplies to contractors in the southern region of the United States. Each month, the IT division at Webster prints monthly statements and sends them to the accounts receivable (AR) department, where a clerk mails them to the customers. Webster's customers mail their payments back to Webster, where a clerk in AR batches the checks and sends them to the cashier. The AR clerk then uses the payment stub to enter the payments into the computer, where the AR master data is updated to record the payment.

   b.   Construct a context diagram based on the table you prepared in part (a).

SP 4-2   Prepare a physical DFD based on the output from Short Problem 4-1.

SP 4-3   a.   Prepare an annotated table of entities and activities based on the output from Short Problems 4-1 and 4-2. Indicate on this table the groupings, bubble numbers, and bubble titles to be used in preparing a level 0 logical DFD.

   b.   Prepare a logical DFD (level 0 only) based on the table you prepared in part (a).

SP 4-4   Construct a systems flowchart based on the narrative and the output from Short Problems 4-1 through 4-3.

SP 4-5   A description of 14 typical information processing routines is given here, along with 10 numbered segments from systems flowcharts (**Figure 4.14**).

   Match the flowcharting segments with the descriptions to which they correspond. Four descriptions will be left blank.

   a.   Data stored on a disk is sorted and placed on another disk.

   b.   A report is printed from the contents of a disk.

   c.   Documents are manually posted to a paper ledger.

   d.   Magnetic tape input is used to update master data kept on a disk.

   e.   A printed output document is filed.

   f.   Two documents are sent to an external entity.

   g.   Data on source documents are keyed to an offline disk.

   h.   Programmed edits are performed on key input, the data entry clerk investigates exceptions and keys in corrections, and then data on the disk are updated.

   i.   Input stored on two magnetic disks is merged.

j.   The computer prepares a report that is sent to an external entity.

k.   Output is provided to a display device at a remote location.

l.   A batch total of input documents is compared to the total reflected on an error and summary report produced after the documents were recorded.

m.   Data are keyed from a remote location.

n.   Data on a magnetic tape are printed during an offline operation.

FIGURE 4.14   Flowchart Segments for Short Problem 4-5

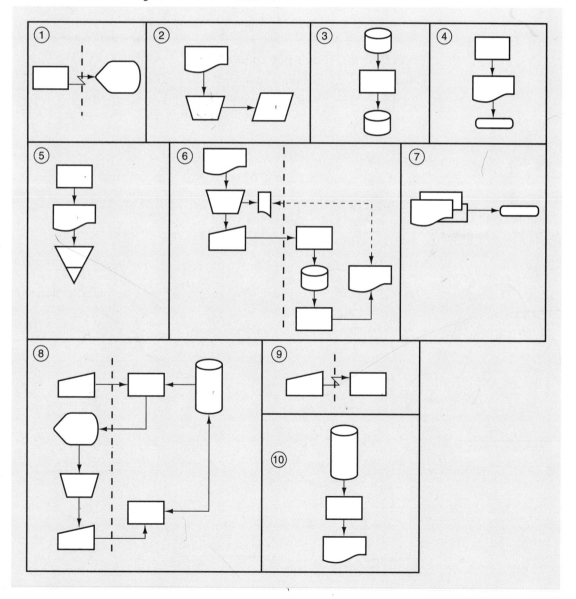

Problems

P 4-1 Prepare a narrative to describe the system depicted in the physical DFD in **Figure 4.15**.

P 4-2 Prepare a narrative to describe the system depicted in the logical DFD in **Figure 4.16**.

P 4-3 Prepare a narrative to describe the system depicted in the flowchart in **Figure 4.17** (pg. 138).

Note for Problems 4-4 through 4-7: These problems are based on the following narratives of processes in two fictional companies. Good Buy, Inc. describes the sales process at good-buy.com and Millennium Insurance Company describes an automobile insurance order entry and billing system. If you want to test your documentation skills beyond these problems, there are narratives at the end of Chapters 10 through 14.

Good Buy, Inc. (good-buy.com)

Good Buy, Inc. (a fictitious company) sells a variety of consumer products through its Web site, good-buy.com. Good Buy's IT infrastructure consists of a front-end Web server that interacts with customers and a back-end

FIGURE 4.15 Physical DFD for Problem 4-1

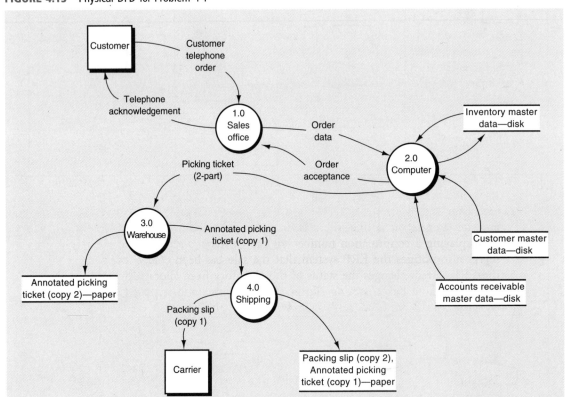

FIGURE 4.16   Logical DFD for Problem 4-2

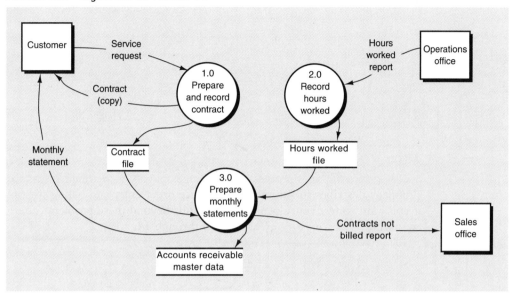

ERP system that manages the inventory and performs other typical ERP functions. The sales order process begins when a customer logs on to the good-buy.com Web site. The Web server requests the current Good Buy online catalog from the ERP system, which sends the catalog to the Web server, and the server displays it to the customer. The customer selects the items and quantities that he wants to purchase; the Web server edits the customer input for accuracy (e.g., ensures that all required fields have been selected or filled in) and sends this list on to the ERP system, where the requested quantities of inventory are allocated for the sale. The ERP sends back to the Web server the quantities that have been allocated, and the Web server displays this information on the customer's screen. The customer verifies that the order is correct and completes the sale by entering his shipping and credit card information. The Web server edits this data for accuracy (e.g., ensures that all required fields have been selected or filled in and that the length of the entered credit card number is correct) and sends the credit card information and amount of the sale on to the credit card company. The credit card company sends back a verification number, and the Web server notifies the customer that the sale has been completed by displaying a confirmation number on the customer's screen. The Web server also notifies the ERP system that the sale has been completed, and the ERP system changes the status of the inventory from allocated to sold, prints a picking ticket/packing slip in the warehouse, and records (on the enterprise database) a sale and an accounts receivable from the credit card company.

Millennium Insurance Company

Millennium Insurance Company of Asheville, North Carolina, processes its automobile insurance policies on a batch-oriented computer system with magnetic disk storage. Customers send requests for auto insurance into the

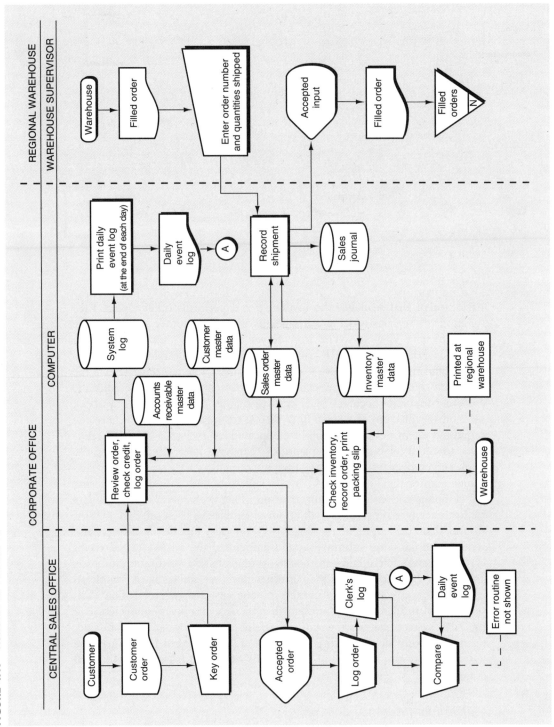

FIGURE 4.17 Flowchart for Problem 4-3

Asheville sales office, where sales clerks prepare policy request forms. They file a copy of the form and forward the original to the input preparation section, where data entry clerks use networked PCs to key and key-verify the data contained on the documents to a disk ("policy requests").

Each evening, computer operations retrieves the policy request data from the network, edits the data on the computer for accuracy (e.g., all required fields completed), sorts the data in policy number sequence, and prints a summary report listing the edited policy requests (there is an error routine, not described here, for those requests that do not pass the computer edits). The summary report is sent to the sales office, where the sales clerks compare the report to the copy of the policy request form that they previously filed. If everything checks out, they notify computer operations to go ahead with processing. When notified, computer operations processes the correct policy request data against the policyholder master data to create a new policy record. Each evening, a disk, which was created during the processing run, is used to print premium notices that are sent to the customer.

TABLE 4.3   Table of Entities and Activities for Problem 4-9

Entities	Para		Activities	
Sales rep	2	2.	Enter customer order data.	*1.0 Capture customer order.*
Sales rep laptop	2	3.	Add order to daily orders file.	
	2	4.	Print customer order (2 copies).	
Sales rep	2	6.	File copy 2 of the order.	
Sales rep laptop	3	7.	Retrieve day's orders from the daily orders file.	*2.0 Record customer order.*
Computer	3	9.	Calculate totals.	
	3	10.	Record orders (and totals) in customer orders file.	
Computer	3	11.	Display customer orders (with totals) to order entry clerk.	
Order entry clerk	4	12.	Review orders.	*3.0 Edit customer order.*
	4	13.	Compare totals.	
		14.	Initiate computer process.	
Computer	4	16.	Validate customer name and address.	
	4	17.	Check inventory availability and pricing.	
	4	18.	Compare credit limit to order, sales orders, and accounts receivable.	
Computer	5	20.	Record customer orders on sales order master file.	*4.0 Record sales order.*
	5	21.	Reduce inventory balances.	
	5	22.	Print acknowledgement (sales order copy 1) and picking ticket (sales order copy 2).	

P 4-4   a. Prepare a table of entities and activities for Good Buy, Inc. or Millennium Insurance Company.

b. Construct a context diagram based on the table you prepared in part (a).

P 4-5   Prepare a physical DFD based on the output from Problem 4-4.

P 4-6   a. Prepare an annotated table of entities and activities based on the output from Problems 4-4 and 4-5. Indicate on this table the groupings, bubble numbers, and bubble titles to be used in preparing a level 0 logical DFD.

b. Prepare a logical DFD (level 0 only) based on the table you prepared in part (a).

P 4-7   Construct a systems flowchart based on the narrative and the output from Problems 4-4 through 4-6.

P 4-8   Refer to Figure 4.11 (pg. 124), the level 0 DFD of Suprina's order entry system.

a. Construct a diagram 1 that explodes process 1.0, "Capture customer order," down to the next level.

b. Construct a diagram 2 that explodes process 2.0, "Record customer order," down to the next level.

c. Construct a diagram 3 that explodes process 3.0, "Record sales order," down to the next level.

P 4-9   **Table 4.3** on page 139 depicts a different logical grouping of activities than does Table 4.2 (pg. 123). Construct a logical DFD (level 0) based on Table 4.3.

CHAPTER 5

Database Management Systems

Learning Objectives

After reading this chapter, you should be able to:

- Describe the limitations of traditional application approaches to managing data.
- Analyze the advantages gained by using the centralized database approach to managing data.
- Create normalized tables in a relational database.
- Use entity-relationship diagrams in database design and implementation.
- Explain the importance of advanced database applications in decision support and knowledge management.

ERPs contain databases with, on average, thousands of data tables, holding up to terabytes (10^{12} bytes) of data in total. Many ERPs also include data warehouses with petabytes (10^{15} bytes) of data. As an auditor, where would you begin auditing such a massive amount of data? As a consultant or designer, how would you advise a client about implementing or using such a complex system? How would you even begin such tasks? First, some basic knowledge is needed to work with databases as accountants (whether in the role of an auditor, consultant, or designer). Fortunately, you will probably never have to do these tasks or make these decisions alone. Nevertheless, you need to have a general understanding of what is needed to complete such tasks. You need to understand the basics of how databases are designed if you participate in auditing businesses that use information systems built on large databases. In today's business environment, that is essentially all businesses. To advise clients about implementing business information systems as consultants, you must have a detailed working knowledge of what kinds of information systems and databases are available and what they are capable of doing.

Synopsis

In this chapter, you will learn about the approaches that organizations use to process business event data. These events, as you learned in Chapter 2, include but are not limited to sales, purchases, cash receipts, and cash disbursements. In this chapter, you will learn how data from business events are recorded and processed using differing accounting systems designs. As business events occur, data are processed and recorded. In a traditional manual accounting system, or in an automated system designed in the format of a manual accounting system, the accounting data are recorded in journals and classified in ledgers. Increasingly, however, accounting systems are built on underlying databases of business event data. In these databases, accounting information (along with other business information) is stored in database tables. Accounting reports, such as financial statements, and traditional accounting records, such as journals and ledgers, are generated from the information stored in these database tables. As a result, accounting information has gone from being a primary input of business data to being one of many outputs. In a database accounting system, data management is broken into two functions, the creation and maintenance of master data (see Figure 2.4 on pg. 48) and the recording of business event data (see Figure 2.5 on pg. 49). You will learn the basic elements of database design and implementation that organizations use when they create databases for their accounting information. In some larger organizations, the business event data is copied periodically into a separate database (a *data warehouse*) where it is stored. Managers can gain important insights by analyzing this collected historical data with multidimensional analytic tools and exploratory techniques (called *data mining*). In some companies, these data warehouses are combined with business event databases to create sophisticated reporting systems that help managers make better decisions. These systems include decision support systems, executive information systems, group support systems, and expert systems. Many of these advanced systems use software tools called *intelligent agents*. Finally, you will learn about knowledge management systems that combine event processing databases, data warehouses, and decision support systems, and make the combined knowledge contained in these systems available across the organization.

Introduction

Organizations engage in various business processes and events, such as hiring employees, purchasing inventory, making sales, and collecting cash from customers. As you learned in Chapters 1 and 2, the activities that occur during the execution of these business processes are called *events*.[1] Among the most important elements in any organization's information systems, whether those systems deal with accounting information or other information that managers use to make decisions, are the data describing these events that are stored in those systems. This is the *business event data* first described in Chapter 3.

As an aspiring decision maker, you should know that no matter what career path you take, data and databases will become an integral part of your day-to-day work. In this chapter, the major approaches used to manage data are described and compared. You will learn about the benefits and costs of alternative methods for collecting, storing, and using business data.

Two Approaches to Business Event Processing

As we begin, let's describe the processing of business event data. First, we know that as organizations engage in business processes, such as purchasing inventory, several business events, such as preparing a purchase order and receiving the goods, occur. Second, as these business events occur, business event data is captured to describe the *who, what,*

---

[1] As noted in previous chapters, transactions are those events that have an accounting impact and result in entries in the general ledger.

where, and *when* about that event. In the following sections, you will learn about the *applications approach* and the *centralized database²* *approach* (sometimes referred to as simply the *database approach*) to capturing and storing that business event data.

The Applications Approach to Business Event Processing

Figure 5.1 compares the applications approach (discussed in this section) with the centralized database approach to business event processing (discussed in the next section). **Figure 5.2** (pg. 144) contains the record layouts for the files in Figure 5.1, part (a).

FIGURE 5.1   Two Approaches to Business Event Processing

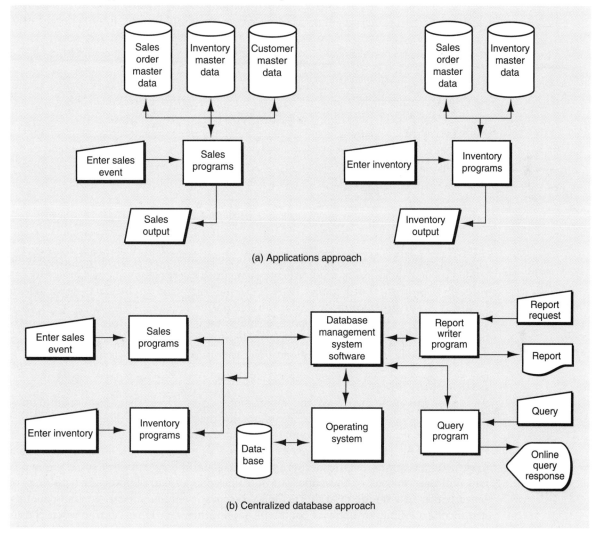

(a) Applications approach

(b) Centralized database approach

---

²We define a "database" as a collection of data within one or more files and a "centralized database" as a collection of data within an interconnected series of files. The files in a database need not be interconnected. For example, a professor's "student database" may consist of several Excel spreadsheets kept at work and home. The spreadsheets need not be directly connected and can contain different data. Accordingly, application approaches involve databases strictly speaking but do not consist of centralized databases.

FIGURE 5.2   Record Layouts Under an Applications Approach to Business Event Processing

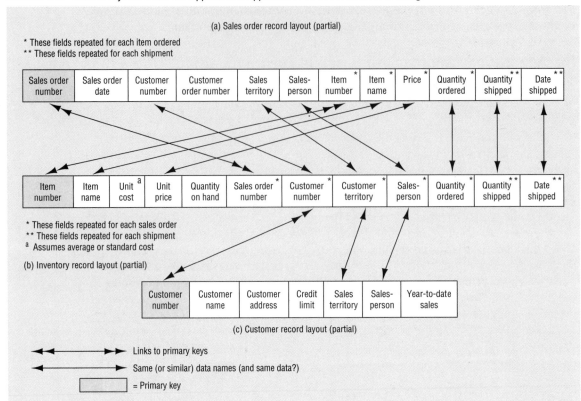

Before databases became widely used in business information systems, organizations tended to view their data as a subordinate element to the program that used the data. As you can see in part (a) of Figure 5.1 (pg. 143), the traditional **applications approach to business event processing** view concentrates on the process being performed. In this case, data play a secondary or supportive role to the programs that run in each application system. Under this approach, each application collects and manages its own data, generally in dedicated, separate, physically distinguishable files for each application.

Data Redundancy

An important consequence of the applications approach is that **data redundancy**, data stored in multiple locations, occurs among the various files. For example, notice the redundancies (indicated by double-ended arrows) depicted in the record layouts in Figure 5.2. This redundancy increases labor and storage costs because redundant data must be entered into the system more than once, and the system must store and maintain multiple versions of the same data in different files. In addition, data residing in separate files may not be shareable among applications because of software and data format incompatibilities or network communication difficulties. However, the worst consequence of using an applications approach is that the redundant data stored in multiple files can become inconsistent when information is updated in one file and not in other files where it also resides.

In Chapter 1, you learned about horizontal (business operations) and vertical (managerial decision support) information flows. The data in Figure 5.2 have two purposes. The data (1) mirror and monitor the business operations (the *horizontal information flows*) and (2) provide the basis for managerial decisions (the *vertical information flows*). In addition to data derived from the horizontal flows, managers often use data unrelated to event data processing, that is, data about phenomena outside the organization. Stock exchange data and information about the overall economy are examples of such additional data. These data are collected and generally stored in the organization's database alongside the business event related data.

Consider the following example: A manager asked that a sales application be designed to perform sales analysis and generate reports such as product sales by territory, by customer, or by salesperson. To do this, the sales application stores data for sales territory and salesperson in the sales order record shown in part (a) of Figure 5.2. Assume that a different manager asked to have the inventory application conduct similar analyses. To do this, the inventory application stores similar (and redundant) data about territory and salesperson such as that depicted in part (b) of Figure 5.2. As implied by Figure 5.1, part (a) (pg. 143), the sales data in the inventory file—including customer territory and salesperson—can be updated by the sales application or updated separately by the inventory application. This creates a condition in which similar information about the same fact is stored in different files. This condition violates the *integrity* of the data. As a second example, assume that a sales manager wants to know all the products that a particular customer has purchased (perhaps so the company can promote those products that the customer is no longer buying). Given the record layouts depicted in Figure 5.2, the information can be obtained by sorting the inventory or sales order data by customer number. Alternatively, the company may have collected these data in the customer master data (in part [c] of Figure 5.2). In all of these examples, the data are difficult and expensive to obtain. Also, if the applications were not originally designed to yield these data, the applications approach to business event processing makes it difficult to add these data after the fact.

The Centralized Database Approach to Business Event Processing

The preceding examples have all involved business event data related to selling merchandise. The applications approach leaves us with similar problems for *standing data*. In Figure 5.2, you can see the redundancies among the three files with respect to master file standing data such as customer number, territory, and salesperson. These fields could easily take on different values for the same facts over time as changes are made in one file but not all files in which the data are stored. The **centralized database approach to business event processing**, in which facts about events are stored in relational database tables instead of separate files, solves many of the problems caused by data redundancy. You will learn about the centralized database approach in the next section, and then you can return to Figure 5.2 and see how these data are handled in a centralized database approach, rather than an application approach.

Databases and Business Events

Traditional file management approaches that focus on an applications approach to data management are often sufficient to support a conventional applications approach to processing business event data. The use of centralized databases has improved the efficiency of processing business event data by eliminating data redundancies and improving data integrity. However, the big change that databases have helped make possible is the creation of integrated business information systems that include data about all of a company's operations in one massive collection of relational tables (in a centralized database or in a set of databases that are linked to each other). Multiple users from throughout the organization can view and aggregate *event* data in a manner most conducive to their needs.

Enterprise
Systems
At the heart of this movement is a fundamental shift in the view of information processing in business organizations. Traditionally, organizational information systems have been focused on capturing data for the purpose of generating reports and using the reporting function to support decision making. Increasingly, management's view is shifting to one of viewing information systems processing as a decision-support activity first and a reporting function second. This perspective leads to a focus on aggregating and maintaining data in an original form from which reports can be derived, but users also can access and manipulate data using their own models and their own data aggregations. In Chapter 2, you learned about strategic shifts in information design, including the trend toward the use of enterprise systems that might include one or more ERP systems, CRM systems, and other special-purpose systems. Some of these systems include their own databases, but most are built on existing relational databases, which are typically centralized databases.

Database Management Systems (DBMSs)

A **database management system (DBMS)** is a set of integrated programs designed to simplify the tasks of creating, accessing, and managing a centralized database. DBMSs integrate a collection of files that are independent of application programs and are available to satisfy a number of different processing needs. Organizations use DBMSs to coordinate the activities of their many functional areas. The DBMS, containing data related to all of an organization's applications, supports normal data processing needs and enhances the organization's management activities by providing data useful to managers (i.e., information). Enterprise databases are a type or subset of DBMS. This use is consistent with the meaning intended by most computer users and developers.

Logical versus Physical Database Models

The concept underlying the centralized database approach to business event processing is to decouple the data from the system applications (i.e., to make the data independent of the application or other users). This decoupling, called **data independence**, is a major difference between the centralized database approach and the applications approach. Systems that use this decoupled approach are often referred to as having a **three-tier architecture**, with the three tiers being the user or presentation tier, the application or business logic tier (also called "middleware"), and the data or database tier. Recall that in the applications approach, the data is subordinate to, or dependent upon, the application program that uses the data. As a result, in the applications approach, there are only two tiers. Therefore, as reflected in part (b) of Figure 5.1 (pg. 143), in a three-tier architecture, the data can become the focus of attention. Several other aspects of the centralized database approach are noteworthy:

- The database is now shared by multiple system applications that support related business processes, as shown at the left of Figure 5.1, part (b).
- In addition to being used by application programs, the data can be accessed through two other user interfaces that are built into most database management software: (1) *report generation*, the creation of onscreen or printed summaries of specific data, as shown in the upper-right portion of part (b), and (2) ad hoc user inquiries, also called *queries*, which allow users to ask questions about the data in the database handled through *query language* software, depicted in the lower-right portion of part (b).
- Two layers of software are needed to translate user views into instructions for retrieving the data from the physical location in which it is stored (e.g., a

computer's disk drive). The distinction between the way a user thinks of the data in a database, called a user's *logical view*, and the way the data is actually stored on the computer hardware, called the *physical view* of the data, is important for computer scientists who develop database software, but it is not very important for accountants and managers who use the software because the DBMS includes the software that handles this translation automatically. Some of the more technical design issues of DBMSs are described in **Technology Summary 5.1**.

Figure 5.3 (pg. 148) depicts how a database might look if the data from Figure 5.2 (pg. 144) were stored in a database that used a relational structure, which is the most common type of database structure used in businesses today. The data from our three files are now stored in four tables: CUSTOMERS (instead of the customer master data), INVENTORY_ ITEMS (instead of the inventory master data), and SALES_ORDERS

Technology Summary 5.1

DATABASE MANAGEMENT SYSTEMS (DBMSs)

As described earlier, a DBMS is a set of integrated programs designed to simplify the tasks of creating, accessing, and managing a database. The DBMS performs several functions, including but not limited to the following:

- Defining the data
- Defining the relations among data
- Interfacing with the *operating system* for storage of the data on the *physical* media
- Mapping each user's view of the data

In the language of DBMS, a schema is a complete description of the configuration of record types, data items and the relationships among them. The schema defines the *logical* structure of the database. The schema, therefore, defines the organizational view of the data. A subschema is a description of a *portion* of a schema. The DBMS maps each user's view of the data from subschemas to the schema. In this way, the DBMS provides flexibility in identifying and selecting records. Each of the many database users may want to access records in a certain way. For example, the credit department would need to know credit limits for customers, whereas the sales manager might want to know sales information by customer. The following figure portrays the schema–subschema relationship.

A chief advantage of a DBMS is that it contains a query language (also called a data manipulation language, or DML), which is a language much like ordinary language. A query language is used to access a database and to produce inquiry reports. These languages allow nontechnical users to bypass the programmer and to access the database directly. Deriving data from the database using a query does not replace applications programs, which are still required to perform routine data processing tasks. However, when information is needed quickly or when a manager wants to browse through the database combining data in a variety of ways, the query facility of a DBMS is a vast improvement over the traditional method of requesting that a program be written to generate a report. Later in this chapter and in Chapter 6, you will see examples of SQL (*Structured Query Language*), the de facto standard for DBMS query languages.

A DBMS normally contains a number of security controls to protect the data from access by unauthorized users as well as from accidental or deliberate alteration or destruction. A DBMS also includes software that allows the data to be simultaneously shared by multiple users. This software often allows managers to manage access rights for specific users. For example, all employees can view employee names and addresses, but only specific authorized users can view employee's pay rates.

Customer number	Customer name	Customer address	Credit limit	Sales-person	Sales territory	Year-to-date sales

(a) Schema

Customer number	Customer name	Credit limit

(b) Credit department subschema

Customer number	Customer name	Sales-person	Sales territory	Year-to-date sales

(c) Sales manager subschema

and SALES_LINES (these two tables replace the sales order master data). These tables are *logical views* of data that are *physically* stored in a database. Users can access the data in the tables by:

- Formulating a query
- Preparing a report using a report writer
- Including a request for data within an application program

FIGURE 5.3   Record Layouts as Tables

Shaded_Attribute(s)	= Primary Key

CUSTOMERS

Cust_Code	Cust_Name	Cust_City	Credit_Limit	Sales_YTD	Sales_Person
ETC	Bikes Et Cetera	Elgin	10000.00	9561.55	Wilke
IBS	Inter. Bicycle Sales	New York	5000.00	4191.18	Breitenstein
RODEBYKE	Rodebyke Bic. & Mopeds	San Jose	2000.00	1142.50	Goodall
STANS	Stan's Cyclery	Hawthorne	10000.00	8330.00	Garcia
WHEEL	Wheelaway Cycle Center	Campbell	10000.00	6854.00	Garcia

INVENTORY_ITEMS

Item_Number	Item_Name	Qty_On_Hand	Unit_Cost	Unit_Price
1000-1	20 in. Bicycle	247	55.00	137.50
1001-1	26 in. Bicycle	103	60.00	150.00
1002-1	24 in. Bicycle	484	60.00	150.00
1003-1	20 in. Bicycle	4	24.37	60.93
1280-054	Kickstand	72	6.50	16.25
2010-0050	Formed Handlebar	90	4.47	11.25
3050-2197	Pedal	23	0.75	1.88
3961-1010	Tire, 26 in.	42	1.45	3.13
3961-1041	Tire Tube, 26 in.	19	1.25	3.13
3965-1050	Spoke Reflector	232	0.29	0.63
3970-1011	Wheel, 26 in.	211	10.50	25.00

SALES_ORDERS

SO_Number	Cust_Code	Cust_Order_Number	SO_Date
1010	WHEEL	453	061205
1011	ETC	347	061205
1012	WHEEL	56-6	061205
1013	IBS	3422	061205
1014	ETC	778	061205
1015	WHEEL	5673	061206
1016	ETC	3345	061206

SALES_LINES

SO_Number	Item_Number	Qty_Ordered	Sales_Price	Qty_Shipped
1010	1000-1	5	137.50	0
1010	2010-0050	2	11.25	0
1011	1001-1	10	127.50	8
1011	1002-1	5	150.00	4
1012	1003-1	5	60.93	0
1012	1001-1	10	127.50	5
1013	1001-1	50	78.30	0
1014	1003-1	25	37.42	0
1015	1003-1	25	37.42	0
1016	1003-1	5	60.93	0
1016	3965-1050	50	33.00	0
1016	3961-1041	5	3.13	0
1016	1000-1	4	137.50	0

These three methods are depicted in Figure 5.1, part (b) (pg. 143). In some cases, a user formulates a query and enters it to receive the query results immediately on the computer screen. In other cases, queries are placed into onscreen forms or reports that are generated by software within the DBMS. A third alternative is to include queries in the program code that use the data in the DBMS. In the second and third cases, users might not be aware that a query was operating to help them obtain the information. They simply open the form, print the report, or run the program.

Overcoming the Limitations of the Applications Approach

Earlier in this chapter, you learned about some of the limitations of the applications approach to business event processing. In this section, you will learn how the centralized database approach can overcome these limitations. You also will learn about other advantages of the centralized database approach. Of course, the centralized database approach has its own limitations. You will learn about those in this section also.

- *Eliminating data redundancy:* With the centralized database approach to business event processing, an item of data is stored only once. Applications that need data can access the data from the central database. For example, in Figure 5.1, part (a), multiple versions of the inventory master data are present, whereas in part (b), only one exists. Further, Figure 5.2 (pg. 144) depicts the same data elements on more than one file, whereas Figure 5.3 shows each data element only once. An organization using the applications approach to business event processing must incur the costs and risks of storing and maintaining these duplicate files and data elements. `Controls`

- *Ease of maintenance:* Because each data element is stored only once, additions, deletions, or changes to the database are accomplished easily. Contrast this to the illustration in Figure 5.2, where changes in a salesperson, territory, or customer combination would require changes in three different files.

- *Reduced labor and storage costs:* By eliminating redundant data, storage space is reduced, which results in associated cost savings. However, in most database installations, this savings is *more than offset* by the additional costs of DBMS software.

- *Data integrity:* This advantage, like several others, results from eliminating data redundancy. As mentioned earlier, storing multiple versions of the same data element is bound to produce inconsistencies among the versions. For instance, the salesperson and sales territory data might differ among their many versions, not only because of clerical errors but also because of timing differences in making *data maintenance* changes. Inconsistent data could also result from the timing differences that can occur during *business event processing* of the inventory master data by the sales and inventory applications. With only one version of each data element stored in the database, such inconsistencies are no longer a threat. `Controls`

- *Data independence:* The centralized database approach allows applications and databases to exist independently. Accordingly, the database can be modified or changed without affecting applications using that database. For instance, a company may decide to change from an Oracle database to an SQL Server database, yet the company's applications (e.g., sales) will continue to be able to use the new database as easily as the previous one. Similarly, data independence allows multiple application programs to use the data concurrently. The data can be accessed in several ways (e.g., through applications processing, online query, and report writing programs), and the access can be quickly changed by modifying the definition of the tables or views. With the traditional applications approach to business event processing, the programs would need revisions to provide access to more or less data.

- *Privacy:* The security modules available in most DBMS software include powerful features to protect the database against unauthorized disclosure, alteration, or destruction. Control over data access can typically be exercised down to the data element level. Users can be granted access to data for reading or updating (add, revise, delete) data. Other ways to implement security include *data classification* (i.e., data objects are given classification levels, and users are assigned clearance levels) and *data encryption* (discussed in Chapters 8 and 9). DBMSs also allow you to set up *passwords* (discussed in Chapter 8) as a control.

Despite the many advantages of using a DBMS instead of an application approach, some organizations do not use a DBMS. A DBMS can be expensive to implement. In general, a DBMS requires more powerful, and thus more expensive, hardware. The DBMS itself costs money. Hiring people to maintain and operate the database can be more expensive than hiring application maintenance programmers. Also, drawbacks exist that are related to operating the DBMS. Operational issues can include the following:

- Although database sharing is an advantage, it carries a downside risk. If the DBMS fails, all of the organization's information processing halts.
- Having all your data in a single centralized database increases the potential magnitude of the damage that can happen should unauthorized access to the database occur, compared to having data distributed over several databases.

- Because all applications depend on the DBMS, *Continuous Data Protection (CDP)* and *contingency planning* (discussed in Chapter 8) are more important than in the applications approach to business event data processing.
- When more than one user attempts to access data at the *same* time, the database can face "contention" or "concurrency" problems. Procedures such as *record locking* or *field locking* can mitigate these problems, but these solutions are not foolproof. Further discussion of this topic is beyond the scope of this book.
- Territorial disputes can arise over who "owns" the data. For instance, disputes can arise regarding who is responsible for data maintenance (additions/deletions/ changes) to customer data. The sales department might think it should own those data, but the credit department and the accountants managing accounts receivable might argue with that contention.

To cope with these and other problems, most companies that have adopted the centralized database approach have found it necessary to create a database administrator function. In most organizations, the database administrator is responsible for administrative and technical issues related to the DBMS.

Database Essentials

The design and implementation of a DBMS can be a more complex process than creating specific applications with subordinate data. To understand how the centralized database approach works, you need some background information in database essentials. You will learn about logical database structures and gain an understanding of some key database elements in this section. You also will be introduced to the process of designing and implementing a database. Chapter 6 includes a more detailed treatment of database design, implementation, and use.

Logical Database Models

Four types of logical DBMS models exist: hierarchical, network, relational, and object-oriented. As a *designer* or *user* of an AIS, you will participate in the selection of the

DBMS for your organization, and the choice from among these logical models will affect the speed and flexibility of the DBMS. In addition, as a user or auditor of business information systems, your effective use of a DBMS often depends on your understanding of these logical models. Of these four DBMS models, you will probably work only with relational and object-oriented databases because hierarchical and network databases are now obsolete and likely to be encountered only in *legacy systems*.

The first DBMSs used a **hierarchical database model**. In this model, records are organized in a pyramid structure. The records at or near the top of the structure contain records below them. This structure works well for simple situations. For example, a bank that wants to record information about its customers and their accounts could use a hierarchical DBMS. The top-level records may hold information about customers. The next level down could include records with information about accounts. A customer might have a savings account, a checking account, and a loan account. All of a customer's accounts would be below that customer record in the hierarchy. The next level down may include records that stored information about transactions in each account.

In a hierarchical DBMS, records that are included in a record one level above them are called **child records** of that upper-level record. **Parent records** include the lower-level child records. A child of a parent record can be the parent of another child record. Each parent record can have many child records, but each child record can have only one parent record. In the bank example, the customer records would be the parent records of the child account records, which in turn would be the parent records of the child records that stored information about account increases and decreases.

In their heyday, hierarchical DBMSs were ideal for implementing accounting systems because the charts of accounts used in most accounting systems are branching structures that allow child records to have only one parent record. Therefore it is not surprising that general ledger systems and accounting departments were among the first business functions to be computerized. Hierarchical DBMSs work well for such simple data structures; however, they fall apart quickly when the data becomes more complex. For example, the hierarchical bank example DBMS described previously could not handle joint accounts unless the joint owners were considered a single entity. To handle more complex data structures, database researchers created a different database model. In the **network database model**, a child record can have more than one parent record. This was a significant improvement over the early hierarchical designs. Network DBMSs were adopted by a number of organizations that had been frustrated by the limitations of hierarchical DBMSs. The wholesale move to network DBMSs was interrupted, however, by the development of a vastly more flexible model, the relational database.

Relational Database Model

In a **relational database model**, data are logically organized in two-dimensional tables. Each individual fact or type of information (i.e., *entity*) is stored in its own table. The relational model was developed using a branch of mathematics called *set theory*. In set theory, a two-dimensional collection of information is called a *relation* (thus the name "relational"). However, today most people call these collections of information "tables." A relational DBMS allows users to query the tables to obtain information from one or more tables in a very flexible way. The tables in Figure 5.3 (pg. 148) are relational tables.

The relational structure is attractive from a user's standpoint because end users often think of the data they need as a table. This mental picture translates well to the logical data model of a relational DBMS. The capability of a relational DBMS to handle complex queries also is important. Although the relational model is considered to be a dramatic improvement over the network and relational models, it does have two disadvantages. First, a relational DBMS requires much more computer memory and processing time than the earlier models. Increases in computer processing speeds as well as a steady decrease in hardware costs have reduced the impact of this first disadvantage. The second disadvantage is that the relational model, as originally conceived, allows only text and numerical information to be stored in the database. It did not allow the inclusion of complex object types in the database such as graphics, audio, video, or geographic information. The desire to include these complex objects in databases led to the development of object-oriented databases.

Object-Oriented Database Model

Both simple and complex objects can be stored in an **object-oriented database model**. Earlier data models were designed to store text-based data (which includes numbers). In *object-oriented* data models, other types of data can be stored. For example, video clips or pictures can be stored in an object-oriented database. Object-oriented databases include abstract data types that allow users to define characteristics of the data to be stored when developing an application. This overcomes the limitations of relational databases. Relational databases limit the types of data that can be stored in table columns. Instead of tables, an object-oriented DBMS stores data in objects.

An object can store attributes (similar to the attributes stored in table columns in a relational database) and instructions for actions that can be performed on the object or its attributes. These instructions are called *encapsulated methods* ("encapsulated" because they are included as part of the object). Objects can be placed in a hierarchy so that other objects lower in the hierarchy (subclass objects) can obtain (inherit) attributes from objects higher in the hierarchy (superclass objects). **Figure 5.4** shows three objects in an object-oriented DBMS. The superclass object EMPLOYEE provides the same set of attributes to both subclasses—MANAGER and ADMIN_STAFF. In other words, every MANAGER would have a Name, Address, and Employee_No (as would every ADMIN_STAFF). Objects are drawn using a rectangle with rounded corners, which is divided into three parts: the object name, the attributes, and any encapsulated methods.

FIGURE 5.4 Object-Oriented Database Model

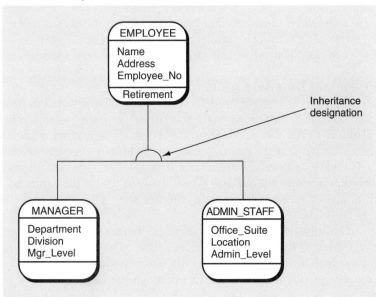

For example, in Figure 5.4, Retirement is an encapsulated method for calculating an employee's current retirement pay and benefits.

Although many researchers have argued that object-oriented DBMSs are superior to relational DBMSs, most organizations still use relational DBMSs. The main advantage of an object-oriented model is to store complex data types. In recent years, **object-relational databases** have been developed. This combined structure includes a relational DBMS framework with the capability to store complex data types. Although developers continue to refine object-oriented DBMSs, most companies seem to be satisfied with relational *or* object-relational DBMSs at this time. The next section describes some of the important elements of relational databases.

Elements of Relational Databases

Although many vendors offer DBMS software products, all DBMSs have the same essential elements. In this section, you will learn about these elements and some important concepts that underlie database design and implementation.

The elements that make up all DBMSs include **tables**, a place to store data; **queries**, tools that allow users to access the data stored in various tables and to transform data into information; **forms**, onscreen presentations that allow users to view data in tables or collected by queries from one or more tables and input new data; and **reports**, which provide printed lists and summaries of data stored in tables or collected by queries from one or more tables. Note how these four DBMS elements equate to the four components of Chapter 1's functional model of information systems (Figure 1.3, pg. 14): Forms are used to input data; queries are used to process data into information; tables are used to store data; and reports are used to display output (i.e., information).[3] You can easily see how the functional model provides the conceptual architecture for DBMSs.

The most important step in creating a useful database is designing the tables properly. Each database table only stores data about one specific thing or entity. It might be a person, such as a customer; an object, such as inventory; or an event, such as a sale. You are probably familiar with spreadsheet software. In spreadsheet software, the main element of the user interface is a worksheet that has rows and columns.

A database table is like a worksheet in that it has rows and columns, but it is unlike a worksheet in that a database table has very strict rules about what can be put in those rows and columns. In a database table, a specific row contains all the information about a particular instance of the type of thing stored in the table. For example, the first row in the CUSTOMERS table (Figure 5.3, pg. 148) stores all of the information about the customer Bikes Et Cetera. No other row can contain information about that customer. Database table columns each store one specific attribute of the type of things stored in the table. For example, the column labeled Cust_Name in the CUSTOMERS table in Figure 5.3 stores all of the customer names. No customer name can ever appear in any other column.

A spreadsheet cell (the intersection of a row and a column) can hold text, numbers, a formula, a graphic, a command button, a chart, or any of a number of different types of data. A cell in a database table can only hold the type of data allowed in its column (all of which must be alphanumeric, i.e., text or numbers) and must contain the value of that specific attribute for the instance of the item recorded in its row. For example, the first row of the SALES_LINES table (Figure 5.3) contains a number, 137.50, in the

---

[3]Forms can also be used to display output.

Sales_Price column. This column contains the sales price of each item on each sales order. The values in this column must be numbers, and the numbers must each have two decimal places. The number in the first row is the sales price for each of the five Item Number 1000-1 products that were sold on sales order number 1010. This fact is stored in this row and column and does not appear anywhere else in the database.

Each row in a database must be unique; that is, no other row can exist in the table that stores identical information. Each row must include a unique identifier that serves as an address for the row. This unique identifier is called the table's **primary key**, and its value is often stored in the first column of the table. In Figure 5.3 (pg. 148), you can see that the primary key of the CUSTOMERS table is the first column of the table, labeled Cust_Code. Some tables use two or more columns in combination to provide a primary key for each row. This type of key is called a **composite primary key**. The SALES_LINES table in Figure 5.3 has a composite primary key formed by combining the first two columns in that table. Note that each of the first two columns individually contains nonunique values in some rows, but when the two columns are combined, the resulting values across both columns are unique for all rows in the table.

The primary key fields in tables must be unique identifiers, which can present problems for database designers who are not very careful in creating the values to be used in these fields. For example, a designer who wants to create a primary key for an employee table might be tempted to use employees' last names as the value. As soon as the business hires more than one person with the same last name, the primary key becomes unworkable. Because the requirement that primary key fields contain unique values is so important, most database designers create an artificial value for each row in each table. They do this by following procedures for classifying and coding as described in **Technology Summary 5.2**. DBMSs have many built-in tools for creating tables and enforcing the strict rules on the columns and rows. After the tables have been properly designed, the DBMS helps to enforce the design by using these tools. First, however, the tables need to be designed in accordance with the relational model. This design task is the subject of the next two sections.

Normalization in Relational Databases

Two approaches are used in designing a relational database: bottom-up and top-down. You will learn about top-down design in the next section. In the bottom-up design approach, the designer identifies the attributes that are of interest and organizes those attributes into tables. Referring to Figure 5.3, you can see that the attributes of sales events might include such things as customer name, customer city, salesperson, credit limit, inventory item name, unit cost, unit price, sales order number, and so on.

Controls

When converting manual (or paper-based) business processes into computerized processes, a common way to execute the bottom-up approach is to first collect all of the paper forms, reports, and other documents currently used in the business processes. Then, the computer system is designed so that all of these documents can be completed electronically. A limitation of this approach is that one tends to simply automate current practices without leveraging the capabilities that computer technology has to improve those practices. Another pitfall with an automation approach is that it is very easy to overlook the fact that controls that were effective in a manual system may not be effective in an automated system. Thus, the need for new computer-oriented controls may be ignored.

The structure of the tables must comply with several rules, called **normal forms**, that include specifications that must be met by relational database tables. Following the normal forms yields tables that prevent errors (also called **anomalies**) that otherwise might occur when adding, changing, or deleting data stored in the database.

Applying the normal forms to collections of data transforms tables that are not in normal form into tables that comply with the rules. The resulting tables are said to be "in normal form." There are six levels of normal form, but business systems usually work well if they comply with the first three. A table that is in first normal form (1NF) is usually preferable to a table that is not in 1NF; a table in second normal form (2NF) is preferred to a table in 1NF; and a table in third normal form (3NF) is

---

Technology Summary 5.2

CLASSIFYING AND CODING

Classifying and coding data are important elements of any database design. Classifying is the process of grouping or categorizing data according to common attributes. Your college or university probably has numerous occasions to classify you (and your peers who have the same characteristics) according to class (freshman, sophomore, etc.), housing (resident versus commuter), financial aid status, major, class enrollment (e.g., all students enrolled in section 001 of AC 322), and so forth.

To classify students into meaningful categories, schools do not create computer records that include values such as "junior," "resident," "work study assigned to department X," or "20-meal plan." To be efficient, they use a shorthand substitute for these long labels. The creation of these substitute values, or codes, is called coding. Many coding schemes exist; the following list outlines the most common and useful examples. The accompanying figure illustrates five common coding types.

- *Sequential coding:* Sequential coding (also known as serial coding) assigns numbers to objects in chronological sequence. This coding scheme provides limited flexibility. Additions can be made only at the end of the sequence; deletions result in unused numbers unless the numbers are recycled; and the codes tell nothing about the objects' attributes.
- *Block coding:* In block coding, groups of numbers are dedicated to particular characteristics of the objects being identified. This provides some improvement over sequential coding. For example, in the universal product codes (UPCs) that supermarkets and other retailers use, the first block of five digits represents the manufacturer, and the second block of five digits designates the product. However, within each block, no significance is given to any of the digits. For example, Kellogg's has a manufacturer's code of 38000, whereas Ralston Purina's code is 17800. Cracklin' Oat Bran (Kellogg's) has a 04510 product identifier, which appears to have no relationship to Ralston's Wheat Chex code, 15011. Within each block of digits, numbers are usually assigned sequentially (see the employee example in the accompanying figure), which means that block coding may

have the same limitations related to additions and deletions as sequential coding.
- *Significant digit coding:* Significant digit coding assigns meanings to specific digits. The accompanying figure shows how this method can be used for inventory items. Parts of the inventory item number describe the product group, the product type (part, subassembly, or end-item), the warehouse in which the part is stored, and a unique number that identifies the specific item.
- *Hierarchical coding:* Like significant digit codes, hierarchical codes also attach specific meaning to particular character positions. Hierarchical coding orders items in descending order, where each successive rank order is a subset of the rank above it. Reading from left to right in a hierarchical code, each digit is a subcategory of the digit to its immediate left. The five-digit postal ZIP code illustrated in the accompanying figure shows the hierarchical elements in this type of coding.
- *Mnemonic coding:* Computers are good at handling numeric data, and typically the previous coding schemes use numbers. Most humans, however, have trouble learning and remembering strings of numbers. In mnemonic coding, some or all of the code is made of letters. The word *mnemonic* comes from the Greek *mnemonikos,* "to remember," and means "assisting or related to memory." The accompanying figure shows a mnemonic code used for college courses.
- *Other coding schemes:* Other coding schemes can be useful in creating primary key fields in databases. A check digit is a code that includes an extra digit that can be used to check the accuracy of the code. The extra digit is computed by applying a mathematical formula to the primary code. For example, a bank account number of 1234-0784 might have an extra digit of 9 (it might appear on the account as 1234-0784-9). The number 9 is calculated from the other numbers using a formula. In this case, the formula is the sum of the last four digits $(0 + 7 + 8 + 4 = 19)$ minus the sum of the first four digits (e.g., $1 + 2 + 3 + 4 = 10$). If a data entry clerk enters the first eight digits incorrectly, the check digit will likely be different. The formulae used in practice are much more complex, but they work much the same as in this example.

(Continued)

Technology Summary 5.2 (Continued)		

Coding Type	Everyday Example(s)	Example Based on Employee ID Codes
A. Sequential (serial)	• Student ID numbers • Ticket taken to identify your turn to be waited on at the supermarket deli counter	001 = first employee hired 002 = second employee hired • • etc. •
B. Block	Universal product code (UPC): (a) 73805 80248 Manufacturer Product code identifier	001-100 fabricating department employees 101-200 assembly department employees • • etc. • Within department blocks, codes are usually assigned to individual employees on a sequential basis.
C. Significant digit	Inventory item: 16 2 17 4389 Product Warehouse group Part, subassembly Unique item or end-item identifier	2 0 4 623 • • • • • • — Unique • • • employee Work Pay rate identifier center code Exempt or nonexempt
D. Hierarchical	Postal ZIP Codes: 0 18 90 • • • Section of Region Locality country within (e.g., town) section within region	01 3 9 623 • • — Unique Company • • employee division • • identifier Plant within Department division within plant
E. Mnemonic	College course numbering: AC 340 = Accounting Information Systems EN 101 = English Composition	D V T 623 • • • — Unique • • • employee • • • identifier DBA Veteran Tenured terminal degree

NOTE:

(a) The universal product code (UPC) is *physically* implemented through bar codes attached to the product or its container. Therefore ⟶

0   3
73805 80248

preferred to a table in 2NF. The goal of normalization is to produce a database model that contains relations that are in 3NF. The normal forms are inclusive, which means that each higher normal form includes all lower normal forms. That is, a table in 3NF is in 1NF and in 2NF. Two concepts are essential to an understanding of normal forms: functional dependence and primary keys.

Functional Dependence and Primary Keys

An attribute (a column in a table) is **functionally dependent** on a second attribute (or a collection of other attributes) if a value for the first attribute determines a single value for the second attribute at any time. When functional dependence exists, the first attribute determines the second attribute.

Consider a table that contains information about purchases in two columns, one for purchase order number (PO_Num) and another for purchase order date (PO_Date).

A value in PO_Date does not determine the value in PO_Num because a particular date could have several purchase orders (and thus, several distinct values for PO_Num) associated with it. In this case, PO_Num is not functionally dependent on PO_Date. However, PO_Date is functionally dependent on PO_Num because the value in PO_Num will always be associated with a single value for PO_Date; the value will always be the date on which that purchase order was issued.

The second concept that is essential to understanding normalization is that of the primary key. Although you know from its definition earlier in this chapter that a primary key contains a value that uniquely identifies a specific row in a table, the use of this concept in normalization requires that you learn a more formal specific definition. A candidate attribute (a column or collection of columns) in a table is that table's primary key if:

- All attributes in the table are functionally dependent on the candidate attribute.
- No collection of other columns in the table, taken together, has the first property.

First Normal Form (1NF)

An **unnormalized table** contains repeating *attributes* (or *fields*) within each *row* (or *record*). We call these repeated attributes "repeating groups." **Figure 5.5** is an unnormalized table because it contains repeating groups. Each sales order occupies one row, but then Item_Number, Item_Name, Qty_Ordered, Cust_Code, and Cust_Name are repeated as many times as necessary.

A table is in **first normal form (1NF)** if it does not contain repeating groups. Transforming this table into 1NF requires the removal of the repeating groups. **Figure 5.6** (pg. 158) shows the table SALES_ORDERS in 1NF. Instead of one row with repeating groups, each sales order is represented in the number of rows required. For example, sales order 1010 now has two rows, rather than the one row it had in Figure 5.5. The primary key for the new table is a combination of SO_Number and Item_Number. Recall that a primary key that is formed by the combination of two or more columns is called a *composite primary key*. The simpler table structure shown in Figure 5.6 solves a big problem. If a table has repeating groups, the designer must decide in advance how many repeats to allow by allocating separate columns for repeating attributes in the table design. The risk is always that the

FIGURE 5.5   Unnormalized Relation

SALES_ORDERS

SO_Number	Item_Number	Item_Name	Qty_Ordered	Cust_Code	Cust_Name
1010	2010-0050	Formed Handlebar	2	WHEEL	Wheelaway Cycle Center
	1000-1	20 in. Bicycle	5	WHEEL	Wheelaway Cycle Center
1011	1002-1	24 in. Bicycle	5	ETC	Bikes Et Cetera
	1001-1	26 in. Bicycle	10	ETC	Bikes Et Cetera
1012	1003-1	20 in. Bicycle	5	WHEEL	Wheelaway Cycle Center
	1001-1	26 in. Bicycle	10	WHEEL	Wheelaway Cycle Center
1013	1001-1	26 in. Bicycle	50	IBS	Inter. Bicycle Sales
1014	1003-1	20 in. Bicycle	25	ETC	Bikes Et Cetera
1015	1003-1	20 in. Bicycle	25	WHEEL	Wheelaway Cycle Center
1016	3961-1041	Tire Tube, 26 in.	5	ETC	Bikes Et Cetera
	3965-1050	Spoke Reflector	50	ETC	Bikes Et Cetera
	1003-1	20 in. Bicycle	5	ETC	Bikes Et Cetera
	1000-1	20 in. Bicycle	4	ETC	Bikes Et Cetera

FIGURE 5.6   Relation in First Normal Form (1NF)

Shaded_Attribute(s) = Primary Key					

SALES_ORDERS					
SO_Number	Item_Number	Item_Name	Qty_Ordered	Cust_Code	Cust_Name
1010	2010-0050	Formed Handlebar	2	WHEEL	Wheelaway Cycle Center
1010	1000-1	20 in. Bicycle	5	WHEEL	Wheelaway Cycle Center
1011	1002-1	24 in. Bicycle	5	ETC	Bikes Et Cetera
1011	1001-1	26 in. Bicycle	10	ETC	Bikes Et Cetera
1012	1003-1	20 in. Bicycle	5	WHEEL	Wheelaway Cycle Center
1012	1001-1	26 in. Bicycle	10	WHEEL	Wheelaway Cycle Center
1013	1001-1	26 in. Bicycle	50	IBS	Inter. Bicycle Sales
1014	1003-1	20 in. Bicycle	25	ETC	Bikes Et Cetera
1015	1003-1	20 in. Bicycle	25	WHEEL	Wheelaway Cycle Center
1016	3961-1041	Tire Tube, 26 in.	5	ETC	Bikes Et Cetera
1016	3965-1050	Spoke Reflector	50	ETC	Bikes Et Cetera
1016	1003-1	20 in. Bicycle	5	ETC	Bikes Et Cetera
1016	1000-1	20 in. Bicycle	4	ETC	Bikes Et Cetera

designer will not allocate enough columns. With tables in 1NF, the designer does not need to speculate because the table expands vertically to accommodate any number of items.

Second Normal Form (2NF)

Although the table shown in Figure 5.6 is in 1NF, it still has problems. The table includes the following *functional dependencies*:

- Item_Number functionally determines Item_Name. Therefore, item names, such as "26 in. Bicycle," are repeated several times. This data redundancy should be eliminated.
- Cust_Code functionally determines Cust_Name.
- The combination of SO_Number and Item_Number together functionally determine Item_Name, Qty_Ordered, Cust_Code, and Cust_Name.
- These dependencies cause several problems, called **update anomalies**:
- *Update:* A change to the name of any item requires not one change but several. Each row in which any item, such as the 26 in. Bicycle, appears must be changed if the description is updated.
- *Inconsistent data:* Nothing is preventing an item from having several different names in different rows of the table.
- *Additions:* If a user tries to add a new inventory item to the database, a problem arises. Because the primary key to the table is the item number *and* the sales order number, a user cannot add a new inventory item to the database unless it has a sales order. This is an impossible requirement for a business, which would want to have information about inventory items stored in its database before accepting orders to sell those inventory items.
- *Deletions:* Deleting an inventory item from the database (by deleting its row) could cause the table to lose the information it has stored about all sales orders that contained that item.

These problems arise because we have an attribute, Item_Name, that is dependent on a portion of the primary key, Item_Number, *not* on the entire key. Database designers call this problem a **partial dependency**.

A table is in **second normal form (2NF)** if it is in 1NF and has no partial dependencies; that is, no non-key attribute is dependent on only a portion of the primary key. An attribute is a **non-key attribute** if it is not part of the primary key. For instance, in Figure 5.6, Item_Name, Quantity_Ordered, Cust_Code, and Cust_Name are non-key attributes.

A designer would perform two steps to get this 1NF table into 2NF. First, create a new table for each subset of the table that is partially dependent on a part of the composite primary key (i.e., SO_Number and Item_Number). In this case, that procedure would yield two new tables, one with SO_Number as its primary key (a SALES_ORDERS table) and another with Item_Number as its primary key (an INVENTORY_ITEMS table). Second, place each of the non-key attributes that are dependent on a part of the composite primary key into the table that now has a primary key that is the field on which the non-key attribute is partially dependent. For example, the Item_Name field is partially dependent on the Item_Number field portion of the composite primary key, so it would be moved into the new INVENTORY_ITEMS table. This transformation yields the three tables shown in **Figure 5.7**.

With this set of three tables, the *update anomaly* problems mentioned earlier are resolved. Users can add inventory items without having a sales order by adding them to the table INVENTORY_ITEMS. Because item names are stored only once, the potential for inconsistencies no longer exists, and updates to names require only one change. Finally, users can delete inventory items from the database and not lose any sales order information.

Third Normal Form (3NF)

Before proceeding to third normal form, we need one more definition. A **transitive dependency** exists in a table when a non-key attribute is functionally dependent on another non-key attribute (of course, the second non-key attribute will be dependent on the primary key). If you examine the table SALES_ORDERS in Figure 5.7, you

FIGURE 5.7   Relations in Second Normal Form (2NF)

Shaded_Attribute(s) = Primary Key

SALES_ORDERS

SO_Number	Cust_Code	Cust_Name
1010	WHEEL	Wheelaway Cycle Center
1011	ETC	Bikes Et Cetera
1012	WHEEL	Wheelaway Cycle Center
1013	IBS	Inter. Bicycle Sales
1014	ETC	Bikes Et Cetera
1015	WHEEL	Wheelaway Cycle Center
1016	ETC	Bikes Et Cetera

SALES_ORDER *line item* INVENTORY

SO_Number	Item_Number	Qty_Ordered
1010	2010-0050	2
1010	1000-1	5
1011	1002-1	5
1011	1001-1	10
1012	1003-1	5
1012	1001-1	10
1013	1001-1	50
1014	1003-1	25
1015	1003-1	25
1016	3961-1041	5
1016	3965-1050	50
1016	1003-1	5
1016	1000-1	4

INVENTORY_ITEMS

Item_Number	Item_Name
1000-1	20 in. Bicycle
1001-1	26 in. Bicycle
1002-1	24 in. Bicycle
1003-1	20 in. Bicycle
1280-054	Kickstand
2010-0050	Formed Handlebar
3050-2197	Pedal
3961-1010	Tire, 26 in.
3961-1041	Tire Tube, 26 in.
3965-1050	Spoke Reflector
3970-1011	Wheel, 26 in.

will notice that the values in Cust_Name are functionally dependent on Cust_Code, which is a non-key attribute. Thus, a transitive dependency exists in this table.

Some of the customer names—Wheelaway Cycle Center, for example—are repeated several times. This transitive dependency causes these *update anomalies*:

- *Update:* A change to the name of any customer could require not one change but several. The user would have to change each row in which any customer appears. For example, changing Wheelaway's name would require changing three rows in the SALES_ORDERS table.
- *Inconsistent data:* Nothing in this design prevents users from entering several different names for a single customer.
- *Additions:* A new customer cannot be added to the database unless the customer already has a sales order. Good internal control dictates that an authorized customer should exist before a sales order can be created for that customer.
- *Deletions:* If a user deletes a sales order from the database, the name of a customer might be erased from the database.

These problems arise because the transitive dependency exists in the table SALES_ORDERS. To summarize, a table is in **third normal form (3NF)** if it is in 2NF and has no transitive dependencies.

Figure 5.8 contains the 3NF tables that are the final result of the normalization process. The tables in Figure 5.8 are free of the anomalies outlined earlier. Users can add customers without sales orders. Because customer names are stored only once, each customer has only one name, and updates to names require only one change. Finally, users can delete customers from the database without regard to the sales order information.

Using Entity-Relationship Models

Although it is possible to create a workable database design using a bottom-up approach as previously described, most database professionals prefer to use a top-down approach, described in this section, as a first step in creating a new database. Although the bottom-up approach is useful for checking the results obtained with a top-down approach, and the bottom-up approach is easier to learn and understand, the top-down approaches usually result in a better database design. The top-down approach is sometimes referred to as an *event-driven approach* because it attempts to describe all aspects of the business events and processes under consideration, rather than focus on how users currently interact with these events and processes (which is the bottom-up or *user-driven approach*). By considering all possible aspects of an event, even those not presently used by the business, it is easier to overcome the tendency to automate current practices rather than making changes that will lead to improvements in the system and potential computer-oriented controls. For example, an event-driven approach to "customer records" would look at the benefit of recording different types of customer information than had been previously recorded. An example might include collecting new data about customers' backgrounds to help marketing increase the effectiveness of the advertising budget.

A **data model** depicts user requirements for data stored in a database. There are a number of approaches to data modeling, any of which can be used to implement top-down database design. The most popular data modeling approach is **entity-relationship modeling**, in which the designer identifies the important things (called **entities**) about which information will be stored[4] and then identifies how the things

---

[4]Notice that this definition of entity—including events as it does—is broader than that introduced in Chapter 1.

FIGURE 5.8   Relations in Third Normal Form (3NF)

```
Shaded_Attribute(s) = Primary Key
```

SALES_ORDERS

SO_Number	Cust_Code
1010	WHEEL
1011	ETC
1012	WHEEL
1013	IBS
1014	ETC
1015	WHEEL
1016	ETC

CUSTOMERS

Cust_Code	Cust_Name
ETC	Bikes Et Cetera
IBS	Inter. Bicycle Sales
RODEBYKE	Rodebyke Bic. & Mopeds
STANS	Stan's Cyclery
WHEEL	Wheelaway Cycle Center

INVENTORY_ITEMS

Item_Number	Item_Name
1000-1	20 in. Bicycle
1001-1	26 in. Bicycle
1002-1	24 in. Bicycle
1003-1	20 in. Bicycle
1280-054	Kickstand
2010-0050	Formed Handlebar
3050-2197	Pedal
3961-1010	Tire, 26 in.
3961-1041	Tire Tube, 26 in.
3965-1050	Spoke Reflector
3970-1011	Wheel, 26 in.

SALES_ORDER *line item* **INVENTORY**

SO_Number	Item_Number	Qty_Ordered
1010	2010-0050	2
1010	1000-1	5
1011	1002-1	5
1011	1001-1	10
1012	1003-1	5
1012	1001-1	10
1013	1001-1	50
1014	1003-1	25
1015	1003-1	25
1016	3961-1041	5
1016	3965-1050	50
1016	1003-1	5
1016	1000-1	4

are related to each other (called **relationships**). Next, the designer draws a diagram of the relational model by applying some simple rules. Because this diagram includes entities and relationships, it is called an **entity-relationship model**. You will often see "entity-relationship" abbreviated as E-R. The **E-R diagram** (also called an **entity-relationship diagram**) reflects the system's key entities and the relationships among those entities. The E-R diagram represents the data model. Database designers use standard symbols when creating E-R diagrams; however, several sets of standard symbols do exist. This book uses one of the more popular sets of symbols, but you should keep in mind that you might see E-R diagrams in other books or in your practice of accounting that differ from the diagrams used here. **Figure 5.9** (pg. 162). shows an E-R diagram in the form that we will be using in this book.

Most E-R diagrams use rectangles, connecting lines, and diamonds. The rectangles represent entities, and the connecting lines represent relationships. The diamonds are used to show the characteristics of relationships. In the E-R diagram shown in Figure 5.9, the entities include ORDERS, INVENTORY, CUSTOMERS, and SALES. The connecting lines show the five relationships in the data model. These relationships are between ORDERS and INVENTORY, ORDERS and CUSTOMERS, ORDERS and SALES, INVENTORY and SALES, and CUSTOMERS and SALES. The diamonds on the connecting lines provide some information about the relationships between the entities. For example, the relationship between ORDERS and CUSTOMERS occurs because orders are received from customers.

FIGURE 5.9 Entity-Relationship (E-R) Diagram

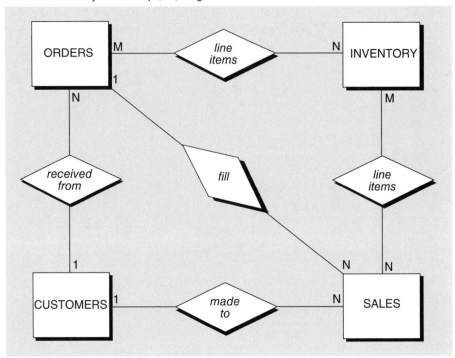

The first step in E-R modeling is to determine users' requirements for the database (typically by using either a top-down approach or a bottom-up approach). This process is often incorporated into a process called *systems analysis* and is usually conducted by a person called a *systems analyst*. To discover user requirements, the systems analyst conducts interviews and observations and reviews existing system documentation. To document the existing system and the user's requirements for the new database, the analyst prepares narratives and diagrams, one of which is the E-R diagram.

Part of the information collected by the analyst is the structure of the data being used in the activities of the organization. This information leads the analyst through three steps. First, the analyst identifies the entities. Second, the analyst identifies the relationships between the entities and learns more about the characteristics of those relationships. Finally, the analyst uses the information about the entities and relationships (which is summarized in the E-R diagram) to create database tables and define connections among those tables.

Identify Entities

The analyst first examines existing system documentation and talks with users to learn which entities are important to the business processes about which the database will store information. Any "thing" that is an important element in the business process can be modeled as an entity. However, if only one instance of a thing occurs in the process, it is not modeled as an entity. Entities become tables, and if there is only one instance of a thing, you do not need a table to store information about it. For example, if a small business has one sales manager, it does not need a table to store information about its sales managers. A larger company with several sales managers would probably want to use a table because it has multiple instances of the thing "sales manager."

Accounting researchers have identified categories of entities that commonly occur in systems that track accounting information. These categories include resources, events, and agents. **Resources** are assets (tangible or intangible) that the company owns. Resources include things such as inventory, equipment, and cash. **Events** are occurrences related to resources that are of interest to the business. Events include orders, sales, and purchases. **Agents** are people or organizations that participate in events. Agents can be part of the company, or they can be external to the company. Agents include customers, employees, and vendors.

This modeling approach, called REA for Resources-Events-Agents, is an excellent example of how a model can simplify a complex problem. When using the REA model to design a database, we know—even before drawing the first E-R diagram or laying out the first relational table—that all of the tables in the database will be R, E, or A tables. Thus, when considering business processes, which can be extremely confusing at first glance, we know that by relying on the REA model, we have only to identify resources (e.g., inventory and cash), events (e.g., purchase orders and customer inquiries), and agents (e.g., employees and suppliers). According to the REA model, nothing else in the processes is (or should be) relevant for our database. The REA model has thereby made what might at first seem an impossibly complex task (designing a database for a business) into something manageable. You will find a more detailed discussion of REA modeling in Chapter 6.

Identify the Relationships That Connect the Entities

Next, the analyst identifies the relationships between and among the entities. The *relationships* are shown in the E-R diagram as connecting lines with diamonds that describe the nature of the relationship. Figure 5.9 shows an E-R diagram of a simple sales and order entry database. In this figure, you can see that relationships can exist between the following:

- Two events, such as SALES fill ORDERS
- An agent and an event, such as ORDERS are received from CUSTOMERS or SALES are made to CUSTOMERS
- A resource and an event, such as ORDERS have line items INVENTORY or INVENTORY has line items SALES

Characteristics of Relationships

The diamond on the left side of the diagram in Figure 5.9 includes one characteristic of the relationship between ORDERS and CUSTOMERS: It shows that an order is received from a customer. The formal notation for this relationship characteristic is "ORDERS are *received from* CUSTOMERS."

A person reading the diagram could be confused by the diagram and want to interpret its meaning as "CUSTOMERS are *received from* ORDERS." However, most users who are familiar with the business processes being modeled can usually interpret the diagram correctly because they know the context of the relationship.

In addition to the description of the relationship that appears in the diamond, each relationship has a characteristic, called a **cardinality**, that shows the degree to which each entity participates in the relationship. A full discussion of cardinalities is complex and not really necessary for an understanding of E-R modeling. However, you should know that the discussion here is limited in scope and that you might see different notations used in practice to describe relationship cardinalities.

The **maximum cardinality** is a measure of the highest level of participation that one entity can have in another entity. In the cardinality notation used in this book, a maximum cardinality can have a value of "one" or "many." A value of one is shown as the digit "1," and a value of many is shown as the letter "N" or the letter "M." For example, the letter "N" beneath the ORDERS rectangle in Figure 5.9 (pg. 162) means that each customer may have many (more than one) orders, and the "1" above the CUSTOMERS rectangle means that each order is from only one customer. In reading this E-R diagram, you would say "the relationship between customers and orders is one-to-many." You could also say "the relationship between orders and customers is many-to-one."

In a relational database, a relationship between the entities is one of three types (common notation is shown in parentheses): one-to-many (1:N), many-to-many (M:N), or one-to-one (1:1). A many-to-one (N:1) relationship is the same as a one-to-many relationship but stated in reverse.

In Figure 5.9, you can see that each inventory item can have many orders, and each order can have many inventory items. This relationship has a many-to-many (M:N) cardinality. The relationship between INVENTORY and SALES is also many-to-many (there can be many inventory items in a sale, and each sale can have many inventory items).

The third cardinality, one-to-one, means that an instance of an entity is related to one specific instance of another entity. This cardinality is easier to visualize using tables. Recall that each entity in the E-R model will become a table in the database. If two entities (tables) have a one-to-one relationship, each row in the first table will be related to one (and only one) row in the second table. An analyst who identifies a one-to-one relationship will, in most cases, simply combine the two tables into one.

The E-R diagram in Figure 5.9 reflects only part of an organization's business processes. An organization would require more data than just the customers, orders, inventory, and sales shown in this diagram. It would require data related to purchases, payments, payroll, and so on. Before going on to the next step, the analyst would confirm the accuracy of the E-R diagram with the people in the organization who will use the database.

Create Tables and Relationships

Having completed a data model that captures users' requirements, the analyst continues the data modeling process by transforming the data model into a *logical* design for the database. This logical design takes the user requirements and converts them into a usable database. This database design includes a definition of each table in the database and how each table is related to other tables in the database.

Figure 5.10 is the logical design for our database. It is the data model in Figure 5.9 implemented in a relational database. The analyst can create this logical model from the E-R diagram by following these five steps:

1. Create a relational table for each entity. In Figure 5.10, CUSTOMERS, INVENTORY, ORDERS, and SALES are the entity tables. Tables must be uniquely named.

2. Determine a *primary key* for each of the entity tables. The primary key must uniquely identify each row within the table, and it must contain a value in each row. A customer code or number (Cust_Code), stock number (Item_Number), and order number (SO_Number) are commonly used to identify customers, items of inventory, and orders. The SALES table uses the date (YYMMDD), followed by a three-digit sequentially assigned serial number (the *unique* portion of the Shipment_Number) to represent each shipment record (row).

3. Determine the *attributes* for each of the entities. An attribute is sometimes called a *field* and is represented in a database table as a column. The accepted custom

among relational database designers is to put the primary key attribute in the first column of the table. User requirements determine the other attributes. The other columns shown in these entity tables contain typical attributes, but you will see different attributes included in databases used by different organizations. Attributes (columns) must have unique names within each table.

4. Implement the relationships among the entities. This is accomplished by assuring that the primary key in one table also exists as an attribute in every table (entity)

FIGURE 5.10   Relational Database

Shaded_Attribute(s) = Primary Key

CUSTOMERS

Cust_Code	Cust_Name	Cust_City	Credit_Limit	Sales_YTD	Sales_Person
ETC	Bikes Et Cetera	Elgin	10000.00	9561.55	Wilke
IBS	Inter. Bicycle Sales	New York	5000.00	4191.18	Breitenstein
RODEBYKE	Rodebyke Bic. & Mopeds	San Jose	2000.00	1142.50	Goodall
STANS	Stan's Cyclery	Hawthorne	10000.00	8330.00	Garcia
WHEEL	Wheelaway Cycle Center	Campbell	10000.00	6854.00	Garcia

INVENTORY

Item_Number	Item_Name	Qty_On_Hand	Unit_Cost	Unit_Price
1000-1	20 in. Bicycle	247	55.00	137.50
1001-1	26 in. Bicycle	103	60.00	150.00
1002-1	24 in. Bicycle	484	60.00	150.00
1003-1	20 in. Bicycle	4	24.37	60.93
1280-054	Kickstand	72	6.50	16.25
2010-0050	Formed Handlebar	90	4.47	11.25
3050-2197	Pedal	23	0.75	1.88
3961-1010	Tire, 26 in.	42	1.45	3.13
3961-1041	Tire Tube, 26 in.	19	1.25	3.13
3965-1050	Spoke Reflector	232	0.29	0.63
3970-1011	Wheel, 26 in.	211	10.50	25.00

ORDERS

SO_Number	Cust_Code	Cust_Order_Number	SO_Date
1010	WHEEL	453	061205
1011	ETC	347	061205
1012	WHEEL	56-6	061205
1013	IBS	3422	061205
1014	ETC	778	061205
1015	WHEEL	5673	061206
1016	ETC	3345	061206

SALES

Shipment_Number	Invoice_Number	SO_Number	Cust_Code
021207028	35	1011	ETC
021207042	36	1012	WHEEL

ORDERS *line items* **INVENTORY**

SO_Number	Item_Number	Qty_Ordered	Sales_Price
1010	1000-1	5	137.50
1010	2010-0050	2	11.25
1011	1001-1	10	127.50
1011	1002-1	5	150.00
1012	1003-1	5	60.93
1012	1001-1	10	127.50
1013	1001-1	50	78.30
1014	1003-1	25	37.42
1015	1003-1	25	37.42
1016	1003-1	5	60.93
1016	3965-1050	50	33.00
1016	3961-1041	5	3.13
1016	1000-1	4	137.50

SALES *line items* **INVENTORY**

Shipment_Number	Item_Number	Qty_Shipped
021207028	1001-1	8
021207028	1002-1	4
021207042	1001-1	5

for which there is a relationship specified in the E-R diagram. Implementing the many-to-many relationships requires the creation of tables, called *relationship tables* or *junction tables*. Relationship (junction) tables are tables with *composite* primary keys that connect (join) tables in a many-to-many relationship. This is necessary because relational DBMSs cannot model a many-to-many relationship directly. Each many-to-many relationship must be modeled as a pair of one-to-many relationships. For example, the SALES and INVENTORY relationship (M:N) is modeled as two (1:N) relationships. One of these relationships is between SALES and the relationship table titled "SALES *line items* INVENTORY," and the other is between INVENTORY and "SALES *line items* INVENTORY." Relationship tables always have composite primary keys that are a combination of the primary keys of the entity tables that participate in the M:N relationship.

5. Determine the *attributes*, if any, for each of the relationship tables. Some relationship tables only need the columns that make up their composite primary keys. Other relationship tables provide a way to store interesting information that depends on the combination of the attributes contained in their composite primary keys. The two relationship tables shown in **Figure 5.11** (pg. 172), each have additional attributes. For example, the "SALES *line items* INVENTORY" table includes the attribute Qty_Shipped. This attribute stores the quantity of each item on a particular sale. This value is determined jointly by the Shipment_Number and the Item_Number, which are the two attributes that make up the table's composite primary key.

Using Databases and Intelligent Systems to Aid Decision Makers

Using databases can help organizations track accounting information better. Another major benefit of having information stored in a database is that it is easier to access the information in new and creative ways. This type of information access can help managers make better decisions. Each day, hundreds of thousands of decisions are made in business organizations. In this section, you will learn about the information tools (generically referred to as **decision aids**) that can help decision makers: *decision support systems, executive information systems, group support systems, expert systems,* and *intelligent agents*. Decision aids may be defined as computerized tools used to assist decision makers and, in some instances, even replace the decision maker.

As you learned earlier in this book (Chapter 1), many decisions—particularly important decisions made by high-level management—are predominantly unstructured. Four levels of expertise can be applied to these decision situations:

- Managers can make the decision without assistance, using their expertise.
- The decision maker can be assisted by problem-solving aids such as manuals and checklists. For example, an information systems auditor will use an *internal control questionnaire* to evaluate controls to ensure a comprehensive review.
- The checklists and manuals might be automated. An automated internal control questionnaire can incorporate thousands of factors, relationships, and rules of thumb. This automated expertise can assist the auditor in arriving at a conclusion regarding the effectiveness of the controls.
- The system itself can replace the decision maker, as when an *expert system* monitors the activity in a production line and adjusts the machinery as required.

Decision Aids: Decision Support Systems, Executive Information Systems, and Group Support Systems

Many automated tools—decision aids—are available to assist or replace the decision maker. Decision aids may be classified as being model-driven, data-driven, communications-driven, document-driven, or knowledge-driven.[5] Most *decision support systems (DSS)* and *executive support systems (ESS*; also called *executive information systems, or EIS)* combine two or more of these types of decision aids. For example, **Technology Summary 5.3** (pg. 168) describes DSS and EIS that assist the manager by combining current and historical facts, numerical data, and statistics—from both inside and outside the organization—and by converting these data into information useful in making the decision.

Here is a comparison that shows the differences between DSS and EIS. A manager could use a spreadsheet—a typical component of DSS—to calculate variances and to compare them to variances from a previous period. This information might help the manager measure current performance against budget. With the DSS, the decision maker prepares a presentation in a format that is suitable for *him or her* for *this* decision at *this* point in time. In contrast, an EIS would have its presentation formats programmed in advance. An executive using an EIS turns on the computer each morning and views a screen that contains icons for EIS applications that are available. An executive who wants to examine sales trends would click the "sales trends" icon. The EIS might ask some questions, such as the period of time and the geographical area to be used in the analysis, but the EIS would follow its programmed instructions to retrieve data and present the output, most likely in the form of graphs depicting sales trends. This sales trend information might alert the executive to some problem, that is, the *intelligence* step in a decision. To determine what to do, the executive might successively request more detailed information, a process known as "drill down."

DSS and EIS are similar in that neither tells the decision maker what to do; both primarily provide views for interpreting the information. However, users generally use DSS to arrive at estimated or "recommended" solutions to problems being considered. Statistical methods such as regression analysis are common ways of arriving at these solutions. EIS are rarely used in this manner. They are mainly about collecting and presenting information desired by an executive, and less about doing additional processing and calculations. EIS are more likely to have the ability to drill down (e.g., go from the summarized information to the primary documents from which it came) than are DSS. But no matter what type of decision aid is being used, the knowledge and experience required to analyze the information, to make the judgments, and to take the actions required reside with the decision maker. These two types of decision aids are discussed in more detail in Technology Summary 5.3.

DSS and EIS help managers, who typically work alone, make decisions. **Group support systems (GSS)**, also called **group decision support systems (GDSS)**, are computer-based systems that support collaborative intellectual work such as idea generation, elaboration, analysis, synthesis, information sharing, and decision making. GSS use technology to solve the time and place dimension problems associated with group work. That is, a GSS creates a "virtual meeting" for a group. While "attending" this meeting, members of the group work toward completing their tasks and achieving the group's objectives. **Technology Application 5.1** (pg. 169) discusses how GSS can help auditors detect fraud by facilitating *brainstorming*.

---

[5]Power, D., "What Is the Expanded DSS Framework?" *DSS News,* 5(1), January 4, 2004.

DECISION SUPPORT SYSTEMS AND EXECUTIVE INFORMATION SYSTEMS

Decision support systems (DSS) are information systems that assist managers with unstructured decisions by retrieving and analyzing data for purposes of identifying and generating useful information. DSS possess interactive capabilities, aid in answering ad hoc queries, and provide data and modeling facilities (generally through the use of spreadsheet models or statistical analysis programs) to support nonrecurring, relatively unstructured decision making. The main components of DSS appear in the accompanying figure. Notice that the data made available to the decision maker include both internal data from the enterprise database and data obtained from outside the organization, such as Dow Jones financial information.

DSS can provide the required relevant data and can model, simulate, and perform "what-if" analysis. DSS are superior to normal computer programs because DSS can work on loosely defined tasks, in areas of high uncertainty, and in situations where user requirements and data are in a constant state of change. Thus, to some extent, DSS can imitate human decision making when confronting situations that are complex and ambiguous. This ability in computers is often referred to as artificial intelligence.

Over the years, the term *DSS* has become synonymous with financial modeling and ad hoc querying. To support managers at the top echelon of the organization, executive information systems (EIS) have been developed (these also are called executive support systems, or ESS). These systems combine information from the organization and the environment, organize and analyze the information, and present the information to the manager in a form that assists in decision making.

Most EIS have highly interactive graphical user interfaces (GUIs). The typical EIS presents output using text, graphics, and color; has multiple presentation formats; and can be tailored and customized for each executive. The complexity of these systems has greatly increased in recent years as they have expanded to include the support of crisis management and as sources of information for dealing with media questioning during such crises. This expansion in complexity has been dovetailed with the development of data warehouses and can be used to search for data needed to answer questions during unexpected crises.

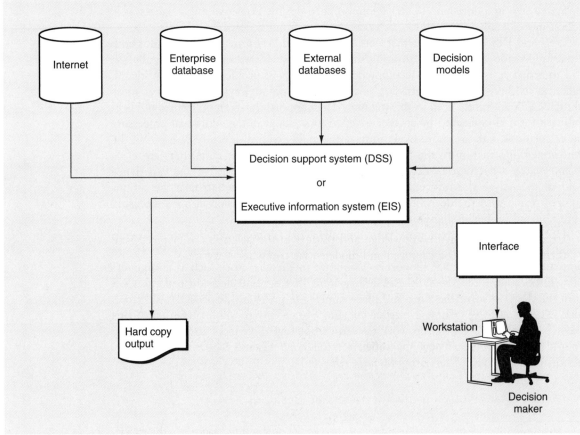

Technology Application 5.1

GSS, AUDIT TEAMS, AND BRAINSTORMING

Following such well-publicized corporate scandals as Enron and WorldCom, the American Institute of Certified Public Accountants (AICPA) issued Statement on Auditing Standards (SAS) No. 99, *Consideration of Fraud in a Financial Statement Audit*, in 2002. This new standard revised existing fraud guidelines, specifically requiring auditors to conduct fraud "brainstorming" meetings during audit engagements. Brainstorming can be defined as a method for freely and creatively generating as many ideas as possible without undue regard for their practicality or realism. According to SAS 99, the objectives of fraud brainstorming are to identify fraud risk factors in the company being audited and to stress to audit team members the importance of a "questioning mind" and "professional skepticism."

Generally, audit teams conduct these brainstorming sessions in face-to-face meetings. In such meetings, the auditors come together in a common location to share ideas, discuss alternatives, and reach a consensus regarding how to conduct the audit so as to have the best possible chance of detecting fraud. An alternative to meeting face-to-face is for the audit team members to interact using computer-mediated communication. Group support systems (GSS)

are one such tool for computer-mediated communication. Not only can GSS overcome space and time limitations (i.e., the audit team members do not have to physically meet in the same room), they can provide a well-structured communication environment in which team members can jointly discuss and generate ideas and arrive at decisions they agree upon.

Recent accounting research has compared the relative effectiveness of face-to-face to computer-mediated brainstorming meetings, finding that in most circumstances audit team brainstorming meetings using computer-mediated communication outperform teams conducting face-to-face meetings. In face-to-face meetings, team members must wait for their turn to speak. In addition, social etiquette generally requires members to pay attention to the person speaking. These aspects of face-to-face meetings can interfere with the brainstorming process, resulting, for example, in fewer ideas being generated. However, in a brainstorming team using computer-mediated communication, team members can make their inputs simultaneously, allowing for a freer flow of ideas, with more ideas being produced.

Source: Lynch, A., Murthy, U., and Engle, T., "Fraud Brainstorming Using Computer-Mediated Communication: The Effects of Brainstorming Technique and Facilitation," *The Accounting Review*, 84(4): 1209–1232, 2009.

Expert Systems

Many decision-making situations can benefit from an even higher level of support than that provided by DSS, EIS, or GSS. Managers can use **expert systems (ES)** in these situations. Expert systems may be appropriate in situations that have the following characteristics:

- Decisions are extremely complex.
- Consistency of decision making is desirable.
- The decision maker wants to minimize time spent making the decision while *maximizing* the quality of the decision.
- Experts familiar with the knowledge and context of the decision are involved, and their knowledge can be captured and modeled via computer software.

Companies sometimes use ES as a part of a downsizing strategy. In downsizing, much of an organization's collective knowledge and experience can be lost because employees with the most seniority and the highest pay are often the first to go. These employees often are exactly the people who have accumulated vast amounts of knowledge about the business and expertise in making decisions using that knowledge. The increasing complexity of the business organization and its operations, along with the trend toward decentralization, also prompt companies to implement expert systems. ES can be used to:

- Capture and retain the expertise of the retiring employees.
- Distribute the expertise to the remaining employees.
- Distribute the expertise to the employees who cannot obtain timely access to the expert.

- Train new employees.
- Guide human experts by suggesting trends, asking questions, highlighting exceptions, and generally serving as an "electronic colleague."

The benefits derived—increased productivity, improved decision making, competitive advantage, and so on—from an ES must exceed the costs of developing and maintaining the system. A company also must be able to identify and extract the expertise required and to enter that expertise into the ES's knowledge base. Therefore, companies must carefully choose the areas in which they use ES.

Neural networks (NN) are computer hardware and software systems that mimic the human brain's ability to recognize patterns or predict outcomes using less-than-complete information. For example, NN are used to recognize faces, voices, and handwritten characters. NN also are used to sort good apples from bad, to detect fraudulent users of credit cards, and to manage investment funds.

Given a volume of data, ES make decisions by using the knowledge acquired from outside experts. NN, on the other hand, derive their knowledge from the data. For example, an ES designed to predict bankruptcy would have a knowledge base that included the rules that experts have used to predict bankruptcy. A rule might be: "If the current ratio is less than X, and interest has not been paid on long-term debt, then bankruptcy is likely." NN, on the other hand, would be given data on firms that have gone bankrupt and firms that have not (using an expert to decide which data are relevant). NN sift through the data and decide how to determine whether a firm will go bankrupt. NN develop their own knowledge base and continue to learn as they process additional data. This knowledge base includes an understanding of the patterns underlying the data and the logic necessary to reconstruct the patterns to solve future problems. **Technology Application 5.2** offers some examples of NN used in business today. The capability of NN to discover patterns in large quantities of data makes them useful in decision making and performing well in areas that are difficult for ES, DSS, or EIS.

Technology Application 5.2

USES OF NEURAL NETWORKS

These examples of NN will help you understand how they operate and how useful they can be:

- At VISA, NN are used to prevent/detect fraud by comparing customers' typical spending patterns with individual transactions.
- NN help manage several mutual funds, including the Standard & Poor's Neural Fair Value 25, a fund that since inception has consistently beat the Standard & Poor's 500 Stock Index.
- NN help with real estate location and appraisal by reviewing data from hundreds of houses and analyzing the data in many different ways. NN can be used by auditors to forecast a client's earnings and expenses. By comparing the forecast to actual results, the auditor can make a judgment as to the reasonableness of the actual results. The forecasted earnings also can indicate to the auditor if the client is likely to continue as a going concern.
- NN help cost accountants/consultants determine optimal resource allocation and production schedules. The manipulation of the hundreds of variables and constraints has traditionally been undertaken using operations research models.

NN have become so common that they are emerging as the tool of choice for fraud detection and order checking. Future applications will likely move toward more intelligent versions that will require even less user intervention.

Source: http://corporate.visa.com, August 2006; "A 'Neural' Approach to the Market," *BusinessWeek Online*, May 8, 2006, www.businessweek.com; for more information on these and other related topics, see the American Association of Artificial Intelligence at www.aaai.org.

In the discussion of decision aids up to this point, we have treated them as off-the-shelf software that users acquire and use "as is." However, with minimal IT expertise (e.g., a basic working knowledge of spreadsheets), any user can design a decision aid. **Technology Application 5.3** (pg. 172) gives an example of building a fairly simple decision aid using Excel.

Intelligent Agents

One of the greatest growth areas in intelligent systems currently underway is the development and application of *intelligent agents*. An **intelligent agent** is a software program that may be integrated into DSS or other software tools (such as word processing, spreadsheet, or database packages).

Like any agent, an intelligent agent works on your behalf. Once set in motion, intelligent agents (sometimes called "bots," short for "robots") continue to perform their tasks without further direction from the user. Search engines frequently incorporate intelligent agents. For example, Google's "Shopping" feature will search for products and prices from Internet vendors, keeping you from the time-consuming task of finding specific vendors and hunting down the products at their sites. Intelligent agents are also used in EIS for collecting specific information from the Internet or large data warehouses. After the sought-after information has been found, the EIS user is notified by the computer and can then view the results using a preformatted presentation.

An intelligent agent might provide automated assistance or advice on the use of the software into which it is embedded, identify factors that should be considered when using a system for decision making, or present a list of common responses made by other users. Most *intelligent agents* are designed to learn from the actions of the system's user and to respond based on the user's inputs or usage patterns.

Here is a summary of what you have read in this section regarding systems that provide intelligence-based assistance to the management decision maker:

- To overcome the roadblocks to quality decision making, managers use decision support systems (DSS), executive information systems (EIS), group support systems (GSS), expert systems (ES), neural networks (NN), and intelligent agents.
- DSS structure the available data to provide information about alternative courses of action without offering a solution. DSS work well with unstructured or semi-structured problems that have a quantifiable dimension.
- EIS use menus, graphics, and color to provide a friendly interface to DSS for executives who want to minimize their interaction with the system.
- GSS facilitate group interaction and group consensus building.
- ES apply expertise extracted from a human expert to provide specific recommendations on problems or decisions.
- Both DSS and ES can assist a user in problem solving but in different ways. A DSS is a *passive tool*; it depends on the human user's knowledge and ability to provide the right data to the system's decision model. An ES is an *active* teacher or partner that can guide the user in deciding what data to enter and in providing hints about further actions that are indicated by the analysis to date.
- NN supplement ES in areas where expertise has not yet been captured. By examining the data, NN can identify and replicate the patterns that exist.
- ES can automate portions of the decision-making activity. They can function independently and actually make the decision, or they can assist the decision maker and recommend a course of action. The goal of ES is not to replace people. These systems make it possible for valuable expertise to be available in multiple locations.
- Intelligent agents can be embedded in software to perform tasks for you or help you more effectively complete certain tasks.

BUILD-YOUR-OWN-DECISION-AID

Using computers to help us make decisions is popularly portrayed as a complex and mysterious process. Movies in the '60s and '70s, for example, would show scientists in white lab coats feeding questions into large mainframe computers covering entire walls. The scientist would then step back, and the computer would take over—lights would flash on and off, tape reels would spin back and forth, and out would pop the answer. **Figure 5.11** gives some idea of the working environment of mainframe computing in its early days.

Today, working with computerized *decision aids* (also called *decision support systems*) is almost the opposite of this outdated image. Decision aid users are typically very involved with the process from beginning to end. They often set up the underlying decision model, enter and work with the data to get it in proper shape for processing by the decision model, and often have to try variations of "the question" to find a version that can be "answered" by the computer. Generally, the computer does not provide an answer per se but only information to help the user decide on the best solution. Despite these constant interactions with the decision aid, the process is often quite simple.

The following is a real-world example of using computers as decision aids to help with decision making. Two professors were given 30 research papers, along with reviews of the papers from other professors, and asked to decide on 6 of the 30 to be presented at a conference. To come up with this list of six papers, they decided to rank the research papers based on the evaluations from reviewers of the papers, usually two reviewers per paper. The reviewers had evaluated each paper on several criteria (e.g., readability, relevance to accounting practice, interest to accounting academics, and accuracy of analysis). Reviewers also gave an overall "thumbs up/thumbs down" for each paper in terms of its presentation-worthiness at the conference. Unfortunately, rarely did reviewers of a paper agree on all, if any, of the criteria. Often, reviews were even in opposite directions. The two professors therefore had to attempt to form an overall impression of the reviews for each paper and then for each paper relative to the other 29 papers—and finally reach an agreement between themselves. After three days of concentrated work, they came up with a ranking and the list of the six top papers.

Afterwards, one of the professors, with an interest in decision aids, decided to set up a "simple" decision model for this problem using Excel, as shown in **Figure 5.12**. He assigned weights to the various criteria used by the reviewers. The professor decided against using equal weights for all of the criteria because he believed that the criteria should not be considered equally important in arriving at

FIGURE 5.11 The IBM 709—Large, General-Purpose Digital Computer Designed to Solve Complex Commercial and Scientific Problems (1957)

Source: Courtesy of IBM Archives (www-03.ibm.com/ibm/history/exhibits/mainframe/mainframe_2423PH709.html)

(Continued)

Technology Application 5.3 (Continued)

FIGURE 5.12 Excel Decision Model Example

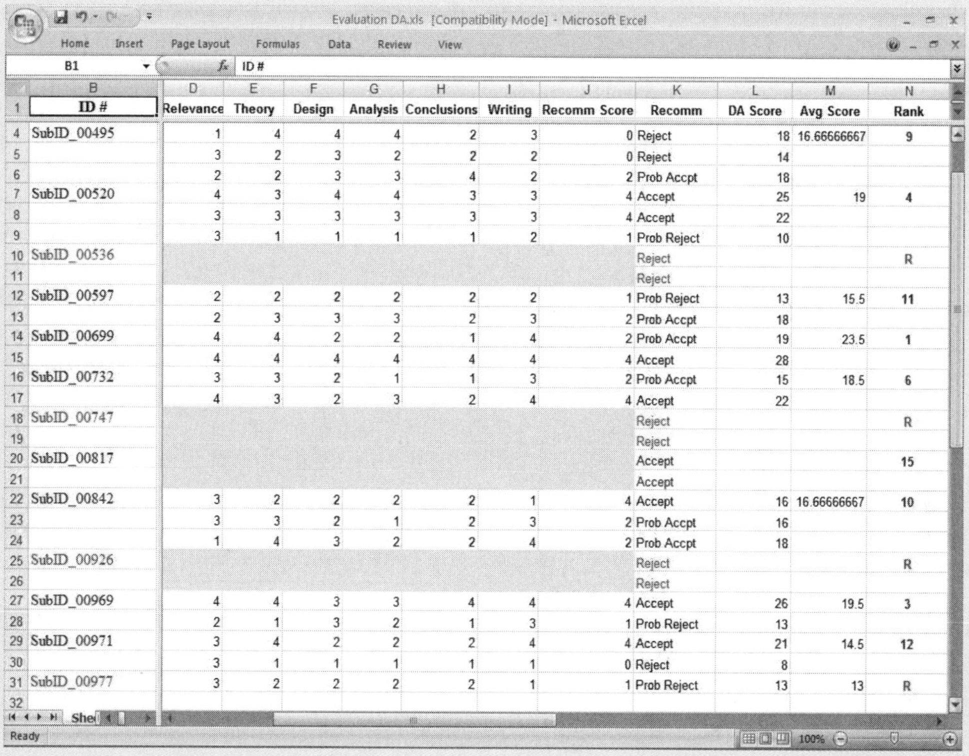

	ID #	Relevance	Theory	Design	Analysis	Conclusions	Writing	Recomm Score	Recomm	DA Score	Avg Score	Rank
4	SubID_00495	1	4	4	4	2	3	0	Reject	18	16.66666667	9
5		3	2	3	2	2	2	0	Reject	14		
6		2	2	3	3	4	2	2	Prob Accpt	18		
7	SubID_00520	4	3	4	4	3	3	4	Accept	25	19	4
8		3	3	3	3	3	3	4	Accept	22		
9		3	1	1	1	1	2	1	Prob Reject	10		
10	SubID_00536								Reject			R
11									Reject			
12	SubID_00597	2	2	2	2	2	2	1	Prob Reject	13	15.5	11
13		2	3	3	3	2	3	2	Prob Accpt	18		
14	SubID_00699	4	4	2	2	1	4	2	Prob Accpt	19	23.5	1
15		4	4	4	4	4	4	4	Accept	28		
16	SubID_00732	3	3	2	1	1	3	2	Prob Accpt	15	18.5	6
17		4	3	2	3	2	4	4	Accept	22		
18	SubID_00747								Reject			R
19									Reject			
20	SubID_00817								Accept			15
21									Accept			
22	SubID_00842	3	2	2	2	2	1	4	Accept	16	16.66666667	10
23		3	3	2	1	2	3	2	Prob Accpt	16		
24		1	4	3	2	2	4	2	Prob Accpt	18		
25	SubID_00926								Reject			R
26									Reject			
27	SubID_00969	4	4	3	3	4	4	4	Accept	26	19.5	3
28		2	1	3	2	1	3	1	Prob Reject	13		
29	SubID_00971	3	4	2	2	2	4	4	Accept	21	14.5	12
30		3	1	1	1	1	1	0	Reject	8		
31	SubID_00977	3	2	2	2	2	1	1	Prob Reject	13	13	R
32												

the final list of six papers. For example, the overall evaluation of presentation-worthiness by each reviewer was assigned a higher weight than the specific criteria. There were also weight differences among these remaining specific criteria; for example, relevance to the accounting practice was more important (and therefore had a higher weight in the Excel spreadsheet) than readability. It took several hours to set up this decision model in Excel and type in the data from the reviewers. However, running the model took only a few seconds—and the list of the top six papers produced by the Excel decision model was exactly the same as that arrived at by the two professors after three days of work!

One thing to note about this Excel-based decision aid is how it differs from basic "what-if" analysis using spreadsheets. This decision aid—as is true of many types of decision aids, but not all—was meant to be a simplified model of the decision-making processes of the two professors. That is, the model was attempting to imitate human thought processes. It was not meant to do anything the professors couldn't do. The advantage of such decision aids, as is evident from the preceding anecdote, is that computerized models can usually solve problems in less time. The Excel decision aid arrived at the list of six top papers in a matter of hours (including model setup and data entry times), in contrast to the several days required by the two professors. Also, after the model with its various decision weights is in place in the software, the decision making will be completely consistent in regard to the model, whereas people tend to be inconsistent, even when using their own decision-making models. Finally, it should be noted that there are other types of decision aids and decision support systems that assist decision making by supplementing human thought processes instead of imitating them. For example, they may perform complex statistical calculations far beyond what we are able to do ordinarily.

Data Warehouses

Two contemporary concepts that are driving many new DBMS implementations in organizations are *data warehousing* and *data mining*.

Data warehousing is the use of information systems facilities to focus on the collection, organization, integration, and long-term storage of entity-wide data. Its purpose is to provide users with easy access to large quantities of varied data from across the organization for the sole purpose of improving decision-making capabilities. A data warehouse is typically created by copying data periodically—sometimes as often as several times in one day—from the transaction (or operational) databases into a separate database where it is stored. In this separate database, external data (nonorganizational data, such as industry data or government statistics) may be included to improve the usefulness to decision makers.

Managers can gain important insights by analyzing this data warehouse with multidimensional analytical tools and exploratory techniques, for example, the intelligent agents or bots mentioned earlier. Such techniques, called data mining, refer to the exploration, aggregation, and analysis of large quantities of varied data from across the organization. *Data mining* is used to better understand an organization's business processes, trends within these processes, and potential opportunities to improve the effectiveness and efficiency of the organization. However, successful data mining requires training and expertise. Because of the large amounts of data used in data mining, it is far too easy, if one isn't careful with the methods applied, to identify relationships between factors that appear to be relevant but in fact are not (called "spurious correlations"), as the following Dilbert cartoon illustrates.

Copyright ⓒ 2000 United Feature Syndicate, Inc.
Redistribution in whole or in part prohibited

Control and Audit Implications

In one sense, a data warehouse is simply a type of database; that is, it is a platform for storing, accessing, and retrieving data. Thus, data warehousing and data mining are dependent on the massive data integration and data independence made possible through database technology. However, in general usage, *databases* and *data warehouses* are distinguished, especially in business information systems. Large ERP systems, for example, often have both an operational database (in the terabyte range) for transaction processing and a data warehouse (in the petabyte range) to support management's tactical and strategic decision making. Besides these functional and size distinctions between databases and data warehouses, there are also important structural differences. Databases, which are generally relational, are highly normalized and emphasize data integrity because their primary mission is to support business transactions. One way this is done is through the use of cardinalities and primary keys. (See Technology Application 6.1, pg. 199, in Chapter 6 for an example.)

On the other hand, data warehouses, which are primarily meant for decision support, require speed of data retrieval to perform data analysis. Because the data in data warehouses often come from many sources that may have different underlying ways of organizing data, data integrity is usually relaxed in data warehouses. In fact, incoming data are often deliberately de-normalized to allow for more complete access and quicker retrieval. For analysis purposes, it is generally more important that all possible data are included during processing and analysis than that all included data are of the highest integrity. In operational settings, these priorities are usually reversed—data integrity is more important than speed of data retrieval. This trade-off should sound familiar to you. It is basically a variation of the "relevance versus reliability" issue that accounting has recognized and struggled with for decades (see Chapter 1, Figure 1.6, pg. 20). Thus, for internal control and audit purposes, you can immediately see that an operational database must be approached (e.g., audited) much differently than a data warehouse. For instances, if assuring the information in a report based on data from a data warehouse (using data mining), the auditor must be especially attentive to the possibility that "bad data" were included during processing due to weak data integrity. Garbage in, garbage out (GIGO) is a long-standing warning in information systems.

Knowledge Management Systems

Knowledge management is the process of capturing, storing, retrieving, and distributing the knowledge of the individuals in an organization for use by others in the organization to improve the quality and efficiency of decision making across the firm. The primary enabler of *knowledge management* efforts is information technology, in particular, database technology. Knowledge management systems may be thought of as the logical next step after the DBMS in business information systems. Databases store data that are turned into information by various users. **Knowledge** refers to information that has been formatted and distributed in accordance with an organization's standards. A company's knowledge may be found in untraditional forms, such as an audio-visual file containing a CEO's speech at a shareholders' meeting. These documents and files are a company's collective, and often proprietary, knowledge base (analogous to a database). When a company uses information technology to help capture, store, organize, present, distribute, and control access to this knowledge base, then the resulting system is called a knowledge management system.

The difference between "knowledge" and "information" is not always clear. The following classic definition of "knowledge" may help:

> Knowledge is a fluid mix of framed experience, values, contextual information, and expert insight that provides a framework for evaluating and incorporating new experiences and information. It originates and is applied in the minds of knowers. In organizations, it often becomes embedded not only in documents or repositories but also in organizational routines, processes, practices, and norms.[6]

Probably more important than understanding formal definitions that differentiate "information" from "knowledge" is an awareness that technologies developed and used for handling something (i.e., "knowledge") users understand are different from the traditional output of databases (i.e., "information"). Such knowledge management systems are primarily concerned with collecting and organizing the output of traditional

---

[6]Davenport T., and Prusak L., *Working Knowledge* (Boston, MA: Harvard Business School Press, 1998): 5.

databases, for example, reports, memos, and financial statements. Knowledge management systems provide an extension to the traditional uses of databases.

Effective knowledge management means that an organization must be able to connect the knowledge of one individual with other individuals in the firm who need the same knowledge. This "capture and distribute" need is generally well served by the existing databases, although sometimes the capabilities of the database are expanded with object-oriented features (e.g., storing video and audio files). Employees can access a database to contribute knowledge or extract knowledge from anywhere in the world. Databases also provide a mechanism for orderly storage and retrieval of the captured knowledge.

Summary

In this chapter, you learned how organizations use databases to store information about business events such as sales, purchases, cash receipts, and cash disbursements. You learned how data from these events are recorded and processed in database systems.

You learned about the types of databases and the basic elements of database design that organizations use when they create databases for their accounting information, including normalization and entity-relationship data modeling. You learned that larger organizations store information in data warehouses and that managers can gain important insights by analyzing the information in data warehouses. You learned that many companies combine their data resources with decision-support systems, executive information systems, group decision systems, and other advanced technology-based systems to improve decision making and operations.

Key Terms

applications approach to business event processing, 144

data redundancy, 144

centralized database approach to business event processing, 145

database management system (DBMS), 146

data independence, 146

three-tier architecture, 146

schema, 147

subschema, 147

query language, 147

data manipulation language (DML), 147

hierarchical database model, 151

child records, 151

parent records, 151

network database model, 151

relational database model, 151

object-oriented database model, 152

object-relational databases, 153

tables, 153

queries, 153

forms, 153

reports, 153

primary key, 154

composite primary key, 154

normal forms, 154

anomalies, 154

classifying, 155

coding, 155

sequential coding, 155

serial coding, 155

block coding, 155

significant digit coding, 155

hierarchical coding, 155

mnemonic coding, 155

check digit, 155

functionally dependent, 156

unnormalized table, 157

first normal form (1NF), 157

update anomalies, 158

partial dependency, 158

Review Questions

RQ 5-1 What is a database?

RQ 5-2 What is data redundancy? Explain why it is important in business information systems.

RQ 5-3 How can storing the same facts in different computer files potentially affect the integrity of data?

RQ 5-4 What are the most important limitations of the applications approach to business information system design?

RQ 5-5 How are the applications approach and the centralized database approach to business event processing similar? How are they different?

RQ 5-6 What are the limitations of the centralized database approach to business information systems?

RQ 5-7 What are the main ways users can access information stored in a DBMS?

RQ 5-8 What are the main advantages and disadvantages of using a centralized database approach when designing and implementing business information systems?

RQ 5-9 What are the four main elements in a relational database?

RQ 5-10 What is a primary key? What is a composite primary key?

RQ 5-11 What are the five primary schemes for coding data?

RQ 5-12 What is the purpose of database normalization in a relational database?

RQ 5-13 Explain the concept of functional dependence.

RQ 5-14 What is a partial dependency?

RQ 5-15 What is an entity in an entity-relationship model (E-R model)? How does it differ from the concept of "entity" used in creating data flow diagrams?

RQ 5-16 What is the cardinality of a relationship in a relational database?

RQ 5-17 Explain when a database designer might use a relationship table in constructing a relational database.

RQ 5-18 What factors distinguish DSS from EIS?

RQ 5-19 Describe the basic differences between ES and NN.

RQ 5-20 What role do intelligent agents play in the operation of a decision-support system?

RQ 5-21 Why have knowledge management systems become so important to businesses in recent years?

RQ 5-22 What is a knowledge base? How is it different from a database?

RQ 5-23 Why are data warehouses important to decision makers?

Discussion Questions

DQ 5-1 What are the basic components of a database management system (DBMS)? Discuss the relationship between the components of DBMS and the functional model of information systems discussed in Chapter 1.

DQ 5-2 How has the technological availability and implementation of DBMSs benefited decision makers in organizations?

DQ 5-3 What is data independence? Why is it important in a comparison of the application and centralized database approaches to storing data?

DQ 5-4 How is a DBMS different from a database?

DQ 5-5 What are the differences between a logical view and a physical view of a database? Which would be more important for accountants who are involved in the design of a database that will store business event information?

DQ 5-6 What is three-tier architecture? What are some of its advantages over two-tier architecture?

DQ 5-7 What problems are solved by transforming a set of relational tables from second normal form (2NF) to third normal form (3NF)?

DQ 5-8 What are the different logical database models (or structures)?

DQ 5-9 "The centralized database approach to data management is a good alternative to using enterprise systems such as ERP and CRM." Do you agree? Discuss fully.

DQ 5-10 Why have object-oriented databases not replaced relational databases in business information system applications?

DQ 5-11 Demonstrate your understanding of some of the coding schemes discussed in Technology Summary 5.2 (pp. 155–156) by indicating which type of code is represented by each of the following. You should be prepared to explain and defend your answers.

    a. The student ID codes used at your college.

    b. MICR codes used by the banking industry.

    c. The customer codes used in Figure 5.3 (pg. 148).

DQ 5-12 What are the comparative advantages of the various data *coding* types discussed in Technology Summary 5.2 (pp. 155–156) when applied to each of the following? Discuss fully.

a. Employee ID numbers

b. Customer ID numbers

c. Vendor ID numbers

d. The general ledger chart of accounts

Short Problems

SP 5-1   Create an E-R diagram with maximum cardinalities for the shipping of inventory to customers. Show this diagram as an REA model identifying resources, events, and agents.

SP 5-2   *Note*: This short problem is a continuation of SP 5-1. Using the E-R diagram in from SP 5-1, write a description for each of the relationships in the diagram. In your description, include the cardinalities. For example, you might describe the relationship between CUSTOMERS and SHIPMENTS as: "Shipments are made to customers. A customer may receive many (N) shipments, but each shipment is for only one (1) customer."

SP 5-3   *Note*: This short problem is a continuation of SP 5-1. Implement the E-R diagram from SP 5-1 as tables in a database software package, such as Access. Once the tables are created, link the tables together in relationships. Finally, populate the tables with several instances of each entity. To do this, it will be necessary to identify typical attributes for each entity. Obtain a printout of the tables and their relationships.   `ACCESS`

SP 5-4   *Note*: This short problem is a continuation of SP 5-3. Using database software (e.g., Access) and the database tables implemented in SP 5-3, run a query identifying customers by name and the inventory item(s) they received by description. Obtain a printout of the query design and the results.   `ACCESS`

Problems

Notes regarding Problems 5-1 through 5-5

These problems should be completed with a database software package, such as Access. For Problems 5-1 through 5-3, you may use data that you (or your instructor) have downloaded from an accounting database. Problem 5-4 provides an alternative to Problems 5-1 through 5-3 by using the database structure and sample data from Figure 5.10 (pg. 165). This problem also may be completed using the software of your choosing.

P 5-1   Before starting this problem, you should consult the customer master data record layout in Figure 5.2 (pg. 144).   `ACCESS`

Using the database software indicated by your instructor:

a. Create the "structure" for the records in the customer data. Use Figure 5.2 as a general guide to the data elements to be included in the customer records. However, observe the following specific requirements:

(1) For the customer address, use five separate fields, one each for street address, additional address information (e.g., apartment number), city, state, and ZIP code.

(2) Provide for three additional data elements that are not shown in Figure 5.2 (pg. 144) (because they normally would be accessed from other files)—open sales orders, back orders, and accounts receivable balance.

b. If the software package supports a function to design input screens, create the screen format to be used for entering customer data.

c. Create example customer records and enter them into the database. Use a variety of names, street addresses, states, ZIP codes, open sales order amounts, accounts receivable balances, and credit limits. (The number of records will be indicated by your instructor.)

d. Obtain a printout of the database records.

P 5-2 *Note*: This problem is a continuation of Problem 5-1.

a. "Search" the database for all customers with a specific state (choose a state that is common to at least two but not to all of your customers). Obtain a printout of your search algorithm and a list of customers whose records met the search parameter.

b. "Sort" the database in *descending* order of credit limit amounts. Obtain a printout of your sort algorithm and a printout of the sorted list of customers.

c. Create a "Customer Status Report" (the report title). Observe the following specific requirements:

(1) Provide column headings, in left-to-right order, for customer name, credit limit, accounts receivable balance, open orders, and back orders.

(2) For each state, print subtotals of the accounts receivable balance, open orders, and back orders columns.

P 5-3 *Note*: This problem is a continuation of Problem 5-1.

a. Write a "program" to enter customer order amounts into the database and to have the system either warn the user if the new order places the customer over his or her credit limit or advise the user if the credit limit is not exceeded.

b. Test the program developed in (a) by entering the amounts of customer order business event data (use a variety of order amounts and different customers so that you test all possible combinations of variables involved in the credit-checking algorithm). (The number of order business event data will be indicated by your instructor.) Obtain hard copy evidence of the results of your testing.

P 5-4 Using the database structure and sample data in Figure 5.10 (pg. 165) as a starting point (rather than Figure 5.2), complete the requirements of Problems 5-1 through 5-3 (or whatever portions of those problems your instructor may indicate).

P 5-5 Use the database structure and sample data in Figure 5.10 to:

a. Combine the tables to obtain a complete record of orders and shipments. Obtain a printout of the algorithm(s) used to combine the tables and a printout of the list of these records.

b. Write a query that selects the inventory items for which there is no order. Obtain printouts of the algorithm(s) you used and a list of the selected records.

c. Select those orders that have not yet been shipped (i.e., open orders). Obtain printouts of the algorithm(s) you used and a list of the selected records.

d. Calculate the total value (price) of the inventory items that are on hand. Sort the items in descending order of value. Obtain printouts of the algorithm(s) you used and a list of the selected records.

P 5-6   A local accounting firm that is growing rapidly has asked for your help. The firm has four partners who are primarily responsible for developing new business. In addition to developing new business, the partners are very busy with their management tasks, so the partners need an easy way to record their new business development activities that does not take too much time or effort. The managing partner of the firm has asked you to develop a database that will help the four partners track their new business development efforts. After talking with the managing partner, you decide that the following information needs to be included in the database:

ACCESS

*   Identity of the partner who is developing the new business lead, including the partner's first name, middle initial, last name, and four-digit employee ID number.
*   Identity of the client or potential client for which the work would be done, including the company name, the key contact persons at the company, and the company's address (street address, city, state, and ZIP code).
*   Information about each new business lead, including the type of new business (the firm classifies its work into the following categories: audit, accounting, tax compliance, tax research, litigation support, and other consulting) and an estimate of the revenue the firm could derive from the new business.
*   Information about each contact made to develop each new business lead, including the date of the contact, how much time the partner spent on the contact (in hours), and a brief summary of important points discussed.

Required:

Using the bottom-up approach described in this chapter, design a set of relational database tables that will include all needed information. Be sure that the tables are in 3NF. Your instructor might have you create the tables and their relationships in a DBMS such as Microsoft Access and enter a few rows of data into each table.

P 5-7   Review the E-R diagram in **Figure 5.13** (pg. 182) and:

a. List the resources, events, and agents that are represented as entities in this diagram.

b. Write a description for each of the six relationships in the diagram. In your description, include the cardinalities. For example, you might describe the relationship between VENDORS and PURCHASE

FIGURE 5.13 Entity-Relationship (E-R) Diagram for Problem 5-7

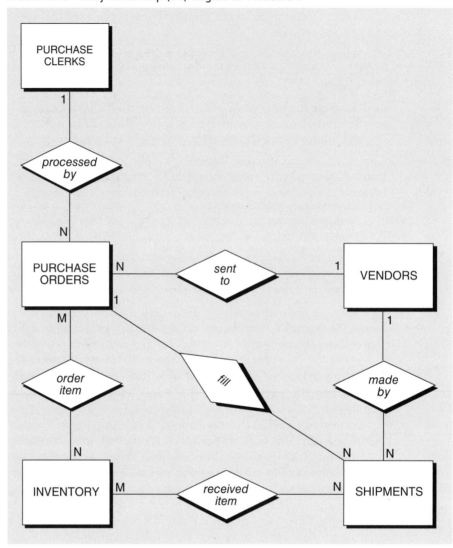

ORDERS as: "Purchase orders are sent to vendors. A vendor may receive many (N) orders, but each purchase order is for only one (1) vendor."

P 5-8   This problem asks you to research the literature for applications of intelligent systems. Your instructor will guide you regarding the number of pages required for each part.

a. Develop a paper that outlines the use of ES in accounting and tax applications. Your paper should describe at least two ES and should describe the benefits and costs of the systems.

b. Develop a paper that describes how EIS may be implemented (e.g., using *digital dashboards*). Include examples (including images) of the systems you find.

FIGURE 5.14 Unnormalized Relation for Problem 5-9

SOFTWARE							
PACKID	TAGNUM	COMPID	INSTDATE	SOFTCOST	EMPNUM	EMPNAME	LOCATION
AC01	32808	M759	9/13/06	754.95	611	Dinh, Melissa	Accounting
DB32	32808	M759	12/13/06	380.00	611	Dinh, Melissa	Accounting
	37691	B121	06/15/06	380.00	124	Alvarez, Ramon	Sales
DB33	57772	C007	05/27/06	412.77	567	Feinstein, Betty	Info Systems
WP08	37691	B121	06/15/06	227.50	124	Alvarez, Ramon	Sales
	57772	C007	05/27/06	170.24	567	Feinstein, Betty	Info Systems
WP09	59836	B221	10/30/06	35.00	124	Alvarez, Ramon	Home
	77740	M759	05/27/06	35.00	567	Feinstein, Betty	Home

KEY:

PACKID = Software package identification code   **SOFTCOST** = Cost of the particular package installed
TAGNUM = Fixed asset inventory tag number   **EMPNUM** = Employee identification code
COMPID = Computer model   **EMPNAME** = Employee name
INSTDATE = Date software was installed on the computer   **LOCATION** = Location of the computer

Source: Table and data adapted from Philip J. Pratt and Joseph J. Adamski, *Database Systems Management and Design*, 3rd ed. (Danvers, MA: Boyd & Fraser Publishing Company, 1994): 218, with permission of Boyd & Fraser Publishing Company. All rights reserved.

    c.   Develop a paper that describes an accounting application of a NN. (The application you choose should not be one already described in the chapter.) Your paper should include at least one system and should include the positive and negative implications of using the application you selected.

P 5-9   Transform the database structure that appears in **Figure 5.14** into 3NF. Be sure to show your intermediate steps of 1NF and 2NF.

P 5-10   **Figure 5.15** (pg. 184) is a sample from a spreadsheet used to record donors for a small college. You have been asked to design and implement a database to allow easy inputting, updating, and reporting of contribution data. `ACCESS`

    a.   Transform the structure into 3NF providing the intermediate steps of 1NF and 2NF.

    b.   Use a DBMS (such as Access) to implement your structure.

P 5-11   Use the Internet to research the database integration features of an ERP software package and a CRM software package. The number of pages will be indicated by your instructor.

    a.   Learn about the ERP products of SAP and the CRM products of Oracle's Siebel. Select one specific product offered by each company and determine whether it includes its own database or must be used with an existing database. If the product requires an existing database, identify which DBMSs the product can use. Summarize your findings in a written report.

    b.   Discuss the advantages and disadvantages of stand-alone CRM and ERP packages versus integrated packages. Your sources should include information on CRM software packages that are stand-alone and integratable.

P 5-12   Technology Summary 5.2 (pp. 155–156) uses examples of employee ID codes to illustrate five data coding types. Refer to those examples. Create *student* ID codes that illustrate each of the five coding schemes. Discuss the strengths and weaknesses of each example.

FIGURE 5.15 Unnormalized Relation for Problem 5-10

GIFT DATE	DONOR NAME	DONOR NUMBER	RECEIPT NUMBER	FUND ID	FUND NAME	AMOUNT
12/5/2009	A. Eddy	109	1201	10	Academic Excellence	$100
				40	Athletic Scholarships	$100
12/17/2009	B. Lester	116	1317	99	Unrestricted Gift	$500
12/17/2009	B. Green	102	1318	40	Athletic Scholarships	$50
				60	Department of Accounting	$100
				10	Academic Excellence	$100
12/19/2009	R. Curtis	210	1411	10	Academic Excellence	$500
				60	Department of Accounting	$500
12/31/2009	G. Smith	221	1573	60	Department of Accounting	$1,000
				40	Athletic Scholarships	$25

Source: Table and data adapted from Philip J. Pratt and Joseph J. Adamski, *Database Systems Management and Design*, 3rd ed. (Danvers, MA: Boyd & Fraser Publishing Company,1994): 218, with permission of Boyd & Fraser Publishing Company. All rights reserved.

P 5-13 Use the Internet to research knowledge management systems. Specifically, (1) find one example of a knowledge management system, (2) identify the provider or vendor, (3) provide the Web site URL, and (4) list the features of the system found that help an organization manage its knowledge. Write up your findings. The number of pages will be indicated by your instructor.

P 5-14 Using a spreadsheet (e.g., Excel), design a decision aid to help you complete the following task.

You are looking for a new apartment and decided to go through a realtor instead of shopping for the apartment through advertisements. Cain Realty provided you with the following list of 7 available apartments in the area you specified. The apartments have been evaluated by Cain Realty using 12 different criteria (listed as 2–13 on the spreadsheet in **Figure 5.16**). Here are some suggestions on how to set up your decision aid: (1) Decide which of the 12 factors you want to include in your decision model. (2) For each factor selected in step (1), decide how much decision weight you want to assign it relative to the other factors. Suggestion: You may want to distribute the decision weights so that they add up to 100 (i.e., 100%). Be prepared to discuss and justify your decisions about factors and weights, especially in comparison to the factors and weights used by other students.

FIGURE 5.16 Table of Data Provided by Cain Realty

	A	B	C	D	E	F	G	H
1	APARTMENT	1	2	3	4	5	6	7
2	Rent relative to average rent	over	over	under	under	under	under	under
3	Size of apartment	cramped	cramped	spacious	spacious	spacious	spacious	spacious
4	Age	old	old	old	new	new	new	new
5	Size of safety deposit required	large	large	large	large	small	small	small
6	Distance from university	far	far	far	far	far	near	near
7	Washer and drier included	no	no	no	no	no	no	yes
8	Hi-speed Internet connection included	yes	yes	yes	yes	yes	yes	no
9	Discount for first time renters	yes	yes	yes	yes	yes	no	no
10	Private parking spot provided	yes	yes	yes	yes	no	no	no
11	Reputation of management	good	good	good	bad	bad	bad	bad
12	Workout facility/indoor pool	yes	yes	no	no	no	no	no
13	Average utilities bill	low	high	high	high	high	high	high
14								

CHAPTER 6

Relational Databases and SQL

Learning Objectives

After reading this chapter, you should be able to:

- Understand basic aspects of business intelligence (BI) and appreciate its importance to the business community.
- Understand the techniques used to model complex accounting phenomena in an entity-relationship (E-R) diagram.
- Develop E-R diagrams that model effective accounting database structures using the Resources-Events-Agents (REA) approach.
- Recognize the components of relational tables and the keys to effective relational database design.
- Understand the use of structured query language (SQL) commands to create relational tables during implementation of the model.
- Manipulate relational tables to extract the necessary data during decision making.

Each year, Ringnes AS in Norway distributes over half a billion bottles of beer, soft drinks, and water. Running such a distribution system was a quite a challenge to Ringnes' management. To handle this challenge, Ringnes, teaming up with IBM, installed a tracking system using radio frequency identification (RFID) technology. RFID tags were placed in bottle containers in delivery trucks, and antennas for capturing information from the containers' tags were located at the main gate and various loading docks of the distribution facility. The information captured through the RFID tracking system was then made available to managers through near-real-time, Web-based business intelligence (BI) "dashboard" displays. Managers could now see, for example, how many and which trucks are inside and outside the facility, and their load status (full, empty, or being loaded). As a result, they could more efficiently control usage of containers, trucks, and loading docks during operations. Managers could immediately identify and correct distribution weaknesses and inefficiencies. (Another BI dashboard was put in the facility's cafeteria for viewing by any interested employee.) Furthermore, through additional analysis of this data using various BI tools, valuable intelligence was derived for tactical and strategic planning. For example, managers were able to discover which loading docks were used the most, which were used the least, and how much time each dock spent loading and unloading. This intelligence, in turn, allowed managers to plan the most efficient use of the different loading docks.[1]

> As you can see from the above example, one of the newest and most exciting developments in today's business information systems is *business intelligence (BI)*. BI builds on many prior business information technologies—for example, enterprise systems, ERP systems, databases, data warehouses, spreadsheets, advanced data analysis tools, and various modeling techniques—and integrates them to provide managers with state-of-the-art decision-making support. Ultimately, however, the value of the decisions made by managers using BI depends on the nature of the data in the system, consistent with the long-standing computer science adage: "GIGO—garbage in, garbage out." To keep a company competitive, decision makers must base their decisions on as much data and as many different types of data as possible.

The REA approach to developing models of accounting databases ensures that a system captures all data related to business events (such as issuing a purchase order), not just the accounting transactions. Such additional data are often referred to as "nonfinancial" data because they do not affect account balances in the financial statements. Examples of nonfinancial data include surveys of customer satisfaction, phone logs of customer queries, records of employee training, and information about how well vendors meet delivery deadlines. Note that none of these are measured as monetary values. Capturing relevant data, combined with a method of extracting and analyzing that data, such as SQL, helps managers manage operations to achieve organization objectives. Over time, as business information systems have increased in capacity and capability, nonfinancial data have played an increasingly important role in business decision making, especially at strategic levels. It also reduces the risk of fraud, and if fraud does occur, it makes the work of a forensic accountant much more productive.

Synopsis

In this chapter, we provide a brief introduction to business intelligence (BI), explaining its use and internal control implications. Next, we describe the Resources-Events-Agents (REA) approach for developing models of accounting databases and using those models to build relational databases. We also describe SQL (structured query language), a database query language used to construct and manipulate relational databases.

You will learn to develop complex entity-relationship (E-R) diagrams, integrate REA concepts with E-R diagrams, and create and manipulate relational databases with SQL. These advanced database techniques provide the foundation for understanding how ERP systems (including BI modules added onto the ERP systems) are constructed and how they function in a business environment. Advanced database skills will aid you in designing effective business information systems, finding the data you need to perform various business tasks, and creating reports that provide your data in an easy-to-use format. At the conclusion of your study of this chapter, you should understand how enterprise databases are constructed and used in modern organizations.

Enterprise Systems

---

[1] From material dated April 29, 2009, at www.ibm.com/us/en/, accessed March 1, 2010.

Introduction

In earlier chapters, you learned that organizations need well-designed information and DBMSs to effectively support decision making. You learned how to create data models using both bottom-up and top-down approaches and learned about alternative types of DBMSs.

In this chapter, our goal is to increase your knowledge of DBMSs, data modeling, DBMS implementation, and query languages. We begin with a discussion of BI, a current decision support system for mangers that relies heavily on database technologies, data modeling, and advanced data analysis techniques. Then we proceed with a more in-depth discussion of entity-relationship (E-R) modeling and the REA approach to designing data models for accounting systems. This discussion is followed by an exploration of the key components and concepts underlying relational DBMSs and how to build a working set of relational tables from an E-R model. We then examine the core commands in SQL for purposes of creating and manipulating relational databases.

We have discussed the importance of data to organizations in the information age, as well as a shift in the focus of organizations from using information for operational control toward the use of information in decision-support applications. Information systems today must effectively collect, organize, and integrate the data necessary to support decision making. BI is a prime example of this trend in the development of business information technology. The successful accountant of tomorrow will manage the creation of *data warehouses* and effectively use tools such as *data mining* to gather information that will help managers make better decisions using such tools as *BI*.

Business Intelligence (BI)

In its first 2010 issue, *Computerworld* ranked business intelligence (BI) as one of the top six "key areas" of current developments in business information technology.[2] While there are many divergent definitions for BI, the consensus points to the following common aspects:

- Having access to massive amounts of data, often stored in *data warehouses* (see Chapter 5), is a prerequisite to BI.
- Data are frequently from a wide variety of sources, inside and outside the company, and cover a wide range of data types—financial and nonfinancial, accounting and non-accounting.
- Turning these data into information to support management decision making is the primary goal of BI.
- On the technological side, most BI uses spreadsheets as an easy-to-use tool for managers to view the data pulled from the large databases.
- On the conceptual side, BI uses simplified business models to help managers make sense of the large amounts of data available (see more on *models* in the following section and Chapter 5 on *modeling*).
- BI is usually implemented into an existing information system as an add-on and therefore does not require an extensive or complete overhaul of the information system.

---

[2]Mary Brandel, "6 Hot Skills for 2010," *Computerworld* (January 4, 2010): 31.

In essence, **business intelligence (BI)** uses state-of-the-art information technologies for storing and analyzing data to help managers make the best possible decisions for their companies. Unlike enterprise systems, which focus primarily on assisting companies in running their day-to-day operations and transactions, BI systems are specifically designed to support managers in making tactical and strategic decisions. Of course, as noted in Chapter 2, enterprise systems have always provided management with some degree of decision support. Accordingly, BI should probably be seen as a natural extension of enterprise systems, and not as a completely new development. In fact, BI is often installed into an existing ERP as an additional module.

Enterprise Systems

Through its use of spreadsheets, BI can improve internal controls within a company, since this use of spreadsheets entails a more thorough integration of spreadsheets into the overall enterprise system than is usually the case. A 2004 PricewaterhouseCoopers study of spreadsheet use found that spreadsheets are frequently used offline relative to the company's enterprise systems, thus bypassing the company's online internal controls.[3] For example, data is downloaded from the enterprise system (with its numerous integrated controls) into a spreadsheet that is not an integrated part of the enterprise system. In one such case, this study found an error from offline spreadsheet analysis that resulted in a $1 billion financial statement error. By increasing spreadsheet use within the system (i.e., online), BI increases the available control a company can exert over spreadsheet use, which in turn increases its compliance with the Sarbanes-Oxley Act (Section 404).

Controls

SOX

REA Modeling

In Chapter 5, you learned some basic E-R modeling concepts, including *entities* and *attributes*. In this section, you will gain a deeper understanding of how database designers use the REA model to identify entities and attributes for accounting applications.

A **model** is a simplified representation of a complex entity or phenomenon. Models can be very useful for identifying important aspects of an entity and for discarding details that are irrelevant and distracting, making it easier to decide what data to capture about the entity in the database.

Entities and Attributes

Extending the concepts from Chapter 5, an entity in an accounting system can be classified as a *resource*, *event*, or *agent* about which data are collected. You learned that resources could include merchandise inventory, equipment, and cash. Events might include orders, sales, and purchases. Agents can be people such as customers and employees; agents also can be organizations, such as corporate vendors. An entity may also be described as anything in which we are interested that exists independently. An **instance** of an entity is one specific thing of the type defined by the entity. For example, the agent entity EMPLOYEE in a small company with three employees might have instances of Marge Evans, Roberto Garcia, and Arte Singh. In a relational database, the entity is represented as a table, and the three instances of the entity are represented as rows in that table.

---

[3]"The Use of Spreadsheets: Considerations for Section 404 of the Sarbanes-Oxley Act," Pricewaterhouse-Coopers LLP (July 2004).

FIGURE 6.1 Attribute Hierarchy for the Entity CLIENT

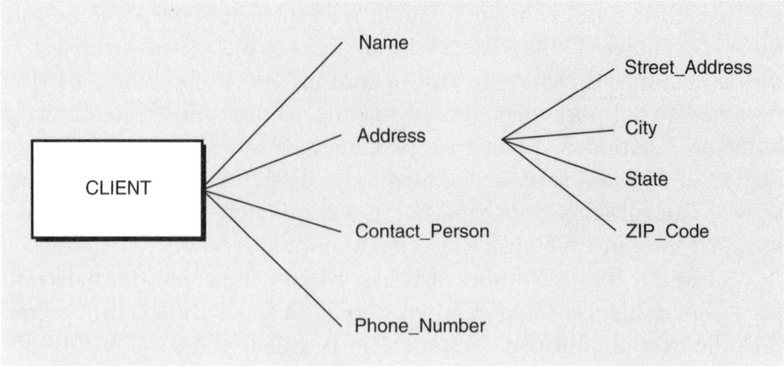

To understand which entity we are capturing in our database and, likewise, to identify that unique entity when we retrieve the data, we need to describe the entity in detail. *Data models* describe entities by capturing their essential characteristics. Recall from Chapter 5 that data models are used to identify user requirements for data in a database. From a business perspective, this identification is important because many business users (e.g., managers) require data to help them achieve company objectives and monitor company performance.

The essential characteristics of an entity are its attributes. An **attribute** is an item of data that characterizes an entity or relationship. **Figure 6.1** displays an attribute hierarchy for the agent entity CLIENT. To fully describe a CLIENT, we need to record several attributes such as Name, Address, Contact_Person, and Phone_Number. Sometimes attributes are a combination of parts that have unique meanings of their own. As you can see in Figure 6.1, the attribute Address can include several independent subattributes such as Street_Address, City, State, and ZIP_Code. Such attributes, those that consist of multiple subattributes, are referred to as **composite attributes**. The degree to which a database designer breaks down attributes is a matter of judgment. For example, the attribute Street_Address could be broken down into further subattributes such as Street_Number, Street_Name, Street_Type (road, avenue, lane, etc.), and Street_Directional_Suffix (N, S, E, NE, etc.). Although an important goal of attribute identification is to break the attributes down into small components, attributes do not need to be broken into the smallest possible units in every case.

Note that an important assumption lies behind our specification of the attributes for the agent entity CLIENT. We have assumed that a common set of attributes exists for each instance of CLIENT. That is, every client has a name, address, contact person, and phone number. To design an effective data model, you must learn to identify the complete set of entities and the attributes that fully describe each entity. The REA approach helps the designers of accounting databases identify a complete set of entities. It is important that the attributes allow the user of a database to uniquely identify each entity in the database.

To achieve the objective of uniquely identifying each entity to be stored in our database, it is necessary that one or more attributes be identified that will allow the user to access the entity the user is seeking. A **key attribute** is the attribute whose value is unique (i.e., different) for every entity that will ever appear in the database and is the most meaningful way of identifying each entity. This key attribute becomes the primary key (as discussed in Chapter 5). For our CLIENT agent entity, we might be tempted to use Name for the key attribute, but alphabetic-based attributes such as names are tricky because computers do not consistently distinguish between (or fail to distinguish between) uppercase and lowercase letters. Further, spellings and full names can be troublesome in that one user might view the company name as "Arnold Consultants," whereas another user might use the full name, "Arnold Consultants, LLP." Similar problems can arise with company names such as "The Final Authority." A well-intentioned data entry clerk might enter that name as "Final Authority, The" or simply "Final Authority" after concluding that the article "The" is not an important part of the company name. Most designers would use a numeric-valued or a non-naming alphabetic attribute. For instance, an internally generated client number could be assigned to each instance in the CLIENT table. A numeric form using a *sequential coding* scheme might assign a number such as "12345." A non-naming alphabetic form using *block coding* to categorize companies by the first letter of a company's name might assign an alphanumeric such as "A1234" for the client number.

Figure 6.2, part (a), shows one common set of symbols that are used to represent entities and attributes in E-R diagrams. In Figure 6.2, part (b), the rectangle is used to represent the CLIENT agent entity. To map the attributes of an entity, we attach an oval to the entity (i.e., the rectangle) by means of a connector line for each attribute, as shown in part (a). Notice in part (b) that we have added an oval for each of the attributes shown in Figure 6.1. For the composite attribute Address, we use the same oval connectors for each of the subattributes of the main attribute. Note that we have

FIGURE 6.2   Symbols Used in E-R and REA Diagrams

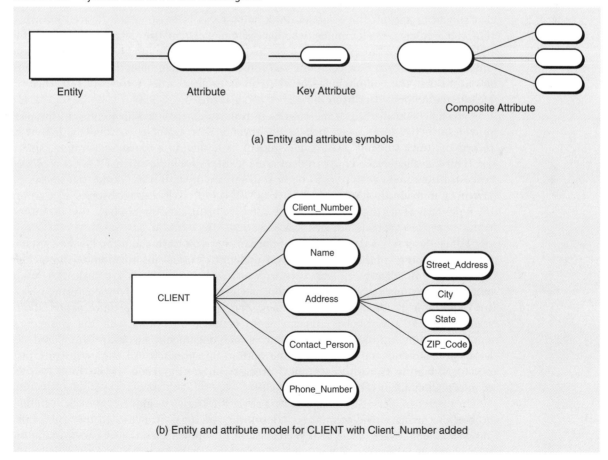

(a) Entity and attribute symbols

(b) Entity and attribute model for CLIENT with Client_Number added

added a new attribute to the set of attributes shown in Figure 6.1—Client_Number. This attribute is the CLIENT entity's key attribute. The underline beneath the attribute name documents its selection as the key attribute.

Relationships

In Chapter 5, we defined relationships as associations between entities. As you have learned, a database includes multiple entities. However, to make the data stored in entities available to users who might want to reconstruct descriptions of various business events, the entities must be logically linked to represent the relationships that exist between them. The ease with which a user can extract related data from a database is heavily dependent on the quality of the design of these logical links—that is, effective identification of the relationships between different entities. These relationships map and define the way in which data can be extracted from the database. The mapping of the relationships between entities (i.e., development of the E-R diagram) provides a roadmap for getting from one piece of data in the database to another related piece of data—much as a road map in an atlas might show you how to drive from one city to another. Thus, when implemented into relational database software (e.g., Microsoft Access), the CLIENT entity will become a CLIENT table, and the various attributes shown in Figure 6.2 (pg. 191) will become fields in that table. Note, however, that there will not be an "address" attribute (i.e., column) but only individual attributes (i.e., columns) for "street_address," "city," "state," and "ZIP_code."

A three-step strategy is generally most effective in identifying all the relationships that should be included in a model. First, identify users' existing and desired information requirements to determine whether relationships in the data model can fulfill those requirements. For example, if users had been previously filling out paper purchase order forms, then the new computerized information system being implemented needs to ensure that—at a minimum—the electronic purchase order forms will reference or include the relevant data from the earlier paper forms.

Second, evaluate each of the entities in pairs to determine which entity in the pair provides a better location to include an attribute. For example, it would be better to record and track students' majors in a student table than in a course registration table.

Third, evaluate each entity to determine if there would be any need for two occurrences of the same entity type to be linked. For example, if a car dealer tracks cars in inventory individually (by serial number or VIN) but tracks car accessories as a group (by type, such as driving lights), then the database being used should have two inventory tables—one for cars and another for accessories.

When designing a database, it is important that you learn about the business events that occur in the company and that you understand users' information requirements. This helps you identify all the ways in which different entities are related to each other in the company. This information will give you an idea of which relationships are required in the data model. The most common way to gather information about relationships in a particular company is to conduct interviews with the company's employees. You can also collect the forms and documents currently being used, as noted in Chapter 5 when discussing the bottom-up approach. All employees (not just managers) who work with the business process you are modeling can be good sources of information about relationships.

In the remainder of this chapter, we use an illustrative example of the client billing process that many public accounting, consulting, and legal firms use. In this client billing system, employees of the firm keep track of how much time they spend working on each client. Each employee fills out a weekly time sheet to record the time spent on each client. The hours spent on each client are then multiplied by the employee's billable rate for each hour worked. The cumulative fees for all employees' work are then used to generate a bill for each client. The business process here is the capture of all information necessary to track employees' work hours and client billing information.

Examine **Figure 6.3** briefly before we go on. The figure includes information about three entities and their attributes. Using the REA approach, we have identified one event and two agents that participate in the business process of billing for professional services. The WORK_COMPLETED entity is an event. The CLIENT and EMPLOYEE entities are agents. No resources are tracked in this data model for the client-billing business process.

Desirable linkages between entities will often be easy to recognize when the relationship defines an attribute. If our billing system requires that we know for which client an employee has worked, the entity representing work completed needs to include a client number. This client number links the WORK_COMPLETED entity to the CLIENT entity, which provides a full description of the attribute denoted by client number in WORK_COMPLETED. As you can see in Figure 6.3, part (a), CLIENT is an entity and not an attribute of WORK_COMPLETED. However, CLIENT does improve the description of an attribute for the work completed—the client for whom the work was performed. This descriptive value suggests that a relationship exists between the CLIENT entity and the entity capturing the completed work, as shown in Figure 6.3, part (a). Hence, we often can identify the need for defining relationships (such as Works_For) by examining the prescribed entities as pairs (in this case, we examined the pair CLIENT and WORK_COMPLETED) to identify logical linkages that would improve the description of an entity's attributes.

Another type of relationship is displayed in Figure 6.3, part (b). The relationship Supervises is called a *recursive relationship*. A **recursive relationship** occurs between two different instances of an entity. For example, most organizations have relationships

FIGURE 6.3 Relationship Types in the REA Model of the Client-Billing Business Process

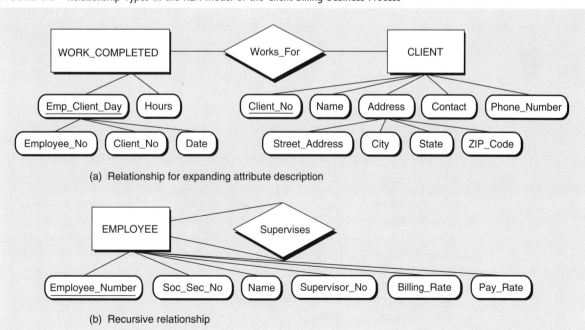

(a) Relationship for expanding attribute description

(b) Recursive relationship

among employees in which one employee supervises other employees. This relationship is often important in business processes and in decision-making contexts. Thus, this relationship should be represented in our database. Figure 6.3 (pg. 193), part (b) shows how a recursive relationship is displayed in an REA data model diagram. One tempting alternative is to represent supervisors and their supervised employees as separate entities in the model. Unfortunately, this separate entity approach yields data redundancies when the supervisor is supervised by a third employee. Thus, it is easier and more logically correct to use a recursive relationship to the entity EMPLOYEE. In this recursive relationship, a link is created between the employee who is being supervised and another employee who is the supervisor. In Figure 6.3, part (b), the diamond represents the recursive relationship, Supervises, just as it would be used to show any relationship (such as the Works_For relationship in part [a]).

Model Constraints

In this section, we explore the various types of relationships that can occur and discuss the constraints used to specify such relationships. In Chapter 5, we briefly explored three different relationship types: 1:N (one-to-many), M:N (many-to-many), and 1:1 (one-to-one). You learned in Chapter 5 that the degree of these three relationship types is called *cardinality*.

Figure 6.4, part (a) is an REA diagram that shows the maximum cardinalities for the Works relationship between the agent entity EMPLOYEE and the event entity WORK_COMPLETED in the client billing business process. The "1" above the left line of the relationship indicates that one employee performs each completed work entry. The "N" above the right line indicates that an employee can perform many work entries.

To determine the cardinality of a relationship, ask yourself the question, "How many items (records) in this entity could be related to any one item (record) in the other entity—one or many?" The answer determines that half of the cardinality ratio, and then the same question is asked in the reverse direction of the relationship to determine the other half of the cardinality ratio. In our example, we take the relationship in Figure 6.4, part (a), and ask the question, "How many work completed entries can an employee have?" The answer is many, based on the attributes specified for WORK_COMPLETED in Figure 6.3, part (a), which indicates that a given occurrence in the WORK_COMPLETED entity relates to one employee's time spent on a given client in a single time period. The question is then reversed to ask, "How many

FIGURE 6.4   Relationship Constraints in the Client Billing Business Process

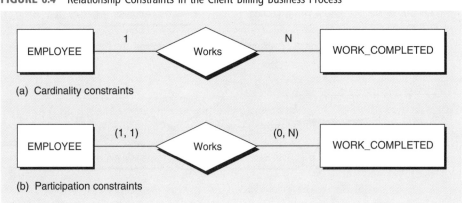

(a) Cardinality constraints

(b) Participation constraints

employees can provide a specific work completed entry?" The maximum number will be one. Hence, the cardinality of the relationship is specified as one-to-many and is indicated on the diagram with the "1" and "N" notation. Most DBMSs include a feature that enforces maximum constraints. In other words, the DBMS will ensure that data are never entered that connect more than one employee to a single work completed entry.

Cardinality is the most common constraint specified in E-R diagrams. The other meaningful constraint that may be specified is participation. The **participation constraint** specifies the degree of minimum participation of one entity in the relationship with the other entity. This constraint is either 1 or 0, meaning that a relationship between the two entities is either mandatory (1) or optional (0). In Figure 6.4, part (b), the *participation constraints* appear in the diagram. In the Works relationship, not every employee will have completed a billable work activity. Some employees are new and are not yet billable, and others might have nonclient service responsibilities, such as training or new business development. The "many" cardinality that appears in part (a) of the diagram only specifies the maximum participation in the relationship, not the minimum. The minimum participation in the relationship can be zero or one. The notation (0, N) on the line on the right in part (b) reflects the range of zero to many occurrences of work being completed on client projects, where the numbers reflect (minimum, maximum). The notation (1, 1) on the line on the left side in part (b) illustrates that for any given occurrence of work completed for a client, the maximum of one employee providing the specific service still holds. In this case, the minimum also will be one because an employee must perform a particular occurrence of the completed work. The (1, 1) relationship reflects the fact that there is a required participation of one, and only one, employee.

Although the participation constraint provides more information, it is still used less frequently than the cardinality constraint. In this book, we present the diagrams using the maximum cardinality and omit the participation (or minimum) constraints. You should know that both types of constraints and notation are used because, as a member of the development team, as an auditor, or as a user, you will need to communicate using the methods selected by the organization with which you are working. Minimum constraints are especially useful in designing tables so that **null** values (fields with missing values) occur infrequently. (Null values waste memory space and may cause problems when running queries.) Minimizing null values, however, requires using a new set of rules for the creation of additional tables, which we will not cover in this text. We will simply comment that relational tables function well without observing the minimum constraint rules as long as the rules relating to cardinality (or maximum) constraints are applied. It should also be noted that while maximum and minimum constraints can often be determined by logic or common sense, they frequently can be determined only by referencing the company's specific way of running its business. For example, it is up to management (not logic) whether the relationship between "salesperson" and "sales region" is 1:M, M:N, 1:1, or M:1—all of these relationships are logically feasible.

REA Data Models and E-R Diagrams

You now have all of the basic knowledge you need to develop effective REA models and their representations in E-R diagrams. You should be ready to start developing an integrated database model. Each of the data model segments included in Figure 6.1 (pg. 190), Figure 6.2 (pg. 191), Figure 6.3 (pg. 193), and Figure 6.4 are parts of REA data models.

A fundamental requirement for moving toward an event-driven model, such as REA, is the complete integration of data related to an organization's business events.

Although the development of a full, comprehensive integrated data model for an entire organization is a major undertaking, you can use your data-modeling skills to explore the integration of two business processes: client billing and human resources.

Two of the main objectives in the development of an REA model are (1) to identify the data required by managers and other users to perform effectively and (2) to integrate the data in a way that allows those users to efficiently access the information needed. **Figure 6.5** presents the integrated REA data model for the billing and human resources business processes. Follow along with the REA diagram as we discuss the data relationships in the following scenario.

In a service organization such as a public accounting or consultancy firm, billing clients requires that the firm track the person-hours spent by each employee who is providing service. To execute the client billing process effectively, the database must capture data about all employees who provided client services. The database must record each employee's work for a specific client. Each employee can have a different billing rate for his or her time. To meet the needs of the billing process, the database must aggregate each employee's time worked, each employee's billing rate, and sufficient information about the client to deliver the billing statement. Three entities are

FIGURE 6.5   An Integrated REA Model for the Client Billing and Human Resources Processes

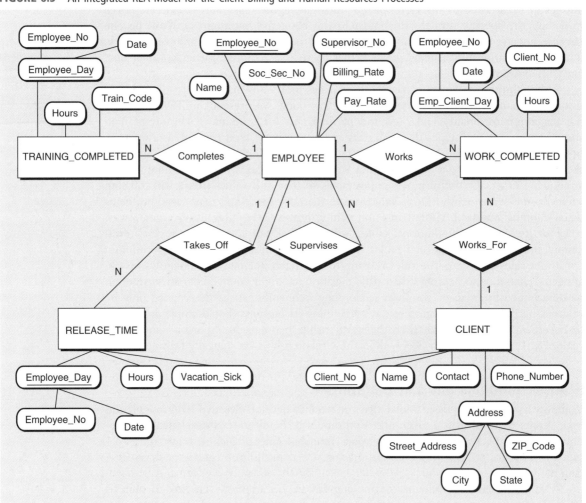

involved in the billing process: the agent EMPLOYEE, the agent CLIENT, and the event WORK_COMPLETED. Note in Figure 6.5 that the three entities for the billing process are linked together on the right half of the diagram. The linkages allow us to pull together information related to the employees' hours worked on a specific client, their billing rates, and the contact address for sending the billing statement.

Service businesses also are interested in tracking employee work activities as part of the human resources process. The human resources process includes payroll activities, employee education and development, and other activities. To complete the payroll process, information is needed regarding work hours completed, pay rate, vacation time, sick days, and training time. Using the REA approach, we can identify two additional entities, the events RELEASE_TIME and TRAINING_COMPLETED, which are added to the model that also includes the previously identified agent entity EMPLOYEE and event entity WORK_COMPLETED. These four entities enable the database to aggregate the information it needs to determine the employee's pay rate, hours worked, hours spent in training, and hours of sick time and vacation time used.

The human resources department needs information about employee education and development so it can monitor training activities and ensure that the employee is receiving enough continuing education to comply with state licensing requirements and the firm's policies. Human resources also will monitor the percentage of billable hours the employee has accumulated as a measure of job performance. To accomplish these activities, human resources must be able to link data about completed work activities and training programs to specific employees. This information can be drawn from the agent entity EMPLOYEE, the event entity TRAINING_COMPLETED, and the event entity WORK_COMPLETED. Human resources can use this information to accumulate a given employee's training record and calculate that employee's percentage of hours worked that were billable hours.

Note that Figure 6.5 shows only a small part of the overall enterprise model that integrates all information across the entire organization. The REA model effectively integrates the data required for the firm's business processes. For example, all four entities in Figure 6.5 are directly or indirectly linked to each other. As other business processes are examined, modeled, and integrated, the REA data model will continue to expand through an explosion of entities and relationships. Many organizations have moved toward integration of all data across the organization. These integrated enterprise models are the foundations for implementing enterprise systems, which you learned about in Chapter 2.

Enterprise Systems

In the following sections, we describe how to implement the REA data model in a relational database system. Subsequently, we examine the use of SQL to create and manipulate the database.

Relational Databases

We briefly demonstrated the use of the *relational databases* in Chapter 5. In this section, we expand our examination of relational databases and explore a few of the more technical issues. Despite a push toward *object-oriented databases*, relational database–driven legacy systems exist in most large organizations, and the effort to switch them over to object-oriented databases is cost prohibitive. Many of these **legacy systems** (i.e., systems that have existed in an organization over a long period of time and were developed using an organization's previous computer hardware and software platforms) have been functioning reliably for decades. As an alternative to making costly changes to object-oriented databases, relational database vendors are providing modified versions of their software that support objects within the relational structure. Relational-based DBMSs likely will remain dominant for at least the near future.

Our exploration of relational databases is divided into two segments. First, we look at the basic concepts that underlie relational databases. Then we explore the task of mapping REA data models into relational database tables and relationships.

Relational Database Concepts

Relational databases often are perceived by users as a collection of tables. This is a reasonable perception because the logical view of the data is a tabular type format referred to as a *relation*. A **relation** is a collection of data representing multiple occurrences of a resource, event, or agent. These relations correspond to the entities in the E-R model and the REA model.

Figure 6.6 displays an example relation along with labels for each of the components (or attributes) of a relation. Consistent with a tabular representation, a relation consists of rows and columns. Rows are sometimes referred to as *tuples,* and columns are referred to as *attributes*. A **tuple** is a set of data that describes a single instance of the entity represented by a relation (e.g., one employee is an instance of the EMPLOYEE relation). Attributes, as in an E-R model, represent an item of data that characterizes an object, event, or agent. Attributes are often called *fields*.

In viewing the relation in Figure 6.6, note that the data contained in the table do not appear to be in any particular order. In a relational database model, no ordering is given to the tuples contained within a relation. This is different from the traditional file structures and the database models that existed before the relational model that you learned about in Chapter 5. In those systems, sequence or keyed locations could be critical. The ordering of the tuples in a relational database is unimportant because the tuples are recalled from the database by matching an attribute's value with some prescribed value or through a query in which the ordering of the output could be established on any attribute (e.g., a query could sort on the Pay_Rate or Billing_Rate attribute).

To identify a tuple uniquely, each tuple must be distinct from all other tuples. This means that each tuple in a relation must be identified uniquely by a single attribute or some combination of multiple attributes. In each table, a *primary key* is specified to uniquely identify each tuple in the relation. Notice in Figure 6.6 that Employee_Number is the primary key, which is unique for each tuple.

Controls

Additionally, constraints should be implemented to ensure that the *referential integrity* of the database is maintained. **Referential integrity** specifies that for every attribute

FIGURE 6.6 Example of a Relation (EMPLOYEE) and Its Parts

EMPLOYEE	Employee_Number	Soc_Sec_No	Name	Supervisor_No	Billing_Rate	Pay_Rate
	B432	305-45-9592	Carl Elks	A632	57.00	2,500
	A491	350-97-9030	Janet Robins	A632	57.00	2,500
	A632	125-87-8090	Greg Kinman	B122	100.00	4,500
	B011	178-78-0406	Christy Bazie	A632	57.00	2,600
	B122	123-78-0907	Elaine Kopp	Null	150.00	7,000
	A356	127-92-3453	John Mast	A632	57.00	2,600

value in one relation that has been specified to allow reference to another relation, the tuple being referenced must remain intact. For example, consider the relation EMPLOYEE in Figure 6.6. You might recall that EMPLOYEE was involved in a recursive relation in Figure 6.3, part (b) (pg. 193). In that recursive relation, Supervisor_No is used to reference the Employee_No of the supervising employee. If the tuple for Greg Kinman were deleted from the database, four other employees would no longer have a valid Supervisor_No (because the Supervisor_No would be referencing a tuple that no longer exists). Thus, a *referential integrity constraint* would require the user to reassign the four employees to a new supervisor before the tuple for Greg Kinman could be deleted. Most DBMS software products have built-in mechanisms for enforcing referential integrity. See **Technology Application 6.1** for a more detailed discussion of how referential integrity and primary keys can serve as controls.

Technology Application 6.1

CONTROL ASPECTS OF PRIMARY KEYS

As noted earlier, primary keys can be used to link relational database tables together. A major benefit of such links is that data from separate tables can be extracted and combined for further analysis and reporting. For example, a marketing department might use demographic data from a customer table along with date, time, and location data from a sales table to identify buying patterns that in turn can help with decisions concerning advertising strategies. Such decisions are likely to affect the advertising budget and the use of company assets. As you will see in Chapter 7, one of the three primary objectives for controls is to monitor how well a company uses its resources.

On a more technical level, primary keys can also provide important controls for preventing assets and resources from being lost or stolen. Consider the following example using Microsoft Access. Victoria's Movie Rental is a small local business that rents hard-to-find movies, usually older releases not available in major movie rental stores. Victoria has automated her business using Access. For the revenue processes, she has set up separate relational tables for (1) customers, (2) inventory of movies, (3) renting movies to customers, and (4) returning of rented movies. (In an REA model, note that customers would be an agent, inventory would be a resource, and renting and returning movies would be two events.) The Access screenshot in **Figure 6.7** shows these tables and their links using primary keys. The primary keys are shown as key symbols. In this illustration, the links between tables create a control feature that Access calls *referential integrity*, as shown by the 1 and ∞ (i.e., infinity) symbols. Access Help defines

FIGURE 6.7   A Relationship with Cardinalities in Microsoft Access DBMS

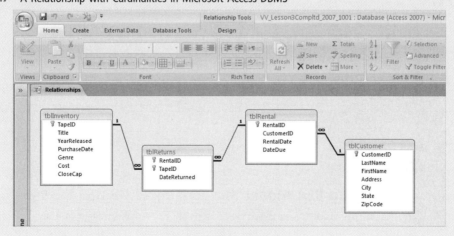

(Continued)

Technology Application 6.1 (Continued)

referential integrity as "rules that you follow to preserve the defined relationships between tables when you add, update, or delete records." As a control, referential integrity helps Victoria safeguard her movie assets. For example, if someone not in the customer table wanted to rent a movie, the presence of referential integrity would prevent this transaction from occurring. It would not allow a new rental event (with this customer) to be entered into the rental table until a customer record for this person is first entered into the customer table. **Figure 6.8** shows the warning that Access gives the database user when trying to rent a movie to someone not in the customer table.

This aspect of referential integrity can protect the movies assets in several ways. In case the movie is not returned in a reasonable amount of time, customer data would allow Victoria to contact the customer about the situation. Further, if credit card information is included in the customer record, the replacement cost of the lost movie could be charged to the customer (provided the legal requirements governing the transaction were met; e.g., the customer was informed that this is company policy).

A database cannot have referential integrity without primary key links. However, tables can be linked together using primary keys without enforcing referential integrity. Notice the absence of any 1 and ∞ symbols in the following Access screenshot (**Figure 6.9**). Without referential integrity, it would be possible to rent a movie to a customer who is not in the customer table and thereby risk losing the movie (the company asset) without recourse.

FIGURE 6.8 A Warning ("Caution") Pop-Up in Microsoft Access DBMS

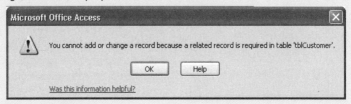

FIGURE 6.9 A Relationship without Cardinalities in Microsoft Access DBMS

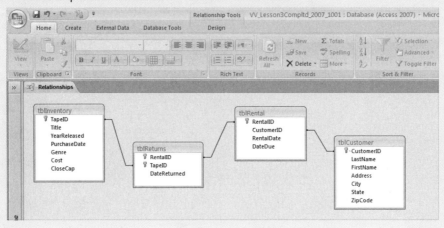

Mapping an REA Model to a Relational DBMS

So far in this chapter, we have discussed the development of REA models and the foundations for implementing good relational database models. It is now time to put these two concepts together. This process is referred to as *mapping* an REA model onto a logical database model—in this case, the relational data model.

In Chapter 5, we outlined a simple five-step process for creating tables and relationships based on an E-R diagram. We will now expand the five-step process to develop a well-constrained relational database implementation. To aid in the comparability with our original discussion, we will reintroduce each of the five steps in the context of the discussion on this expanded mapping methodology. Follow along as we map the REA diagram in Figure 6.5 (pg. 196) to the relational database schema in **Figure 6.10**.

1. *Create a separate relational table for each entity:* This is a logical starting point whenever mapping an REA model onto a relational database model. As a starting point in this process, it is generally useful to first specify the database schema before proceeding to expand the relations to account for specific tuples. Notice that each of the entities in Figure 6.5 has become a relation in Figure 6.10. To complete the schema, however, steps 2 and 3 also must be completed.

2. *Determine the primary key for each of the relations:* The primary key must uniquely identify any row within the table.

3. *Determine the attributes for each of the entities:* Note in Figure 6.5 that a complete REA model includes specification of all attributes, including the key attribute. This eliminates the need to do this during development of the relations. Rather, the focus is on step 2 and is simply a matter of determining how to implement the prescribed key attribute within a relation. With a single attribute specified as the key, the key attribute specified in the REA model is matched to the corresponding attribute in the relation (e.g., Employee_No in the EMPLOYEE agent entity shown in Figure 6.5 and the EMPLOYEE agent relation in Figure 6.10).

   To create a *composite primary key*, you simply break the key down into its component subattributes. For instance, in the implementation of the WORK_COMPLETED event relation, Employee_No, Date, and Client_No are three

FIGURE 6.10 Schema for the Client Billing and Human Resources Portion of the Database

CLIENT

Client_No	Name	Street_Address	City	State	ZIP_Code	Contact	Phone_Number

WORK_COMPLETED

Employee_No	Date	Client_No	Hours

EMPLOYEE

Employee_No	Soc_Sec_No	Name	Supervisor_No	Billing_Rate	Pay_Rate

TRAINING_COMPLETED

Employee_No	Date	Hours	Train_Code

RELEASE_TIME

Employee_No	Date	Hours	Vacation_Sick

distinct attributes in the relation but also combine to form the composite primary key. Similarly, in the event relations TRAINING_COMPLETED and RELEASE_TIME, attributes Employee_No and Date combine to form the composite primary key Employee_Day. The completed schema, reflecting the attributes and primary keys, is presented in Figure 6.10 (pg. 201). Note the direct mapping between the entities and attributes in the REA model and the relations and attributes, respectively, in the relational schema.

4. *Implement the relationships among the entities by ensuring that the primary key in one table also exists as an attribute in every table for which there is a relationship specified in the REA diagram:* With the availability of the full REA model, the mapping of the relationships in the model to the relationships in the relational schema is straightforward. References to the key attributes of one entity are captured by including a corresponding attribute in the other entity that participates in the relationship. These primary key attributes are commonly referred to as **foreign keys** when inserted into other tables to establish links. All of the relationships in this example are 1:N relationships, which simplifies the process. Let's consider how the different degrees of relationships (i.e., cardinality constraints) can affect the mapping of relationships to the schema.

- One-to-many (1:N or N:1) relationships are implemented by including the primary key of the table on the one side of the relationship as an attribute (i.e., foreign key) in the table on the many side of the relationship. This is the situation we have for all the relationships in Figure 6.5 (pg. 196). The links between these relations in the schema are drawn in **Figure 6.11**. Note that Client_No in CLIENT and Employee_No in EMPLOYEE provide the links to WORK_COMPLETED. Similarly, Employee_No in EMPLOYEE provides links to TRAINING_COMPLETED and RELEASE_TIME. The recursive

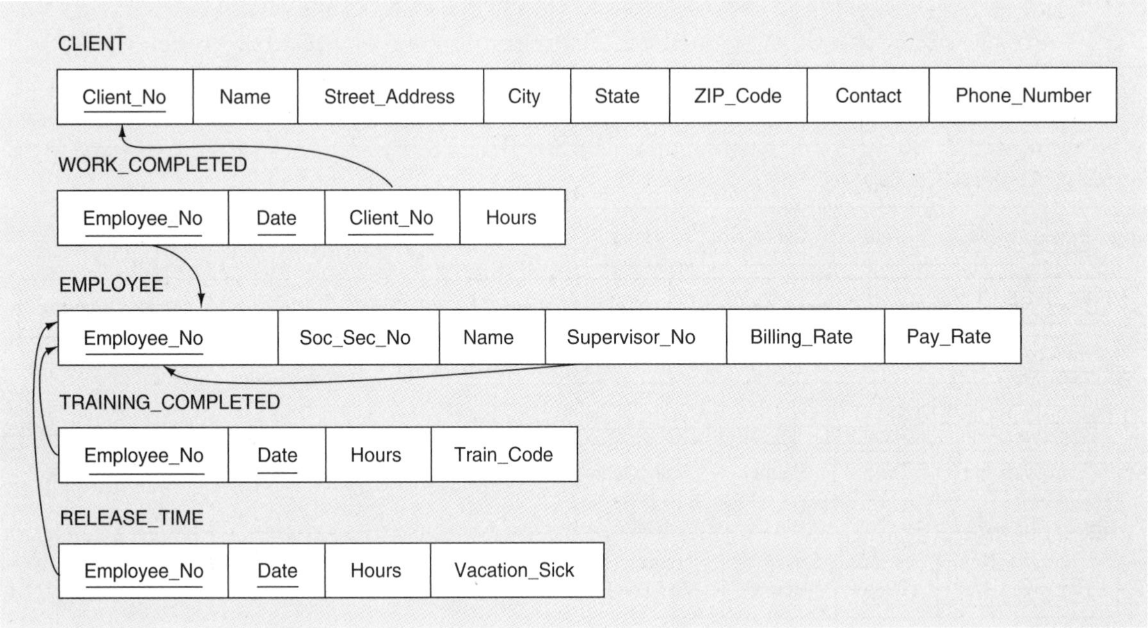

FIGURE 6.11 Referential Constraints for the Relational Schema

relationship with EMPLOYEE uses Supervisor_No to identify the correct EMPLOYEE as the supervisor.

- One-to-one (1:1) relationships are even easier. You can follow the same steps used for 1:N relationships, but you can start with either table. For example, if currently one entry in WORK_COMPLETED is sufficient to finish any client project, then a 1:1 relationship exists between WORK_COMPLETED and CLIENT. In this situation, we could still select the Client_No in CLIENT to establish the primary key (Figure 6.11). Starting with CLIENT has an advantage: If a client engagement in the future might require more than one entry in WORK_COMPLETED to finish or more than one employee to complete, using Client_No in the CLIENT table would still work (i.e., it would form the many dimension shown for the relationship Works_For in Figure 6.5, pg. 196).

- Many-to-many (M:N) relationships are implemented by creating a new relation whose primary key is a composite of the primary keys of the relations to be linked. In our model, we do not have any M:N relationships, but if we had not needed to record the Date and Hours in the WORK_COMPLETED entity, that entity would not have existed. Still, we would need a relationship between the EMPLOYEE and CLIENT entities, which would then be an M:N relationship. This creates problems because tables that have been normalized (as discussed in Chapter 5) cannot store multiple client numbers in a single EMPLOYEE tuple. Similarly, a single CLIENT tuple cannot store multiple employee numbers. In that situation, we would need to develop a relation to link the EMPLOYEE and CLIENT relations (**Figure 6.12**). This new relation would have a composite key consisting of Employee_No from EMPLOYEE and Client_No from CLIENT—similar to the composite key in the existing relation, WORK_COMPLETED (Figure 6.10, pg. 201).

- Beyond concerns over meeting the constraint requirements for primary keys, we also must ensure adherence to the referential integrity constraints. We identify the referential integrity constraints by locating the corresponding attribute in each relation that is linked via a relationship. We then determine which of the relations contain the tuple that—if the reference attribute were deleted or changed—would jeopardize the integrity of the database. In Figure 6.11, the arrow represents referential integrity constraints; the destination of the arrow is

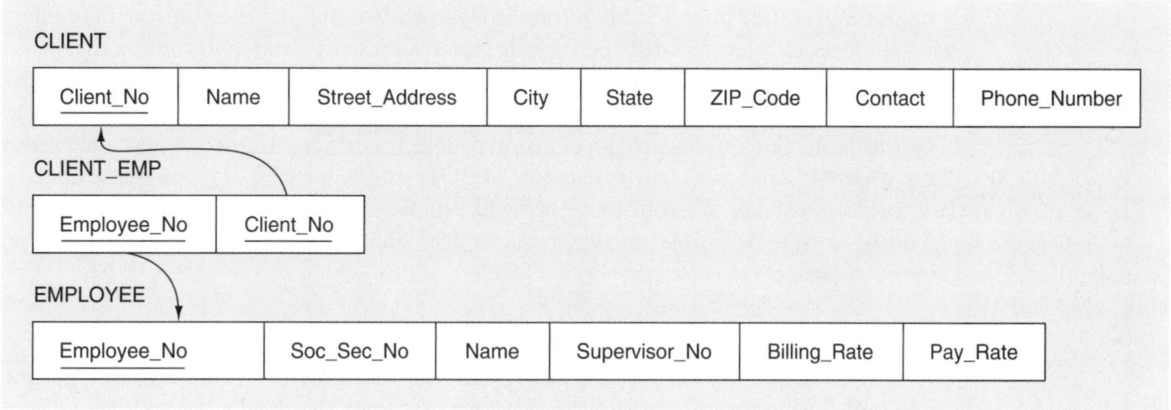

FIGURE 6.12 Linking Two Relations in a Many-to-Many Relationship

the attribute that must be controlled to achieve referential integrity. In other words, changing the attribute to which the arrow points could cause an attribute not to have a matching value in the attribute at the source of the arrow. To achieve referential integrity, constraints should be established that ensure Employee_No is not altered or deleted for any EMPLOYEE until the referencing attri bute values for the Employee_No attributes in WORK_COMPLETED, TRAINING_ COMPLETED, and RELEASE_TIME have first been corrected. A similar constraint should be placed on Client_No in CLIENT until Client_No has been corrected in WORK_COMPLETED. Technology Application 6.1 (pp. 199-200) illustrates how referential integrity can serve as an effective control on an operational level.

- It should be noted that merely placing a *foreign key* in a table does not automatically establish a relationship between tables. You must explicitly link the tables from primary key to foreign key.

5. *Determine the attributes, if any, for each of the relationship tables:* Again, in the extended version of the REA model, the attributes map directly to the relations. The implementation of the schema is shown in **Figure 6.13**.

SQL: A Relational Database Query Language

In this section, you will learn how SQL can be used to create a database, store data in the new database, and manipulate the data stored in the database. Our intention in this section is to introduce you to SQL. There are many important functions and commands that we will not cover. (For SQL functions and commands not reviewed in this section, use the Help function in Microsoft Access.)

SQL is a powerful database language that can be used to define database systems, query the database for information, generate reports from the database, and access databases from within programs using embedded SQL commands. It has become the de facto standard database language—evidenced by continual efforts by the industry to provide standardization guidelines for vendors and the number of variations of the language that exist in databases from supercomputers to personal computers. SQL has become so critical to many business organizations that more and more software is being developed to provide intelligent interfaces that help the user generate queries more quickly. Using such an interface, a user enters a description of the output desired, and the system generates an SQL query. However, these query utilities can be risky to use because they do not always generate the SQL query intended; therefore, it is imperative that the user thoroughly understand the queries to ensure that the intended data is properly extracted from the database.

SQL is increasingly becoming a survival tool among accounting and business professionals. After you complete your study of the material presented here, you should have the basic skills necessary to develop your own databases and retrieve data from many different databases. Our discussion of SQL will begin with the commands necessary to create databases. From there, we will explore the basic querying commands that will allow us to update the database, retrieve data, and generate reports.

Constructing Relational Databases

The first command of interest in creating the database structure is the CREATE command, which we will use to create the relations that form the database structure. Browse the queries in **Figure 6.14** (pg. 206) before reading the following discussion.

Use Figure 6.14 (pg. 206) to follow the steps for creating a database structure with SQL as discussed next. To create a relation, follow these steps:

1. Assign the relation a name (which we have already done for our relations in defining the schema in Figure 6.10, pg. 201).
2. Assign each attribute a name. Again, in the schema demonstrated in Figure 6.10, we have already given our attributes names.

FIGURE 6.13 Implementation of the Relational Schema

EMPLOYEE	Employee_No	Soc_Sec_No	Name	Supervisor_No	Billing_Rate	Pay_Rate
	B432	305-45-9592	Carl Elks	A632	57.00	2,500
	A491	350-97-9030	Janet Robins	A632	57.00	2,500
	A632	125-87-8090	Greg Kinman	B122	100.00	4,500
	B011	178-78-0406	Christy Bazie	A632	57.00	2,600
	B122	123-78-0907	Elaine Kopp	Null	150.00	7,000
	A356	127-92-3453	John Mast	A632	57.00	2,600

TRAINING_COMPLETED	Employee_No	Date	Hour	Train_Code
	A356	070823	8	32
	B011	070823	8	32
	B432	070823	8	32
	A491	070823	8	32
	A356	070824	8	32
	B011	070824	8	32
	B432	070824	8	32
	A491	070824	8	32
	A356	070825	8	32
	B011	070825	8	32
	B432	070825	8	32
	A491	070825	8	32

RELEASE_TIME	Employee_No	Date	Hour	Vacation_Sick
	B011	070826	8	V
	B011	070827	8	V

CLIENT	Client_No	Name	Street_Address	City	State	ZIP_Code	Contact	Phone_Number
	A12345	Arnold, LLP	11 Nayatt Dr.	Barrington	RI	02806	V. Arnold	401-792-8341
	F11555	Fleet Services	10 Mission Rd.	Providence	RI	02835	R. Grass	401-774-9843
	H12456	Hasbro, Inc.	4516 Burton Pike	Providence	RI	02844	T. Bayers	401-837-2132

WORK_COMPLETED	Employee_No	Client_No	Date	Hours
	B122	F11555	070823	8
	A632	F11555	070823	8
	B122	F11555	070824	8
	A632	F11555	070824	8
	B122	F11555	070825	8
	A632	F11555	070825	8
	B122	H12456	070826	8
	A632	H12456	070826	8
	A356	F11555	070826	8
	B432	H12456	070826	8
	A491	H12456	070826	8
	B122	F11555	070827	8
	A632	H12456	070827	8
	A356	F11555	070827	8
	B432	H12456	070827	8
	A491	H12456	070827	8

3. Specify the data type for each attribute. Data type descriptions generally include some combination of alphanumeric (e.g., with letters and/or symbols) or numeric values. Alphanumeric types include CHAR (for fixed-length strings) and VAR-CHAR (for varying length alphanumeric strings). Numeric data types include INTEGER and FLOAT (which has a floating decimal point).

Controls

4. Specify constraints, when appropriate, on the attributes. Most notably, we need to make sure that the primary key values are not left empty (i.e., null); otherwise, there will be no key value by which to identify and pull the tuple's record from the database. We may want to require that other attributes be assigned some value rather than having the option of being null. In each of these cases, we can assign a value of NOT NULL as the constraint.

In Microsoft Access, you can create a relation (and state other SQL commands) by doing the following:

1. Open or create an Access database file.
2. In the Create tab, select the Query Design function. Close the Show Table window.
3. In the Design tab, select the Data Definition function.
4. Type the SQL command (for example, those shown in Figure 6.14) in the blank field where the cursor is blinking. When done, select the Run function to execute the command.

The previous conventions are applied in Figure 6.14 to generate the relations specified in our earlier defined schema in Figure 6.10 (pg. 201). Carefully study how the

FIGURE 6.14 SQL Commands for Creating Database Relations

```
CREATE TABLE EMPLOYEE           (Employee_No      Char(4)        NOT NULL,
                                 Soc_Sec_No       Char(11)       NOT NULL,
                                 Name             VarChar(25)    NOT NULL,
                                 Supervisor_No    Char(4),
                                 Billing_Rate     Float,
                                 Pay_Rate         Float;

CREATE TABLE TRAINING_COMPLETED (Employee_No      Char(11)       NOT NULL,
                                 Train_Date       Integer        NOT NULL,
                                 Hour             Integer,
                                 Train_Code       Integer);

CREATE TABLE RELEASE_TIME       (Employee_No      Char(11)       NOT NULL,
                                 Release_Date     Integer        NOT NULL,
                                 Hour             Integer,
                                 Vacation_Sick    Char(1));

CREATE TABLE CLIENT             (Client_No        Char(6)        NOT NULL,
                                 Name             VarChar(25),
                                 Street_Address   VarChar(30),
                                 City             VarChar(15),
                                 State            Char(2),
                                 ZIP_Code         Integer,
                                 Contact          VarChar(25)    NOT NULL,
                                 Phone_Number     VarChar(12));

CREATE TABLE WORK_COMPLETED     (Employee_No      Char(11)       NOT NULL,
                                 Client_No        Char(6)        NOT NULL,
                                 Work_Date        Integer        NOT NULL);

ALTER TABLE WORK_COMPLETED
ADD COLUMN                       Hours            Integer;
```

various conventions have been applied. For instance, note in the EMPLOYEE relation that we have assigned a fixed-length character value (11 characters) for the attribute Soc_Sec_No. This accommodates the use of the hyphens in the number. In many cases, a company might choose to omit the hyphens and even reflect the social security number as a numeric. Also, note that despite our longest employee name currently being 13 characters, we have allowed a variable length alphanumeric field of 25 characters to accommodate longer names that may be entered in the future.

At the bottom of Figure 6.14, note that we demonstrate a new command— ALTER. ALTER is SQL's way of recognizing that we may not always get the permanent design of a relation right the first time. In this way, additional attributes can be added to a relation in the future. In our case, we are adding an attribute column for hours worked.

Populating the Database

Our next concern is loading data into the structure we just created with the CREATE command. This is accomplished using the INSERT command to add new tuples to a relation. In the future, a user might want to DELETE or UPDATE the data stored within relations. Thus, data can be changed in the database in three ways (i.e., INSERT, DELETE, and UPDATE). We will review these commands in this section.

The INSERT command is used to add a single tuple to an existing relation. Hence, when you create a relational database using SQL, you must first use the CREATE command to generate the structure of the relation and then use the INSERT command to enter the current data into the structure. The INSERT command in its simplest form only requires the user to specify the SQL table and the values to be inserted for each attribute if a value is provided for every attribute. This simple form of the INSERT command is demonstrated in **Figure 6.15** (pg. 208) by the command to enter the first tuple into the EMPLOYEE table—that is, the values for Carl Elks. This form of the command also is demonstrated in Figure 6.15 for entering the first record of the remaining tables.

If values are not entered for all attributes of a given tuple, then the INSERT command must be specified more clearly. Namely, when the table is specified in the INSERT command, the attributes for which values are being provided must be specified. If you study Figure 6.15 again, you will notice that when we enter the fifth EMPLOYEE tuple, we specify the attributes to receive values because Elaine Kopp, as the top-level manager, has no supervisor specified—that is, Supervisor_No is NULL.

The DELETE command is, of course, the flip side of the INSERT command and is the method by which we delete a tuple from a relation. The DELETE command requires specification of the table name and inclusion of a WHERE condition, which is used to identify the unique tuple(s) for deletion. For instance, if the EMPLOYEE named Elaine Kopp decided to leave the firm, we could enter the following command to delete her from the EMPLOYEE table:

Controls

```
DELETE FROM     EMPLOYEE

WHERE           Employee_No = 'B122'
```

The last command of interest in this segment is UPDATE. The UPDATE command is used when we want to change one or more attribute values for one or more tuples in a table. To accomplish a change of an attribute value, the UPDATE command must be able to identify the table with the value to be updated, the new values to be placed in the database, and the conditions for identifying the correct tuple for UPDATE. To make the change, we identify the tuple using the WHERE condition we just used for deletion, and we change the existing values by using a SET command to set the new values for the database.

For example, let's assume that our firm has decided to give Elaine Kopp a raise so that she will stay as an employee. We need to place her new Pay_Rate of $7,500 in her record in the database. To accomplish this, we execute the following UPDATE command:

```
UPDATE          EMPLOYEE

SET             Pay_Rate=7500

WHERE           Employee_No ='B122'
```

Basic Querying Commands

Queries of the database are driven by SELECT commands that allow us to develop elaborate conditions for narrowing our data search to a very narrow view. In their simplest form, SELECT commands retrieve the values for a list of attributes from the tuples of a single relation. In their most complex form, SELECT commands allow us to join data across multiple tables to link specific pieces of information that are of

FIGURE 6.15 SQL Commands to Add Data to the Database

```
INSERT INTO     EMPLOYEE
VALUES          ('B432','305-45-9592','Carl Elks','A632',57,2500)

INSERT INTO     EMPLOYEE
VALUES          ('A491','350-97-9030','Janet Robins','A632',57,2500)

INSERT INTO     EMPLOYEE
VALUES          ('A632','125-87-8090','Greg Kinman','B122',100,4500)

INSERT INTO     EMPLOYEE
VALUES          ('B011','178-78-0406','Christy Bazie','A632',57,2600)

INSERT INTO     EMPLOYEE (Employee_No, Soc_Sec_No, Name, Billing_Rate, Pay_Rate
VALUES          ('B122','123-78-0907','Elaine Kopp',150,7000)

INSERT INTO     EMPLOYEE
VALUES          ('A356','127-92-3453','John Mast','A632',57,2600)

INSERT INTO     TRAINING_COMPLETED
VALUES          ('A356',990823,8,32)
        :              :      :    :
        :              :      :    :

INSERT INTO     RELEASE_TIME
VALUES          ('B011',990826,8,'V')
        :              :      :    :
        :              :      :    :

INSERT INTO     CLIENT
VALUES          ('A12345','Arnold,LLP','11 Nayatt Dr.','Barrington','RI',02806,
                'V. Arnold','401-792-8341')
        :              :      :    :
        :              :      :    :

INSERT INTO     WORK_COMPLETED
VALUES          ('B122','F11555',990823,8)
        :              :      :    :
        :              :      :    :
```

interest. In the following discussion, we outline the foundations from which such complex queries can be generated.

The SELECT statement consists of three parts: (1) a list of attributes that we want to SELECT from the database, (2) a list of tables where these attributes can be found, and (3) a WHERE clause that sets the conditions under which attribute values are to be retrieved. For instance, if we wanted to retrieve a list of all employees with a pay rate over $3,000, we would issue the following SELECT command:

```
SELECT        Name

FROM          EMPLOYEE

WHERE         Pay_Rate>3000
```

SQL would first locate the table named EMPLOYEE and then search all the tuples to identify any with a Pay_Rate greater than 3000. From the identified tuples, the SELECT attributes are extracted, and the values are returned to the screen. The following are the results of this query based on the values shown in Figure 6.13 (pg. 205):

```
Greg Kinman

Elaine Kopp
```

Often, a user will want to aggregate data from more than one table. If we go back to our original reasons for designing this database, one goal was to facilitate the billing process. To process client billing, we need a combination of data from the EMPLOYEE, WORK_COMPLETED, and CLIENT relations. From the EMPLOYEE relation, we need information on Billing_Rate for each record of WORK_COMPLETED. From the CLIENT relation, we need data for Name, Street_Address, City, State, ZIP_Code, and Contact to send the bill to the correct client. From the WORK_COMPLETED relation, we will match the previously noted information with the records of employees' completed work to provide line item detail on the date and hours of work completed. The SELECT command to aggregate the data for the billing for Hasbro, Inc., could be as follows:

```
SELECT       CLIENT.Name, Street_Address, City, State, ZIP_Code, Contact,
             Date, Hours, Billing_Rate

FROM         EMPLOYEE, CLIENT, WORK_COMPLETED

WHERE        EMPLOYEE.Employee_No=WORK_COMPLETED.Employee_No AND
             CLIENT.Client_No='H12456' AND WORK_COMPLETED.Client_No ='H12456'
```

Note the new conventions we have added in this query. First, in the SELECT attribute list, we used CLIENT.Name to identify the client name. The table name is attached to the front of the attribute name because the attribute Name is ambiguous—that is, SQL would not be able to tell if we wanted the Name attribute from the EMPLOYEE or the CLIENT relation. We did the same thing in the WHERE clause for Client_No. In fact, the rule is that any time we reference an attribute in a SELECT statement and the attribute name appears in more than one relation in the table list specified on the FROM list, we must use the table name extension as a prefix to the attribute name.

The other convention is the use of AND in the WHERE clause. We use connectors such as AND to link multiple conditions that must all be met when selecting tuples from one or more tables. The most common other connector is the OR connector, which allows for a tuple to be selected if either condition in the WHERE clause is true.

One final note on querying regards the output that comes from the previous query. As shown in **Figure 6.16** (pg. 210), this query would attach the client name and address

FIGURE 6.16 Generation of Client Billing Information (Single-Query Approach)

Name	Street_Address	City	State	ZIP_Code	Contact	Date	Hours	Billing_Rate
Hasbro, Inc.	4516 Burton Pike	Providence	RI	02844	T. Bayers	070826	8	150.00
Hasbro, Inc.	4516 Burton Pike	Providence	RI	02844	T. Bayers	070826	8	100.00
Hasbro, Inc.	4516 Burton Pike	Providence	RI	02844	T. Bayers	070826	8	57.00
Hasbro, Inc.	4516 Burton Pike	Providence	RI	02844	T. Bayers	070826	8	57.00
Hasbro, Inc.	4516 Burton Pike	Providence	RI	02844	T. Bayers	070827	8	100.00
Hasbro, Inc.	4516 Burton Pike	Providence	RI	02844	T. Bayers	070827	8	57.00
Hasbro, Inc.	4516 Burton Pike	Providence	RI	02844	T. Bayers	070827	8	57.00

to every line of output generated when a row of WORK_COMPLETED is identified. Hence, for the seven lines of completed work that are returned in the query, there is a repetitive return of the client name and address each time. In this case, where the name, address, and contact person will be the same for every query response, it makes more sense to split the query into two parts. First, we identify the client billing address information.

Then, in a second query, we pull out the multiple lines of billing information for completed work. This two-query approach and the related output are demonstrated in **Figure 6.17**.

FIGURE 6.17 Generation of Client Billing Information (Double-Query Approach)

```
SELECT      Name, Street_Address, City, State, ZIP_Code, Contact
FROM        CLIENT
WHERE       Client_No='H12456'
```

Output

Name	Street_Address	City	State	ZIP_Code	Contact
Hasbro, Inc.	4516 Burton Pike	Providence	RI	02844	T. Bayers

```
SELECT      Date, Hours, Billing_Rate
FROM        EMPLOYEE, WORK_COMPLETED
WHERE       EMPLOYEE.Employee_No=WORK_COMPLETED.Employee_No AND
            Client_No='H12456'
```

Output

Date	Hours	Billing_Rate
070826	8	150.00
070826	8	100.00
070826	8	57.00
070826	8	57.00
070827	8	100.00
070827	8	57.00
070827	8	57.00

Summary

The information needs and wants of users continue to escalate in the business world, as evidenced by the recent rise of business intelligence (BI) data analysis tools and modules. As a result of these demands, database integration has clearly become the norm rather than the exception. The focus is no longer on finding places in the business where implementing databases is useful. This is now a prerequisite for a company to compete and survive. Instead, the focus has shifted to finding ways to integrate as much of the organization's data as possible into a single logical database so that business decision makers can extract information to make the best decisions possible. This shift in focus offers new opportunities and challenges for accountants as they strive to continue as the primary information providers in organizations.

With these opportunities and challenges come huge responsibilities. The very lifeblood of an organization today often resides in a database that contains all the organization's information. If the database is destroyed and cannot be recovered, the organization might not survive in today's business environment. Likewise, if competitors or other unauthorized persons gain access to the data, the organization's capability to compete can be jeopardized.

Safeguarding data while providing information to users who need it is not a simple task. In Chapters 7, 8, and 9, our discussion will shift to the issues surrounding data reliability, access, and security. You will learn about procedures that organizations implement to ensure the reliability of information that is updated or added to the database. You will also learn about safeguarding the data and maintaining backups of data so that if something should happen to the database, it can be recovered in a timely manner to allow the organization to carry on its operations. These are truly challenging but exciting times for accountants who are prepared to operate in an information systems environment.

Key Terms

business intelligence, 189

model, 189

instance, 189

attribute, 190

composite attributes, 190

key attribute, 190

recursive relationship, 193

participation constraint, 195

null, 195

legacy systems, 197

relation, 198

tuple, 198

referential integrity, 198

foreign keys, 202

Review Questions

RQ 6-1   What is business intelligence (BI)?

RQ 6-2   What is an entity? Distinguish an *entity* and an *instance* of an entity.

RQ 6-3   What is an attribute?

RQ 6-4   What is a key attribute (e.g., a primary key)? What coding techniques can be used to create good primary key attributes?

RQ 6-5   What is a relationship?

RQ 6-6   What are the three steps in the strategy to effectively identify all the relationships that should be included in a model? What is the most common way to gather information about the relationships?

RQ 6-7   What are the characteristics of recursive relationships that distinguish them from other types of relationships?

RQ 6-8   Describe a situation in which one entity has minimum participation in its relationship with another entity.

RQ 6-9   How can an REA model help an organization improve the level of data integration it achieves across multiple business processes?

RQ 6-10 What is a relation? What is a tuple?

RQ 6-11 What is referential integrity? Give an example of how it may be implemented in a DBMS.

RQ 6-12 What is a composite primary key?

RQ 6-13 What is a foreign key?

RQ 6-14 What is the difference in implementation of a one-to-many and a one-to-one relationship in a relational database model?

RQ 6-15 What is SQL? In general terms, how can it be used?

RQ 6-16 What are the three ways to use SQL to change data in a database?

RQ 6-17 What are the three components of the SQL SELECT statement?

RQ 6-18 How do you create SQL commands in Microsoft Access?

Discussion Questions

DQ 6-1   What is the relationship between business intelligence (BI) and enterprise systems, especially ERP systems?

DQ 6-2   What is a model? How is modeling a database or information system useful and important from a business or accounting perspective?

DQ 6-3   Discuss how you determine the placement of primary keys in relational tables to link the tables to each other.

DQ 6-4   How can primary keys and the linking of tables in a relational database affect controls?

DQ 6-5   Several steps are required when designing a database. List and describe the *main* steps of this process.

DQ 6-6   Refer to Figure 6.12 (pg. 203). To implement a many-to-many (M:N) relationship between two relations, the figure demonstrates creating a new relation with a composite key made up of the primary keys (Client_No and Employee_No) of the relations to be linked. As an alternative, you might be tempted to simply add the fields Employee_No to the Client relation, and Client_No to the Employee relation. Discuss the reporting problems that might occur with that alternative strategy.

DQ 6-7   Although today's enterprise systems incorporate many of the REA concepts, many organizations continue to use legacy systems. Why do you believe this is true? (Although the obvious answer is in the chapter, you may want to look to other sources to support your answer.)

DQ 6-8   Although SQL is the de facto standard database language, there are many variations of the language. Using the Internet (or other sources), answer the following questions. What is a de facto standard? Provide examples (other than SQL) of such standards. How does SQL (the *primary* database language) being a *de facto* standard affect you, in your role as an information user?

Short Problems

SP 6-1   Develop an REA data model for ordering inventory. Consider this a single event. You will need to identify the associated resource(s) and agent(s).

SP 6-2   Develop the REA data model from Short Problem 6-1 into an E-R diagram with maximum cardinalities. Assume that each inventory item can be order multiple times.

Note: Short Problem 6-3 and Short Problem 6-4 should be completed with a database software package such as Access.

SP 6-3   Using SQL commands, create a vendor table and purchase order table, and populate them with data.   `ACCESS`

SP 6-4   Using the vendor and purchase order tables from Short Problem 6-3 and SQL commands, create a query to find out the date of each purchase order and the vendor by name each purchase order was sent to.   `ACCESS`

SP 6-5   Examine **Figure 6.18**, which contains the REA model for Winston Industrial Supply (WIS). The model is partially completed; it includes all entities and relationships, but it does not include cardinalities or descriptions of the relationships (which would appear in diamonds on the connecting lines between entities). WIS sells replacement parts for packaging machinery to companies in several states. WIS accepts orders via telephone, fax, and mail. When an

FIGURE 6.18   Partially Completed REA Model of the Winston Industrial Supply Sales Business

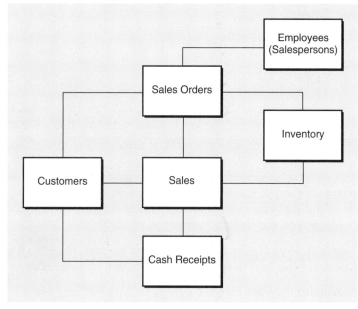

order arrives, one of the salespersons enters it as a sales order. The sales order includes the customer's name and a list of the inventory items that the customer wants to purchase. This inventory list includes the quantity of each inventory item and the price at which WIS is currently selling the item. When the order is ready to ship, WIS completes an invoice and records the sale. Sometimes, inventory items that a customer has ordered are not in stock. In those cases, WIS will ship partial orders. Customers are expected to pay their invoices within 30 days. Most customers do pay on time; however, some customers make partial payments over two or more months. List each entity in the REA model, and identify it as a resource, event, or agent. Redraw the REA model to include the diamonds for each relationship and include an appropriate description in each diamond.

SP 6-6 Examine the REA model for Winston Industrial Supply that appears in Figure 6.18 (pg. 213). Determine the maximum cardinalities for each of the eight relationships indicated in the model. State any assumptions you needed to make, and be prepared to defend the rationale for your selection.

SP 6-7 Examine the REA model for Winston Industrial Supply that appears in Figure 6.18. For each of the six entities in the model, list the attributes that a database designer should include in each table. Identify primary key attributes with (PK) and composite primary key attributes with (CPK). State any assumptions you needed to make, and be prepared to defend the rationale for the attributes you have chosen.

Problems

P 6-1 What SQL command(s) would you use to add the date on which an employee was hired to the EMPLOYEE table represented in Figure 6.13 (pg. 205)? Name this new attribute Employment_Date. Assume that the employees were hired on the following dates, using a year-month-day format as YYYYMMDD:

- Carl Elks 19990522
- Janet Robins 20010105
- Greg Kinman 19971125
- Christy Bazie 20020801
- Elaine Kopp 20060916
- John Mast 19951209

P 6-2 Human Resources department needs the work time, vacation time, and sick time for Janet Robins (see the EMPLOYEE table in Figure 6.13). What SQL command(s) would you use to extract this information from the tables in Figure 6.13?

Note: These problems should be completed with a database software package such as Access. For Problems 6-3 and 6-4, you may use data that you (or your instructor) have downloaded from an accounting database. Problem 6-5 demonstrates the interaction between an application software system and the database.

P 6-3 Using the information from Figure 6.12 (pg. 203) and Figure 6.13 create the database in the software package of your choice. This will require three steps:

- Implement the relations from Figure 6.13.
- Insert the data from Figure 6.13 into the relational tables.

- Print the data from each of the relations to test for successful implementation.

P 6-4   *Note:* This problem is a continuation of Problem 6-3 but requires access to the Internet, a site for posting the database on the Web, and an understanding of Internet access.

    a.   Take the database developed in Problem 6-3 and place it on the Internet (or your instructor may provide the same).

    b.   Access the database from your local computer using the appropriate address for the database. (Your software must be capable of using Internet addresses for locating the data.)

    c.   Use a series of queries similar to that in Figure 6.17 (pg. 210) to pull down the billing information for Fleet Services.

P 6-5   *Note:* This problem is a continuation of Problem 6-3 but requires use of a spreadsheet package that is capable of reading data from your database package (e.g., Excel can import data from an Access database).

    a.   Using your spreadsheet package, construct SQL queries (or use the software's menu generation for queries) to import the billing information for Fleet Services.

    b.   Develop a report format for using the information from your queries to generate a nice-looking report in your spreadsheet package.

    c.   Document the queries used in your spreadsheet package to access the data and explain what each step of the queries does.

P 6-6   Using the REA model in Figure 6.18 (pg. 213) and your answers to Discussion Questions 6-2, 6-3, and 6-4, create a database for WIS in the software package of your choice. This will require that you do the following:

    a.   Create tables for each of the relations you identified in Discussion Question 6-1 that include the attributes you identified in Review Question 6-3.

    b.   Insert a few tuples of sample data that you devise.

    c.   Print the data from each of the relations to test for successful implementation.

P 6-7   The following E-R diagram (**Figure 6.19**) represents students registering for classes for a single semester. Assume that the Registration "table" can hold a complete history of each individual student's registration events. For example, if James has registered for six semesters while attending the university, then the Registration table will contain six separate records (rows) for James.

    a.   Determine the maximum cardinalities for the E-R diagram.

    b.   Then provide primary keys for each table and show how the tables would be linked together in a relational database such as Microsoft Access.

FIGURE 6.19   E-R Diagram of Students Registering for Classes

Enterprise Risk Management

Controlling Information Systems: Introduction to Enterprise Risk Management and Internal Control

Learning Objectives

After reading this chapter, you should be able to:

- Summarize the eight elements of COSO's Enterprise Risk Management—Integrated Framework.
- Understand that management employs internal control systems as part of organizational and IT governance initiatives.
- Describe how internal control systems help organizations achieve objectives and respond to risks.
- Describe fraud, computer fraud, and computer abuse.
- Enumerate control goals for operations and information processes.
- Describe the major categories of control plans.

The 21st century started with a bang, followed by a whimper! We are now in midst of an economic recession—the "whimper"—probably second in magnitude only to the Great Depression of the 1930s. One of the key elements of this recession was the collapse of the financial services industry that was caused, in many cases, by failure to adequately assess the risks associated with various investment strategies. Also, several years before the beginning of the current recession, news of widespread business scandals and corruption—the "bang"—blazed across worldwide media at the speed of light. CPA firms, investors, lenders, managers, and innocent bystanders were deeply affected by the discovery, nature, and extent of corporate malfeasance and recession. The direct injuries sustained by corporate stakeholders were staggering, and the collateral damage inflicted on the public was frightening. Reports of corporate shenanigans and failed financial institutions dominated newspaper headlines. These included the Enron Corporation, Arthur Andersen, WorldCom, Adelphia Communications, Tyco International, Global Crossing, Quest Communications, Merrill Lynch, Bear Stearns, and Lehman Brothers. These business scandals and disasters have had a very significant impact on the accounting profession, as we shall discuss in this chapter. One can only wonder how the 2007 recession, which was also largely the result of questionable business practices and inadequate risk assessment, will affect accounting, auditing, and taxation.

In response to the notable business and audit failures uncovered in the early part of the twenty-first century, the U.S. Congress passed the Sarbanes-Oxley Act of 2002 (SOX) to mandate improved organizational governance. These improvements included auditor independence, composition and responsibilities of boards of directors and management, and enhanced financial disclosures. Of particular interest for our discussions in this chapter are the requirements related to internal control. SOX Section 404 required that management and auditors document, test, and report on the effectiveness of internal controls over financial reporting.

SOX

In complying with SOX, the vast majority of organizations discovered that they had simultaneously improved decision making, obtained process efficiencies, engendered greater public confidence in their financial reporting, and improved their overall value. For example, studies have shown that better organizational governance has led to higher credit ratings and lower interests rates, which increase profits. These value improvements were in addition to regulatory compliance required by SOX, and, hopefully, they reduce the chance of more frauds such as Enron. In this chapter, you will learn how organizational governance processes can improve organization performance and value while reducing fraud. You will see how COSO's *Enterprise Risk Management—Integrated Framework* can guide an organization's governance processes, including entity-wide risk assessment, which could have reduced the financial sector failures noted earlier. And, finally, you will learn how *internal control*—a key component of governance and risk management—helps organizations achieve objectives, respond to risks, prevent fraud, and provide a means to detect fraud.

Synopsis

Can an organization operate without good governance processes? Yes—but the chances of positive outcomes are much greater with governance processes that select objectives, establish processes to achieve the objectives, and monitor progress. Can these processes work toward achieving objectives without controls? Perhaps—but the odds are not very good! In this chapter, as well as in Chapters 8 and 9, we make the case that controlling business processes is a critically important element of organizational governance and enterprise risk management. Controls provide reasonable assurance that objectives are achieved and that responses to risks are carried out. These chapters should provide you with a solid foundation for the later study of the controls for specific business processes that are covered in Chapters 10 through 15.

Controls

We placed a Controls icon at the head of this synopsis to emphasize that the content of this chapter is almost entirely about controls. In this chapter, we consider the importance of controls in organizations that are tightly integrated internally, such as with *enterprise systems*, or have multiple connections to their environment, such as *e-business* architectures. Managers of these organizations must be confident that each component of the organization performs as expected; otherwise, chaos will prevail, and business partnerships will fail. In particular, organizations engaged in e-business must have internal control processes in place to reduce the possibilities of fraud and other disruptive events and to ensure compliance with applicable laws and regulations. For example, when engaged in Internet-based commerce, the organization may need to ensure the security of its own database, as well as the security of communication networks it operates in conjunction with trading partners; also, e-business firms might have to comply with relevant privacy-related laws and regulations. We begin by discussing organizational governance.

Enterprise
Systems

E-Business

FIGURE 7.1 Objective Setting

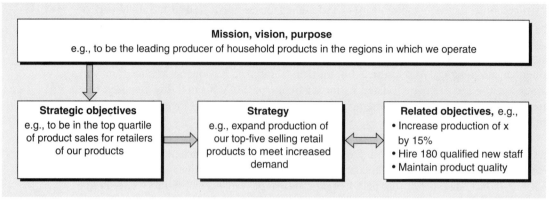

Source: Adapted from *Enterprise Risk Management—Integrated Framework, Application Techniques*, p. 20.

Organizational Governance

Organizational governance is a process by which organizations select objectives, establish processes to achieve objectives, and monitor performance. Objective setting includes defining mission, vision, purpose, and strategies to establish relationships such as those depicted in **Figure 7.1**. Processes to achieve the objectives (see "Related Objectives" in Figure 7.1), including essential internal controls and monitoring activities, are then designed and implemented. For example, production processes to produce product x—or increase its production—are put in place, as are processes to screen and hire new staff and to acquire the raw materials that will be necessary for production. Finally, internal control and monitoring activities are implemented—as separate functions or as part of these processes—to review performance and provide feedback to provide a reasonable assurance that objectives are being achieved. Has production increased by 15 percent? Did we hire 180 new staff, and are they qualified? Is product quality being maintained?

Doesn't this seem to make sense? If you were running an organization, wouldn't you want to have objectives and relationships such as those depicted in Figure 7.1? Wouldn't you want them clearly and explicitly defined so you know what to aim for? Wouldn't you want to establish processes, controls, and monitoring mechanisms to see that your organization's objectives were being accomplished? Well, yes, but good governance isn't as easy in practice as it might sound. A quick Internet search for definitions of governance should indicate the expansive nature of governance. For example, you might find descriptions that include "efficient management," "incentive mechanisms," "organization design, including the distribution of rights and responsibilities for managers, boards, and other stakeholders," "rules and procedures for making decisions," "fairness, transparency, and accountability," and "return on investment/value creation." And so we need guidance to implement an effective governance process. In the next section, we describe *Enterprise Risk Management*, a framework that has proven to be an effective process for organizational governance.

Enterprise Risk Management (ERM)

"**Enterprise Risk Management (ERM)** is a process, effected by an entity's board of directors, management, and other personnel, applied in strategy settings and across the enterprise, designed to identify potential events that may affect the entity, and manage risk to be within its risk appetite, to provide reasonable assurance regarding the achievement of entity objectives."[1] The framework from which this definition is quoted[2] was developed to help management identify, assess, and manage risk. The ERM framework addresses four categories of management objectives:

- *Strategic:* High-level goals aligned with and supporting its mission.
- *Operations:* Effective and efficient use of its resources.
- *Reporting:* Reliability of reporting.
- *Compliance:* Compliance with applicable laws and regulations.[3]

The eight components that comprise the ERM framework are described in **Exhibit 7.1**. The ERM process, and indeed the organizational governance process, begins with the first ERM component, *internal environment*, within which decisions are made about how an organization is to think about integrity, ethical values, risk (i.e., risk philosophy), how much risk they will be willing to accept (i.e., risk appetite),

EXHIBIT 7.1 Components of Enterprise Risk Management

- *Internal environment:* The internal environment encompasses the tone of an organization and sets the basis for how risk is viewed and addressed by an entity's people, including risk management philosophy and risk appetite, integrity and ethical values, and the environment in which they operate.
- *Objective setting:* Objectives must exist before management can identify potential events affecting their achievement. ERM ensures that management has a process in place to set objectives and that the chosen objectives support and align with the entity's mission and are consistent with its risk appetite.
- *Event identification:* Internal and external events affecting achievement of an entity's objectives must be identified, distinguishing between risks and opportunities. Opportunities are channeled back to management's strategy or objective-setting processes.
- *Risk assessment:* Risks are analyzed, considering likelihood and impact, as a basis for determining how they should be managed. Risks are assessed on an inherent and a residual basis.
- *Risk response:* Management selects risk responses—avoiding, accepting, reducing, or sharing risk—developing a set of actions to align risks with the entity's risk tolerances and risk appetite.
- *Control activities:* Policies and procedures are established and implemented to help ensure the risk responses are effectively carried out.
- *Information and communication:* Relevant information is identified, captured, and communicated in a form and timeframe that enable people to carry out their responsibilities. Effective communication also occurs in a broader sense, flowing down, across, and up the entity.
- *Monitoring:* The entirety of ERM is monitored, and modifications are made as necessary. Monitoring is accomplished through ongoing management activities, separate evaluations, or both.

Source: *Enterprise Risk Management—Integrated Framework, Executive Summary* (New York: Committee of Sponsoring Organizations of the Treadway Commission, 2004): 5–6.

---

[1]*Enterprise Risk Management—Integrated Framework, Executive Summary* (New York: Committee of Sponsoring Organizations of the Treadway Commission, 2004): 4.

[2]The framework was issued by the Committee of Sponsoring Organizations of the Treadway Commission (COSO). COSO was originally formed in 1985 to sponsor the National Commission on Fraudulent Financial Reporting, which studied the causal factors that can lead to fraudulent financial reporting. Five organizations comprise COSO: American Institute of CPAs (AICPA), American Accounting Association (AAA), Institute of Internal Auditors (IIA), Institute of Management Accountants (IMA), and Financial Executives Institute (FEI).

[3]*Enterprise Risk Management—Integrated Framework, Executive Summary* (New York: Committee of Sponsoring Organizations of the Treadway Commission, 2004): 5.

mechanisms for oversight by the board of directors, organization design, and assignment of authority and responsibility. Reports suggest that this is the area in which managements at Enron, WorldCom, Adelphia, and others got started on the wrong foot.

After establishing its internal environment, an organization then moves on to *objective setting* (second ERM component) to define the relationships such as those depicted in Figure 7.1 (pg. 220). *Strategic* objectives are established as well as related objectives for *operations*, *reporting*, and *compliance*. Risk appetite guides strategy setting to balance, for example, growth, risk, and return. Risk appetite drives risk tolerances—acceptable levels of variation in achieving objectives. For example, the tolerance for the hiring objective in Figure 7.1 might be that we hire between 165 and 200 qualified new staff.

After an organization has its strategy and objectives in place, it must engage in *event identification* (third ERM component) to identify risks and opportunities that would affect achievement of its objectives. **Risks** are those events that would have a negative impact on organization objectives, and *opportunities* are events that would have a positive impact on objectives. Risks require assessment and response, whereas opportunities are channeled back to the strategy-setting process. For example, a new market opportunity might have opened up that management could decide to pursue.

After risks are identified, the organization must perform *risk assessment* (the fourth ERM component) to determine the effect that risks may have on achievement of objectives. There are two factors to be considered: likelihood and impact. *Likelihood* is the possibility that an event will occur, and *impact* is the effect of an event's occurrence. For example, there might be a 75 percent chance that an event will occur, whereas the impact of the occurrence might be a loss of $50,000. Inherent risk exists in the absence of any actions that management might take to reduce likelihood or impact. The financial services industry firms that failed in 2008 either did not identify the investment risks they were facing or did not adequately respond to those risks.

In *risk response* (the fifth ERM component), management selects from one of four response types. We can *avoid* a risk by leaving the activity that is giving rise to the risk. For example, if selling in a particular market poses unacceptable risk, we might get out of that market. We can *reduce* a risk by taking actions that reduce the likelihood of an event (e.g., institute fire-prevention programs) or reduce the impact (e.g., install sprinklers). We can *share* a risk by, for example, buying insurance or outsourcing the activity. Finally, we can *accept* a risk by taking no action (i.e., there is no cost-beneficial response). Residual risk is the risk that remains after one of these responses is chosen. **Exhibit 7.2** describes, with a little more detail, an approach to calculating *residual risk* that takes into account the probability that a risk will occur, the amount of any loss that would result, and the cost of the control response. **Exhibit 7.3** on page 224 depicts the elements of a risk assessment and risk response process for a financial reporting objective, an example of a related objective (Figure 7.1).

Control activities, the sixth ERM component, are policies and procedures that help ensure that risk responses are carried out. In some cases, the control is itself the risk response. Control activities, or simply controls or internal controls, will be described later in this chapter and in Chapters 8 through 15. These controls include approvals, authorizations, verifications, reconciliations, reviews of operating performance, security procedures (e.g., access restrictions), supervision, audit trails, and segregation of duties. The risk responses in Exhibit 7.3 are controls that seek to reduce the related risks.

The *information and communication* component (the seventh ERM component) argues that pertinent information must be identified, captured, and communicated in a form and time frame that enable people to carry out their responsibilities. Effective communication requires that appropriate, timely, and quality information from internal and external sources flows down, up, and across the entity to facilitate risk management and intelligent decision making. Personnel must understand their role in enterprise management and how individual activities relate to the work of others. For example, the *systems flowcharts* introduced in Chapter 4 are an extremely effective means for depicting the actions and *control activities* related to each entity (e.g., person, department, computer) in a business process. With this information, personnel can appreciate their role in responding to risks and helping the organization achieve its objectives.

Monitoring is the eighth and final component of ERM, but it should not be considered a final activity. The ERM *process* and its components are evaluated—via ongoing management activities, separate evaluations, or both—to determine its effectiveness and to make necessary modifications. For example, business processes put in place to accomplish objectives are reviewed to determine their effectiveness (e.g., has the output of the production process increased by 15 percent as indicated in Figure 7.1, pg. 220)? Controls implemented to respond to risks must be reviewed to determine that the activities have been performed and to determine whether additional actions must be taken to respond

---

EXHIBIT 7.2   Risk Assessment and Residual Risk

A dilemma exists regarding the costs and benefits of risk responses. An organization strives to have enough control to ensure that its objectives are achieved. At the same time, the organization does not want to pay more for the controls than can be derived from their implementation. For example, suppose an organization installs a sophisticated fire-prevention and fire-detection system. This control should reduce the possibility of a fire that could destroy an organization's physical assets. If the fire-prevention system costs more than the assets being protected, however, the system obviously is not worthwhile from a financial perspective.

Many risk assessment models are used to determine whether a control should be implemented. As a practical matter, it is difficult to determine the amount to spend on a particular control or set of controls because an organization cannot afford to *prevent* all losses. One method that *can* be used is conceptually simple:

1. Estimate the annual dollar loss that would occur (i.e., the impact) should a costly event, say a destructive fire, take place. For example, say that the estimated loss is –$1,000,000.
2. Estimate the annual probability that the event will occur (i.e., the likelihood). Suppose the estimate is 5 percent.
3. Multiply item 1 by item 2 to get an initial *expected gross risk* (loss) of –$50,000 (–$1,000,000 × 0.05), which is the maximum amount or upper limit that should be paid for controls, and the related risk reduction offered by such controls, in a given year. Next, we illustrate a recommendation plan using one *corrective* control, a fire insurance policy, and one *preventive* control, a sprinkler system.

4. Assume that the company would pay $1,000 annually (*cost of control*) for a $20,000 fire insurance policy (*reduced risk exposure due to control*). The estimated monetary damage remains at $1 million and *expected* gross risk (loss) remains at –$50,000 because there is still a 5 percent chance that a fire could occur. But the company's *residual expected risk* exposure is now –$31,000 [–$50,000 + ($20,000 – $1,000)]. Our *expected* loss is reduced by the amount of the insurance policy (less the cost of the policy).
5. Next, you recommend that the company install a sprinkler system with a five-year annualized cost (net present value) of $10,000 each year to install and maintain (*cost of control*). At this point, you might be tempted to say that the company's *residual expected risk* just increased to –$41,000 (–$31,000 – $10,000), but wait! The sprinkler system lowered the likelihood of a damaging fire from 5 to 2 percent. In conjunction with this lower probability, the insurance company agreed to increase its coverage to $30,000 while holding the annual premium constant at $1,000.
6. Thus, the *residual expected risk* exposure is –$1,000, calculated as follows: Expected gross risk (–$20,000, or –$1,000,000 × 0.02) plus the insurance policy ($30,000) equals a gain of $10,000, but we must subtract the insurance premium ($1,000) and the sprinkler system ($10,000), leaving the residual expected risk at –$1,000.

Hence, *residual expected risk* is a function of *initial expected gross risk*, *reduced risk exposure due to controls*, and *cost of controls*. After all this, however, a large dose of management judgment is required to determine a *reasonable* level of control.

to the risk (e.g., has someone followed up on open POs as indicated in Exhibit 7.3, and is the residual risk as expected?). As a final example, the *event identification* process must be monitored to determine that evolving events have been identified and evaluated. As an organization and its environment change, controls often become less effective.

In conclusion, let's summarize ERM and revisit our initial proposition, that ERM is a process for *organizational governance*. ERM is a process, or framework, by which organizations create value for their stakeholders by establishing objectives and identifying and managing risks that might result in failure to achieve objectives. ERM is, therefore, a process for organizational governance. Now we move on to a discussion of SOX, the law the U.S. Congress responded with in reaction to the governance failures that manifested themselves at the start of the 21st century.

The Sarbanes-Oxley Act of 2002

SOX   As a result of Enron, WorldCom, Tyco, and the other business scandals noted in the introduction to this chapter, the federal government was forced to interject its will into organizational governance. Why? Because these business entities failed to enact and enforce proper governance processes throughout their organizations, and as a result, some employees boldly violated ethical codes, business rules, regulatory requirements, and statutory mandates, resulting in massive frauds. Investors and lenders lost huge sums of money, and public trust in corporate managers, public accounting firms, and

EXHIBIT 7.3 Objectives, Risks, and Responses

Reporting Objective	Asset acquisitions and expenses entered for processing are valid, all entered (complete), and entered accurately.				
Target	Errors in monthly statements are less than $100,000.				
Tolerance	Errors less than $110,000.				
Risks	**Inherent risk assessment**		**Risk response (examples)**	**Residual risk assessment**	
	Likelihood	Impact		Likelihood	Impact
Vendors are paid from statements as well as invoices, resulting in duplicate payments (validity).	Possible	Minor $5,000–$15,000	Compare vendor name and number with those on file to detect duplicate invoices.	Unlikely	Minor $5,000–$7,500
Vendor invoices are not received prior to monthly cutoff (completeness).	Almost certain	Moderate $10,000–$25,000	Produce listings of unmatched POs (no invoice) and follow up.	Possible	Minor $2,500–$7,500
Vendor invoice amounts are captured incorrectly (accuracy).	Possible	Minor $5,000–$15,000	Programmed edit checks, including tests for blank fields and for reasonable quantities and amounts.	Unlikely	Minor $2,500–$7,500

Source: Adapted from *Enterprise Risk Management—Integrated Framework, Application Techniques* (New York: Committee of Sponsoring Organizations of the Treadway Commission, 2004): 64.

federal regulators had been severely, perhaps irreparably, harmed. The federal government's duty is to protect its citizens from such abuses; accordingly, one of the measures taken by Congress was to pass the Sarbanes-Oxley Act of 2002 (SOX), bringing about some of the most significant changes to federal securities laws since the Securities Act of 1933 and the Securities Exchange Act of 1934.

This section is aimed at placing SOX into the context of organizational governance. We highlight SOX here—you will undoubtedly hear more about it in your financial accounting and auditing classes—because of the critical role that SOX has had in changing the way we design, implement, and evaluate systems of internal control. Also, as noted previously, internal control is an essential element in managing the *risks* that may prevent achieving organizational objectives. The basic elements of SOX are outlined in **Exhibit 7.4** (pg. 226).

The key provisions of SOX are that SOX created a new accounting oversight board (the PCAOB), strengthened auditor independence rules, increased accountability of company officers and directors, mandated upper management to take responsibility for the company's internal control structure, enhanced the quality of financial reporting, and put teeth into white-collar crime penalties. Of particular note to students of AIS, Section 201 of the act prohibits audit firms from providing a wide array of nonaudit services to audit clients; in particular, the act prohibits consulting engagements involving the design and implementation of financial information systems. Does this suggest that CPA firms will no longer offer systems-related consulting engagements? No—it means that CPA firm A cannot offer such services to audit client X, but CPA firm B can provide these services to client X. Thus, in all likelihood, nonaudit engagements of this nature will swap around among CPA firms—not disappear altogether.

Section 404, which mandates the annual filing of an internal control report to the SEC, is also of particular interest to you as AIS students as we introduce the concept of internal control. It is Section 404 that has received the most press as companies and their auditors have struggled to comply with its requirements. Section 404, the SEC's Interpretive Guidance,[4] and PCAOB Auditing Standard No. 5 (AS5)[5] require that the management of each audited (i.e., publicly traded) company:

* Evaluate the design of the company's controls to determine whether they adequately address the risk that a material misstatement of the financial statements would not be prevented or detected in a timely manner.
* Gather and evaluate evidence about the operation of its controls. The nature and extent of this evidence is to be aligned with its assessment of the risk associated with those controls.
* Present a written assessment of the effectiveness of internal control over financial reporting.
* Subsequently, as part of the annual audit, each company's independent auditor must test and report on the effectiveness of the company's system of internal controls.

To identify the key controls over financial reporting, management and the independent auditor may document relevant processes. This documentation should help in understanding the flow of transactions from initiation through recording and reporting and the related control activities. To do so, they may use a variety of tools, including the narratives and *systems flowcharts* described in Chapter 4 of this book. To assess the

---

[4]SEC Release No. 33-8810, June 27, 2007.

[5]"Auditing Standard No. 5—An Audit of Internal Control Over Financial Reporting That Is Integrated with an Audit of Financial Statements," PCAOB, July 12, 2007.

EXHIBIT 7.4 Outline of the Sarbanes-Oxley Act of 2002

The Sarbanes-Oxley Act of 2002 (SOX) affects corporate managers, independent auditors, and other players who are integral to capital formation in the United States. This omnibus regulation will forever alter the face of corporate reporting and auditing. SOX titles and key sections are outlined here:

- *Title I—Public Company Accounting Oversight Board:* Section 101 establishes the Public Company Accounting Oversight Board (PCAOB), an independent board to oversee public company audits. Section 107 assigns oversight and enforcement authority over the board to the Securities and Exchange Commission (SEC).
- *Title II—Auditor Independence:* Section 201 prohibits a CPA firm that audits a public company from engaging in certain non-audit services with the same client. Most relevant to AIS is the prohibition of providing financial information systems design and implementation services to audit clients. Section 203 requires audit partner rotation in their fifth, sixth, or seventh year, depending on the partner's role in the audit. Section 206 states that a company's chief executive officer (CEO), chief financial officer (CFO), controller, or chief accountant cannot have been employed by the company's audit firm and participated in an audit of that company during the prior one-year period.
- *Title III—Corporate Responsibility:* Section 302 requires a company's CEO and CFO to certify quarterly and annual reports. They are certifying that they reviewed the reports; the reports are not materially untruthful or misleading; the financial statements fairly reflect in all material respects the financial position of the company; and they are responsible for establishing, maintaining, and reporting on the effectiveness of internal controls, including significant deficiencies, frauds, or changes in internal controls.
- *Title IV—Enhanced Financial Disclosures:* Section 404 requires each annual report filed with the SEC to include an internal control report. The report shall state the responsibility of management for establishing and maintaining an adequate internal control structure and procedures for financial reporting. The report must also contain management's assessment, as of the end of the company's fiscal year, of the effectiveness of the internal control structure and procedures of the company for financial reporting.[a] Section 406 requires that companies disclose whether or not they have adopted a code of ethics for senior financial officers. Section 407 requires that companies disclose whether or not their audit committee

contains at least one member who is a financial expert. Section 409 requires that companies disclose information on material changes in their financial condition or operations on a rapid and current basis.

- *Title V—Analysts' Conflicts of Interests:* Requires financial analysts to properly disclose in research reports any conflicts of interest they might hold with the companies they recommend.
- *Title VI—Commission Resources and Authority:* Section 602 authorizes the SEC to censure or deny any person the privilege of appearing or practicing before the SEC if that person is deemed to be unqualified, have acted in an unethical manner, or have aided and abetted in the violation of federal securities laws.
- *Title VII—Studies and Reports:* Authorizes the Government Accountability Office (GAO) to study the consolidation of public accounting firms since 1989 and offer solutions to any recognized problems.
- *Title VIII—Corporate and Criminal Fraud Accountability:* Section 802 makes it a felony to *knowingly* destroy, alter, or create records or documents with the intent to impede, obstruct, or influence an ongoing or contemplated federal investigation. Section 806 offers legal protection to whistleblowers who provide evidence of fraud. Section 807 provides criminal penalties of fines and up to 25 years imprisonment for those who knowingly execute, or attempt to execute, securities fraud.
- *Title IX—White-Collar Crime Penalty Enhancements:* Section 906 requires that CEOs and CFOs certify that information contained in periodic reports fairly presents, in all material respects, the financial condition and results of the company's operations. The section sets forth criminal penalties applicable to CEOs and CFOs of up to $5 million and up to 20 years in prison if they knowingly or willfully falsely so certify.
- *Title X—Corporate Tax Returns:* Section 1001 conveys a "sense of the Senate" that the corporate federal income tax returns are signed by the CEO.
- *Title XI—Corporate Fraud and Accountability:* Section 1102 provides for fines and imprisonment of up to 20 years for individuals who corruptly alter, destroy, mutilate, or conceal documents with the intent to impair the document's integrity or availability for use in an official proceeding, or to otherwise obstruct, influence, or impede any official proceeding. Section 1105 authorizes the SEC to prohibit anyone from serving as an officer or director if the person has committed securities fraud.

[a]Until the issuance of Auditing Standard No. 5 ("An Audit of Internal Control Over Financial Reporting That Is Integrated with an Audit of Financial Statements," PCAOB, July 12, 2007), Section 404 required that the company's independent auditors attest to and report on the assessments made by company management regarding the internal control structure and the company's procedures for financial reporting.

Source: 107 P.L. 204, § 1, 116 Stat. 745, July 30, 2002.

effectiveness of the internal controls system design and to identify the key controls to be tested to determine the operating effectiveness of the system of internal controls, companies and their auditors often use matrices such as those introduced later in this chapter and demonstrated in Chapters 9 through 15. These matrices match controls to the objectives that they purport to achieve.

Business process management (BPM) (Technology Summary 2.3, pg. 41) often facilitates the implementation and assessment of a system of internal controls. With BPM, manual processes are automated, and all such processes perform consistently. The BPM engine handles the connections between processes to maintain the integrity of data moved among these processes. Management control policies are defined in the database of business rules, and these rules are executed consistently, which leaves an audit trail of activities to demonstrate that the controls were performed. This latter feature helps both management and auditors in their assessment of the operating effectiveness of the system of internal controls and provides evidence of compliance with rules and regulations.

How has the implementation of SOX Section 404 affected the performance of organizations and their systems of internal controls? The answer depends on who you talk to and their frame of reference. One study reports that first-year SOX Section 404 costs averaged $1.5 million for smaller companies (market capitalization between $75 million and $700 million) and $7.3 million for larger companies.[6] Another asserts that the total costs for SOX in 2006 will exceed $6 billion.[7] Concerns have also been raised that, in order to avoid the costs of complying with the various SOX requirements, many small U.S. companies have gone private and numerous foreign firms have removed their stocks from American exchanges. Additionally, the average "listing premium" (the benefit a company receives by listing its stocks on American exchanges) dropped by 19 percent between the passing of SOX (2002) and the beginning of the current recession (2007).[8]

On the other side of the issue, we see reports that companies have used information obtained during their SOX 404 compliance activities to improve processes, reduce risks, and build better businesses. Indeed, compliance efforts have revealed weaknesses in controls and business processes, and organizations have taken these findings and corrected problems, optimized their system of internal control, and improved processes. Investors have observed and acted on SOX 404 reports. For example, one report showed that the average share price gain of companies that had corrected internal control problems—from 2004 to 2005—exceeded overall market gains and trailed only slightly the average gain of companies that had no reported problems in 2004 or 2005.[9] Finally, with the issuance of the SEC Interpretative Guidance and the implementation of AS5, we should see significantly reduced company costs, including audit fees, because auditors no longer opine on the effectiveness of management's internal controls reporting process, and because both management and auditors are to assess internal controls with a more risk-based approach, thus reducing the number of controls that need to be documented, evaluated, and tested.

---

[6]"Sarbanes-Oxley Section 404 Cost and Implementation Issues: Survey Update," Washington, DC: CRA International, December 8, 2005.

[7]Kevin Reilly, "AMR Research Estimates Sarbanes-Oxley Spending Will Exceed $6 Billion in 2006," AMR Research, November 29, 2005.

[8]William A. Niskanen, "Enron's Last Victim: American Markets," *New York Times*, January 3, 2007.

[9]David Reilly, "Checks on Internal Controls Pays Off," *Wall Street Journal*, May 8, 2006: C3.b n.

Defining Internal Control

In the preceding sections, we discussed internal control from several points of view. For organizational governance, internal controls (or control activities, or simply controls) are implemented to help ensure that risk responses are effectively carried out, or the controls themselves are the responses to risks. Also, as we have just discussed, internal control is the subject of SOX Section 404. But what do we mean by *internal control*? Up to now we have only alluded to this term's meaning. In the next two sections, we describe definitions of internal control found in the authoritative literature and then offer our own working definition.

The COSO Definition of Internal Control

Earlier in this chapter, we introduced *Enterprise Risk Management—Integrated Framework* and the organization that issued that framework, the Committee of Sponsoring Organizations of the Treadway Commission (COSO). In 1992, the COSO organization introduced a framework, *Internal Control—Integrated Framework*, which itself became known as "COSO." The definition of internal control contained in COSO has become widely accepted and is the basis for definitions of control adopted for other international control frameworks:[10]

> Internal control is a process—effected by an entity's board of directors, management, and other personnel—designed to provide reasonable assurance regarding the achievement of objectives in the following categories:
>
> * Effectiveness and efficiency of operations
> * Reliability of financial reporting
> * Compliance with applicable laws and regulations[11]

Figure 7.2 depicts the influence that this definition has had on authoritative auditing and control literature. In 1995, Statement on Auditing Standards No. 78 (SAS No. 78), "Consideration of Internal Control in a Financial Statement Audit: An Amendment of Statement on Auditing Standards No. 55," adopted the COSO definition of internal control.

SOX

COSO describes five interrelated components of internal control:[12]

* *Control environment:* Sets the tone of an organization, influencing the control consciousness of its people. It is the foundation for all other components of internal control, providing discipline and structure. (AS5, paragraph 25 emphasizes the importance of the control environment to effective internal control over financial reporting.)
* *Risk assessment:* The entity's identification and analysis of relevant risks to the achievement of its objectives, forming a basis for determining how the risks should be managed. (Risk assessment is the core of effective compliance with SOX Section 404.)

---

[10]The influence of the COSO definition of internal control is apparent in the definitions adopted by the following: (a) the *Turnbull Report* published as *Internal Control: Revised Guidance for Directors on the Combined Code* (London: Financial Reporting Council, October, 2005); (b) *Guidance on Assessing Control* (Toronto, Ontario: Canadian Institute of Chartered Accountants, 1999); (c) *COBIT 4.1: Control Objectives for Information and Related Technology* (Rolling Meadows, IL: IT Governance Institute, 2007); and (d) *King II Report on Corporate Governance for South Africa 2002* (Johannesburg: Institute of Directors in South Africa, 2002).

[11]*Internal Control—Integrated Framework—Framework Volume* (New York: Committee of Sponsoring Organizations of the Treadway Commission 1992): 1.

[12]*Internal Control—Integrated Framework—Framework Volume* (New York: Committee of Sponsoring Organizations of the Treadway Commission, 1992): 2–3.

FIGURE 7.2   COSO Influence on Defining Internal Control

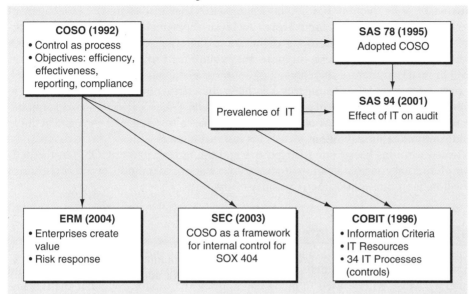

- *Control activities:* The policies and procedures that help ensure that management directives are carried out. (Chapters 8 and 9 introduce two categories of controls activities—pervasive and general controls in Chapter 8 and business process/application controls in Chapter 9. The controls are applied to the business processes in Chapters 10–15.)
- *Information and communication:* The identification, capture, and exchange of information in a form and time frame that enables people to carry out their responsibilities. (For business processes, this communication often takes the form of process narratives, systems flowcharts, written policies and procedures, etc.)
- *Monitoring:* A process that assesses the quality of internal control performance over time. (This is a key element in the long-term success of a system of internal control. It includes but is not limited to organizational governance, management's compliance with SOX Section 404, the activities of internal and external auditors, and certain control activities.)

As the influence of IT over information systems, financial reporting, and auditing became clearer, the IT auditing and auditing communities responded. In 1996, the Information Systems Audit and Control Association (ISACA) issued COBIT (Control Objectives for Information and Related Technology), with a definition of internal control that closely paralleled COSO.[13] COBIT's 34 IT processes form the basis of our discussion of pervasive and general controls in Chapter 8. In 2001, the Auditing Standards Board issued Statement on Auditing Standards No. 94 (SAS No. 94), "The Effect of Information Technology on the Auditor's Consideration of Internal Control in a Financial Statement Audit." SAS No. 94 provided guidance on how an organization's IT might affect any of COSO's five components of internal control. This standard guides auditors in understanding the impact of IT on internal control and assessing IT-related control risks.

---

[13]COBIT version 4.1 was released in 2007 by an ISACA sister organization, the IT Governance Institute.

SOX

On June 27, 2007, the SEC issued revised guidance related to management's implementation of SOX Section 404.[14] The ruling states that management's assessment of the effectiveness of internal control over financial reporting must be made in accordance with a suitable framework's definition of internal control, such as COSO. PCAOB Auditing Standard No. 5 repeats the requirement to use a framework such as COSO in its description of the conduct of an integrated audit under SOX 404. Finally, you may have noticed the similarity of the eight components of ERM outlined in Exhibit 7.1 (pg. 221) and the five components of COSO. The ERM framework emphasizes the compatibility of ERM and COSO and suggests that organizations and auditors should continue to use COSO as a basis for internal control.

Armed with this background perspective and the importance of COSO in the definition of internal control, let's now proceed to a working definition of internal control that will be used throughout the remainder of the text.

Working Definition of Internal Control

Given the prominence of COSO in developing these ideas and in defining internal control, we offer the following definition of control (as also defined in the Preface and Chapter 1), which will be used to guide our study of the topic throughout the remainder of the book:

> **Internal control** is a process—effected by an entity's board of directors, management, and other personnel—designed to provide reasonable assurance regarding the achievement of objectives in the following categories:
>
> - Effectiveness and efficiency of operations
> - Reliability of reporting
> - Compliance with applicable laws and regulations

SOX

The common ground on which we have developed our working definition of internal control includes the following points of general agreement:

- Consult the definition of ERM (pp. 220–221) and COSO's definition of internal control and notice that both refer to internal control as a process for accomplishing objectives. In general, a **process** is a series of actions or operations leading to a particular and usually desirable result. Results could be risk management as described by ERM, effective internal control as proposed by COSO, or a specified output of an operations process for a particular market or customer.
- As noted in Title IV of SOX (Exhibit 7.4, pg. 226), establishing and maintaining a viable internal control system is *management's* responsibility. In fact, ultimate ownership of the system should rest with the CEO. Only if the primary responsibility for the system resides at the top can control effectively permeate the entire organization.
- The strength of any internal control system is largely a function of the people who operate it. In other words, no matter how sound the control *processes* may be, they will fail unless the personnel who apply them are competent and honest. Because internal control is so people-dependent, we explore the ethical dimensions of control more fully later in the chapter. Ethics must be a central concern when designing an effective internal control system.

---

[14]SEC Release No. 33-8810, June 27, 2007.

- Partly because it depends on people to operate it and partly because it comes only at some cost to the organization, internal control cannot be expected to provide *absolute*, 100 percent assurance that the organization will reach its objectives. Rather, the operative phrase is that it should provide *reasonable assurance* to that effect.

Let's summarize some of what you have learned so far. Organizational governance, as implemented with a framework such as ERM, begins with establishing mission, vision, and purpose; then, strategy and objectives directed at the mission are established (Figure 7.1, pg. 220). Next, events that could affect achieving objectives, including opportunities and risks, are identified. After assessing risks and deciding how to respond to the risks, controls are put in place to ensure that responses to the risks are carried out. COSO and our own definition of internal control jump in at this point by describing internal control as a process for achieving objectives. We conclude then by saying that the purpose of internal control is to provide reasonable assurance that objectives are achieved and that risk responses are carried out.

How do we determine whether a system of internal control is designed well and can help an organization achieve objectives and respond to risks? Typically, a key tool in the assessment of a system of internal control is a *matrix* such as that depicted in **Figure 7.3**.

Figure 1.7 in Chapter 1 (pg. 23) depicted a similar matrix for assessing achievement of qualities of information such as timeliness (i.e., effectiveness), validity, accuracy, and completeness (i.e., reliability of reporting). The concept here is the same and will be repeated several times in this book. Figure 7.3 shows that we have established five high-level categories of objectives, and we have listed a sample of the processes/controls that address these objectives (from the definition of ERM). The check marks show which processes address which objectives. You can see, for example, that processes 2 and 3 are directed at effectiveness of operations. If you go back to the example in Figure 7.1 this objective—which if accomplished would lead to effective operations—might be to increase production of product x by 15 percent.

If we want to assess the *design* of the system of internal control, we use this matrix to simply ask the question, "Can these processes/controls provide reasonable assurance that the objectives are achieved?" An organization should have at least one process for each objective. Otherwise, the organization *may* achieve its objectives, but the odds are

FIGURE 7.3 Matrix for Evaluating Internal Controls

Processes (with controls)	Objectives				
	Strategy setting	Effectiveness of operations	Efficiency of operations	Reliability of reporting	Compliance with laws and regulations
Process 1	✓			✓	
Process 2		✓			✓
Process 3		✓	✓	✓	
Process n	✓				✓

not very good. In this example, we would ask if these processes and controls can provide reasonable assurance that production can be increased by 15 percent.

The assessment concludes with recommendations for changes to the processes and controls that might be necessary. Such recommendations must be made very carefully because there are many cost-benefit factors to consider. Changes can include changes to process activities (i.e., purchasing raw materials) or changes to process controls (i.e., approving purchase orders). If changes in the process do not reduce the variance from objectives, changes to process objectives (e.g., increase production by only 5 percent) might also be considered.

Because control is an ongoing process, there are periodic iterations of the steps just outlined. For example, as we will discuss next with regard to fraud, periodic reviews are conducted to determine the effectiveness of fraud-prevention programs.

Fraud and Its Relationship to Control

SOX

In this section, we discuss fraud, computer fraud, and computer abuse, as well as emphasize that an organization's system of internal control must be designed to address the risks of fraud. **Fraud** is a deliberate act or untruth intended to obtain unfair or unlawful gain. Since fraud, by definition, involves a false representation, one can see why it is such an important concern in AIS. Fraud always entails manipulating *information* for criminal purposes. Management's legal responsibility to prevent fraud and other irregularities is implied by laws such as the Foreign Corrupt Practices Act,[15] which states that "a fundamental aspect of management's stewardship responsibility is to provide shareholders with reasonable assurance that the business is adequately controlled." Notice that Title XI of the Sarbanes-Oxley Act specifically addresses corporate fraud.

The accounting profession has been proactive in dealing with corporate fraud. For example, one outcome of an antifraud program is Statement on Auditing Standards No. 99 (SAS No. 99), "Consideration of Fraud in a Financial Statement Audit." SAS No. 99 emphasizes brainstorming fraud risks (Technology Application 5.1, pg. 169), increasing professional skepticism, using unpredictable audit test patterns, and detecting management override of internal controls. The SEC's interpretive guidance regarding management's report on internal control over financial reporting states that "Management's evaluation of risk of misstatement should include consideration of the vulnerability of the entity to fraudulent activity...."[16] Regarding the independent auditor, AS5 states, "When planning and performing the audit of internal control over financial reporting, the auditor should take into account the results of his or her fraud risk assessment."[17]

Why are Congress, the accounting profession, the financial community, and others so impassioned about the subject of fraud? This is largely because of some highly publicized business failures in recent years that caught people completely by surprise because the financial statements of these businesses showed that they were prospering. When these firms, such as Enron, went "belly-up," it was discovered that the seeming prosperity was an illusion concocted by "cooking the books" (i.e., creating false and misleading financial statements).

---

[15]See the Foreign Corrupt Practices Act (FCPA) of 1977 (P.L. 95-213).

[16]SEC Release No. 33-8810, June 27, 2007, paragraph II.A.1.a.

[17]"Auditing Standard No. 5—An Audit of Internal Control Over Financial Reporting That Is Integrated with an Audit of Financial Statements," PCAOB, July 12, 2007, paragraph 14.

Technology Summary 7.1

2010 ACFE REPORT TO THE NATION ON OCCUPATIONAL FRAUD AND ABUSE

Between January 2008 and December 2009, the Association of Certified Fraud Examiners (ACFE) gathered information from Certified Fraud Examiners (CFEs) from 106 nations about fraud cases that they had personally investigated. The median loss of the 1843 cases of fraud (over 40 percent of the cases were from the United States) reported by the CFEs was $160,000. Nearly one quarter of these cases caused at least $1 million in losses. In the report summarizing these frauds, we learn the following:

- Respondents estimated that the typical organization lost 5 percent of its annual revenues to fraud, which, if projected to the entire global economy, would total $2.9 trillion in total losses.

- The typical fraud was under way 18 months before being detected.

- Frauds were more likely to be detected by tips (e.g., through hotlines such as those required by SOX) than through audits or internal controls. Small businesses—those with fewer than 100 employees—suffer disproportionately larger losses.

- Over 80 percent of the frauds were committed by individuals in accounting, operations, sales, executive/upper management, customer service, or purchasing.

- The most common red flags displayed by fraud perpetrators were living beyond their means (43 percent of cases) and experiencing financial difficulties (36 percent of cases).

- Small businesses are disproportionately victimized by fraud (31 percent of cases) due to relatively weak anti-fraud controls.

Source: *2010 ACFE Report to the Nation on Occupational Fraud and Abuse* (Austin, TX: Association of Certified Fraud Examiners, 2010).

Aside from some widely reported cases, is fraud really that prevalent in business? First, **Technology Summary 7.1** describes the highlights of a report issued by the Association of Certified Fraud Examiners. Notice the total estimated fraud losses and the disproportionate number of frauds committed against small businesses. Second, **Technology Summary 7.2** (pg. 234) describes the results of the 2009 Global Economic Crime Survey conducted by PricewaterhouseCoopers (PwC). This study concludes that fraud controls, while absolutely necessary, must be backed by a strong ethical culture, a broad risk management program, the right "tone at the top" in upper management, and strong sanctions for *any* fraud (i.e., building a "zero tolerance culture"), regardless of the position of the perpetrator.

We can also see from the PwC report that fraud is indeed a worldwide problem and that it is increasing, especially during periods of economic crisis. We can see from both reports that the losses are significant. Furthermore, the two reports agree that internal controls and audits are not sufficient to detect fraud. Fraud-prevention programs and detection measures, such as hotlines, are necessary to address the risk of fraud. The implication is clear: A system of internal control, including an ongoing *process* of review, can reduce the incidence of fraud.

Implications of Computer Fraud and Abuse

Now let's turn our attention to computer fraud and abuse. The proliferation of computers in business organizations, and the connection of those computers to each other and to the Internet, has created expanded opportunities for criminal infiltration. Computers have been used to commit a wide variety of crimes, including identify theft, fraud, larceny, and embezzlement. In general, computer-related crimes have been referred to as *computer fraud*, *computer abuse*, or *computer crime*. Some of these frauds are more prevalent when an organization is engaged in e-business. For example, an organization that receives payment via credit card, where the credit card is not present during the transaction (e.g., sales via Web site or telephone), absorbs the loss if a transaction is fraudulent. To prevent these losses, the organization may install controls, such as anti-fraud software, to detect attempts to make unauthorized use of credit cards. Let's now examine some of these fraud techniques and the means for coping with them.

E-Business

Technology Summary 7.2

GLOBAL ECONOMIC CRIME SURVEY 2009

In 2009, PricewaterhouseCoopers conducted its fifth biennial Economic Crime Survey. Key findings, based on interviews of 3,037 companies in 54 countries, include the following:

- 30 percent of companies reported frauds in the previous 12 months, with 43 percent reporting an increase in the incidences of fraud compared to one year earlier.
- Larger companies reported a greater number of frauds.
- Collateral damage—described as damage or significant damage to their business (e.g., lower employee morale or strained

business relationships)—was reported by 100 percent of those respondents who had suffered fraud.

- The single most effective fraud detection method was internal audit, at 17 percent, followed by internal tip offs (16 percent) and fraud risk management (14 percent).
- There was a strong correlation between fraud risk-management activities and higher chances of detecting frauds.
- Accounting fraud was second only to asset misappropriation as the type of fraud most reported, the percentages being 38 and 67, respectively. Furthermore, accounting fraud increased over the past two years, while asset misappropriation declined.

Source: PricewaterhouseCoopers, *Global Economic Crime Survey 2009*, November 2009.

Computer crime includes crime in which the computer is the target of the crime or the means used to commit the crime.[18] The majority of computer crimes fall into these two basic types:

- The computer is used as the *tool* of the criminal to accomplish the illegal act. For instance, the perpetrator could illegally access one or more banking systems to make unauthorized transfers to a foreign bank account and then go to the other country to enjoy the ill-gotten gain.
- The computer or the information stored in it is the *target* of the criminal. *Computer viruses* fall into this category.

E-Business

Technology Summary 7.3 describes types of **malware**—short for *mal*icious soft*ware*—which is software designed specifically to damage or disrupt a computer system. **Technology Summary 7.4** on page 236 provides a brief presentation of computer viruses, perhaps the most common type of malware. *Computer hacking*, another category of computer abuse, is discussed in Chapter 8. All of these techniques are major concerns to organizations engaged in e-business because they affect the actual and perceived reliability and integrity of their electronic infrastructure. Be aware of two things: Insiders commit over half of computer crimes,[19] and the methods listed are by no means exhaustive.

Before leaving this section, let's make a few other points. First, systems have been manipulated in a number of different ways in perpetrating computer crimes. Manipulation of event-related data (i.e., the adding, altering, or deleting of events) represents one frequently employed method of committing computer fraud.

Second, regardless of the method used in committing computer crime, we must not overlook the real issue. Computer crime represents an interesting example of a process failure. It characterizes a poorly controlled process. Process failure can usually be corrected by a conscientious application of appropriate control plans. For example,

---

[18]We use the terms *computer crime*, *computer abuse*, and *computer fraud* interchangeably. Technically, they refer to slightly different concepts, but we do not need to distinguish among them for your discussions here.

[19]For example, in the *CSI Survey 2009: The 14th Annual Computer Crime and Security Survey* (Computer Security Institute, 2009), 55 percent of respondents believed that at least some of the computer security attacks that they experienced were perpetrated by insiders. This is a significant increase from what was reported in the *CSI Survey 2008* (Computer Security Institute, 2008), which showed 49 percent for these types of attack.

Technology Summary 7.3

MALICIOUS SOFTWARE

- *Salami slicing:* Unauthorized instructions are inserted into a program to systematically steal very small amounts, usually by rounding to the nearest cent in financial transactions such as the calculation of interest on savings accounts. A dishonest programmer includes an instruction that if the amount of interest to be credited to the account is other than an even penny (e.g., $2.7345), the excess over the even amount (.0045) is to be credited to account number 673492, which just happens to be his own. Although each credit to his account is minute, the total can accumulate very rapidly. (This technique was portrayed in the 1999 movie *Office Space.*)

- *Back door:* During the development of a program, the programmer may insert a special code or password that enables him to bypass the security features of the program to access the program for troubleshooting or other purposes. These are meant to be removed when the programmer's work is done, but sometimes they aren't and can be used by the programmer or others to attack the program.

- *Trojan horse:* A module of unauthorized computer code is covertly placed in a seemingly harmless program. The program executes its intended function, while the malicious code performs an unauthorized act such as destroying your hard disk. Trojan horses, such as *spybots* that report on Web sites that a user visits, and *key-loggers* that log keystrokes and send the information back to clients, can be inadvertently downloaded by visiting a criminal's bogus Web site or clicking on a hyperlink in, for example, an e-mail. This link then sends you to a bogus Web site. This latter technique is often used in *phishing* e-mails.

- *Logic bomb:* Code, secretly inserted into a program, is designed to execute (or "explode") when, for example, a specific date or event occurs (i.e., a delayed-action *Trojan horse* or *computer virus*). The code may display a harmless message, or it could cause a disaster, such as shutting a system down or destroying data.

- *Worm:* This type of *computer virus* replicates itself on disks, in memory, and across networks. It uses computing resources to the point of denying access to these resources to others, thus effectively shutting down the system.

- *Zombie (zombie agent, zombie network):* This program secretly takes over another Internet-attached computer and then uses that computer to launch attacks that can't be traced to the zombie's creator. Zombies are elements of the *denial-of-service attacks* discussed in Chapter 8.

---

inadequately controlled changes to programs (see *program change* controls in Chapter 8) have allowed programmers to insert malicious code such as Trojan horses and logic bombs into legitimate programs to perpetrate major frauds. If access to the computer programs and data are protected, frauds can be prevented.

Finally, as seductive as the topic of computer fraud and abuse is for students, you should not leave this section with the mistaken impression that controls are important simply because they can protect against "rip-offs." It has been estimated that losses due to accidental, nonmalicious acts far exceed those caused by willful, intentional misdeeds. Therefore, you should recognize that the computer must be protected by a system of controls capable not only of preventing crimes but also of minimizing simple, innocent errors and omissions.

Ethical Considerations and the Control Environment

Before discussing our framework for analyzing a system of internal control, let's pause to examine the very underpinnings of the system—namely, its ethical foundation. COSO places integrity and ethical values at the heart of what it calls the *control environment* (captured in ERM as *internal environment*). In arguing the importance of integrity and ethics, these frameworks make the case that the best-designed control systems are subject to failure caused by human error, faulty judgment, circumvention through collusion, and management override of the system. COSO, for example, states that:

> Ethical behavior and management integrity are products of the "corporate culture." Corporate culture includes ethical and behavioral standards, how they are communicated, and how they are reinforced in practice. Official policies specify what

management wants to happen. Corporate culture determines what actually happens and which rules are obeyed, bent, or ignored.[20]

There is some evidence to suggest that companies with formal ethics policies might even lower their internal control costs. Cases in point: The business and audit failures noted at the beginning of this chapter arose primarily because upper management did not establish or reinforce ethical corporate cultures across their organizations; in some cases, managers willfully violated any semblance of ethical behavior.

Management is responsible for internal control and can respond to this requirement legalistically or by creating a control environment. That is, management can follow the "letter of the law" (its form), or it can respond *substantively* to the need for control (its spirit). The **control environment** reflects the organization's (primarily the board of directors' and management's) general awareness of and commitment to the importance of control throughout the organization. In other words, by setting the example and by

---

Technology Summary 7.4

COMPUTER VIRUSES

A computer virus is program code that can attach itself to other programs (including macros within word processing documents), thereby "infecting" those programs and macros. Viruses can *reproduce themselves* in a manner analogous to biological viruses. Viruses are activated when you run an infected program, open an infected document, or boot a computer from an infected disk. Computer viruses alter their "host" programs, destroy data, or render computer resources (e.g., disk drives, processors, networks) unavailable for use.

Some viruses are fairly innocent—they might merely produce a message such as "GOTCHA" or play "The Blue Danube" through the computer's speakers. Other viruses can be more harmful. Some viruses will delete programs and files; some will even format your hard drive, thus wiping away all stored data! Viruses also can overload networks with "messages," making it impossible to send or receive e-mail or to connect to external sources, such as the Internet. Finally, denial-of-service attacks, in which hackers continuously deluge Web servers with high volumes of messages, can render a server so busy handling the onslaught of messages that legitimate customers are prohibited from gaining access and conducting business with the companies.

Viruses can enter an organization through software that is shared through the exchange of storage media (i.e., peer-to-peer

technologies), Web server vulnerabilities, and e-mail. Such exchanges allow viruses to quickly become an epidemic, much like a biological virus. The real fear that can cause information systems managers to lose sleep, of course, is that the virus will then spread to the organization's networks (and networked computing resources) and destroy the organization's most sensitive data or result in denial of service to customers.

How extensive is the virus problem? Respondents of the 2009 CSI computer crime survey[a] reported that viruses represented 64 percent of detected computer crimes, up from 50 percent in 2008. At 64 percent, viruses were the most prevalent computer threat to organizations in terms of monetary losses, followed by theft of laptops and mobile devices (42 percent) and insider abuses of net access and email (30 percent). Kaspersky Labs, Inc. reports that there were 500,000 virus-type incidents in 2006 and that the number is expected to increase steadily in the future[b].

How do you protect your computer from a viral infection? By improving methods that legitimate users use to gain access—such as stronger passwords, biometrics, and smartcards. Typical defensive technologies, such as antivirus software and firewalls, should also be used in combination with personnel policies, practices, and training, file attachment filtering, and so on. Many of these are discussed in Chapter 8.

[a]CSI Survey 2010: The 14th Annual Computer Crime and Security Survey (Computer Security Institute, 2010).
[b]Ben Worthen, "Business Technology: Hacker Camps Train Network Defenders; Sessions Teach IT Pros to Use Tools of the Online Criminal Trade," *Wall Street Journal* (April 1, 2008): B.6.

---

[20]*Internal Control—Integrated Framework—Framework Volume* (New York: Committee of Sponsoring Organizations of the Treadway Commission, 1992): 20.

addressing the need for control in a positive manner at the top of the organization, management can make an organization *control conscious*.

For instance, reward systems might consider ethical, legal, and social performance, as well as the "bottom line."[21] Imagine the temptation to circumvent the control system or to "bend the rules" that could result from a reward system that pressures employees to meet unrealistic performance targets—such as happened at Enron Corporation—or that places upper and lower limits on employee bonus plans. Strategies should be developed that do not create conflicts between business performance and legal requirements. Finally, management should consistently find it unacceptable for personnel to circumvent the organization's system of controls, and, as importantly, the organization *should impose stiff sanctions for such unacceptable behavior*. These actions are included in what some call the "tone at the top" of the organization.

One tangible way an increasing number of companies have articulated the ethical behavior expected of employees is to develop corporate *codes of conduct* that are periodically acknowledged (i.e., signed) by employees. The codes often address such matters as illegal or improper payments; conflicts of interest; insider trading; computer ethics, including personal use of office e-mail systems and Internet connections; and software piracy.

A Framework for Assessing the Design of a System of Internal Control

In this final major section of this chapter, we begin our presentation of a framework for assessing the design of a system of internal control, including defining control goals and controls plans. We continue to employ a matrix to assist us in our analysis. We call this particular type of matrix a **control matrix**, which is a tool designed to assist you in evaluating the potential effectiveness of controls in a business process by matching control goals with relevant control plans. To focus our discussion throughout the rest of the chapter, we will apply control concepts to the Suprina Company order entry process that we first saw in Chapter 4. The Suprina systems flowchart is depicted in **Figure 7.4** on page 238 and the associated narrative is included in **Exhibit 7.5** on page 239. Before proceeding, be sure to reacquaint yourself with the Suprina process.

As a manager, what are your concerns about this process? That is, what are your objectives and the related risks? Let's review a few concerns:

- We want all of the orders to be entered in a timely manner, but orders might be lost, stolen, or delayed.
- We want all of the orders to be recorded correctly, but we might miss some orders, record orders we didn't get from a customer, or record order amounts incorrectly.
- We want all inventory changes to be recorded correctly (i.e., correct item and amount).
- We want to accomplish all this with a minimum of resources such as the sales reps, order entry clerks, and the computer in Figure 7.4.

A recurring theme throughout this text has been that an organization defines objectives, assesses risks, and then establishes processes and controls to provide reasonable assurance that those objectives are achieved (and that there is an appropriate response

---

[21]COSO even goes so far as to suggest that responsibility for internal control should be an explicit or implicit part of everyone's job description.

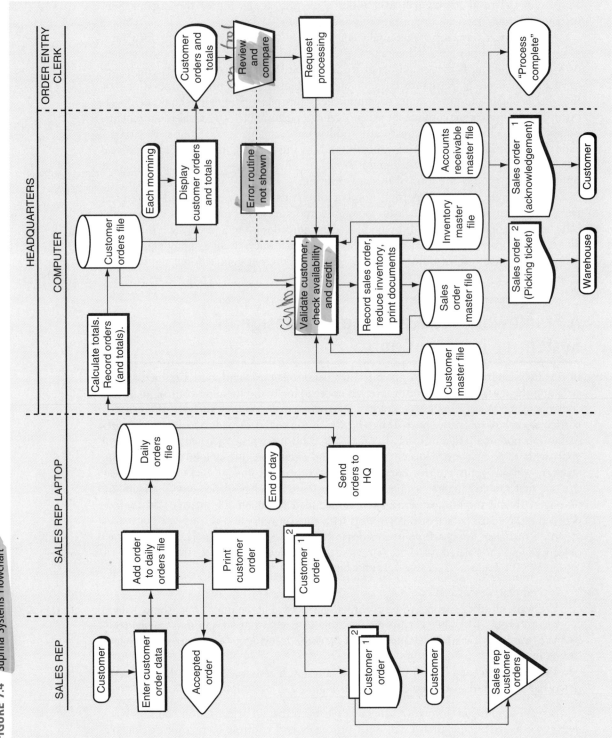

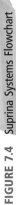

FIGURE 7.4 Suprina Systems Flowchart

EXHIBIT 7.5   Suprina Company System Narrative

Suprina Athletic Supply Company specializes in selling sporting goods, gymnasium equipment, and other athletic supplies to high schools, colleges, and universities. Customers give their orders to the company's sales representatives at customer locations using the following procedures.

At the customer locations, Suprina's sales representatives enter customer orders on their laptop computers, where they are added to the daily orders file. Once entered, two copies of the order are printed and the sales rep gives copy 1 to the customer and retains copy 2 for his files.

At the end of each day the laptop retrieves the day's orders and sends them to the computer at Suprina headquarters. The computer calculates various totals, such as number of orders and number of line items on those orders, and records those totals with the orders in the customer order file.

Each morning, the computer at Suprina headquarters displays the customer order file (with totals) to the order entry clerk

(also at Suprina headquarters). The clerk reviews the orders and compares the totals for each sales rep's orders with the overall totals that the computer has provided. After being notified by the clerk, the computer begins processing the customer orders by performing a series of programmed edits as follows: Data from the customer master file is accessed to validate customer name and address. The inventory master file is accessed to check for inventory availability and pricing. The customer's credit limit (from the customer master file) is then compared to the amount of the order, outstanding sales orders (sales order master file), and accounts receivable balances. If any orders fail these edits, the clerk is notified.

Customer orders that pass these tests are then recorded on the sales order master file and the inventory balances are reduced. Two copies of the sales order are printed and sent to the customer (copy 1, an order acknowlededgment) and to the warehouse (copy 2, a picking ticket).

to the risks). Refer, for example, to Figure 1.7 in Chapter 1 (pg. 23), Exhibit 7.3 (pg. 224), and Figure 7.3 (pg. 231). The purpose of internal control as defined in this text is consistent with that theme. The purpose is to provide reasonable assurance of achieving objectives in three categories: *operations* (efficient and effective), *reporting* (i.e., reliable), and *compliance* with applicable laws and regulations. For our control framework, we convert those three categories into control goals for two categories, *operations process control goals* (for efficiency and effectiveness) and *information process control goals* (for reliable reporting).[22] Notice that these two categories correspond to operations and information processes in Figure 1.4 (pg. 16).[23] Control goals are business process objectives that an internal control system is designed to achieve. **Figure 7.5** on page 240 depicts the breakdown of these goals as column headings on a portion of our control matrix. **Table 7.1** on page 241 provides an overview of the *generic* control goals of the *operations process* and *information process*. In the following paragraphs, we discuss each goal, and ask you to follow Figure 7.5, Table 7.1, and Figure 7.4 in the process.

Control Goals of Operations Processes

The first control goal, *ensure effectiveness of operations*, strives to ensure that a given operational process (e.g., Suprina's order entry process) is fulfilling the purpose for which it was intended. Notice that we must itemize the specific *effectiveness (i.e., operations process) goals* to be achieved. In Figure 7.5, we show two examples (i.e., timely acknowledgement and customer creditworthiness). These goals are created by people and are therefore

---

[22]We include *compliance with applicable laws, regulations*, and *contractual agreements* as one of the goals of each operations process to which such laws, regulations, or agreements might be appropriate. For instance, compliance with the Robinson/Patman Act is shown as a legitimate goal of the order entry/sales system process in Chapter 10.

[23]For simplicity, our analysis of controls does not include the third business process component, the management process.

FIGURE 7.5 Control Goals for the Suprina Order Entry Process

Control Goals of the Suprina Order Entry Process							
Control Goals of the Operations Process			Control Goals of the Information Process				
Ensure effectiveness of operations	Ensure efficient employment of resources (e.g., people and computers)	Ensure security of resources (e.g., inventory, customer master data)	For the customer order inputs, ensure:			For the sales order and inventory master data, ensure:	
A B			IV	IC	IA	UC	UA

Effectiveness goals include:

A – Provide timely acknowledgement of customer orders

B – Provide assurance of customer's creditworthiness

IV = Input Validity

IC = Input Completeness

IA = Input Accuracy

UC = Update Completeness

UA = Update Accuracy

subjective, so no uniform set of operations process goals exists. In each of the business process chapters, we provide a representative listing of effectiveness goals.

The next goal, *ensure efficient employment of resources*, can only be evaluated in a relative sense. For example, to determine efficiency in achieving Suprina's effectiveness goal to provide an acknowledgement in a timely manner, we would need to know the cost of the people and computer equipment required to accomplish this goal. If the costs are more than the benefits obtained (e.g., improved customer relations, and reduction of incorrect or denied orders), then the system might be considered *in*efficient. Likewise, if the Suprina process costs more to operate than a process in a similar organization, we might also judge the system to be *in*efficient.

Let's now discuss the last operations process control goal in Table 7.1: to *ensure security of resources*. As noted in the table, organizational resources take many forms, both physical and nonphysical. Since the advent and proliferation of computer systems, information has become an increasingly important resource. For example, Suprina's customer data represents an important resource for this company. The data tell Suprina who their customers are, where they are located, how much they have purchased in the past, and so on. It would not be good for Suprina if, for example, this data fell into the hands of a competitor. Suprina must protect all of its resources, both tangible and intangible. In addition to the inventory and customer master data, other resources—for other business processes—include cash and raw materials inventory, accounts receivable master data, accounts payable master data, and inventory master data.

Control Goals of Information Processes

A glance at Table 7.1 and Figure 7.5 reveals that the first three control goals related to the information process deal with entering event-related data into a system. Recall from Chapter 1 that data input includes *capturing* data (e.g., completing a source document such as a customer order). Also, data input includes, if necessary, *converting* the data to *machine-readable form* (e.g., for Suprina, keying the customer order data). Therefore, *event data* are the targets of the *input* control goals shown in Table 7.1 and Figure 7.5.

Recall from Chapter 1 that only actual authorized events have validity. To illustrate the importance of achieving the first control goal, *ensure input validity*, assume that Suprina's order entry clerk requested processing of 50 customer orders. Further assume that two of the 50 orders are fictitious (e.g., they were not given to a sales rep by an existing Suprina customer). What is the effect of processing the 50 orders, including the two fictitious orders? First, the sales order and inventory master data have been corrupted by the addition of two bogus orders. Second, if not detected and corrected, goods will be picked and possibly shipped to a bogus customer. The goods will be lost and no payment is likely to be forthcoming. These errors will result in unreliable financial statements—overstated accounts receivable and sales—and other erroneous system outputs (e.g., sales reports, accounts receivable agings).[24]

TABLE 7.1 Control Goals

Control Goal	Definitions	Discussion
Control Goals of Operations Processes		
Ensure *effectiveness of operations* by achieving selected *goals* for the operations process.	Effectiveness: A measure of success in meeting one or more *goals* for the *operations process*.	If we assume that one of Suprina's goals is to acknowledge customer orders in a timely manner, the operations process is effective if orders are acknowledged with a copy of the customer order when the order is taken by the sales rep.
Ensure efficient employment of resources (e.g., people, computers).	Efficiency: A measure of the productivity of the resources applied to achieve a set of goals.	The cost of the people, computers, and other resources needed to process customer orders each day.
Ensure *security of resources* (e.g., cash, data assets, inventory).	Security of resources: Protecting an organization's resources from loss, destruction, disclosure, copying, sale, or other misuse.	Physical (e.g., inventory) and nonphysical (e.g., information) resources are available when required and put only to authorized use.
Control Goals of Information Processes		
Ensure input validity (IV).	Input validity: Input data are appropriately authorized and represent actual economic events and objects.	Only customer orders received from actual customers should be input into the Suprina process.
Ensure input completeness (IC).	Input completeness: All valid events or objects are captured and entered into a system once and only once.	All valid customer orders are entered into the Suprina process once and only once.
Ensure input accuracy (IA).	Input accuracy: All valid events must be correctly captured and entered into a system.	The customer, item numbers, quantities, and prices must be keyed correctly into the sales rep laptops.
Ensure update completeness (UC).	Update completeness: All events entered into a system must be reflected in the respective master data once and only once.	All customer orders entered must be recorded in the sales order and inventory master data once and only once.
Ensure update accuracy (UA).	Update accuracy: Data entered into a system must be reflected correctly in the respective master data.	All customer orders entered must be correctly recorded in the sales order and inventory master data.

---

[24]Under generally accepted accounting principles (GAAP), a shipment to a bogus customer, a shipment for which payment is unlikely, cannot be recognized as revenue and recorded as an account receivable.

To discuss the second information process goal, *ensure input completeness*, let's return to the Suprina example and suppose that there are 48 *valid* orders to be processed (we'll ignore the two fictitious orders in this example), but the order entry clerk makes a mistake and only requests the processing of 38 orders. What is the effect of processing 38 orders, rather than the original 48? First, the sales order master data will be incomplete; that is, it will fail to reflect the true number of orders. Second, picking tickets will not be prepared for the 10 missing orders, leading to lost sales and poor customer relations. Notice that by failing to input these 10 documents Suprina loses sales and the resulting revenue and profits. But the financial statements are still accurate because there was no accounting transaction (i.e., no shipment, no billing, and no cash receipt). In some cases there can be fraudulent, intentional misstatements of the accounting data by omitting some events such as liabilities.

The goal of *input completeness* is concerned with the actual number of events or objects to be processed. Particular questions relative to this goal include the following:

- Is *every* event or object captured (e.g., are source documents prepared for every valid event or object)?
- Is every captured event or object *entered into the computer* (or manually recorded in the books of original entry) and selected for processing? This latter failure was the breakdown in the Suprina example of 10 orders not being processed.
- Is each captured event or object entered and processed only once? If the sales clerk requested processing of the 38 orders more than once (let's ignore the missing 10), we would have a failure of the input completeness control goal.
- When dealing with input completeness, we are concerned with the documents or records representing an event or object, not the *correctness* or *accuracy* of the document or record. Accuracy issues are addressed by the third information process goal. Input completeness simply means that *all* of the events or objects that should be processed (i.e., the valid events and objects) are processed once and only once.

The third information process goal, *ensure input accuracy*, relates to the various data items that usually constitute a record of an event, such as a source document. To achieve this goal, we must minimize discrepancies between data items entered into a system and the economic events or objects they represent. Mathematical mistakes and inaccurate transcription of data from one document or medium to another may cause accuracy errors. Again, let's return to the Suprina example. Suppose that one of the *valid* orders is from Acme Company, customer 159, for 200 baseballs. The sales rep mistakenly enters the customer number as 195, resulting in Ajax Inc. (rather than Acme) submitting an order for 200 baseballs. Missing data fields on a source document or computer screen represent another type of accuracy error. For Suprina, the absence of a customer number on an order would result in a lost sale (i.e., orders that can't be shipped to a particular customer). We consider this type of system malfunction to be an accuracy error rather than a completeness error because the mere presence of the source document suggests that the event itself has been captured and that the input data are, by our definition, therefore complete.

Two critical questions must be asked concerning the goal of input accuracy:

- Is the initial capturing of data correct (e.g., are data recorded accurately on source documents)?
- Is the entered data correct (e.g., are data transcribed or recorded in the books of original entry or correctly converted from source documents into machine-readable form)? Again, the Suprina example of keying an incorrect customer number was an inaccurate input.

To achieve the goal of input accuracy, we must capture and enter into a system all important data elements. Thus, all important data elements must be identified for each economic event or object that we want to include in a system's database. In general, you should find the following guidelines helpful in identifying important data elements:

- All financial data elements are usually important, such as numbers that enter into a calculation. For a Suprina order, the amount ordered, selling price, discount, and net sales amount are crucial.
- Reference numbers, such as those for inventory items, customer numbers, and general ledger coding, are important. Among other reasons, accurate reference numbers are crucial to the proper *classification* of items in the financial statements.
- Dates are also very important so that we can determine that events are recorded in the proper time period. For instance, if a shipment made by Suprina on December 29th was recorded as shipped on December 30th, would you as an auditor be concerned? Possibly, but not nearly as concerned as you would be if the order was shipped on January 2nd and was recorded as shipped on December 31st (assuming that Suprina's year-end is December 31st). Notice that this accuracy error causes sales to be invalid in December (the order was not shipped in December) and incomplete in January (a shipment that occurred in January has not been recorded in January).

Now let's examine the last two information process control goals shown in Table 7.1 and Figure 7.5 (pp. 241 and 240). These goals deal with updating *master data*. As you learned in Chapter 3, master data update is an information-processing activity whose function is to incorporate new data into existing master data. You also learned that there are two types of updates that can be made to master data: *information processing* and *data maintenance*. You also should remember from Chapter 3 that master data updates resulting from information processing are analogous to the *posting* step in a manual bookkeeping cycle. In this textbook, we emphasize information processing; therefore, our analysis of the internal controls related to data updates is restricted to data updates from information processing.

In a manual-based system, the goals of *ensure update completeness* and *ensure update accuracy* relate to updating various ledgers (e.g., the accounts receivable subsidiary ledger) for data items entered into the books of original entry (e.g., the sales and cash receipts journals). In Suprina's process, the goal of *ensure update completeness* relates to recording all customer orders in the sales order and inventory master data for *all* customer orders recorded in the customer orders file. The goal of *ensure update accuracy* relates to correctly recording (e.g., correct customer, correct items and quantities) customer orders in the sales order and inventory master data.

After valid data have been *completely* and *accurately* entered into a computer (i.e., added to event data such as Suprina's daily orders file on each sales reps laptop), the data usually go through a series of processing steps. Several things can go wrong with the data after they have been entered into a computer for processing. Accordingly, the goals of update completeness and accuracy are aimed at minimizing processing errors.

In general, an awareness of the following types of processing errors should assist you in achieving the goals of update completeness and update accuracy:

- *Programming errors:* For example, logical or technical errors may exist in the program software. (For instance, instead of reducing inventory for each order, the inventory balances were increased.)
- *Operational errors:* For example, today's customer orders may be processed against an out-of-date (yesterday's) sales order master data. Or we may fail to execute some intermediate steps in a process. This may happen if input data is used for

Enterprise Systems

more than one application, and we fail to use the inputs for all of the intended processes. (Note that this should not be a problem with enterprise systems where one input automatically impacts all relevant applications.) Finally, some applications (such as in banking) process "memo" updates during the day to immediately reflect activity, such as cash withdrawals. The "real" updates take place overnight in a batch process. If we fail to properly execute the overnight process, the updates may be incomplete or inaccurate.

These two examples present illustrations of how things can go wrong while updating master data, even when the data are valid, complete, and accurate at the input stage. Controls that ensure *input* accuracy and completeness do not necessarily ensure *update* accuracy and completeness. We should note, however, that if the events or transactions are processed using an *online real-time (OLRT) processing* system such as the one depicted in Figure 3.5 (pg. 75) the input and update will occur nearly simultaneously. This will minimize the possibility that the update will be incomplete or inaccurate. This is NOT the case with the Suprina process, where the input to the customer orders file is not immediately followed by the update to the sales order and inventory master data; the order entry clerk must request the processing step that causes the sales order and inventory master data updates.

Note that we do *not* have a separate goal for *update validity* as we do for update completeness and update accuracy. There would be invalid updates only if the input completeness or update completeness control goals are not met (i.e., inputs or updates are to be processed once and only once).

Control Plans

Control plans reflect information-processing policies and procedures that assist in accomplishing control goals. Control plans can be classified in a number of different ways that help us understand them. **Figure 7.6** shows one such classification scheme. The fact that the *control environment* appears at the top of the hierarchy illustrates that it comprises a multitude of factors that can either reinforce or mitigate the effectiveness of the pervasive and application control plans.

The second level in the Figure 7.6 control hierarchy consists of pervasive control plans. **Pervasive control plans** relate to a multitude of goals and processes. Like the control environment, they provide a climate or set of surrounding conditions in which the various business processes operate. They are broad in scope and apply equally to all business processes; hence, they *pervade* all systems. **General controls**—also known as **IT general controls**—are applied to all IT service activities. For example, preventing unauthorized access to the computer system would protect all of the specific business processes that run on the computer (such as order entry/sales, billing/accounts receivable/cash receipts, inventory, payroll, etc.). We discuss pervasive control plans and general controls/IT general controls in Chapter 8.

SOX   PCAOB Auditing Standard No. 5, paragraphs 22–27, includes these first two levels within what the standard describes as "entity-level-controls." These include controls such as the control environment and general controls (they use the term IT general controls). The standard emphasizes the pervasive effect that entity-level controls have on the achievement of control objectives and the effectiveness of specific controls, such as business process controls. Many of these entity-level controls, including IT general controls, such as controls over computer program development, program change controls, controls over computer operations, and access to programs and data, are discussed in Chapter 8.

Business process control plans are applied to a particular business process, such as billing or cash receipts. **Application controls** are automated business process controls contained within IT application systems (i.e., computer programs).[25] Business process control plans and application controls are introduced in Chapter 9 and discussed

FIGURE 7.6   A Control Hierarchy

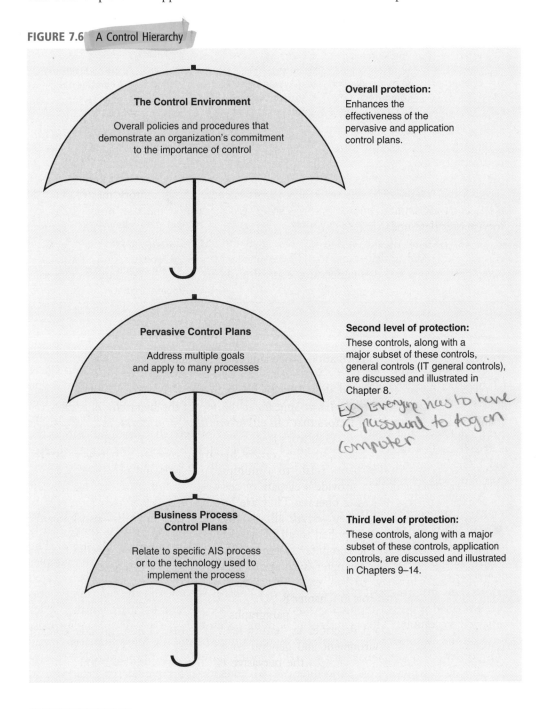

The Control Environment

Overall policies and procedures that demonstrate an organization's commitment to the importance of control

Overall protection:
Enhances the effectiveness of the pervasive and application control plans.

Pervasive Control Plans

Address multiple goals and apply to many processes

Second level of protection:
These controls, along with a major subset of these controls, general controls (IT general controls), are discussed and illustrated in Chapter 8.

EX) Everyone has to have a password to log on computer

Business Process Control Plans

Relate to specific AIS process or to the technology used to implement the process

Third level of protection:
These controls, along with a major subset of these controls, application controls, are discussed and illustrated in Chapters 9–14.

---

[25]We use business process controls as the general category of controls for business processes that includes manual controls and application (i.e., automated) controls. Other frameworks might refer to manual application controls and automated application controls. In any case, business processes have manual and automated controls.

FIGURE 7.7 Suprina Control Matrix

Recommended control plans	Control Goals of the Suprina Order Entry Process								
	Control Goals of the Operations Process			Control Goals of the Information Process				
	Ensure effective-ness of operations	Ensure efficient employment of resources (e.g., people and computers)	Ensure security of resources (e.g., inventory, customer master data)	For the customer order inputs, ensure:			For the sales order and inventory master data, ensure:	
	A	B			IV	IC	IA	UC	UA
P-1:	P-1					P-1			
P-n:		P-n						P-n	

Effectiveness goals include:

A – Provide timely acknowledgement of customer orders

B – Provide assurance of customer's creditworthiness

IV = Input validity

IC = Input completeness

IA = Input accuracy

UC = Update completeness

UA = Update accuracy

further in Chapters 10 through 14. We will use a control matrix, such as that in **Figure 7.7**, to match business process controls to the goals that we discussed previously. As you will learn in Chapter 9, a control matrix such as this will allow us to assess the effectiveness of design of the system of internal control by examining, easily, which goals are being addressed and which goals are not. See the cross-reference examples within the matrix (e.g., P-1 under A and IC, and P-n under efficient employment of resources and UC). Be careful, however, to use this matrix only to assess business process controls. You will learn more about this in Chapter 9.

Another useful and common way to classify controls is in relation to the timing of their occurrence. **Preventive control plans** stop problems from occurring. **Detective control plans** discover that problems have occurred. **Corrective control plans** rectify problems that have occurred. Let's use the Suprina process again to illustrate. The programmed edits, such as validation of the customer name and address, are examples of *preventive* controls; customer orders with incorrect customer data would be rejected before they are processed further. A *detective* control is shown in the Suprina process at the manual process (trapezoid symbol) labeled "Review and compare" in the Order entry clerk column. The comparison is done to ensure that no discrepancies exist between the customer orders displayed by the computer and the totals that accompany those orders. If discrepancies are *detected*, Suprina should have a procedure for resolving the discrepancy. This procedure would constitute a *corrective* control, which, although not shown in Figure 7.4 (pg. 238), is alluded to with the annotation "Error routine not shown."

Obviously, if we had our choice, we would implement preventive controls because, in the long run, it is less expensive and less disruptive to operations to prevent, rather than to detect and correct, problems. However, because no control can be made to be 100 percent effective, we need to implement a combination of preventive, detective, and corrective controls. Furthermore, it should go without saying that detective control plans often can help to prevent or deter fraudulent or careless acts. That is, if someone knows that plans exist to detect or uncover fraud and carelessness, such knowledge can serve as one additional preventive measure.

Summary

In the introduction and in the section on fraud, we gave some alarming examples of fraud and computer crime incidences. Future managers must confront these problems much more directly than have their predecessors, particularly in light of recent business and audit failures, which gave rise to the Sarbanes-Oxley Act. Also, as computer-based systems become more sophisticated, managers must continually question how such technological changes affect the system of internal controls. For example, some companies have already implemented paperless (totally electronic) information systems. Others employ electronic data interchange (EDI) technology, which we discussed in Chapter 3. The challenges to future managers are to keep pace with the development of these types of systems and to ensure that changes in any process are complemented by enhancements in the company's system of internal control.

Minimizing computer fraud and abuse is only one area of concern for today's managers. An organization's stakeholders—investors, customers, employees, taxpayers, government, and so on—have recently raised a number of *organizational governance* issues to demonstrate their interest in and concern over how well organizations are being managed. For example, these stakeholders are asking how well the board of directors (BOD) governs its own performance and that of the organization's managers. In addition, how do the BOD and management implement *and demonstrate* that they have control over their operations? We submit that only through an effective system of internal control can these and other matters be adequately addressed and suitably resolved.

Key Terms

organizational governance, 220

Enterprise Risk Management (ERM), 220–221

risks, 222

internal control, 230

process, 230

fraud, 232

computer crime, 234

malware, 234

computer virus, 236

control environment, 236

control matrix, 237

control goals, 239

effectiveness, 241

efficiency, 241

security of resources, 241

input validity, 241

input completeness, 241

input accuracy, 241

update completeness, 241

update accuracy, 241

control plans, 244

pervasive control plans, 244

general controls, 244

IT general controls, 244

business process control plans, 245

application controls, 245

preventive control plans, 246

detective control plans, 246

corrective control plans, 246

Review Questions

RQ 7-1   Describe organizational governance.

RQ 7-2   Describe Enterprise Risk Management (ERM).

RQ 7-3   Describe the eight elements of ERM.

RQ 7-4   Describe and compare risks and opportunities.

RQ 7-5   Describe four risk responses.

RQ 7-6   What gave rise to the Sarbanes-Oxley Act of 2002 (SOX)?

RQ 7-7   What are the key provisions of SOX?

RQ 7-8   What is COSO?

RQ 7-9   Describe the elements common to most current definitions of internal control.

RQ 7-10 What is the relationship between fraud and internal control?

RQ 7-11 What is computer crime?

RQ 7-12 What is malware? Name and explain three types of malware.

RQ 7-13 What is a computer virus?

RQ 7-14 Explain what is meant by the *control environment*. What elements might comprise the control environment?

RQ 7-15 Explain how business ethics relate to internal control.

RQ 7-16 a. What are the three generic control goals of operations processes?

        b. Explain the difference between the following pairs of control goals: (1) ensure effectiveness of operations processes and ensure efficient employment of resources; (2) ensure efficient employment of resources and ensure security of resources.

RQ 7-17 a. What are the five generic control goals of information processes?

        b. Explain the difference between the following pairs of control goals: (1) ensure input validity and ensure input accuracy; (2) ensure input completeness and ensure input accuracy; (3) ensure input completeness and ensure update completeness; and (4) ensure input accuracy and ensure update accuracy.

RQ 7-18 What are the differences among the control environment, a pervasive control plan, and a business process control plan?

RQ 7-19 Distinguish among preventive, detective, and corrective control plans.

Discussion Questions

DQ 7-1   Recently, the U.S. federal government and the American Institute of Certified Public Accountants (AICPA) have taken aggressive steps aimed at ensuring the quality of organizational governance. What are these changes, how might they change organizational governance procedures, and do you believe that these actions will really improve internal control of business organizations?

DQ 7-2   "Enterprise Risk Management is a process for organizational governance." Discuss why this might be correct and why it might not.

DQ 7-3   "If it weren't for the potential of computer crime, the emphasis on controlling computer systems would decline significantly in importance." Do you agree? Discuss fully.

DQ 7-4   Provide five examples of potential conflict between the control goals of ensuring effectiveness of operations and of ensuring efficient employment of resources.

DQ 7-5   Discuss how the *efficiency* and *effectiveness* of a mass-transit system in a large city can be measured.

DQ 7-6   "If *input data* are entered into the system completely and accurately, then the information process control goals of *ensuring update completeness* and *ensuring update accuracy* will be automatically achieved." Do you agree? Discuss fully.

DQ 7-7   "Section 404 of SOX has not been a good idea. It has been too costly and it has not had its intended effect." Do you agree? Discuss fully.

DQ 7-8   How does this text's definition of internal control differ from COSO? How does it differ from the controls that are subject to review under Section 404 of SOX?

DQ 7-9   What, if anything, is wrong with the following control hierarchy? Discuss fully.

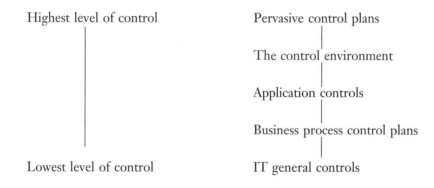

Highest level of control

Lowest level of control

Pervasive control plans

The control environment

Application controls

Business process control plans

IT general controls

Short Problems

SP 7-1   Provide a comparison of the internal control frameworks of COSO's ERM and SAS 78. Discuss (in a manner prescribed by your professor) the implications to independent auditors of the differences.

SP 7-2   List 1 has six terms from this chapter, Chapter 1, or Chapter 3; List 2 contains five definitions or explanations of terms.

Match the definitions with the terms by placing a *capital* letter from List 1 on the blank line to the left of its corresponding definition in List 2. You should have one letter left over from List 1.

List 1—Terms

A. Input validity
B. Preventive control plan
C. Operations process effectiveness goal
D. Business process control plan

E. Control environment

F. Information processing update (of master data)

List 2—Definitions

_____ 1. The process of modifying the master data reflects the results of new events.

_____ 2. A control designed to keep problems from occurring.

_____ 3. A control goal of the information process that is directed at ensuring that fictitious or bogus events are not recorded.

_____ 4. A goal of an operations process that signifies the very reason for which that process exists.

_____ 5. The highest level in the control hierarchy; a control category that evidences management's commitment to the importance of control in the organization.

SP 7-3 List 1 has six terms from this chapter, Chapter 1, or Chapter 3; List 2 contains five definitions or explanations of terms.

Match the definitions with the terms by placing a _capital_ letter from List 1 on the blank line to the left of its corresponding definition in List 2. You should have one letter left over from List 1.

List 1—Terms

A. Input accuracy

B. Pervasive control plan

C. Application control

D. Control goals

E. Risk

F. Data maintenance update (of master data)

List 2—Definitions

_____ 1. The process of modifying a master data store's _standing data_.

_____ 2. An automated control that is exercised within a business process as that process' events are processed.

_____ 3. An event that may cause an organization to fail to meet its objectives.

_____ 4. Objectives to be achieved by the internal control system.

_____ 5. A control that addresses a multitude of goals across many business processes.

SP 7-4 Investigate the internal controls in one of the following (ask your instructor which): a local business, your home, your school, or your place of employment. Report (in a manner prescribed by your instructor) on the controls that you found and the goals that they were designed to achieve.

Problems

P 7-1 In the following first list are 12 examples of the items described in the second list.

Match the two lists by placing the capital letter from the first list on the blank line preceding the description to which it best relates. You should have two letters left over from List 1.

List 1—Examples

A. Business process (i.e., manual) control
B. Application (i.e., automated) control
C. Preventive control
D. Detective control
E. Corrective control
F. Control environment
G. Input validity
H. Input completeness
I. Input accuracy
J. Update completeness
K. Update accuracy
L. Efficient use of resources

List 2—Descriptions

_____ 1. Insurance policy reimburses a company for losses due to a fire in a warehouse.

_____ 2. Shipping notices have a serial number that is tracked to ensure that they are all input.

_____ 3. Computer reviews each input to ensure that all required data are included.

_____ 4. Inventory movements are tracked with a scanner to reduce manual counting.

_____ 5. Purchase orders are signed to approve the purchase.

_____ 6. Computer operators verify dates and serial numbers of master data stores to ensure that the proper version is used.

_____ 7. Count inventory items every year to ensure that inventory records are accurate.

_____ 8. A clerk reviews customer orders to ensure that they have been prepared properly.

_____ 9. Visitors must be approved by a security guard before entering a building.

_____ 10. A code of conduct must be read and signed by all new employees.

P 7-2   Conduct research to determine management's responsibility for establishing and maintaining an adequate system of internal control. Create a written report, in a manner prescribed by your instructor, describing applicable statutory and professional guidance, the implications of internal control obligations, and how management should discharge its internal control responsibilities.

P 7-3   Following is a list of eight generic control goals from the chapter, followed by eight descriptions of either process failures (i.e., control goals not met) or instances of successful control plans (i.e., plans that helped to achieve control goals).

List the numbers 1 through 8 on a solution sheet. Each number represents one of the described situations. Next to each number:

a. Place the *capital* letter of the control goal that *best* matches the situation described.

b. Provide a one- or two-sentence explanation of how the situation relates to the control goal you selected. If you select more than one control goal for a situation, provide an explanation for each that you select.

Hint: Some letters may be used more than once. Conversely, some letters may not apply at all.

Control Goals

A. Ensure effectiveness of operations
B. Ensure efficient employment of resources
C. Ensure security of resources
D. Ensure input validity
E. Ensure input completeness
F. Ensure input accuracy
G. Ensure update completeness
H. Ensure update accuracy

Situations

1. XYZ Co. prepares customer sales orders on a multipart form, one copy of which is sent to its billing department, where it is placed in a temporary file pending shipping notification. Each morning, a billing clerk reviews the file of open sales orders and investigates with the shipping department any missing shipping notices for orders entered 48 hours (or more) earlier.

2. Referring to situation 1, once a shipping notice is received in the billing department, the first step in preparing the invoice to the customer is to compare the unit prices shown on the sales order with a standard price list kept in the billing department.

3. At Otis Company, the accounts receivable master data is updated at the end of each day from payment data contained on the cash receipts event data store. At the completion of the update run, the difference between the total dollar value of accounts receivable before and after the update run is compared to the total dollars of payments being processed.

4. MiniScribe Corporation recorded as sales some shipments of disk drives between their warehouses. These disks drives had not been ordered by anyone and were still the property of MiniScribe.

5. An accounts payable clerk at Woburn Company enters vendor invoices into the computer. When the invoices for a particular day were entered, the computer noted that vendor invoice 12345 appeared twice. The computer rejected the second entry (i.e., the duplicate, the invoice with the same number).

6. In entering the invoices mentioned in situation 1, the data for the payment terms were missing from invoice 12349 and therefore were not keyed into the computer.

7. Instead of preparing deposit slips by hand, Lenox Company has them generated by the computer. The company does so to speed up the deposit of cash (speedy deposit being an objective at Lenox).

8. In a typical cash receipts process, one of the earliest processes is to endorse each customer's check with the legend, for example, "for deposit only to ABC Company."

P 7-4   In the following first list are 10 examples of the items described in the second list.

Match the two lists by placing the *capital* letter from the first list on the blank line preceding the description to which it best relates. You should have two letters left over from List 1.

List 1—Examples

A. Fire extinguishers
B. Deleting an inactive customer's record from customer master data
C. Ensure input validity
D. Ensure security of resources
E. Computer virus
F. Management philosophy and operating style
G. Accounts receivable subsidiary ledger in a manual system
H. Customer name and address
I. The process of increasing customer balances for sales made
J. Cash receipts journal in a manual system

List 2—Descriptions

_____ 1. *Event data* in a computer system.

_____ 2. A control goal of the *information process*.

_____ 3. An element included in the *control environment*.

_____ 4. An element of *standing data*.

_____ 5. A control goal of an *operations process*.

_____ 6. An instance of *data maintenance*.

_____ 7. *Master data* in a computerized system.

_____ 8. An illustration of an *information processing update* (of master data).

P 7-5   The CFO of Amerigein Corporation is very uncomfortable with its current risk exposure related to the possibility of business disruptions. Specifically, Amerigein is heavily involved in e-business, and its internal information systems are tightly interlinked with its key customers' systems. The CFO has estimated that every hour of system downtime will cost the company about $10,000 in sales. The CFO and CIO have further estimated that if the system were to fail, the average downtime would be 1 hour per incident. They have anticipated that Amerigein will likely experience 50 downtime incidents in a given year due to internal computer system problems and another 50 incidents per year due to external problems—specifically, system failures with the Internet service provider (ISP). Currently, Amerigein pays an annualized cost of $150,000 for redundant computer and communication systems, and $100,000 for ISP support just to keep the total expected number of incidents to 100 per year.

Required:

a. Given the information provided thus far, how much ($) is the company's current *expected residual risk*?

b. A further preventive control would be to purchase and maintain more redundant computers and communication lines where possible, at an annualized cost of $100,000, which would reduce the expected number of downtime incidents to 15 per year due to internal computer system problems. What would be the dollar amount of Amerigein's current *residual expected risk* at this point?

c. An external threat still prevails; that is, the ISP could cause the business interruption. Hence, another preventive control would be to increase the annual service fee the company pays to its ISP to a higher level of guaranteed service, based on the following schedule:

Would you purchase a higher level of service from the ISP? If so, what level of service would you purchase? Please defend your answer both quantitatively and qualitatively.

Guaranteed Maximum Number of Downtime Incidents per Year	Annual Cost of Service Support
50	$100,000 (current contract)
40	$150,000
30	$200,000
20	$300,000
10	$425,000
0	$550,000

P 7-6   **Figure 7.8** depicts the adaptation of a sample control matrix from a PricewaterhouseCoopers guide for Section 404 of the Sarbanes-Oxley Act of 2004.[26] We have added some data from the Suprina Company example to the first row of the matrix. Compare the elements in Figure 7.8 to those in Figure 7.7 (pg. 246). What is similar? What is different?

FIGURE 7.8 PwC Sample Control Matrix for Problem 7-6

Subprocess	Control Objective	Description and Frequency of Control Activity	Financial Statement Area	Information Processing Objectives (C, A, V, R)[1]	Assertions (CO, EO, RO, VA, PD)[2]	P or D[3]	A or M[4]
Customer credit check	Provide assurance of customer's creditworthiness	Compare customer's credit limit to the amount of the order, outstanding sales orders, and accounts receivable balances.	None	V	EO, RO, VA	P	A

[1]Completeness (C), accuracy (A), validity (V), and restricted access (R).

[2]Completeness (C), existence or occurrence (EO), rights and obligations (RO), valuation and allocation (VA), and presentation and disclosure (PD).

[3]Preventive (P) or detective (D) control.

[4]Automated (A) or manual (M) control.

---

[26]*Sarbanes-Oxley Act: Section 404 Practical Guidance for Management* (PricewaterhouseCoopers, July 2004): 105.

CHAPTER 8

Controlling Information Systems: Introduction to Pervasive Controls

Learning Objectives

After reading this chapter, you should be able to:

- Describe the major pervasive controls that organizations employ as part of their internal control structure.

- Explain how pervasive controls help ensure continuous, reliable operational and IT processes.

- Appreciate how an organization must plan and organize all resources, including IT resources, to ensure achievement of its strategic vision.

- Overview the major controls used to manage the design and implementation of new processes, especially new IT processes.

- Appreciate the integral part played by the monitoring function in ensuring the overall effectiveness of a system of internal controls.

Walter Pavlo, Jr., helped embezzle $6 million from MCI Communications Inc. and received 2 and a half years in jail for doing so. Pavlo, who oversaw one of the collections departments at MCI, handled as much as $2 billion in delinquent accounts receivables each year. He was pressured by his supervisors to keep the bad debt expenses resulting from unpaid receivables off MCI's books. In response to this steady pressure, Pavlo decided to collude with a friend to concoct a scheme for fraudulently eliminating these bad debts while embezzling money for themselves. The friend posed as an investor willing to cover the receivables of some of MCI's worst customers—those who racked up huge phones bills without paying them. In return for cancelling their debts, Pavlo and his friend convinced these customers to make much-reduced payments into an offshore account in the Cayman Islands. In less than a year, the two embezzlers received $6 million in cash from customers. Pavlo's share was about $700,000. Pavlo said that as long as he told his bosses what they wanted to hear regarding these bad debts, they didn't look too closely at how he achieved the desired results. He said that this lax supervision by his bosses, along with a loose and ineffective internal oversight system, made it easy to embezzle the money. The scheme worked until internal auditors caught a discrepancy in one of the payments. In addition to the jail term, divorce and bankruptcy resulted from Pavlo's crimes.[1]

In January 2008, Jerome Kerviel, a trader for Société Générale bank, caused losses at the bank totaling $7.2 billion by creating fake trades to offset losing trades. Bank

---

[1] J. Napsha, "Embezzling from MCI Easy, Ex-Con Says," *Pittsburgh Tribune-Review*, March 27, 2008.

officials say that Kerviel closed the trades just two to three days before the banks' control programs would have triggered an audit notice. He was able to hack into the bank's computers, override various program change and access controls, and eliminate trade size controlsand credit controls. Kerviel also misappropriated and used passwords from colleagues. Until January 2008, Kerviel was thought to be a diligent employee and refused his supervisor's attempts to get him to take his annual vacation.[2]

In 2008, contractors with the federal government passport office wrongfully accessed information about three presidential candidates. Accessed data included names, social security numbers, birth dates, and previous travel. The contractors had no business with this data and were not authorized to view the data obtained. The incidents also raised questions as to whether the information may have been accessed for political purposes. This access was a failure of the passport office to comply with applicable privacy laws and regulations.[3]

SOX

These stories introduce the subject of this chapter because they are all significant failures of pervasive controls. PCAOB Auditing Standard No. 5, paragraph 24 includes pervasive controls within "entity-level controls" and emphasizes how these controls affect the achievement of control objectives and the more specific business process and application controls.[4] The standard goes on to give examples of entity-level controls, including controls over the organization's structure and environment, controls over major policies, controls over computer processing, and controls that ensure monitoring of other controls.

The control failures discussed previously each relate to one or more of the pervasive controls discussed in this chapter as follows:

- The failure at MCI showed significant weaknesses in management's supervision of an employee. It also illustrates how harmful pressure from the top can be if not carefully monitored, and how damaging collusion can be to the effectiveness of controls.
- The failure at Société Générale bank resulted from significant weaknesses in personnel policies, access controls, and program change controls.
- The failure at the passport office is related to weaknesses in computer processing controls. The contractors at the passport office should not have been able to access the data on the presidential candidates.
- Finally, all of these control problems resulted from monitoring failures where the company's management failed to ensure that controls that should have been in place were operating properly.

Synopsis

Controls

In this chapter we describe four important pervasive controls that comprise a major element in *organizational governance* and *IT governance* initiatives. These controls protect an organization's resources, ensure that business processes operate as planned, assist in the achievement of an organization's objectives, and ensure effective IT operations. The four pervasive controls we discuss in this chapter are: organizational design with a focus on segregation of duties, corporate policies with a focus on personnel policies, monitoring controls, and IT general controls.

[2]J. Goldfarb, D. Cass, and C. Sanati, "Too Many Days on the Job," *The Wall Street Journal*, January 29, 2008, p. C14.

[3]E. Bazar and M. Bello, "State Dept. Investigating Passport-Data Snooping," *USA Today*, March 21, 2008.

[4]"Auditing Standard No. 5—An Audit of Internal Control Over Financial Reporting That Is Integrated with an Audit of Financial Statements," PCAOB, November 9, 2007.

Introduction

In Chapter 7, we discussed *organizational governance* and *Enterprise Risk Management (ERM)* as important organizational governance processes. Recall that an organization establishes a system of controls to provide reasonable assurance that organizational objectives will be achieved (or, alternatively, that risks will be reduced or avoided). In Chapter 7, we also introduced the concept of a control hierarchy that started with the control environment at the highest level, proceeding to more specific control plans. This chapter addresses the second highest level of control plans: *pervasive control plans*, which we defined in Chapter 7 as those that relate to a multitude of control goals and processes. The controls can apply to both manual and automated processes.

Pervasive controls are particularly important because they relate to a multitude of control goals and processes, not just one. Furthermore, pervasive control plans influence the effectiveness of the control plans at lower levels of the control hierarchy: *business process control plans* and *application control plans*. For example, an IT general control plan that restricts access to data and programs stored on a computer can reduce the possibility that computer-based data (e.g., payroll or accounts receivable) will be altered without proper authorization. Thus, the IT general control (restricting access to the computer) will have an impact on *any* application control intended to ensure the reliability of *any* related data. Similarly, a personnel control plan that ensures the hiring of qualified people will have an impact on any control plan for the process or processes that the employee performs.

Organizational Design Control Plans

Organization design involves the creation of roles, processes, and formal reporting relationships in an organization. One aspect of organizational design includes establishing departmental relationships, including the degree of centralization in the organization. Another aspect involves personnel reporting structures such as chain of command and approval levels. An example of organizational design has the upper management of a company reporting to the board of directors. Another example is separation of operating units (e.g., sales, production) from accounting units. Organizational design is a key component of a company's internal control structure.

When organizations are improperly structured, the potential for fraud exists. For example, the CEO and CFO of WorldCom, Inc. thwarted the system of internal controls by authorizing, executing, and recording false accounting transactions that resulted in bogus inflated revenues totaling around $11 billion. The board of directors, which was supposed to serve as a "watchdog" over upper management, was so passive that it failed to uncover the fraud that was taking place under its very nose.[5] The entire system of organizational design apparently imploded at WorldCom.

The Segregation of Duties Control Plan

One of the most important control aspects of organizational design is segregation of duties. **Segregation of duties** consists of separating the four basic functions of event processing:

- *Function 1:* Authorizing events.
- *Function 2:* Executing events.

---

[5]Jim Hopkins, "Report: WorldCom Board Passive," *USA Today—Business*, June 10, 2003.

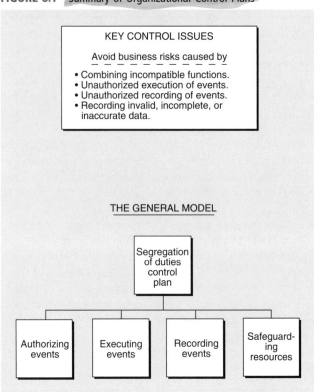

FIGURE 8.1 Summary of Organizational Control Plans

The General Model figure contains:

KEY CONTROL ISSUES

Avoid business risks caused by
- Combining incompatible functions.
- Unauthorized execution of events.
- Unauthorized recording of events.
- Recording invalid, incomplete, or inaccurate data.

THE GENERAL MODEL

Segregation of duties control plan

- Authorizing events
- Executing events
- Recording events
- Safeguarding resources

- *Function 3:* Recording events.
- *Function 4:* Safeguarding resources resulting from consummating events.

The concept underlying segregation of duties is simple enough. Through the design of an appropriate organizational structure, no single employee should be in a position both to perpetrate and to conceal frauds, errors, or other kinds of system failures. **Figure 8.1** summarizes a general model of the segregation of duties control plan. Segregation of duties applies to classic accounting transactions, such as a cash disbursement or credit sale, but also to other events and activities, such as planning a company dinner or implementing a new general ledger system. For example, meeting planners generally execute a company dinner, yet they must get approval from senior management for the event, expenses, location, guest list, and so on. In addition, the event must be deemed safe and secure for employees, and cost-beneficial to the company and its stakeholders. Thus, segregation of authorization, execution, recording, and safeguarding applies even to a company dinner. To summarize, no matter what the "event," for proper control, more than one person must be involved, and functions must be separated.

Table 8.1 illustrates segregation of duties for a traditional accounting transaction. Examine the top half of the table, which defines the four basic functions. Controls to prevent *unauthorized* execution of events help prevent *fraud* by ensuring that only *valid* events are recorded. Therefore, Function 1, authorizing events, takes on particular significance in our segregation of duties model. Control plans for authorizing or approving events empower individuals or computers to initiate events and to approve actions taken subsequently in executing and recording events. The bottom half of the

TABLE 8.1 Illustration of Segregation of Duties

Function 1	Function 2	Function 3	Function 4
Authorizing Events	Executing Events	Recording Events	Safeguarding Resources Resulting from Consummating Events
Activities • Approve phases of event processing.	• Physically move resources. • Complete source documents.	• Record events in books of original entry. • Post event summaries to the general ledger.	• Physically protect resources. • Maintain accountability of physical resources.
Example: Processing a credit sales event			

Activities
• Approve customer credit.
• Approve picking inventory and sending inventory to shipping department.
• Approve shipping inventory to customer.
• Approve recording accounting entries.
	Physical Movement Resources
	• Pick inventory from bins.
	• Move inventory from warehouse to shipping department.
	• Ship inventory to customer.
	
	Complete Source Documents
	• Complete sales order.
	• Complete shipping document.
	• Complete invoice.
		Record Event Details
		DR AR–A/R Subsidiary Ledger
		   CR Sales–Sales Journal
		
		DR Cost of Goods Sold-Inventory Ledger
		   CR Inventory–Inventory Ledger
		
		Post Event GL Summaries
		DR AR
		   CR Sales
		
		DR Cost of Goods Sold
		   CR Inventory
			Physically Protect
			• Safeguard inventory while in storage at warehouse, while in transit to shipping department, and while being prepared for shipment to customer.
			
			Maintain Accountability
			• Examine and count inventory periodically, and compare physical total to recorded total.

table extends the coverage of segregation of duties by illustrating the processing of a credit sales event.

Let's examine Table 8.1 as a means of better understanding the control notion underlying segregation of duties. Ideal segregation of duties requires that different units (departments) of an organization carry out each of the four phases of event processing. In this way, *collusion* would need to occur between one or more persons (or departments) to exploit the system and conceal abuse. Whenever collusion is necessary to commit a fraud, a greater likelihood exists that the perpetrators will be deterred by the risks associated with getting another individual involved in the fraud. Thus, at a minimum, an organization must be large enough to support at least four independent units to implement segregation of duties *effectively*. For example, the *customer service department* might be responsible for accepting customer orders and completing sales orders. The *credit department* might be responsible for determining the existence of customers and approving their creditworthiness. The *warehouse* might be responsible for safeguarding inventory while it is being stored. The *shipping department* might be responsible for protecting inventory while it is awaiting shipment and for executing the shipment.

However, it is possible to go a step further in implementing segregation of duties and making controls even more effective. A company can do this by assigning more than one person to a single function—for example, by having two employees authorize the release of a purchase order or requiring dual signatures on checks. Of course, these procedures usually increase the overall number of employees involved in the business processes, thereby raising labor costs. As with most business decisions, it is necessary to conduct cost-benefit analysis when making decisions about the degree to which a company should implement segregation of duties. So how would we accomplish segregation of duties in small organizations that have few employees? Perhaps we don't—or at least not as completely as we would like. At a minimum, we should strive to separate the most critical duties. For example, in inventory, we should separate record keeping from physical custody. Also, in this kind of environment, we would place greater reliance on management supervision, ownership involvement in the day-to-day operations of the business, and personnel control plans aimed at hiring honest employees. These alternative control plans are commonly called *compensatory controls*.

E-Business

On the other hand, for large companies with highly automated e-business processes, how do we accomplish segregation of duties? For example, in some e-business trading partner arrangements, a retail store's computer is authorized to automatically send a stock replenishment order to a vendor when shelf inventory runs low. The vendor's computer automatically causes the goods to be shipped to the retail store. In turn, the retail store's computer automatically pays the vendor after the goods have been received. In this example, computer-based rules authorized the purchase, movement, and receipt of goods and payment for the goods. These procedures receive management authorization when the system is approved during initial development or when the system is changed.

SOX

Although consolidating authorization, execution, and recordkeeping functions within a software program may appear to be a bad idea, doing so may actually serve to *increase* internal control. For example, automated credit checks to *authorize* sales will—if the programs are tested and implemented properly—be *consistently* performed on *every* sale. The sales order will not be prepared (i.e., *executed*) and sent to shipping unless the credit check has been performed. Finally, the sale will not be *recorded* unless an authorized person (e.g., a shipping clerk) enters the shipment. The system can also keep a record of when and by whom each step was performed. Thus, during a SOX 404 review of internal controls, this automated segregation of duties can be tested to determine that the controls are in place (i.e., they are in the programs) and have been performed (the audit trail). This automation of segregation of duties may provide a more *efficient* and *effective* system of internal control in automated processes.

Enterprise Systems

To further ensure appropriate segregation of duties, large companies with highly automated systems are purchasing and installing Segregation of Duties (SOD) software such as *Symantec Corp.'s Security Information Manager (SSIM)* and *Control Compliance Suite* and *Approva's Authorization Insight*. This software works with major ERP systems (e.g., SAP, Oracle, PeopleSoft) and, after it is set up for a company, it monitors user access levels across the system to prevent, detect, and correct segregation of duties conflicts and inappropriate access to sensitive transactions.[6]

Personnel Policy Control Plans

A **policy** is a plan or process put in place to guide actions and thus achieve goals. The term *policy* applies to company activities in a variety of areas. For example, most companies have personnel, customer relations, and approval level policies. Policies differ from law. Whereas law can compel behaviors and enforce penalties for noncompliance (e.g., a law requiring the payment of taxes), policies merely guide behavior toward the actions that are most likely to achieve desired goals. One major policy area that significantly affects internal control in an organization is the area of personnel policies.

All personnel must be managed to maximize their contributions to the organization. Specific attention must be paid to recruitment, promotion, personnel qualifications, training, backup, performance evaluation, job change, and termination. An organization

---

[6]Thomas Hoffman, "Calibrating Toward Compliance," *Computerworld*, February 6, 2006, pp. 21–24.

that does not have a critical mass of honest, competent employees will find it virtually impossible to implement other control plans.

Personnel control plans help to protect an organization against certain types of risks. For example, hiring incompetent employees could result in time and money being wasted on futile training programs. Alternatively, offering employment to an individual unqualified to fill a position may preclude efficient, effective operations or, if the person cannot follow instructions, may lead to inaccurate information processing. Hiring an employee with a prior record of dishonesty exposes the organization to a greater possibility of *fraud*.

Figure 8.2 summarizes a number of personnel control plans aimed at mitigating the effects of these types of risks. As you study each plan, think of the risks that the plan can prevent or the control goal that could be achieved by implementing the plan.

FIGURE 8.2 Summary of Personnel Control Plans

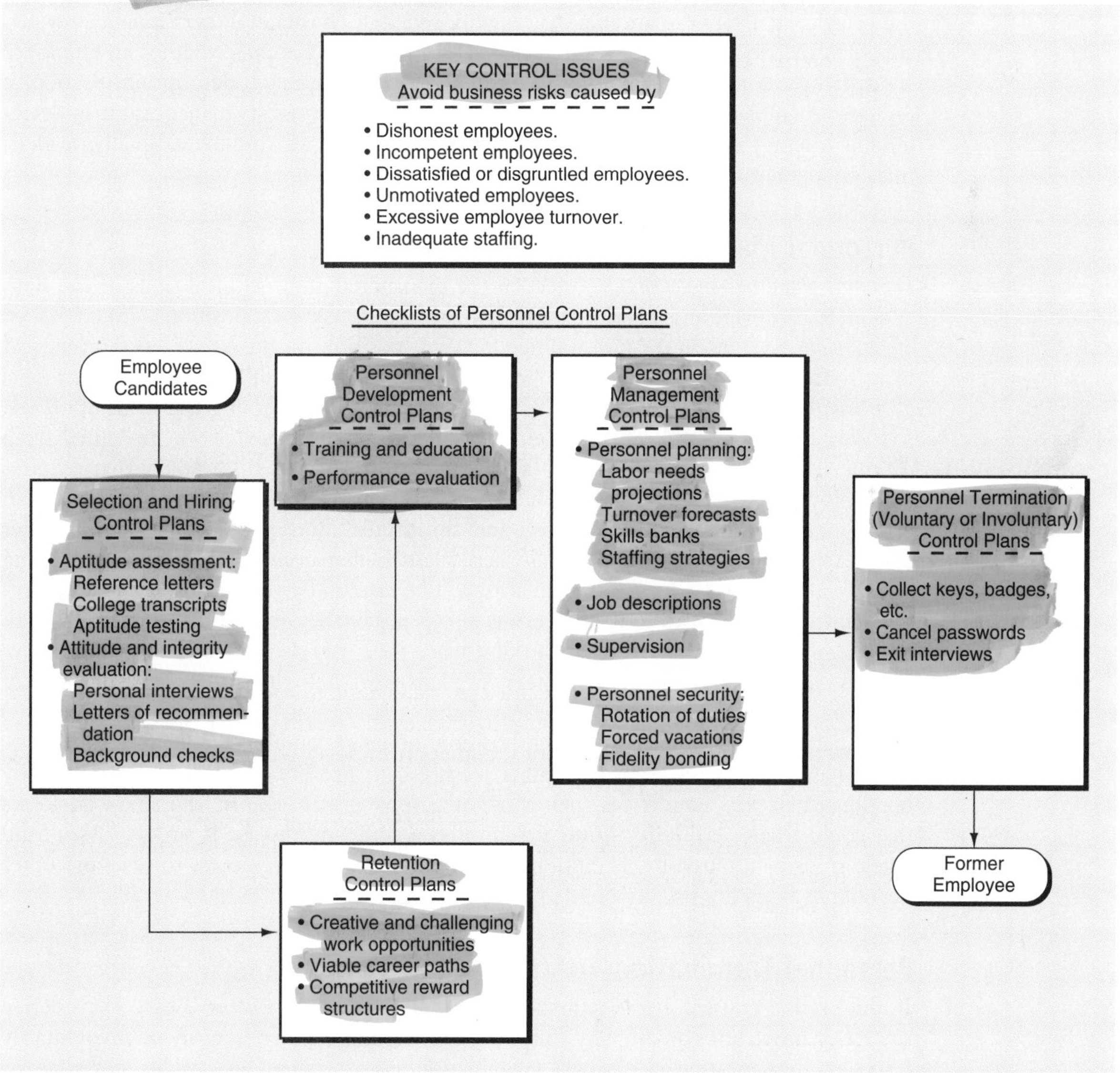

Selection and Hiring Control Plans

Candidates applying for positions should be carefully screened, selected, and hired. A multitude of control plans exist for selection and hiring. Companies choose which plans to employ based on the salary level and job duties for the position for which the candidate is applying.

Retention Control Plans

Retaining qualified personnel can be even more difficult than hiring them. Companies should make every effort to provide creative and challenging work opportunities and, when possible, to offer open channels to management-level positions.

Personnel Development Control Plans

Training must be regular, not haphazard. Deficiencies noted in an employee's background should be rectified through proper training or education. Training must be a top priority in arranging an employee's work schedule. In general, performance reviews are performed for at least four reasons. First, a review determines whether an employee is satisfying the requirements of a position as indicated by a job description. Second, it assesses an employee's strengths and weaknesses. Third, it assists management in determining whether to make salary adjustments and promote an employee. Finally, it identifies opportunities for training and for personal growth.

Personnel Management Control Plans

Personnel planning control plans project future managerial and technical skills of the staff, anticipate turnover, and develop a strategy for filling necessary positions. *Job description control plans* lay out the responsibilities for each position on an organization chart and identify the resources to be used in performing those responsibilities. *Supervision control plans* involve the processes of approving, monitoring, and observing the work of others.

Personnel security control plans help prevent the organization's own personnel from committing acts of fraud or theft of assets. **Rotation of duties** is a policy that requires an employee to alternate jobs periodically. **Forced vacations** is a policy that requires an employee to take leave from the job and substitutes another employee in his or her place. The control notion underlying these plans is that if an employee is perpetrating some kind of irregularity, that irregularity will be *detected* by the substitute (i.e., a detective control). Furthermore, if these plans are in place, they should act as a deterrent to the irregularity ever occurring in the first place (i.e., a preventive control). In addition to these control considerations, the two plans also help lessen the disruption that might be caused when an employee leaves the organization. Because another person(s) is familiar with the job duties of each position, no single employee is irreplaceable.

What if personnel security control plans fail to prevent employee dishonesty? By bonding their key employees, many organizations insure against the financial losses that could result. A **fidelity bond** indemnifies a company in case it suffers losses from defalcations committed by its employees. Employees who have access to cash and other negotiable assets are usually bonded.

Personnel Termination Control Plans

In this section you will learn about *personnel termination control plans*. These plans define the set of procedures a company follows when an employee voluntarily or involuntarily leaves an organization. Voluntary termination occurs when an employee retires or leaves to pursue other opportunities. Involuntary termination occurs when an employee is laid off or fired for cause. Termination control plans are particularly important when employees are fired for cause because the employee is likely to be upset or angry and thus likely to do damage to the organization. Termination can be immediate, or companies can require notice. Immediate termination is appropriate when the employee can damage property or perhaps steal sensitive information. Notice is appropriate when staffing is an issue or the employee needs to train a replacement. Termination control plans include collecting any items displaying the company's identification (e.g., letterhead), reclaiming office and building keys, and removing password access to data.

Monitoring Control Plans

Monitoring in an internal control system means assessment by management to determine whether the control plans in place are continuing to function appropriately over time. It further involves making sure that any control weaknesses are communicated to responsible parties on a timely basis and that the responsible parties take appropriate action. The Committee of Sponsoring Organizations of the Treadway Commission (COSO) believes that monitoring has often been underused by organizations.[7] Ineffective monitoring can result in a failure of the control system itself or, less severely, in a failure to implement control plans to correct identified problems.

Monitoring consists of two parts: The first is putting controls in place to periodically follow up on the operation of control plans. The processes include determining a *baseline* to know when a control is operating effectively, to identify if there is a *change* in a process or a control plan itself, and to periodically *test* that a control is operating. For example, a control *baseline* for a sales process might be the expected number of credit/collection failures in a given period. Monitoring *change* would include observation of the addition of a new sales outlet with different order entry procedures or noticing an increase in turnover in the sales entry department. These changes may indicate that the control processes need to be retested and that monitoring should be increased.

The second part of monitoring is ensuring that appropriate *communications* are taking place. A control weakness should be reported to the person responsible for the control's operation and at least one person at a higher level. In one of our earlier examples (the trader for Société Générale), an employee was not taking required vacation days. His immediate supervisor knew of this control weakness, but no monitoring was in place to make sure that personnel higher than the direct supervisor were aware of the violation of the forced vacation control plan.

Monitoring control plans differ from normal control plans in that they verify the operation of the normal control plans. A normal control plan only serves to detect and correct errors. Monitoring control plans lead to the identification of the root cause of the error and ideally the implementation of normal control plans to prevent future errors. Continuing our example of the forced vacation control plan, monitoring that control plan would involve creating a periodic exception report listing all employees who have not taken vacations within a specified time frame and ensuring that report was reviewed and acted upon by management. To further illustrate the difference between normal control plans and monitoring control plans, let's take the control plan of implementing an employee code of conduct. Writing and distributing the code of

---

[7]*Internal Control—Integrated Framework: Guidance on Monitoring* (New York: Committee of Sponsoring Organizations of the Treadway Commission, September 2007).

conduct outlining appropriate employee behavior is a normal control plan; a monitoring control plan would involve periodically collecting and reviewing letters signed by the employees that they have read, understand, and will follow the code of conduct.

IT General Controls and the COBIT Framework

We have discussed *organizational governance* as the processes employed by organizations to select objectives, establish processes to achieve objectives, and monitor performance. **IT governance** is a process that ensures that the enterprise's IT sustains and extends the organization's strategies and objectives.[8]

How important is IT to supporting organizational objectives? What are management's concerns about IT? Two recent surveys should give you some idea of the answers to these questions and highlight how critical IT is to most, if not all, businesses. The first, a 2009 survey by The Standish Group, revealed these top 10 IT management concerns, all about IT's capability to support an organization's vision and strategy (listed in order of importance):[9]

1. Decline in IT investments by companies due to the current economic recession
2. Overall security of IT assets, especially due to the threats from viruses, hackers, and malicious behavior
3. Need for project management leadership
4. Increasing demand for green computing (or enviro-computing)
5. Regulatory compliance, especially with such federal regulations as GAAP, FDA, HIPAA, Sarbanes-Oxley, and SAS 70
6. Growing use of service-oriented architectures (SOA) (discussed in Chapter 3), primarily in regard to how to take advantage of this trend for one's own company
7. Optimizing IT use to compensate for the current decline in IT budgets during the present economic downturn (related to number 1 above)
8. Maintaining IT readiness, including disaster recovery planning
9. Managing business processes to align organizations with the needs of clients and to increase organizational innovation, flexibility, and integration with technology
10. Increasing the use of open source programs (in which the source code is available without cost) and standard infrastructures (in which the same IT components are used throughout the organization)

If we focus on IT security concerns (number 2 in the list above), a recent survey by The Ponemon Institute of 577 IT security professionals reported the following top eight concerns (again in order of importance):[10]

1. Data breaches
2. Cyber crimes, including cyber attacks
3. Workforce mobility
4. Outsourcing
5. Cloud computing
6. Mobility devices, including laptops and cell phones

---

[8]Adapted from *COBIT 4.1: Control Objectives for Information and Related Technology* (Rolling Meadows, IL: IT Governance Institute, 2007): 5.

[9]Jim Johnson, "Top 10 CIO Concerns for 2009," *SoftwareMag.com*, September 2009 (www.softwaremag.com/l.cfm?doc=1230-9/2009, last accessed February 4, 2010).

[10]"2009 Security Mega Trends Survey," The Ponemon Institute LLC, November 2008.

7. P2P (person-to-person) file sharing
8. Web 2.0, e.g., blogs and social networking sites

These concerns are addressed by IT general controls as part of the IT governance process. We begin our coverage of these control issues by introducing a hypothetical computer system. This system has multiple connections among the IT resources within and outside the organization. We then outline the personnel who operate the hypothetical computer system and the functions these personnel perform. After introducing the system and personnel, we discuss the COBIT framework and *IT general controls*.

A Hypothetical Computer System

IT resources are typically configured with some or all of the elements shown in **Figure 8.3**, which we will use to focus our discussions. This computer system consists of one or more *servers* clustered together and housed in a computer room within the organization's headquarters. This computer is connected to printers, external storage devices, and PCs, usually called *clients*, located within the building, and to PCs located in the organization's other facilities. All of these connections are via networks, often referred to as *local area networks (LANs)* or *wide area networks (WANs)*. Finally, computer facilities operated by other organizations are connected, perhaps via the *Internet* and through *firewalls*, to the internal servers, PCs, and other equipment.

FIGURE 8.3 A Hypothetical Computer System

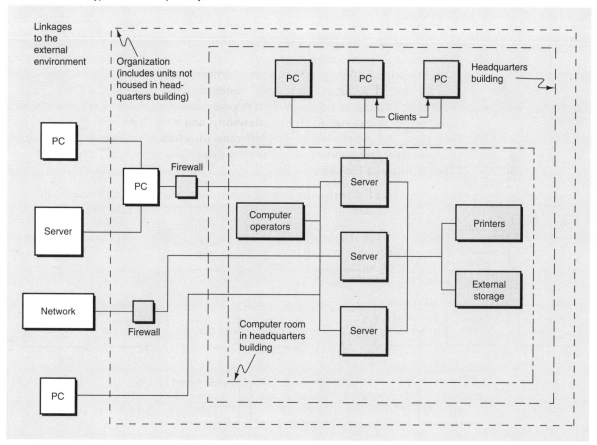

Controlling the operation of this configuration provides many challenges to the organization. To support organizational objectives and to provide an environment in which business process control plans can be effective, we must determine how we can protect the computer from misuse, whether intentional or unintentional, from inside and outside the organization. Additionally, how do we protect the computer room, the headquarters building, and the rooms and buildings in which other connected facilities are located? In the event of a disaster, do we have plans in place for continuing our operations? What policies and procedures should be established (and documented) to provide for efficient, effective, and authorized use of the computer? What measures can we take to help ensure that the personnel who operate and use the computer are competent and honest? Answers to these and similar questions run to the heart of *IT general controls*.

The Information Systems Organization

Before we begin the discussion of IT general controls, however, we need to take a look at the information systems organization, which is the department or function that develops and operates an organization's information system. The function (department) is composed of people, procedures, and equipment, and is typically called the *information systems department*, *IS department*, or *IT department*. **Figure 8.4** depicts a typical IT department.

FIGURE 8.4 Information Systems Organization

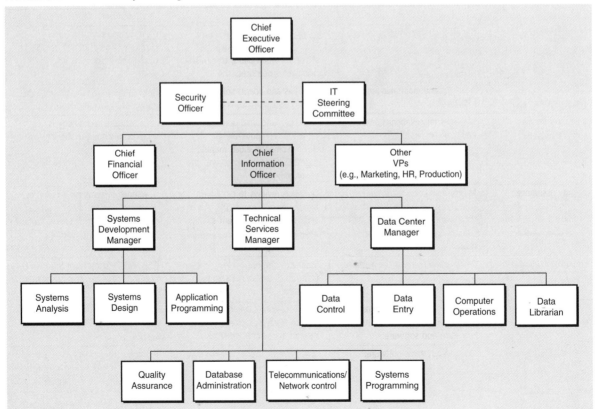

Table 8.2 outlines the principal responsibilities, major duties, and key control concerns related to each functional box depicted in Figure 8.4. We include key control concerns in Table 8.2 to increase your appreciation of how control issues relate to particular functional activities and to the organization of the information system as a whole.

Take time to thoroughly study Figure 8.4 and Table 8.2 so that you have a good understanding of the principal responsibilities, major duties, and key control concerns of each functional title. Although titles may vary from company to company, the

TABLE 8.2 Summary of IT Organization Functions

Functional Title (see Figure 8.4)	Principal Responsibilities	Major Duties	Key Control Concerns
Steering committee	Guide and advise IT.	Prioritize and select IT projects and resources.	Organization and IT strategic objectives are misaligned.
Security officer	Ensure the security of all IT resources.	Physical security (e.g., building and computer) and logical security (enterprise data).	Disasters (e.g., hurricanes, terrorist attacks, power outages, fires, hackers).
Chief information officer (CIO)	Efficient, effective operation of IT. Alignment of IT resources and organization objectives.	Plans IT acquisition and development; controls IT operations.	IT function fails to support organization's mission.
Systems development manager	Delivers cost-effective, bugfree applications.	Supervises applications systems development; sets and monitors multiple project deadlines.	Systems development can develop and implement systems without management or user approval.
Systems analysis	Studies information-related problems and proposes solutions.	Analyzes existing system; writes specifications.	Combining analysis with programming or design precludes containment of analysis errors.
Systems design	Converts analyst's specifications into a design.	Devises program specifications, report layouts, data requirements, implementation plans, tests plans, and user procedures.	Combining design with programming or analysis precludes containment of design errors.
Application programming	Develops and maintains application software.	Modifies and adapts software.	Programmers can easily access programs and data.
Technical services manager	Manages miscellaneous specialized and technical functions.	Manages functional units such as networks, computer-aided design/computer-aided manufacturing (CAD/CAM), and systems programming.	Access to this technology is a vulnerable point in the information system.
Quality assurance	Maintains quality management standards and systems. Ensures continuous improvement of systems development and data quality.	Conducts reviews to determine adherence to IT standards and procedures and achievement of IT objectives.	Developed systems fail to achieve objectives. Projects not completed on time and within budgets. Data fail to satisfy quality criteria.
Database administration (DBA)	Designs and controls the database.	Maintains database software; monitors and controls access to the database.	DBA is the central point from which to control data and is a central point of vulnerability.
Telecommunications/ network control	Installs and supports organizational telecommunications and network hardware and software.	Acquires, installs, maintains, and secures telecommunications and network hardware and software.	Less than optimal performance of telecommunications and networks. Security breaches.
Systems programming	Maintains systems software.	Modifies and adapts systems software, including operating systems and various utility routines.	Systems programmers can easily access applications programs and data.

(continued)

TABLE 8.2   Summary of IT Organization Functions (*continued*)

Functional Title (see Figure 8.4)	Principal Responsibilities	Major Duties	Key Control Concerns
Data center manager	Plans, controls, and delivers IT production activities.	Monitors computer operations; hires, schedules, and oversees personnel on multishift operations.	Systems development activities undertaken by operations personnel can bypass normal controls.
Data control	Routes all work into and out of the data center; corrects errors; monitors all error correction.	Checks input and output batches for validity, completeness, and accuracy; distributes output.	An independent data control function ensures valid, complete, and accurate processing.
Data entry	Prepares input for computer processing.	Keys data directly into computer; uses offline devices to record data on magnetic or optical disks.	High risk of data conversion errors, which have pervasive impact.
Computer operations	Provides efficient and effective operation of the computer equipment.	Mounts tapes, disks, and other media; monitors equipment operation.	An operator allowed to program the computer can make unauthorized software changes.
Data librarian	Maintains custody of and controls access to programs, files, and documentation.	Issues programs, data, and documentation to authorized users; maintains record of data, program, and documentation usage.	Controlled access to data, programs, and documentation reduces unauthorized program changes and unauthorized computer operations.

functionality of the positions remains stable; for example, the Chief Information Officer might also be called the Vice President of IT, or the Chief Technology Officer. Also, note the difference between the two types of programming: Application programming produces software that provides services to the user (e.g., sales, accounting, HR), whereas systems programming produces software that manages computer hardware (e.g., accessing data on servers, printing).

The COBIT Framework

SOX

In Chapter 7, we discussed COSO as a general framework for internal control. COSO is also the framework suggested by the PCAOB as a suitable framework to guide management's assessment of internal control for SOX Section 404. However, the PCAOB made no such recommendation for IT controls. Nevertheless, one framework that has been widely adopted for IT governance and IT controls is **COBIT** (Control Objectives for Information and Related Technology). COBIT was developed by the IT Governance Institute to provide guidance to managers, users, and auditors on the best practices for the management of information technology. According to COBIT, IT resources (i.e., applications, information, infrastructure, and people) must be managed by IT control processes to ensure that an organization has the information it needs to achieve its objectives.[11] COBIT thus supports IT governance by providing a framework to ensure that:

- IT is aligned with the business.
- IT enables the business and maximizes benefits.

---

[11]*COBIT 4.1: Control Objectives for Information and Related Technology* (Rolling Meadows, IL: IT Governance Institute, 2007): 12.

- IT resources are used responsibly.
- IT risks are managed appropriately.[12]

Because we use the COBIT framework to organize the control processes described in this chapter, we should include here the COBIT definition for control:

> The policies, procedures, practices, and organizational structures designed to provide reasonable assurance that business objectives will be achieved and that undesired events will be prevented or detected and corrected.[13]

Let's compare this definition to those proposed by COSO and this textbook. Notice that all three definitions refer to the achievement of objectives. The COBIT definition adds the idea that controls should address "undesired events." This is similar to our assertion here and in Chapter 7 that internal controls—and in this particular instance, IT processes—should reduce the possibility that risks will occur.

COBIT's Four Broad IT Control Process Domains

COBIT groups IT control processes into four broad domains: (1) Plan and Organize, (2) Acquire and Implement, (3) Deliver and Support, and (4) Monitor and Evaluate. **Figure 8.5** on page 270 depicts the relationship of these four domains and lists the IT control processes within each domain, for a total of 10 processes. Notice that the Monitor and Evaluate domain provides feedback to the other three domains.

Before we move on to a discussion of the 10 IT control processes, let's discuss the concept of a control process. First, a "control process" could easily be, and often is, referred to as a "management practice." The latter terminology emphasizes management's responsibility for control in the organization. Second, the prominence of "process" in this terminology reminds us that control is an ongoing activity. Within each process, there are specific plans or activities that an organization undertakes to achieve its goals.[14]

Plan and Organize Domain

Within the Plan and Organize domain are processes to develop the strategy and tactics for realizing an organization's IT strategy. The overriding goal of these processes is to identify ways that IT can best contribute to the achievement of the organization's objectives. After a strategic vision is set, management must communicate the vision to affected parties (inside and outside the organization) and put in place the IT organization and technology infrastructure that enables that vision. The Plan and Organize domain also includes processes that identify and address threats and IT requirements to address those threats. Finally, this domain includes efforts to identify and take advantage of emerging information technology to gain competitive advantage.

IT Process 1: Establish Strategic Vision for Information Technology

Management of the information services function should adopt a process for developing a strategic plan and for converting that plan into short-term goals. The information

---

[12]*COBIT 4.1: Control Objectives for Information and Related Technology* (Rolling Meadows, IL: IT Governance Institute, 2007): 6.

[13]*COBIT 4.1: Control Objectives for Information and Related Technology* (Rolling Meadows, IL: IT Governance Institute, 2007): 13.

[14]COBIT uses the term "IT processes" to refer to "IT control plans." While we retain that terminology here, you should consider the terms "control plans" and "control processes" to be equivalent.

systems strategic planning effort must ensure that the organization's strategic plan is supported and that information technology is used to the best advantage of the organization. An organization wants to be sure that the information systems function is prepared to anticipate the competition's actions and to take advantage of emerging information technology. An organization must establish links between organizational and information systems strategic planning to ensure that strategies plotted in the organizational plan receive the IT support they need.

Strategic planning processes, and corresponding activities within IT process 1, include the following:

1. *A summary of the organizational strategic plan's goals and strategies, and how they are related to IT:* This information is included to provide a framework for the strategic IT plan and to make sure that the IT plan is directed toward achieving organizational objectives.
2. *IT goals and strategies, and a statement of how each will support organizational goals and strategies:* These strategies include a description of major information subsystems

FIGURE 8.5 Four Broad IT Control Process Domains (from COBIT) and 10 Important IT Control Processes

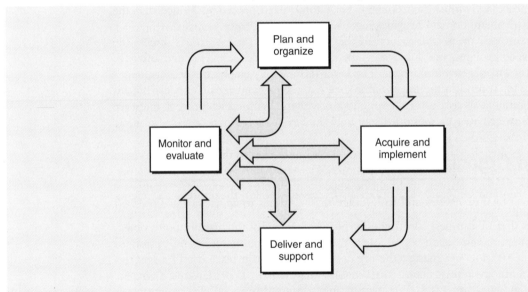

IT Control Processes and Domains

Domain	Plan and Organize	Acquire and Implement	Deliver and Support	Monitor and Evaluate
IT Control Process	1. Establish strategic vision for IT. 2. Develop tactics to plan, communicate, and manage realization of the strategic vision.	3. Identify automated solutions. 4. Develop and acquire IT solutions. 5. Integrate IT solutions into operational processes. 6. Manage changes to existing IT systems.	7. Deliver required IT services. 8. Ensure security and continuous service. 9. Provide support services.	10. Monitor and evaluate the processes.

and applications. Mission-critical applications—those IT applications central to the successful competitive performance of the organization—must be separately identified and monitored.

3. *An information architecture model encompassing the corporate data model and the associated information systems:* Plans for any new lines of business, such as e-business, or changes in business processes, such as changeover to an enterprise system, will require new data and relationships among the data. These data elements and relationships must be incorporated into the organization's information architecture model.

E-Business

Enterprise Systems

4. *An inventory of current IT capabilities:* The inventory should include hardware (computers and networks), software, personnel (quantities and skills), application systems, usage rates, strengths, and weaknesses. This inventory should address both primary and backup facilities. A process must be in place to review IT capabilities to ensure that there is adequate technology to take advantage of emerging technology.

5. *Acquisition and development schedules for hardware, software, and application systems and for personnel and financial requirements:* These should be stated in detail for the following one or two years and should provide a basis for specific actions and for control.

6. IT-related requirements to comply with industry, regulatory, legal, and contractual obligations, including safety, privacy, transborder data flows, e-business, and insurance contracts: To avoid fines, sanctions, and loss of business, the organization must maintain procedures to ensure awareness and compliance with these obligations.

E-Business

7. IT risks and the risk action plan: To ensure the achievement of IT objectives, in support of business objectives, and to respond to threats to the provision of IT services, management should establish a risk-assessment framework, including risk identification, measurement, actions, and the formal acceptance and communication of the residual risk.

8. Process for modifying the plan to accommodate changes to the organization's strategic plan and changes in IT conditions: The strategic IT plan should not be a static document. Rather, it should be kept up to date to accommodate changes in organizational objectives and to leverage opportunities to apply information technology for the strategic advantage of the organization.

IT Process 2: Develop Tactics to Plan, Communicate, and Manage Realization of the Strategic Vision

To ensure adequate funding for IT, controlled disbursement of financial resources, and effective and efficient use of IT resources, an organization must manage IT resources by using IT capital and operating budgets, by justifying IT expenditures, and by monitoring costs (in light of risks).

To ensure the overall effectiveness of the IT function, management must establish a direction and related *policies* that are consistent with the *control environment* established by the organization's senior management. Then these policies must be communicated (internally and externally) to obtain commitment and compliance. These policies address such aspects as departmental codes of conduct/ethics, quality standards, personnel policies, and security/disclosure policies. Personnel policies are particularly important in the IT department. Because of the extensive technical skills required, IT personnel have been in high demand over the past decade or two. This high demand could easily cause managers to overlook organizational hiring policies or termination policies. However, incompetent or disgruntled IT personnel can cause a lot of damage in a short time. For example, computer operations personnel could intentionally or unintentionally erase large amounts of stored data in a matter of minutes, or computer programmers could destroy programs or documentation. Thus, while all departments within a company should implement personnel policies, rigorous application of these policies is particularly important in IT.

To ensure that projects are undertaken in order of importance, completed on time, and completed within budget, management must establish a project-management framework to ensure that project selection is in line with plans and that a project-management methodology is applied to each project undertaken.

Finally, similar to other departments, IT departments must be designed properly and implement policies to ensure that IT services are delivered in an efficient and effective manner. IT departments must employ *organizational design* principles such as appropriate reporting structures and *segregation of duties*.

The entire IT organization acts in a service capacity for other operating units *across* the organization. In this role, it should be limited to carrying out function 3 in Table 8.1 (pg. 259), *recording* events. Approving and executing accounting transactions along with safeguarding non-IT assets should be carried out by departments other than IT. This arrangement allows for the effective implementation of segregation of duties *across* the organization. As we described earlier in this chapter, it sometimes seems that this functional division is violated; for instance, some IT systems appear to authorize and execute events: The computer might be programmed to create a PO, approve payment, and create a check after a receipt notice is entered. However, in this example, the authorization actually occurred when the appropriate manager developed and implemented the computer-based rules, and the safeguarding of assets (inventory received) was in the hands of the receiving function. Any requests to change the computer-based rules must be restricted to authorized persons who are not part of IT.

We also have organizational control plans and segregation of duties that must occur *within* the IT department. While users own the transaction processing application, data and control processes, the IT department is responsible for making the applications work to the satisfaction of the users. Thus, the IT department has responsibility for implementing and updating programs based on authorized user requests, processing data for users accurately and completely, and protecting data and computer equipment. When looking at these responsibilities of the IT department, remember it is important to segregate the four basic functions of events: authorizing events, executing events, recording events, and safeguarding resources. Within the IT department, these responsibilities are treated as events and must be appropriately divided. For example, programmers should not be able to authorize a program change, write the code to change the program, run a program, or have unlimited access to data. If they could, a programmer might authorize a change to the payroll program to double his salary each pay period, execute that change into the computer program code, then run the program, and hide the overpayment by changing the data.

Let's go back to the organizational chart of our hypothetical IT department (Figure 8.4, pg. 266) and the summary of organizational functions (Table 8.2, pp. 267–268). At the top of the chart and figure, we see the IT steering committee. This committee should consist of about seven executives from major functional areas of the organization, including the CIO; report to senior management; and meet regularly. This **IT steering committee** coordinates the organizational and IT strategic planning processes and reviews and approves the strategic IT plan. The steering committee guides the IT organization in establishing and meeting user information requirements and in ensuring

TABLE 8.3   Illustration of Segregation of Duties *within* the IT Department

Function 1	Function 2	Function 3	Function 4
Authorizing Events	**Executing Events**	**Recording Events**	**Safeguarding Resources Resulting from Consummating Events**
• Approve IT activities and budgets.	• Create or update programs.	• Process data received from user departments.	• Protect data and computer equipment.
IT personnel			
• Steering committee • Chief Information Officer	• Systems development manager • Systems analysis, design and programming • Systems Programming	• Data center manager • Data control • Data preparation • Computer operations	• Security officer • Technical service manager • Quality assurance, database administrator, and telecommunications • Data librarian

the effective and efficient use of its resources. The steering committee and the CIO are the main authorizing bodies within the IT department.

Also at the top of the chart and table is the security officer. The **security officer** is charged with safeguarding the IT organization and does so by (1) establishing employee passwords and access to data and (2) making sure the IT organization is secure from physical threats. The security officer might also monitor employees' network access, grant security clearance for sensitive projects, and work with human resources to ensure that interview practices, such as thorough background checks, are conducted during the hiring process. The data librarian also assists in protecting data and separating key functions. For example, a librarian function grants access to stored data and programs to authorized personnel only. This separation reduces the risk of unauthorized computer operation or unauthorized programming by operators. Librarian controls, combined with restricting access to the database and making the security officer responsible for assigning passwords, are critical to separating key functions within IT and protecting computing resources.

The development and programming activities are the main events that the IT department "executes." However, as noted earlier, its main service to other departments is recording transaction events.

Previously, Table 8.2 (pp. 267–268) described the major duties of the other personnel in the IT department. Now **Table 8.3** shows the segregation of these duties *within* the IT department.

Acquire and Implement Domain

Processes within the Acquire and Implement domain are designed to identify, develop or acquire, and implement IT solutions. Failure to successfully execute these processes can lead to significant risks throughout the organization. For example, if we do not correctly determine the requirements for a new information system *and* see that those requirements are satisfied by the new system, the new system could cause us to violate accounting standards or perform calculations incorrectly. Or we may not complete the development on time, putting us at a competitive disadvantage if our competition implements such a system first. Finally, should we fail to implement proper controls for the new system, we could experience several risks, including erroneous financial reporting, fraud, and loss of resources. This domain also includes changes to existing systems. As business requirements change or software becomes obsolete, the existing system must be modified to keep meeting user requirements.

Thus, the Acquire and Implement domain includes what is often referred to the **systems development life cycle (SDLC)**. The SDLC covers the progression of information systems *through* the systems development process, from birth, through implementation, to ongoing use and modification. Our discussion of this domain is brief here because these processes are analyzed in depth in Chapter 17.

IT Process 3: Identify Automated Solutions

An organization's SDLC must include procedures to define information requirements, formulate alternative courses of action, perform feasibility studies, and assess risks. These solutions should be consistent with the strategic IT plan and the technology and data infrastructure. At the completion of this process, an organization must decide what approach will be taken to satisfy users' requirements, and whether it will develop the IT solution in-house or will contract with third parties for all or part of the development.

IT Process 4: Develop and Acquire IT Solutions

After an IT solution has been determined and approved, then application software and infrastructure must be acquired or developed. We use application software as the general term for the software that is used to facilitate the execution of a given business process. However, a business process may use more than one application. For instance, an order-to-cash process might have one application for customer relationships, one for sales orders, and another for customer payments. In all likelihood, these applications would be linked to one another; nevertheless, they might actually represent three distinct applications.

Develop and Acquire Application Software

Design specifications include those for inputs, outputs, processes, programs, and stored data. To ensure that applications will satisfy users' IT requirements, an organization's SDLC should include procedures to compare design specifications to user requirements. The specifications should be developed with systems users and be approved by management and user departments.

Acquire Technology Infrastructure

The SDLC should include procedures to ensure that platforms (hardware and systems software) support the new or modified application. Further, an assessment should be made of the impact of new hardware and software on the performance of the overall system. Finally, procedures should be in place to ensure that hardware and systems software are installed, maintained, and changed to continue to support business processes.

Develop Service-Level Requirements and Application Documentation

Enterprise Systems

E-Business

To ensure the ongoing, effective use of IT, the organization's SDLC should provide for the preparation and maintenance of service-level requirements and application documentation. *Service-level requirements* include such items as availability, reliability, performance, capacity for growth, levels of user support, disaster recovery, security, minimal system functionality, and service charges. As IT organizations become larger and more complex, especially those that must implement and operate enterprise systems, these service-level requirements become important methods for communicating the expectations of the business units for IT services. If the organization is engaged in e-business, these service-level requirements become benchmarks for services on a Web site or with business partners engaged in e-commerce.

The SDLC should include processes to ensure that comprehensive documentation is developed for each application to enable the effective use, operation, and maintenance of the application. *Application documentation* typically includes the following:

- *Systems documentation:* Provides an overall description of the application, including the system's purpose; an overview of system procedures; and sample source documents, outputs, and reports.
- *Program documentation:* Provides a description of an application program and usually includes the program's purpose; program flowcharts; source code listings; descriptions of inputs, data, and outputs; program test data and test results; and a history of program changes and approvals of such changes.
- *Operations run manual:* Gives detailed instructions to *computer operators* and to *data control* about a particular application. These manuals typically specify input source, form, and when received; output form and distribution; and computer operation instructions, including setup, required data, restart procedures, and error messages.
- *User manual:* Describes user procedures for an application. These instructions, which assist users in preparing inputs and using outputs, include a description of the application, procedures for completing source documents, instructions on how to input data to the computer, descriptions of manual files and computerized data, instructions on how to perform manual and automated processing, explanations of controls (including how to detect and correct errors), and procedures for distributing and using normal outputs.
- *Training material:* Helps users learn their jobs and perform consistently in those jobs.

IT Process 5: Integrate IT Solutions into Operational Processes

To ensure that a new or significantly revised system is suitable, the organization's SDLC should provide for a planned, tested, controlled, and approved conversion to the new system. After installation, the SDLC should call for a review to determine that the new system has met users' needs in a cost-effective manner.

IT Process 6: Manage Changes to Existing IT Systems

To ensure processing integrity between versions of systems and to ensure consistency of results from period to period, changes to the IT infrastructure (hardware, systems software, and applications) must be managed via change request, impact assessment, documentation, authorization, release and distribution policies, and procedures.

Program change controls provide assurance that all modifications to programs are authorized and documented, and that the changes are completed, tested, and properly implemented. Changes in documentation should mirror the changes made to the related programs. Improper change controls could allow a programmer to change, for example, the payroll program so that salaries for all programmers are increased each pay period. **Figure 8.6** on page 276 depicts the stages through which programs should progress to ensure that only authorized and tested programs are placed in production. Notice in this figure that separate organizational entities are responsible for each stage in the change process.

These controls take on an even higher level of significance with *enterprise systems*. The challenges are the result of the interdependence of the business processes and the complexity of these processes and their connections. Should unauthorized or untested changes be made to such systems, the results could be disastrous. For example, assume that a change is made to the inventory module of an ERP system without testing to see the impact that change will have on the sales module used to enter customer orders. Because these two modules work together, and orders from customers for inventory

Enterprise Systems

FIGURE 8.6 Illustration of Program Change Controls

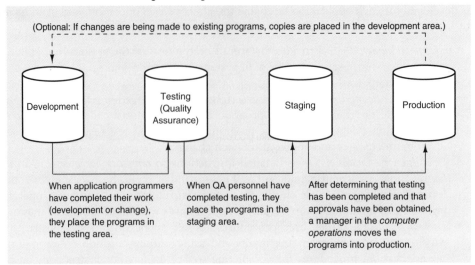

cannot be processed without the inventory module, changes to either module must be carefully planned and executed.

Deliver and Support Domain

The Deliver and Support domain includes processes to deliver required IT services efficiently and effectively; that is, management wants to know that IT services are delivered in line with business priorities and in a cost-effective manner. To deliver services efficiently and effectively means that application programs and data must be available as needed to keep the organization running smoothly. Further, systems and data must be secured because computing resources that are unavailable for any reason can lead to lost revenues as well as increased costs. Finally, unauthorized use of the computing resources can lead to fraud or violations of laws and regulations, such as those related to privacy.

IT Process 7: Deliver Required IT Services

This process includes activities related to the delivery of the IT services that were planned in the Plan and Organize domain, and developed and implemented in the Acquire and Implement domain. **Table 8.4** describes some of the key service-delivery activities.

IT Process 8: Ensure Security and Continuous Service

In addition to managing ongoing IT operations, the IT function must ensure that computing resources are operational and secured. To ensure computing resources are operational, IT management must plan for increases in required capacity or losses of usable resources. To ensure that computing resources are secured—that is, not lost, altered, or used without authorization—management should establish a process to account for all IT components. Processes should be in place to identify, track, and resolve problems in a timely manner. Two important aspects of this process are discussed in the following sections: ensure continuous service and secure IT assets.

TABLE 8.4   Delivering Required Services

Activity	Discussion
Define service levels.	The minimum levels of the quantity and quality of IT services must be defined so that the quality of service can be evaluated. For example, a minimum response time should be established.
Manage third-party services.	Processes must be in place to identify, manage, and monitor nonentity IT resources, for example, processes for reporting problems with slow response times.
Manage IT operations.	Standard procedures for IT operations must be established, including procedures for staffing, job scheduling, and preventive maintenance.
Manage data.	Management must establish a combination of pervasive and application controls to protect data.
Identify and allocate costs.	Management should identify the costs of providing IT services and should allocate those costs to the users of those services.

Ensure Continuous Service

These control plans are directed at potentially calamitous disruptions of business processes that could imperil the organization's very survival. Catastrophes such as hurricanes, earthquakes, terrorist attacks, strikes, fires, and power outages have struck fear in the hearts of many executives that their firms may be destroyed by natural or man-made disasters. **Business continuity planning** (also known as **disaster recovery planning**, **contingency planning**, and **business interruption planning**) is a process that identifies events that may threaten an organization and provides a framework to ensure that the organization will continue to operate when the threatened event occurs or will resume operations with a minimum of disruption. It is important for organizations and IT operations to implement business continuity plans.

A number of business continuity planning models are available. The model we describe was developed by the Business Continuity Institute.[15] Think about a wagon wheel, with a center hub and five spokes. The first element, the business continuity management (BCM) program, serves as the hub that glues the entire business continuity lifecycle together.

1. *BCM policy and program management* (the hub of the wheel previously described): Provides the framework around which the BCM is designed and built. Defines the scope of the BCM plan and assigns the BCM team responsibilities. The BCM team should be ready to respond in an emergency.
2. *Understanding the organization:* Understand the organization and the urgency with which activities and processes need to be restored if they are interrupted. Perform a business impact analysis to identify what constitutes a business interruption and the maximum tolerable period of business interruption at which the BCM becomes active.
3. *Determine business continuity strategies:* Define alternative operating methods to be used after an interruption. Key decisions include the desired recovery time, the distance to recovery facilities—and for data storage—the personnel to be involved, the supporting technologies that will be used, and the impact on stakeholder partners and contractors.

---

[15]"Good Practice Guidelines (2008)," Business Continuity Institute. Available, as of February 2010, at www.thebci.org.

4. *Developing and implementing a BCM response:* Formalize a response plan, determine how to define and handle crises and incidents, and create incident response teams and related communication networks.

5. *Exercising, maintenance, and review:* Exercising involves rehearsing the plan with affected parties, testing the technology and other business continuity systems. Maintenance means keeping the plan up to date when business processes and risks change. Both the testing and updating need to be reviewed to make sure that the plan is operating effectively.

6. *Embedding BCM in the organization's culture:* Design and deliver education, training, and awareness so that employees are ready to respond to the BCM in an effective manner.

E-Business

For our discussions, we want to focus on those elements of business continuity planning that relate to business processes, especially those supported by IT. However, business continuity management reaches beyond IT to providing continuity planning for resources (e.g., people, supplies, documentation) residing in all operational business units of the organization. Also, the plan may extend beyond the organization for key resources provided by third parties. You also might note that we should plan contingencies for important *processes* rather than individual *resources*. Thus, we would develop a contingency plan for our Internet presence rather than for the specific computers, networks, and software that enable that presence.

In the remainder of this section, we describe the major strategies that are used to provide for the continuity of IT services. Two major elements are required. First, we must have the programs, data, and documentation necessary to continue or resume operations. Second, we must have alternative computer facilities and related resources (e.g., electricity, personnel, and communications) that can be used should the primary facilities and resources become unavailable. The strategy chosen for one often coincides with the strategy for the other.

To have data, programs, and documentation ready to continue operations, we must *periodically* make a copy called a **backup**. Backups should be stored in a secure location at a distance from the primary facility. Data files are often backed up to tapes or disks and may be transported to a third-party facility. The process whereby we restore the lost data and resume operations is called **recovery**. In this case, we use the backup data to restore the lost data and to resume operations. In general, such procedures are called "backup and recovery."

E-Business

Recovery can occur at a company location or at an alternative processing site. Companies determine their alternative processing needs by performing a *risk assessment* to determine the likelihood that their systems will become unavailable, the losses that could result, and the costs they are willing to incur to address the risks. Some organizations, especially organizations such as airlines and those with significant e-business operations, need to keep their systems and Internet commerce sites online at all times or must have instant recovery from an interruption. Even less IT-oriented organizations cannot operate for extended periods of time without their application systems; without them, they cannot manufacture goods, accept customer orders, or order raw materials.

Organizations that must ensure *continuous operations* may maintain and operate two or more sites that separately contain identical equipment and identical copies of all programs, data, and documentation. Should the primary facility become unavailable, one of the secondary sites takes over, sometimes automatically and without noticeable delay. In these situations, data must be replicated in real time on both systems. This data replication strategy is called **Continuous Data Protection (CDP)**, whereby all data changes are date stamped and saved to secondary systems as the changes are happening. Notice that this process is not the periodic backup of files mentioned previously but is a process for continuous and immediate replication of any data changes. The site that maintains copies of the primary site's programs and data is a **mirror site**.

For many organizations, it is not cost-effective to maintain duplicate computer facilities, although they still need CDP. These organizations might contract with third parties such as U.S. Data Trust Corporation or Iron Mountain, Inc. for **electronic vaulting**. Electronic vaulting is a service whereby data changes are automatically transmitted over the Internet on a continuous basis to an off-site server maintained by a third party. When needed, the backed-up data can be retrieved from the electronic vault to recover from a data loss at the primary computer facility or to resume interrupted operations at an alternative facility.

E-Business

For those companies that determine their risks are not high enough to use a *mirror site* or *electronic vaulting*, a good strategy is to make arrangements with hardware vendors, service centers, or others for the standby use of compatible computer equipment. These arrangements are generally of two types—*hot sites* or *cold sites*. A **hot site** is a fully equipped data center, often housed in bunker-like facilities, that can accommodate many businesses and that is made available to client companies for a monthly subscriber fee. Less costly, but obviously less responsive, is a **cold site**. A cold site is a facility usually comprised of air-conditioned space with a raised floor, telephone connections, and computer ports into which a subscriber can move equipment. The disaster recovery contractor or the manufacturer provides the necessary equipment. Obviously, it is necessary to have a contract for the delivery of the replacement equipment to ensure that it will be available when needed. A company that contracts for either a hot site or a cold site should expect some delay in getting operations up and running after a disaster strikes as, at a minimum, it must relocate operations to that site. In the aftermath of Hurricane Katrina, some organizations found that hot sites got very heavy usage because so many firms had simultaneously declared disasters.

We conclude this section with a discussion of a serious threat that can affect the capability of Internet-based businesses such as eBay and Amazon.com to ensure continuous service to their customers. **Technology Summary 8.1** describes this phenomenon, *denial-of-service attacks*, and the processes that might be put in place to detect and correct them to ensure that organizations achieve the level of service that they require.

E-Business

Technology Summary 8.1

DENIAL-OF-SERVICE ATTACKS

In a denial-of-service attack, a Web site is overwhelmed by an intentional onslaught of thousands of simultaneous messages, making it impossible for the attacked site to engage in its normal activities. A distributed denial-of-service attack uses many computers (called *zombies*; see Technology Summary 7.3 on pg. 235 in Chapter 7) that unwittingly cooperate in a *denial-of-service attack* by sending messages to the target Web sites. Unfortunately, the distributed version is more effective because the number of computers responding multiplies the number of attack messages. Also, because each computer has its own IP address, it is more difficult to detect that an attack is taking place than it would be if all the messages were coming from one address. Denial-of-service attacks can be categorized into four levels, with progressively more severe consequences: (1) inundating the server with bogus requests; (2) consuming CPU cycles, memory, and other resources; (3) disabling Web traffic by misconfiguring routers; and (4) sending mail-bombs to individuals, lists, or domains.

Currently, no easy *preventive* controls exist. To *detect* a denial-of-service attack, Web sites may employ *filters* to sense the multiple messages and block traffic from the sites sending them, and *switches* to move their legitimate traffic to servers and Internet service providers (ISPs) that are not under attack (i.e., *corrective*). However, attackers can hide their identity by creating false IP addresses for *each* message, making many filtering defenses slow to respond or virtually ineffective. An organization might also carry insurance to reimburse it for any losses suffered from an attack (i.e., *corrective*).

Secure IT Assets

As we saw above in the recent "Security Mega Trends" survey by The Ponemon Institute, data breaches are the number one concern of IT security professionals. The same research group found that, from 2005 through 2008, more than 250 million customer records had been lost or stolen. In 2008, the various financial consequences averaged over $200 per record.[16] We frequently read about such data breaches in the news. For example, a laptop belonging to Fidelity Investments was stolen that contained the personal information, including social security numbers, of 196,000 current and former Hewlett-Packard, Co. employees.[17] Similarly, TJX, the parent company of TJ Maxx, Marshalls, and other discount stores, reported that hackers broke into its computer network and stole at least 45.7 million credit card numbers.[18] In early 2009, a possible data breach of payment cards even larger than that of TJX was reported. In this case, Heartland Payment Systems disclosed that hackers may have accessed over 100 million credit and debit card transactions.[19]

What's the problem here? Management has a legal responsibility to protect an organization's assets, including informational assets. For example, the unauthorized disclosure of financial information (i.e., nonpublic data) is a violation of federal securities laws. It may also violate various other laws and regulations, such as the Health Insurance Portability and Accountability Act (HIPAA) of 1996, which places restrictions on the use, handling, and disclosure of individually identifiable health information. In the case of TJX, the Federal Trade Commission was involved because it was a retail store failure. And as a further result of these kinds of problems, major credit card companies have developed their own standards for security and insisted that companies who accept their cards comply with their standard. **Technology Summary 8.2** describes these standards.

To ensure that organizational information is not subject to unauthorized use, disclosure, modification, damage, or loss, management should implement logical and physical access controls to ensure that access to computing resources—systems, data, and programs—is restricted to authorized users for authorized uses by implementing two types of plans:

- Control plans that restrict physical access to computer facilities
- Control plans that restrict logical access to stored programs, data, and documentation

E-Business **Figure 8.7** (pg. 282) shows the levels (or layers) of protection included in each of these categories. Use Figure 8.7 as a road map for the discussion that follows. As you study this section, consider how much more important these controls become when the organization engages in e-business and has electronic connections to customers and business partners.

Control Plans for Restricting Physical Access to Computer Facilities. Naturally, only authorized personnel should be allowed access to the computer facility. As shown in Figure 8.7, control plans for restricting physical access to computer facilities encompass

---

[16]"Fourth Annual US Cost of Data Breach Study," The Ponemon Institute LLC, January 2009.

[17]Jennifer Levitz and John Hechinger, "Laptops Prove Weakest Link in Data Security," *The Wall Street Journal*, March 24, 2006, pp. B1, B2.

[18]Pereira, Joseph, "How Credit-Card Data Went Out Wireless Door, Biggest Known Theft Came from Retailer with Old Weak Security," *The Wall Street Journal*, May 4, 2007, pp. A1, A12.

[19]Byron Acohido, "Hackers Breach Heartland Payment Credit Card System," *USA Today*, January 20, 2009. Available, as of February 2010, at www.usatoday.com/money/perfi/credit/2009-01-20-heartland-credit-card-security-breach_N.htm.

Technology Summary 8.2

PAYMENT CARD INDUSTRY (PCI) DATA SECURITY STANDARDS

Retailers have struggled with a variety of credit card data breaches leading to identity theft and illicit credit card charges. Breaches of customer information were estimated to have cost approximately $12.5 billion dollars in 2008. As a result of these breaches and in response to retailer complaints over multiple standards, the major credit card companies (Visa, MasterCard, American Express, Discover) developed a joint set of "best practices" security protocols (the PCI standard) in 2006. The PCI standard applies to all businesses accepting payment by credit card, which includes most retail and service businesses worldwide. Businesses that do not comply with the standard may lose the ability to accept credit cards and may face financial penalties.

The standard is built around six areas, as follows:

1. **Build and Maintain a Secure Network**
   1.1. Install and maintain a firewall configuration to protect cardholder data.
   1.2. Do not use vendor-supplied defaults for system passwords and other security parameters.

2. **Protect Cardholder Data**
   2.1. Protect stored cardholder data.
   2.2. Encrypt transmission of cardholder data across open, public networks.

3. **Maintain a Vulnerability Management Program**
   3.1. Use and regularly update anti-virus software.
   3.2. Develop and maintain secure systems and applications.

4. **Implement Strong Access Control Measures**
   4.1. Restrict access to cardholder data by business need-to-know.
   4.2. Assign a unique ID to each person with computer access.
   4.3. Restrict physical access to cardholder data.

5. **Regularly Monitor and Test Networks**
   5.1. Track and monitor all access to network resources and cardholder data.
   5.2. Regularly test security systems and processes.

6. **Maintain an Information Security Policy**
   6.1. Maintain a policy that addresses information security.

Sources: Joseph Pereria, "Credit-Card Security Falters," *The Wall Street Journal*, April 29, 2008, p. A9; "Fourth Annual US Cost of Data Breach Study," The Ponemon Institute LLC, January 2009; "The PCI Data Security Standard," available, as of February 2010, at www.pcisecuritystandards.org/.

---

three layers of controls. The outermost layer restricts access to the facility itself (e.g., fences), the next layer restricts access to the building (e.g., locked doors), and finally the last layer restricts access to the computer facility or the computer itself (e.g., employee badges). One important type of control for the computer facility is a biometric identification system. Although not foolproof, the technology has improved dramatically in recent years, leading to the widening use of such systems in practice. The most common biometric devices read fingerprints. In fact, biometric fingerprint identification is used to secure physical access to many types of facilities and devices such as laptops and PDAs. Biometric identification is expanding rapidly and could be soon used instead of keys even for homes and cars.[20]

Although controls for restricting physical access to computer facilities seem straightforward and are generally accepted as good practice, they are not always effectively implemented. A recent robbery at a large Web hosting facility was a wake-up call for IT managers.[21] Robbers stole equipment and data from CI Host Inc. by entering the building via a fire escape, bypassing a security guard, and forcing the night operator to open the data center. Incidents like this and pressure from clients are forcing data center managers to increase the physical security of data centers. Actions include hiding data centers underground or at remote, hard-to-approach locations, using

---

[20]Ann Keeton, "Fingerprints Give a Hand to Security, Verifying Identities Through Biometrics Is Poised to Expand," *The Wall Street Journal*, April 12, 2007, p. B4.

[21]Patrick Thibodean, "Robbery Alters Thinking on Data Center Security," *Computerworld*, January 14, 2008.

multiple biometric access devices, and implementing tripwires that notify authorities if a breach has occurred.[22]

Control Plans for Restricting Logical Access to Stored Programs, Data, and Documentation. At the beginning of this section, we listed several security failures. Although some of those failures involved lost hardware (e.g., laptops), others were failures to protect the data itself. In an *online* environment, **access control software** ensures that (1) only authorized users gain access to a system through a process of *identification* (e.g., a unique account number for each user) and *authentication* (e.g., a password to verify that users are who they say they are), (2) restricts authorized users to specific data they require

FIGURE 8.7 Restricting Access to Computing Resources—Layers of Protection

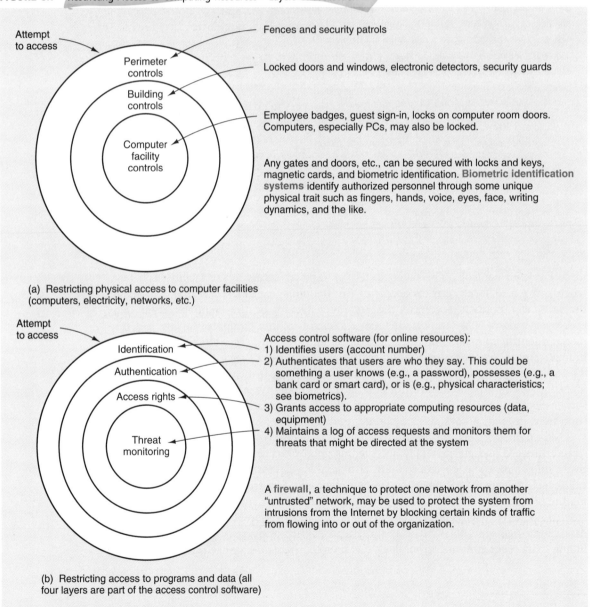

Fences and security patrols

Locked doors and windows, electronic detectors, security guards

Employee badges, guest sign-in, locks on computer room doors. Computers, especially PCs, may also be locked.

Any gates and doors, etc., can be secured with locks and keys, magnetic cards, and biometric identification. **Biometric identification systems** identify authorized personnel through some unique physical trait such as fingers, hands, voice, eyes, face, writing dynamics, and the like.

(a) Restricting physical access to computer facilities (computers, electricity, networks, etc.)

Access control software (for online resources):
1) Identifies users (account number)
2) Authenticates that users are who they say. This could be something a user knows (e.g., a password), possesses (e.g., a bank card or smart card), or is (e.g., physical characteristics; see biometrics).
3) Grants access to appropriate computing resources (data, equipment)
4) Maintains a log of access requests and monitors them for threats that might be directed at the system

A **firewall**, a technique to protect one network from another "untrusted" network, may be used to protect the system from intrusions from the Internet by blocking certain kinds of traffic from flowing into or out of the organization.

(b) Restricting access to programs and data (all four layers are part of the access control software)

[22]J. Nicholas Hoover, "Next-Gen Data Centers," *Information Week*, March 3, 2008, pp. 38–44.

and sets the action privileges for that data (e.g., read, copy, write data), and (3) monitors access attempts and violations. These steps are depicted in part (b) of Figure 8.7.

The first step, identification and authentication, involves what is commonly known as the user ID and password. However, passwords are a notoriously weak method for authenticating user identification because, for ease of use, most people choose simple passwords. Free software already exists that can decode simple word passwords in seconds. Employees should be trained to use longer passwords and those made up of random characters, including letters, numbers, and symbols. Employees should also be instructed not to write down or divulge their passwords. The best way to mitigate password risk is to put in additional authentications, such as a *biometric identification system* (i.e., something they are) or a *smartcard* (i.e., something they have) that users must use along with their passwords and user IDs.[23]

In addition to access control software, most companies employ a firewall as part of their access control. A firewall is simply a program or hardware device that filters the information coming through the Internet connection into a private network or computer system. If an incoming packet of information is flagged by the filters, it is not allowed through (Figure 8.7).

The final part of access control software is the **intrusion-detection system (IDS)**, which logs and monitors who is on or trying to access the network. Typical user behavior is accumulated in *user profiles*. Subsequently, when usage patterns differ from the normal profile, the exceptional activity is flagged and reported. IDSs can be used to detect attacks from outside the organization, such as *denial-of-service attacks*, or from inside the organization, as when authorized users attempt to undertake unauthorized actions. Organizations not wanting to wait until an unauthorized activity *has* occurred might employ an **intrusion-prevention system (IPS)** to actively block unauthorized traffic using rules specified by the organization.

The primary plans for restricting access in an *offline* environment involve the use of *segregation of duties*, *restricting physical access to computer facilities*, *program change controls*, and *library controls*. The first three plans have been defined and discussed in previous sections. **Library controls** restrict access to data, programs, and documentation. Library controls are provided by a *librarian function*, a combination of people, procedures, and computer software that serves two major purposes. First, library controls limit the use of stored data, programs, and documentation to authenticated users with authorized requests. Second, they maintain the storage media (e.g., disks, tapes).

In *online* environments, librarian software is used to restrict access to online programs, data, and documentation. For example, the software will keep track of the many versions of event and master data and ensure that the latest versions of such data are used. The software can also permit appropriate access to development, testing, staging, and production versions of programs (Figure 8.6, pg. 276).

Another option for protecting data is to encrypt it. **Data encryption** is a process that employs mathematical algorithms and encryption keys to encode data (i.e., change unencoded data, called plaintext, to a coded text form, called ciphertext) so that it is unintelligible in its encrypted form. Thus if the access control software, firewall, IDS, IPS, and data librarian all fail, unauthorized users still cannot read the data. The crux of conventional encryption procedures is a *single key* used both by the sender to encrypt the message and by the receiver to decrypt it. A major drawback to such systems is that the key itself has to be transmitted by secure channels. If the key is not kept secret, the security of the entire system is compromised. **Public-key cryptography** helps to solve this problem by employing a pair of matched keys for each system user, one private (i.e.,

---

[23]Ben Worthen, "Hacker Camps Train Network Defenders, Sessions Teach IT Pros to Use Tools of the Online Criminal Trade," *The Wall Street Journal*, April 1, 2008, p. B6.

known only to the party who possesses it) and one public. The public key corresponds to but is not the same as the user's private key. As its name implies, the public key is assumed to be public knowledge and could even be published in a directory. *Public-key cryptography* and a related technique, *digital signature*, are described in Appendix 9A. Besides public-key cryptography, there are other complex algorithms and encryption key techniques currently in use that are much more powerful than a single key cipher. These techniques are beyond the scope of this textbook.

Before we leave this section, let's briefly explore a topic that always receives much media attention, *computer hacking*. In spite of significant efforts by a multitude of entities (companies, police entities, software developers), hacking is growing. Current statistics show that 70 percent of all e-mail is spam (unwanted), the number of Web sites used to trick users into giving up personal data has quintupled in the past year, and the number of viruses designed to take over, shut down, or steal data from computers continues to grow at an astounding rate.[24] In simple terms, **computer hacking and cracking** reflects the intentional, unauthorized access to an organization's computer system, accomplished by bypassing the system's access security controls. Generally, a **hacker** is someone who simply gets a kick out of breaking into a computer system but does not hold malicious intentions to destroy or steal. We use the term **cracker** when the motive is crime, theft, or destruction. Hackers *and* crackers use a variety of techniques to break into computer systems. Some of these techniques are listed in **Table 8.5**.

Control Plans for Physical Protection of IT Assets. To protect the IT facilities against man-made and natural hazards, the organization must install and regularly review suitable environmental and physical controls. These plans reduce losses caused by a variety of physical, mechanical, and environmental events. Fire and water damages represent major threats to most businesses, as do power outages and lax data backup procedures. **Table 8.6** summarizes some of the more common controls directed at these environmental hazards.

The advanced state of today's hardware technology results in a high degree of equipment reliability; unless the system is quite old, hardware malfunctions are rare. Even if a malfunction occurs, it is usually detected and corrected automatically. In addition to relying on the controls contained within the computer hardware, organizations should perform

TABLE 8.5 Hacking Techniques

Technique Name	What the Hacker Does
Shoulder Surfing	Watches the user type in passwords or user IDs or listens as they give account information over the phone.
Scavenging or Dumpster Diving	Searches through rubbish for system information such as passwords.
Smoozing	Calls and requests a password based on some pretext.
Password Cracking	Uses software to decode passwords. Programs match an encrypted version of a password to a list generated using common encryption algorithms.
Phishing	Sends out an e-mail pretending to be a legitimate business asking for information about your account.
Spyware	Gets a user to load software that captures user names, passwords, and other information.

[24]Bob Keefe, "New Kind of Hacker, Web Insecurity Worsens: Not Just kids; Big Bucks, Small Risk Entice Criminals," *The Atlanta Journal and Constitution*, April 13, 2008, pp. C1, C4.

TABLE 8.6   Environmental Controls

Environmental Hazard	Controls
Fire	Smoke detectors, fire alarms, fire extinguishers, fire-resistant construction materials, insurance
Water damage	Waterproof ceilings, walls, and floors; adequate drainage; water and moisture detection alarms; insurance
Dust, coffee, tea, soft drinks	Regular cleaning of rooms and equipment, dust-collecting rugs at entrances, separate dust-generating activities from computer, do not allow food/drink near computers, good housekeeping
Energy increase, decrease, loss	Voltage regulators, backup batteries and generators

regular **preventive maintenance** (periodic cleaning, testing, and adjusting of computer equipment) to ensure their equipment's continued efficient and correct operation.

IT Process 9: Provide Support Services

To ensure that users make effective use of IT, management should identify the training needs of all personnel, internal and external, who use the organization's IT services, and should see that timely training sessions are conducted. To effectively use IT resources, users often require advice and may require assistance to overcome problems encountered in using those resources. This assistance is generally delivered via a **help desk** function.

Monitor and Evaluate Domain

As noted previously, monitoring involves two phases: The first is putting controls in place to periodically follow up on the operation of control plans. The second part of monitoring is ensuring that appropriate *communications* are taking place. Monitoring IT uses the same phases but focuses on the performance of IT services and controls. Monitoring IT may be performed as a self-assessment activity within IT by an entity's internal/IT audit group, by an external organization such as a public accounting firm, or by an IT security company.

IT Process 10: Monitor and Evaluate the Processes

To ensure the achievement of IT process objectives, management should establish a system for defining performance indicators (service levels), gathering data about all processes, and generating performance reports. Management should review these reports to measure progress toward identified goals. Outside confirmation based on an independent review should be used on a regular basis.

The American Institute of Certified Public Accountants (AICPA) and Canadian Institute of Chartered Accountants (CICA) have developed a set of professional assurance and advisory services based on a common set of Trust Service Principles and Criteria, which are outlined in **Table 8.7** (pg. 286). These principles and criteria apply to WebTrust and SysTrust engagements, among others.

E-Business

The WebTrust (version 3.0) family of services offers best practices and e-business solutions related to business-to-consumer and business-to-business electronic commerce. Some of the services within the family include WebTrust Confidentiality, WebTrust Online Privacy, and WebTrust Consumer Protection.

SysTrust (version 2.0) is an assurance service designed to test and monitor the reliability of an entity's information system and databases, including ERP systems.

TABLE 8.7 Trust Services Principles and Criteria

Principle	Description
Security	Determines whether the system is protected against unauthorized access (both physical and logical).
Availability	Determines whether the system is available for operation and use as committed or agreed.
Processing Integrity	Determines whether processing is complete, accurate, timely, and authorized.
Confidentiality	Determines whether business information designated as confidential is protected as committed or agreed.
Privacy	Personal information is collected, used, retained, disclosed, and destroyed in conformity with the commitments in the entity's privacy notice and with criteria set forth in generally accepted privacy principles issued by the AICPA and CICA.

Source: As of August 16, 2010, www.aicpa.org/InterestAreas/InformationTechnology/Resourses/TrustServices/Pages/default.aspx.

As you can see, the accounting profession is very involved with not only the Monitor and Evaluate domain (Figure 8.5, pg. 270) but also the Plan and Organize, Acquire and Implement, and Deliver and Support domains outlined in the COBIT framework.[25]

We will conclude our discussion of pervasive control plans by looking at some of the control concerns surrounding one of the more recent developments in business IT environment—*cloud computing*. (See Chapter 1 for an introduction to cloud computing.) In general, it is cloud computing's flexibility and loosely structured network that is both its strength and its weakness. In this discussion, we will focus on the weaknesses. The following lists some of the main control concerns with cloud computing:[26]

- Support and overall control of the cloud computing services are largely in the hands of the third-party cloud service provider. There is typically no 24/7 on-call support, with one-hour response time common.
- Much of the cloud communication occurs over the Internet. Unless a secure network connection or encrypted line is used, the communication is in clear text with associated security risks.
- Cloud users commonly use browsers, including older versions that have known security vulnerabilities.
- Cloud service providers' employees might have loosely controlled access to sensitive data stored on their servers.
- Cloud services have been known to go down for up to an hour and some start-up cloud vendors have even failed.

As with any new IT development, there are pros and cons in adopting it for use, especially in a business environment. The relative weights of the pros and cons need to be evaluated before committing to using the IT, and pervasive and lower level controls should be implemented to deal with risks from the cons.

---

[25]These services are introduced in Chapter 1.

[26]This following discussion is based on Sailesh Gadia, "Cloud Computing: An Auditor's Perspective," *ISACA Journal*, Vol. 6, November 2009, pp. 24–28.

Summary

In this chapter, we discussed four important categories of pervasive control plans: organization design, policies, monitoring, and IT general controls. To put these control plans into perspective once again, return to the hierarchy shown in Figure 7.6 (pg. 245). Note that pervasive control plans provide a second umbrella of protection, in addition to the control environment, over all AIS business processes. Pervasive control plans are particularly important because they operate across all business processes and affect a company's capability to meet a multitude of control goals.

In Chapter 9, we will begin to examine the third level in the hierarchy, business process control plans and application controls, by looking at those controls associated with the technology used to implement a business process. Then, in Chapters 10 through 15, we continue the coverage of the business process control plans and application controls by examining those related to each specific business process.

Key Terms

segregation of duties, 257

policy, 260

rotation of duties, 262

forced vacations, 262

fidelity bond, 262

monitoring, 263

IT governance, 264

COBIT, 268

IT steering committee, 272

security officer, 273

systems development life cycle (SDLC), 274

program change controls, 275

business continuity planning, 277

disaster recovery planning, 277

contingency planning, 277

business interruption planning, 277

backup, 278

recovery, 278

Continuous Data Protection (CDP), 278

mirror site, 279

electronic vaulting, 279

hot site, 279

cold site, 279

denial-of-service attack, 279

distributed denial-of-service attack, 279

biometric identification systems, 282

access control software, 282

firewall, 282

intrusion-detection system (IDS), 283

intrusion-prevention system (IPS), 283

library controls, 283

data encryption, 283

public-key cryptography, 283

computer hacking and cracking, 284

hacker, 284

cracker, 284

preventive maintenance, 285

help desk, 285

Review Questions

RQ 8- 1   What are the four major categories of pervasive controls? Why would the PCAOB refer to these controls as entity level?

RQ 8- 2   What are the differences among a pervasive control plan, a business process control plan, an application control plan, and an IT control process?

RQ 8-3   Segregation of duties consists of separating what four basic functions? Briefly define each function.

RQ 8-4   Describe some compensating controls that can be used to reduce exposures when it is not possible to properly segregate duties in a small organization.

RQ 8-5   What are policy controls plans? How do policies differ from laws?

RQ 8-6   Describe one specific control for each of the following categories of personnel control plans: hiring, retention, development, management, and termination.

RQ 8-7   Why should an organization conduct monitoring activities? Who should conduct monitoring activities? What are the two major steps in monitoring?

RQ 8-8   What is IT governance?

RQ 8-9   What are the principal responsibilities, major duties, and key control concerns of *each* functional position pictured in Figure 8.4 on page 266 (i.e., the organization chart of an IT organization)?

RQ 8-10   What is the COBIT framework? How does it differ from the COSO framework?

RQ 8-11   Name the four IT resources as delineated by COBIT.

RQ 8-12   How does the COBIT framework define control?

RQ 8-13   What are the four IT control process domains?

RQ 8-14   What is the purpose of the strategic IT plan?

RQ 8-15   What are the major elements of the strategic IT plan?

RQ 8-16   What functions within the IT organization should be segregated?

RQ 8-17   What is the systems development life cycle (SDLC)?

RQ 8-18   What types of documentation constitute a well-documented application? Describe each type.

RQ 8-19   What are the four stages through which a program should move as it is being developed? Who should have responsibility for each of those phases?

RQ 8-20   What steps are commonly included in a business continuity planning methodology?

RQ 8-21   Describe backup and recovery.

RQ 8-22   Describe continuous data protection (CDP), a mirror site, and electronic vaulting.

RQ 8-23   What is the difference between a *hot site* and a *cold site*?

RQ 8-24   Describe a *denial-of-service attack*. What controls are recommended to detect or correct such an attack?

RQ 8-25   Describe the three layers of controls for restricting physical access to computer facilities.

RQ 8-26   Explain *biometric identification systems*.

RQ 8-27   Describe the four layers of controls for restricting logical access to stored programs, data, and documentation.

RQ 8-28   Distinguish *firewalls*, *intrusion detections systems (IDS)*, and *intrusion prevention systems (IPS)*.

RQ 8-29   Describe *library controls*.

RQ 8-30   What is *data encryption*? What is the *key* in encryption? What is the *algorithm* in encryption? What is public-key cryptography?

RQ 8-31   Define computer *hacking* and *cracking*, and explain how they undermine resource security.

RQ 8-32   Provide three examples of hacking techniques. Which technique do you think is most prevalent?

RQ 8-33   a.   What *kinds* of damage are included in the category of environmental hazards?

b.   What control plans are designed to *prevent* such hazards from occurring?

c.   What control plans are designed to *limit losses* resulting from such hazards or to recover from such hazards?

Discussion Questions

DQ 8-1   "The Enterprise Risk Management (ERM) framework introduced in Chapter 7 can be used by management to make decisions on which controls in this chapter should be implemented." Do you agree? Discuss fully.

DQ 8-2   "In small companies with few employees, it is virtually impossible to implement the *segregation of duties* control plan." Do you agree? Discuss fully.

DQ 8-3   "No matter how sophisticated a system of internal control is, its success ultimately requires that you place your trust in certain key personnel." Do you agree? Discuss fully.

DQ 8-4   "If personnel hiring is done correctly, the other personnel control plans are not needed." Do you agree? Discuss fully.

DQ 8-5   "Monitoring must be performed by an independent function such as a CPA." Do you agree? Discuss fully.

DQ 8-6   Compare and contrast the COBIT definition of control in this chapter (pg. 269) with definitions in Chapter 7 for ERM (pp. 220–221), the COSO definition of internal control (pg. 228), and this textbook's definition of internal control (pg. 230).

DQ 8-7   A key control concern described in Table 8.2 (pp. 267–268) regarding the systems development manager is that "systems development can develop and implement systems without management approval." Discuss a control described in this chapter that reduces the risk that unauthorized systems will be implemented.

DQ 8-8   Debate the following point: "*Business continuity planning* is really an IT issue."

DQ 8-9   "Contracting for a *hot site* is too cost-prohibitive except in the rarest of circumstances. Therefore, the vast majority of companies should think in terms of providing for a *cold site* at most." Discuss fully.

DQ 8-10   "Preventing the unauthorized disclosure and loss of data has become almost impossible. Employees and others can use iPods, flash drives, cameras, and PDAs, such as BlackBerries and Treos, to download data and remove it from an organization's premises." Do you agree? Describe some controls from this chapter that might be applied to reduce the risk of data disclosure and loss for these devices.

DQ 8-11 Your boss was heard to say, "If we implemented every control plan discussed in this chapter, we'd never get any work done around here." Do you agree? Discuss fully.

DQ 8-12 For each of these control plans, suggest a monitoring activity:

a. Credit approval

b. Removal of terminated employee access to computer systems

c. New employee background check

Short Problems

SP 8-1 The following is a list of six control plans from this chapter.

Control Plans

A. Service level agreements
B. Library controls
C. Security guards
D. User manuals
E. Biometric identification systems
F. Program change controls

The following is a list of five situations that have control implications.

Control Situations

1. Henry and Edward have been friends for many years. Henry works in the shipping department at Superior Company, an electronics wholesaler, and Edward is unemployed. To make a little money, Edward "borrowed" Henry's employee badge (it has a magnetic strip on the back to open doors at Superior Company), and used the badge to access the Superior warehouse and steal some electronics gear.

2. At Capstone Company, most transaction processing is automated. When an inventory item reaches its reorder point, the computer automatically prints a purchase order for the economic order quantity (EOQ). A programmer, who was in collusion with CubicArm, Inc., the vendor that supplied several parts, altered the computer program and the inventory master data for those parts. He reduced the EOQ and made certain program alterations, so that items supplied by CubicArm were ordered more often than Capstone required them.

3. The customer service representatives at Gamma Supplies, a catalog sales company, have been complaining that the computer system response time is very slow. They find themselves apologizing to customers who are waiting on the phone for their orders to be completed.

4. The data entry clerk in the accounts payable department at Lloyd Company did not have detailed instructions for completing the input form for approved vendor invoices. To speed up data entry, he let all of the date information default from the current day's date. As a result, several invoices were paid late, and Lloyd Company lost cash discounts on several other vendor payments.

5. During a normal workday, Bill, who was not an employee, entered Rowley Company's offices and was able to find and remove some computer printouts containing user IDs and other sensitive information. He later used that information to gain access to Rowley's computer system.

Match the five situations with a control plan that would *best* prevent the system failure from occurring. Because there are six control plans, you should have one letter left over.

SP 8-2   The following is a list of six control plans from this chapter.

Control Plans

A. Firewall
B. Access control software
C. Personnel termination control plans
D. Personnel selection and hiring control plans
E. Rotation of duties and forced vacations
F. Continuous data protection

The following is a list of five situations that have control implications.

Control Situations

1. Therese is employed in the personnel department at Lisieux Company. From the computer in her office, Therese was able to access the order entry system at Lisieux and entered some orders for goods to be shipped to her cousin.
2. A hacker accessed the Web site at Vandalia, Inc. and changed some of the graphics. Confused by these changes, some customers took their business elsewhere.
3. Martha Dawson, the company cashier, was known throughout the company as a workaholic. After three years on the job, Martha suddenly suffered heart problems and was incapacitated for several weeks. While she was ill, the treasurer temporarily assumed the cashier's duties and discovered that Martha had misappropriated several thousand dollars since she was hired.
4. During a severe ice storm, an employee at Goldmeyer Company was keying data at one of the computers in the order entry department. After about an hour of data entry, ice buildup on power lines caused a company-wide power failure. When power was restored, the employee had to rekey all the data from scratch.
5. The résumé of an applicant for the job of controller at Gordon's Bakery showed that the candidate had graduated, some 10 years earlier, magna cum laude from Excellentia State University (ESU) with a major in accounting. ESU's accounting program was well respected, and Gordon's Bakery had hired several ESU graduates over the years. In his second month on the job, the new controller became tongue-tied when the CFO asked him a technical question about earnings per share reporting. When later it was discovered that the controller's degree from ESU was in mechanical engineering, he was dismissed.

Match the five situations with a control plan that would *best* prevent the system failure from occurring. Because there are six control plans, you should have one letter left over.

SP 8-3 1. Using a key of 2, and an algorithm of add and subtract from alternating letters starting with addition, encrypt the word "accounting."
2. Using a key of 3 and an algorithm of add and subtract from alternating letters starting with subtraction, encrypt your professor's last name.

SP 8-4 Research the Internet, newspapers, magazines, and journals to find a recent fraud case involving IT and pervasive controls failure. Develop a report (format and length to be determined by your instructor) briefly describing the case, what pervasive controls failed, and how they failed. Also, list any lower-level (i.e., business process and application) controls affected by the pervasive controls failure. Be sure to include your sources.

Problems

P 8-1 The following is a list of 10 common security problems. For each problem, describe why it is a problem, and choose a control plan from this chapter that would prevent or detect the problem from occurring.

A. Criminals posing as small business owners obtained names, addresses, and social security numbers from an organization whose business is to give such information only to legitimate customers who have a right to the data.

B. An executive of a financial services firm implements a wireless network so that she can work at home from anywhere in her house. After setting up the network, she logs on using the default password.

C. An organization's top salesman uses a consumer-grade instant messaging (IM) client (e.g., AOL Instant Messaging). Such clients bypass anti-virus and spam software, don't have auditing and logging capabilities, and allow users to choose their IM names.

D. A financial analyst's laptop was stolen from his car. The laptop contained the names and social security numbers of 27,500 current and former employees.

E. To keep track of the passwords used to access various computer systems, employees create Word documents listing their passwords and store the document with the name "passwords.doc."

F. Backup disks that included information on 3.9 million credit card customers were lost in transit to a credit bureau. Data included names, social security numbers, account numbers, and payment histories.

G. Private and sensitive information is sent to multiple persons via e-mail. The e-mails include all addressee names within the e-mail address list.

H. An individual made millions by purchasing bank account information from eight employees of various banks. He had approximately 540,000 accounts in his database. Some bank employees were accessing up to 300 customer accounts each week to obtain the account information that they were selling.

I. A third-party processor of credit card transactions allowed an unauthorized individual to infiltrate its network and access cardholder data.

J. An individual sold his cell phone on eBay. The cell phone contained hundreds of confidential business-related e-mails.

P 8-2   Listed here are 20 control plans discussed in the chapter. On the blank line to the left of each control plan, insert a P (preventive), D (detective), or C (corrective) to classify that control most accurately. If you think that more than one code could apply to a particular plan, insert all appropriate codes and briefly explain your answer:

Code		Control Plan
_____	1.	Library controls
_____	2.	Program change controls
_____	3.	Fire and water alarms
_____	4.	Fire and water insurance
_____	5.	Install batteries to provide backup for temporary loss in power
_____	6.	Backup and recovery procedures
_____	7.	Service level agreements
_____	8.	IT steering committee
_____	9.	Security officer
_____	10.	Operations run manuals
_____	11.	Rotation of duties and forced vacations
_____	12.	Fidelity bonding
_____	13.	Personnel management (supervision)
_____	14.	Personnel termination procedures
_____	15.	Segregation of duties
_____	16.	Strategic IT plan
_____	17.	Disaster recovery planning
_____	18.	Restrict entry to the computer facility through the use of employee badges, guest sign-in, and locks on computer room doors
_____	19.	Access control software
_____	20.	Personnel development controls

P 8-3   The following is a list of 12 control plans from this chapter.

Control Plans

A. Firewall
B. Backup batteries and generators
C. Insurance
D. Employee badges, guest sign-in, locks on computer room doors
E. Hot site
F. Intrusion detection systems
G. Off-site storage of backup computer programs and data
H. Training (personnel development)
I. Personnel termination procedures
J. Security guards
K. Program change controls
L. Operations run manuals

The following is a list of 10 situations that have control implications.

Situations

1. The computer users at the Identity Company do not know how to use the computer very well.
2. A computer hacker created a program to generate random user IDs and passwords. He used the random number program to access the computer system of Samson, Inc.
3. During the nightly computer run to update bank customers' accounts for deposits and withdrawals for that day, an electrical storm caused a temporary power failure. The run had to be reprocessed from the beginning, resulting in certain other computer jobs not being completed on schedule.
4. A fire destroyed part of the computer room and the adjacent library of computer disks at Petunia, Inc. It took several months to reconstruct the data from manual source documents and other hard copy records.
5. A competitor flooded the Wolfeson Company Web server with false messages (i.e., a denial-of-service attack). The Web server, unable to handle all of this traffic, shut down for several hours until the messages could be cleared.
6. A group of demonstrators broke into a computer center and destroyed computer equipment worth several thousand dollars.
7. A computer programmer at Dover Company was fired for gross incompetence. During the two-week notice period, the programmer destroyed the documentation for all programs that he had developed since being hired.
8. A computer operator experienced an abnormal ending during the nightly run of updates to the inventory master data. In a state of panic, he woke his supervisor from a sound sleep at 4:00 a.m. to get help in getting the job restarted.
9. A disgruntled programmer at the Going Company planted a logic bomb in the computer program that produced weekly payroll checks. The bomb was triggered to go off if the programmer were ever terminated. When the programmer was fired for continued absenteeism, the next weekly payroll run destroyed all the company's payroll master data.
10. The computer systems at Club, Inc. were destroyed in a recent fire. It took Club several days to get its IT functions operating again.

Match the 10 situations with a control plan that would *best* prevent the system failure from occurring. Because there are 12 control plans, you should have two letters left over.

P 8-4   Assume that accounts payable are processed on a computer and that the options in the accounts payable system module are as follows:

1. Maintain vendor master data (i.e., add, change, or delete vendors in the vendor master data).
2. Record vendor invoices.
3. Record vendor credit memos.
4. Select vendor invoices for payment.
5. Print checks.
6. Record payments.
7. Print accounts payable reports.

Further assume that personnel in the accounts payable department include the department manager and two clerks, M. Matthew and J. Mark.

By placing a "Y" for yes or an "N" for no in the following table, show which users, if any, should (or should not) have access to each of the seven accounts payable options. Make and state whatever assumptions you think are necessary. In one or two paragraphs, explain how your matrix design would optimize the segregation of duties control plan.

Option	Manager	Matthew	Mark
1	___	___	___
2	___	___	___
3	___	___	___
4	___	___	___
5	___	___	___
6	___	___	___
7	___	___	___

P 8-5   Personnel at Victorian Company must perform the following functions:

1. Receive checks and remittance advice from customers.
2. Approve vendor invoices for payment and prepare checks.
3. Approve credit memoranda for customer sales returns.
4. Record collections on account from customers.
5. Record customer sales returns.
6. Make daily deposits of cash receipts.
7. Sign payment checks and mail them to vendors.
8. Record cash payments to vendors.
9. Record purchase returns and allowances.
10. Reconcile the bank account each month.

Victorian has three employees, Nathan, Jordyn, and James, any of whom is capable of performing any of the 10 functions.

Explain how you would divide the 10 functions among the three employees to optimize the segregation of duties control plan discussed in the chapter. Consider only control aspects when allocating the duties. In other words, ignore factors such as the workload of each employee, except that any one employee should be assigned a minimum of two functions. Your solution should also include a one-paragraph explanation of how your design accomplishes the control goals that segregation of duties is supposed to achieve.

P 8-6   List A contains the COBIT domains, List B contains the 10 COBIT processes, and List C contains 20 specific controls plans (there are two plans listed for each process). Each list is in alphabetical order. Match processes to domains and plans to processes, and place in the correct order.

List A: COBIT Domains

1. Acquire and Implement domain.
2. Deliver and Support domain.

3. Monitor and Evaluate domain.
4. Plan and Organize domain.

List B: COBIT Processes

1. Deliver Required IT Services.
2. Develop and Acquire IT Solutions.
3. Develop Tactics to Plan, Communicate, and Manage Realization of the Strategic Vision.
4. Ensure Security and Continuous Service.
5. Establish Strategic Vision for Information Technology.
6. Identify Automated Solutions.
7. Integrate IT Solutions into Operational Processes.
8. Manage Changes to Existing IT Systems.
9. Monitor and Evaluate the Processes.
10. Provide Support Services.

List C: Control Plans

1. A new system requirements definition document.
2. A post implementation review.
3. A process for testing a new system.
4. A process to select and prioritize user requests for system changes.
5. A quality assurance plan.
6. An assessment of how new hardware might affect existing hardware.
7. An inventory of IT capabilities.
8. An IT security audit.
9. Application documentation.
10. Biometric security devices.
11. Complete a disaster recovery plan.
12. Define service levels.
13. Feasibility studies.
14. Help desk.
15. Perform preventive maintenance.
16. Program change testing.
17. Report on response times.
18. Segregation of duties within the IT department.
19. Statement of IT goals and strategies.
20. User training classes.

P 8-7   AS5 outlines the processes for "An Audit of Internal Control Over Financial Reporting That Is Integrated with an Audit of Financial Statements." Paragraph 24 of this document lists eight entity-level controls. Entity-level controls are comparable to the pervasive controls covered in this chapter.

List A contains Entity-Level Controls from AS5, and List B contains specific control plans. Match the control plans to the correct entity-level controls.

List A: Entity-Level Controls

1. Controls related to the control environment.
2. Controls over management override.
3. The company's risk assessment process.

4. Centralized processing and controls, including shared service environments.
5. Controls to monitor the results of operations.
6. Controls to monitor other controls, including activities of the internal audit function, the audit committee, and self-assessment programs.
7. Controls over the period-end financial reporting process.
8. Policies that address significant business control and risk management practices.

List B: Specific Control Plans

A. A file of signed code of conduct letters.
B. A report of all employees not taking required vacation days.
C. A report on IT risks and a risk action plan.
D. Access control software.
E. A systems development life cycle methodology (SDLC).
F. Budgetary controls.
G. Development of a business interruption plan.
H. Establishment of a code of conduct.
I. Not covered.
J. Program change controls.
K. Segregation of duties.
L. Selection and hiring control plans.
M. Service-level agreements and reporting processes.
N. Supervision.
O. Use of control frameworks such as COBIT and COSO.

P 8-8   Examine the last column in Table 8.2 (pp. 267–268) for the following personnel only: security officer, Chief Information Officer (CIO), systems development manager, quality assurance, and systems programming.

For each of the five functions, list *one* control plan from this chapter that would address the control concern described in the last column of Table 8.2 (pp. 267–268) for that function. Explain how the plan might address the concern mentioned. Do not use the same plan twice; use five different plans.

P 8-9   Research the Internet, newspapers, magazines, and journals to find recent incidences of outages of one or more Web sites. Develop a report (format and length to be determined by your instructor) providing a general overview of the incident(s), including any necessary background information, and describing how long the site(s) were not available and how they came to be out of service. Describe in your report which controls would have *prevented*, *detected*, or *corrected* the outages. Be sure to include your sources.

P 8-10   Research the Internet, newspapers, magazines, and journals to find recent incidences of *denial-of-service attacks* on one or more Web sites. Develop a report (format and length to be determined by your instructor) providing a general overview of the incident(s), including any necessary background information, and describing how long the site(s) were not available and how they came to be out of service. Describe in your report the controls which would have *prevented*, *detected*, or *corrected* the attacks and resulting outages. Be sure to include your sources.

P 8-11   The AICPA has adopted a framework called Trust Services Principles and Criteria.

a.   Look up this framework on the Internet and explain each of the principles.

b.   What types of assurance services are already based on the Trust Service Principles and Criteria?

c.   Create two additional services, not already in place or under consideration by the AICPA, which can use Trust Services Principles and Criteria. For each additional service you recommend, explain which principles and criteria would apply, how, and why.

CHAPTER 9

Controlling Information Systems: Business Process and Application Controls

Learning Objectives

After reading this chapter, you should be able to:

* Complete the steps in the control framework and prepare a control matrix.
* Write explanations that describe how the business process and application controls introduced in this chapter accomplish control goals.
* Describe the importance of business process and application controls to organizations with enterprise systems and those engaging in e-business.

How well do you believe that Fortune 1000 companies manage their critical data? What percentage of that critical data do you think is accurate—99 percent, 95 percent, or 90 percent? According to Gartner, Inc., only 75 percent of critical data within Fortune 1000 companies is accurate. Furthermore, only 34 percent of executives responding to a 2004 PricewaterhouseCoopers survey said that they had confidence in the quality of their corporate data.[1] What is the result of this problem? Internal operations that depend on accurate data do not perform as planned. For example, can we manage our inventory if we don't know exactly how much we have and where it is? Inaccurate financial reporting, uncollectible receivables, and overpayments to vendors are other problems caused by inaccurate data.

What is going on here? Haven't we had enough experience using computers to capture and store data in such a way that we have accurate data? Although we do know how, we do not pay sufficient attention to the controls that are needed to capture and maintain accurate data. This chapter introduces you to business process and application controls that can be applied across many types of processes to ensure that an information system captures only legitimate (i.e., *valid*) data, captures it once and only once (i.e., *complete*), and that data is captured correctly (i.e., *accurate*) so that the data supports an organization's operations (i.e., *effectiveness*), protects its resources (i.e., *security of resources*), and does so with minimal use of an organization's resources (i.e., *efficiency*).

---

[1]Kym Gilhooly, "Dirty Data Blights the Bottom Line," *Computerworld*, November 7, 2005, pp. 23–24.

Controls

This chapter presents a conceptual framework for the analysis of controls in business processes. We apply the control framework by describing business process and application controls that may be found in any business process. These controls will help us *prevent* (or *detect* or *correct*) the data quality issues plaguing organizations throughout the world.

Enterprise Systems

Many of the controls described in this chapter provide assurance about the quality of the data entry process. Such controls take on increased importance with *enterprise systems* because they *prevent* erroneous data from entering the system and negatively impacting the many tightly connected processes that follow the initial entry of the data. For example, good controls over the entry of customer orders will help us perform the activities that follow the recording of that order, including the shipment; update to the inventory balance; customer invoicing; general ledger entries for sales, accounts receivable, inventory, and costs of goods sold; and the inventory replenishment process.

E-Business

Good data entry controls also are important for those engaging in *e-business*. For example, if we receive customer orders electronically, our systems must have sufficient controls within them so that they accept only authorized and accurate order data and record that data once and only once. If we don't have these controls, we may not make shipments, make inaccurate or duplicate shipments, or make shipments to those who have no intention of paying for the goods being shipped.

Introduction

Having covered the control environment in Chapter 7 and pervasive and general controls (and IT general controls) in Chapter 8, we are now ready to move to the third level of control plans appearing in the hierarchy shown in Figure 7.6 (pg. 245)—business process and application control plans. We start by defining the components of a control framework and introducing the tools used to implement it. Then we apply the control framework to two generic business processes that include controls that may be found in any information system. In Chapters 10 through 16, we will examine controls that might be found in particular business processes (e.g., order entry/sales, billing, accounts receivable, etc.).

The Control Framework

In this section, we formally introduce the control framework that we began to discuss in Chapter 7 in the section titled "A Framework for Assessing the Design of a System of Internal Control" (pp. 237–242). We recommend that you review those pages now. The control framework provides you with a structure for analyzing the internal controls of business organizations. However, structure alone is of little practical value to you. To make the framework functional, you need to become familiar with, and comfortable in using, the tools for implementing the framework. Chapter 4 introduced you to one of the key tools—the systems flowchart. Now we tell you more about a related tool—the control matrix.

The Control Matrix

SOX

As noted in Chapter 7, a *control matrix* is a tool designed to assist you in evaluating the potential effectiveness of controls in a particular business process by matching control goals with relevant control plans. PCAOB Auditing Standard No. 5 calls this "Effectiveness of Control Design." Assessing the effectiveness of control design is required to comply with SOX Section 404. When management and independent auditors perform this assessment, they often use a control matrix such as the one used in our control framework.[2]

Figure 9.1, an extension of Figure 7.7 (pg. 246), presents a "bare-bones" outline of the control matrix. This control matrix includes the explanation of cell entries in

FIGURE 9.1 Suprina Control Matrix

Recommended control plans (b)	Control Goals of the Suprina Order Entry Process								
	Control Goals of the Operations Process (a)				Control Goals of the Information Process (a)				
	Ensure effectiveness of operations		Ensure efficient employment of resources (e.g., people and computers)	Ensure security of resources (e.g., inventory, customer master data)	For the customer order inputs, ensure:			For the sales order and inventory master data, ensure:	
	A	B			IV	IC	IA	UC	UA
Present Controls									
P-1: Enter data close to the location where the customer order is prepared	P-1 (c)		P-1			P-1	P-1		
P-2: Customer credit check		P-2		P-2	P-2				
Missing Controls									
M-1: Agreement of run-to-run totals								M-1	M-1
M-2: Programmed edit checks			M-2				M-2		

Effectiveness goals include:

A – Provide timely acknowledgement of customer orders

B – Provide assurance of customer's creditworthiness

IV = input validity

IC = input completeness

IA = input accuracy

UC = update completeness

UA = update accuracy

Note: Four elements of the control matrix

(a) Control goals

(b) Recommended control plans

(c) Cell entries

(d) Explanation of cell entries (Exhibit 9.1)

---

[2]Some auditors use a control checklist or questionnaire for this assessment. The matrix, being two-dimensional rather than one-dimensional, facilitates a matching of controls and objectives.

Exhibit 9.1. **Figure 9.2** is the "annotated" systems flowchart for the Suprina order entry process that is produced when we complete the steps in the control framework. The control matrix provides a means to explain and analyze the controls that have been annotated on a systems flowchart.

We cannot overemphasize that our intent in Figure 9.1 is not to have you learn about the control goals and control plans for an order entry process. Those are covered in Chapter 10. Rather, we are giving you an overview of the control matrix elements and how they relate to each other, and walking you through the steps in preparing the matrix. Please follow along in Figure 9.1 as we describe how to prepare the control matrix.

Steps in Preparing the Control Matrix

Step I. *Specify control goals.* These goals are listed across the top of the matrix; they should be familiar to you from discussions in Chapter 7, where we showed them in Figure 7.5 (pg. 240). Recall from Chapter 7 that we filled in the top row of the matrix by following these steps:

1. *Identify operations process control goals:* As we noted in Chapter 7, our control framework subdivides operations process control goals into effectiveness of operations, efficient employment of resources, and security of resources (Table 7.1, pg. 241).

EXHIBIT 9.1 Explanation of Cell Entries for Control Matrix in Figure 9.1 (d)

P-1: *Enter data close to the location where the customer order is prepared.*

- *Effectiveness goal A, efficient employment of resources:* Use of this strategy places the sales reps in a position to process customer orders immediately, and being familiar with the orders allows the them to input the orders more quickly, which leads to timely acknowledgements and more orders processed by each sales rep (efficiency).
- *Customer order input completeness:* By having the sales reps enter the order data rather than forwarding to a data entry function, the risk of orders getting lost should be reduced.
- *Customer order input accuracy:* Because the sales reps are familiar with the type of data being entered and can correct any input errors "on the spot," input accuracy should be improved.

P-2: *Customer credit check.*

- *Effectiveness goal B:* The credit check is performed by ascertaining that the amount of the customer order (plus the amount of any open sales orders and the amount of any outstanding receivables balance) falls within the credit limit established by the credit department. If the request falls outside the limit, then the control terminates the sale.

- *Security of resources:* Termination of orders exceeding credit limits ensures that the organization protects its resources by dealing only with customers who have demonstrated an ability to satisfy their liabilities.
- *Sales order input validity:* Valid sales orders include those that fall within authorized credit limits.

M-1: *Agreement of run-to-run totals.*
Note: We assume that batch totals could be prepared for the customer orders when she requests processing of those orders and that these totals are compared to the updates made to the sales order master and inventory master files.

- *Update completeness, update accuracy:* Agreement of the batch totals ensures that all orders submitted for processing by the order entry clerk result in updates to the sales order master and inventory master data files, which are made once and only once (completeness) and are made correctly (accuracy).

M-2: *Programmed edit checks.*
Note: We assume that the orders could be edited on the sales rep laptop for *reasonableness* of the input order quantities.

- *Efficient employment of resources:* Programmed edit checks provide quick, low-cost editing of input data.
- *Customer order input accuracy:* By editing input data and rejecting erroneous data, input accuracy is improved.

By reviewing the systems flowchart and other information about the business process, we determine the following specifics:

a. *Effectiveness goals*

    i. *Effectiveness* goals describe measures of success for the operations process. These are developed during an enterprise's risk-management process. For example, see "Related Objectives" in Figure 7.1 (pg. 221).

    ii. Because these goals might be difficult for you to derive without an organizational context, we will recommend some sample effectiveness goals for each process discussed in this text.

    iii. For the Suprina order entry process, we include only two examples here: Goal A—Provide timely acknowledgement of customer orders, and Goal B—Provide assurance of customer's creditworthiness.[3] Other effectiveness goals would be shown as Goals C, D, and so forth.

FIGURE 9.2   Suprina Company Annotated Systems Flowchart

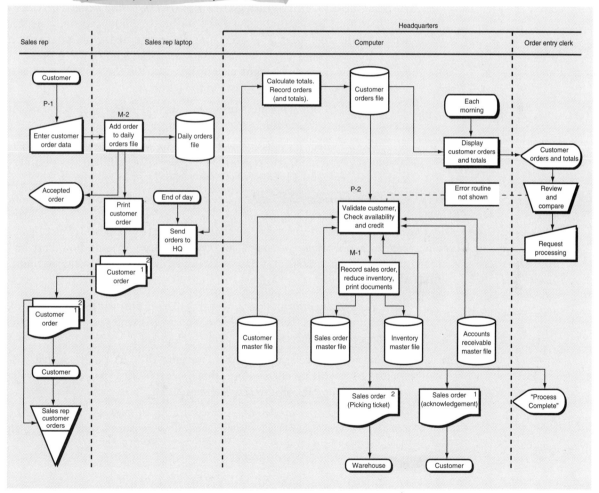

---

[3]Remember that one of the goals of any business process may be to comply with applicable laws, regulations, and contractual agreements. Depending on the particular process being analyzed, we tailor the matrix to identify the specific law, regulation, or agreement with which we desire to achieve compliance.

b. *Efficiency goals*

    i.   Efficiency control goals relate to ensuring that resources used in the business process are being employed in the most productive manner.

    ii.   In parentheses, notice that we have listed two resources of the order entry process for which efficiency is applicable—people and computers. In fact, people and computers would always be considered in the efficiency assessments related to accounting information systems.

    iii.   In other business processes, such as receiving goods and supplies, we might also be concerned with the productive use of equipment such as trucks, forklifts, and handheld scanners.

c. *Security goals*

    i.   *Security* control goals relate to protecting entity resources from loss, destruction, disclosure, copying, sale, or other misuse. These are meant to manage risks identified in the enterprise risk-management process.

    ii.   In parentheses, we have included two resources of the order entry process that must be secured—inventory and information (customer master data). With any business process, we are concerned with information that is added, changed, or deleted as a result of executing the process, as well as assets that are brought into or taken out of the organization as a result of the process, such as cash and inventory.

    iii.   With regard to other business processes, such as cash receipts, we might include accounts receivable master data and cash.

    iv.   *Note:* Security over hard assets used to execute business processes, such as computer equipment, trucks, and loading docks, is handled through pervasive, general, and IT general controls (discussed in Chapter 8).

2. *Identify information process control goals:* As noted in Chapter 7, our control framework (Table 7.1, pg. 241) subdivides information process control goals into input control goals (*input validity*, *input completeness*, and *input accuracy*) and update control goals (*update completeness* and *update accuracy*). By reviewing the systems flowchart and other information about the business process, we determine the following specifics:

a. *Input goals*

    i.   *Input* goals of the information process relate to ensuring input validity (IV), input completeness (IC), and input accuracy (IA) with respect to all business process data entering the system.

    ii.   For Suprina's process, we review the systems flowchart and see that customer orders will be entered into the system. Notice that we specifically name the input data on the control matrix.

    iii.   For other business processes, such as hiring employees, we would be concerned with other inputs, such as employee, payroll, and benefit plan data.

b. *Update goals*

    i.   The purpose of the *update* control goals of the information process is to ensure the update completeness (UC) and update accuracy (UA) of the business process input data. Note that these goals only apply when there is a periodic process—that is, a delay between input and update. When there is an immediate process, the UC and UA columns on the control matrix are shaded to indicate that they do not apply to the process because the input and update of master data are simultaneous, and no additional controls, beyond those controlling the input, are required to ensure UC and UA.

ii.   For the Suprina order entry process, we see that the customer order data are coming from customers and are used to update the sales order master and inventory master data. Notice that we list these *master data* on the control matrix.

iii. Other business processes, such as cash payments, would involve different update concerns, such as vendor, payroll, or accounts payable master data.

Step II. *Identify recommended control plans* for the business process under evaluation. This step focuses on the nature and extent of control plans that should be in place to accomplish our objectives and to reduce residual risk to an acceptable level. In the final analysis, the comfort level that management and auditors reach with respect to residual risk is a matter of professional judgment.

For a given business process, each control goal should be addressed by one or more control plans. For instance, one or more control plans should cover the effectiveness goals (A and B), the efficiency goal, the security goal, and each of the information process goals (IV, IC, IA, UC, and UA). The following advice will help you to structure your thinking with regard to control plans. Perhaps the most difficult part of this process, the preparation of a control matrix, is identifying controls that should be in place (we call these *present controls*) and those controls that are not in place but should be (we call these *missing controls*). Follow along as we describe a process to help you complete this task:

1. *Identify "Present" Control Plans and annotate them on the systems flowchart:* Start on the upper-left column of the systems flowchart (which should be the start of the process) and identify controls that seem to accomplish one or more of the control goals. As a general rule, each process symbol in the flowchart should be associated with one or more controls. Accordingly, for each process symbol, ask yourself, "Does this process involve a control to help me to protect a resource?" or "Does this process involve a control to improve the accuracy of the input?" and so on. There may, of course, be controls not directly associated with process symbols in the flowchart (for example, input formats on documents), but rarely should there be process symbols not involving controls. Controls will fall into two categories: the generic controls that we describe later in this chapter that apply to all or most business processes, and the controls that relate to a specific business process. These latter controls will be introduced in Chapters 10 through 16.

    a.   Reviewing the Suprina systems flowchart (Figure 9.2, pg. 303), you will find that the first process is entitled "Enter customer order data." Can this help us accomplish a control goal? As we will learn later in the chapter, the location of the data entry process can be important. In this case, by entering the customer orders on their laptops, sales reps can ensure more timely inputs, enter the orders in an efficient manner, and reduce the number of lost and incorrect orders. Because this process appears on the flowchart, this control plan already exists, meaning that it is *present* as opposed to *missing*. Accordingly, we *annotate* the systems flowchart with a P-1—a *P-* indicating that it is *present*, and a *1* because it is the *first* present control plan on the flowchart.[4]

---

[4]The numbering for present and missing controls is used only to cross-reference the flowchart and control matrix. The sequence of the numbers is not significant.

b. Continue reviewing the systems flowchart by following its sequential logic, annotating the flowchart with P-2, P-3, and so on until you have accounted for all *present* control plans. Notice in Figure 9.2 that we have found two present controls, P-1 and P-2. There are more, but we are trying to keep the example simple for now.

2. *Evaluate "Present" Control Plans:* Write the control number (P-1, P-2, P-3, through P-*n*) and name of each control plan in the left-hand column of the control matrix. Then, starting with P-1, look across the row and determine which control goals the plan addresses, and then place a P-1 in each *cell* of the matrix for which P-1 is applicable. It is common for a given control plan to address more than one control goal. Continue this procedure for each of the *present* control plans. Simultaneously, in the section below the matrix (Exhibit 9.1, pg. 302), describe *how* the control plan addresses each noted control goal. When you are learning this process, writing these explanations will cause you the most difficulty. Yet we believe this element is the most important part of the matrix because the purpose of the matrix is to relate plans to goals. Unless you can explain the association between plans and goals, there's a good possibility you may have guessed at the cell entry. Sometimes you'll guess right, but it's just as likely you'll guess wrong. Don't play the guessing game! Be prepared to defend your cell entries.

   a. To illustrate, we list the two illustrative control plans (P-1 and P-2) for the order entry process at Suprina in the left column of Figure 9.1 (pg. 301).

   b. P-1 (Enter data close to the location where the customer order is prepared) provides timely acknowledgements (effectiveness goal A), is efficient, and ensures input completeness and input accuracy.

   c. P-2 (Customer credit check) provides assurance of customer creditworthiness (effectiveness goal B), secures inventory from being shipped to those who won't pay, and ensures input validity by determining that the order falls within authorized credit limits.

3. *Identify and evaluate "Missing" Control Plans:* The next step in assessing control plans is to determine whether additional controls are needed to address missing control goal areas, strengthen present control plans, or both.

   a. *Examine the controls matrix* to see if there are any control goals (operations or information) that no present control plan is addressing. If so, you need to do the following:

      i. In the left-hand column of the matrix, number the first missing control plan as M-1 (i.e., *M-* for *missing* and *1* because it is the *first* missing plan identified), and label or title the plan.

      ii. Across the matrix row, place M-1 in each cell for which the missing control is designed.

      iii. In the explanation section below the matrix (such as Exhibit 9.1), explain how the missing control will address each noted control goal.

      iv. *Annotate* the systems flowchart with M-1 where the control should be inserted.

      v. If there are still control goals for which there is no control plan, develop another plan (M-2), and repeat the four previous steps (i through iv). Continue this procedure until each control goal on the matrix is addressed by at least one control plan.

vi. For this step we have noted one missing control plan (M-1), although there may be more. Recall that the purpose of this chapter is to offer guidelines for creating a controls matrix, not to completely analyze Suprina's order entry process. For missing control plan M-1, we note that by agreeing run-to-run totals at the point that the sales order master and inventory master files are updated, we can ensure that these data stores are updated completely and accurately.

b. *Analyze the systems flowchart for further risk exposures:* Even though all of the control goals on the matrix are now addressed by one or more control plans, it is worthwhile to closely scrutinize the systems flowchart at least one more time. Such analysis can reveal areas where further controls are needed. Although all of the control goals on the matrix have one or more associated control plans, it may be necessary to add more control plans or strengthen existing plans to further reduce residual risk to an acceptable level in certain areas. Our missing control M-2 falls into this category. Well-designed systems of internal control should perform edits on inputs as early in the process as possible. It is for this reason that we have added control M-2 to complement the edits, such as P-2, that will be performed later in the process. We note that Suprina should perform programmed edits on the sales rep laptops to mitigate risks related to efficiency and input accuracy. It takes training and experience (and usually teamwork) to effectively spot risks and weaknesses of this nature. In Chapters 10 through 16, you will learn more about how to make such critical internal control assessments.

When your assessment leads you to the identification (and correction) of control weaknesses, as reflected in missing control plans or recommendations for strengthening present control plans, you are essentially recommending remedial changes to the system (if necessary) to correct deficiencies in the system.

In addition to telling you about the control strengths and weaknesses of a particular system, a completed matrix and annotated systems flowchart also facilitates your evaluation from the perspectives of *control effectiveness* (are all the control goals achieved?), *control efficiency* (do individual control plans address multiple goals?), and *control redundancy* (are too many goals directed at the same goal?).

Exhibit 9.2 (pg. 308) summarizes the steps we have just undertaken in preparing the illustrative control matrix in Figure 9.1 (pg. 301), the related explanations (Exhibit 9.1, pg. 302), and the annotated systems flowchart (Figure 9.2, pg. 303). Combined with the preceding discussion and illustration, the steps should be self-explanatory. You should take time now to study each of the steps to make sure that you have a reasonable understanding of them.

Sample Control Plans for Data Input

In the preceding section, we described the framework used to analyze business process and application controls. The framework consists of two main elements: specifying control goals and recommending control plans. For the remainder of this chapter, we describe generic controls that apply to many business processes. Knowing these controls will help you identify present and missing controls. In the following sections, we describe two methods for processing input data: (1) manual and automated data entry and (2) data entry with batches of input data. For both of these methods, we describe the processing logic, present a systems flowchart, and describe and analyze the controls with a control matrix and control explanations.

EXHIBIT 9.2 Steps in Preparing a Control Matrix

Step I *Specify control goals:* Review the systems flowchart and related narrative description to become familiar with the system under examination. Identify the business process (e.g., cash receipts); the key relevant resources (e.g., cash, accounts receivable master data); the input (e.g., the remittance advice); storage, if any, for the input data (e.g., cash receipts event data); and the master data being updated (e.g., accounts receivable master data). With regard to the business process under consideration:

1. Identify operations process control goals:
    a. Effectiveness goals (there may be more than one)
    b. Efficiency goals (usually people and computers)
    c. Security goals (consider all affected data and tangible assets)
2. Identify information process control goals:
    a. Input goals (validity, completeness, and accuracy)
    b. Update goals (completeness and accuracy), if the process is periodic

Step II *Identify recommended control plans:* List a set of recommended control plans that are appropriate for the process being analyzed. The list should include both plans related to the operations process (e.g., the order entry process) and those related to the information processing methods (e.g., data entry controls, batch controls). In Figure 9.1 (pg. 301) and Exhibit 9.1 (pg. 302), we presented only two illustrative *present* plans for Suprina's system and two *missing* plans.

1. *Identify present control plans and annotate them on the systems flowchart* by placing P-1, P-2, through P-*n* beside all present controls. Start on the upper-left column of the flow-chart, and follow the sequential processing logic of the flowchart.
2. Evaluate *present* control plans by placing the number and name of the plan on the control matrix, entering the control plan number in the matrix cells for each appropriate control goal, and explaining, in the section below the matrix, how each control addresses each control goal where a cell entry was made.
3. Identify and evaluate *missing* control plans (M-1, M-2, through M-*n*).
    a. Examine the control matrix to determine whether there are any control goals for which no control plan exists. If so, develop a control plan designed to minimize associated risks (i.e., address control goals). Explain the nature and extent of the missing plan in the section below the matrix. Repeat this procedure until all control goals on the matrix are addressed by one or more control plans.
    b. Analyze the systems flowchart for further risk exposures for which you would recommend adding additional controls or strengthening existing controls. Note any further additions or refinements on the control matrix using the same procedures described for present or missing controls plans.

Perhaps the most error-prone and inefficient steps in an operations or information process are the steps during which data is entered into a system. Although much has been done to improve the accuracy and efficiency of the data entry process, numerous problems remain, especially when humans enter data into a system. Thus we begin our discussion of process controls by describing those controls that improve the data entry process.

As you study these controls, keep in mind the following improvements that have been made to address the errors and inefficiencies of the data entry process:

- The data entry process may be automated. Documents containing bar codes and OCR encoding may be scanned, or radio frequency identification (RFID) readers may be used to obtain data from RFID chips.[5] This automation reduces or eliminates manual keying.

E-Business
- Business events, such as purchases, may be initiated in one (buying) organization and transmitted to another (selling) organization via the Internet or *electronic data interchange (EDI)*. In this case, the receiving (selling) organization need not enter the data at all.

Enterprise Systems
- The multiple steps in a business process may be tightly integrated, as in an enterprise system. In these cases, the number of data entry steps is greatly reduced. For example, there may be no need to enter a shipment (sale) into the billing system because the billing system has been integrated with the shipping system.

___

[5]See Chapter 10 for an explanation of bar codes and scanning and Chapter 12 for an explanation of RFID.

Control Plans for Manual and Automated Data Entry

In this section, we introduce you to a hypothetical system that employs manual and automated data entry techniques. We describe the system, walk you through its systems flowchart, list and explain the control plans associated with these data entry methods, and incorporate those plans into a control matrix for the system.

System Description and Flowchart

Figure 9.3 shows an annotated systems flowchart for a hypothetical system that we will use to describe our first set of controls. The processing starts in the first column to the left in Figure 9.3 with the input document. Let's assume that the document is designed to facilitate the data entry process and that it includes the signature of an authorizing

FIGURE 9.3 Systems Flowchart: Manual and Automated Data Entry

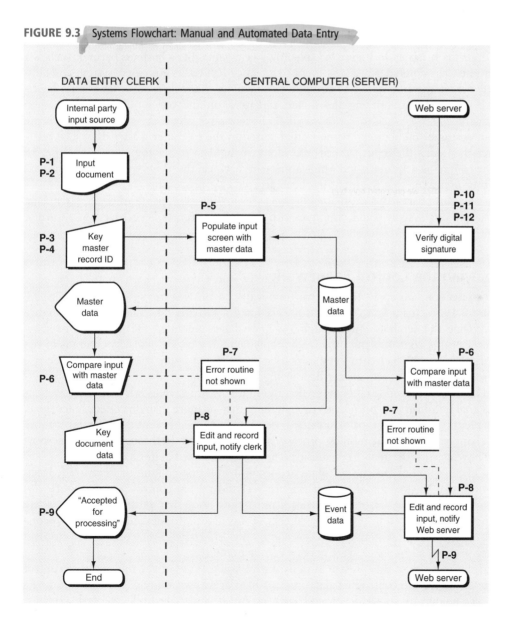

individual. The data entry program presents the clerk with a preformatted input screen and then prompts the clerk to enter certain data into fields on that screen, starting with the IDs, or codes, for some master records (e.g., customer code, item numbers).

In response to keying the master record IDs, the computer populates the input screen with master data, such as a customer record. The data entry clerk compares the display to the input document to determine that the correct code has been entered. Corrective measures may be taken (see "Error routine not shown"), such as entering a corrected code. The data entry clerk would then enter the remaining data, such as the codes for the items that the customer has ordered (the computer would display the inventory master data as each item number is entered, and the clerk would compare each display to the input document). The computer then edits the input and records the input (if the data passes the edits; otherwise, an error routine is activated), and then displays a message to the clerk indicating that the input has been accepted for processing.

On the right side of the central computer column we see an automated data entry process that roughly parallels the manual entry by the data entry clerk, with a few exceptions. As mentioned previously, automated data entry may be via RFID, OCR, bar codes, EDI, or the Internet. In Figure 9.3 (pg. 309), we assume that a business partner, such as a customer, has entered a business event (e.g., an order) on its computer system and submitted it via the Internet. The computer determines that this is an order from a legitimate customer by verifying the digital signature on the order. The computer then compares the input data to the master data. For example, the computer might match the input customer number and name to that stored in the customer master data. The computer then edits the input, records the input (if the data passes the edits; otherwise, an error routine is activated), and sends a message back via the Web server to the business partner indicating that the input has been accepted for processing.

Our flowchart stops at this point *without* depicting the update of any master data. Certainly our system could continue with an update process. We have not shown it here so that we can concentrate on the *input* controls.

Applying the Control Framework

In this section, we apply the control framework to the generic system just described. **Figure 9.4** presents a sample control matrix for the systems flowchart shown in Figure 9.3. Using the symbols P-1 through P-12, we have annotated the flowchart to show where specific control plans are already implemented. The UC and UA columns in the matrix have been shaded to emphasize that they do not apply to this analysis because there is no update of any master data in Figure 9.3.

Under the operations process section of Figure 9.4, we have shown only one effectiveness goal for illustrative purposes—though there may be more than one effectiveness goal. We identify the goal as Goal A: Ensure *timely* input of (blank) event data (whatever those data happen to be). In the business process chapters (Chapters 10 through 14), we will show you how to tailor the goals to the business processes discussed in those chapters.

The recommended control plans are listed in the first column in Figure 9.4. Keep in mind that the systems flowchart (Figure 9.3) and related control matrix (Figure 9.4) are shown here for illustrative purposes only; thus, they may be incomplete in some respects. To help you in future assessments of this nature, we next present a list of controls that are representative of those commonly associated with controlling the data entry process, all of which were applied to our example.

The purpose of this presentation is to give you a sense of the multitude of control plans available for controlling data input. Once again, we remind you that the plans are *not* unique to a specific process such as order entry/sales, billings, cash receipts, and so forth. Rather, they apply to *any* data entry process. Therefore, when the technology of a system is appropriate, these controls should be incorporated into the list of recommended control plans. Recall that in the previous section of this chapter, you were instructed to look for controls that seem to address the control goals

FIGURE 9.4   Control Matrix for Manual and Automated Data Entry

Data Entry

Recommended Control Plans	Control Goals of the Operations Process			Control Goals of the Information Process (a)				
	Ensure Effectiveness of Operations	Ensure Efficient Employment of Resources (people, computers)	Ensure Security of Resources (event data, assets)	For the (blank) inputs, ensure:			For the (blank) master data, ensure:	
	A			IV	IC	IA	UC	UA
Present Controls								
P-1: Document design	P-1	P-1				P-1		
P-2: Written approvals			P-2	P-2				
P-3: Preformatted screens	P-3	P-3				P-3		
P-4: Online prompting	P-4	P-4				P-4		
P-5: Populate input screens with master data	P-5	P-5		P-5		P-5		
P-6: Compare input data with master data	P-6	P-6		P-6		P-6		
P-7: Procedures for rejected Inputs					P-7	P-7		
P-8: Programmed edit checks	P-8	P-8				P-8		
P-9: Confirm input acceptance					P-9			
P-10: Automated data entry	P-10	P-10				P-10		
P-11: Enter data close to the originating source	P-11	P-11			P-11	P-11		
P-12: Digital signatures			P-12	P-12		P-12		
Missing Controls								
None noted								

Possible effectiveness goals include the following:

A = Ensure timely input of (blank) event data.

See Exhibit 9.3 for a complete explanation of control plans and cell entries.

IV = input validity

IC = input completeness

IA = input accuracy

UC = update completeness

UA = update accuracy

(e.g., effectiveness, efficiency, input accuracy). Begin at the upper-left column of the flowchart, and look for such controls. Then follow along with us as we trace the processing logic by following the flow of work activities. We first define and explain these controls and then summarize, in **Exhibit 9.3** (pp. 316–317) each cell entry in Figure 9.4 (pg. 311), the control matrix:

- **Document design** (Exhibit 9.3 and Figure 9.4, P-1): A control plan in which a source document is designed to make it easier to prepare the document initially and later to input data from the document into a computer or other input device. In our example, we assume that the organization has properly designed this document to facilitate the data preparation and data entry processes.
- **Written approvals** (Exhibit 9.3 and Figure 9.4, P-2): These take the form of a signature or initials on a document to indicate that someone has authorized the event. This control ensures that the data input arises from a valid business event and that appropriate authorizations have been obtained. Another control aspect of approving an input document is that such an approval segregates authorizing events from recording events (as discussed in Chapter 8).

Note: In some situations, we might use **electronic approvals**, whereby business events are routed, using a computer system's *workflow* facility, to persons authorized to approve the event. For example, purchase requisitions might be routed for approval to those with budgetary authority.

- **Preformatted screens** (Exhibit 9.3 and Figure 9.4, P-3): Control the entry of data by defining the acceptable *format* of each data field. For example, the screen might force users to key exactly nine alphabetic characters in one field and exactly five numerals in another field. Or the system may provide drop-down lists of data that are acceptable for a given field, such as shipping methods and sales terms. To facilitate the data entry process, the cursor may *automatically move* to the next field on the screen. The program may require that certain fields be completed, thus preventing the user from omitting any *mandatory* data. Finally, the system may *automatically populate* certain fields with data, such as the current date, sales tax rates, and other terms of a business event. This reduces the number of keystrokes required, making data entry quicker and more efficient. Also, with fewer keystrokes and by using the default data, fewer keying mistakes are expected, which makes data entry more accurate. To ensure that the system has not provided inappropriate defaults, the clerk must compare the data provided by the system with that of the input.
- **Online prompting** (Exhibit 9.3 and Figure 9.4, P-4): Requests user input or asks questions that the user must answer. For example, after entering all the input data for a particular customer order, you might be presented with three options: "Accept" the completed screen, "Edit" the completed screen, or "Reject" the completed screen. By forcing you to stop and accept the data, online prompting is, in a sense, advising you to check your data entries before moving on. In addition, many systems provide *context-sensitive help*, whereby the user is automatically provided with, or can ask for, descriptions of the data to be entered into each input field.
- **Populate input screens with master data** (Exhibit 9.3 and Figure 9.4, P-5): The clerk enters the identification code for an entity, such as a customer, and the system retrieves data about that entity from the master data. For example, in our earlier example of entering a customer order, the user might be prompted to enter the customer ID (code). Then, by accessing the customer master data, the system

automatically provides data such as the customer's name and address, the salesperson's name, and the sales terms. This reduces the number of keystrokes required, making data entry quicker and more efficient. With fewer keystrokes and using the existing data, fewer keying mistakes are expected. To enable this control, numeric, alphabetic, and other designators are usually assigned to entities such as customers, vendors, and employees.

- **Compare input data with master data** (Exhibit 9.3 and Figure 9.4, P-6): Comparisons performed manually or by the computer to determine the accuracy and validity of input data. Here are just three types of comparisons that can be made:

  a. *Input/master data match:* These edits test that the correct identification (ID) code has been manually entered. For example, a clerk keys in a customer number, and the system displays this record on the input screen. The clerk then matches the customer data, such as name and address, to the input document. In a similar manner, the clerk could read the name and address back to a customer who is on the phone.

  b. *Input/master data dependency checks:* These edits test whether the contents of two or more data elements or fields on the event data bear the correct logical relationship. For example, input customer orders can be tested to determine whether the salesperson works in the customer's territory. If these two items don't match, there is some evidence that the customer number or the salesperson ID was input erroneously.

  c. *Input/master data validity and accuracy checks:* These edits test whether master data supports the validity and accuracy of the input. For example, this edit might prevent the input of a shipment when no record of a corresponding customer order exists. If no match is made, we may have input some data incorrectly, or the shipment might simply be invalid. We might also compare elements *within* the input and master data. For example, we can compare the quantities to be shipped to the quantities ordered. Quantities that do not match *may* have been picked from the shelf or entered into the computer incorrectly.

- **Procedures for rejected inputs** (Exhibit 9.3 and Figure 9.4, P-7): Designed to ensure that erroneous data (i.e., data not accepted for processing) are corrected and resubmitted for processing. To make sure that the corrected input does not still contain errors, the corrected input data should undergo all routines through which the input was processed originally. A "suspense file" of rejected inputs is often retained (manually or by the computer) to ensure the timely clearing of rejected items. To reduce the clutter in the simple flowcharts in this text, we typically depict such routines with the annotation "Error routine not shown" and provide no further details.

- **Programmed edit checks** (Exhibit 9.3 and Figure 9.4, P-8): Automatically performed by data entry programs upon entry of the input data. Erroneous data may be highlighted on the input screen to allow the operator to take corrective action immediately. For automated data entry, rejected business events may be listed in a summary report periodically produced by the computer. Programmed edits can highlight actual or potential input errors and allow them to be corrected quickly and efficiently. The most common types of programmed edit checks are the following:

  a. **Limit checks** test whether the contents (e.g., values) of the data entered fall within predetermined limits. The limits may describe a standard range (e.g., customer numbers must be between 0001 and 5000, months must be 01 to 12) or maximum values (e.g., no normal hours worked greater than 40 and no overtime hours greater than 20). A variation of this control is a **reasonableness check** that compares entered data with a calculated amount (not a predetermined amount) to discover inputs that *may* be incorrect. For example, the amount of an item ordered by a customer is compared to the total amount of that item purchased in the previous 12 months. The computer would then ask the data entry clerk to verify that this is *really* the amount being ordered.

b. **Document/record hash totals** reflect a summarization of any numeric data field within the input document or record, such as item numbers or quantities on a customer order. The totaling of these numbers typically serves no purpose other than as a control. Calculated before and then again after entry of the document or record, this total can be used to determine that the applicable fields were entered accurately.

c. **Mathematical accuracy checks** compare calculations performed manually to those performed by the computer to determine whether a document has been entered correctly. For this check, the user might enter the individual items (e.g., quantity purchased, unit cost, tax, shipping cost) on a document, such as an invoice, and the total for that document. Then the computer adds the individual items and compares that total to the one input by the user. If they don't agree, something has likely been entered erroneously. Alternatively, the user can review the computer calculations and compare them to totals prepared before input.

d. **Check digit**, as noted in Chapter 5, is an extra digit added to the identification number of entities such as customers and vendors. More than likely, you have a check digit as part of the ID on your ATM, credit, and debit cards. The check digit is calculated originally by applying a formula to an identification number; the check digit then is appended to the identification number. Whenever a data entry person enters the identification number later, the computer program applies the mathematical formula to determine that the number was input correctly. If the program does not calculate the original check digit, it is likely that the number has not been input correctly.

- **Confirm input acceptance** (Exhibit 9.3 and Figure 9.4, P-9): This control causes the data entry program to inform the user that the input has been accepted for processing. The program may flash a message on the screen telling a user that the input has been *accepted*, or it might display a number assigned to the event. For example, after input of a customer order, the computer might display the internal sales order number that will be used to track the sale. To complete the control, the data entry clerk might write that number on the customer's order or read the number to the customer who is on the phone. For automated inputs, the computer might send the number back to the originator, such as when a confirmation number is sent back to you after you enter an order on a Web site.

- **Automated data entry** (Exhibit 9.3 and Figure 9.4, P-10): This is a strategy for the capture and entry of event-related data using technology such as OCR, bar codes, RFID, and EDI. These methods use fewer human resources and capture more data in a period of time than is possible with manual entry. By eliminating the keying errors that can occur in manual data entry, these methods improve the accuracy of the entered data. Finally, in some cases, the input method can validate the authenticity of the input. For example, when the RFID chip on a box is read, we know that the box exists.

- **Enter data close to the originating source** (Exhibit 9.3 and Figure 9.4, P-11): This is a strategy for the capture and entry of event-related data close to the place and time that an event occurs. *Online transaction entry (OLTE)* and *online real-time processing (OLRT)* are examples of this processing strategy. When this strategy is employed, databases are more current, and subsequent events can occur in a *timelier* manner. Because data are not transported to a data entry location, there is less risk that inputs will be lost. Also, the input can be more accurate because the data entry person may be in a position to recognize and immediately correct input errors. Finally, some efficiency can be gained by reducing the number of entities handling the event data or by shifting the data entry outside the organization to a business partner (e.g., customers enter orders on the Web).

- **Digital signatures** (Exhibit 9.3 and Figure 9.4, P-12): This technology validates the identity of the sender and the integrity of an electronic message to reduce the risk that a communication was sent by an unauthorized system or user or was intercepted or modified in transit. To appreciate how digital signatures work, you first must understand the basic mechanics of *data encryption* (Chapter 8) and *public key cryptography* (Appendix 9A, pg. 326).

  E-Business

  Now that you are armed with an understanding of the basic fundamentals of these control plans, look at Exhibit 9.3 (pg. 316) and decide if you agree with (and understand) the relationship between each plan and the goal(s) that it addresses. Remember, your ability to explain the relationships among plans and goals is more important than rote memorization.

  Before we leave this discussion of controls for manual and automated data entry, let's go back to a topic that we introduced in Chapter 7 and then briefly discussed in Chapter 8. In Auditing Standard No. 5, the PCAOB asserted that auditors must consider the impact that entity-level controls (i.e., control environment, pervasive, general, and IT general controls) can have on business process controls and application controls. **Technology Summary 9.1** (pg. 318) describes the impact that the pervasive, general, and IT general controls described in Chapter 8 can have on the effectiveness of controls in this chapter, specifically the controls in Figures 9.3 (pg. 309) and 9.4 (pg. 311), and Exhibit 9.3.

  SOX

Control Plans for Data Entry with Batches

In this section, we introduce you to a hypothetical system in which we use the example of a shipping and billing process to illustrate certain points. The distinguishing control-related features in this system are that it processes event data in batches, uses *batch totals* as a major control, and produces an *exception and summary report* at the end of major processing steps. Once again, we describe the system, walk you through its systems flowchart, list and explain the control plans associated with batch-oriented systems, and incorporate those plans into a control matrix for the system.

System Description and Flowchart

Figure 9.5 (pg. 319) shows the systems flowchart for our hypothetical batch processing system. Follow along in the flowchart as we describe the system and discuss some of the assumptions we used in its creation.

Processing begins in the first column of the flowchart with picking tickets that have been received in the shipping department from the warehouse. Let's assume that accompanying these picking tickets are goods that are about to be shipped to customers. Upon receipt of the picking tickets, a shipping department employee assembles them into groups or batches of 25 and calculates batch totals (the nature of the totals that could be taken is discussed in the next section).

EXHIBIT 9.3 Explanation of Cell Entries for the Control Matrix in Figure 9.4

P-1: *Document design.*

- *Effectiveness goal A, efficient employment of resources:* A well-designed document can be completed more quickly (*effectiveness goal A*) and can be prepared and entered into the computer with less effort (efficiency).
- *Input accuracy:* We tend to fill in a well-designed document completely and legibly. If a document is legible, data entry errors will occur less frequently.

P-2: *Written approvals.*

- *Security of resources, input validity:* By checking to see that approvals are present on all input documents, we reduce the possibility that invalid (unauthorized) event data will be input and that resources can be used without approval.

P-3: *Preformatted screens.*

- *Effectiveness goal A, efficient employment of resources:* By structuring the data entry process, automatically populating fields, and preventing errors, preformatted screens simplify data input and save time (*effectiveness goal A*), allowing a user to input more data over a period of time (efficiency).
- *Input accuracy:* As each data field is completed on a preformatted screen, the cursor moves to the next field on the screen, thus preventing the user from omitting any required data. The data for fields that are automatically populated need not be manually entered, thus reducing input errors. Incorrectly formatted fields are rejected.

P-4: *Online prompting.*

- *Effectiveness goal A, efficient employment of resources:* By asking questions and providing online guidance, this plan ensures a quicker data entry process (*effectiveness goal A*) and allows the user to input more data over a period of time (efficiency).
- *Input accuracy:* The online guidance should reduce input errors.

P-5: *Populate input screens with master data.*

- *Effectiveness goal A, efficient employment of resources:* Automatic population of inputs from the master data results in fewer keystrokes, which should improve the speed and productivity of the data entry personnel.
- *Input validity:* The code entered by the user calls up data from existing records (e.g., a customer record, a sales order record), and those data establish authorization for the input event. For example, without a customer record, a customer order cannot be entered.

- *Input accuracy:* Fewer keystrokes and the use of data called up from existing records reduce the possibility of input errors.

P-6: *Compare input data with master data.*

- *Effectiveness goal A, efficient employment of resources:* Events can be processed on a timelier basis and at a lower cost if errors are detected and prevented from entering the system in the first place.
- *Input validity:* The edits identify erroneous or suspect data and reduce the possibility of the input of invalid events.
- *Input accuracy:* The edits identify erroneous or suspect data and reduce input errors.

P-7: *Procedures for rejected inputs.*

- *Input completeness, input accuracy:* The rejection procedures (i.e., "Error routine not shown" annotations) are designed to ensure that erroneous data not accepted for processing are corrected (accuracy) and resubmitted for processing (completeness).

P-8: *Programmed edit checks.*

- *Effectiveness goal A, efficient employment of resources:* Event data can be processed on a timelier basis (*effectiveness goal A*) and at a lower cost if errors are detected and prevented from entering the system in the first place (efficiency).
- *Input accuracy:* The edits identify erroneous or suspect data and reduce input errors.

P-9: *Confirm input acceptance.*

- *Input completeness:* By advising the user that input has been accepted, this confirmation helps ensure input completeness.

P-10: *Automated data entry.*

- *Effectiveness goal A, efficient employment of resources:* Inputs are entered more quickly and with fewer personnel resources than are inputs entered manually.
- *Input accuracy:* By eliminating manual keying and using scanning and other technology, the input accuracy is improved.

P-11: *Enter data close to the originating source.*

- *Effectiveness goal A, efficient employment of resources:* This strategy processes events immediately (i.e., no time taken to send to a data entry location). Being familiar with the input

(continues)

EXHIBIT 9.3   Explanation of Cell Entries for the Control Matrix in Figure 9.4 (*continued*)

may allow the user to input the events more quickly. Finally, some efficiency can be gained by reducing the number of entities handling the event data or by shifting the data entry outside the organization to a business partner (e.g., customers enter orders on the Web).

- *Input completeness:* Because the inputs are captured at the source, they are less likely to be lost as they are transported to the data entry location.
- *Input accuracy:* Because operations personnel or business partners are familiar with the event being entered, they are

less likely to make input errors and can more readily correct these errors if they occur.

P-12: *Digital signatures.*

- *Security of resources, input validity:* Digital signatures authenticate that the sender of the message has authority to send it and thus prevent the unauthorized diversion of resources. This also determines that the message itself is genuine.
- *Input accuracy:* Detects messages that have been altered in transit, thus preventing input of inaccurate data.

The batch of documents is then scanned. As the batch is recorded, the data entry program calculates one or more totals for the batch and displays those batch totals to the shipping clerk. The clerk determines whether the displayed totals agree with the ones previously calculated. If they don't, an error-correcting routine (see "Error routine not shown") is performed. This process is repeated throughout the day as picking tickets are received in the shipping department.

Periodically, the shipment data is sent to the computer for processing by the shipment programs. This program records the inputs on the sales event data (sales journal) and updates the accounts receivable master data to create a new open receivable. Invoices are printed and sent to the customer. Packing slips are printed and sent to the shipping department, where they are matched with the picking ticket before the goods are sent to the customer. "Further processing" includes packing and shipping the goods.

One of the system outputs is usually an **exception and summary report**. This report reflects the events—either in detail, summary, or both—that were accepted or rejected by the system. Even though the keyed inputs were edited and validated, some data still could be rejected at the update stage of processing, where the computer *compares the input data with the master data*. In our system, a clerk in shipping compares the totals on this report to the input batch totals. Finally, picking tickets and packing slips are compared to ensure that they agree and that no picking tickets remain unshipped for an unduly long period of time.

Applying the Control Framework

In this section, we apply the control framework to the batch processing system just described. **Figure 9.6** (pg. 320) presents a completed control matrix for the systems flowchart shown in Figure 9.5 (pg. 319), which has been annotated to show the location of recommended control plans that exist in the system (codes P-1, P-2, …, P-5). We also have some control plans that we *assume* are missing (codes M-1 and M-2) because the process description did not mention them specifically.

In Figure 9.4 (pg. 311), we could not complete certain parts of the top of the control matrix. However, for this example, we know the nature of the input (i.e., picking tickets), the resources that are to be protected (i.e., the inventory and the accounts receivable master data), and the data store that is to be updated (i.e., the accounts receivable master data). Therefore, we have completed these elements in Figure 9.6.

In this section, we discuss each of the recommended control plans listed in the first column of the matrix. First we describe how the plans work, and then, in **Exhibit 9.4** (pg. 324) we explain the cell entries appearing in the control matrix. Be sure to trace each plan to the flowchart location where it is implemented (or could be implemented in the case of a missing plan).

Before we start, let's explain what we mean by *batch controls*. **Batch control plans** regulate information processing by calculating control totals at various points in a processing run and subsequently comparing these totals. When the various batch totals fail to agree, evidence exists that an event description(s) may have been added (validity exposure), lost or processed more than once (completeness exposure), or changed (accuracy exposure). Once established, batch totals can be reconciled manually, or the computer can reconcile them. In general, for batch control plans to be effective, we must ensure that:

- *All* documents are batched; in other words, the batch totals should be established close to the time that the source documents are created or are received from external entities.

Technology Summary 9.1

CONSIDERING THE EFFECT OF ENTITY-LEVEL CONTROLS ON THE BUSINESS PROCESS CONTROLS AND APPLICATION CONTROLS IN FIGURE 9.3

The two types of business process controls in Figure 9.3 (pg. 309) are manual controls and automated controls (also known as application controls). The effectiveness of these controls can depend on the operation of several controls described in Chapter 8. In this summary, we examine some of those relationships.

MANUAL CONTROLS

There are four controls in Figure 9.3 that depend, somewhat, on the ability, training, and diligence of the data entry personnel. First, *written approvals* will only be effective if the data entry clerk looks for the approval, knows which approvals are valid, and rejects input documents that are not properly approved. Second, when the data entry clerk *compares input data with master data*, we expect that the clerk will know when the inputs don't match the master data and will take action to correct errors that are discovered. Third, to complete the *procedures for rejected inputs*, the data entry clerk must know how to correct the error and must follow through to re-input the corrected document. Fourth, although the computer will *confirm input acceptance*, we must rely on the clerk to wait for the confirmation before moving on to the next input.

What controls in Chapter 8 will improve the effectiveness of these manual controls? There are several examples that we can give. There must be a *segregation of duties* between the person authorizing the input document and the data entry clerk. The organization should employ *selection and hiring* controls to ensure the hiring of quality personnel. All personnel, including data entry clerks, should receive relevant *training and education* to make sure that they *can* perform their required functions, and they should receive *performance evaluations* to determine that they *do* perform their required functions. Finally, data entry clerks must be provided with *application documentation* explaining how to perform their required functions.

AUTOMATED CONTROLS

All of the controls that are performed by the computer system (i.e., application controls) depend on the general controls (also known as IT general controls or ITGCs) in Chapter 8. Those controls include *electronic approvals*, *compare inputs with master data*, *programmed edit checks*, and *digital signatures*. How do we know that these controls and the other automated controls are working as planned? First, we need to know that the programs will perform the controls as designed. Second, we need to know that the stored data used by the computer when executing these controls is valid and accurate. We can ask such questions as, "Will the business event be routed to the correct person for approval?" and "Is the person logged on as the approver really that person or an imposter?" and "Is the stored customer record—used to validate an input—a valid record, or has it been added by an unauthorized person?"

On which general controls from Chapter 8 do we rely for these automated controls to be effective? There are several examples that we can give. Programs must be developed using a *systems development life cycle (SDLC)* methodology to ensure that user requirements, including controls, are built into the computer programs. Before being implemented, these programs must be tested and approved using *program change controls* to ensure that the program performs as expected and that no unauthorized elements have been included in the programs that might, for example, bypass controls. Finally, access to computer facilities, programs, and data must be restricted to prevent loss or destruction of these assets, or unauthorized changes to the programs and data. A combination of physical access controls, including *perimeter controls*, *building controls*, and *computer facility controls*, and logical access controls, including *firewalls*, *access control software*, and *intrusion detection systems (IDS)*, must be in place to protect the computing resources.

- *All* batches are submitted for processing; batch transmittals and batch logs are useful in protecting against the loss of entire batches.
- *All* differences disclosed by reconciliations are investigated and corrected in a timely manner.
- *All* batches are accepted by the computer; the user should be instrumental in performing this checking.

Batch control procedures must start by grouping event data and then calculating a control total(s) for the group. For example, Figure 9.5 shows the shipping department employee preparing batch totals for the picking tickets documents before they are scanned.

Several types of batch control totals can be calculated, as discussed in the following paragraphs. You will note in the following discussion that certain types of batch totals are better than others in addressing the information process control goals of input validity, input completeness, and input accuracy.

Document/record counts are simple counts of the number of documents entered (e.g., 25 documents in a batch). This procedure represents the minimum level required to control *input completeness* (i.e., input the document once). It is not sufficient if there are multiple parts to an event. For example, consider a sales document that can include one

FIGURE 9.5   Systems Flowchart: Data Entry with Batches

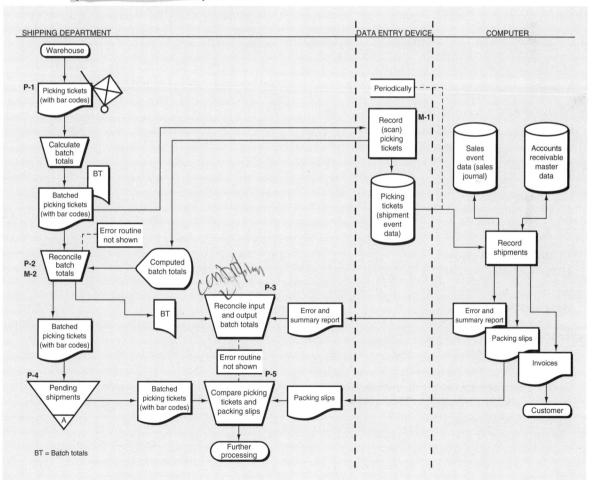

or more items (say, one television set and three chairs). A document/record count would not reflect the number of individual items sold, but rather, only the one document. This total would not be enough to ensure input accuracy. Also, because one document could be intentionally replaced with another, this control is not effective for ensuring input *validity* and input *completeness* (i.e., the insertion of a duplicate document, a completeness violation, or the insertion of a bogus document, a validity violation).

Item or line counts are counts of the number of items or lines of data entered, such as a count of the number of different items on a sales document. By reducing the possibility that line items or entire documents could be added to the batch or not be input, this control improves input *validity*, *completeness*, and *accuracy*. Remember, an extra, bogus event record is a validity violation, a missing or duplicated event record is a *completeness* error, and an event record with missing data is an *accuracy* error. With

FIGURE 9.6   Control Matrix for Data Entry with Batches

	Control Goals of the Shipping Business Process							
	Control Goals of the Operations Process			Control Goals of the Information Process				
Recommended Control Plans	Ensure Effectiveness of Operations	Ensure Efficient Employment of Resources (people, computers)	Ensure Security of Resources (inventory, AR master data)	For the picking ticket inputs, ensure:			For the AR master data, ensure:	
	A			IV	IC	IA	UC	UA
Present Controls								
P-1: Turnaround documents	P-1	P-1		P-1		P-1		
P-2: Manually reconcile batch totals				P-2	P-2	P-2		
P-3: Agree run-to-run totals (reconcile input and output batch totals)			P-3	P-3	P-3	P-3	P-3	P-3
P-4: Review tickler file (file of pending shipments)	P-4				P-4		P-4	
P-5: One-for-one checking (compare picking tickets and packing slips)			P-5	P-5	P-5	P-5	P-5	P-5
Missing Controls								
M-1: Sequence check				M-1	M-1			
M-2: Computer agreement of batch totals	M-2	M-2		M-2	M-2	M-2		

Possible effectiveness goals include the following:

A = Ensure timely input and processing of picking tickets.

See Exhibit 9.4 for a complete explanation of control plans and cell entries

IV = input validity
IC = input completeness
IA = input accuracy
UC = update completeness
UA = update accuracy

these type totals, there are no absolute guarantees as to accuracy because we could input the required number of lines but make errors in entering a line.

Dollar totals are a summation of the dollar value of items in the batch, such as the total dollar value of all remittance advices in a batch. By reducing the possibility that entire documents could be duplicated, added to a batch, or lost from a batch, or that dollar amounts are incorrectly input, this control improves input *validity*, *completeness*, and *accuracy*.

Hash totals are a summation of any numeric data existing for all documents in the batch, such as a total of customer numbers or purchase order numbers, in the case of sales documents. Unlike dollar totals, hash totals normally serve no purpose other than control. Hash totals can be a powerful batch control because they can determine whether inputs have been altered (accuracy), added (validity), duplicated (completeness), or deleted (completeness). These *batch* hash totals operate for a batch in a manner similar to the operation of *document/record hash totals* (a type of *programmed edit check*) for individual inputs.

Now that we have introduced batch totals, we can describe the controls in Figures 9.5 (pg. 319) and 9.6. As we did previously with the controls for automated and manual data entry, we begin by defining and explaining the controls plans in Figures 9.5 and 9.6 and then summarize, in Exhibit 9.4 (pg. 324), each cell entry in Figure 9.6, the control matrix.

- **Turnaround documents** (Exhibit 9.4 and Figure 9.6, P-1): These are used to capture and input a *subsequent* event. Picking tickets, inventory count sheets, and remittance advice stubs attached to customer invoices are all examples of turnaround documents. For example, we have seen picking tickets that are printed by the computer, used to pick the goods, and sent to shipping, where the *bar code* on the picking ticket is scanned to trigger the recording of the shipment. Thus, turnaround documents can facilitate *automated data entry*, described in Exhibit 9.3 (pp. 316–317) and Figure 9.4 (pg. 311), P-10. Turnaround documents can be used for the input of individual items, rather than batches. In such cases, the scanning computer displays the scanned data, such as items and quantities to be shipped, to the data entry clerk or shipping clerk. If the data has been scanned correctly, the clerk need only press one key or click the mouse button to record the input.

Although technically the following control (key verification) is missing from the process depicted in Figure 9.5, we would not advocate that it be added in this instance because we prefer to scan the documents to enhance the validity and accuracy of the data entry process. However, key verification is occasionally applied to the input of low-volume, high-value batches of events and should be described here so that you know about this powerful control.

- **Key verification**: This takes place when input documents are keyed by one individual and then rekeyed by a second individual. The data entry software compares the second keystrokes to the strokes keyed by the first individual. If there are differences, it is assumed that one person misread or miskeyed the data. Someone, perhaps a supervisor or the second clerk, would determine which keying was correct, the first or the second, and make corrections as appropriate to ensure that the input is accurate. Key verification is depicted in Figure 4.7, part (e) (pg. 111).

We notice, at this point, that a sequence check is not applied to the input documents. Read on about a type of control that could have been applied at this point:

- **Sequence checks** (Exhibit 9.4 and Figure 9.6, M-1): Whenever documents are numbered sequentially—either assigned a number when the document is prepared or received from an external source or the input document is *prenumbered*—a *sequence check* can be applied to those documents to determine that all documents have been processed (*completeness*) and that no extra documents have been processed (*completeness*, if a duplicated document, or *validity*, if a bogus document). One of two kinds of sequence checks may be used—either a batch sequence check or a cumulative sequence check.

In a **batch sequence check**, the event data within a batch are checked as follows:

1. The range of serial numbers constituting the documents in the batch is entered.
2. Each individual serially prenumbered document is entered.
3. The computer program sorts the input documents into numerical order; checks the documents against the sequence number range; and reports missing, duplicate, and out-of-range data.

If the documents come from an external source, and we cannot control the serial numbers of the input data, we can assign numbers to the items as the batch is prepared for processing.

A slight variation on the batch sequence check is the cumulative sequence check. The **cumulative sequence check** provides input control in those situations in which the serial numbers are assigned within the organization (e.g., sales order numbers issued by the sales order department) but are not entered in perfect serial number sequence (e.g., picking tickets do not necessarily arrive at the shipping department in sequence). In this case, the matching of individual event data (picking ticket) numbers is made to a file that contains *all* document numbers (all sales order numbers). *Periodically*, reports of missing numbers are produced for manual follow-up.

Reconciling a checkbook is another example of a situation in which numbers (the check numbers) are issued in sequence. When we receive a bank statement, the batch may not contain a complete sequence of checks. Our check register assists us in performing a cumulative sequence check to make sure that all checks are eventually cleared.

- **Manually reconcile batch totals** (Exhibit 9.4 and Figure 9.6, P-2): The **manual reconciliation of batch totals** control plan operates in the following manner:

  1. One or more of the batch totals are established manually (e.g., in the shipping department in Figure 9.5.
  2. As individual event descriptions are entered (or scanned), the data entry program accumulates independent batch totals.
  3. The computer produces reports (or displays) at the end of either the input process or the update process, or both. The report (or display) includes the relevant control totals that must be manually reconciled with the totals established prior to the particular process.
  4. The person who reconciles the batch total (e.g., the shipping department employee in Figure 9.5) must determine why the totals do not agree and make corrections as necessary to ensure the integrity of the input data.

We notice, at this point, that the clerk must perform a manual reconciliation of the batch totals. Read on about a more efficient means for performing that reconciliation:

- **Computer agreement of batch totals** (Exhibit 9.4 and Figure 9.6, M-2): This control plan does not exist in Figure 9.5 and therefore is shown as a missing plan. Note in Figure 9.5 where we have placed the M-2 annotation. The **Computer agreement of batch totals** plan is pictured in **Figure 9.7** and works in the following manner:

  1. First, one or more of the batch totals are established manually (i.e., in the user department in Figure 9.7).
  2. Then the manually prepared total is entered into the computer and is written to the computer batch control totals data.

FIGURE 9.7 Computer Agreement of Batch Totals Control Plan

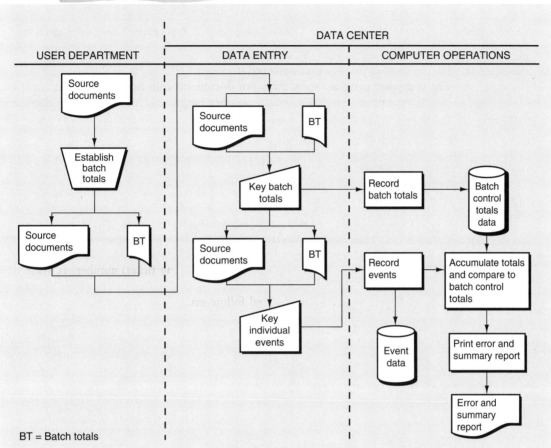

BT = Batch totals

3. As individual source documents are entered, a computer program accumulates independent batch totals and compares these totals to the ones prepared manually and entered at the start of the processing.

4. The computer prepares a report, which usually contains details of each batch, together with an indication of whether the totals agreed or disagreed. Normally, batches that do not balance are rejected, and discrepancies are manually investigated. Such an analysis would be included in a report similar to the "Error and summary report" in Figures 9.5 (pg. 319) and 9.7.

- **Agree run-to-run totals (reconcile input and output batch totals)** (Exhibit 9.4 and Figure 9.6 (pg. 320), P-3): This is a variation of the reconciliation/agreement of batch totals control. We **agree run-to-run totals** by reconciling totals prepared before a computer process has begun to totals prepared at the completion of the computer process. The totals may be prepared and reconciled either manually or by the computer. The post-process controls are often found on an *error and summary* report (i.e., totals prepared by the computer). When totals agree, we have evidence that the input *and* the update took place correctly. This control is especially useful when there are several intermediate steps between the beginning and the end of the process, and we want to be assured of the integrity of each process.

- **Review tickler file (file of pending shipments)** (Exhibit 9.4 and Figure 9.6, P-4): A **tickler file** is a manual file of documents, or a computer file, that contains business

EXHIBIT 9.4 Explanation of Cell Entries for the Control Matrix in Figure 9.6

P-1: *Turnaround documents.*

- *Effectiveness goal A, efficient employment of resources:* By scanning the picking ticket, we reduce the amount of data that must be input to record the shipment and improve the speed (effectiveness) and productivity of the data entry personnel (efficiency).
- *Input validity:* The turnaround documents were printed in a different functional area. This separates event authorization (as reflected by the picking ticket) from execution of the shipment (as represented by the packing slips).
- *Input accuracy:* Using a prerecorded bar code to trigger the event reduces the possibility of input errors.

P-2: *Manually reconcile batch totals.*

- *Input validity, input completeness, input accuracy:* Agreement of the batch totals at this point ensures that only valid source documents comprising the original batch have been input (input validity), that all source documents were input once and only once (input completeness), and that data elements appearing on the source documents have been input correctly (input accuracy).

P-3: *Agree run-to-run totals (reconcile input and output batch totals).*

- *Security of resources, input validity:* By determining that updates to the accounts receivable master data reflect goods picked and about to be shipped, we reduce the possibility of recording an invalid sales event and shipping to customers who did not order, and will not pay for, the goods.
- *Input completeness, input accuracy, update completeness, update accuracy:* By comparing totals prepared before the input to those produced after the update, we ensure that all events were input once and only once (input completeness), all events were input correctly (input accuracy), all events were updated to the master data once and only once (update completeness), and all events were updated correctly to the master data (update accuracy).

P-4: *Review tickler file (file of pending shipments).*

- *Effectiveness goal A, input completeness, update completeness:* A file of picking tickets is retained in shipping awaiting packing slips. If the packing slips are received in a timely manner, and the corresponding picking tickets are removed from the Pending Shipments file, we can ensure that goods will be shipped in a timely manner and that the picking

tickets were indeed input and the master data updated. If picking tickets do not receive packing slips within a reasonable period of time, then an inquiry procedure is initiated to determine the nature and extent of the delay.

P-5: *One-for-one checking (compare picking tickets and packing slips).*

- *Security of resources, input validity:* By matching details on the picking tickets with the data on the packing slips produced by the computer, we reduce the possibility that an invalid sales event has been recorded and that we will not ship goods to customers who did not order, and will not pay for, the goods.
- *Input completeness, input accuracy, update completeness, update accuracy:* By matching details on the picking tickets (i.e., the inputs) with the details on the packing slips produced by the computer, we ensure that all events were input once and only once (input completeness), all events were input correctly (input accuracy), all events were updated to the master data once and only once (update completeness), and all events were updated correctly to the master data (update accuracy).

M-1: *Sequence check.*

- *Input validity, input completeness:* By comparing an expected sequence of documents to those actually input, sequence checks can detect a document not in the original sequence (i.e., possibly an invalid document) or a second occurrence of a particular document number (i.e., documents input more than once), and they can detect missing document numbers (i.e., documents that were not input).

M-2: *Computer agreement of batch totals.*

- *Effectiveness goal A, efficient employment of resources:* Had the computer been used to reconcile the control totals, the processing of the events would have been completed more quickly and with less human effort.
- *Input validity, input completeness, input accuracy:* Regarding these control goals, the effect of this control is the same as P-2. Agreement of the batch totals at this point would have ensured that only valid source documents comprising the original batch had been input, that all source documents were input once and only once, and that data elements appearing on the source documents had been input correctly.

event data that is pending further action. Such files must be reviewed on a regular basis for the purpose of taking action to clear items from that file. Figure 9.5 shows a file of picking ticket items that should be shipped ("Pending Shipments" file), but tickler files also may be computer records reflecting events that need to be completed, such as open sales orders and open purchase orders. If tickler file documents remain in the file for an extended period of time, the person or computer monitoring the file determines the nature and extent of the delay. In our example, after packing slips are received, the picking tickets are compared to their associated packing slips and removed from the Pending Shipments file. We are classifying this as a present control because we are assuming that the shipping clerk periodically reviews the file looking for picking tickets that have been pending for too long.

- **One-for-one checking (compare picking tickets and packing slips)** (Exhibit 9.4 and Figure 9.6, P-5): **One-for-one checking** is the detailed comparison of the individual elements of two or more data sources to determine that they agree. This control is often used to compare a source document to an output produced later in a process. Differences may indicate errors in input or update. If the output cannot be found for comparison, there is evidence of failure to input or process the event. This procedure provides detail as to *what* is incorrect within a batch. Because it's very expensive to perform, one-for-one checking should be reserved for low-volume, high-value events.

Now that we have examined what each of the recommended control plans means and how each operates, we can look at how the plans meet the control goals. Exhibit 9.4 explains the relationship between each control plan and each control goal that it helps to achieve. As you study Exhibit 9.4, we again urge you to concentrate your energies on understanding these relationships.

Summary

In this chapter, we began our study of business process control plans, the third level in the control hierarchy shown in Figure 7.6 in Chapter 7 (pg. 245). Our study of business process control plans will continue in Chapters 10 through 14, in which we will apply the control framework and explore those controls that are unique to each business process. **Exhibit 9.5** provides a framework for determining how well these pervasive, general, business process, and application controls can perform. That is, this framework helps us

SOX

EXHIBIT 9.5   Level of Assurance Provided by Internal Controls

The degree of assurance, the quality, and the effectiveness of internal controls may be based on several factors:

Less Assurance	Greater Assurance
Manual control	Automated control
Control is performed by a junior, inexperienced person	Control is performed by an experienced manager
Detective control	Preventive control
Single control	Multiple, overlapping controls
Control checks some items (sampling)	Control checks all items
Control takes place after the event occurs	Control takes place as the event occurs

Source: Adapted from *Sarbanes-Oxley Act: Section 404, Practical Guidance for Management*, PricewaterhouseCoopers, July 2004, pp. 52–53.

determine the "effectiveness of the design of controls" required by the PCAOB in Auditing Standard No. 5.

Before we leave this chapter, let's address one more aspect of business process controls and application controls. Many of these controls attempt to detect data that *may* be in error. For example, a *reasonableness check* may reject a price change that is beyond a normal limit (e.g., percent of existing price), even though the price change has been authorized and correctly entered. As another example, perhaps a customer order is rejected because it does not pass the credit check, but it might be in the best interest of the company to permit the sale. In these cases, we need to be able to *override* the control and permit the event to process. If our control system is to remain effective, these overrides must be used sparingly and securely (e.g., requiring a *password* or signature to effect the override). Finally, a record of all overrides should be periodically reviewed to determine that the override authority is not being abused.

Key Terms

document design, 312

written approvals, 312

electronic approvals, 312

preformatted screens, 312

online prompting, 312

populate input screens with master data, 312

compare input data with master data, 313

procedures for rejected inputs, 313

programmed edit checks, 313

limit checks, 313

reasonableness check, 314

document/record hash totals, 314

mathematical accuracy checks, 314

confirm input acceptance, 314

automated data entry, 314

enter data close to the originating source, 314

digital signatures, 315

exception and summary report, 317

batch control plans, 318

document/record counts, 319

item or line counts, 320

dollar totals, 321

hash totals, 321

turnaround documents, 321

key verification, 321

sequence checks, 321

batch sequence check, 322

cumulative sequence check, 322

manual reconciliation of batch totals, 322

computer agreement of batch totals, 322

agree run-to-run totals, 323

tickler file, 323

one-for-one checking, 325

Appendix 9A

Public Key Cryptography and Digital Signatures

E-Business

As we noted in Chapter 8, a conventional *data encryption* procedure involves a *single key* that is used both by the sender to encrypt the message and by the receiver to decrypt it. A major drawback to single key systems is that you need a different key for each trading partner. Another disadvantage is that the key itself has to be transmitted by secure channels. If the key is not kept secret, the security of the entire system is compromised. *Public key cryptography* helps to solve this problem by employing a *pair* of matched keys for each system user, one private (i.e., known only to the party who possesses it) and one public. The public key corresponds to, but is not the same as, the user's private key. As its name implies, the public key is assumed to be public knowledge and even could be published in a directory, in much the same way as a person's telephone number.

Figure 9.8 illustrates how public key cryptography is used both to *encrypt* messages (part [a] of the figure) and to *authenticate* a message by appending a *digital signature* to it (part [b] of the figure). Note that although we show both parts (a) and (b) being executed, in practice, the parts are separable. That is, a message could be encrypted as shown in part (a) without having a digital signature added to it. Digital signatures enhance security by ensuring that the message comes from an authorized source and that the message has not been changed during transmission.

The figure tells the story, so we discuss it only briefly. First note that Sally Sender and Ray Receiver each have a *pair* of keys. In part (a), Ray's *public* key is used to encrypt messages sent to him from any source. Privacy/confidentiality of the messages is ensured because only Ray's *private* key can decrypt the messages. The private decryption key does

FIGURE 9.8   Illustration of Public Key Cryptography and Digital Signatures

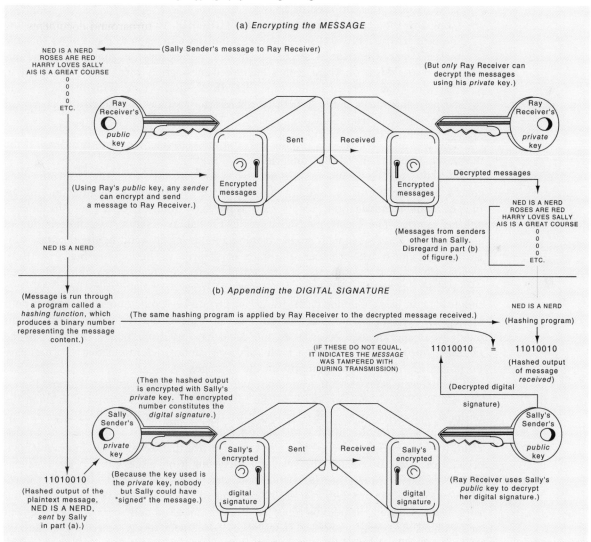

not have to be transmitted; it is always in Ray's exclusive possession. This process ensures that only Ray can read messages encrypted with his *public* key.

In part (b), Sally first uses a hashing function to translate the plaintext message that is being sent to Ray into a binary number. Any message *other* than NED IS A NERD would not "hash" into the number 11010010. By then using her *private* key to encrypt the binary number, Sally, in effect, has digitally "signed" the message. On the right side of part (b), Ray Receiver employs Sally's *public* key to decrypt her "signature." Because no public key except Sally's will work to decode the "signature," Ray knows that the message comes from her. Note that *anyone* could use Sally's *public* key to decode her signature, but that is not important because all they would get is the number 11010010, and that number cannot be used to recreate (reverse engineer) the original message. The object is not to keep the hash number secret or private but rather to *authenticate* that it was Sally, and *only* she, who "signed" the message.

To ensure the *integrity of the message* (received in part [a] of the figure), Ray does the following:

- Runs the decrypted message, NED IS A NERD, through a hashing function—the same hashing function used by Sally.
- Compares the decoded digital signature (11010010) with the hashed output of the message *received* (11010010). If the two numbers don't agree, Ray knows that the message is not the same as the one Sally sent. For example, assume that Ted Tamperer was able to intercept Sally's encrypted message in part (a) and change it so that when Ray decoded it, he read NED IS A NICE GUY. This message would *not* hash into the number 11010010; therefore, it would not match the decrypted digital signature from Sally.

The process, then, tells us if Sally sent the message (i.e., authentication) *and* if the message has been changed (i.e., integrity).

E-Business
Digital signatures facilitate e-business when they are used to create electronic cash, checks, and other forms of payment and to replace handwritten signatures on a multitude of business and legal documents, such as purchase orders, checks, court documents, and tax returns. The Electronic Signatures in Global and National Commerce Act of 2000 makes contracts "signed" by electronic methods legally valid in all 50 states. This law was designed to accelerate the rate of growth of business-to-business (B2B) *e-business* by allowing companies to immediately execute documents online. However, we need to distinguish an "electronic signature" from the "digital signature." We can simply sign an electronic document using our private key. When opened with our public key, the receiver knows that we signed the document. But we cannot ensure confidentiality of the message because anyone could have used our public key to open the message. Furthermore, without a hash total, we cannot determine that the message/document was not changed (integrity of the message).

Digital signatures also offer an additional benefit to e-business transactions. Buyers and sellers of goods and services over the Internet can only feel comfortable about the business transaction if one party is sure that the other party will not renege on the agreement. One way for a party to back off from an agreement is to repudiate or disclaim the agreement. If the other party cannot prove that a legally binding agreement took place in the first place, the reneging party might be successful. To ward off this threat, digital signatures are used to ensure *nonrepudiation*; that is, digital signatures offer the necessary proof that a legal "meeting of the minds" took place, as neither party can successfully dispute or repudiate the existence and authenticity of a document or signature. As noted previously, if we open a document using someone's public key, we know that they signed that document.

One final thought—for public key cryptography to be effective, the *private* keys must be kept *private*. To do that, we can employ a variety of techniques, some of which were introduced in Chapter 8. For example, the private key might be kept within a protected computer or device such as a *cryptographic box*. Access to the device, and to the private key, must then be protected with *passwords* or other *authentication* procedures.

One such procedure involves the use of a thumbprint reader or retinal imager attached to the computer. With such devices, users must put their thumb onto the reader or eye into an imager before the private key can be used to "sign" a message. The thumbprint reader and retinal imager are examples of the *biometric identification systems* introduced in Chapter 8.

Review Questions

RQ 9- 1   Explain the difference between the category of business process control and application control covered in this chapter and the business process controls and application controls to be covered in Chapters 10 through 16.

RQ 9- 2   Describe the relationship between the *control matrix* and the *systems flowchart*.

RQ 9- 3   How could the control matrix be used to recommend changes in the system to improve control of that system?

RQ 9- 4   How would the control matrix be useful in evaluating control *effectiveness*, control *efficiency*, and control *redundancy*? Include in your answer a definition of these three terms.

RQ 9- 5   What are the steps involved in preparing a control matrix?

RQ 9- 6   Describe the four common *programmed edit checks*.

RQ 9- 7   How do the 12 control plans listed in Figure 9.4 (pg. 311) work?

RQ 9- 8   Name and explain four different types of batch totals that could be calculated in a batch processing system.

RQ 9- 9   How do the seven control plans (five present, two missing) listed in Figure 9.6 (pg. 320) work?

RQ 9- 10   Referring to Appendix 9A, distinguish among data encryption, public key cryptography, and digital signatures.

Discussion Questions

DQ 9-1   Discuss why the control matrix is custom-tailored for each business process.

DQ 9-2   Explain why input controls are so important. Discuss fully.

DQ 9-3   In evaluating business process controls and application controls, some auditors differentiate between the point in the system at which the control is "established" and the *later* point at which that control is "exercised." Speculate about the meaning of the terms "*establish a control*" and "*exercise a control*" by discussing those terms in the context of:

    a.   Batch total procedures

    b.   Turnaround documents

    c.   Tickler files

DQ 9-4   "The mere fact that event data appear on a prenumbered document is no proof of the validity of the event. Someone intent on defrauding a system by introducing a fictitious event probably would be clever enough to get access to the prenumbered documents or would replicate those documents to make the event appear genuine."

a.   Do you agree with this comment? Why or why not?

b.   Without prejudice to your answer to part (a), assume that the comment is true. Present (and explain) a "statement of relationship" between the control plan of using prenumbered documents and the information system control goal of event "validity."

DQ 9-5   Describe situations in your daily activities, working or not, where you have experienced or employed controls discussed in this chapter.

DQ 9-6   Refer to Exhibit 9.5 (pg. 325). For each pair of factors, describe why you believe the factor in the right column provides a higher level of assurance. That is, why do these factors indicate a stronger control?

DQ 9-7   Referring to Appendix 9A, discuss fully the following statement: "Protecting the private key is a critical element in public key cryptography."

DQ 9-8   On October 2, 2002, a clerk at Bear Stearns had erroneously entered an order to sell nearly $4 billion worth of securities. The trader had sent an order to sell $4 million worth. Only $622 million of the orders were executed, and the remainder of the orders was canceled prior to execution. Reports stated that it was a human error, not a computer error and that it was the fault of the clerk, not the trader. What is your opinion of these reports? What controls could have *prevented* this error?

DQ 9-9   "Technology Summary 9.1 (pg. 318) seems to indicate that the business process and application control plans in this chapter cannot be relied on." Do you agree? Discuss fully.

DQ 9-10   "If a business process is implemented with OLRT processing, we do not need to worry about update completeness and update accuracy." Do you agree? Discuss fully.

Short Problems

SP 9-1   The following is a brief description of the financial statement assertions from PCAOB Interim Auditing Standards Section AU 326, Evidential Matter:

A. *Existence or occurrence:* Assets or liabilities of the entity exist at a given date (existence) or recorded transactions have occurred during a given period (occurrence). For example, management asserts that finished goods inventories in the balance sheet are available for sale. Similarly, management asserts that sales in the income statement represent the exchange of goods or services with customers for cash or other consideration.

B. *Completeness:* Transactions and accounts that should be presented in the financial statements are so included. For example, management asserts that all purchases of goods and services are recorded and are included in the financial statements. Similarly, management asserts that notes payable in the balance sheet include all such obligations of the entity.

C. *Rights and obligations:* Assets are the rights of the entity and liabilities are the obligations of the entity at a given date. For example, management asserts that amounts capitalized for leases in the balance sheet represent the cost of the entity's rights to leased property and that the corresponding lease liability represents an obligation of the entity.

D. *Valuation or allocation:* Asset, liability, equity, revenue, and expense components have been included in the financial statements at appropriate amounts. For example, management asserts that property is recorded at historical cost and that such cost is systematically allocated to appropriate accounting periods. Similarly, management asserts that trade accounts receivable included in the balance sheet are stated at net realizable value.

E. *Presentation and disclosure:* Particular components of the financial statements are properly classified, described, and disclosed. For example, management asserts that obligations classified as long-term liabilities in the balance sheet will not mature within one year. Similarly, management asserts that amounts presented as extraordinary items in the income statement are properly classified and described.

Match each of these five assertions with *all* of the input control goals that apply. Write a one- or two-sentence explanation of each matching entry.

Assertions

A. Existence or occurrence
B. Completeness
C. Rights and obligations
D. Valuation and allocation
E. Presentation and disclosure

Control Goals

1. Input validity (IV)
2. Input completeness (IC)
3. Input accuracy (IA)

SP 9-2   **Figure 9.9** (pg. 332), depicts the transmission of an electronic message incorporating public key cryptography, encryption, and digital signatures. Answer the following questions related to that figure:

1. Can anyone read the message? Why?
2. Can Sally be sure the message is from Harry? Why?
3. Is the digital signature message (containing the hash total calculated by Harry) secret? Why?
4. Could anyone other than Harry send the digital signature message?
5. How does Sally know that the message has not been corrupted in transit?
6. Which question, or questions, above are related to authenticity?
7. Which question, or questions, above are related to integrity?
8. Which question, or questions, above are related to confidentiality?

FIGURE 9.9 Electronic Message Diagram to Accompany Short Problem 9-2

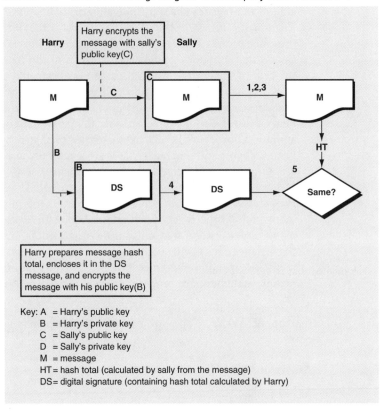

SP 9-3 **Figure 9.10** lists 10 control plans from this chapter and three control goals for the information process. Fill in the table cells, as appropriate, to indicate which control plans can accomplish which control goals. Number your entries, and describe the reason for your entry (i.e., why the control can accomplish the goal). Some rows (controls) will have more than one entry. We have completed two entries for you as an example.
Example answers:

1. A well-designed document can be filled in completely and legibly and be input to the computer with fewer errors.
2. Approvals indicate authorization for a document or business event, thus reducing the possibility of processing invalid events.

Problems

P 9-1 The narrative and systems flowchart for the Causeway Company cash receipts system are included in **Exhibit 9.6** and **Figure 9.11** (pg. 334), respectively.

Using Exhibit 9.6 and Figure 9.11, do the following:

a. Prepare a control matrix, including explanations of how each recommended control plan helps to accomplish—or would accomplish in the case of missing plans—each related control goal. Your choice of recommended control plans should come from Figure 9.4 (pg. 311)/Exhibit 9.3

FIGURE 9.10   Table to Accompany Problem SP 9-3

Control Plan	Input Validity	Input Completeness	Input Accuracy
Document design			1
Written approvals	2		
Preformatted screens			
Limit check			
Confirm input acceptance			
Digital signature			
Reconciliation of batch totals (document count)			
Turnaround documents			
Sequence check			
Populate input screens with master data			

(pp. 316–317) or Figure 9.6 (pg. 320)/Exhibit 9.4 (pg. 324), as appropriate. Be sure to tailor the matrix columns to conform to the specifics of the Causeway system. In doing so, assume the following two effectiveness goals only:

- Timely deposit of checks
- Comply with compensating balance agreements with the depository bank

b. Annotate the systems flowchart in Figure 9.11 to show the location of each control plan listed in the control matrix.

P 9-2   The following narrative describes the processing of customer mail orders at ePetID Company:

ePetID Company is a small manufacturing operation engaged in the selling of digital identification chips that can be implanted into household pets,

EXHIBIT 9.6   Causeway Company System Narrative to Accompany Problem 9-1

Causeway Company uses the following procedures to process the cash received from credit sales. Customers send checks and remittance advices to Causeway. The mailroom clerk at Causeway endorses the checks and writes the amount paid and the check number on the remittance advice. Periodically, the mailroom clerk prepares a batch total of the remittance advices and sends the batch of remittance advices to accounts receivable, along with a copy of the batch total. At the same time, the clerk sends the corresponding batch of checks to the cashier.

In accounts receivable, a clerk enters the batch into the computer by keying the batch total, the customer number, the invoice number, the amount paid, and the check number. After verifying that the invoice is open and that the correct amount is being paid, the computer updates the accounts receivable master data. If there are any discrepancies, the clerk is notified.

At the end of each batch (or at the end of the day), the computer prints a deposit slip in duplicate on the printer in the cashier's office. The cashier compares the deposit slip to the corresponding batch of checks and then takes the deposit to the bank.

As they are entered, the check number and the amount paid for each receipt are logged on a disk. This event data is used to create a cash receipts listing at the end of each day. A summary of customer accounts paid that day is also printed at this time. The accounts receivable clerk compares these reports to the remittance advices and batch totals and sends the total of the cash receipts to the general ledger office.

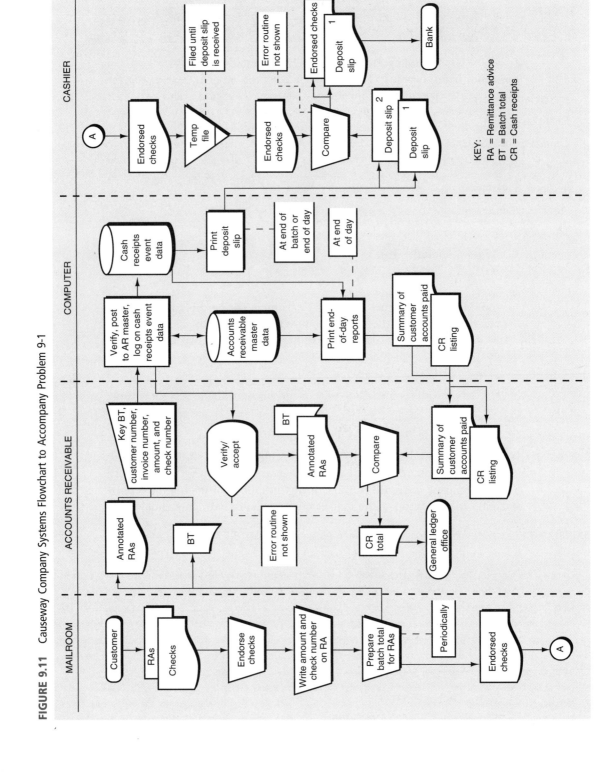

FIGURE 9.11 Causeway Company Systems Flowchart to Accompany Problem 9-1

such as cats and dogs. Customers (e.g., veterinary clinics, animal hospitals) send orders by mail to the sales order department, where sales order clerks open the orders and review them for accuracy. For each order, the clerks enter the customer number, and the computer displays the customer record. The clerk matches the customer information on the screen with the customer order. Assuming that they match, the clerk enters the items and quantities being ordered. The computer edits the order by comparing the input data to customer and inventory master data. Assuming that the order passes the edits, the computer records the order on the sales event data and the sales order master data, and then updates the inventory to allocate the ordered inventory. As the order is recorded, it is printed on a printer in the warehouse (the picking ticket). A copy of the sales order is also printed in the sales order department and is sent to the customer (a customer acknowledgement).

(Complete only those requirements specified by your instructor.)

a. Prepare a table of entities and activities.

b. Draw a context diagram.

c. Draw a physical data flow diagram (DFD).

d. Prepare an annotated table of entities and activities. Indicate on the table the groupings, bubble numbers, and bubble titles to be used in preparing a level 0 logical DFD.

e. Draw a level 0 logical DFD.

f. Draw a systems flowchart.

g. Prepare a control matrix, including explanations of how each recommended existing control plan helps to accomplish—or would accomplish in the case of missing plans—each related control goal. Your choice of recommended control plans may come from Figure 9.4/Exhibit 9.3 or Figure 9.6/Exhibit 9.4, as appropriate. Be sure to tailor the matrix columns to conform to the specifics of the ePetID Company system. In doing so, assume the following two operations process goals only:

  • To provide timely acknowledgement of customer orders
  • To provide timely shipment of goods to customers

h. Annotate the systems flowchart prepared in requirement (f) to show the location of each control plan listed in the control matrix.

P 9-3   The following is a list of 12 control plans from this chapter:

Control Plans

A. Batch sequence check
B. Confirm input acceptance
C. Programmed edit checks
D. Manual agreement of batch totals
E. Online prompting
F. Cumulative sequence check
G. Electronic approvals
H. Document design

I. Procedures for rejected inputs
J. Compare input data with master data
K. Turnaround documents
L. Digital signatures

The following is a list of 10 system failures that have control implications.

System Failures

1. At Holeriver Company, customer orders are received in the mail in the sales department, where clerks enter individual orders online and then file the completed orders. For each order, the customer should receive an acknowledgement. When the customer fails to receive an acknowledgement, the customer calls to inquire. Inevitably, the sales clerk will find the customer's order filed with other customer orders that had been entered into the computer.

2. At Prairie Inc., data entry clerks receive a variety of documents from many departments throughout the company. In some cases, unauthorized inputs are keyed and entered into the computer.

3. The tellers at Dixie Bank have been having difficulty reconciling their cash drawers. All customer transactions such as deposits and withdrawals are entered online at each teller station. At the end of the shift, the computer prints a list of the transactions that have occurred during the shift. The tellers must then review the list to determine that their drawers contain checks, cash, and other documents to support each entry on the list.

4. Data entry clerks at Courage Company use networked PCs to enter batches of documents into the computer. Recently, a number of errors have been found in key numeric fields. The supervisor would like to implement a control to reduce the transcription errors being made by the clerks.

5. At Dulce Inc., clerks in the accounting offices of Dulce's three divisions prepare prenumbered general ledger voucher documents. Once prepared, the vouchers are given to each office's data entry clerk, who keys them into an online terminal. The computer records whatever general ledger adjustment was indicated by the voucher. The controller has found that several vouchers were never recorded, and some vouchers were recorded twice.

6. Purchase orders at Etronics Corp. are prepared online by purchasing clerks. Recently, the purchasing manager discovered that many purchase orders are being sent for quantities far greater (i.e., incorrect quantities) than would normally be requested.

7. At David Brothers, Inc., a clerk on the trading floor mistakenly entered the dollar amount of a trade into the box on the computer screen reserved for the number of shares to be sold, and then transmitted the incorrect trade to the stock exchange's computer.

8. At Jefferson Company, clerks in the cash applications area of the accounts receivable office open mail containing checks from customers. They prepare a remittance advice (RA) containing the customer number, invoice numbers, amount owed, amount paid, and check number. Once prepared, the RAs are sent to a clerk who keys them into the

computer. The accounts receivable manager has been complaining that the RA entry process is slow and error-prone.

9. Rudolf Company enters shipping notices in batches. Upon entry, the computer performs certain edits to eliminate those notices that have errors. As a result, many actual shipments never get recorded.

10. Jamie the hacker gained access to the computer system of National Bank and entered the data to transfer funds to his bank account in the Turks and Caicos Islands.

Match the 10 system failures with a control plan that would *best* prevent the system failure from occurring. Because there are 12 control plans, you should have two letters left over.

P 9-4   The following is a list of 12 control plans from this chapter:

Control Plans

A. Limit checks
B. Tickler files
C. Public key cryptography
D. Compare input data with master data
E. Batch sequence check
F. Manual reconciliation of batch totals (document/record counts)
G. One-for-one checking
H. Manual reconciliation of batch totals (hash totals)
I. Turnaround documents
J. Procedures for rejected inputs
K. Digital signatures
L. Confirm input acceptance

Listed here are 10 definitions or descriptions of control plans.

Definitions or Descriptions

1. Determines if a customer number has been input correctly.
2. Ensures that transmitted messages can be read only by authorized receivers.
3. A control plan that cannot be implemented unless source documents are prenumbered or numbered before input.
4. In systems where accountable documents are not used, this control plan helps ensure input completeness by informing the data entry person that data have been accepted for processing by the computer system.
5. Used to detect changes in batches of events to ensure the validity, completeness, and accuracy of the batch.
6. Used to determine that a message has not been altered and has actually been sent by the person claiming to have sent the message.
7. A file of open sales orders that is periodically reviewed to ensure the timely shipment of goods.
8. Sales orders are compared to packing slips and the goods to determine that what was ordered is what is about to be shipped.
9. A system output becomes an input source in a *subsequent* event.
10. A type of programmed edit check that is similar to a reasonableness check.

Match the 10 definitions or descriptions with a control plan that *best* matches the definition. Because there are 12 control plans, you should have two letters left over.

P 9-5   **Figure 9.12** is a systems flowchart for the first few steps in an order entry process. Some but not all of the controls have been annotated on the flowchart. **Figure 9.13** is a partially completed control matrix for the system in Figure 9.12. Some controls are not on the matrix at all. For some controls, not all of the cells have been completed. **Exhibit 9.7** is a partially completed set of explanations of the cell entries in Figure 9.12.

Required:

a.   Annotate the flowchart to indicate additional present and missing controls. (Some controls that are on the matrix are not annotated on the flowchart. Others are missing from both the flowchart and the matrix.)

FIGURE 9.12   Flowchart to Accompany Problem 9-5

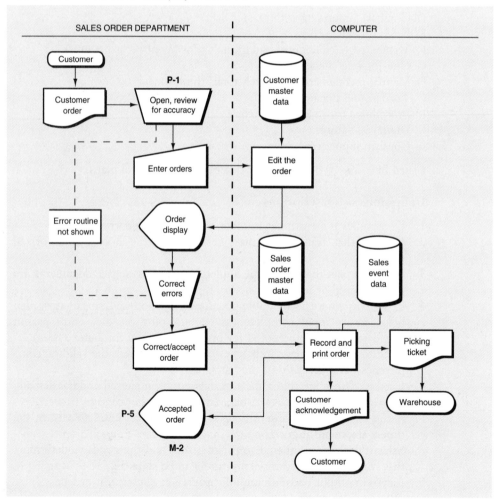

FIGURE 9.13   Control Matrix for Figure 9.12 to Accompany Problem 9-5

Recommended Control Plans	Control Goals of the Order Entry Business Process								
	Control Goals of the Operations Process				Control Goals of the Information Process				
	Ensure effectiveness of operations		Ensure efficient employment of resources (people, computers)	Ensure security of resources (inventory, customer master data)	For the sales order inputs (i.e., customer orders) ensure:			For the sales order master data, ensure:	
	A	B			IV	IC	IA	UC	UA
Present Controls									
P-1: Review document for accuracy									
P-4: Procedures for rejected input									
P-5: Confirm input acceptance									
Missing Controls									
M-2: Manual reconciliation of batch totals				M-2	M-2	M-2	M-2		

Possible effectiveness goals Include following:

A = Provide timely acknowledgement of customer orders.

B = Provide timely shipment of goods to customers.

See Exhibit 9.7 for a complete explanation of control plans and cell entries.

IV = input validity

IC = input completeness

IA = input accuracy

UC = update completeness

UA = update accuracy

    b. Complete the control matrix by adding new controls (ones you added to the flowchart or ones that were on the flowchart but not on the matrix) and by adding cell entries to controls that are already on the matrix.

    c. Complete the control explanations to reflect changes that you made to the flowchart and matrix.

P 9-6   Technology Summary 9.1 (pg. 318) describes the impact that pervasive and general controls from Chapter 8 can have on the effectiveness of controls in Figure 9.3 (pg. 309), Figure 9.4 (pg. 311), and Exhibit 9.3 (pp. 317–317) (i.e., controls for manual and automated data entry). Prepare a comparable summary that describes the impact that pervasive and general controls from Chapter 8 can have on the effectiveness of controls in Figure 9.5 (pg. 319), Figure 9.6 (pg. 320), and Exhibit 9.4 (pg. 324) (i.e., controls over data entry with batches).

EXHIBIT 9.7   Explanation of Cell Entries for the Control Matrix in Figure 9.13 to Accompany Problem 9-5

P-1: *Review document for accuracy.*

P-2: *Preformatted screens.*

- *Effectiveness goals A and B, efficient employment of resources:* By structuring the data entry process, automatically populating fields, and preventing errors, preformatted screens simplify data input and save time (*effectiveness goals A and B*), allowing a user to input more data over a period of time (efficiency).

- *Input accuracy:* As each data field is completed on a preformatted screen, the cursor moves to the next field on the screen, thus preventing the user from omitting any required data set. The data for fields that are automatically populated need not be manually entered, thus reducing input errors. Incorrectly formatted fields are rejected.

P-4: *Procedures for rejected inputs.*

P-5: *Confirm input acceptance.*

M-2: *Manually reconcile batch totals.*

- *Security of resources:* Agreement of the batch totals at this point would ensure that only valid source documents have been input and that invalid picking tickets have not been sent to the warehouse leading to inappropriate shipments of inventory.

- *Input validity, input completeness, input accuracy:* Agreement of the batch totals at this point would ensure that only valid source documents comprising the original batch have been input (input validity), that all source documents were input (input completeness), and that data elements appearing on the source documents have been input correctly (input accuracy).

- *Update completeness, update accuracy:* Reconciliation of batch totals from before input to those after update would ensure a complete and accurate update of the master data.

Business Processes

CHAPTER 10

The Order Entry/Sales (OE/S) Process

Learning Objectives

After reading this chapter, you should be able to:

- Describe the relationship between the OE/S process and its business environment.
- Illustrate the potential of the OE/S process to assist management decision making.
- Summarize how ERP add-ons, e-business, and other technologies can improve the effectiveness and efficiency of the OE/S process.
- Depict the typical logical and physical characteristics of the OE/S process.
- Prepare a control matrix for some typical OE/S processes, including explanations of how business process control plans can accomplish OE/S operations and information process control goals.

Time was, when if you wanted to buy a product, you would go to the seller's (i.e., vendor's) location and pick up the item—or place an order for future pick-up or delivery. You can picture this for a builder or electrician picking up lumber or electrical fixtures. Using an alternate process, a sales representative for the vendor might visit you at your business to take your order. When geography made such personal contact infeasible, you might call in your order or send a paper order via the mail, or possibly by fax. Such orders could be written by hand, typed, or printed by your computer's purchasing system (we won't go back so far that there is no computer involved!). When the order arrived at your vendor, it was probably entered into your vendor's computerized sales system.

Some business partners still communicate that way today. What does it cost? One estimate is that it costs the vendor between $60 and $200 to process the paper order—more towards the higher end if errors are made entering the data into the computer or if the document gets lost. How much can automation reduce this cost? Again, one estimate is that 70 percent of the costs can be saved.[1]

These manual processes changed as business relationships changed and as more advanced technology became available. Competition and productivity imperatives stressed automation and enhanced customer service. Companies could no longer afford to manually enter customer orders; it was too time consuming, costly, and error prone. Competitive pressures permitted customers to demand timely processing and delivery and

[1]Jean-Michel Bérard, "Automated Sales Order Processing: How Manufacturers Improve Customer Service While Cutting Cost," accountingsoftware411.com, posted September 22, 2009, accessed September 23, 2009.

on-demand information about their orders. At the same time, the selling organization's own marketing personnel wanted to know who they were selling to and why. Many questions were asked: Who are our customers? Where do we find them? How do they find us? What products do they want? What products don't they want and why? What do customers consider good service? What do customers consider a good experience? How do we keep the customers who are profitable and part with those that are not?

What are the technologies, then, that can automate these processes, reduce costs, enhance information availability, and satisfy the other requirements of the buyer and seller? In this chapter we will discuss several, including *Enterprise Systems* (Chapter 2), *EDI* (Chapter 3), *cloud computing* (Chapter 3), and some of the systems, introduced in Chapter 2, that are offered via cloud computing, such as *CRM*, *CSS*, and *SFA*. Several other technologies are introduced in this chapter, including electronic data capture, *digital image processing*, and *Web 2.0*. These technologies support the order entry and sales process, as well as the remainder of the *order-to-cash process* (the *billing/accounts receivable/cash receipts process*) and the *purchase-to-pay process*.

Synopsis

In business process analysis and design, we must carefully consider the business process as a whole, including all the interrelated parts that work toward the common purpose of meeting business process requirements. We follow this model in examining each of the business processes that enable organizations to successfully achieve their organizational goals. Accordingly, in Chapters 10 through 15 we will explore the following topics for each business process:

- Process definition and functions
- Organizational setting of the process
- Technologies, including e-business and enterprise systems, used to implement the process   *E-Business*
- Decision making supported by the information system   *Enterprise Systems*
- Logical process features
- Logical database design
- Physical process features
- Control analysis applied to the process (including an examination of process goalss)   *Controls*

Introduction

The order entry/sales (OE/S) process includes the first four steps in the *order-to-cash process* shown in Figure 2.7 (pg. 53) in Chapter 2, presales activities, sales order processing, picking and packing the goods, and shipping. The last two steps in Figure 2.7, billing and processing the customer payment, are described in Chapter 11, in the *billing/accounts receivable/cash receipts process*.

As we noted in Chapter 1, a complete study of AIS requires that you understand both the *operations process* and *information process* functions of each business process. The operational aspects of the OE/S process are critical to the success—in fact, the very survival—of businesses today and in the future. Many organizations focus the bulk of their investment in strategic information systems on supporting OE/S process effectiveness. Why? Because customers want to place their orders quickly and easily. They want immediate pricing and material availability information. They expect convenient and timely access to information about their order from order initiation, through product delivery, and until after the bill has been paid! This is why later sections of the chapter discuss the vital topics of *decision making*, satisfying customer needs, employing technology to gain competitive advantage, and other issues that transcend the mere processing of business events and accounting transactions.

Process Definition and Functions

The **order entry/sales (OE/S) process** is an interacting structure of people, equipment, activities, and controls that is designed to achieve certain goals. The primary function of the OE/S process is to create information flows that support the following:

- Repetitive work routines of the sales order department, credit department, and shipping department[2]
- Decision needs of those who manage various sales and marketing functions

Let's quickly examine each of these functions. First, the OE/S process supports the repetitive work routines of the sales order, credit, and shipping departments by capturing, recording, and communicating sales-related data. For example, we need to know the identity of the customer and what the customer has ordered. These data will be used to determine the total amount of the order; to decide, if relevant, whether credit should be granted; and to inform workers in the warehouse that certain goods need to be picked and transported to the shipping department. Additional discussions and illustrations of this function will be provided throughout the chapter.

Second, the OE/S process supports the decision needs of various sales and marketing managers. Obviously, in addition to these managers, any number of people within a given organization may benefit from information generated by the OE/S process. Later sections discuss the relationship between the OE/S process and managerial decision making and provide some examples of related information that might facilitate decision making.

Organizational Setting

In this section, we take both a horizontal and a vertical view of how the OE/S process fits into the organizational setting of a company. The horizontal perspective will enhance your appreciation of how the OE/S process relates to the repetitive work routines of the sales order, credit, and shipping departments. Conversely, the vertical perspective will sharpen your understanding of how the OE/S process relates to managerial decision making within the marketing function.

---

[2]To focus our discussion, we have assumed that these departments are the primary ones related to the OE/S process. For a given organization, however, the departments associated with the OE/S process may differ.

FIGURE 10.1   A Horizontal Perspective of the OE/S Process

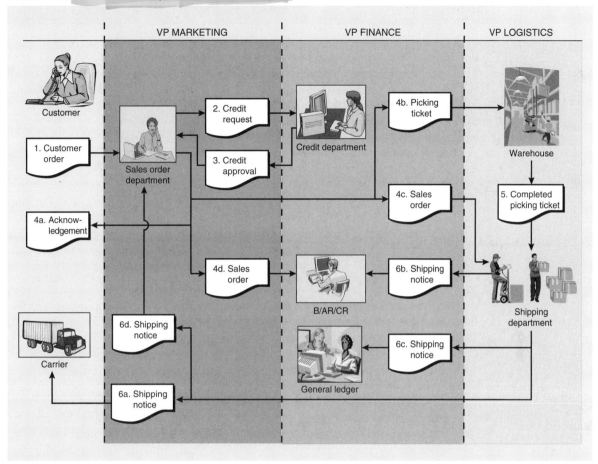

A Horizontal Perspective

Figure 10.1 and **Table 10.1** (pg. 346) present a horizontal view of the relationship between the OE/S process and its organizational environment. The figure shows the various information flows, depicted as documents, generated or captured by the OE/S process. The information flows are superimposed onto the organizational structures that are related to the OE/S process and the multiple entities with which the OE/S process interacts (customers, carriers, other business processes such as *billing/accounts receivable/cash receipts* *[B/AR/CR]* and *general ledger*).

As you examine this figure and the number of interacting organizational units, consider again the discussion of *value chain* in Chapter 2. The ultimate goal of the activities depicted in Figure 10.1 is to create value for the customer. Organizations usually assign an owner to this process (often called the order-fulfillment process) to coordinate the activities to ensure that customer value expectations are met. The order-fulfillment process owner must balance the goals of making goods available in a timely manner with the goal of maximizing profit. To do so, the process owner must ensure, for example, that just enough inventory is carried to meet expected demand; that customer orders are relayed accurately and promptly; and that customers receive the right goods in the right condition, on time, and at the expected price.

TABLE 10.1 Descriptions of Horizontal Information Flows

Flow No.	Description
1	Customer places order.
2	Sales order department requests credit approval from credit department.
3	Credit department informs sales order department of disposition of credit request.
4	Sales order department acknowledges order to the customer (4a), and notifies the warehouse (4b), shipping (4c), and the B/AR/CR process (4d) of the sales order.
5	Warehouse sends completed picking ticket to shipping.
6	Shipping department informs carrier (6a), B/AR/CR process (6b), the general ledger process (6c), and the sales order department (6d) of the shipment.

Figure 10.1 (pg. 345) and Table 10.1 reveal six information flows that function as vital communications links among the various operations departments, business processes, and external entities. We briefly explain each flow here to give you a quick introduction to the OE/S process. Although Figure 10.1 depicts these flows using a document symbol, most of them can be implemented using electronic communications (e.g., *workflow*) and data stored in an enterprise database.

- Flow 1 apprises representatives in the sales order department of a customer request for goods. This information flow might take the physical form of a telephone call, an EDI transmission, an entry on a Web site, or a faxed or mailed *customer order*.
- Flows 2 and 3 represent the credit check. These flows could be a form sent to and from the credit department, a phone call, a look-up on a customer's master data, or a request routed to an authorized individual by a system's *workflow* module to have the credit authorized via an *electronic approval*.
- Flow 4a could be a form sent to the customer, a confirmation number delivered via a Web site or read by a sales clerk over the phone, or an EDI transmission. With flow 4b, the warehouse picks the goods. Flow 4c informs workers in the shipping department of a pending shipment; this communication facilitates the operational planning and related activities associated with the shipping function. This information flow might take the form of a copy of a *sales order*, or it might be an electronic image appearing on a computer workstation located in the shipping department. Flow 4d informs the billing department that a shipment is pending (and that an invoicing process will soon be required).
- Flow 5 accompanies the goods from the warehouse to shipping.
- The shipping department prepares the shipping notice (flows 6a–6d) after matching flow 4c and flow 5. Flow 6a identifies the goods and their destination for the carrier. The billing department begins the invoicing process after matching flow 4d and flow 6b. The general ledger uses flow 6c to update inventory and costs of goods sold for the shipment.[3]

As we will note again later, two important activities precede all of these flows in a typical commercial operation where goods are sold to ongoing customers. *Data maintenance* must be performed to create a customer master record, including a credit limit. Data maintenance must also be performed to create one or more inventory master records, including sales prices.

---

[3]The timing of the recording of the shipment and the related billing transaction in the general ledger may depend on how close together those two activities occur and the specific software employed.

FIGURE 10.2   A Vertical Perspective of the OE/S Process

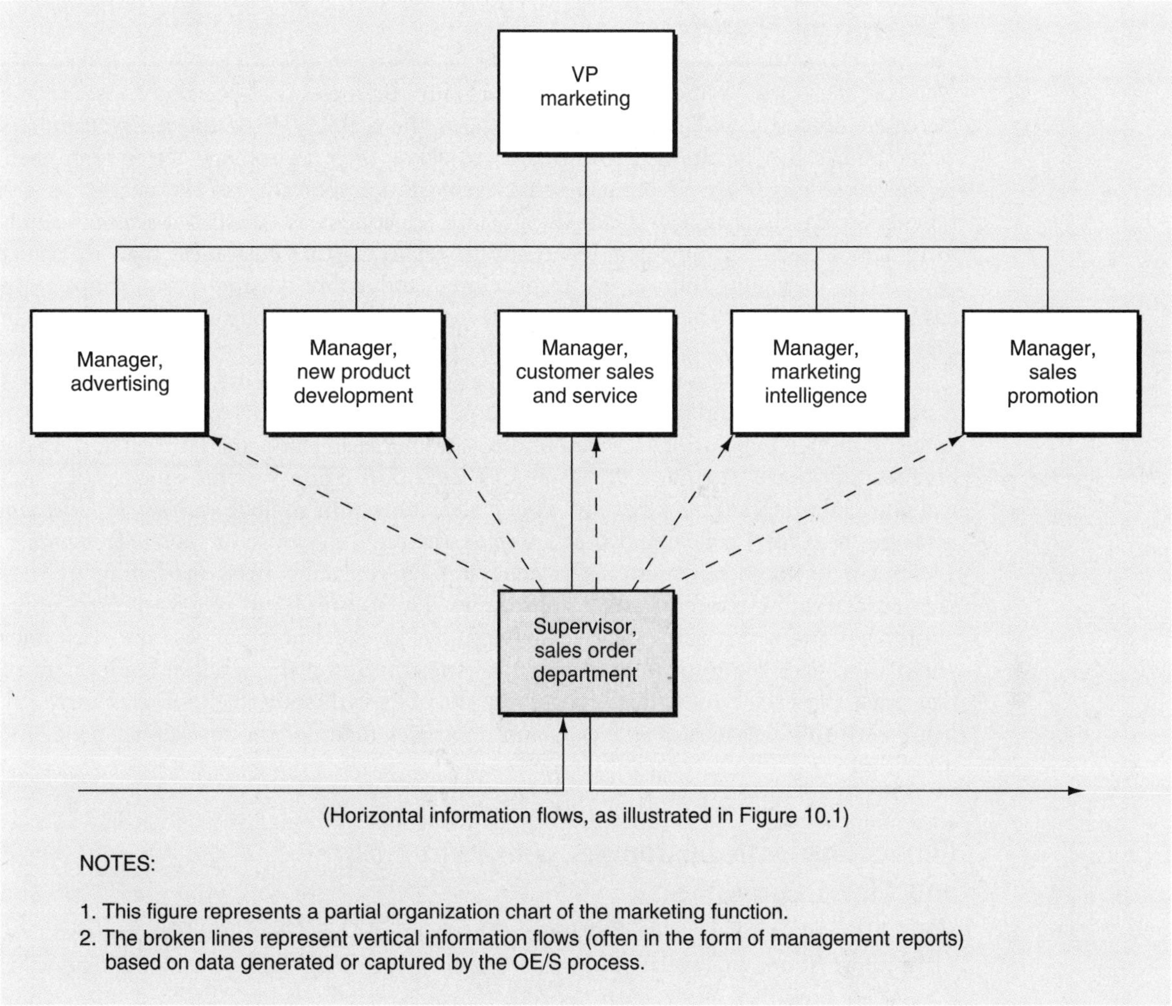

(Horizontal information flows, as illustrated in Figure 10.1)

NOTES:

1. This figure represents a partial organization chart of the marketing function.
2. The broken lines represent vertical information flows (often in the form of management reports) based on data generated or captured by the OE/S process.

A Vertical Perspective

To understand the relationship between the OE/S process and managerial decision making, you need to become familiar with the key players involved in the marketing function. **Figure 10.2** presents these players in the form of an organization chart. Take some time now to study the chart.

As the figure illustrates, sales-related data are captured in the sales order department and then flow vertically (in a summarized format) to managers housed within the marketing organizational structure. Much of this information was traditionally based on sales-related events and was captured through the use of a sales order form or through entry of sales data directly into a database. However, as organizations become increasingly focused on customers, the information needs for decision making are less accounting entry–oriented and more focused on customer characteristics, needs, and preferences, as described at the start of this chapter. The next section provides an overview of the relationship between management decision making and the OE/S process, and how information technology facilitates the demands of decision makers.

Managing the OE/S Process: Satisfying Customer Needs

One of the most critical success factors for businesses, especially those facing increased domestic and global competition, is their ability to know their customers better and, armed with such knowledge, to serve their customers better than their competition. Firms are recognizing that their most important asset—one that is not capitalized on the balance sheet—is a happy customer. A satisfied customer tends to remain a customer, and it is less costly to retain existing customers than to attract new ones. Certainly, efforts to form closer and more lasting partnerships with customers would top the priority list of several of the marketing managers shown in Figure 10.2 (pg. 347).

Enterprise Systems

What does this situation mean for the OE/S process? Most importantly, it has expanded the type and amount of data collected by the OE/S process regarding a firm's customer population. To respond to the increasing information demand, many organizations have expanded the scope of their information systems to assist decision making in the marketing function. This expansion might include *customer relationship management (CRM) systems* and *Web 2.0* tools, operated in-house or via *cloud computing*. The focus of these new systems is generally on replacing mass marketing or segmented marketing strategies with approaches that use new and more powerful computing resources to zero in on increasingly smaller portions of the customer population, with the ultimate aim being to concentrate on the smallest component of that population—the individual consumer. We start with some technologies currently being used to satisfy customer needs and to answer many of the marketing managers' questions.

Connecting with Customers with Web 2.0 and Cloud Computing

E-Business

Web 2.0 is a set of tools that allow people to build social and business connections, share information, and collaborate on projects online. These tools include blogs, wikis (i.e., Web sites that allow users to add, delete, and edit content), social-networking (e.g., Facebook and Twitter) and other online communities, and virtual worlds.[4] These tools can be used by marketing managers to connect with customers, to learn what they like and don't like, and about new products that they want. Such connections can build loyalty, increase sales, and help develop new and improved products. Twitter, for example, can be used to get the word out about promotions in a timely fashion. Facebook and Twitter can be used to offer exclusive discounts and to hold countdowns and contests. Finally, companies can use these tools to let consumers know what is still in stock and what is going fast.[5] **Technology Application 10.1** describes some uses of Web 2.0 tools that have been reported.

Trust has become the real differentiator with consumers in the *Web 2.0* world. As trust increases, it becomes more unlikely that a customer will leave; they don't want to start building trust all over again. Transparency is one way to build this trust. Transparency includes tracking orders; following up on e-mails and phone calls; viewing an

---

[4]Salvatore Parise, Patricia J. Guinan, Bruce D. Weinberg, "The Secrets of Marketing in a Web 2.0 World," *Wall Street Journal*, December 15, 2008, p. R4.

[5]Samantha Murphy, "Wrapping Up the E-Shopping Season," *Chain Store Age*, December 2009, p. 46.

organization as one entity, including catalog, phone, Web site, or e-mail; and using customer feedback innovation, and R&D.[6] Top-ranked global brands are highly active in the social Web. For example, Coca-Cola's Facebook fan page is used for fans to share stories, leave comments, and receive messages sent from the brand. Leading companies are rated highest in terms of level of engagement. Also, there is a positive correlation between social engagement and financial performance.[7]

Cloud computing is often used to facilitate connections to customers, to improve customer service, to reduce costs, and to improve process timeliness. **Technology Application 10.2** (pg. 350) describes a few examples of cloud computing.

Technology Application 10.1

USING WEB 2.0 TO INTERACT WITH CUSTOMERS

Case 1

Lion Brand Yarn employees run a blog called "Lion Brand Notebook" that humanizes the company. Testing indicates that customers coming to the Web site from the blog convert to being Lion Brand customers at a rate 41 percent higher than the average site traffic. Also, those that interact with Lion Brand socially are 83 percent more likely to identify as "very loyal" than those not so engaged.

Case 2

A leading greeting card and gift company set up an online community to solicit opinions on greeting card design, gift ideas, and pricing.

Case 3

A large technology company created wikis to improve collaboration with business partners and consumers. For example, after the release of a new piece of software, consumers spotted a problem with it, described ways to deal with it, and finally proposed a way to fix the problem, a solution that the company adopted.

Case 4

A major consumer-electronics company monitors blogs immediately after a new product launch to understand how customers are reacting to the new product.

Case 5

Another company found a popular blogger who had spoken highly of the company's brand. They sent him a free sample of a new product, inviting him to review it. The blogger wrote a favorable review that generated a flood of comments. The result was free publicity and feedback.

Case 6

A consumer-electronics organization created an online community of 50,000 consumers to discuss product development and marketing issues. Community members identified what it was that they were looking for in the company's products, but also suggested innovations to satisfy those needs. The company developed prototypes and received an enthusiastic response from the community. Members asked when they could buy the product and whether they could get first opportunity.

Case 7

Toys "R" Us customers can sign up to receive instant alerts, via Twitter, Facebook, and other social networking sites, or e-mails about deals available in stores and online at toysrus.com. Fans of the Toys "R" Us Facebook fan page can obtain updates on deals, special promotions, coupon offers, and about deals just for members. Facebook fans also receive exclusive previews of some of the biggest sales at Toys "R" Us and are alerted about availability of hard-to-find products.

Sources: Lauren McKay, "Knitting Together a Community of Enthusiasts," *Customer Relationship Management*, January 2010, pp. 46–47; Salvatore Parise, Patricia J. Guinan, and Bruce D. Weinberg, "The Secrets of Marketing in a Web 2.0 World," *Wall Street Journal*, December 15, 2008, p. R4; "Toysrus.com Enhances Gift-Giving Convenience with Mobile Shopping, eGift Cards and Expanded Free Shipping; World's Largest Online Toy Store. Also Makes Deal-Hunting Easy for On-the-Go Shoppers and Introduces Buyer Protection Plan," *PR Newswire*, November 20, 2009.

---

[6]Lauren McKay, "Transparency," *Customer Relationship Management*, December 2008, pp. 24–29.

[7]"Trust Is the New Differentiator," *Customer Relationship Management*, December 2009, pp. 17–18.

Technology Application 10.2

CLOUD COMPUTING AND SALES

Case 1

Avon "sales leaders" had managed 6 million Avon sales representatives with face-to-face meetings and phone conversations. Now, the sales leaders use smartphones and PCs to connect to a cloud-based computing system to keep up-to-date on each sales rep and alert them when the reps have not placed orders recently or have payments overdue.

Case 2

Genentech sales reps use smartphones to access "Peeps," a Facebook-like directory of Genentech staff, to find answers from

Genentech staff with the appropriate expertise to questions that doctors pose during office sales calls. The Genentech sales reps also use their smartphones to connect to other cloud services such as Salesforce.com's sales management service and Google Apps.

Case 3

Coca-Cola Enterprises' 12,000 store merchandisers use smartphones and cloud computing to stay in touch with bosses and the company's information storehouse. At the end of each stop they complete online surveys that give the company a complete picture of sales trends and store manager relationships that they can react to in real time.

Source: Steve Hamm, "Cloud Computing's Big Bang for Business," *Businessweek*, June 15, 2009, pp. 42–48.

Decision Making and Kinds of Decisions

Now let's look at an example of the decisions that marketing managers shown in Figure 10.2 (pg. 347) must confront. As we noted at the start of this chapter, many questions are asked. A few representative questions are the following:

1. Where is sales volume (quantity and dollars) concentrated?
2. Who are the specific major customers (by sales and by profitability), both present and potential?
3. What opportunities exist to sell after-sales services, to cross-sell (offer related products), and to up-sell (offer higher-priced products)?
4. What types of advertising and promotions have the greatest influence on customers?

Could the information system help you obtain the answers? Certainly, at least to the extent that it has captured and stored historical data related to sales events and additional customer information. To answer the first question, you might find a sales report by region helpful. A sales report by customer could provide *some* answers to the second question. An organization's own sales database should provide answers to the third question.

Where might you find answers to questions like the fourth one? It depends. If you want to know which advertising and promotions have had an impact on your own customers, you would need to gather that data as sales take place. Otherwise, you would need to use census reports, market research questionnaires, trade journals, and data collected using social networking and other Web 2.0 tools described in the previous sections. Also, research houses garner vast amounts of information from public records—drivers' licenses, automobile registrations, tax rolls, mortgage registrations, and the like—and sell that information to other companies. In certain industries, the mechanisms to collect data regarding customers, their buying habits, and other demographics have become quite sophisticated. Recent advances in database management systems and the underlying technologies are leading to a focus on the use of *data warehousing* and *data mining* techniques (as discussed in Chapter 5) to support marketing analysis. Let's take a closer look at some of the key technologies supporting these efforts.

Using Data Mining to Support Marketing

Data warehousing applications in organizations are usually viewed as being focused on either operational or analytical applications. Operational applications focus on providing decision makers with the information they need to monitor and control their business processes. For example, an important question might be "how many hours or days does it take to make a shipment after receiving a customer order?" Analytical applications, which include *data mining*, are intended to allow the use of sophisticated statistical and other analytical software to help an organization's members develop insights about customers, processes, and markets. It is important that this analysis include internal data collected from sales events, as well as external data, such as industry data and that collected with Web 2.0 tools. Two analytical applications are discussed in **Technology Application 10.3**.

Enterprise Systems

Data warehousing can be a massive effort for a company. For instance, the New York Stock Exchange (NYSE) has a data warehouse from Netezza Corporation that houses data about deals from its nearly 3,000 companies, an enormous amount of data.[8] This warehouse is used to perform a variety of functions, including tracking the value of a listed company, performing trend analysis, and searching for evidence of fraudulent activity. Prior to implementing this warehouse, the NYSE took six hours to fulfill a query request. Afterwards the time was reduced to 20 seconds! Implementing this warehouse also had a huge impact on the NYSE's capability to comply with numerous financial regulations.

One of the major analytical users of warehouse data is the marketing department. When the marketing department is armed with this massive array of data from which

---

Technology Application 10.3

APPLICATIONS OF DATA MINING

Case 1

Kroger® Company has increased market share in the highly competitive supermarket industry by mining data from its customer loyalty cards. This analysis, conducted by British firm Dunnhumby, has helped drive traffic and increase purchases by optimizing marketing programs. For example, if a customer has a new baby, Kroger will provide coupons for items such as baby wipes and diapers.

Case 2

Barneys New York, the upscale clothing store chain, reports a 10 percent increase in online revenue by using data mining software that finds links between online behavior and greater propensity to buy. Barneys uses a system from Proclivity Systems to analyze data about when a customer visits its site and other demographic information to determine on whom it should focus its e-mail messages. For example, an e-mail message announcing a sale might be sent to those who had purchased certain products in the past, but only when the items were on sale. This has not only increased sales but has increased customer goodwill by showing that Barneys understands its clientele's interests.

Sources: Alexander Eule, "Thriving in Wal-Mart's World," *Barron's*, January 7, 2008, p. 26; Eric A. Taub, "Guessing the Online Customer's Next Want," *The New York Times*, May 19, 2008, p. C6.

---

[8]"Data Analytics Pays Dividends," *IT Week*, May 12, 2008, p. 22.

customer buying habits, characteristics, and addresses can be analyzed and linked, extensive study can be undertaken. Researchers using *neural networks* (discussed in Chapter 5), comprehensive statistical analysis packages, and graphical presentation software can rapidly begin to develop insights about relationships within the marketing information.

Mastering Global E-Business

E-Business

E-business systems can be used to penetrate global markets by allowing trading partners and customers to easily process international orders without a physical presence. E-business systems are broken into two categories: buy-side and sell-side.

Buy-side systems use the Internet to automate and manage purchases and the vendors from which these purchases are made. The predominant technology in this area is *electronic data interchange (EDI)*. Examples of other buy-side e-commerce software applications are supply chain management (SCM) (discussed in Chapter 12, this allows an organization to manage the entire purchase-to-pay business cycle with worldwide trading partners), e-procurement (automates corporate purchasing), and e-sourcing (sets up auctions among various vendors for products and services). Because the buyer often controls the buyer–seller relationship, technology on the sell-side may include whatever is necessary to connect to the buyer. For example, if the buyer wants to send purchase orders via EDI, then the seller must use EDI to receive those orders, or it will lose that business.

Sell-side systems are designed to allow a company to market, sell, deliver, and service goods and services to customers throughout the world via the Internet. Sell-side applications can handle both B2B and B2C business transactions. For instance, sell-side applications can process many customer-related functions, such as catalog browsing, sales, payments, customer support, and analytics. One facet of sell-side systems is *customer relationship management (CRM)* applications. Other examples of sell-side applications include marketing management (used to manage campaigns and promotions), catalog management (allows a company to keep its catalog up-to-date), e-payment (designed to handle global credit authorizations and currency transactions), and order management (administers order information).

Customer Relationship Management (CRM) Systems

Enterprise
Systems

Controls

In Chapter 2, we introduced you to CRM software, along with related *customer self-service (CSS) software*, and *sales force automation (SFA) software*. Recall that CRM software is designed to manage all the data related to customers, such as marketing, field service, and contact management data. CRM has become the focus of ERP vendors who realize the need to tap into this growing market and to integrate CRM data with the other data already residing within the ERP system's database. For example, SAP has developed its own product, and Oracle has acquired the former leader in the CRM software market, Siebel® Systems.

The concept behind CRM is to cultivate customer relationships by prospecting, acquiring, servicing, and retaining customers. Better customer service means happier customers and better sales—particularly repeat sales. Prospecting includes finding new customers or new business with existing customers (e.g., cross-sell, up-sell). In the acquiring phase, potential business is turned into sales, which is followed by service tasks such as providing technical support and handling complaints. Customers are retained if they are serviced well and their changing requirements are anticipated. The following paragraphs describe how CRM systems support the cultivation of the customer relationship. As the following elements become more integrated, we can streamline customer interactions to provide a single face to the customer. As you read, consider how we obtain this data and combine the internal and external data for comprehensive analysis.

CRM contact management features facilitate the recording and storing of information related to each contact the organization has with a client and the context of conversations or meetings. Additionally, each time the client makes contact regarding queries or service help, this information also is recorded (field service records). The result is that a salesperson can review all the historical information before calling on a customer and thus be better prepared to provide that customer with targeted products and services. These systems also support the recording of information about the customer contact, such as spouse's name, children, hobbies, and so on, that helps the salesperson make a more personalized contact with the customer.

At the same time, CRM software supports organizing and retrieving information on historical sales activities and promotions planning. This facilitates matching sales promotions with customers' buying trends and forecasting future sales. This is a particularly crucial area for integration with any existing ERP system because much of the information necessary to support sales analyses comes from data captured during the recording of sales event data in the ERP system. The buzzword for this CRM application is "segmentation," the grouping of customers into categories based on key characteristics. These categories might represent customers likely to respond to a marketing campaign, high-end customers who should receive "high-touch" customer service, and low-end customers who should be directed to self-service options.

A third area that is prevalent in CRMs is support for customer service—particularly automation for operators handling customer support at call-in centers. *Sales-force automation software*, for example, may route calls to a particular sales representative who has previously worked with the customer. The CRM quickly provides the operator with information on the customer's history and usually links the operator with a database of solutions for various problems about which a customer may be inquiring. These solutions may simply be warranty or contract information, or, at a more complex level, solutions to operations or maintenance problems on machinery or equipment. All this information can be efficiently stored in the database for quick retrieval by the system's user.

Another common feature of CRM systems is *customer self-service (CSS) systems*. Recall from Chapter 2 that a CSS system is an extension of a CRM system that allows a customer to complete an inquiry or perform a task within an organization's business process without the aid of the organization's employees. Originally, CSS systems were implemented through the use of automated telephone systems in which the customer selects options and enters account information via the number keys on the telephone. A more recent trend that has received positive public feedback is the move to Internet systems that provide access to customer information. Although these systems tend to take the same time to use as the telephone-based systems, studies show that consumers enjoy Internet-based systems more than the much-maligned phone-based systems. Internet-based systems also bring greater capability to systems. For instance, most of the courier companies (FedEx, UPS, etc.) now allow users to connect through the Internet and identify where their package for delivery is currently located and, if delivered, who signed for the receipt of the package.

E-Business

A major extension to these systems is the interconnection of CSS systems with enterprise systems. In some cases, customers can check their orders as they progress through the manufacturing process or even check inventory availability before placing

Enterprise Systems

orders. Some of the more advanced systems even allow customers to check production planning for future manufacturing to determine whether goods will be available when they are needed.

Why are companies so interested in CSS systems and willing to allow access to information in their internal systems? Quite simply, the payback on such systems is huge considering the reduced number of people needed to staff customer call centers. Reduction of staffing needs for call centers is particularly beneficial because of the high turnover such centers incur due to the high boredom factor associated with the job.

Logical Description of the OE/S Process

Using data flow diagrams (DFDs), this section provides a logical view of a typical OE/S process. Although the narrative highlights certain key points that you should discern from the diagrams, your study of Chapter 4 has equipped you to glean much knowledge simply from a careful study of the diagrams. We conclude the section with a description of the data created or used by the OE/S process.[9]

Logical Data Flow Diagrams

Our first view of the process is a general one. **Figure 10.3** portrays the OE/S process in the form of a *context diagram* and delineates the domain of our study. In examining Figure 10.3, you should observe one input entering the process and six outputs emerging. Also notice the entities with which the OE/S process interacts. Some of these entities reside outside the organization (Customer and Carrier), whereas one is internal to the organization but external to the OE/S process (the Billing/Accounts Receivable/Cash Receipts [B/AR/CR] process).

Notice that this diagram shows the process *after* the "Presales activities" depicted in Figure 2.7 (pg. 53) have taken place. Those activities would include such things as salespersons contacting customers and recording information about that contact in the CRM system, customer inquiries regarding price and availability of goods, customer formal requests for a quote (RFQ), and responses to those with a quotation. The customer order entering our process indicates that a customer has decided to place an order. As noted earlier, this order could be submitted via mail, telephone, fax, EDI, Internet, and so on. This is the beauty of the *logical DFD*; we do not need to know the form by which the order is transmitted, just that it is sent from the customer to the OE/S process.

Figure 10.4 (pg. 356) presents a *level 0 diagram* of the OE/S process. In examining the figure, observe that the inputs and outputs are identical to those presented in Figure 10.3. Recall that this *balancing* of inputs and outputs is an important convention to observe when constructing a set of DFDs. The single bubble in Figure 10.3 has been divided into three bubbles in Figure 10.4, one for each of the three major processes performed by the OE/S process.[10] Additional data flows connecting the

---

[9]As we have indicated in earlier chapters, whenever we show data being stored in separate data stores, you should recognize that such data stores represent a process view of data that in reality may reside in an *enterprise database*.

[10]To focus our discussion, we have assumed that the OE/S process performs three major processes. A given process, however, may perform more or fewer processes than we have chosen to illustrate here.

FIGURE 10.3   The OE/S Process—Context Diagram

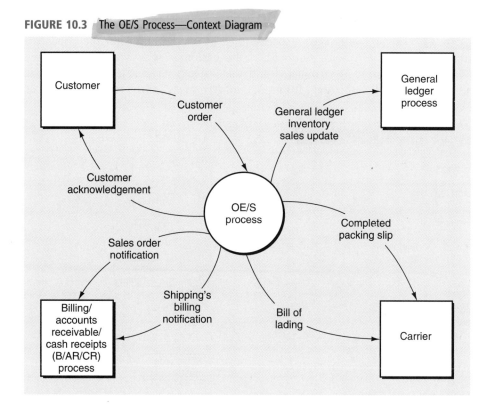

newly partitioned bubbles appear, as do the data stores used to store various sets of data. Take some time now to study the data flows, processes, and data stores shown in Figure 10.4.[11]

Each of the three processes shown in Figure 10.4 will now be decomposed (i.e., "exploded") into lower-level diagrams. **Figure 10.5** (pg. 357) decomposes bubble 1.0 of Figure 10.4. Notice, first, that the inputs and outputs in this figure do not match those for bubble 1.0 in Figure 10.4. We see here the convention, first mentioned in Chapter 4, of showing *reject stubs* only below level 0 DFDs. Therefore, the three flows seen here and not in Figure 10.4 (i.e., two "Reject" stubs and the flow "Back order") do not make these diagrams out of balance.

The customer order is the *trigger* that initiates process 1.1.[12] How does the OE/S process then validate a customer order? First, process 1.1 verifies the availability of the requested inventory by consulting the inventory master data. Recall from Chapter 2 that determining inventory availability—available to promise (ATP)—can be a complicated process that would be facilitated by an enterprise system that can look worldwide within the organization and up and down the supply chain to determine when and from where goods can be delivered. If a sufficient level of inventory is on hand to satisfy the request, the order is forwarded for further processing, as depicted by the data flow "Inventory available order." Conversely, if a customer orders goods that are not in stock, process 1.1 runs a special back order routine. This routine determines the inventory requirement necessary to satisfy the order and then sends the back order request to the purchasing

Enterprise
Systems

---

[11]The line enclosing the right side of the Sales order master data indicates that there is another occurrence of that data store on the diagram.

[12]We use the term *trigger* to refer to any data flow or event that causes a process to begin.

department. This activity is depicted by the "Back order" data flow, which in reality is a specific type of *exception routine* (i.e., a specific type of reject stub). After the goods are received, the order is processed routinely. If the customer refuses to accept a back order, then the sales event is terminated and the order is rejected, as shown by the "Reject" data flow. Information from the order (e.g., sales region, customer

FIGURE 10.4   The OE/S Process—Level 0 Diagram

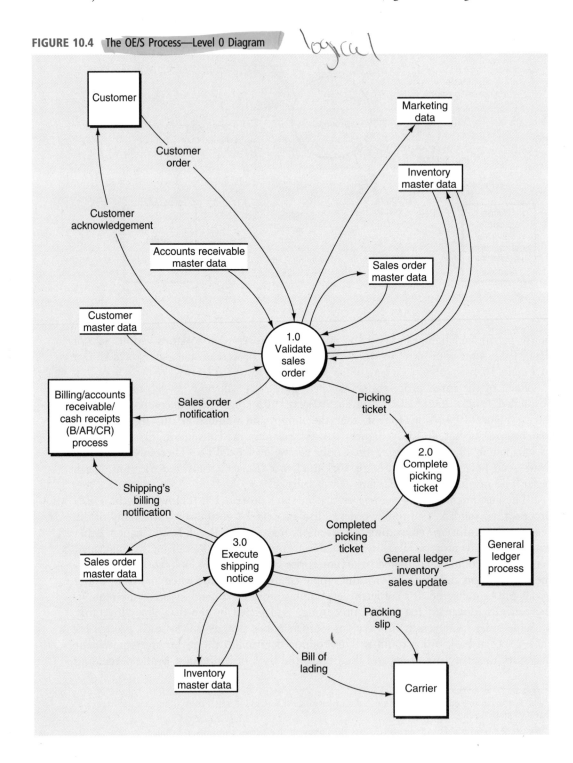

demographics, and order characteristics that reflect buying habits) that has potential value to marketing is recorded in the marketing data store.

After assuring inventory availability, process 1.2 establishes the customer's existence and then evaluates credit with an enterprise system, one record should exist for each customer, wherever the customer is located and from whatever parts of the organization the customer makes purchases. This allows an organization to readily determine the amount of credit available to that customer worldwide. Without this central database, a customer could incur multiple receivable balances that in total exceed an amount the selling organization considers desirable.

Enterprise Systems

Credit can be checked using a variety of techniques from the very simple to the very complex. For example, the amount of the order (e.g., the sum of quantities × the prices that were on "Inventory available order") might be compared to a credit limit stored on the customer master record. This, unfortunately, would allow a customer to submit several orders at or just below their credit limit. The total credit risk would then be greater than desirable. To reduce that risk, the credit check might add the amount of the order to accounts receivable balances and open sales orders (i.e., orders about to be receivables), and compare that total to the credit limit. The flows from the

FIGURE 10.5   The OE/S Process—Diagram 1

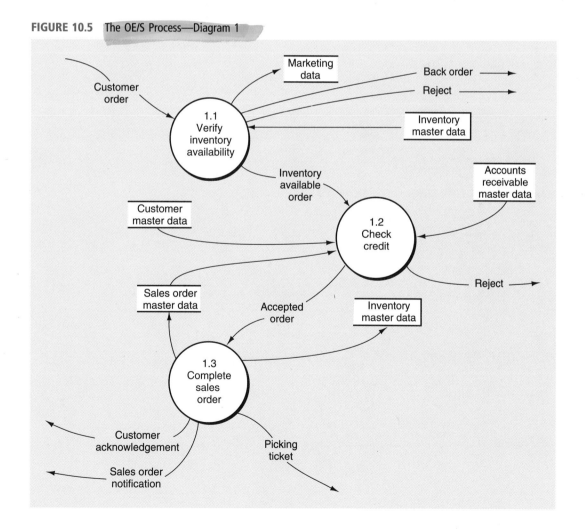

accounts receivable master data and the sales order master data assume this type of credit check. Finally, a customer's credit might be reviewed for each sale. This review might include financial statements and reports from credit rating agencies such as Dun & Bradstreet. This latter credit check would only be used for large sales such as mainframe computers, fleets of automobiles, and the like. However, this type of check might be performed when a customer is first accepted to establish the customer's limit, which is used for each subsequent credit check.

Upon a successful credit approval, process 1.3 performs the following activities simultaneously:

- Updates the inventory master data to allocate the quantity ordered to the sales order. The inventory balance could actually be reduced at this time to save a later update of the inventory master data. (If the inventory is updated at this point, the flow to the general ledger would emanate from this subprocess rather than subprocess 3.2.)
- Updates the sales order master data to indicate that a completed sales order has been created.
- Disseminates the sales order.

Enterprise Systems

The physical means used to disseminate the order may vary from using a multipart sales order form to using electronic images appearing on various computer screens (illustrated in **Figure 10.6**) or as a record in a computer data store. Notice in Figure 10.6

FIGURE 10.6 SAP Sales Order Inquiry Screen

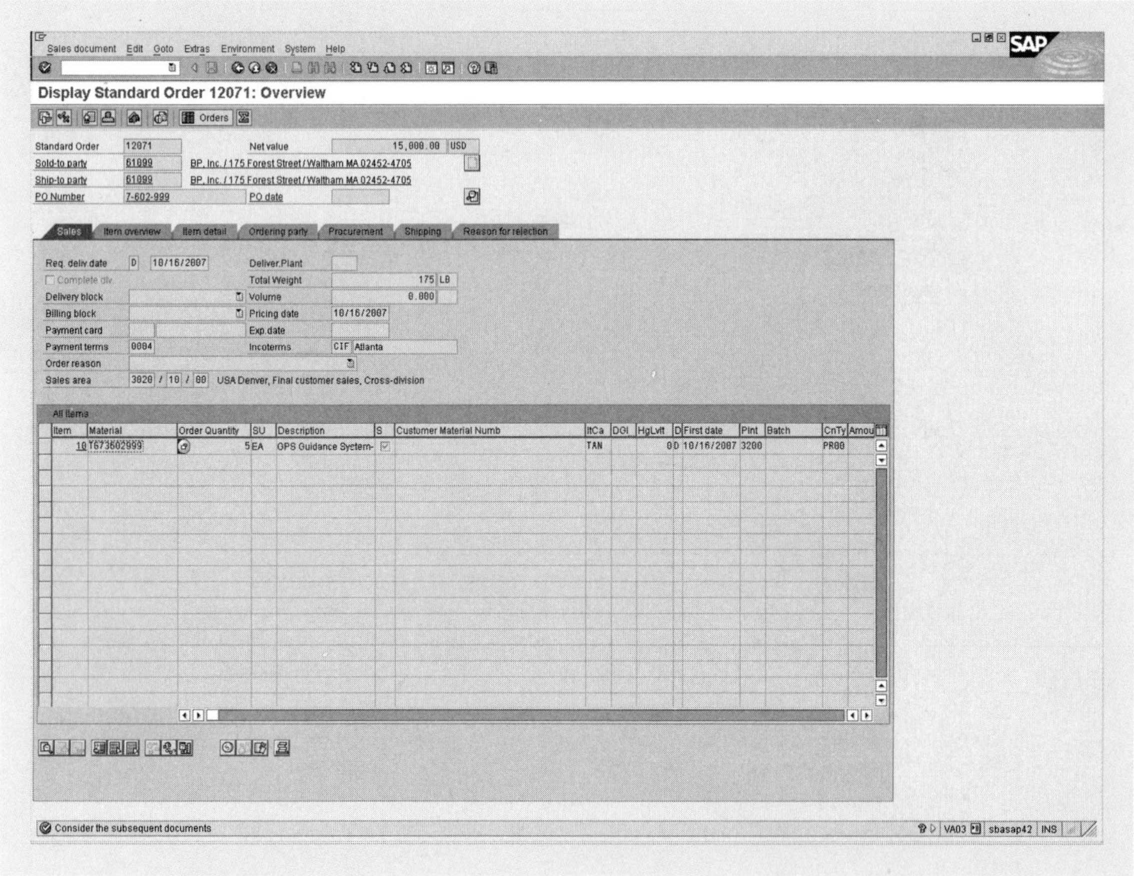

FIGURE 10.7   The OE/S Process—Diagram 2

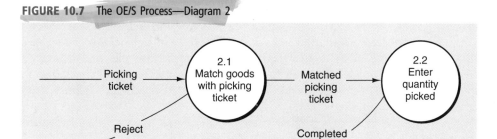

the quantity and nature of information that is available in a sales order record. For example, notice the ship-to party, the customer's PO number, and the required delivery date. The Material number (e.g., TG73602999), Order Quantity, and Description, as well as the net value of the order are shown (the individual selling price is not shown in this view).

Regardless of the physical form used, we generally expect the dissemination of the sales order to include the following data flows:

- A **picking ticket** authorizes the warehouse to "pick" the goods from the shelf and send them to the shipping department. The picking ticket identifies the goods to be picked and usually indicates the warehouse location. This is usually a document printed in the warehouse, but it could be sent to the screen of a handheld device.
- A **customer acknowledgement** is sent to notify the customer of the order's acceptance and the expected shipment date. Again, as noted earlier, this could be sent via a paper document, an EDI transmission, a confirmation number given over the phone or on the Web, and so on.
- A sales order notification is sent to the billing department to notify them of a pending shipment. This could take many forms, including a message received on a computer screen or a report of pending shipments. Or the sales order notification might not be actually "sent" at all. Rather, the computer record of the sales order, accessible to the billing personnel, might be sufficient.

Figure 10.7, a lower-level view of bubble 2.0 of Figure 10.4 (pg. 356), describes activities that normally take place in a warehouse. Warehouse personnel receive a picking ticket, locate the goods, take the goods off the shelf (i.e., "pick" the goods), and match the goods with the picking ticket.

The reject stub coming from bubble 2.1 indicates at least two situations that might occur at this point. First, the goods pulled from the shelf might not be those indicated on the picking ticket (i.e., goods have been placed in the wrong warehouse location). Second, sufficient goods may not exist to satisfy the quantity requested. The second situation may arise when goods have been misplaced or when the actual physical balance does not agree with the perpetual inventory balance indicated in the inventory master data. These predicaments must be resolved, and a back order routine may be initiated to order the missing goods for the customer.

In process 2.2, warehouse personnel write the quantities "picked" on the picking ticket (thus "completing" the ticket) and forward the picking ticket (along with the goods) to the shipping department.

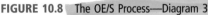

FIGURE 10.8   The OE/S Process—Diagram 3

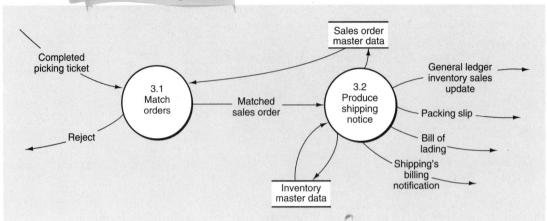

Figure 10.8, a lower-level view of bubble 3.0 in Figure 10.4 (pg. 356), describes activities that normally take place in a shipping department. The figure shows that process 3.1 receives two data flows, namely the completed picking ticket from process 2.2 of Figure 10.7 (pg. 359) and data retrieved from the sales order master data. The shipping clerk matches the quantity of the goods, the quantity on the picking ticket, and the quantity stored in the sales order master data (i.e., the order quantity in Figure 10.6 on pg. 358). Alternatively, the clerk could compare the goods with the quantities on the picking ticket and then enter that quantity (or a corrected quantity) into the computer, where a comparison to the order quantity would take place. If the details agree, the matched sales order is forwarded to process 3.2. If the details of the data flows do not agree, process 3.1 rejects the order and initiates procedures for resolving any discrepancies.

When process 3.2 receives a matched sales order from process 3.1, it produces and disseminates notices of the shipment and updates the sales order and inventory master data. The sales order master data is updated to reflect the fact that the goods have been picked, packed, and shipped. The inventory master data is updated to change the quantity allocated for the sales order to an actual shipment, thus reducing the quantity of inventory on hand (unless the balance was directly reduced in process 1.3 in Figure 10.5 [pg. 357]). We generally expect the dissemination of notices will include the following data flows:

- Shipping notifies billing to begin the invoicing process. This could take many forms, including a message received on a computer screen or a report of shipments that have not been billed.
- A **bill of lading** is used, which is a contract between the shipper and the carrier in which the carrier agrees to transport the goods to the shipper's customer. The carrier's signature on the bill of lading, or the customer's signature on some other form of receipt, substantiates the shipment. A copy of the bill of lading, indicating customer and shipping destination, may be attached to the outside of the package.
- A **packing slip** is inserted into the package (a copy may be attached to the outside of a package) and identifies the customer, the shipment destination, and the contents of the package.
- The flow "General ledger inventory sales update" notifies the general ledger process that inventory has been sold and the cost of goods sold has increased. Even

though this entry (reduce inventory/increase cost of goods sold) may be made directly to the general ledger by the OE/S process, we depict the update as being completed by the general ledger *process*. (As noted earlier, this flow may have emanated from subprocess 1.3 if inventory was to be relieved at that time.)[13]

Logical Data Descriptions

Figure 10.4 shows that the OE/S process employs the following five data stores:

- Customer master data
- Inventory master data
- Marketing data
- Sales order master data
- Accounts receivable master data

The OE/S process is responsible for performing *data maintenance* and *master data updates* on all but the last data store in this list. The accounts receivable master data is the responsibility of the billing/accounts receivable/cash receipts process and will be described in Chapter 11. As noted earlier, before goods can be sold to ongoing customers, data maintenance must be performed to create a customer master record, including a credit limit, and to create one or more inventory master records, including sales prices and warehouse locations. This section discusses the purpose and contents of the first four data stores.

Customer master data contain a record of every customer with whom we are authorized to regularly do business. Each record includes a unique customer number and data that identify the particular characteristics of each customer, such as name, address, telephone number, industry, and so forth. It also stores various credit data. Although customer data may be altered directly during the OE/S process, proper control techniques require that all such master data changes (i.e., data maintenance) be documented, approved, and executed by someone other than the individuals who create sales orders, and that a report of all data changes be reviewed periodically.

Inventory master data contain a record of each item that is stocked in the warehouse or is regularly ordered from a vendor. These records are used to manage inventory, and they are the subsidiary ledger for the inventory account in the general ledger. Each record includes a unique item number, unit of issue, weight, volume, warehouse location, price, cost, and so on.

Earlier, we noted that the *marketing data* is the repository of a variety of sales-oriented data, some of which result from recording sales events (i.e., processed sales orders), and some of which originate from activities that do not culminate in completed sales, such as presales activities. Typically, these data include items discussed in an earlier section, such as economic forecasts, census reports, responses to market research questionnaires, customer buying habits, customer demographics, and the like. Collection and maintenance of these data are activities of the CRM system.

---

[13]In the system shown, after the shipment is recorded, the quantity on hand in the inventory master data (the subsidiary ledger) is reduced for the amount shipped, and the GL is updated (a debit to COGS and a credit to inventory), there is no matching of this expense with any revenue because an invoice has not been recorded. If because of this timing difference there is a material mismatch of revenues and expenses, and the organization needs to close an accounting period and produce financial statement, then an adjusting entry might be made. In other systems, the revenue and expense entries may occur simultaneously.

As shown in the DFDs, records in the **sales order master data** are created on completion of a sales order. Then, after the goods have been shipped, the sales order record is updated. Refer to Figure 10.6 (pg. 358) for examples of the kinds of data that are stored. Depending on how the OE/S process is designed and how many updates take place during the process, the sales order master data may include the time and date of the picking, packing, and shipping of the goods and who completed each step.

Logical Database Design

In Chapter 5, we compared data as it would be stored in a file(s) with that same data when stored in a database, with emphasis on the relational database model (see, in particular, Figures 5.2 and 5.3 on pages 144 and 148, respectively). In this section, we will depict the relational tables for the data we have just mentioned in the discussion of the customer master data and the sales order master data.

To show these relational tables, we should first redraw the E-R diagram appearing in Figure 5.9, pg. 162 in Chapter 5. **Figure 10.9** is our new E-R diagram. It differs from Figure 5.9 in that the SALES event in Chapter 5 now has been divided into three events comprising the sale—namely picking goods (STOCK_PICK event in Figure 10.9), shipping goods (SHIPMENTS event), and billing the customer for the shipment (SALES_INVOICES event). Before proceeding, study Figure 10.9 and compare it to Figure 5.9. From Figure 10.9, we have developed the relational tables appearing in **Figure 10.10** (pg. 364).

Before going on, we should note three things about these figures. First, you should observe that the SALES_RELATIONS relationship and table gradually accumulate a record of the events as they progress from a customer's order through to sending an invoice to the customer. The box around this relationship indicates that we will have a relation in our database for this relationship, whereas the other relationships will not have a corresponding relation. Second, if you look carefully, you will see that some of the relationships, and attributes in the relations, really aren't needed. For example, we actually don't need the *activate* relationship, nor do we need the related sales order number in the STOCK_PICK relation; we can get that from SALES_RELATIONS. As you see, this model is not yet fully normalized. We include the "extra" relationships and redundant attributes to help you see the logical sequence of events. Third, the notes on Figure 10.9 indicate that this is a simplified model. Certainly, realistic models must deal with partial picking, shipping, and invoicing.

Compare the CUSTOMERS relation in Figure 10.10 with the discussion of the customer master data, and observe that the data elements (attributes) are *essentially* the same. Note that the relation allows for both a customer address and a "ship-to" address, each being subdivided into four attributes—street address, city, state, and ZIP code—to facilitate database inquiries using any of these attributes. Now compare the SALES_ ORDERS and SALES_RELATIONS relations to the sales order in Figure 10.6 and the discussion of the sales order master data. Here we see some marked differences. The two sales order tables contain far fewer data elements than the sales order display itself because many of the elements needed to complete the display are available from other relations. Recall that a major advantage of a database approach to data management is the elimination of redundant data items. Therefore, using the Cust_No from SALES_ ORDERS, we can obtain the customer's name, address, ship-to name, ship-to address, and credit terms from the CUSTOMERS relation. Likewise, using Item_No from SALES_ RELATIONS, we can obtain from the INVENTORY relation the description of the goods and unit selling price. Finally, using the primary key from SALES_RELATIONS (i.e., the *combination* of SO_No/Item_No), we can determine the quantity picked/shipped.

FIGURE 10.9   Entity-Relationship (E-R) Diagram for the OE/S Process

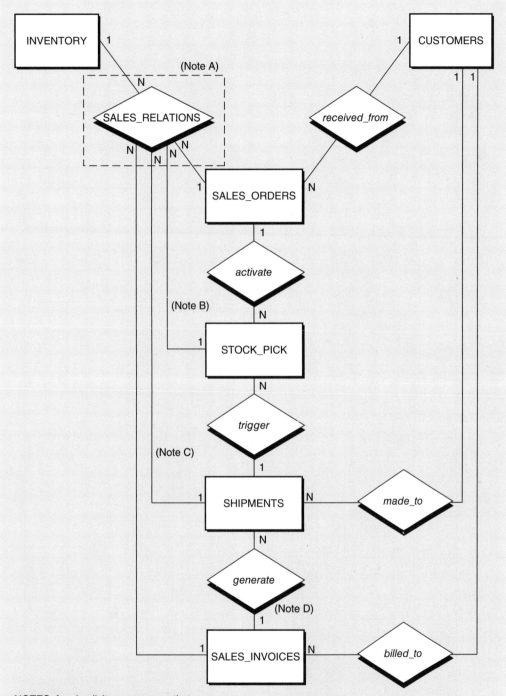

NOTES, for simplicity, we assume that:
A—See page 362 for an explanation of the box around SALES_RELATIONS and why the model is not fully normalized.
B—All goods ordered are picked (no partial picks).
C—All goods picked are shipped (no partial shipments).
D—All shipments are invoiced in full (no partial invoices).

FIGURE 10.10 Selected Relational Tables (Partial) for the OE/S Process

Shaded_Attribute(s)	= Primary Key

CUSTOMERS

Cust_No	Cust_Name	Cust_Street	Cust_City	Cust_State	Cust_ZIP	Ship_to_Name	Ship_to_Street	Ship_to_City	Ship_to_State	Ship_to_ZIP	Credit_Limit	Last_Revised	Credit_Terms
1234	Acme Co.	175 Fifth St	Beaufort	SC	29902	Same	Same	Same	Same	Same	5000	20060101	2/10,n/30
1235	Robbins, Inc	220 North Rd	Columbia	SC	29801	ALine Fabric	2 Main St	Greenwood	SC	29845	10000	20070915	n/60
1236	Jazzy Corp.	45 Ocean Dr	Hilton Hd	SC	29910	Same	Same	Same	Same	Same	0	20070610	COD

SALES ORDERS

SO_No	SO_Date	Cust_No	Cust_PO_No	Cust_PO_Date	Ship_Via	FOB_Terms
5677	20071216	1235	41523	20071212	UPS	Ship Pt
5678	20071216	1276	A1190	20071214	Best way	Ship Pt
5679	20071216	1236	9422	20071216	Fed Ex	Destin

STOCK PICK

Pick_No	Pick_Date	Picked_By	SO_No	Ship_No
9436	20071215	Butch	5676	94101
9437	20071215	Rachel	5677	94102
9438	20071216	Ace	5678	94103

INVENTORY

Item_No	Item_Name	Price	Location	Qty_on_Hand	Reorder_Pt
936	Machine Plates	39.50	Macomb	1,500	950
1001	Gaskets	9.50	Macomb	10,002	3,500
1010	Crank Shafts	115.00	Tampa	952	500
1025	Manifolds	45.00	Tampa	402	400

SHIPMENTS

Ship_No	Ship_Date	Shipped_By	Cust_No	Invoice_No
94101	20071215	Jason	1293	964
94102	20071216	Carol	1235	965
94103	20071216	Jason	1249	966

SALES INVOICES

Invoice_No	Invoice_Date	Invoice_Total	Cust_No
964	20071216	549.00	1293
965	20071216	9575.00	1235
966	20071217	1580.00	1249

SALES RELATIONS

SO_No	Item_No	Qty_Ordered	Pick_No	Qty_Picked	Ship_No	Qty_Shipped	Invoice_No	Qty_Invoiced	Amt_Invoiced
5676	1074	60	9436	60	94101	60	964	60	549.00
5677	1001	100	9437	100	94102	100	965	100	950.00
5677	1010	75	9437	75	94102	75	965	75	8625.00
5678	936	40	9438	40	94103	40	966	40	1580.00

The remainder of Figure 10.10 needs no additional comment, except to note once again that many relations contain relatively few attributes because most of the data needed to complete a picking ticket or shipping notice reside in other relations. For example, an actual picking ticket often takes the physical form of a duplicate copy of the sales order document. The primary item that differentiates the two documents is the warehouse location, which must appear on the picking ticket to facilitate the actual picking of the goods. After the goods are picked, the picking ticket *document* can be *completed* by adding the quantity picked, date picked, and identification of the person who picked the items, which are attributes that appear in the two relations.

Physical Description of the OE/S Process

Before describing a "typical" physical implementation of an OE/S process, let's discuss some key technologies that enable modern sales order processes. These are image-based technologies that facilitate electronic data capture and digital image processing.

Electronic Data Capture

Although a variety of methods exist for capturing data electronically, the interest here is in image-based technologies. Increasingly, these technologies are being used to eliminate the need to key data (a major source of data entry error) and to eliminate voluminous files of paper documents by maintaining electronic copies.[14]

Controls

The most common technology is probably that of bar coding. **Bar code readers** are devices that use light reflection to read differences in bar code patterns to identify a labeled item. Although the most common place for bar code readers is in grocery, department, and other retail stores, warehouses also use bar coding systems extensively for inventory tracking. Similarly, delivery and courier companies, such as FedEx® and UPS™, use such coding systems to track inventory items and packages during shipping transfers.

E-Business

In many cases, bar coding schemes are not feasible. For instance, when customers mail payments, converting payment amounts into bar codes is not necessary. On the other hand, utility and credit card companies frequently ask customers to handwrite the amount of the payment on the remittance slip. In such cases, **optical character recognition** is used—similar to the way bar code readers work—for pattern recognition of handwritten or printed characters. Although such systems have more difficulty than bar code readers in consistently reading data (due mainly to inconsistencies in writing characters), optical character recognition fulfills a need where bar coding is not feasible. Note, however, that both bar code readers and optical character recognition are technologies designed to eliminate the need for individuals to key data and the accompanying potential risk of error.

The third major optical input technology is the *scanner*. **Scanners** are input devices that capture printed images or documents and convert them into electronic digital signals (i.e., into binary representations of the printed image or document) that can be stored on computer media. Scanners are crucial to the increased use of electronic digital imaging to drive business processes and facilitate management decision making.

---

[14]These technologies are key elements of online transaction entry (OLTE) systems introduced in Chapter 3 and the control *automated data* entry introduced in Chapter 9.

Digital Image Processing

E-Business **Digital image processing systems** are computer-based systems for the capture, storage, retrieval, and presentation of images of objects such as pictures and documents. Once the domain of large mainframe computers only, these systems are now easily implemented on personal computer platforms. Because of the quantity of paper documents that typically flow through an organization's business process, the ability to quickly scan, store, add information to, and retrieve documents on an as-needed basis can significantly reduce both labor costs for filing and the physical storage space and structures necessary for storing paper-based files. The following describes the major steps in a typical digital image processing system.

In the *input* stage, *scanners* are used to capture images, such as pictures and documents. In some cases, pieces of data from, or associated with, the object must be manually entered. Examples of data that must be keyed include data from a document that could not be read directly by the OCR incorporated into the scanner, or data needed to identify an image, such as the reference data for a scanned article or the identification of a scanned picture. The stored documents are organized and filed (much like their paper counterparts). Electronic folders are created to store and organize related documents. As a result, the image processes logically parallel the same processes used in traditional paper systems, without the headache of storing the mounds of paper and delivering requested documents by hand across the building or even across the world.

The digital image processing system can make an electronic image instantly available anywhere in the world where a connection to the system can be established. For example, a clerk might input a customer number to obtain a list of related source document images, such as customer orders, for that customer. One of the documents—the one with the sought-after information—is then selected for display. In addition to screen output, images also may be printed.

Enterprise Systems After a document has been input, additional processing may take place. For example, additional data related to the document might be added, or someone might act on data contained in, or associated with, the document. Documents might be routed, using *workflow* components of enterprise systems, to those needing to work on a document. Retrieval and processing capabilities may be incorporated into existing applications. In this way, the images become an integral part of the information system. Recall that in Chapter 5 we discussed the move toward object-oriented databases that are capable of handling object data—such as images—and that we noted the move toward enabling object storage within relational databases. A major part of the demand for object-capable databases is the management of a vast array of document images. Linkage of these images into an enterprise system can make accessibility much greater and easier because the information can readily be distributed throughout the organization to where it is needed.

The OE/S Process

Enterprise Systems We have assumed a particular physical model to illustrate the OE/S process. As you examine the physical features of the process, you should notice a close resemblance between those features and the logical design of the OE/S process, as presented in Figures 10.3 (pg. 355), 10.4 (pg. 356), 10.5 (pg. 357), 10.7 (pg. 359), and 10.8 (pg. 360). You also should see that this system demonstrates the use of an enterprise system and several features of the technology discussed earlier in this chapter. **Figure 10.11** presents a systems flowchart of the model process. Take some time now to examine the flowchart.

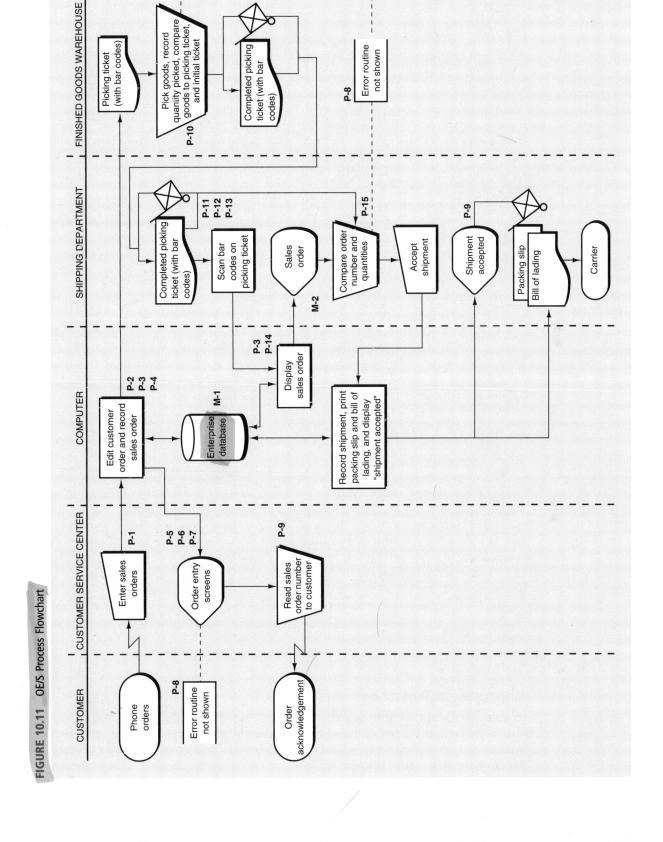

FIGURE 10.11 OE/S Process Flowchart

We start with customer calls received in the customer service center. Customer service representatives (CSRs) may perform a number of services for a customer, such as determining the status of open orders or checking the price and availability of inventory items. Our model assumes that the customer has called in an order; the CSR then invokes the option to enter a sales order and sees a screen much like the one shown earlier in Figure 10.6 (pg. 358). The system then prompts the CSR to enter the *customer number*. If the CSR enters a customer number for which the system has no record, the system rejects the order and the process is terminated.

Assuming the CSR enters a valid customer number, the system automatically retrieves certain *standing data*, such as the customer name, address, and credit terms, from the customer master data. The CSR asks the customer to confirm the name and address to ensure that the correct customer record has been retrieved. Next, the CSR enters the other data in the sales order, guided by the cursor moving to each new position in the *preformatted screen*.

When the CSR enters data for each item ordered, starting with the part number, the system automatically displays the description and price. Finally, the CSR enters the quantity ordered. If the total amount of the current order, any open orders, and the outstanding receivable balance exceeds the customer's credit limit, the operator is warned of this fact, the order is suspended, and the credit rejection procedures are initiated. If the total amount falls within the customer's credit range, the processing continues. Should the balance shown on the inventory data be less than the quantity ordered, back order procedures are initiated.

After the CSR has finished entering the order data, the computer creates a sales order record, updates the inventory master data to allocate the inventory to the sales order, and gives the CSR a sales order number (such as "12071" in Figure 10.6) that the CSR relays to the customer. Simultaneously, a picking ticket, containing a bar code of the sales order number, is printed in the warehouse.

As each item is picked, warehouse personnel insert the picked quantities on the picking ticket. When all the goods have been picked, they compare the goods to the picking ticket, initial the ticket, and then move the goods and the completed picking ticket to the shipping department.

Shipping personnel scan the bar code on the picking ticket to bring the sales order up on their computer screen. After they confirm that this is the correct order and that the quantities are correct, they select the option to record the shipment. This action causes the computer to update the sales order, inventory, and general ledger master data to reflect the shipment and to print a packing slip and bill of lading. The goods are packed, with the packing slip inside, the shipping label (bill of lading) is attached to the box, and the box is given to the carrier for delivery. The completed picking ticket is discarded.

As noted earlier, error routines are initiated if the customer record does not exist, the customer's credit limit is not sufficient, the goods are not available in the requested quantity, the goods picked from the shelf do not agree with the picking ticket, or the goods to be shipped do not match the picking ticket and the sales order.

Management Reporting

In an online system that incorporates an inquiry processing capability, the need for regular preparation of printed management reports is reduced or eliminated. Instead, each manager can use a PC to access a database and retrieve relevant management information. For example, a sales manager could access the marketing database at any time and assess the performance of particular sales people.

FIGURE 10.12   Sample SAP Sales Analysis Report

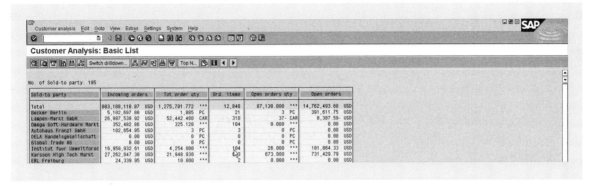

Alternatively, sales reports in many desired formats can be obtained on demand. For example, some of the report options could include sales analyses by part number, product group, customer, or salesperson as well as open order status, sorted and accumulated in a variety of ways. Notice, for example, in Figure 10.6 that the sales area is part of the sales order master data. A manager could run a report analyzing the relative performance of sales areas. **Figure 10.12** illustrates part of one such report. This report can be previewed onscreen as shown and can then be printed, if desired. This report shows sales by customer (sold-to party), including incoming orders; by dollar and quantity; and by the amounts for open orders, that is, those that have not yet been shipped. Monitoring these open orders to ensure prompt shipment is a form of *tickler file*.

Enterprise
Systems

Application of the Control Framework

The methodology for studying application controls was presented in Chapter 9. You might want to review that material before proceeding. In this section, we apply the control framework to the OE/S process. **Figure 10.13** (pp. 370–371) presents a completed *control matrix* for the systems flowchart presented in Figure 10.11 (pg. 367). The *systems flowchart* is annotated to show the location of the various application control plans.[15]

Controls

Control Goals

The control goals listed across the top of the matrix are similar to those presented in Chapters 7 and 9, except that they have been *tailored* to the specifics of this OE/S process.

The following are the *operations process control goals* that are typical for the OE/S process:

- *Effectiveness of operations:* Goals A, B, and C in Figure 10.13 identify three representative *effectiveness goals* for the OE/S process. These goals relate to the reason(s) for

---

[15]The columns for UC and UA are shaded to emphasize that the update goals will not apply in this analysis because the updates are simultaneous with the inputs, and the input controls will address any update completeness and update accuracy issues.

FIGURE 10.13 Control Matrix for the OE/S Business Process

Control Goals of the OE/S Business Process

Recommended control plans	Control Goals of the Operations Process					Control Goals of the Information Process									
	Ensure effectiveness of operations:			Ensure efficient employment of resources (people, computers)	Ensure security of resources (inventory, customer master data)	For sales order inputs (i.e., customer orders), ensure:			For sales order and inventory master data, ensure:		For shipping notice inputs (i.e., shipment data), ensure:			For sales order and inventory master data, ensure:	
	A	B	C			IV	IC	IA	UC	UA	IV	IC	IA	UC	UA
Present Controls															
P-1: Enter customer order close to where the order is received			P-1	P-1			P-1	P-1							
P-2: Customer credit check		P-2			P-2	P-2									
P-3: Populate input screens with master data			P-3	P-3		P-3		P-3			P-3				
P-4: Programmed edit checks			P-4	P-4				P-4							
P-5: Compare input data with master data			P-5	P-5	P-5	P-5									
P-6: Preformatted screens			P-6	P-6				P-6							
P-7: Online prompting			P-7	P-7				P-7							
P-8: Procedures for rejected inputs			P-8	P-8			P-8	P-8				P-8	P-8		
P-9: Confirm input acceptance							P-9					P-9			
P-10: One-for-one checking of picking ticket with the goods			P-10	P-10	P-10						P-10		P-10		

(Continues)

FIGURE 10.13   Control Matrix for the OE/S Business Process (*continued*)

Recommended control plans	Control Goals of the Operations Process					Control Goals of the Information Process									
	Ensure effectiveness of operations:			Ensure efficient employment of resources (people, computers)	Ensure security of resources (inventory, customer master data)	For sales order inputs (i.e., customer orders), ensure:			For sales order and inventory master data, ensure:		For shipping notice inputs (i.e., shipment data), ensure:			For sales order and inventory master data, ensure:	
	A	B	C			IV	IC	IA	UC	UA	IV	IC	IA	UC	UA
P-11: Enter shipment data in shipping			P-11	P-11								P-11	P-11		
P-12: Turnaround document			P-12	P-12							P-12		P-12		
P-13: Automated data entry			P-13	P-13									P-13		
P-14: Independent shipping authorization					P-14						P-14				
P-15: One-for-one checking of goods, picking ticket, sales order					P-15						P-15		P-15		
Missing Controls															
M-1: Independent customer master data maintenance		M-1			M-1	M-1									
M-2: Review open sales orders (tickler file)			M-2									M-2			

Possible effectiveness goals include the following:

A—Provide timely acknowledgement of customer orders

B—Provide assurance of customer's creditworthiness

C—Provide timely shipment of goods to customers.

See Exhibit 10.1 for a complete explanation of control plans and cell entries.

IV = input validity
IC = input completeness
IA = input accuracy
UC = update completeness
UA = update accuracy

which the process exists. Notice that these goals address the issue of satisfying customers, a topic discussed earlier in the chapter, and creditworthiness, a major risk that we face when engaging in credit sales.

- *Efficient employment of resources:* As noted in Chapter 9, people and computers are the resources found in most business processes.
- *Resource security:* Note that in this column, we have named two specific resources that are of concern to the OE/S process. Control plans should be in place to prevent theft or unauthorized sale of merchandise inventory. Equally important are plans designed to preclude unauthorized access to or copying, changing, selling, or destroying customer master data.

The *information process control goals* comprise the second category of control goals in Figure 10.13 (pg. 370–371). To focus our discussion, we have not included other system inputs (i.e., customer inquiries, credit applications, credit-limit changes, and management inquiries). The following are the information process control goals:

- *Input validity (IV):* A *valid* sales order is from an existing, authorized customer—one contained in the customer master data—whose current order falls within authorized credit limits. To be added to the customer master data, a customer should pass an initial credit investigation. By adding the customer to the customer master data, management has provided *authorization* to do business with that customer.
- *Input validity (IV):* A *valid* shipping notice input is one that is supported by both an approved sales order and an *actual* shipment of goods. Failure to achieve these goals may result in loss of goods and overstatement of revenue.
- *Input completeness (IC) and input accuracy (IA) of sales orders and shipping notices:* Failure to achieve these goals may result in inaccurate shipments; shipments not being made, which leads to poor customer service or lost revenue; and shipments made but not recorded, not recorded correctly, or recorded more than once, which leads to errors in revenue, inventory, and accounts receivable.
- *Update completeness (UC) and update accuracy (UA) of the sales order and inventory master data:*[16] We have seen earlier in the chapter that for this particular process the sales order master data is updated at least twice[17]—once when a new sales order is created and later to reflect the shipment of that order. The inventory master data is updated at the same time the sales order is created to allocate the inventory to the sales order and again when the order is shipped to reduce the inventory balance.

Recommended Control Plans

Recall that application control plans include both those that are characteristic of a particular AIS business process and those that relate to the technology used to implement the application. We introduce those new plans here that are particular to the OE/S business process. We first define and explain these controls and then summarize, in **Exhibit 10.1** (pp. 374–376), each cell entry in Figure 10.13 (pp. 370–371) of the control matrix:

---

[16]These update goals will not apply in this analysis because the updates are simultaneous with the inputs, and the input controls will address any update completeness and update accuracy issues.

[17]The sales order could also be updated when a backorder is prepared or cleared, when items are scheduled for delivery, when they are picked, when they are packed, and so on.

- **Customer credit check** (Exhibit 10.1 and Figure 10.13, P-2): This is performed to ensure that an organization does not extend more credit to a customer than is prudent. Balances over this limit may not be collectible and may not be recognizable as a sale under generally accepted accounting principles (GAAP). The credit check may be a simple comparison of the order amount to a credit limit, or the amount ordered might be added to outstanding orders and accounts receivable balances to ensure that the total amount owed by a customer does not exceed an authorized maximum. This control assumes segregation of duties between sales and the function (e.g., credit department) that authorizes and creates customer master records.
- **Compare picking ticket to picked goods** (Exhibit 10.1 and Figure 10.13, P-10): This is an example of *one-for-one checking* that ensures that the correct goods are picked from the shelf and that any errors are detected and corrected in a timely manner (e.g., before the goods get to the shipping department).
- **Independent shipping authorization** (Exhibit 10.1 and Figure 10.13, P-14): This establishes, for the shipping personnel, that someone other than the warehouse personnel authorized the shipment. Typically, this would be accomplished by sending a copy of the sales order from customer service directly to the shipping department or by giving the shipping personnel access to open sales order records on the sales order master data. Without this control, warehouse personnel could cause a shipment by simply sending goods to the shipping department. This control assumes a segregation of duties among sales, the warehouse, and shipping.
- **Compare shipment to sales order and picking ticket** (Exhibit 10.1 and Figure 10.13, P-15): This is an example of *one-for-one checking* that ensures that the shipment will be authorized and accurate. Any discrepancy among these items might indicate an unauthorized or duplicate shipment (no open sales order) or an inaccurate shipment (quantities to be shipped do not agree with the picking ticket or open sales order).
- **Independent customer master data maintenance** (Exhibit 10.1 and Figure 10.13, M-1): This assumes that there is a segregation of duties between the personnel who create the customer record (to authorize sales to the customer) and the personnel who create the sales order (execute the sale). There may be a *written approval* or an *electronic approval* required before a customer record can be created. In this way, we preclude any one person from having the authority to do business with a customer (and approve the credit limit) and creating a sales order for that customer. This control makes the *customer credit check* effective.
- **Review file of open sales orders (tickler file)** (Exhibit 10.1 and Figure 10.13, M-2): This is to detect any shipments that should have taken place. This will ensure that all shipments are made in a timely manner.

Exhibit 10.1 contains a discussion of each recommended control plan listed in the control matrix, including an explanation of how each plan meets the related control goals. As you study the control plans, be sure to see where they are located on the systems flowchart. Also, see whether you agree with (and understand) the relationship between each plan and the goal(s) that it addresses. Remember that your ability to *explain* the relationships between plans and goals is more important than your memorization of the cell entries themselves. For simplicity, we have assumed that most of the plans exist in our system (i.e., are "P" plans), regardless of whether they were specifically mentioned in the narrative or not. One of the control plans described in Chapter 9—namely *digital signatures*—is not used in this particular system because the CSRs communicate directly with the customer on the phone (i.e., their order is not submitted electronically).

EXHIBIT 10.1   Explanation of Cell Entries for Control Matrix in Figure 10.13

P-1: *Enter customer order close to where the order is received.*

- *Effectiveness goals A and C, efficient employment of resources:* Use of this strategy places CSRs in a position to process customer orders immediately, and being familiar with the orders allows the CSRs to input the orders more quickly, which leads to timely acknowledgements and shipments and more orders processed by each representative (efficiency).
- *Sales order input completeness:* By having the CSRs enter the sales data rather than forwarding to a data entry function, the risk of orders getting lost should be reduced.
- *Sales order input accuracy:* Because CSRs are familiar with the type of data being entered and can correct any input errors "on the spot," input accuracy should be improved.

P-2: *Customer credit check.*

- *Effectiveness goal B:* The credit check is performed by ascertaining that the amount of the customer order (plus the amount of any open orders and the amount of any outstanding receivables balance) falls within the credit limit established by the credit department. If the request falls outside the limit, then the control terminates the sale.
- *Security of resources:* Termination of orders exceeding credit limits ensures that the organization protects its resources by dealing only with customers who have demonstrated an ability to satisfy their liabilities.
- *Sales order input validity:* Valid sales orders include those that fall within authorized credit limits (i.e., there is a reasonable expectation of payment).

P-3: *Populate input screens with master data.*

- *Effectiveness goals A and C, efficient employment of resources:* Because the input sales order screens are populated with data from customer and inventory master data, the CSRs use fewer keystrokes for each input (efficiency), enter data more quickly, and provide more timely acknowledgement of customer orders and shipment of goods to customers.
- *Sales order input validity:* If the CSR *correctly* enters a customer code, and the system does not populate the input with customer master data, we presume that there is no matching customer master data and no authorized customer. This prevents the entry of invalid orders.
- *Shipping notice input validity:* When the shipping clerk scans the picking ticket, the system should populate the input with sales order master data. If not, we presume that

there is no matching sales order master data and, therefore, no *authorized* order. This prevents the entry of invalid shipments.

- *Sales order input accuracy:* The automatic retrieval of customer information when the customer code has been entered and inventory data when an item number is entered helps ensure the accuracy of the input data because the CSR keys less data and makes use of the customer and inventory master data that were previously entered and reviewed for accuracy.

P-4: *Programmed edit checks.*
Note: We assume, for example, that input order quantities are edited for *reasonableness.*

- *Effectiveness goals A and C:* By editing and correcting data as it is input, rather than later, we can process orders in a more timely manner.
- *Efficient employment of resources:* Programmed edits provide quick, low-cost editing of input data.
- *Sales order input accuracy:* By editing input data and rejecting erroneous data, input accuracy is improved.

P-5: *Compare input data with master data.*
Note: The CSR compares the screen data to the input customer and item numbers to determine that the numbers were input correctly.

- *Effectiveness goals A and C, efficient employment of resources:* Orders and shipments may be processed more quickly and at a lower cost if errors, such as entering the wrong customer number or wrong item numbers, are detected and prevented from entering the system.
- *Security of resources, sales order input validity:* If there is no customer record in the customer master data, the sale to this customer may not be authorized, and any inventory shipped may be lost.
- *Sales order input accuracy:* By comparing the input data, such as customer number and item numbers, to the data on the screen, the CSR can ensure that data are input correctly.

P-6: *Preformatted screens.*

- *Effectiveness goals A and C, efficient employment of resources:* This simplifies the data entry process, allowing the CSR to enter orders more quickly, which leads to more timely acknowledgements and shipments and allows more orders to be input over a period of time (efficiency).
- *Sales order input accuracy:* Preformatted screens may reduce input errors by populating certain fields and rejecting

(Continues)

EXHIBIT 10.1 Explanation of Cell Entries for Control Matrix in Figure 10.13 (*continued*)

incorrectly formatted fields, thereby preventing the CSR from omitting data or entering data with errors.

P-7: *Online prompting.*

- *Effectiveness goals A and C, efficient employment of resources:* Prompting helps the CSR understand very quickly which data should be entered, which makes the data input process quicker, leads to more timely acknowledgements and shipments, and allows the CSR to input more orders over a period of time (efficiency).

- *Sales order input accuracy:* By forcing the CSR to stop and "accept" the order, online prompting is, in a sense, advising you to check your data entries for accuracy before moving on.

P-8: *Procedures for rejected inputs.*

- *Effectiveness goals A and C, sales order input completeness, sales order input accuracy, shipping notice input completeness, shipping notice input accuracy:* The rejection procedures (i.e., "Error routine not shown" annotations) are designed to ensure that erroneous data not accepted for processing are corrected (accuracy) and resubmitted for processing (completeness) in a timely manner (*effectiveness goals A and C*).

P-9: *Confirm input acceptance.*

- *Sales order input completeness, shipping notice input completeness:* The system tells the CSR and the shipping clerk that the order and the shipment have been accepted.

P-10: *One-for-one checking of picking tickets with the goods.*

- *Effectiveness goal C, efficient employment of resources:* By comparing the goods to the picking ticket (and correcting any picking errors) in the warehouse, rather than later in shipping, we can process shipments in a more timely manner and more efficiently (the warehouse clerk is in a better position to correct picking errors than is the shipping clerk).

- *Security of resources:* By correcting picking errors, we ensure that only goods that were ordered leave the warehouse.

- *Shipping notice input validity, shipping notice input accuracy:* The shipping clerk sends only the quantity of goods that were on the picking ticket, thus ensuring that the goods entered are shipments that will be valid and accurate.

P-11: *Enter shipment data in shipping.*

- *Effectiveness goal C, efficient employment of resources:* Use of this strategy places shipping clerks in a position to process shipments immediately, and being familiar with the shipment allows the clerks to input the shipments more quickly, which leads to timely shipments and more shipments processed by each clerk (efficiency).

- *Shipping notice input completeness:* By having the shipping clerks enter the shipment data rather than forwarding to a data entry function, the risk of shipping notices getting lost should be reduced.

- *Shipping notice input accuracy:* Because shipping clerks are familiar with the type of data being entered and can correct any input errors "on the spot," input accuracy should be improved.

P-12: *Turnaround document (picking ticket).*

- *Effectiveness goal C, efficient employment of resources:* By reducing the amount of data that must be input to record the shipment, we improve the speed and productivity of the shipping personnel.

- *Shipping notice input validity:* The turnaround documents were created at the time the CSR entered the order and were printed in the warehouse. Thus, the shipping clerks are precluded from entering unauthorized shipments.

- *Shipping notice input accuracy:* Using the prerecorded bar code to trigger the event reduces the possibility of input errors.

P-13: *Automated data entry.*

- *Effectiveness goal C, efficient employment of resources:* By reducing the amount of data that must be input to record the shipment, we improve the speed and productivity of the shipping personnel.

- *Shipping notice input accuracy:* Using the prerecorded bar code to trigger the event reduces the possibility of input errors.

P-14: *Independent shipping authorization.*

- *Security of resources:* The system provides the shipping department with an independent authorization (i.e., an open sales order in the enterprise database that was created by the CSR) to ship inventory to a customer. In addition, the plan calls for the system to provide an independent authorization (i.e., a *picking ticket*) to the warehouse to pick goods and send them to the shipping department.

- *Shipping notice input validity:* The shipping department will not record a shipment unless it has received independent authorization to do so. This independent authorization comes in the form of *picking tickets* and the *open sales order* executed by independent functions, the warehouse and the CSR.

(*Continues*)

EXHIBIT 10.1 Explanation of Cell Entries for Control Matrix in Figure 10.13 (*continued*)

P-15: *One-for-one checking of goods, picking ticket, sales order.*

- *Security of resources, shipping notice input validity:* By comparing data on the sales order master data with the data on the *picking ticket* and then comparing these data sets to the actual goods being shipped, this plan ascertains that inventory shipments have been authorized and represent an actual shipment of goods.
- *Shipping notice input accuracy:* By comparing such items as item numbers, quantities, and customer identification, we can ensure that the input of shipping data is accurate.

M-1: *Independent customer master data maintenance.*
Note: We are assuming that this control is missing, even though we are told that there is a credit check and that credit rejection procedures are initiated.

- *Effectiveness goal B:* Only personnel in the credit department, a function that is separate from the sales department, should add new customers to the customer master data.

- *Security of resources:* By precluding sales being made to customers who may not be creditworthy, the organization helps to ensure the security of its resources.
- *Sales order input validity:* Valid sales orders include those that are made to customers for whom management has provided prior *authorization*. This is accomplished here by having the records entered by the credit department.

M-2: *Review open sales orders (tickler file).*

- *Effectiveness goal C:* A tickler file of open sales orders maintained in the enterprise database allows the shipping department to investigate any orders that are open for an unreasonable period of time. Therefore, the plan would provide assurance that goods are shipped to customers on a timely basis.
- *Shipping notice input completeness:* If action is taken to expedite shipments for *all* open sales orders, we ensure that all shipments are recorded.

Summary

E-Business

The OE/S process is critical to revenue generation for the organization, so it is often a priority process for new technology integration. We have discussed one such system in this chapter. You should be aware that different organizations have very differing levels of technology integration in their business processes. As these levels of technology change, the business processes also are altered accordingly. As the business process evolves, so also must the specific internal control procedures necessary to maintain the security and integrity of the process. Keep this in mind as you explore alternative levels of technology. Think about how the control systems change and how the controls in the OE/S process would similarly change given similar technology drivers for the business process.

In this chapter, we presented a technologically advanced order entry and sales system. What's in the future? Well, consider an Internet storefront that many of you use on a regular basis. Buyers can use their PCs to browse through electronic catalogs and compare prices and product specifications, and can make purchases at any hour. And consider that the only recently tapped market of B2B e-commerce is many times larger than predicted. This will mean changes in the types of processes and controls needed to process customer orders.

Consider, for example, the case of L.L. Bean. Leon Leonwood (L.L.) Bean began his business in 1912 with a three-page flyer advertising the Maine Hunting Shoe that he mailed to a list of nonresident Maine hunting license holders. Next came the store, a larger catalog, call-in centers, a toll-free number, 24-hour-a-day store and call-in operations, and finally, a Web site.[18] Recently, L.L. Bean has begun to enhance its Web site and reduce reliance on its catalog. The Web site has been redesigned to make ordering and shipment tracking easier. The site now includes customer ratings and reviews, chatting with call center agents through instant messaging and e-mail, and a "click and call" service that prompts a call within two minutes.[19]

We include here, in **Technology Summary 10.1**, a review of the entity-level controls (e.g., control environment, pervasive controls, and general/IT general controls) that may have an impact on the effectiveness of the OE/S business process controls.

Technology Summary 10.1

CONSIDERING HOW ENTITY-LEVEL CONTROLS AFFECT OE/S BUSINESS PROCESS CONTROLS

The effectiveness of OE/S process controls can depend on the operation of several controls described in Chapter 8. In this summary, we examine some of those relationships.

Segregation of Duties

Several functions in the OE/S process must be segregated for the business process controls to be effective, including the following:

- Authorization to approve credit and create customer master records should be assigned to someone other than those completing the sales orders. For example, customer records might be maintained by a separate function within the marketing department, and the credit limit portion of the record might be maintained by the credit department.
- Before shipping goods, the shipping department checks to see that there is an authorized sales order. This presumes the segregation between marketing (customer sales and service) and logistics (shipping).
- A warehouse function that is separated from the shipping function can provide extra assurance that only authorized and accurate shipments are made. With this organizational setup, the warehouse function must receive a picking ticket directly from customer sales and service, and the shipping function must review an open sales order before shipping any goods.

Additional Manual Controls

Several manual, pervasive, and general controls can affect the performance of the business process controls:

- Counting goods and comparing them to the picking ticket in the warehouse, and counting goods and comparing them to the picking ticket and open sales order in shipping, must be performed well. Supervision of these functions, as well as review of audit trails of accountability documents as goods are exchanged, can ensure the integrity of these processes.
- Physical controls for the perimeter of a warehouse building, as well as the warehouse itself, will reduce the possibility of theft, loss, or destruction of the inventory asset.
- As noted in Technology Summary 9.1 (pg. 318), the performance of these manual controls depends on the quality of the people performing the control activities. Therefore, we expect controls such as *selection and hiring*, *training and education*, *job descriptions*, and *supervision* to be in place.

Automated Controls

All of the OE/S controls performed by the computer depend on the general controls (also known as IT general controls or ITGCs) in Chapter 8. Those controls include *customer credit check*, *programmed edits* (e.g., reasonableness of order amount), and *independent shipping authorization* (e.g., compare input shipment data to open sales orders). We need to know that the programs will perform the controls as designed (e.g., *program change controls*). Also, we need to know that the stored data used by the computer when executing these controls is valid and accurate (e.g., physical and logical access controls). For the OE/S process, we are particularly concerned, for example, with controlled access to the following:

- Customer master records so that one cannot be added without authorization
- Sales order master data so that bogus sales orders cannot be created to force an unauthorized shipment.

---

[18]Company Information at www.llbean.com, accessed March 4, 2010.

[19]"L.L. Bean Follows Its Shoppers to the Web," *Bloomberg Businessweek*, March 1, 2010, p. 43.

Key Terms

order entry/sales (OE/S) process, 344

Web 2.0, 348

picking ticket, 359

customer acknowledgement, 359

bill of lading, 360

packing slip, 360

customer master data, 361

inventory master data, 361

sales order master data, 362

bar code readers, 365

optical character recognition, 365

scanners, 365

digital image processing systems, 366

customer credit check, 373

compare picking ticket to picked goods, 373

independent shipping authorization, 373

compare shipment to sales order and picking ticket, 373

independent customer master data maintenance, 373

review file of open sales orders (tickler file), 373

Review Questions

RQ 10-1 What is the order entry/sales (OE/S) process?

RQ 10-2 What are the major functions performed by the OE/S process? Explain each function.

RQ 10-3 With what internal and external entities does the OE/S process interact?

RQ 10-4 What "key players" would you expect to find in the marketing function's organization chart?

RQ 10-5 Describe Web 2.0. What tools does Web 2.0 include?

RQ 10-6 Describe several ways that *data warehouses* and *data mining* can support the marketing function.

RQ 10-7 Distinguish buy-side and sell-side systems.

RQ 10-8 Discuss how customer relationship management (CRM) systems aid a customer service representative (CSR) in providing service to customers.

RQ 10-9 The following questions concern the logical description of the OE/S process:

    a. What are the three major processes? Describe the subsidiary processes of each major process.

    b. What three exception routines may occur when a customer order is processed?

RQ 10-10 Describe the five master data stores employed by the OE/S process.

RQ 10-11 a. Explain how bar code readers work.

    b. Explain how optical character recognition (OCR) works and how it differs from bar code technology.

    c. Explain how scanners are used to capture data.

RQ 10-12   How is digital image processing used to support the input and management of images and documents?

RQ 10-13   Each of the following questions concerns the control matrix for the OE/S process (Figure 10.13, pp. 370–371) and its related annotated systems flowchart (Figure 10.11, pg. 367):

    a.   What three effectiveness goals does the matrix show?

    b.   In this process, what particular resources do we want to secure?

    c.   What are the two data inputs in this system?

    d.   What constitutes a valid sales order? A valid shipping notice?

RQ 10-14   Describe the key control plans associated with OE/S processes.

RQ 10-15   Describe the impact that entity-level controls (i.e., control environment, pervasive controls, and general/IT general controls) can have on the effectiveness of OE/S business process controls.

Discussion Questions

DQ 10-1   Explain how and where the goals for effectiveness of operations would be shown in the control goal columns of a control matrix prepared for the OE/S process. At a minimum, include the following topics from Chapter 7 in your discussion:

    a.   Differentiate between control goals for the operations process and control goals for the information process.

    b.   Distinguish between effectiveness and efficiency, and between effectiveness and security of resources.

DQ 10-2   "A control plan that helps to attain operational effectiveness by 'providing assurance of creditworthiness of customers' also helps to achieve the information process control goal of sales order input validity." Do you agree? Discuss fully.

DQ 10-3   Examine the systems flowchart in Figure 10.11. Discuss how this process implements the concept of segregation of duties, discussed in Chapter 8. Be specific as to which entity (or entities) performs each of the four processing functions (authorizing, executing, recording, and safeguarding resources) mentioned in Chapter 8 (assuming that all four functions are illustrated by the process).

DQ 10-4   What goals for the OE/S process (both operations process and information process goals) would be more difficult to achieve with an enterprise system?

DQ 10-5   Describe how *data mining* and a *CRM system* might be used by any of the managers depicted in Figure 10.1 (pg. 345), a horizontal perspective of the OE/S process, or in Figure 10.2 (pg. 347), a vertical perspective of the OE/S process.

DQ 10-6   Describe how *Web 2.0* tools might be used by any of the managers depicted in Figure 10.1, a horizontal perspective of the OE/S process, or in Figure 10.2, a vertical perspective of the OE/S process.

DQ 10-7   An *enterprise system* supports a business process by:

    a.   Facilitating the functioning of the business process.

    b.   Providing records that business events have occurred.

    c.   Storing data for decision making.

Describe how the enterprise system depicted in Figure 10.11 (pg. 367) provides support in these three areas.

Short Problems

SP 10-1   Among the three functional entities (marketing, finance, and logistics) shown in Figure 10.1 (pg. 345), what goal conflicts could exist, and how might this affect the results of the OE/S process?

SP 10-2   The chapter presented a brief example of how the OE/S process might or might not support the decision-making needs of marketing managers. For each of the functional positions shown in the organization chart of Figure 10.2 (pg. 347), speculate about the kinds of information each might need to support decision making, and indicate whether the typical OE/S process would provide that information. Be specific.

SP 10-3   Using the following table as a guide, describe for each function from Figure 10.1:

    a.   A risk (an event or action that will cause the organization to fail to meet its goals/objectives)

    b.   A control/process or use of technology that will address the risk

Function	Risks	Controls and Technology
Marketing		
Finance		
Sales Order Department		
Logistics (warehouse and shipping)		

SP 10-4   Assume that a computerized credit-checking procedure operates as follows:

As orders are entered into the computer by a CSR, the computer calculates the total of the customer order and adds to this the customer's outstanding balance from the accounts receivable master data and the customer's outstanding orders on the sales order master data (i.e., orders not yet billed). This total (customer order, open accounts receivable, open sales orders) is then compared to the credit limit stored on the customer master record. If the customer's order would cause the credit limit to be exceeded, the computer displays a warning on the sales representative's screen. The sales representative may choose to cancel the order or to override the credit limit warning. If the representative overrides the warning, the computer accepts and records the order.

Assume that you *cannot* change the computer program (i.e., answer the question based on how the system works now), and discuss the effectiveness of this credit-check procedure. Specifically:

a.   Describe what this credit-checking procedure *does* accomplish.

b.   Describe a weakness in this procedure and a control (remember, assume that you *cannot* change the computer program) that would compensate for that weakness.

SP 10-5   The following is a list of six control plans from this chapter or from Chapter 9.

Control Plans

A. Digital signatures
B. Manually reconcile batch totals
C. Preformatted screens
D. One-for-one checking of the goods, picking ticket, and sales order
E. Independent shipping authorization
F. Turnaround document

The following are six statements describing eith control goal or a system deficiency.

Control Goals or System Deficiencies

1.   Blandford Company receives sales orders on its Web server. Several times each day these are downloaded to the order entry and sales system. During the download process several line items are lost.
2.   When goods arrive from the warehouse at Ludlow Company, the shipping clerk keys in the sales order number to retrieve the sales order. Often, the clerk keys the sales order number incorrectly and the wrong sales order is displayed.
3.   In reviewing the shipping department controls, the internal auditors at Fanning, Inc. believe that they found the potential for fraudulent activity. It looks like the process would allow warehouse employees to ship goods without proper authorization.
4.   Granby Company receives customer orders over the Internet. They are concerned that some orders are fraudulent.
5.   Saunders, Inc. customers are complaining that they are not receiving the items and quantities that they ordered.

Match the five control goals or system deficiencies with a control plan that would *best* prevent the system failure from occurring. Because there are six control plans, you should have one letter left over.

Problems

Note: The first problems in this and several other business process chapters ask you to perform activities that are based on processes of specific companies. The narrative descriptions of those processes (the cases) precede each chapter's problems. If your instructor assigns problems related to these cases, he or she will indicate which of them to study.

CASE STUDIES

CASE A: Office Warehouse, Inc. (Order entry)

Office Warehouse, Inc. is a wholesale distributor of office supplies, such as disks, stationery, file cabinets, and related items. Customers receive an updated catalog annually and place orders over the phone.

When a customer calls in with an order, a clerk asks for the customer ID and name. The clerk keys in the customer number, and the computer retrieves the customer record from the customer database and displays it on the clerk's screen. The clerk compares the customer name to the data on the screen to ensure that the customer is legitimate. If everything checks out, the clerk enters the customer's order. After the order is entered, the computer compares the amount of the order to the available credit to ensure that the purchase does not exceed the credit amount limit.

This results in the creation of an entry in the sales event data store and an allocation of inventory. At the end of the day, the sales event data is processed against the customer data and the inventory data, and the sales order is recorded in the sales order master data store. At the same time, a customer acknowledgement is printed in the mailroom and is mailed to the customer. Also, a picking ticket is printed in the warehouse and will be used to assemble the customer's order.

CASE B: Office Warehouse, Inc. (Shipping)

Before starting this case, review the facts of Case A and see that a picking ticket has been printed in the warehouse and will be used to assemble the customer's order. The completed order (goods and attached picking ticket) is forwarded to the shipping department. The shipping clerk keys the sales order number into the computer, and the order is displayed on the screen. The shipping clerk keys in the items and quantities being shipped, and after the computer displays the shipment data, the clerk accepts the input. After the shipment is accepted, the computer updates the sales order and inventory master data and creates a record for billing (in the billing-due list data store). The computer also prints a packing slip and bill of lading on a printer in the shipping department. These shipping documents and the goods are given to the carrier for shipment to the customer.

CASE C: Bondstreet Company (Order entry and shipping)

The Bondstreet Company sells medical supplies to hospitals, clinics, and doctors' offices. Customers place orders over the phone to the Bondstreet customer fulfillment center. Bondstreet uses an ERP system for all of its business processes.

The sales process starts when the customer calls the Bondstreet fulfillment center and gives his name to the CSR. The CSR keys the customer name into the ERP system, and the system retrieves the customer record and displays that data on the sales order entry screen. The CSR examines the data on the screen to ensure that the correct record has been retrieved. If everything checks out, the CSR enters the items and quantities being requested by the customer. As the order is entered, the computer compares the amount of the order to the available credit to ensure that the purchase does not exceed the credit amount limit and allocates the inventory. After the order has been entered, the clerk saves the order, and the computer creates a sales order record, prints a picking ticket in the warehouse, and displays the sales order number to the CSR. The CSR reads the sales order number to the customer.

In the warehouse, clerks pick the goods from the shelf, record the quantity picked and the lot number on the picking ticket, and bring the goods and attached picking ticket to the shipping department. The shipping clerk scans the sales order number from the picking ticket, and the computer displays the order on the screen. The shipping clerk then scans each item and saves the shipment data. The computer updates the sales order and inventory master data (for lot number and quantity shipped) and creates a record for billing (in the billing-due list data store). The computer also prints a packing slip on a printer in the shipping department that the shipping clerk attaches to the goods and gives the goods to the carrier for shipment to the customer.

CASE D: Polis Grocers, Inc. (Customer order and delivery)

Polis Grocers is an online grocery service that provides home delivery of groceries purchased via the Internet. Polis operates in the greater Chicago area and provides delivery to precertified customers. To be certified, the customer must have a user account with an established credit or charge line and rent a refrigerated unit to store delivered goods at their residence should they not be home at the time of delivery.

To enter an order, the customer must log on to the Polis Web site with a user name and password. Using the customer database, the system confirms that the customer has a refrigerator unit in place and that the customer is in good standing. Once approved, the customer can browse the product list that is generated from the inventory database and add items to the shopping cart. When finished, the customer proceeds to the checkout screen to authorize the billing amount to be charged to her account. When the order is submitted, items are allocated in the inventory database, and a new order is recorded in the order database.

In the warehouse, a clerk downloads an outstanding order from the order database to a handheld computer. The downloaded order provides an electronic picking ticket for use in assembling the customer's order. The clerk reads the order from the handheld computer screen, picks the goods, and scans each item as it is placed in a box. As each item is scanned, the computer updates the inventory and order databases. When the order is completed, the clerk presses a button on the handheld, and the computer prints a barcode on the handheld computer. The clerk attaches the barcode to the outside of the box and places the order on a conveyor belt to delivery services.

In delivery services, the delivery person uses another handheld device to read the barcode and access the sales order information from the order database. The items in the box are rechecked per the order and loaded for delivery to the customer. Keying in the confirmation of the order contents by the delivery person triggers the printing of delivery directions and receipt. Upon delivering the groceries and receipt to the customer, the delivery person once again reads the barcode with the handheld device and presses the button for confirmation of delivery. The completion of the delivery is automatically recorded in the order database. The system at this time also updates the customer's master data for billing purposes.

P 10-1   For the case assigned by your instructor, complete the following requirements:

a. Prepare a table of entities and activities.

b. Draw a context diagram.

c. Draw a physical data flow diagram (DFD).

d. Prepare an annotated table of entities and activities. Indicate on this table the groupings, bubble numbers, and bubble titles to be used in preparing a level 0 logical DFD.

e. Draw a level 0 logical DFD.

P 10-2 For the case assigned by your instructor, complete the following requirements:

a. Draw a systems flowchart.

b. Prepare a control matrix, including explanations of how each recommended existing control plan helps to accomplish—or would accomplish in the case of missing plans—each related control goal. Your choice of recommended control plans could come from Exhibit 10.1 (pp. 374–376) plus any additional technology-related control plans from Chapter 9 that are germane to your company's process. Assume that the effectiveness goals in Figure 10.13 (pp. 370–371) are appropriate for the operations process in the case assigned by your instructor.

c. Annotate the flowchart prepared in part (a) to indicate the points where the control plans are being applied (codes P-1, …, P-*n*) or the points where they could be applied but are not (codes M-1, …, M-*n*).

P 10-3 The following is a list of 12 control plans from this chapter or from Chapters 8 and 9.

Control Plans

A. Enter customer order close to where customer order is prepared
B. Turnaround document
C. Independent shipping authorization
D. Populate input screens with master data
E. One-for-one checking of the goods, picking ticket, and sales order
F. Preformatted screens
G. Confirm input acceptance
H. Reasonableness check
I. Backup procedures (for data)
J. Program change controls
K. Digital signature
L. Personnel termination controls

The following are 10 system failures that have control implications.

System Failures

1. Bob Kyte, a former employee of the Saunders Company, gained access to the order entry department after hours and logged on to the system using his old user ID. He entered an order for a legitimate customer but instructed the system to ship the goods to his home address.
2. Acme Inc.'s field salespeople record customer orders on prenumbered order forms and then forward the forms to central headquarters for processing. Frank Rosen, one of Acme's top salespeople, mailed 40 customer orders to headquarters on one Friday afternoon. Unfortunately, they were misplaced in the mail and did not reach headquarters until two weeks later.

3. At Medford Company, clerks key order data into the order entry system at one of several PCs. In the first week of operations of this system, every sales order produced by the computer was missing the data for the "ship-to" address.

4. At Richmond, Inc., the finished goods warehouse delivers goods to the shipping department, accompanied by the picking ticket. Then the shipping department prepares a packing slip. A recent audit discovered that a dishonest warehouse employee had been forging picking ticket documents, allowing him to have goods shipped to an accomplice.

5. The job of Gladys, a programmer at Tolland, Inc., included doing maintenance programming for the order entry application. Gladys altered the programs so that the credit-checking routine was bypassed for one of the customers, a company owned by her uncle.

6. After receiving goods from the warehouse, with attached picking ticket, shipping clerks at Sandisfield Company key in the sales order number, item numbers, and quantities. The computer then records the picking ticket data and prints a packing slip. Customers have been complaining that the packing slip is not accurate as to items and quantities.

7. Clerks in the shipping department at Quincy, Inc. scan picking tickets to bring up the appropriate open sales order and then scan another bar code on the picking ticket to trigger the recording of the shipment. They then prepare a packing slip, attach it to the box, and put the box on the conveyer to the loading dock. They have discovered that some shipments are not being recorded by the system.

8. Customers of LaFond Company have complained that the goods received are not accurate. Sometimes they receive the wrong goods and sometimes the wrong quantity.

9. Becket Company receives orders from established customers over the Internet. Recently the company has received a number of orders from individuals masquerading as legitimate customers.

10. A recent audit of the order-entry process at Stamford Company determined that the clerks were making many errors in entering data such as the customer's name and address from the customer order documents.

Match the 10 system failures with a control plan that would *best* prevent the system failure from occurring. Write one or two sentences explaining each answer. Because there are 12 control plans, you should have two letters left over.

P 10-4   The following is a list of 12 control plans from this chapter or from Chapters 8 and 9.

Control Plans

A. Customer credit check
B. Review open sales orders (tickler file)
C. Manual reconciliation of batch totals
D. Populate input screens with master data
E. Online prompting
F. Preformatted screens
G. Programmed edit checks (reasonableness check)

H. Library controls
I. Confirm input acceptance
J. Operations run manual
K. Segregation of duties
L. Open sales order data

The following are 10 statements describing either the achievement of a control goal (i.e., a system success) or a system deficiency.

Control Goals or System Deficiencies

1. Results in the efficient employment of resources; when the order entry clerk keys the customer number, the computer supplies the customer name, billing address, and other standing data about the customer.
2. Meets both the effectiveness goal that sales are made only to credit-worthy customers and the information systems control goal of sales order input validity.
3. Helps to achieve the information systems control goal of input accuracy by ensuring that dates are entered as MM/DD/YY.
4. Helps to achieve the information systems control goal of input accuracy by providing interactive dialogue with the data entry person.
5. Results in the efficient employment of resources by providing detailed instructions to computer operations personnel for running production jobs.
6. Addresses the information system control goals of both input accuracy and input completeness.
7. Could have prevented the clerk from entering 10 boxes of an item when a customer ordered 10 each of an item.
8. Can be compared to the goods and the picking ticket to prevent unauthorized shipments.
9. Should prevent unauthorized access to programs, files, and documentation.
10. Helps to ensure that goods are received from the warehouses in a timely manner to help to ensure the effectiveness goal of timely shipment of goods to customers.

Match the 10 control goals or system deficiencies with a control plan that would *best* prevent the system failure from occurring. Because there are 12 control plans, you should have two letters left over.

P 10-5   For Figure 10.4 (pg. 356):
Indicate the sequence of activities by putting numbers next to the data flows. For example, the Customer order in the upper left of the diagram would be number "1." Restart the numbers for each bubble. Assign the same number to simultaneous data flows. For example, several different data flows coming out of bubble 3.0 should get the same number.

- For each process bubble, indicate, by placing a "T" on the flow, the flow that triggers the processing activities.
- Label each flow into and out of the data stores and to and from the other processes. These labels should describe the purpose of the flow.
- Annotate each data store to indicate the data's major elements.
- Include on the diagram one-sentence descriptions of each process bubble's activities.

EXHIBIT 10.2   Lexington Company System Narrative to Accompany Problem 10-6

Lexington Company is a small manufacturing company. Customer mail orders are received in the sales order department, where sales order clerks open the orders and review them for accuracy. The sales order clerks enter the orders into the computer, where they are edited by comparing them to stored customer data. The computer displays the edited order on the clerk's screen. The clerk corrects any errors and accepts the order. The order is then recorded on a sales event data store and the sales order master data store. As the order is recorded, it is printed on a printer in the warehouse (the picking ticket). A copy of the sales order is also printed in the computer room and is sent to the customer (a customer acknowledgement). The warehouse personnel pick the goods, annotate the picking ticket to show what has been picked, attach the picking ticket to the goods, and bring them to shipping. Shipping prepares a three-part bill of lading and gives the goods and copy 1 of the bill of lading to the carrier. The picking ticket and copy 2 of the bill of lading are sent to billing, and copy 3 of the bill of lading is filed in shipping.

P 10-6   The narrative of Lexington Company's sales order entry process and systems flowchart of that process are shown in **Exhibit 10.2** and **Figure 10.14** (pg. 388), respectively. Using Exhibit 10.2 and Figure 10.14, do the following:

a.   Prepare a control matrix, including explanations of how each recommended existing control plan helps to accomplish—or would accomplish in the case of missing plans—each related control goal. Your choice of recommended control plans could come from Exhibit 10.1 (pp. 374–376) plus any additional technology-related control plans from Chapter 9 that are germane to your company's process. Assume that the effectiveness goals in Exhibit 10.1 are appropriate for the Lexington operations process.

b.   Annotate the flowchart in Figure 10.14 to indicate the points where the control plans are being applied (codes P-1, ..., P-n) or the points where they could be applied but are not (codes M-1, ..., M-n).

See Exhibit 10.1 for a complete explanation of control plans and cell entries.

P 10-7   This problem should be completed with database software, such as Microsoft Access. As directed by your instructor, submit the completed database file and the printouts noted below.

1.   Using the E-R diagram in Figure 10.9, select any three or four related entities and implement them as tables using Microsoft Access (or any other database software acceptable to your instructor). Link the tables using the cardinalities shown in the figure. For the tables, you may use attributes shown in Figure 10.10 or create different attributes.

2.   Create forms for each table from part 1 of this problem and use the forms to populate the tables with representative data. Forms should be in good order, readable, and properly formatted. Create at least three records in each table. Print out the populated tables and one instance of each form.

3.   Design three queries using the tables from part 1 of this problem. Print out the output of each query and attach an explanation as to why someone would be interested in the output of each query.

4.   Using the report function in Access, design a report for each query from part 3 of this problem. Reports should be in good order, readable, and properly formatted. Print out each report.

ACCESS

FIGURE 10.14 Lexington Company Systems Flowchart to Accompany Problem 10-6

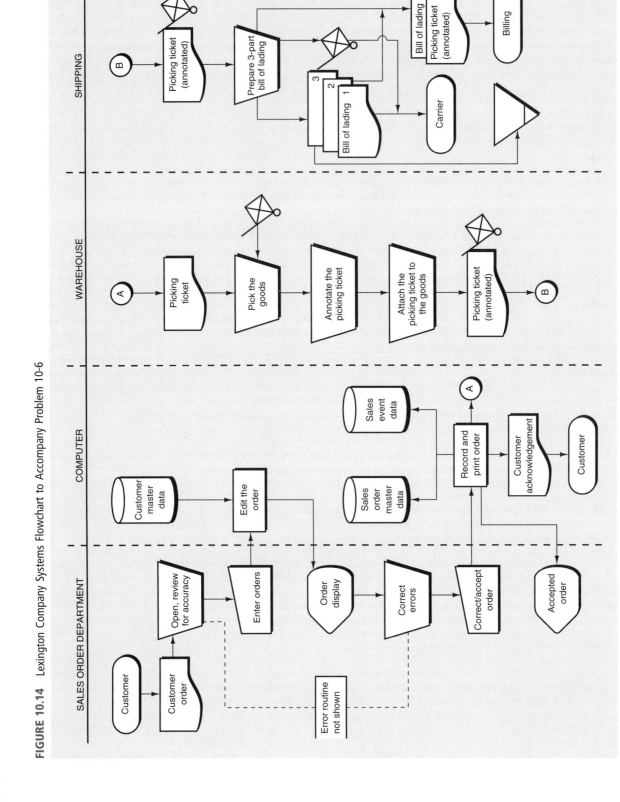

The Billing/Accounts Receivable/Cash Receipts (B/AR/CR) Process

Learning Objectives

After reading this chapter, you should be able to:

- Describe the relationship between the B/AR/CR process and its business environment.
- Illustrate the potential of the B/AR/CR process to assist management decision making.
- Summarize how enterprise systems, e-business, and other technologies can improve the effectiveness of the B/AR/CR process.
- Depict the logical and physical characteristics of the B/AR/CR process.
- Prepare a control matrix for some typical billing and cash receipts processes, including an explanation of how business process control plans can accomplish operations and information process control goals.

Stacey Cox is the vice president and CFO at CableSystems, Inc., an independent provider of cable television and high-speed Internet services.[1] Stacey has developed a new way to bill customers and receive payments. This is how Stacey, in her own words, described the proposed system to Chuck Wild, the president and CEO of CableSystems, and other VPs.

For some time now, we have known that we need to reduce the number of days between the date customers are billed each month and the date the customers' payments become available to CableSystems.[2] This is what I propose.

Each month we will place customer bills on our Web site and send an e-mail telling each customer that his or her bill is there. This is called *electronic bill presentment*.

Customers will log on to our Web site, view the bill, and execute payment. This is called *electronic bill payment*.

Because customers will receive their bills more quickly and make their payments in a timelier manner, the cash flow for CableSystems will improve, and we will have

---

[1] The story of CableSystems, Inc. and the cast of characters are disguised and adapted from a number of sources describing electronic bill presentment and payment (EBPP) services for B2C billing processes at real-world companies. In Chapter 13, we describe electronic invoice presentment and payment (EIPP), the B2B equivalent of EBPP.

[2] This is commonly referred to as days sales outstanding (DSO) and is a key measure of the effectiveness of the B/AR/CR process.

additional funds available to invest in new technology and programming. In addition, the costs associated with preparing and sending bills will be reduced by about 12 percent.

Dora Wolman, the VP of marketing, liked the idea of customers coming to the Web site each month. CableSystems could place advertising on the site to encourage customers to buy additional goods and services.

Bill Shuman, the VP and CIO, added that the Web site also could be designed to provide customer information and services. For example, customers could review their bills and send e-mails to customer service if they wanted to dispute any portion of it. Dora particularly liked Bill's idea because she has been trying to reduce the billing-related calls to the customer service center.

By the end of the meeting, the group decided that the development of an electronic bill presentment and payment (EBPP) system would create great advantages for CableSystems, Inc. Chuck thanked Stacey for her presentation and gave the go-ahead for the project.

Synopsis

This chapter covers the billing/accounts receivable/cash receipts (B/AR/CR) process. A close relationship exists between this process and the order entry/sales (OE/S) process you studied in Chapter 10. In fact, many firms do not distinguish the two processes as clearly as we do in this book. And, as noted in Chapter 10, the expense (shipment) and revenue (billing) transaction may be performed at the same time. Some would also describe this combination of the OE/S and B/AR/CR processes as the "revenue cycle." In combination, the OE/S and B/AR/CR processes comprise the order-to-cash process depicted in Figure 2.7 on pg. 55 in Chapter 2.

Enterprise
Systems

E-Business

Controls

This chapter first defines the B/AR/CR process and describes its activities. In addition to recording the relevant business events, we emphasize the importance of this process in meeting customer needs and show how companies have used the B/AR/CR process to gain competitive advantage. This includes exploring the technologies used to leverage the process and to compete in an increasingly *enterprise systems* and *e-business* driven environment. Based on this business environment, we explore the imprint of the B/AR/CR process on the organization, again taking both a horizontal and a vertical perspective. We follow this with a discussion of both the logical and physical process implementation. As in Chapter 10, *control* issues are dispersed throughout the chapter and are summarized by using the control framework of Chapter 9.

Introduction

The OE/S process performs the critical tasks of (1) processing customer orders and (2) shipping goods to customers. The B/AR/CR process completes the order-to-cash process by accomplishing three separate yet related functions: (1) billing customers, (2) managing customer accounts, and (3) securing and recording payment for goods sold or services rendered.

The **billing/accounts receivable/cash receipts (B/AR/CR) process** is an interacting structure of people, equipment, activities, and controls designed to create information flows and records that accomplish the following:

- Support the repetitive work routines of the credit department, the cashier, and the accounts receivable department.[3]
- Support the problem-solving processes of financial managers.
- Assist in the preparation of internal and external reports.

First, the B/AR/CR process supports the repetitive work routines of the departments listed by capturing, recording, and communicating data resulting from the functions of billing customers, managing customer accounts, and collecting amounts due from customers. Next, the B/AR/CR process supports the problem-solving processes involved in managing the controller and treasury functions. For example, the credit manager, reporting to the treasurer, might use an accounts receivable aging report in making decisions about extending further credit to customers, dunning[4] customers for payment, or writing off worthless accounts. Finally, the B/AR/CR process assists in the preparation of internal and external reports, including GAAP-based financial statements.

The B/AR/CR process occupies a position of critical importance to an organization. For example, an organization needs a rapid billing process, followed by close monitoring of receivables, and a quick cash collections process to convert sales into working resources (e.g., cash) in a timely manner. Keeping receivables at a minimum should be a major objective of a B/AR/CR process. Although we tend to associate the B/AR/CR process with mundane recordkeeping activities, the process also can be used to improve customer relations and competitive advantage. We discuss more about the strategic importance of the B/AR/CR process later in this chapter. First, let's take a look at the organizational aspects of the B/AR/CR process.

Organizational Setting

Figure 11.1 (pg. 392) and **Table 11.1** (pg. 393) present a horizontal view of the relationship between the B/AR/CR process and its organizational environment. The figure shows typical information flows,[5] depicted as documents, generated or captured by the B/AR/CR process. The flows are superimposed onto the organizational structures related to the B/AR/CR process and the entities with which the B/AR/CR process interacts (customers, banks, and other business processes such as OE/S, general ledger, etc.). Take some time now to review the information flows of Figure 11.1.[6]

---

[3]To focus our discussion, we have assumed that these departments are the primary ones related to the B/AR/CR process. For a given organization, however, the departments associated with the B/AR/CR process may differ.

[4]Dunning is a pressing, usually written, demand for payment.

[5]As described in this chapter, organizations can receive payments directly from their customers or indirectly via banks and other service providers. In Figure 11.1 and Table 11.1 and throughout most of this chapter we describe the latter approach with payment notification coming from the bank. Case studies included in the problems at the end of the chapter depict cash receipts processes in which payments are received directly from customers.

[6]Figure 11.1 and Table 11.1 do not depict the flows associated with managing customer accounts during the time between the billing and cash receipts processes. Those flows and processes are depicted in Figure 11.6 on pg. 404.

Figure 11.1 and Table 11.1 reveal five information flows that function as vital communications links among various operations departments, business processes, and external entities. Although Figure 11.1 depicts the flows using a document symbol, most of them can be implemented using electronic communications (e.g., *workflow*) and data stored in the enterprise database.

We briefly explain each flow here to give you a quick introduction to the B/AR/CR process:

- Flow 1 apprises the billing section of the accounts receivable department that a shipment has taken place. The shipping notice need not be a document; billing might be "informed" via *workflow* or a computer batch file of shipping notices. Alternatively, the billing process may be automatically triggered by the shipment—and thus a continuous flow, without interruption, between the OE/S and B/AR/CR processes.
- Flow 2a is the invoice going to the customer. This could be a mailed paper invoice or an "electronic bill/invoice presentment." Flows 2b and 2c "inform" (via documents or electronic notices) the payment applications and general ledger

FIGURE 11.1   A Horizontal View of the B/AR/CR Process

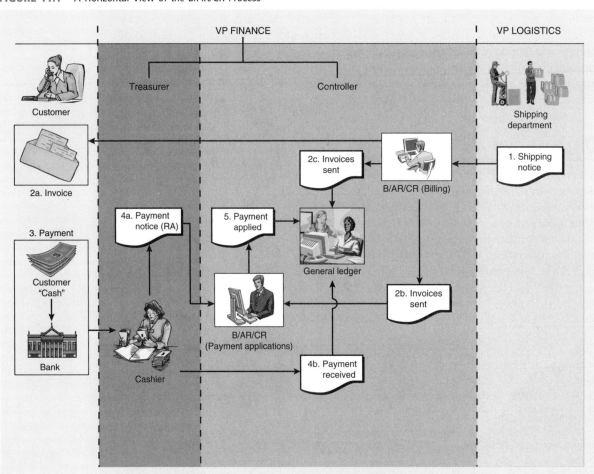

TABLE 11.1 Description of Horizontal Information Flows

Flow No.	Description
1	Shipping department informs the accounts receivable department (billing section) of shipment.
2	Accounts receivable department (billing) sends invoice (2a) to customer, accounts receivable department (payment applications [2b]), and general ledger process (2c).
3	Customer makes payment to bank and bank notifies cashier of the payment. This notice includes the amount received—and deposited—as well as details from the RA (e.g., customer, invoice number[s], amounts paid).
4	Cashier informs accounts receivable department (payment applications [4a]) of the payment details from the RA and general ledger process (4b) of payment amounts/deposits.
5	Accounts receivable (payment applications) informs general ledger process of payment posted AR.

departments/processes that an invoice has been sent. The general ledger uses flow 2c to update sales and accounts receivable for the sale.[7]

- Flow 3 is the customer payment, shown as going to the bank as a check or possibly as an "electronic bill/invoice payment." The bank then notifies the cashier of the payment. As noted in Table 11.1, this notice includes the amount received—and deposited—as well as details from the RA (e.g., customer, invoice number[s], amounts paid).

- In flow 4a, the cashier "informs" the payment applications process of the payment details from the RA. In flow 4b, the cashier informs the general ledger process of the payment amounts/deposits. Again, these flows could be electronic.

- After matching flows 2b and 4a, the payment applications section posts the payment to the customer's account and notifies the general ledger via flow 5. After matching flows 5 and 4b, the general ledger updates accounts receivable and cash (and cash discounts) for the payment.

Let's examine the important control features implicit in the assignment of responsibilities in Figure 11.1. First, we see that the billing function receives external *authorization* to begin the billing process in the form of a notice from the sales order department that a sales order has been approved (see flow 4d in Figure 10.1 on pg. 345). Then we see the notification from logistics (flow 1 in Figure 11.1) that goods have actually been shipped. Also note the separation of the key players within the finance function, the treasurer and the controller. Most organizations divorce the operational responsibility over the security and management of funds (treasurer) from the recording of events (controller). For example, we see that the payment applications section within the controller's area (*recording* the payment) is separated from the cashier within the treasurer area (*custody* of the cash—in this case "custody" is via a direct relationship with the bank and control of the bank accounts).

Controls

Using Technology to Optimize Cash Resources

The B/AR/CR process provides several opportunities to cut costs and accelerate cash flows through emerging technologies and improved management processes. The goal for

---

[7]As noted in Chapter 10, the timing of the recording in the general ledger of this billing transaction and the related shipment transaction may depend on how close together these two activities occur and the software employed.

treasurers, who are responsible for managing an organization's cash resources, is to make funds available so that they can be used to acquire revenue-generating assets, be invested to earn interest, or be used to reduce debt, thus saving interest charges. Of course, before cash can be invested or used for debt reduction, it first must be received and deposited. The overall management objective is to reduce costs and shorten, as much as possible, the time from the beginning of the selling process to the ultimate collection of funds. Therefore, we want to direct technology and management processes at billing, cash receipts, or both.

In the billing process, the cash management goal is to get invoices to customers as quickly as possible, with the hope of reducing the time it then takes to obtain customer payments. Having the B/AR/CR process produce invoices *automatically* helps ensure that invoices are sent to customers shortly after the goods have been shipped. **Technology Summary 11.1** describes *electronic bill presentment and payment (EBPP)* systems, introduced at the start of the chapter in the CableSystems story, which help achieve more timely billing *and* cash receipts at reduced cost.

EBPP is much more likely in the B2C space, where the billing organization can expect consumers to go to a number of Web sites to pay their bills (or use a consolidating service or online banking service). In the B2B space, where the term is *electronic invoice presentment and payment (EIPP)*, the biller may not be in a position to require that vendors pay using a particular method. This will be explored further in Chapter 13.

In those cases where *electronic bill payment* does not follow *electronic bill presentment*, the treasurer must implement other methods to reduce potential delays in collecting/

Technology Summary 11.1

Electronic Bill Presentment and Payment (EBPP) Systems

Electronic bill presentment and payment (EBPP) systems are B2C systems that use a Web site to post customers' bills and to receive their electronic payments. Two major types of EBPP systems exist. One is the *biller direct method*, whereby a company posts its bills/invoices to its own Web site (or to a Web site hosted for it by a third party) and sends an e-mail notification to its customers telling them that their bill has been posted. Customers log on to the Web site, access their accounts, and decide what and how much to pay.[a] The details of the payment, such as customer name, customer number, debit card, credit card, or bank account number, and amount to be paid, are captured at the Web site and sent to a third-party payment processor. The processor sends back a verification that allows the billing company to reduce the receivable (by posting an *expected* payment to the accounts receivable master data) and to notify the customer that the payment has been accepted.

At the end of each day, the third-party processor consolidates all bank transfer type payments made that day for each client (i.e., the biller organizations) and clears the payments through the ACH Network (see Technology Summary 11.2 on pg. 396).[b] At the conclusion of the clearing process, each biller receives a file from its bank containing a list of the customer payments (customer name, customer number, items paid, and amount). When the payment file is received from the bank, the biller companies change their accounts receivable data to reflect that an expected payment has been received.

The second EBPP method is the *consolidation/aggregation method*, in which bills are not posted to the billing company's Web site but are posted to a Web site hosted by the billing company's own bank or by a company such as Fiserv (see www.fiserv.com). This method allows a customer to go to one site to pay bills received from many companies. With the consolidation method, the bill payer would log on to one site to pay all of their bills, rather than a site for each bill. After the bill payer logs on and decides what and how much to pay, the payment proceeds as it would under the direct biller method.

Notes:
[a]Payment options include credit card, debit card, or other electronic funds transfer.
[b]Other settlement methods would be used for credit or debit card payments.

depositing customer cash receipts and having those receipts clear the banking system. The treasurer's goal is to reduce float and hasten the availability of good funds. **Float**, when applied to cash receipts, is the time between the payment by the customer and the availability of good funds. **Good funds** are funds on deposit and available for use. Float is a real cost to a firm and may be measured by the firm's marginal borrowing rate, assuming some type of borrowing occurs to finance the float period.[8]

The following procedures, mostly applicable in the retail/consumer space, are designed to reduce or eliminate the float associated with cash receipts:

- A **credit card** is a method of payment whereby a third party such as a bank removes from the collector the risk of not collecting the amount due from a customer. The collecting company submits the charges to the credit card company for reimbursement. The credit card company bills the cardholder. Payment to the collector is immediate, thus reducing float and hastening the availability of good funds. The credit card process is depicted in **Technology Summary 11.2** (pg. 396).

- A **debit card** is a form of payment authorizing the collector to transfer funds electronically from the payer's bank account to the collector's bank account. Some collectors find the notion of direct debit attractive because it represents the elimination of *float*. Debit cards are processed, and fees (i.e., 2 percent) collected, in a manner similar to that described in Technology Summary 11.2. In 2008, U.S. banks collected more than $20 billion in these so-called interchange fees for debit card transactions.[9]

- Many of us, as consumers, have experienced a portion of the EBPP system, electronic bill payments, when we pay our bills using our bank's Web site or services such as those offered by Quicken. This method varies from EBPP in that we are not presented with an electronic bill. Or, if we are, we choose not to pay that bill at the biller's Web site. Even though we don't pay at the biller's Web site, this method still serves to accelerate cash flow and reduce processing costs for the collecting organization.

- *Customer self-service systems* may also serve to accelerate payments when customers— businesses or consumers—log on to a biller's Web site to obtain information about a bill, get errors corrected, and resolve disputes, leading to a more timely payment.

- *Mobile person-to-person money transfers* use mobile phones to make payments between individuals. After signing up for the service with a bank or other provider, a person can use a telephone number or e-mail address to send money to anyone. The sender's bank account is debited for the amount of the payment plus a nominal fee and the recipient may get the payment deposited to their bank account, credit card, or prepaid card.[10]

Technology Summary 11.3 (pg. 397) discusses other solutions that organizations have used to shorten float, improve Internet business practices, or achieve other economies.

The electronic payment methods described here can accomplish two goals for the collecting organization: accelerating cash flows and reducing the cost of processing

---

[8]Float is more of a problem in countries such as the United States where payments are often made with paper checks or their equivalent. In many countries, payments are mostly electronic, and float is not a concern.

[9]Lloyd Constantine, "Let's End the Debit Card Fee-for-All," *Businessweek*, October 26, 2009, p. 73.

[10]Amy Feldman, "Buddy, Can You E-Mail Me 100 Bucks?" *Businessweek*, November 23, 2009, p. 68.

Technology Summary 11.2

Credit Card Transaction Flow

A credit card transaction occurs (see the following diagram) when a cardholder purchases something from a merchant who has contracted with an acquirer, such as First National Merchant Solutions (www.firstmerchantservices.com) or First Data Corporation (www.firstdatacardprocessing.com). When the merchant swipes the card through the POS terminal, the acquirer obtains authorization for the transaction from the card issuer through the card association, verifying that the cardholder has sufficient credit for the transaction. After the card issuer approves the transaction, the acquirer "acquires" the transaction from the merchant and then transmits it to the applicable card association, which then routes the transaction information to the card issuer. Upon receipt of the

transaction, the card issuer delivers funds to the acquirer via the card association. Generally, the acquirer funds the merchant after receiving the money from the card association. Each participant in the transaction receives compensation for processing the transaction. For example, in a transaction using a Visa or MasterCard for $500.00 with a merchant "discount rate" (i.e., fee) of 2 percent, the card issuer will fund the association $492.50 and bill the cardholder $500.00 on its monthly statement. The card association will retain assessment fees of $0.50 and forward $492.00 to the acquirer. The acquirer will retain $2.00 and pay the merchant $490.00. The $7.50 retained by the card issuer is referred to as interchange, which, like assessment fees, is set by the card association.

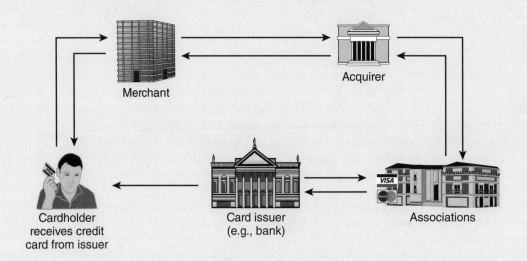

Source: Adapted from description at www.firstnationalmerchants.com/ms/html/en/market_solutions/cnp_tran_flow.html (available as of June 2008).

payments. But, as noted in Technology Summary 11.3, over 30 billion paper checks, with a value over $41 trillion, were paid in the United States in 2006. Currently, about 70 percent of B2B payments are made with paper checks.[11] Businesses often prefer checks because they are comfortable with the check-clearing process and because some alternative payment methods, such as credit and debit cards, come with the interchange fee of 2 percent noted earlier. In the United States, checks are cleared with no transaction fee.

There is evidence, however, that the number of checks is declining. For example, the payments study cited earlier reported that checks had declined by 6.4 percent from 2003 to 2006.[12] In addition, there is evidence outside the United States that paper

---

[11]Steve Bills, "Clearing House to Spur Electronic-Pay Transition," *American Banker*, December 3, 2009, p. 1.

[12]"The 2007 Federal Reserve Payments Study," December 10, 2007, accessed at www.federalreserve.gov on March 12, 2010.

Technology Summary 11.3

Accelerating Cash Receipts

Electronic funds transfer (EFT) is a general term used to describe a variety of procedures for transmitting cash funds between entities via electronic transmission instead of using paper checks. EFT includes wire transfers, credit and debit card processing, as well as payments made via the ACH Network. In 2006, there were 62.7 billion electronic payments, valued at over $34 trillion, processed in the United States. These included 21.7 billion credit card (value $2.1 trillion), 25.3 billion debit card ($1 trillion), and 14.6 billion ACH Network ($31 trillion) payment transactions. This compares to 30.6 billion paper checks valued at $41.7 trillion.[a] Notice especially the dominant place that paper checks have over electronic payments in the value processed and the value of ACH payments among other electronic payments.

The Automated Clearing House (ACH) Network is a *batch processing* system for the interbank clearing of electronic payments. ACH Network payments include credit (i.e., the receiver's account is credited) transactions, such as payroll direct deposit and social security payments paid by the U.S. government, as well as debit (i.e., the receiver's account is debited) transactions, such as mortgages, loans, and insurance premiums. As noted earlier, EBPP systems use the ACH Network to settle some payments.

The number of payments processed by the ACH Network increased from 14.6 billion in 2006 to 18.2 billion in 2008, including over 78 million check conversions, a new electronic payment method whereby paper checks are converted to ACH debit payments.[b]

Another method for accelerating cash receipts is to employ a lockbox for processing customer payments. A lockbox is a postal address maintained by a third party—typically a bank—which is used solely for the purpose of collecting checks. The bank constantly processes the lockbox receipts, providing a quick update to the firm's bank balance, making funds available for use more quickly. To provide the collecting company with the information to update customer accounts, the lockbox bank sends the company the remittance advices (RAs), or *digital images* of the RAs; photocopies of the checks, or *digital images* of the checks; and a listing, or electronic transmission, of the remittance details, prepared by *scanning* the RAs or by keying the remittance data. The lockbox allows the company to post cash receipts more rapidly, at reduced cost, and with more accuracy.

With a lockbox, a bank can process payments more quickly than most organizations because they have specialized resources to open the mail; encode the checks with *magnetic ink character recognition (MICR)* to indicate the amount of the payment; scan the checks to obtain details such as check number, account number (both encoded on the check using MICR codes when the check is printed), and amount of the check; and scan the RAs to obtain details such as customer number, invoice number being paid, and amount of the payment.

Finally, *remote deposit capture* uses scanners to capture check images and to use those images, instead of the paper check, to make a deposit to a checking, savings, or money market account. This service has been available to businesses and is now available to consumers. USAA, for example, allows customers to deposit checks using iPhone or Android apps or other approved scanning devices.[c]

Notes:
[a] "The 2007 Federal Reserve Payments Study," December 10, 2007, accessed at www.federalreserve.gov on March 12, 2010.
[b] "NACHA Reports More than 18.2 Billion ACH Payments in 2008." Press release, April 6, 2009, accessed at www.nacha.org on March 12, 2010.
[c] See USSA Deposit@Mobile and USAA Deposit@Home at www.usaa.com, accessed on March 11, 2010.

checks are in decline. For example, the UK Payments Council has set October 31, 2018, as the final day that paper checks will be processed by the UK's central cheque clearing service.[13] Even with this evidence of declining check use, solutions to float and cost issues associated with paper checks are desirable and are available. One set of solutions involves the ACH Network, which has added the check conversion process noted above as well as other electronic payment enhancements. Another solution is the Check Clearing for the 21st Century Act (also known as Check 21). **Technology Summary 11.4** (pg. 398) explains Check 21, which was first introduced in Chapter 3 when we discussed *electronic document management (EDM)*. Almost 99 percent of paper checks are now

---

[13] "UK Card Use Hastening Death of Checks," *Cardline*, December 25, 2009, p. 2.

Technology Summary 11.4

Check 21

The Check Clearing for the 21st Century Act (Check 21) allows banks to exchange check images electronically. The act does not require that banks exchange check images; it does require that they be able to accept copies of original checks, called "substitute checks" or "image-replacement checks." Before Check 21, paper checks were flown around the country, from bank to bank, to complete the check-clearing process. During the time that this process took to complete, the payer's account had not been charged for the check (i.e., float). With Check 21, check-clearing time is significantly reduced, as is the cost of handling the paper checks.

When a check is received for deposit at a bank, it is scanned on both sides to create an image of the check to be sent, as needed, to the originator of the check. At the same time, an electronic file containing the check details is used to clear the check. The check-clearing process, therefore, can be immediate or up to one day, as compared to several days before Check 21.

---

processed as images. Since the implementation of Check 21, the U.S. Federal Reserve has reduced the number of paper-check processing facilities from 43 to a single site in Cleveland, Ohio.[14]

The Fraud Connection

The B/AR/CR process provides a prime opportunity to manipulate final results. For example, organizations can inflate revenues and accounts receivable by inadvertently, or intentionally, violating revenue recognition rules prescribed by generally accepted accounting principles (GAAP). One such scheme involves recording as sales, shipments to distributors that are expected to be returned in subsequent periods. Another scheme involves the improper recording of sales returns. Other schemes involve booking revenues on shipments of products held in a warehouse until buyers are ready to take delivery (known as "bill-and-hold" schemes). In some cases, these accounting treatments are questionable; in some cases, they are found to be fraudulent.

Controls

There are also many examples of fraud involving cash—not surprising, as this is the most liquid of a company's assets. Without recounting all such cases here, we will mention that in most of them, improper *segregation of duties* occurred between the functions of handling cash (*custody of resources*) and *recording* cash transactions. Where inadequate segregation of duties exists, and payments are made directly to the billing organization, a common scheme for misappropriating cash involves lapping customer accounts. **Lapping** is a fraud by which funds being paid by one customer are stolen, and the theft is covered up by applying funds received from another customer to the first customer's account. Funds from a third customer are applied to the second customer's account, and so on. This fraud might work as follows:

1. Wanda Wayward is the bookkeeper for Honest Harry's House of Horticulture (4Hs). She also handles cash for the company.
2. Wanda pockets cash received on account from customer A. She neither deposits the cash to 4Hs' bank account nor records it as received from A.
3. So that customer A will not complain that the cash payment was never credited to their account, Wanda deposits cash that is later received from customer B but credits A's account for the payment.

---

[14]"Federal Reserve Banks Complete Check Processing Infrastructure Changes," *US Fed News Service, Including US State News*, March 10, 2010.

4. So that customer B will not complain that their payment was not credited to their account, Wanda deposits cash that is later received from customer C but credits B's account for the payment. And on it goes.

Some lapping scams have become so large and unmanageable for the perpetrator to keep covered up that there simply weren't enough hours available in the working day for the dishonest employee to manipulate the accounting records. The embezzler had to take the records, such as aged trial balances, home at night and doctor them there. Controls to *prevent* or *detect* this fraud include *rotation of duties* and *forced vacations*. Perpetrators will be reluctant to attempt this fraud if they know that they cannot continue the scheme, or that the scheme will be detected when they are replaced by another employee. Obviously, the ultimate *preventive* control for lapping includes segregation of duties, such as having checks sent directly to a bank (i.e., a *lockbox*), or using electronic bill/invoice payments so that checks cannot be manipulated.

Logical Process Description

The principal activities of the B/AR/CR process are to bill customers, collect and deposit cash received from those customers, record the invoices and cash collections in customer subsidiary ledgers, and inform the general ledger process to make entries for sales and cash receipts. In addition to the billing (B) and cash receipts (CR) functions, the B/AR/CR process *manages customer accounts* (AR). Activities normally included in this process are sales returns and allowances and bad debts, as well as sending periodic statements to customers.

Logical Data Flow Diagrams

As you learned in Chapter 4 and saw applied in Chapter 10, our first view of the process is a general one, shown in the form of a *context diagram*. For the B/AR/CR process, that view appears in **Figure 11.2** (pg. 400). Take some time to examine this figure and to note the external entities with which this process interacts and the data flows running to and from those entities. As noted earlier, we assume that customers send payments to banks or other service providers and that notifications of payments come from the bank.

Now let's explode Figure 11.2 into the level 0 diagram reflected in **Figure 11.3** (pg. 401). In this expanded view of the process, we see that the single bubble in Figure 11.2 has become three process bubbles. We also see the event and master data for this process. At this point, review Figure 11.3 and compare it to Figure 11.2 to confirm that the two figures are "in balance" with each other.

We will now decompose each of the three processes shown in the level 0 diagram into their lower-level diagrams. **Figure 11.4** (pg. 402) decomposes bubble 1.0 of Figure 11.3.

Most of Figure 11.4 should be self-explanatory. Therefore, we will comment only briefly on it. As you saw in Chapter 10, when the OE/S process produces a *sales order*, it notifies the B/AR/CR process to that effect. This is the flow "Sales order notification."[15]

When *triggered* by the data flow, "Shipping's billing notification" (i.e., the shipping notice), process 1.1 validates the sale by comparing the details on the sales order

---

[15]Please recognize that, *physically*, this data flow could take the form of an open sales order (i.e., an order not yet shipped) in a *sales order master data store* or SALES_ORDERS relational table, both of which you saw in Chapter 10.

FIGURE 11.2 B/AR/CR—Context Diagram

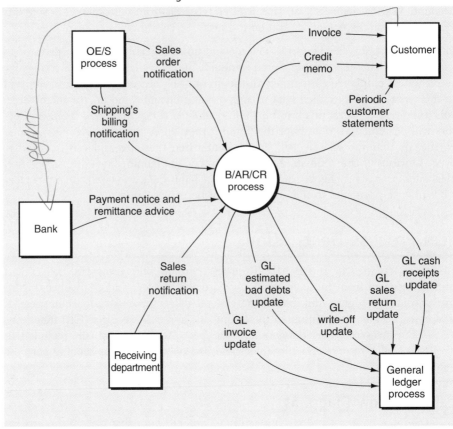

notification to those shown on shipping's billing notification. Essentially, this is a comparison of the order (what was supposed to be shipped) with the shipment (what was shipped). If discrepancies are noted, the shipping notice is rejected, as shown by the reject stub coming from bubble 1.1. Rejected notices are processed later, through a separate *exception routine*.

If the data flows match, process 1.1 sends a validated shipping notification to process 1.2. Process 1.2 then performs the following actions:

- Obtains from the customer master data certain standing data, such as the bill-to address, needed to produce the invoice.
- Creates the invoice and sends it to the customer.
- Updates the accounts receivable master data.
- Adds an invoice to the sales event data (i.e., the sales journal). This could be used for a *periodic* update of the GL for a number of sales events. (However, as shown here, there is an update of the GL for each sale as it occurs.)
- Notifies the general ledger process that a sale has occurred (GL invoice update). This is an *immediate* update of the GL for a single sale.[16]

---

[16]As discussed earlier in this chapter and in Chapter 10, the billing (revenue) transaction described here and the matching shipment (expense) transaction described in Chapter 10 could be processed simultaneously. The choice depends on how close in space and time the shipping and billing actives occur and the software employed.

In the next section, we discuss *accounts receivable master data* and *sales event data*. Before proceeding, let's take a brief look at the information content of an invoice. **Figure 11.5** (pg. 403) shows the display of a typical invoice record.

The **invoice** is a business document—either paper or electronic transmission—used to notify the customer of an obligation to pay the seller for the merchandise (or service) ordered and shipped (or provided, if a service). Notice that the top portion of the

FIGURE 11.3   B/AR/CR Process—Level 0 Diagram

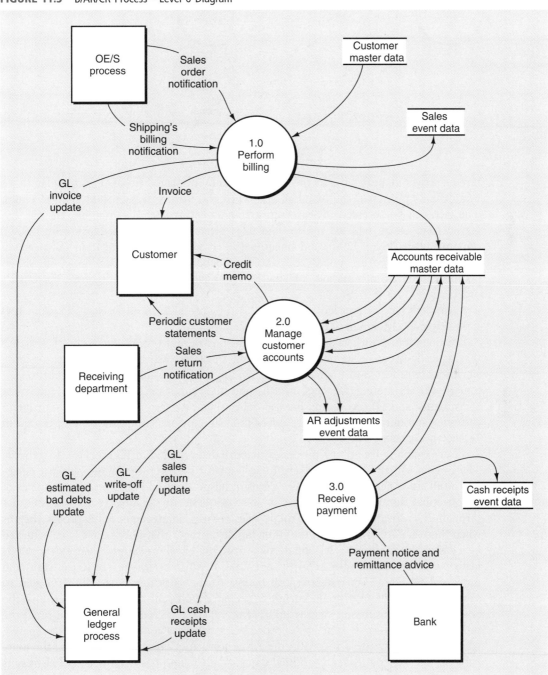

FIGURE 11.4   B/AR/CR Process—Diagram 1

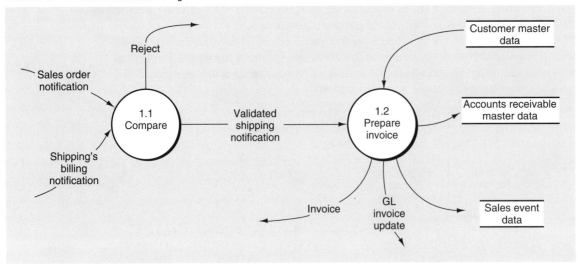

invoice screen identifies the invoice line item being displayed (Item 10; subsequent lines would be 20, 30, etc.), the material, and when the invoice was created and by whom. The tabs can be accessed to learn more about this invoice. For example, on the displayed Item Detail tab, we can see the sales order number (Sales Document 12071), shipping plant (Plant 3200), and quantity (Billed Quantity 5). The Item Partners tab shows who ordered the goods and who should be billed. The Conditions tab shows pricing and terms information, and the PO Data tab provides details of the customer's order.

Now let's take a closer look at process 2.0 in Figure 11.3 (pg. 401). **Figure 11.6** (pg. 404) is the lower-level diagram of that process.

As mentioned earlier, managing customer accounts involves an array of activities that typically occur between customer billing and later cash collection. Three of those activities are reflected in Figure 11.6: (1) sending periodic statements of account to customers, (2) accounting for sales returns and allowances or other accounts receivable adjustments, and (3) accounting for bad debts. The tasks required to properly maintain customer accounts can be fairly resource intensive for an organization, as discussed in **Technology Summary 11.5** (pg. 405).

Let's examine briefly the processes that are diagrammed in Figure 11.6. In general, adjustments will always be necessary to account for sales returns, allowances for defective products or partial shipments, reversals of mispostings and other errors, estimates of uncollectible accounts, and write-offs for bad debt. In Figure 11.6, processes 2.1 through 2.3 relate to just one of these, sales returns adjustments. This process begins when there is notification from the receiving department that goods have been returned by a customer. Subprocess 2.1 obtains data from the *accounts receivable master data* to validate the return. If the sales return is not valid, it will be rejected (see Reject stub) and processed through a separate *exception routine*. If the sales return is valid, it is sent to subprocess 2.2, where a credit memo is prepared and sent to the customer, and the accounts receivable master data is updated to reflect the credit. At the same time, the validated sales return is sent to subprocess 2.3, where a journal voucher is prepared, which is used to create a record in the AR adjustments event data store (i.e., the journal), and the general ledger is notified that a credit memo has been issued. This results in updates to sales returns and allowances and to AR.

Process 2.4 is triggered by a periodic review of aging details obtained from the accounts receivable master data. **Figure 11.7** (pg. 406) is an example of aging details, showing the amounts owed (Due, Past Due, Total OI [open items]) by each customer. You can also see that amounts due are grouped into intervals such as 0–30 days, 31–60 days, and 61–90 days. Such groupings are also available for each customer. This report would be used to identify and follow up on late-paying customer accounts. One of two types of adjustments might result from this review:

- The recurring adjusting entry for *estimated* bad debts.
- The periodic write-off of "definitely worthless" customer accounts. These might, for example, be those receivables over 120 days.

Note that, regardless of type, adjustments such as those in bubbles 2.1, 2.2, 2.3, and 2.4 are recorded in the event data, updated to customer balances in the accounts receivable master data, and summarized and posted to the general ledger master data by the general ledger process.

Like process 2.4, bubble 2.5, "Prepare customer statements," also is triggered by a periodic event that recurs at specified intervals—often on a monthly basis in practice. Details of unpaid invoices are extracted from the accounts receivable master data and are summarized in a statement of account that is mailed (or sent electronically) to customers. The statement typically reports activity for the period, such as payments made

FIGURE 11.5 Sample SAP Invoice Data Screen

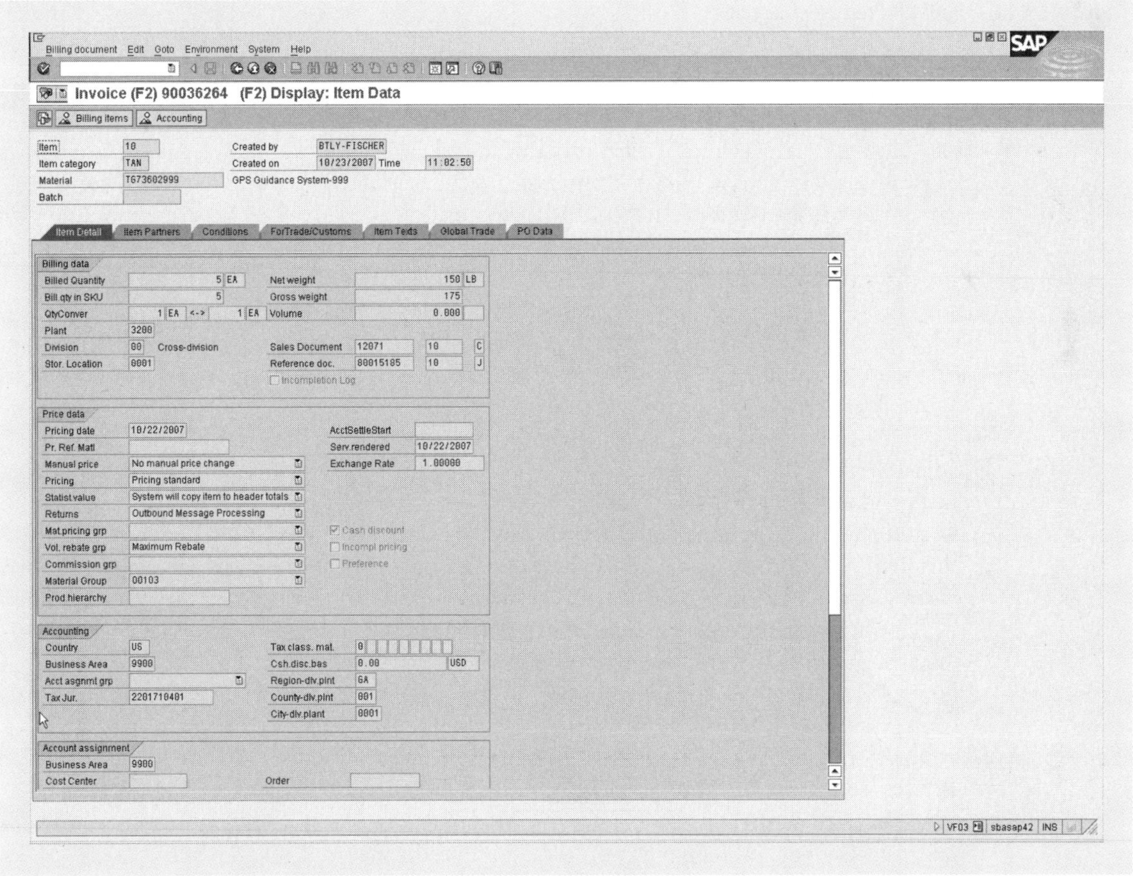

and new charges incurred; confirms the balance owed; and reminds the customer that payment is due (or overdue). Therefore, it serves both operating and control purposes.

Take some time now to track all these activities in Figure 11.6 (pg. 404). Resolve any questions you may have before moving on.

Figure 11.8 (pg. 407), a lower-level diagram of process 3.0, "Receive payment," in Figure 11.3 (pg. 401), completes our analysis of the events comprising the B/AR/CR process. In this diagram, we see our earlier activities culminate in the collection of cash from customers.

The payment notice and remittance advice data trigger the *receive payment* process. A **remittance advice (RA)** is a business document used by the payer to notify the payee of the items being paid. The RA can take various forms. For instance, it may be a copy of the invoice, a detachable RA delivered as part of a statement periodically sent to the customer (often a "stub" attached to the invoice or statement, a *turnaround document*), or a stub attached to the payer's check. In any case, B/AR/CR uses the RA to initiate the recording of a payment.

Upon receipt of the payment notice and RA from the bank, process 3.1 first validates the remittance by comparing the payment notice to the RA. Mismatches are rejected for later processing. If the payment notice and RA agree, the validated remittance is sent to process 3.2, which uses the RA to update the *accounts receivable master data* to reflect the customer's payment and records the collection in the *cash receipts events data* (i.e., the cash receipts journal could be used for a *periodic* update of the GL

FIGURE 11.6   B/AR/CR Process—Diagram 2

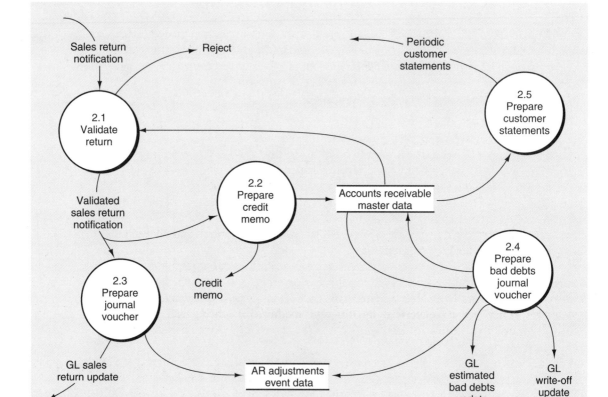

Technology Summary 11.5

Managing Customer Accounts

The management of customers' accounts and the corresponding collection of accounts receivable can be a time-consuming and resource-intensive process. Because orders frequently involve multiple shipments and multiple billing arrangements, sorting all the supporting documentation to accurately bill customers and at the same time handle subsequent queries can be difficult for many organizations. But, as noted earlier, it is through effective billing processes, open receivables monitoring, and timely cash collections that an organization can attain its goals regarding days sales are outstanding (DSO), a key measure of effectiveness of the B/AR/CR process. Many organizations have passed on the problem of managing AR and ensuring timely collections by selling their accounts receivable (i.e., factoring) to another organization that then manages the accounts and receives the payments.

Several best practices have been employed within organizations to optimize the B/AR/CR processes. For example, incentives for prompt payment, such as a 2 percent discount if paid in 10 days, are often provided to customers through the terms of the sale. Also, an organization should avoid the conditions that can lead to a customer contesting, and thereby delaying payment on, an invoice. Customers can dispute such issues as price, quantity, lack of a purchase order reference on the invoice, and quality of the product or service. Reducing these errors and providing processes for investigating and quickly resolving these disputes will accelerate collections. Dispute resolution processes may include using *workflow* systems and *EDM systems* to route customer disputes to those who can best resolve the dispute with the information necessary to investigate the problem.

The EBPP and EIPP services described in this chapter and Chapter 13 are used to accelerate the billing (i.e., *electronic bill/invoice presentment*) and cash receipts (i.e., *electronic bill/invoice payment*) processes. These services also provide a means for business partners to access up-to-date information via the Internet. Providing current information, to both suppliers and buyers, on all the data related to an invoice can facilitate the reconciliation of these data to reduce collection delays that can result from incomplete or inconsistent information. The result should be improved efficiency and increased cash flow for the collecting organization.

for a number of cash receipts events), and notifies the general ledger process of the amount of cash deposited. This is an *immediate* update of the GL for a single cash receipt. Process 3.2, which is a controller function, is typically performed by the payment applications section of the accounts receivable department.

Logical Data Descriptions

Five data stores appear in Figure 11.3 (pg. 401). The *customer master data* was described in Chapter 10. In this section, we describe the other four. The **accounts receivable master data** is a repository of all unpaid invoices issued by an organization and awaiting final disposition. As the invoice is created, a record of the receivable is entered in the master data. Subsequently, the records are updated—that is, the receivable balance is reduced—at the time that the customer makes the payment. As you learned in the previous section, the records also could be updated to reflect sales returns and allowances, bad debt write-offs, or other adjustments.

The accounts receivable master data provides information useful in minimizing outstanding customer balances and in prompting customers to pay in a timely manner. Two types of accounts receivable systems exist: the *balance-forward system* and the *open-item system*. They are characterized by different methods of storing and reporting information, and they result in different formats for the periodic customer statements produced from the master data.

In a **balance-forward system**, accounts receivable records consist of a customer's balance, categorized as current and past due, and current account activity, including such items as current charges, finance charges for past-due balances, and payments. Monthly statements display previous balance, payments, and balance forward, to which are added any new charges to derive the total balance due. Each month, unpaid current balances are rolled into the past-due balances. Electric and gas utility companies typically use balance-forward systems. For an electric bill, for example, the only details supporting the amount of current charges are beginning and ending meter readings, total kilowatt-hours used for the period, and rate(s) per kwh.

In the balance-forward system, customers usually pay from the periodic statement rather than paying individual invoices, and payments are simply posted to the customer's account balance. In contrast, the **open-item system** is more complex and is appropriate in situations where invoices are prepared and sent for each sale (i.e., each shipment), and the customer typically makes payments for specific invoices when those invoices are due. The accounts receivable master data is organized so that each record consists of individual open invoices, against which payments and other adjustments are applied.

On the periodic customer statement of account, invoices (new or settled in the current period) are listed, along with payment details. Also, each open invoice is grouped by aging category and aged individually. Monthly, or at specified times, the customer accounts are aged, and an aging schedule, such as the one depicted in Figure 11.7, is printed.

Three event data stores are depicted in Figure 11.3 (pg. 401). First, the **sales event data** store contains invoice (i.e., sales) records. These records are created as

FIGURE 11.7 Sample Accounts Receivable Aging Report in SAP

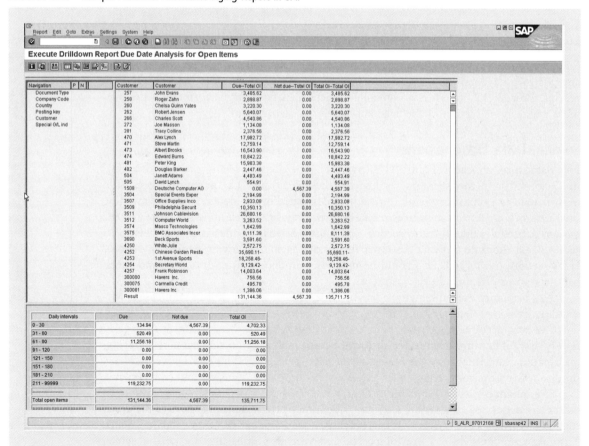

FIGURE 11.8   B/AR/CR Process—Diagram 3

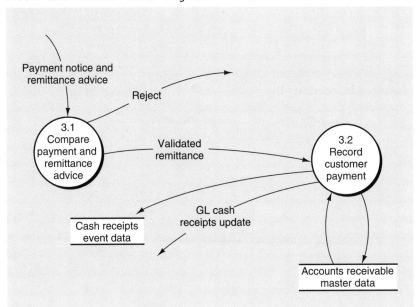

the process prepares and sends an invoice. In a manual process, the sales event data store is called a *sales journal*, with which you may be familiar from earlier accounting courses.

The **accounts receivable (AR) adjustments events data** store is created as sales returns, bad debt write-offs, estimated doubtful accounts, or similar adjustments are processed. As in any event data, the records in this data store are typically keyed by date. The other essential data elements usually include journal voucher number, customer identification, adjustment type, account(s) and amount(s) to be debited, account(s) and amount(s) to be credited, and authorization indicators (i.e., approval code, signature, or the like).

The **cash receipts event data** store, created when customer payments are recorded, contains the details of each payment as reflected on the *RA* accompanying a payment. In a manual process, the cash receipts event data store is called a *cash receipts journal*. Accordingly, each record in this data store normally shows the date the payment is recorded, customer identification, invoice number(s) and gross invoice amount(s), cash discount(s) taken on each invoice, net invoice amount(s), check amount, and check number.

Logical Database Design

We now look at how B/AR/CR data are structured, assuming a *centralized database approach* to data management is employed. To keep the discussion simple, we will look at only two basic economic events as they relate to this process: billing and cash receipts. We also examined billing in Chapter 10 because that event is the bridge between the OE/S process and the B/AR/CR process. We will not cover adjustments resulting from sales returns, bad debt write-offs, and estimated doubtful accounts. **Figure 11.9** (pg. 408) illustrates an E-R diagram of the billing and cash receipts events.

FIGURE 11.9 Entity-Relationship (E-R) Diagram (Partial) for the B/AR/CR Process

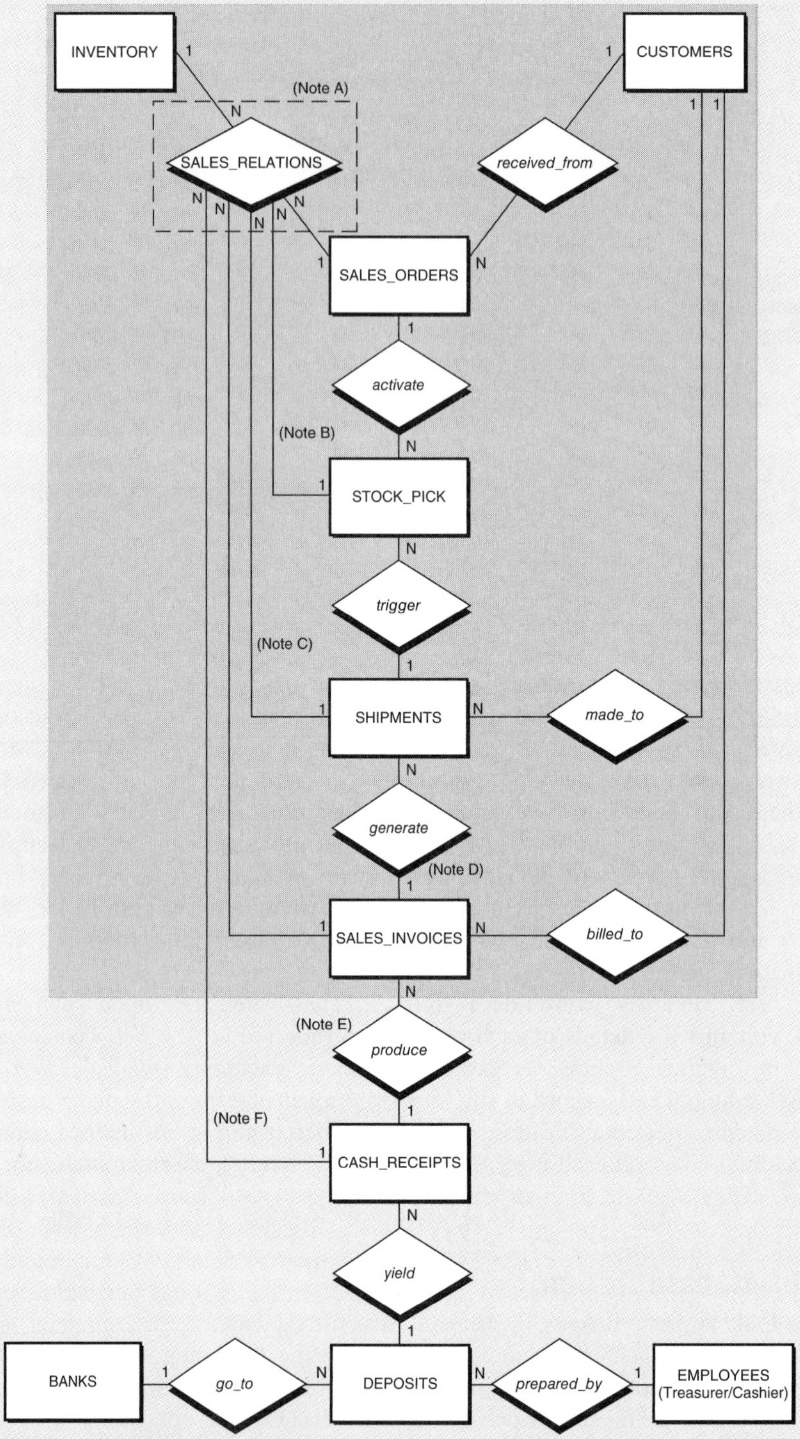

NOTES, for simplicity, we assume that:

A—See page 409 for an explanation of the box around SALES_RELATIONS and why the model is not fully normalized.

B—All goods ordered are picked (no partial picks).

C—All goods picked are shipped (no partial shipments).

D—All shipments are invoiced in full (no partial invoices).

E—The difference between SALES_INVOICES and CASH_RECEIPTS represents account receivable and/or deferred income.

F—A single cash receipt (remittance advice) could pay for several invoices, but there are no partial payments (all invoices are paid in full).

The shaded portion at the top of the diagram is repeated from Chapter 10 (Figure 10.9 on pg. 363). To the entities from Figure 10.9, we have added the CASH_RECEIPTS, DEPOSITS, BANKS, and EMPLOYEES entities. As in Figure 10.9, the SALES_RELATIONS relationship accumulates a record of events as they progress. In this case, we add the cash receipts event to this relationship. Recall from Figure 10.9 that this relationship already has accumulated a record of the SALES_ORDERS, STOCK_PICK, and SHIPMENTS, which we repeat here to emphasize that the invoice is generated after the goods are ordered, picked, and shipped. The box around this relationship indicates that we will have a relation in our database for this relationship, while the other relationships will not have a corresponding relation.

As with Figure 10.9, the model in Figure 11.9 is not fully normalized yet. We include the "extra" relationships and redundant attributes to help you see the logical sequence of events. Also, the notes on Figure 11.9 indicate that this is a simplified model. Certainly, realistic models must deal with partial picking, shipping, invoicing, and payments.

Finally, notice the interesting phenomenon in note E. There is *no separate accounts receivable* entity! Rather, accounts receivable balances (or deferred revenue balances) at any point in time are computed as the *difference* between the continuous events, SALES_INVOICES and CASH_RECEIPTS.[17]

Let's next translate the E-R diagram into relations (i.e., relational tables); **Figure 11.10** (pg. 410) is designed to do that.

We repeat here from Figure 10.10 (pg. 364), the CUSTOMERS, INVENTORY, SALES_ORDERS, STOCK_PICK, SHIPMENTS, SALES_INVOICES, and SALES_RELATIONS relations to emphasize the connections (linkages) among relations and to remind you that before invoicing a customer, we first have accepted a customer's sales order, picked the goods, and shipped the goods to the customer.

To simplify the tables, we have assumed that each inventory line item picked and shipped is billed at a single unit sales price from the INVENTORY relation. Further, SALES_INVOICES ignores freight, sales taxes, or other items that might be billed to a customer. Using the SALES_INVOICES relation and extracting other data, as needed, from other relations, contemplate how you would prepare the invoice *document* to be sent to the customer.

The CASH_RECEIPTS and the attributes added to the end of the SALES_RELATIONS relation (i.e., Remit_No and Remit_Amt) substitute for the cash receipts data and RA data discussed in the preceding section. For simplicity, we have ignored customer cash discounts in the relations shown. First, note that Remit_No in SALES_INVOICES allows us to associate cash receipts with particular customers for the purpose of monitoring customer accounts and assessing any needed bad debt adjustments. In addition, Invoice_No in SALES_RELATIONS can be used to apply collections against specific open invoices (as in an *open-item accounts receivable system*, for instance). Finally, the linkages among CASH_RECEIPTS, SALES_RELATIONS, SALES_INVOICES, and CUSTOMERS can be used to determine customer accounts receivable balances at any moment in time, as shown in the E-R diagram and as explained previously.

---

[17]In "The REA Accounting Model: A Generalized Framework for Accounting Systems in a Shared Environment" (*The Accounting Review*, July 1982, pp. 554–578), William E. McCarthy describes what is portrayed here as a process of producing information "snapshots" from records of continuing activities.

FIGURE 11.10 Selected Relational Tables (Partial) for the B/AR/CR Process

Shaded Attribute(s) = Primary Key

CUSTOMERS

Cust_No	Cust_Name	Cust_Street	Cust_City	Cust_State	Cust_ZIP	Ship_to_Name	Ship_to_Street	Ship_to_City	Ship_to_State	Ship_to_ZIP	Credit_Limit	Last_Revised	Credit_Terms
1234	Acme Co.	175 Fifth St	Beaufort	SC	29902	Same	Same	Same	Same	Same	5000	20060101	2/10,n/30
1235	Robbins, Inc	220 North Rd	Columbia	SC	29801	ALine Fabric	2 Main St	Greenwood	SC	29845	10000	20070915	n/60
1236	Jazzy Corp.	45 Ocean Dr	Hilton Hd	SC	29910	Same	Same	Same	Same	Same	0	20070610	COD

INVENTORY

Item_No	Item_Name	Price	Location	Qty_on_Hand	Reorder_Pt
936	Machine Plates	39.50	Macomb	1,500	950
1001	Gaskets	9.50	Macomb	10,002	3,500
1010	Crank Shafts	115.00	Tampa	952	500
1025	Manifolds	45.00	Tampa	402	400

SALES_ORDERS

SO_No	SO_Date	Cust_No	Cust_PO_No	Cust_PO_Date	Ship_Via	FOB_Terms
5677	20071216	1235	41523	20071212	UPS	Ship Pt
5678	20071216	1276	A1190	20071214	Best way	Ship Pt
5679	20071216	1236	9422	20071216	Fed Ex	Destin

STOCK_PICK

Pick_No	Pick_Date	Picked_By	SO_No	Ship_No	Invoice_No
9436	20071215	Butch	5676	94101	964
9437	20071215	Rachel	5677	94102	965
9438	20071216	Ace	5678	94103	966

SHIPMENTS

Ship_No	Ship_Date	Shipped_By	Cust_No	Invoice_No
94101	20071215	Jason	1293	964
94102	20071216	Carol	1235	965
94103	20071216	Jason	1249	966

CASH_RECEIPTS

Remit_No	Dep_No	Total_Rec	Remit_Date
9529	116-334	549.00	20080110
9530	116-335	369.28	20070110

BANKS

Bank_No	Bank_Name
2239	Acme
2240	Benton

SALES_RELATIONS

SO_No	Item_No	Qty_Ordered	Pick_No	Qty_Picked	Ship_No	Qty_Shipped	Invoice_No	Qty_Invoiced	Amt_Invoiced	Remit_No	Remit_Amt
5676	1074	60	9436	60	94101	60	964	60	549.00	9529	549.00
5677	1001	100	9437	100	94102	100	965	100	950.00		
5677	1010	75	9437	75	94102	75	965	75	8625.00		
5678	936	40	9438	40	94103	40	966	40	1580.00		

SALES_INVOICES

Invoice_No	Invoice_Date	Invoice_Total	Cust_No	Remit_No
964	20071216	549.00	1293	9529
965	20071216	9575.00	1235	
966	20071217	1580.00	1249	

DEPOSITS

Deposit_No	Dep_Date	Deposit_Amt	Emp_No (Treasurer/Cashier)	Bank_No
116-334	20080112	549.00	D762	2239
116-335	20080112	369.28	D762	2239

Types of Billing Systems

In general, two kinds of billing systems exist. In a **post-billing system**, invoices are prepared after goods have been shipped and the sales order notification (i.e., sales order) has been matched to shipping's billing notification (i.e., shipping notice). The data flow diagrams (DFDs) in this section and in Chapter 10 assume a post-billing system.

In a **pre-billing system**, invoices are prepared immediately on acceptance of a customer order—that is, after inventory and credit checks have been accomplished. Pre-billing systems often occur in situations where there is little or no delay between receipt of the customer's order and its shipment. In such systems, there is no separate sales order document as such; copies of the invoice serve as the picking ticket, packing slip, and other functions required by the OE/S process. In other words, the customer is billed (and the inventory, accounts receivable, and general ledger master data are updated) at the time the customer order is entered. However, the customer copy of the invoice is not released until shipment has been made. For this type of system to operate efficiently, the inventory control system must be very reliable. If an order is accepted, and an item then turns out to be unavailable, all accounting entries would have to be reversed.

Physical Description of the Billing Process

Enterprise Systems

Figure 11.11 (pg. 412) presents a physical description of the billing process. From Chapter 10, you should have a good understanding of the order entry and shipping activities leading up to the billing process. Take time now to review the flowchart for general ideas. You will notice a close resemblance between the physical features of this process and the logical design of the billing process as presented in Figures 11.2 (pg. 400), 11.3 (pg. 401), and 11.4 (pg. 402). You should also see that this system demonstrates the use of an enterprise system and several features of the technology discussed earlier in this chapter.

The Billing Process

At the time the sales order was recorded in the order entry department, the billing section of the accounts receivable department was "notified" that a sales order had been created. This notification is shown on the DFDs in Chapter 10 and in Figures 11.2, 11.3, and 11.4 as the data flow "Sales order notification." In Figure 11.11, this notification is simply a sales order master record (with status indicating the order has not been shipped) on the enterprise database. Queries and reports (not shown in Figure 11.11) could be run to get a listing of these sales orders. Such listings would be most useful in the warehouse and shipping department to ensure timely picking and shipment of customer orders.

Throughout the day, as shipments are recorded in the shipping department, the billing section is "notified" by the shipping department. This notification is shown on the DFDs in Chapter 10 and in Figures 11.2, 11.3, and 11.4 as the data flow "Shipping's billing notification." Again, in Figure 11.11, this notification is simply a change to the sales order master record (with the new status indicating that the order has been shipped but not yet billed) on the enterprise database.

In the billing section, a clerk periodically requests a list of sales orders that have been shipped but have not been billed. In the SAP system, this is called the "Billing Due List." The clerk reviews this list, selects the items that are to be billed, prepares batch totals, and executes the billing run.

The billing program creates an electronic invoice;[18] updates the accounts receivable master data, the sales event data, and the general ledger master data to reflect the sale; and notifies the billing clerk that the run has been completed. The billing clerk compares the previously calculated batch total to the totals provided by the billing program to ensure that the billing run processed all of the selected shipments correctly.

FIGURE 11.11   Systems Flowchart of the Billing Process

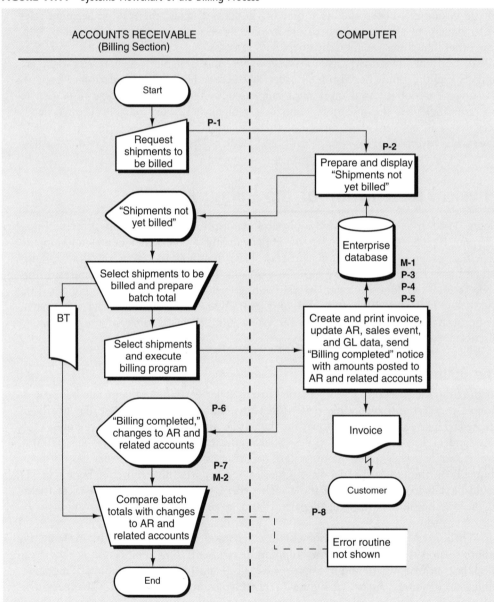

---

[18]The billing program could mail and print an invoice.

FIGURE 11.12 Control Matrix for the Billing Business Process

	Control Goals of the Billing Business Process									
	Control Goals of the Operations Process					Control Goals of the Information Process				
Recommended Control Plans	Ensure effectiveness of operations			Ensure efficient employment of resources (people, computers)	Ensure security of resources (accounts receivable master data)	For completed shipping notice inputs, ensure:			For the accounts receivable and master data, ensure:	
	A	B	C			IV	IC	IA	UC	UA
Present Controls										
P-1: Review shipped not billed sales orders (tickler file)	P-1						P-1			
P-2: Compare input shipping notice to sales order master data						P-2		P-2		
P-3: Independent billing authorization						P-3				
P-4: Check for authorized prices, term, freight, and discounts						P-4		P-4		
P-5: Independent pricing data			P-5			P-5				
P-6: Confirm input acceptance							P-6			
P-7: Reconcile input and output batch totals						P-7	P-7	P-7		
P-8: Procedures for rejected inputs							P-8	P-8		
Missing Controls										
M-1: Confirm customer accounts regularly		M-1				M-1	M-1	M-1		
M-2: Computer agreement of batch totals				M-2		M-2	M-2	M-2		

Possible effectiveness goals include the following:

A = Bill customers promptly upon evidence of shipment.

B = Provide for query and reporting functions that support accountability and meet specific problem-solving requirements (e.g., accounts receivable listings by invoice due date, aging reports).

C = Comply with the fair pricing requirements of the Robinson-Patman Act.

See Exhibit 11.1 for a complete explanation of control plans and cell entries.

IV = input validity
IC = input completeness
IA = input accuracy
UC = update completeness
UA = update accuracy

Selected Process Outputs

A variety of outputs (documents, statements, and reports) are generated during normal processing runs or during special report-generation runs. The key "document" produced by the process depicted in Figure 11.11 (pg. 412) is the invoice.

Another important document, the *customer monthly statement*, is prepared periodically, typically at the end of each month, from data appearing in each customer's accounts receivable master data record. Earlier in the chapter, we included the sending of periodic customer statements as part of the function of *managing customer accounts*. Because any physical implementation of the managing customer accounts process (i.e., the "AR" in the B/AR/CR process) would be highly redundant of the logical diagram in Figure 11.6 (pg. 404), we will not present a physical description of the AR process in this chapter.

Other analyses and reports can be prepared as needed by management. For example, if an accounts receivable aging report were desired, the relevant account data would be extracted from the accounts receivable master data. Figure 11.7 (pg. 406) illustrated a typical accounts receivable aging report.

Application of the Control Framework for the Billing Process

Controls

In this section, the control framework is applied to the billing process. **Figure 11.12** (pg. 413) presents a completed *control matrix* for the systems flowchart depicted in Figure 11.11. Figure 11.11 is annotated to show the location of the control plans keyed to the control matrix.

Control Goals

The control goals listed across the top of the matrix are similar to those presented in Chapters 7, 9, and 10, except that they have been tailored to the specifics of the billing process.

The *operations process control goals* that are typical of the billing process are the following:

- *Effectiveness of operations:* Goals A through C in Figure 11.12 identify three representative *effectiveness goals* for the billing process. Goals A and B address the issues related to cash flow and management of customer accounts discussed earlier in the chapter. In addition, as mentioned in Chapters 7 and 9, the control matrices in this text incorporate as one of the effectiveness goals, when applicable, the COSO report's goal of complying with laws, regulations, and contractual agreements. For this reason, we include goal C for the billing process—comply with the fair pricing requirements of the Robinson-Patman Act of 1936. Briefly stated, the act makes it illegal for a seller to charge different prices to two competing buyers under identical circumstances unless the seller can justify the pricing differential based on differences in its cost to manufacture, sell, and deliver the goods.
- *Efficient employment of resources:* As noted in Chapter 9 and reinforced in Chapter 10, people and computers are the resources found in most business processes.
- *Resource security:* As mentioned in Chapter 9, the resource security column should identify only the assets that are *directly* at risk. For that reason, cash is not listed because it is only indirectly affected by the validity of the billings. The resource that is of interest here is the accounts receivable master data. Controls should prevent unauthorized access, copying, changing, selling, or destruction of the accounts receivable master data.

The *information process control goals* comprise the second category of control goals in Figure 11.12. To focus our discussion, we have limited our coverage of process inputs to just the shipping notice (i.e., the shipments not yet billed) and have not included other process inputs, such as customer inquiries regarding account balances and management inquiries. The information process control goals are the following:

- *Input validity (IV):* Valid shipping notice inputs are those that are properly authorized and reflect actual credit sales; for example, a shipping notice should be supported by a valid sales order and a real shipment, and the invoice should be prepared using authorized prices, terms, freight, and discounts. If a billing process is completed without a real shipment (a genuine sale), revenues will be overstated.
- *Input completeness (IC) of shipping notices:* Failure to achieve this goal may result in billings not being completed, which leads to lost opportunity to obtain reimbursement for the sale, and understated revenue. Should shipping notices be processed more than once, there would be overstated revenue and poor customer service.
- *Input accuracy (IA) of shipping notices:* Inaccurate billings will cause errors in customers' accounts and the GL accounts for revenue and accounts receivable.
- *Update completeness (UC) and update accuracy (UA) of the sales order and accounts receivable master data:*[19] The accounts receivable master data is updated to create a record of the open invoice, and the sales order master data is updated to reflect that the shipment has been billed. This will preclude duplicate (i.e., an update completeness violation) invoices.

Recommended Control Plans

Recall that application control plans include both those that are characteristic of a particular AIS business process and those that relate to the technology used to implement the process. Many of the plans listed in Figure 11.12 and **Exhibit 11.1** (pp. 417) were discussed in Chapter 9, including an explanation of how each plan helps to attain specific control goals. That discussion will not need repeating here except to point out, as necessary, how and where the plan is implemented in the billing process pictured in Figure 11.11. If you cannot explain in your own words the relationship between the plans and goals, you should review the explanations in Chapter 9.[20]

There are a few new plans that are particular to the billing business process. We first define and explain these controls and then summarize, in Exhibit 11.1, each cell entry in Figure 11.12, the control matrix:

- *Review shipped not billed sales orders (tickler file)* (Exhibit 11.1 and Figure 11.12, P-1): By monitoring the sales orders that have been shipped but not yet billed, we can ensure that all shipping notices are billed in a timely manner.
- *Compare input shipping notice to sales order master data* (Exhibit 11.1 and Figure 11.12, P-2): This is an example of *compare input data to master data*, which ensures that the invoice, accounts receivable, and revenue accurately reflect the items and quantities ordered by, and shipped to, the customer.
- **Independent billing authorization** (Exhibit 11.1 and Figure 11.12, P-3): This establishes, for the billing personnel, that the shipment is supported by an actual

---

[19]These update goals do not apply in this analysis because the updates are simultaneous with the inputs, and the input controls address any update completeness and update accuracy issues.

[20]Other controls from Chapter 9 that we could have analyzed here include preformatted screens, online prompting, and programmed edit checks.

sales order. Typically, this would be accomplished by sending a copy of the sales order from customer service directly to the billing department or by giving the billing personnel access to open sales order records on the sales order master data (i.e., the sales order data used in control P-2). Without this control, billing inputs might be for shipments never requested by a customer. This control assumes a *segregation of duties* among sales (customer service), shipping, and billing.

- **Check for authorized prices, terms, freight, and discounts** (Exhibit 11.1 and Figure 11.12, P-4): This ensures that invoices, accounts receivable, and revenue reflect prices, terms, freight, and discounts authorized by management. Profitability may be affected by failure to employ these authorized data.
- **Independent pricing data** (Exhibit 11.1 and Figure 11.12, P-5): This assumes that a *segregation of duties* exists between those who approve unit prices and those involved in the selling function, such as customer sales representatives and billing clerks. Typically, selling prices will be obtained from inventory master data, a source for those prices that is *independent* of those in the selling functions.
- **Confirm customer accounts regularly** (Exhibit 11.1 and Figure 11.12, M-1): The customer can be used as a means of controlling the billing process; the customer can review the report of open invoices to determine that the invoices are valid and accurate.

Exhibit 11.1 contains a discussion of each recommended control plan listed in the control matrix in Figure 11.12, including an explanation of how each plan meets the related control goals. As you study the control plans, be sure to see where they are located on the systems flowchart. Also, see whether you agree with (and understand) the relationship between each plan and the goal(s) that it addresses. Remember that your ability to *explain* the relationships between plans and goals is more important than your memorization of the cell entries themselves.

Physical Description of the Cash Receipts Process

Enterprise Systems

Figure 11.13 (pg. 418) presents a physical description of the cash receipts process. From earlier in this chapter, you should have a good understanding of the billing process leading up to processing cash receipts. Take some time now to review the flowchart for general ideas. You should notice a close resemblance between the physical features of this process and the logical design of the billing process as presented in Figures 11.2 (pg. 400), 11.3 (pg. 401), and Figure 11.8 (pg. 407). You should also see that this system demonstrates the use of an enterprise system and several features of the technology discussed earlier in this chapter.

As discussed earlier, the procedures employed in collecting cash can vary widely. For example, some companies ask customers to mail checks along with RAs to the company; others ask customers to send payments to a designated bank *lockbox*; in e-commerce environments, some form of *electronic bill payment* such as electronic funds transfer is generally used. Figure 11.13 depicts a process in which customer payments are sent to a *lockbox*.

The cash receipts process begins each morning when the lockbox at the bank sends a file of remittance data processed the previous day.[21] The ERP system automatically saves this file in the enterprise database. For each payment, this file contains a customer number, invoice number, and amount paid. Totals in this file include hash totals for

---

[21]For this example, we show a lockbox that processes, typically, checks from customers. ACH payments, ACH check conversions, and other electronic payments would be handled in a similar manner.

EXHIBIT 11.1   Explanation of Cell Entries for the Control Matrix in Figure 11.12

P-1: *Review shipped not billed sales orders (tickler file).*

- *Effectiveness goal A, shipping notice input completeness:* By monitoring the sales orders that have been shipped but not yet billed, we can ensure that *all* shipping notices are billed in a *timely* manner.

P-2: *Compare the input shipping notice to the sales order master data.*

- *Shipping notice input validity and input accuracy:* This comparison can ensure that a sales order exists that corresponds to the shipping notice (validity) and that the items and quantities shipped, and for which an invoice will be prepared, are the same as the items and quantities on the sales order.

P-3: *Independent billing authorization.*

- *Shipping notice input validity:* Comparison of sales orders, entered by a sales representative, with shipping notifications entered by shipping, verifies that each shipment is supported by a valid sales order.

P-4: *Check for authorized prices, terms, freight, and discounts.*

- *Shipping notice input validity and input accuracy:* We see prices, terms, freight, and discounts being calculated during the billing process using *authorized* data in the enterprise database. This will ensure that the invoices will be accurate as to these elements and will reflect criteria approved by management (validity).

P-5: *Independent pricing data.*

- *Effectiveness goal C:* The independent pricing of orders, using prices approved by management, helps to ensure that the company does not engage in discriminatory pricing practices in violation of the Robinson-Patman Act.
- *Shipping notice input validity:* Automatic pricing presumes that previously authorized prices are used in the billing process.

P-6: *Confirm input acceptance.*

- *Shipping notice input completeness:* By advising the billing clerk that input has been accepted, we can ensure that all shipping notices are processed (i.e., input completeness).

P-7: *Reconcile input and output batch totals.*

- *Shipping notice input validity, input completeness, and input accuracy:* The billing clerk reconciles the input batch totals to the totals produced by the computer after the updates have occurred. If we assume that the batch total is either a dollar total or a hash total, we are justified in making cell entries in all three columns: *input validity* (only legitimate shipments were submitted to the billing process), *input completeness* (all shipments were submitted to the billing process and submitted only once), and *input accuracy* (the invoices and updates to accounts receivable and revenue correctly reflect the items and quantities that were shipped).

P-8: *Procedures for rejected inputs.*

- *Shipping notice input completeness and input accuracy:* We presume that corrective action will be taken to investigate all rejected items, remedy any errors (accuracy), and resubmit the corrected input for reprocessing (completeness).

M-1: *Confirm customer accounts regularly.*
    Note: Most organizations send statements, but that process is beyond the scope of that depicted in Figure 11.11 (pg. 412), so we have marked this as missing.

- *Effectiveness goal B:* The customer statements and summary reports produced with them provide the reporting and accountability functions suggested by goal B.
- *Shipping notice input validity, input completeness, and input accuracy:* The customer can be used as a means of controlling the billing process. By sending regular customer statements, we use the customer to check that invoices were valid, complete (not duplicated), and accurate.

M-2: *Computer agreement of batch totals.*
    Note: This control does not appear in the flowchart, nor is it mentioned in the physical process description narrative.

- *Efficient employment of resources:* Computer agreement of batch controls improves efficiency through automation of the process.
- *Shipping notice input validity, input completeness, and input accuracy:* If the computer reconciles the input batch totals with the totals calculated after the updates have occurred, and if those totals are either dollar or hash totals, we can ensure that only legitimate shipments were submitted to the billing process (validity), all shipments were submitted to the billing process (completeness), they were submitted only once (completeness), and the invoices and updates to accounts receivable and revenue correctly reflect the items and quantities that were shipped (accuracy).

customer number and invoice number and the total of the payments. The bank also sends an e-mail containing these same totals. A clerk in the cashier's office requests that the ERP system display the totals in the remittance file and manually compares these totals to those in the e-mail.

If the totals agree, the clerk e-mails the validated totals to a clerk in the payment applications section of the accounts receivable department. The payment applications clerk requests that the ERP system edit the remittance advice data. The editing process verifies the correctness of the remittance data by matching the input remittance data to the open invoice data that reside on the *accounts receivable master data* in the *enterprise database*. The edit process verifies that the customer account number, invoice number, and amount due are correct and that any cash discounts taken by the customer are

FIGURE 11.13 Systems Flowchart of the Cash Receipts Process

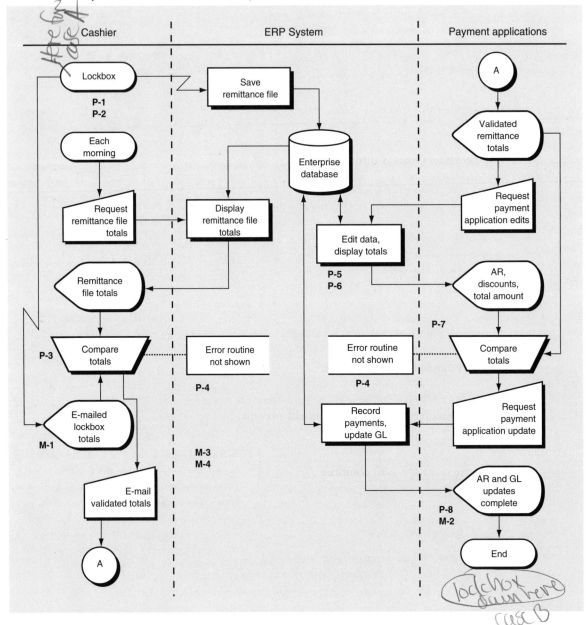

legitimate (i.e., they have been *authorized*). The computer displays the totals that will be recorded to accounts receivable and discounts, and the total amount that will be recorded as paid. The clerk compares these totals to those obtained from the e-mail and remittance file. If these agree, the clerk requests that the ERP system apply the payments by updating accounts receivable and the general ledger (cash, accounts receivable, discounts) for this batch. The computer notifies the clerk when this process is complete.

Application of the Control Framework for the Cash Receipts Process

In this section, the control framework is applied to the cash receipts process. **Figure 11.14** (pg. 420) presents a completed *control matrix* for the annotated systems flowchart depicted in Figure 11.13. Figure 11.13 is annotated to show the location of the control plans keyed to the control matrix.

> Controls

Control Goals

The control goals listed across the top of the matrix are similar to those presented in Chapters 7, 9, and 10, and Figure 11.12 (pg. 413) except that they have been tailored to the specifics of the cash receipts process.

The *operations process control goals* that are typical of the cash receipts process are the following:

- *Effectiveness of operations:* Goals A through C in Figure 11.14 are three representative *effectiveness goals* for the cash receipts process. Goals A and B address the issues related to cash flow and management of customer accounts discussed earlier in the chapter. In addition, as mentioned in Chapters 7 and 9, the control matrices in this text incorporate as one of the effectiveness goals, when applicable, the COSO report's goal of complying with laws, regulations, and contractual agreements. We assume that the company whose process appears in Figure 11.13 has loan agreements with its bank that require it to maintain certain minimum cash balances—known as compensating balances—on deposit. For that reason, effectiveness goal C—"Comply with compensating balance agreements with our depository bank"—appears in Figure 11.14.
- *Efficient employment of resources:* As noted in Chapter 9, reinforced in Chapter 10, and for the billing process earlier in this chapter, people and computers are the resources found in most business processes.
- *Resource security:* As mentioned in Chapter 9, the resource security column should identify assets that are at risk. The resources of interest here are cash and the accounts receivable master data. Controls should prevent the loss of cash and the unauthorized accessing, copying, changing, selling, or destruction of the accounts receivable master data.

The *information process control goals* comprise the second category of control goals in Figure 11.14. To focus our discussion, we have limited our coverage of process inputs to just the RAs (i.e., the cash receipts) and have not included other process inputs, such as customer inquiries regarding account balances and management inquiries. The information process control goals are the following:

- *Input validity (IV):* Valid RA inputs (i.e., cash receipts) are those that represent funds *actually received* and for which cash discounts have been *authorized* and *approved*. If a cash receipts process is completed without actual funds, assets will be misstated (AR too low and cash too high).

FIGURE 11.14   Control Matrix for the Cash Receipts Process

	Control Goals of the Cash Receipts Business Process								
	Control Goals of the Operations Process				Control Goals of the Information Process				
Recommended control plans	Ensure effectiveness of operations			Ensure efficient employment of resources (e.g., people and computers)	Ensure security of resources (e.g., cash, accounts receivable master data)	For the remittance advice inputs (i.e., cash receipts), ensure:			For the accounts receivable master data, ensure:
	A	B	C			IV	IC	IA	UC	UA
Present controls										
P-1: Lockbox	P-1		P-1	P-1	P-1	P-1		P-1		
P-2: Enter cash receipts close to where cash is received	P-2		P-2	P-2				P-2		
P-3: Manually reconcile batch totals				P-3	P-3	P-3	P-3	P-3		
P-4: Procedures for rejected inputs							P-4	P-4		
P-5: Edit cash receipts for accuracy				P-5				P-5		
P-6: Compare input data with master data	P-6			P-6		P-6	P-6			
P-7: Manually reconcile batch totals				P-7		P-7	P-7	P-7		
P-8: Confirm input acceptance							P-8		P-8	
Missing controls										
M-1: Compare amount deposited to amount in remittance file					M-1	M-1		M-1		
M-2: Manually reconcile input and output totals									M-2	M-2
M-3: Reconcile bank account regularly					M-3	M-3		M-3		
M-4: Monitor open accounts receivable	M-4	M-4	M-4			M-4	M-4	M-4	M-4	M-4

Effectiveness goals include:

A – Optimize cash flow by minimizing overdue accounts and reducing the investment in accounts receivable.

B – Provide for querying and reporting functions that support accountability and meet specific problem-solving requirements (e.g., accounts receivable listings by invoice due date, cash on deposit by bank).

C – Comply with compensating balance agreements with our depository bank.

See Exhibit 11.2 for a complete explanation of cell entries

IV = input validity
IC = input completeness
IA = input accuracy
UC = update completeness
UA = update accuracy

- *Input completeness (IC) of RAs:* Failure to achieve this goal may result in loss of accountability for the cash. RAs not processed or processed more than once would lead to customer balances that do not reflect payments made.
- *Input accuracy (IA) of RAs:* Inaccurate cash receipts processing will cause errors in customer accounts and in the GL accounts for accounts receivable, discounts, and cash.
- *Update completeness (UC) and update accuracy (UA) of the accounts receivable master data:*[22] The accounts receivable master data must be updated completely and accurately to reflect the fact that the customer has made a payment.

Recommended Control Plans

Recall that application control plans include both those that are characteristic of a particular AIS business process and those that relate to the technology used to implement the process. Many of the plans listed in Figure 11.14 and **Exhibit 11.2** (pp. 422–423) were discussed in Chapter 9, including an explanation of how each plan helps to attain specific control goals. That discussion will not need repeating here except to point out, as necessary, how and where the plan is implemented in the cash receipts process pictured in Figure 11.13 (pg. 418). If you cannot explain in your own words the relationship between the plans and goals, you should review the explanations in Chapter 9.

A few new plans are particular to the cash receipts business process. Some of these controls only apply if checks are received in the billing organization, while others only apply when various *electronic bill/invoice payment* methods are employed. We first define and explain these controls and then summarize, in Exhibit 11.2, each cell entry in Figure 11.14, the control matrix:

- **Immediately endorse incoming checks:** When checks are received within the billing organization, they must be protected from being fraudulently appropriated (*security of resources*). This requires that the checks be restrictively endorsed as soon as possible following their receipt in the organization. The endorsement should indicate that the check is for deposit only, the name of the organization depositing the check, and the account number and bank to which the check is being deposited. A *lockbox* provides even more protection for the cash by having cash receipts sent directly to a bank.
- **Immediately separate checks and remittance advices:** When checks are received in the billing organization, the RAs should be immediately separated from the checks. This will accelerate the deposit and the recording of the RAs because the customer payment can be recorded at the same time that the deposit is being prepared. The faster the checks are deposited, the less chance that the cash can be diverted. Also, if the person posting the RA does not have the check, *lapping* can be prevented.
- *Lockbox* (Exhibit 11.2 and Figure 11.14, P-1): As noted earlier in this chapter, the lockbox is a third-party service that collects and processes checks for an organization. Because the checks are never received in the billing organization, they cannot be fraudulently misappropriated (*security*) or used for a *lapping* scheme. Lockbox deposits are made more quickly and funds become available sooner. Lockbox personnel and processes are able to process payments with great efficiency and accuracy. Finally, the lockbox is unlikely to report remittances that are not supported by a real payment (*validity*).
- *Turnaround documents:* When the remittance advice that accompanies a payment is the stub from a statement or invoice, the entry of the payment data (by scanning, for example) can be much more efficient and accurate.

---

[22]These update goals do not apply in this analysis because the updates are simultaneous with the inputs, and the input controls address any update completeness and update accuracy issues.

- **Reconcile bank account regularly** (Exhibit 11.2 and Figure 11.14, pg. 420, M-3): A bank statement will reflect actual cash deposits and the correct amount of those deposits. These should be reconciled to the cash receipts event data to ensure that all valid deposits were recorded correctly. Ideally, a person who is independent of those who handle and record cash receipts and disbursements should perform the reconciliation. Having a validated record of actual deposits (and withdrawals) serves to secure the cash resource because it is more difficult to divert funds if an accurate, independent record exists.
- **Monitor open accounts receivable** (Exhibit 11.2 and Figure 11.14, M-4): An organization should regularly review accounts receivable aging reports (Figure 11.7, pg. 406) to ensure that cash is received in a timely manner. Follow-up procedures should be undertaken for payments that are overdue, and those that are deemed uncollectible should be written off to ensure that accounts receivable balances are not overstated. Errors in accounts receivable discovered during this follow-up should be corrected immediately.

Each of the recommended control plans listed in the matrix in Figure 11.14 is discussed in Exhibit 11.2. We have intentionally limited the number of plans to avoid redundancy. For instance, we do not include the plan *computer agreement of batch totals*, which is missing from the process. Further, we make no reference to performing *sequence checks* because the turn-around RAs are not received in sequence and, therefore, sequence checks are not relevant to the process under review. In addition to the control plans discussed in Exhibit 11.2, an organization should *reconcile subsidiary ledgers and control accounts regularly*. This control plan is discussed in Chapter 16. Because checks are sent to a *lockbox*, we do not include the controls *immediately endorse incoming checks*, *immediately separate checks and remittance advices*, and *turnaround documents*. Also, you should note that the control plan *confirm customer accounts regularly*, discussed earlier under the control plans for the billing process, serves to check the validity and accuracy of *both* customer billings and cash receipts.

EXHIBIT 11.2 Explanation of Cell Entries for the Control Matrix in Figure 11.14

P-1: *Lockbox.*

- *Effectiveness goals A and C and security of resources:* By having the payments sent directly to the bank, we can ensure a more timely deposit (*goals A and C*) and reduce the possibility of payments being diverted by the organization's own employees (security).
- *Efficient employment of resources:* The lockbox operation is more efficient than would be the handling of payments within the organization.
- *Remittance advice input validity:* By sending deposits directly to the lockbox, the likelihood of invalid deposits being recorded is reduced.
- *Remittance advice input accuracy:* Lockbox technology and personnel training and experience should lead to a more accurate input process than would be the case inside the organization.

P-2: *Enter cash receipts close to where cash is received.*

- *Effectiveness goals A and C:* By entering the RAs at the lockbox, and not sending them on to the billing organization, RAs will be input in a more timely manner.

- *Efficient employment of resources:* The entry of cash receipts at the lockbox provides for a more efficient employment of resources because lockbox personnel are familiar with the process and are able to handle more receipts in a given period.
- *Remittance advice input accuracy:* Because lockbox personnel would have both the check and the paid billing statement (e.g., remittance advice), they would be in a position to correct many input errors on the spot, thereby improving input accuracy.

P-3: *Manually reconcile batch totals.*

- *Security of resources, remittance advice input validity, input completeness, and input accuracy:* By comparing the totals e-mailed from the bank—hash totals of customer number, invoice number, and total payments—with those from the remittance file, we ensure that the remittance data sent from the bank is complete, accurate, and represents real payments (security, validity).

- *Efficient employment of resources:* By detecting any errors now, we preclude lengthy and costly error correction that might otherwise have been needed later in the process.

P-4: *Procedures for rejected inputs.*

- *Remittance advice input completeness and input accuracy:* We presume that corrective action will be taken to investigate all rejected items, remedy any errors (accuracy), and resubmit the corrected input for reprocessing (completeness).

P-5: *Edit cash receipts for accuracy.*

- *Efficient employment of resources:* Programmed edit checks provide quick, low-cost editing of data.
- *Remittance advice input accuracy:* By identifying erroneous or suspect data and preventing these data from entering the system, programmed edit checks help to ensure input accuracy.

P-6: *Compare input data with master data.*

- *Effectiveness goal A, efficient employment of resources:* The computer matching of payments and invoices can ensure that payments are applied more quickly and at a lower cost and prevent errors from entering the system.
- *Remittance advice input validity:* The matching process verifies that any cash discounts deducted by customers have been *authorized*.
- *Remittance advice input accuracy:* Comparison to the accounts receivable master data should reduce input errors (e.g., customer number, invoice number, amount due, authorized discount).

P-7: *Manually reconcile batch totals.*

- *Efficient employment of resources, remittance advice input validity, input completeness, and input accuracy:* By comparing the e-mailed totals to those produced by the computer after the edits, we can detect errors more *efficiently* than we would by examining the detail (or correcting errors later in the process), and determine that no extra inputs were processed (validity), all inputs will be processed once and only once (completeness), and all inputs will be processed correctly (accuracy).

P-8: *Confirm input acceptance.*

- *Remittance advice input completeness and accounts receivable master data update completeness:* By advising the user that input has been accepted, the input confirmation helps ensure input completeness. Because the

confirmation is provided after the AR data is updated, this confirmation ensures update completeness.

M-1: *Compare amount deposited to the amount in the remittance file.*

- *Security of resources, remittance advice input validity, and input accuracy:* The cashier should compare the dollar amounts in the remittance file with amounts actually deposited in the bank to ensure that there is a record of all cash received (security), that funds have actually been deposited for the remittances received from the lockbox (validity), and that the remittance data agrees with the amounts deposited (accuracy).

M-2: *Manually reconcile input and output batch totals.*

- *Accounts receivable update completeness and update accuracy:* The payment applications clerk should compare the RA totals taken after the edit process to those produced by the computer after the batch has been processed to determine that all remittance data was correctly (accuracy) posted to the AR master data once and only once (completeness).

M-3: *Reconcile bank account regularly.*
Note: Most organizations regularly reconcile their bank accounts, but that process is beyond the scope of that depicted in Figure 11.13 (pg. 418), so we have marked this as missing.

- *Security of resources, remittance advice input validity, and input accuracy:* By comparing the bank statement to the cash receipts event data, we can ensure that cash deposits were genuine (validity) and correctly recorded (accuracy). These accurate and valid records allow the organization to control available cash (security).

M-4: *Monitor open accounts receivable.*
Note: Most organizations regularly review aging reports, but that process is beyond the scope of that depicted in Figure 11.13, so we have marked this as missing.

- *Effectiveness goals A, B, and C:* By following up on open accounts receivable, we can optimize cash flows, solve billing and cash receipts processing problems, and ensure that the organization complies with compensating balance requirements of loan agreements with its bank.
- *Remittance advice input validity, input completeness, input accuracy, accounts receivable master data update completeness, and update accuracy:* By following up on open accounts receivable, we can detect and correct any errors that may have previously been made in the cash receipts input and update processes.

Summary

With the conclusion of this chapter, we complete the second business process in the order-to-cash process depicted in Figure 2.7 (pg. 53). In later chapters, we discuss the interaction of the OE/S and B/AR/CR processes with the other key business processes in an organization.

As we did at the end of Chapter 10, we include here, in **Technology Summary 11.6**, a review of the entity-level controls (i.e., control environment, pervasive controls, and general/IT general controls) that may have an impact on the effectiveness of the B/AR/CR business process controls.

Technology Summary 11.6

Considering the Affect of Entity-Level Controls on B/AR/CR Business Process Controls

The effectiveness of B/AR/CR controls can depend on the operation of several controls described in Chapter 8. In this summary, we examine some of those relationships.

Segregation of Duties

Several functions in the B/AR/CR process must be segregated for the business process controls to be effective, including the following:

- Authorization for item pricing, as well as payment terms, freight, and discounts, should be assigned to someone other than those completing the billing process. For example, prices on the inventory master records might be maintained by marketing.
- The billing process assumes that there has been an authorized sales order and an actual shipment. This presumes segregation among sales, shipping, and billing functions.
- Because the cash receipts process handles cash, there should be a segregation of duties between the cashier (treasurer) and cash applications/accounts receivable (controller) to ensure that the cash is not diverted with such techniques as *lapping*.
- The reconciliation of the bank accounts is a key control over the cash receipts process, and this must be performed by someone other than those who handle cash receipts (and disbursements). Otherwise, thefts undertaken during cash processing can be hidden.

Additional Manual Controls

Several manual, pervasive, and general controls can affect the performance of the business process controls:

- An additional control over the cash receipts process is to have two employees present when mail containing cash is opened.

This will preclude theft by either employee, unless they collude to steal the funds.
- In addition to separating the cashier and payment applications functions, *lapping* can be discouraged by *forced vacations* and *rotation of duties* for those handling cash receipts.
- As noted in Technology Summary 9.1 (pg. 318), the performance of these manual controls depends on the quality of the people performing the control activities. Therefore, we expect controls such as *selection and hiring*, *training and education*, *job descriptions*, and *supervision* to be in place.

Automated Controls

All of the B/AR/CR controls performed by the computer depend on the general controls (also known as IT general controls or ITGCs) in Chapter 8. Those controls include *check for authorized prices, terms, freight, and discounts*; *compare inputs with master data* (e.g., compare input shipping notices to sales orders, and compare input RAs to open invoices); and *programmed edit checks*. We need to know that the programs will perform the controls as designed (e.g., *program change controls*). Also, we need to know that the stored data used by the computer when executing these controls is valid and accurate (e.g., physical and logical access controls). For the B/AR/CR process, we are particularly concerned, for example, with controlled access to:

- Prices so that they cannot be changed without authorization
- AR master data so that an open invoice cannot be deleted without a payment having been received
- Sales order master data so that bogus sales orders cannot be created and so that they cannot be changed to falsely indicate that an invoice has been sent.

Key Terms

billing/accounts receivable/cash receipts (B/AR/CR) process, 391

electronic bill presentment and payment (EBPP), 394

float, 395

good funds, 395

credit card, 395

debit card, 395

electronic funds transfer (EFT), 397

Automated Clearing House (ACH) Network, 397

lockbox, 397

lapping, 398

invoice, 401

remittance advice (RA), 404

accounts receivable master data, 405

balance-forward system, 405

open-item system, 406

sales event data, 406

accounts receivable (AR) adjustments events data, 407

cash receipts event data, 407

post-billing system, 411

pre-billing system, 411

independent billing authorization, 415

check for authorized prices, terms, freight, and discounts, 416

independent pricing data, 416

confirm customer accounts regularly, 416

immediately endorse incoming checks, 421

immediately separate checks and remittance advices, 421

reconcile bank account regularly, 422

monitor open accounts receivable, 422

Review Questions

RQ 11-1   What is the billing/accounts receivable/cash receipts (B/AR/CR) process?

RQ 11-2   What primary activities does the B/AR/CR process perform? Explain each activity.

RQ 11-3   With what internal and external entities does the B/AR/CR interact?

RQ 11-4   What functions are typically segregated in the B/AR/CR process?

RQ 11-5   What are electronic bill presentment and payment (EBPP) systems? How do they reduce costs and accelerate cash flows?

RQ 11-6   Describe several ways that companies have reduced the float connected with cash receipts.

RQ 11-7   What is lapping? What controls can prevent or detect lapping?

RQ 11-8   What is an invoice?

RQ 11-9   What is a remittance advice (RA)?

RQ 11-10   What is accounts receivable master data?

RQ 11-11   What are the major features of a balance-forward and an open-item accounts receivable system?

RQ 11-12   What are the differences between a post-billing system and a pre-billing system?

RQ 11-13   What characterizes a valid shipping notice and invoice?

RQ 11-14   What are the key controls associated with the billing business process? Explain each control.

RQ 11-15 What characterizes a valid RA (i.e., cash receipt)?

RQ 11-16 What are the key controls associated with the cash receipts business process? Explain each control.

RQ 11-17 Describe the impact that entity-level controls (i.e., control environment, pervasive controls, general/IT general controls) can have on the B/AR/CR business process controls.

Discussion Questions

DQ 11-1 Develop several examples of possible goal conflicts among the various managers and supervisors depicted in Figure 11.1 (pg. 392).

DQ 11-2 Based on the definition of float presented in the chapter, discuss several possibilities for improving the cash float for your company, assuming you are the cashier.

DQ 11-3 Using Figure 11.6 (pg. 404), speculate about the kinds of data that might be running along the data flow that comes from the accounts receivable master data to bubble 2.1. Be specific, and be prepared to defend your answer by discussing the use(s) to which *each* of those data elements could be put.

DQ 11-4 Discuss the information content of Figure 11.7 (pg. 406). How might this report be used by the credit manager or by the accounts receivable manager? If you were either of these managers, what other reports concerning accounts receivable might you find useful, and how would you use them? Be specific.

DQ 11-5 Consult the systems flowcharts of Figures 11.11 and 11.13 (pp. 412 and 418). Discuss how each of these processes implements the concept of segregation of duties discussed in Chapter 8. For each of the two processes, be specific as to which entity (or entities) performs each of the four data processing functions mentioned in Chapter 8 (assuming that all four functions are illustrated by the process).

DQ 11-6 a. Discuss the conditions under which each of the following billing systems is most appropriate: (1) pre-billing system and (2) post-billing system.

 b. Discuss the relative advantages of each of the billing systems mentioned in part a, from the standpoint of both the selling company and the customer.

DQ 11-7 "Pre-billing sounds like the type of process used for catalog and Internet sales." Do you agree? Discuss fully.

Short Problems

SP 11-1 Describe the relative advantages of electronic bill presentment and payment (EBPP) systems, a lockbox, charge cards, debit cards, and ACH payments from the standpoint of *both* the party making the payment and the party receiving the payment.

SP 11-2 The following process is used by the Otis Company to process cash receipts. Describe the positive and negative elements of this process.

Include operational, information, and control issues. What additions or other changes to the process do you recommend?

> Mail for Otis Company is delivered to Sally, the company receptionist. Sally opens the mail and prepares a daily log of checks received. She sends the RAs to Al, the accounts receivable clerk, and the checks to Tony, the treasurer. Sally files the check log by date. Tony the treasurer prepares a deposit slip in duplicate and endorses the checks. Tony then takes the deposit slip to the bank and files the duplicate slip by date. Al uses the RAs to update the customer accounts to reflect the payment.

SP 11-3   Using the following table as a guide, describe for each function (see Figure 11.1, pg. 392):

a. A risk (an event or action that will cause the organization to fail to meet its goals/objectives).

b. A control/process or use of technology that will address the risk.

Function	Risks	Controls and Technology
Marketing		
Finance		

Billing
   AR (debit)
      Sales (credit)		

Collections
   Cash (debit)
      AR (credit)		

SP 11-4   Redraw the appropriate part of Figure 11.3 (pg. 401), assuming a lockbox system is used. Also, prepare a lower-level DFD for the cash receipts process, using the same assumption.

SP 11-5   The following is a list of six control plans from this chapter or from Chapters 9 and 10.

Control Plans

A. Prenumbered shipping notifications
B. Confirm customer accounts regularly
C. Confirm input acceptance
D. Programmed edits of shipping notification inputs
E. Independent billing authorization
F. Cumulative sequence check

The following five statements describe either the achievement of a control goal (i.e., a system success) or a system deficiency (i.e., a system failure).

Control Goals or System Deficiencies

1. Helps to ensure the validity of shipping notifications.
2. Provides a detective control to help ensure the accuracy of the billing process.
3. Provides a preventive control to help ensure the accuracy of the billing process.
4. In an online environment, helps to ensure input completeness.

5. Helps to identify duplicate, missing, and out-of-range shipping notifications by comparing input numbers to a previously stored number range.

Match the five control goals or systems deficiencies with a control plan that would *best* achieve the desired goal or prevent the system deficiency. A letter may be used only once, with one letter left over.

SP 11-6   The following is a list of six control plans from this chapter or from Chapters 9 and 10.

Control Plans

A. Procedures for rejected inputs
B. Computer agreement of batch totals
C. Document design
D. Review shipped not billed sales orders
E. Turnaround documents
F. Deposit slip file

The following five statements describe either the achievement of a control goal (i.e., a system success) or a system deficiency (i.e., a system failure).

Control Goals or System Deficiencies

1. The shipping clerk could not read the quantity picked that had been written on the picking ticket by the warehouse clerks.
2. In a periodic/batch environment, helps to ensure the information system control goal of input completeness of the shipping notices.
3. Helps to ensure that all shipments are billed in a timely manner.
4. Meets the operations system control goal of efficiency of resource use by reducing the number of data elements to be entered from source documents.
5. Provides an "audit trail" of deposits.

Match the five control goals or system deficiencies with a control plan that would *best* achieve the desired goal or prevent the system deficiency. A letter may be used only once, with one letter left over.

Problems

Note: As mentioned in Chapter 10, the first few problems in the business process chapters are based on processes of specific companies. Therefore, the problem material starts with narrative descriptions of those processes (cases).

CASE STUDIES

CASE A: Fred's Electrical, Inc. (Cash Receipts Process)

Fred's Electrical, Inc. sells electrical parts to electrical contractors in the northwestern United States. Fred's customers mail their payments—attached to the stub (i.e., remittance advice [RA]) from their monthly statement—to Fred's accounts receivable (AR) office. An AR clerk confirms that the check amount agrees with the amount on the RA and sends the checks to the cashier. The AR clerk prepares batch totals of the customer numbers, invoice numbers, and amount paid. The AR clerk then enters the batch totals and RAs into the computer, where the AR master data is updated to record the payment. The computer reconciles the batch totals, confirms job completion, and reports discrepancies, if any, to the AR clerk.

CASE B: Bondstreet Company (Billing and Cash Receipts Processes)

The Bondstreet Company sells medical supplies to hospitals, clinics, and doctors' offices. Bondstreet uses an ERP system for all of its business processes.

The billing process begins each morning when a clerk in the billing section of the accounts receivable department requests that the ERP system display the billing due list on their computer screen. These are the shipments made the previous day from the warehouse at Bondstreet's customer fulfillment center. At the bottom of the list, the computer displays the total number of records in the billing due list, the total number of items that were shipped, and a hash total of the customer numbers. The clerk records these onto a batch total sheet.

The clerk then requests that the ERP system execute the billing program. This program prepares invoice records by accessing the customer data to get the routing information for the electronic invoice and the payment terms to be given to the customer. The program also obtains the prices from the inventory data. Finally, the program examines the sales order data to determine how the shipment was routed so that shipping costs can be added to the invoice. At the end of this process, the computer calculates and displays a total of the number of invoices, the total items being billed, and a hash total of the customer numbers in the batch of invoices.

The billing clerk reconciles the invoice totals with those obtained from the billing due list. If the totals agree, the clerk accepts the batch of invoices. In response, the ERP system updates the sales order to show that the shipment has been billed, closes the billing due list, creates an accounts receivable record, updates the general ledger for the sale, sends an electronic invoice to the customer, and displays a job completed notice on the billing clerk's screen.

The cash receipts process begins each morning when the lockbox at Bondstreet's bank sends a file of remittance data processed the previous day. Bondstreet's ERP system automatically saves this file. For each payment, this file contains a customer number, invoice number, and amount paid. Totals in this file include hash totals for customer number and invoice number and the total payments. The bank also sends an e-mail containing these same totals. A clerk in the cash applications section of the accounts receivable department requests that the ERP system display the totals in the remittance file and manually compares those totals to those in the e-mail.

If the totals agree, the clerk requests that the ERP system apply the payments to the accounts receivable data. The computer examines the terms on the invoice record, calculates the amount that should be paid, and records the payment (again, assuming that the amounts are all correct). The computer displays the totals recorded to accounts receivable and discounts, and the total amount paid. The clerk compares these totals to those obtained from the e-mail and remittance file. If these agree, the clerk requests that the ERP system update the general ledger (cash, accounts receivable, discounts) for this batch.

CASE C: Fairfield Novelties, Inc. (Billing Process)

Fairfield Novelties manufactures and sells novelty items to retail stores. Completed orders (goods and attached sales order) are received in the shipping department from the factory floor. The shipping clerk keys the sales order number into the computer in the shipping department. The computer accesses the sales order on the sales order master data and displays the open sales order. After determining that the correct sales order has been displayed, the shipping clerk keys in the items and quantities being shipped. The clerk reviews the shipment data and, if correct, accepts the input. (*Note:* The remainder of the shipment process is beyond the scope of this case narrative.)

After the shipment data has been accepted, the computer updates the sales order master data to reflect the shipment, creates and records an invoice on the accounts receivable master data, and prints an invoice, in three parts, on the printer in the billing office. A billing clerk signs the invoice, mails copies 1 and 2 to the customer, and files copy 3 by customer name.

CASE D: Fairfield Novelties, Inc. (Cash Receipts Process)

Before starting this case, review the facts in Case B. Assume that customers have been billed and have sent in a payment with copy 3 of the invoice, on which they have filled in the amount remitted. The cash receipts clerk compares the check to the amount written on the invoice and, in a space reserved, enters the amount received so that it can be computer scanned.

Checks and these invoice copies are batched. The invoice copies are sent to the IT department. The deposit slip is prepared, in triplicate, and the checks are deposited. Copies of the batch totals and deposit slip copy 2 are filed separately by date. Copy 3 of the deposit slip is sent to the treasurer's office.

The IT department uses an optical scanner to process the invoice copies. This run occurs each evening at 10 p.m. Customers' accounts are posted, and a cash receipts listing is produced and sent to cash receipts each morning, where it is checked against and filed with the related batch totals. A copy of the cash receipts listing is sent to the treasurer's office.

P 11-1   For the case assigned by your instructor,[23] complete the following requirements:

   a. Prepare a table of entities and activities.

   b. Draw a context diagram.

   c. Draw a physical data flow diagram (DFD).

   d. Prepare an annotated table of entities and activities. Indicate on this table the groupings, bubble numbers, and bubble titles to be used in preparing a level 0 logical DFD.

   e. Draw a level 0 logical DFD.

P 11-2   For the case assigned by your instructor, complete the following requirements:

   a. Draw a systems flowchart.

   b. Prepare a control matrix, including explanations of how each recommended existing control plan helps to accomplish—or would accomplish in the case of missing plans—each related control goal. Your choice of recommended control plans could come from Exhibit 11.1 and/or Exhibit 11.2 (pgs. 417 and 422–423) plus any other control

---

[23]For problems P 11-1 and P 11-2, if the assigned case is an extension of an earlier case, limit your solution to the narrative contained in the assigned case.

plans from Chapters 9 or 10 that are germane to your company's process.

   c. Annotate the flowchart prepared in part a to indicate the points where the control plans are being applied (codes P-1, … , P-n) or the points where they could be applied but are not (codes M-1, … , M-n).

P 11-3   The following is a list of 12 control plans from Chapter 8.

Control Plans from Chapter 8

A. Access control software (i.e., assignment of access rights to employees)

B. Selection, hiring, and supervision of billing clerks to ensure that they can and do carry out their assigned responsibilities

C. Physical controls for perimeter, building, and computer facilities to prevent loss or destruction of the computer resources

D. Preventive maintenance of computer hardware to ensure reliability and availability

E. Systems development life cycle (SDLC), including testing and approval before implementation of new or revised programs

F. Segregate marketing (i.e., authorization of prices) from billing (i.e., authorization of changes to the billing process and programs)

G. Segregate payment applications clerks from AR clerks who resolve customer complaints

H. Segregate cashier who processes cash receipts from the treasurer

I. Segregate controller functions (recordkeeping for AR) from treasurer functions (custody of cash)

J. Continuous data protection (CDP) to ensure availability of sales order and AR master data

K. Controls for physical and logical access to sales order master data to prevent, for example, unauthorized deletion of open sales orders

L. Controls for physical and logical access to accounts receivable master data to prevent, for example, unauthorized deletion of open invoices

The following is a list of 10 B/AR/CR business process controls or deficiencies.

B/AR/CR Business Process Control Plans or Deficiencies

1. Each day, the computer reviews the open sales orders to identify those that have been shipped but not yet billed. This list is presented to the billing clerk for action. Occasionally, the billing clerk does not bother to follow up on open sales orders, and invoices are not sent out in a timely manner.

2. Periodically, the billing program reviews open sales orders (shipped not billed) and prepares and sends invoices. To prevent some invoices from being sent, someone in the organization has changed some sales orders to indicate that they are closed.

3. When an invoice is prepared, the computer should employ authorized prices, terms, freight, and discounts. Customer complaints include incorrect prices on invoices. Research determines that billing clerks are changing prices prior to billing.

4. Prior to releasing a batch of invoices, the billing clerk agrees the batch totals of the shipments to be billed to the totals prepared by the

computer at the end of the invoicing process. The computer totals are often incorrect.

5. Upon receipt in the mailroom, checks are forwarded to the cashier and RAs to the cash applications clerks.

6. The computer prepares an aging of open invoices, and accounts receivable clerks follow up on overdue balances.

7. Turnaround documents (e.g., RAs) are used to record customer payments. The scanner often does not read the remittance data correctly.

8. The treasurer reconciles bank accounts regularly.

9. Monthly statements are printed in the accounts receivable department and mailed to customers.

10. Cash receipts are edited to determine that the customer has taken the appropriate discounts. Exceptions are routed via *workflow* to the supervisor of AR for electronic approval. Sales clerks have been able to approve the taking of unauthorized discounts.

Match the 10 B/AR/CR business process control plans with a pervasive control plan from Chapter 8 that could prevent the deficiencies noted in the preceding list or have an impact on the successful execution of the business process control. Explain the impact that the pervasive control could have.

P 11-4   (*Note:* You can do this problem only if you have access to a computer-based electronic spreadsheet, such as Excel, or to a database software package, such as Access.)

Problem Data

Gateway Industries is a retailer of bicycles and bicycle parts. It sells on credit terms of net 30 days. As of June 30, 20XX, its subsidiary ledger of customer balances reflects the following details:

Customer Name	Invoice Number	Due Date	Invoice Amount	Total Balance
Bikes Et Cetera	1965	2/15/20XX	$1,427.86	
	2016	3/23	721.40	
	2092	4/16	713.49	
	2163	5/14	853.02	
	2184	5/31	562.92	
	2202	6/13	734.47	
	2235	6/20	622.88	$5,636.04
International Bicycle Sales	1993	3/15	$333.24	
	2010	3/20	564.49	
	2112	4/24	400.69	
	2170	5/16	363.60	
	2182	5/31	1,255.91	$2,917.93
Rodebyke Bicycles & Mopeds	2075	4/10	$634.84	
	2133	4/28	370.97	
	2159	5/7	371.49	

Customer Name	Invoice Number	Due Date	Invoice Amount	Total Balance
	2174	5/22	498.75	
	2197	6/8	713.54	
	2222	6/18	451.11	
	Finance Charge	6/30	10.06	$3,050.76
Stan's Cyclery	1974	2/27	$575.00	
	2000	3/18	536.82	
	2019	3/25	641.60	
	2108	4/22	629.94	
	2125	4/26	682.50	
	2164	5/14	292.36	
	2215	6/16	249.04	$3,607.26
Wheelaway Cycle Center	2117	4/25	$819.55	
	2140	5/4	745.54	
	2171	5/16	490.00	
	2178	5/25	587.80	
	2192	6/3	1,045.23	
	2219	6/17	475.87	
	2234	6/20	257.37	
	2250	6/29	700.03	$5,121.39

Using the computer electronic spreadsheet or database software indicated by your instructor, prepare an accounts receivable aging report as of June 30, 20XX. Observe the following specific requirements:

a. In addition to a report heading, the report should contain column headings for:

- Customer name
- Total balance
- Current balance and past-due balance, with supporting columns for 1 to 30 days, 31 to 60 days, 61 to 90 days, over 90 days

b. Each individual open invoice and its due date should be entered into the computer software. However, those details should *not* appear in the report. Instead, for each customer, show the total outstanding balance and the total amount in each age category.

c. Print totals for each money column and verify that the totals of the aging columns cross-add to the grand total of all outstanding balances.

P 11-5   The following is a list of 12 control plans from this chapter or from Chapters 9 and 10.

Control Plans

A. Review shipped but not billed sales orders
B. Confirm customer balances regularly
C. Enter shipping notice close to location where order is shipped
D. Check for authorized prices, terms, freight, and discounts
E. Hash totals (e.g., of customer ID numbers)
F. Computer agreement of batch totals
G. Key verification
H. Compare input sales return notification to AR master data
I. Immediately endorse incoming checks
J. One-for-one checking of checks and RAs
K. Immediately separate checks and RAs
L. Reconcile bank account regularly

The following are 10 system failures that have control implications.

System Failures

1. After goods are delivered to the common carrier, the shipping department at Stanley, Inc. prepares a three-part shipping notice. Copy 2 of the notice is sent to billing to initiate the billing process. Many shipping notices have either been lost in transit or been delayed in reaching the billing section.

2. Bar-Jacob Company was given a refund for a sales return even though the return was received and processed months after the sales terms allowed such a return.

3. Because the mailroom clerks at Holdington Corp. do not take batch totals of incoming customer checks, the cashier has misappropriated several thousand dollars over the years by depositing company checks to his personal bank account.

4. Nichol, Inc. uses periodic processing for entering sales invoice inputs and updating customer accounts. Although it uses certain batch total procedures, Cooper has experienced a number of instances of recording sales invoices to incorrect customer accounts.

5. Grant Company customers send in their payments with an RA on which they write the amount being paid. These amounts often do not agree with the amount of the payment. As a result, the cash and AR balances at Lincoln are not correct.

6. The balances due from customers at Wright Company are months overdue.

7. At Jefferson, Inc., shipping sends shipping notices to the data entry group in data processing, where they are keyed. During the past month, an inexperienced data entry clerk made several errors in keying the shipping notices. The errors were discovered when customers complained about inaccurate invoices.

8. Sales at Macon Corp. have declined considerably compared to those of the preceding year. In an effort to improve the financial statements, the vice president of finance obtained a supply of blank shipping notices on which she fabricated 100 fictitious shipments. She submitted the fictitious documents to the billing department for billing.

9. The mailroom at Gardener Company forwards checks and RAs to the accounts receivable department. A clerk checks the RAs against open

invoices, as reflected on the accounts receivable master data. It is not uncommon for the clerk to note discrepancies, in which case the customer is contacted in an effort to reconcile the differences. After all the discrepancies have been investigated and cleared, the accounts receivable clerk releases the checks to the cashier for deposit.

10. Clerks in the billing department at Canterbury Enterprises, Inc., prepare sales invoices from a copy of the packing slip received from the shipping department. Recently, the company has experienced a rash of customer complaints that the customers have been billed for freight charges, despite the fact that the freight terms were FOB destination.

Match the 10 system failures with a control plan that would *best* prevent the system failure from occurring. Also, give a brief (one- to two-sentence) explanation of your choice. A letter should be used only once, with two letters left over.

P 11-6   Conduct research on electronic bill presentment and payment (EBPP) systems (see Technology Summary 11.1, pg. 394). Write a paper describing the advantages and disadvantages, to both the payer and payee, of the two methods for implementing these systems—the biller direct and the consolidation/aggregation methods.

P 11-7   Redraw the appropriate part of Figure 11.3 (pg. 401) assuming that, in addition to cash collections from charge customers, the organization also has cash sales and receives cash from the sale of equity securities. Prepare a brief, one- to two-sentence defense for each of the changes made.

Do *not* draw an entirely new Figure 11.3. You might want to photocopy the figure from the chapter and then draw your additions and changes on the photocopy.

P 11-8   For Figure 11.3:

a. Indicate the sequence of activities by putting numbers next to the data flows. For example, the "Sales order notification" in the upper left of the diagram would be number "1." Restart the numbers for each bubble. Assign the same number to simultaneous data flows. For example, "Invoice" and "GL invoice update" coming out of bubble 1.0 should get the same number.

b. For each process bubble, indicate, by placing a "T" on the flow, the flow that triggers the processing activities. For example, "Shipping's billing notification" is flow T2 for bubble 1.0.

c. In a separate narrative describe:

- The activities in each process bubble
- Each flow, including its purpose, into and out of the data stores and to and from each process
- Each data store's major elements

P 11-9   Use the DFDs in Figures 11.3, 11.4, 11.6, and 11.8 (pp. 401, 402, 404, and 407) to solve this problem.

Prepare a four-column table that summarizes the B/AR/CR processes, inputs, and outputs. In the first column, list the three processes shown in the level 0 diagram (Figure 11.3). In the second column, list the subsidiary functions shown in the three lower-level diagrams (Figures 11.4, 11.6, and 11.8). For *each* subsidiary function listed in column 2, list the data flow names or the data stores that are inputs to that process (column 3) or outputs of that process (column 4). (See *Note.*) The following table has been started for you to indicate the format for your solution.

Note: To simplify the solution, do *not* show any reject stubs in column 4.

Solution Format Summary of the B/AR/CR processes, subsidiary functions, inputs, outputs, and data stores

Process	Subsidiary Functions	Inputs	Outputs
1.0 Perform billing	1.1 Compare	Sales order notification Shipping's billing notification	Validated shipping notification
	1.2 Prepare invoice	Validated shipping notification Customer master data	... Continue solution ...

P 11-10 This problem should be completed with database software, such as Microsoft Access. As directed by your instructor, submit the completed database file and the printouts noted below.

a. Using the E-R diagram in Figure 11.9 (pg. 408), select any three or four related entities and implement them as tables using Microsoft Access (or any other database software acceptable to your instructor). Link the tables using the cardinalities shown in the figure. For the tables, you may use attributes shown in Figure 11.10 (pg. 410) or create different attributes.

b. Create forms for each table from part 1 of this problem and use the forms to populate the tables with representative data. Forms should be in good order, readable, and properly formatted. Create at least three records in each table. Print out the populated tables and one instance of each form.

c. Design three queries using the tables from part 1 of this problem. Print out the output of each query and attach an explanation as to why someone would be interested in the output of each query.

d. Using the report function in Access, design a report for each query from part 3 of this problem. Reports should be in good order, readable, and properly formatted. Print out each report.

CHAPTER 12

The Purchasing Process

Learning Objectives

After reading this chapter, you should be able to:

- Describe the relationship between the purchasing process and its business environment, including the organization's supply chain.

- Summarize how enterprise systems, e-business, and other technologies can improve the effectiveness of the purchasing process.

- Assess the implications of implementing a supply chain management (SCM) system in a global business environment.

- Depict the logical and physical characteristics of a typical purchasing process.

- Prepare a control matrix for a typical purchasing process, including an explanation of how business process control plans can accomplish operations and information process control goals.

This is a classic story. In the 1980s, Wal-Mart® and Procter & Gamble™ (P&G™) built a software system that linked P&G to Wal-Mart's distribution centers. When a P&G product ran low in a Wal-Mart distribution center, the system sent a message to P&G. Then P&G initiated a shipment to the Wal-Mart distribution center or perhaps to a Wal-Mart store. Enhancements to the system have allowed P&G to know when any P&G product is scanned at the checkout at any Wal-Mart store rather than waiting to be notified of product levels at distribution centers. Purchases, shipments, invoices, and payments are all automatic. As a result, P&G can make and ship products to Wal-Mart in a timely manner, without maintaining excessive inventory. Wal-Mart has less inventory on hand, lower costs (savings passed on from P&G), and higher product availability. P&G, Wal-Mart, and, most importantly, Wal-Mart customers are happier with this system. In this chapter, we will explore the processes, systems, and controls that should be in place to ensure that the purchasing process operates efficiently (i.e., low cost) and effectively (i.e., high customer value). Particular attention will be paid to processes that are used to determine when and how much to purchase.

Synopsis

This chapter presents our third business process, the purchasing process. The purchasing process includes the first three steps—requirements determination, purchase order (PO) processing, and goods receipt—in the *purchase-to-pay process* (see Figure 2.10 on pg. 56). After we introduce the players involved in the purchasing process, we describe an organization's connections to its suppliers and customers (i.e., its supply chain) to set the stage for the complexities of the purchasing process. In addition, we call your attention to the "Physical Process Description" and the "Application of the Control Framework to Purchasing" sections. These sections cover state-of-the-art material on current and evolving technology and provide reading that we hope you will find both interesting and informative.

Introduction

As previously noted, the purchasing process comprises the first three steps in the purchase-to-pay process (Figure 2.10). Let's take a closer look at the purchasing process.

Process Definition and Functions

The **purchasing process** is an interacting structure of people, equipment, activities, and controls that is designed to accomplish the following:

- Handle the repetitive work routines of the purchasing department and the receiving department.[1]
- Support the decision needs of those who manage the purchasing and receiving departments.
- Assist in the preparation of internal and external reports.

First, the purchasing process handles the repetitive work routines of the purchasing and receiving departments by capturing and recording data related to the day-to-day operations of the departments. The recorded data then may be used to generate source documents (such as POs and receiving reports) and to produce internal and external reports.

The purchasing process prepares a number of reports used by personnel at various levels of management. For example, the manager of the purchasing department might use an open PO report to ascertain which orders have yet to be filled.

Before leaving this section, we need to define two terms that we will be using throughout the chapter: *goods* and *services*. *Goods* are raw materials, merchandise, supplies, fixed assets, or intangible assets. *Services* cover work performed by outside vendors, including contractors, catering firms, towel and linen service providers, consultants, auditors, and the like.

Organizational Setting

The purchasing process is closely linked to functions and processes inside and outside the organization. Let's take a look at those links and the impact they have on the operation of the purchasing process.

---

[1]To focus our discussion, we have assumed that these two departments are the primary operating units related to the purchasing process. For a given organization, however, the departments associated with the process may differ.

An Internal Perspective

Figure 12.1 and **Table 12.1** (pg. 440) present an internal view of the relationship between the purchasing process and its organizational environment. They show the various information flows generated or captured by the process. Take some time now to study the figure to get acquainted with the entities with which the process interacts.

Figure 12.1 and Table 12.1 reveal five information flows that function as vital communication links among various departments, business processes, and external entities. We briefly explain each flow here to give you a quick introduction to the purchasing process. Although Figure 12.1 depicts the flows using the document symbol, most of them can be implemented using electronic communications (e.g., workflow) and data stored in the enterprise database.

- Flow 1 is sent to purchasing from the inventory control department (or process), or various departments in the organization, to request a purchase of goods or services. The requests might be routed to purchasing electronically (e.g., *workflow*).[2]

FIGURE 12.1   An Internal Perspective of the Purchasing Process

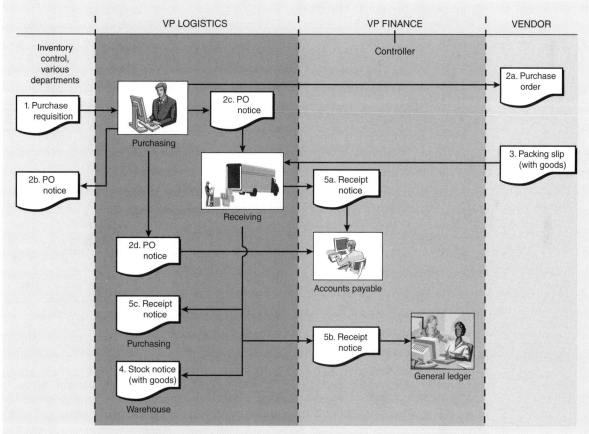

---

[2]In the P&G and Wal-Mart example, shipments are made by P&G without a specific request from Wal-Mart.

TABLE 12.1 Description of Information Flows

Flow No.	Description
1	Purchase requisition sent from inventory control (or various departments) to purchasing
2	PO sent to vendor (2a), inventory control (or various departments) (2b), receiving (2c), and accounts payable (2d)
3	Packing slip (with goods) received from vendor
4	Stock notice (with goods) sent to warehouse
5	Notice of goods receipt sent to accounts payable (5a), general ledger (5b), and purchasing (5c)

- Flow 2a is a PO to a vendor. This could be a mailed, paper PO, or it could be sent electronically (e.g., *EDI*). Flows 2b, 2c, and 2d "inform" (via documents, electronic notices, or changes to the enterprise database) the original requestor (e.g., inventory control, various departments), receiving, and accounts payable that a PO has been sent.
- Flow 3 represents the goods and accompanying packing slip from the vendor to receiving.
- After matching the goods and packing slip to the PO (flow 2c), receiving sends the goods to the warehouse via flow 4.
- Flows 5a, 5b, and 5c "inform" (via documents, electronic notices, or changes to the enterprise database) accounts payable, general ledger, and purchasing that the goods have been received. Accounts payable will match flows 2d and 5a with the vendor invoice, when it is received, to determine that the invoice is valid and accurate. The general ledger uses flow 5b to update the general ledger account for inventory to reflect the increase in inventory on hand. Because we do not have a vendor invoice, we cannot make an entry to the general ledger account for accounts payable. To balance this entry to inventory, the general ledger process will make an entry to a clearing account. We'll discuss this entry later in the chapter and in Chapter 13. Upon receipt of flow 5c, purchasing will "close" the PO.[3]

Let's examine the important control implicit in the assignment of responsibilities in Figure 12.1. First, we see that purchasing receives *authorization* (via the purchase requisition and, if required, approval of the PO) to *execute* and *record* the purchase. The open PO (i.e., flow 2c) *authorizes* receiving to accept the goods. Receiving *executes* the receipts and, along with the warehouse, has *custody* of the goods. The controller/general ledger *records* the increase in inventory.

Organizational Setting and Possible Goal Conflicts

The chief purchasing executive in an organization assumes various titles such as manager of purchasing, director of purchasing, procurement manager, or purchasing agent. We use the term *purchasing manager*. The purchasing manager usually performs major buying activities as well as the required administrative duties of running a department. In many organizations, professional *buyers* do the actual buying. The *receiving supervisor* is responsible for receiving incoming goods, signing the *bill of lading* presented by the carrier or the

---

[3]The timing of the recording in the general ledger of this receipt transaction (i.e., increase inventory) and the related invoice transaction (i.e., increase accounts payable) may depend on how close together these two activities occur and the specific software employed.

supplier in connection with the shipment, reporting the receipt of goods,[4] and making prompt transfer of goods to the appropriate warehouse or department.

The goals of individual managers in this setting may conflict with (i.e., are not in *congruence* with) overall organizational objectives. That is, some of the managers and supervisors shown in Figure 12.1 might be "marching to different drummers." For example, the purchasing manager probably will want to buy in large quantities to take advantage of quantity discounts and to reduce ordering costs. Receiving, inspecting, and storing large quantities of inventory, however, will more than likely present problems for the receiving department supervisor and the warehouse manager.

In addition to goal conflicts between managers, ambiguity often exists in defining goals and successfully meeting those goals. For instance, one of the purchasing goals might be *to select a vendor who will provide the best quality at the lowest price by the promised delivery date.* But what does this goal mean, precisely? Does it mean that a particular vendor must satisfy all three conditions of best quality, lowest price, and timely delivery? Realistically, one vendor probably will not satisfy all three conditions.

Prioritization of goals is often necessary in choosing the *optimal* solution given the various conflicts and constraints placed on the process. This implies that trade-offs must be made in prioritizing among the goals that conflict. For example, if a company operates in an industry that is extremely sensitive to satisfying customer needs, it may be willing to pay a premium price to ensure that it is procuring the best-quality goods and obtaining them when needed.

An External Perspective

Figure 12.2 (pg. 442) presents an external view of the relationship between the purchasing process and its environment. A **supply chain** comprises the connections from the suppliers of merchandise and raw materials through to an organization's customers. These connections include the flow of information, materials, and services. We depict the supply chain as a value system (Figure 2.2, pg. 43) because each player in the supply chain is - performing a set of activities to transform inputs into outputs valued by its customers (i.e., a *value chain*). As discussed in Chapter 2, the value chain within an organization is facilitated by its enterprise system. And you should know that the links between the organizations in the supply chain are normally global, e-business connections.

In our discussion here, we will assume the role of the retailer in Figure 12.2 and not consider the manufacturer. In Chapter 15, we will discuss the role of the manufacturing process in the supply chain. For now, assume we are a retailer, such as Wal-Mart, Target®, or Staples®, and we need to manage the links in our supply chain so that we can get the right goods on our shelves, in the right amount, at the right time, and at minimal cost (i.e., *efficiency*) to create maximum value for our customers (i.e., *effectiveness*). How we do that is discussed next.

Supply Chain Management

Supply chain management (SCM) is the combination of processes and procedures used to ensure the delivery of goods and services to customers at the lowest cost while providing the highest value to the customers. As previously noted, the goal of SCM is to increase product availability while reducing inventory across the supply chain.

Enterprise
Systems

E-Business

---

[4]In this section and in the section describing the logical purchasing process, we assume that the receiving supervisor is also responsible for indicating that services have been received. In practice, the receipt of services might well be reported by various operating departments that have received the service.

FIGURE 12.2 An External Perspective of the Purchasing Process: The Organization's Supply Chain (A Value System)

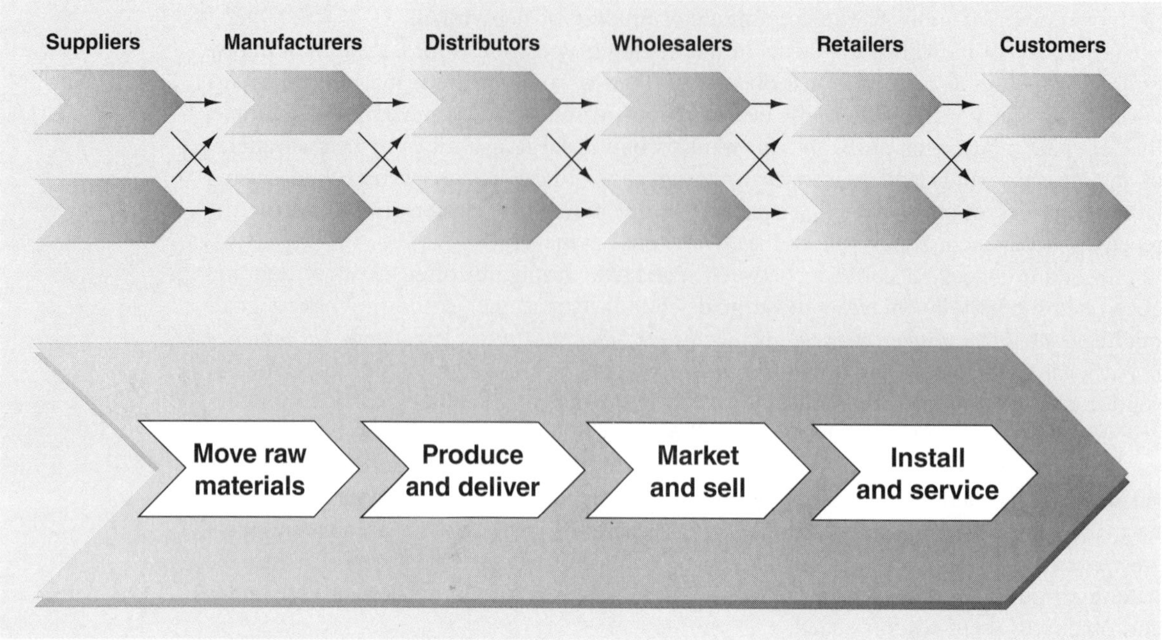

To do this, supply chain partners must coordinate the flow of information and physical goods among members of the supply chain. **Technology Summary 12.1** describes a model for SCM developed by the Supply-Chain Council and adopted by many of the council's nearly 1,000 members.

SCM software helps an organization execute the steps in the supply chain. Software products are available to perform individual functions within each of the five steps in SCM (i.e., the five components in Technology Summary 12.1), and products are available to perform complete steps or several of the steps. The products can be divided into two categories. The first, *supply chain planning* software, accumulates data about orders from retail customers, sales from retail outlets, and data about manufacturing and delivery capability of assisting in planning for each of the SCM steps. The most valuable, and problematic, of these products is demand planning software used to determine how much product is needed to satisfy customer demand.

Enterprise Systems

E-Business

The second category of supply chain software, *supply chain execution* software, automates the SCM steps. ERP software is assigned to this category as it receives customer orders, routes orders to an appropriate warehouse, and executes the invoice for the sale. As previously noted, many of the connections between players in the supply chain are B2B automated interfaces. For example, the sourcing step may be implemented through an automatic order sent to a supplier via the Internet or EDI.

At the beginning of this chapter, we briefly described the advantages that P&G and Wal-Mart achieved by managing their supply chain. In general, management of the supply chain leads to some or all of the following benefits:

- Lower costs to the customer.
- Higher availability of the product. (for the customer, for production, etc.)
- Higher availability leading to lower backorder costs. (e.g., expedited orders)
- Higher responsiveness to customer requests for product customization and other specifications.

Technology Summary 12.1

SUPPLY-CHAIN OPERATIONS REFERENCE-MODEL (SCOR)

The SCOR model is a process reference tool that allows companies to benchmark their supply chain processes and identify how to make improvements in the processes and relationships that a given company has with its partners, suppliers, and customers. The model defines five basic components for SCM:

1. *Plan:* Balance resources with requirements; establish and communicate a plan to source, make, deliver, and, if necessary, return the product or service.

2. *Source:* Select supply sources; procure goods and services; schedule deliveries; receive, verify, and transfer product; authorize payments to suppliers.

3. *Make:* Schedule production, produce and test product, package and release product to deliver.

4. *Deliver:* Process customer inquiries, quotes, and orders; pick, load, and ship product; invoice customers.

5. *Return:* Receive defective or excess products back from customers.

Source: *Supply-Chain Operations Reference-Model: SCOR Version 9.0* (Supply Chain Council, Inc., 2008), accessed at www.supply-chain.org on April 15, 2010.

- Reduced inventories along the supply chain.
- Improved relationships between buyers and sellers.
- Smooth workloads due to planned arrivals and departures of goods, leading to reduced overtime costs.
- Reduced item costs as a result of planned purchases through contracts and other arrangements.
- Increased customer orders due to improved customer responsiveness.
- Reduced product defects through specifying quality during planning and sharing defect information with suppliers during execution.

Are all SCM initiatives successful? No. Here are some things that can go wrong and, in some cases, how to avoid those problems:

Enterprise Systems

- Data are not collected or are not shared across functional boundaries. For example:

  - Up-to-date real-time sales data must be fed to the SCM demand forecasting system. An *enterprise system* and Internet (i.e., B2B) connection typically facilitate this process.

  Controls

  E-Business

  - Supply chain performance is not fed back to the planning system. Again, an enterprise system can relay purchasing, receiving, transportation, and other logistics data.

  - Data such as customer, location, warranty, and service contracts needed for post-customer support are not available. This data must be collected during sales processing and made available to the appropriate functions.

- Data originates at retailers and must be shared across the supply chain, but confused lines of responsibility and lack of trust can lead to a lack of information sharing between supply chain partners. These issues must be worked out in the SCM planning phase.
- Inaccurate data within the supply chain can negatively affect the entire chain. Implementation of the controls, such as those introduced in Chapters 8 and 9 and discussed throughout the business process chapters, should reduce this problem.
- Overreliance on demand forecasting software can lead to inaccurate forecasts. Good demand forecasting requires an intelligent combination of software tools and human experience.
- Competing objectives can lead to unrealistic forecasts. For example, marketing may want a high target to ensure a successful product (i.e., promotion and

production budgets will be based on the forecast). Sales, on the other hand, will be evaluated on its ability to meet sales quotas and wants a lower demand forecast. Deference to the modeling tools and to objective arbitration should reduce this conflict.

Several methods have been developed for managing the supply chain and implementing the SCOR model. **Technology Summary 12.2** describes an evolution of those techniques, and **Technology Summary 12.3** details the most recent, CPFR.

Technology Summary 12.2

SELECTED METHODS FOR INFORMATION SHARING (COLLABORATION) IN THE SUPPLY CHAIN

Collaboration Type	Features	Discussion
Continuous Replenishment (CRP) (also known as Vendor Managed Inventory [VMI] and Supplier Managed Inventory [SMI]).	A vendor (i.e., the seller/supplier) obtains a buyer's current sales, demand, and inventory data in real time and replenishes the buyer's inventory. Sales and demand data may be warehouse withdrawal, production control (for manufacturing), or retail point-of-sale (POS). Data may be sent via EDI or accessed by vendor via a Web interface into the buyer's system (e.g., extranet, actual system) or a hosted hub (e.g., the SAP Inventory Collaboration Hub).	CRP was started in 1987 with P&G shipping Pampers to Wal-Mart. Benefits: • Vendor has less uncertainty and can provide a specified level of service with minimum cost (e.g., inventory, production, freight [expediting]). • Buyer has better balance of inventory cost and customer service (e.g., fewer stock-outs/higher fill rates). • Lower costs are passed on to the partner/customer.
Co-Managed Inventory (a form of CRP).	The vendor replenishes standard merchandise, and the buyer manages the replenishment of promotion merchandise.	In 1992, Wal-Mart added retailer-provided sales forecasts to CRP. The buyer manages exceptions.
Collaborative Forecasting and Replenishment (CFAR) (a precursor of CPFR).	Retailer and manufacturer forecast demand and schedule production jointly.	Starting in 1995/1996, Warner-Lambert and Wal-Mart forecasted the demand for Listerine. Introduces sales forecast collaboration.
Collaborative Planning Forecasting and Replenishment (CPFR).	Collaborative processes across the supply chain using a set of processes and technology models. Trading partners share plans, forecasts, and other data over the Internet. During planning and execution, partners negotiate resolution to exceptions such as: • Dramatic change in plans. • Plans do not match. • Forecast accuracy is out of tolerance. • Overstock and understock conditions	An initiative of the Voluntary Interindustry Commerce Standards (VICS) Association, 1998. Adds planning (joint business plan) to CFAR.

Technology Summary 12.3

CPFR PROCESS

Strategy & Planning

- *Collaboration arrangement:* Set the business goals for the relationship, define the scope of the collaboration, and assign roles, responsibilities, checkpoints, and escalation procedures.
- *Joint business plan:* Identify significant events that affect supply and demand, such as planned promotions, inventory policy changes, store openings/closings, and product introductions.

Demand & Supply Management

- *Sales forecasting:* Project consumer demand at the point of sale.
- *Order planning/forecasting:* Determine future product ordering and delivery requirements based on the sales forecast, inventory positions, transit lead times, and other factors.

Execution

- *Order generation:* Transition forecasts into firm demands.
- *Order fulfillment:* Produce, ship, deliver, and stock products for consumer purchase.

Analysis

- *Exception management:* Monitor planning operations for out-of-bound conditions.
- *Performance assessment:* Calculate key metrics to evaluate the achievement of business goals, uncover trends, or develop alternative strategies.

Source: Collaborative Planning, Forecasting and Replenishment (CPFR®): An Overview, 18 May 2004, accessed at www.vics.org on April 15, 2010.

How does a supply chain operate without using some of the techniques described in Technology Summary 12.2? Generally, not well. Here are some things that can happen:

- An organization in the chain can relay a false demand signal. For example, a retailer could misread retail demand and double its normal order. Assume further that the wholesaler in response doubles its normal order (now four times the retail order) and so on up the chain to the manufacturer and its supplier. The multiplication of these orders up the supply chain can cause wild demand and supply fluctuations known as the **bullwhip effect**.
- Any member of the supply chain can increase its orders for reasons other than an expected increase in demand. For example, a wholesaler might plan a promotion, a retailer might order extra product one month to take advantage of a sale price, or a distributor could increase its order in anticipation of rationing, hoping to lower the reduction that it will receive from its supplier.
- A sales forecast—what a retailer will sell and when they will sell it—is not easily converted into a demand forecast, which is what the retailer will order from its supplier and when. One problem is that the calculations can be staggering. For example, Payless ShoeSource® Worldwide, Inc. must forecast sales and demand for more than 4,600 stores and 2,000 unique brands of footwear in 13 sizes acquired from 200 factories in seven countries. Payless uses SCM software such as i2®'s Merchandise Planner software to crunch the 22 billion variables that are involved.[5]
- Global supply chains, such as those at Payless ShoeSource Worldwide, can add additional stress to supply chain planning and coordination. For example, NCH Corp., an Irving, Texas–based supplier of industrial maintenance products, has 26 sales offices in Europe, each with its own separate, stand-alone system, making sales and demand planning, as well as order generation and order fulfillment,

Enterprise
Systems

---

[5]Marc L. Songini, "Supply Chains Put to the Test of Global Reach," *Computerworld*, May 16, 2005, p. 16.

time-consuming and expensive. The company's solution is to integrate these systems using ERP modules from Oracle.[6]

- Supply chain planning and execution requires that worldwide systems and databases remain available, and the integrity of the data maintained, at all locations at all times. Controls, such as *business continuity planning*, *continuous data protection (CDP)*, and *hot sites*, are essential for addressing systems failures.

As noted in Technology Summaries 12.2 (pg. 444) and 12.3 (pg. 445), SCM solutions can reduce the impact of the *bullwhip effect* and other negative effects of a dysfunctional supply chain by:

- Sharing information such as sales and demand forecasts, sales data, and planned promotions. This allows each member of the supply chain to plan its orders and production.
- Coordinating pricing, transportation, and product ownership.
- Obtaining operational efficiencies by reducing ordering and carrying costs.
- Using technologies such as *bar codes*, *RFID*, and *global positioning systems (GPS)* to track the location of products in production, in warehouses, and in transit, worldwide.

Technology Application 12.1 describes some successful supply-chain collaborations. The collaboration in Case 1 was initiated by a manufacturer, which is less typical than Case 2, in which the retailer has initiated the collaboration.

Technology Application 12.1

Enterprise Systems

E-Business

SUPPLY CHAIN COLLABORATION SUCCESS STORIES

Case 1

Motorola, Inc. offers over 120 models of its mobile phone handsets globally. While Motorola could see how many units its retailers were buying, they could not see what they were selling. Consequently, Motorola had difficulty knowing how many of which models to make and sell. Accurate forecasting was further complicated because one phone model can have multiple SKUs for such variations as GSM, color, dual mode, etc. By implementing CPFR, Motorola was able to reduce forecasting errors to a fraction of their previous levels, reduce inventory at the retailer's distribution centers, reduced stock-out rates by one-third, and reduce inventory held in reserve for retailers by 30 percent. Before CPFR was implemented, retailers sometimes gave Motorola "C", "D," and "F" ratings

in such performance areas as on-time delivery, ease of doing business, stock-outs, and order quality. After CPFR, the same retailers gave Motorola "A" ratings in these areas.

Case 2

BJ's Wholesale Club, Inc. initiated a CPFR program with its supplier Pharmavite LLC, a major supplier of dietary supplements, to reduce inventory levels and increase sales. After implementing CPFR, BJ's reduced on-hand inventory by 30 percent and increased sales by 24 percent. Because Pharmavite had a better insight into BJ's demands, it was able to have the right product at the right time on BJ's shelves and eliminate excess safety stock. The collaboration allowed BJ's and Pharmavite to reduce demand forecast errors, effectively plan sales and promotion volumes, and calculate inventory requirements.

Source: Jerold P. Cerlund, Rajiv Kohli, Susan A. Sherer, and Yuliang Yao, "How Motorola Put CPFR into Action," *Supply Chain Management Review*, October 2007, p. 28; "BJ's Wholesale Achieves Substantial ROI Leveraging JDA Software Solutions to Support CPFR Program," *Business Wire*, January 14, 2008).

---

[6]Gary H. Anthes, "Blind Spots: Uncovering the Holes in Your Global Supply Chain," *Computerworld*, February 20, 2006, pp. 38, 40.

Logical Process Description

The principal activities of the purchasing process are to determine what goods and services need to be ordered; when and how much to order; to prepare and send purchase orders to selected vendors; and to receive goods and services from vendors. Once again, logical DFDs are used to present the basic logical composition of a typical purchasing process. We also discuss the relationship between certain goals of the process and the logical design of the process. This section includes brief discussions of the interfaces between the purchasing and inventory processes. We also describe and illustrate the major data stores in the process.[7]

Discussion and Illustration

Figure 12.3 is the context diagram for our purchasing process. Notice that the process responds to requests for goods and services (i.e., purchase requisitions) received from the inventory process and from various departments; sends a PO to the vendor; and sends notices to other departments and processes. Vendors respond by sending goods and services (with the vendor packing slip), which results in additional notices being sent out to accounts payable, general ledger, and the warehouse. As depicted, we do not see supply chain techniques such as *Vendor Managed Inventory* (*VMI*; see Technology Summary 12.2, pg. 444), by which the vendor would receive inventory and sales data and respond with automatic shipments (i.e., without a purchase order).

Figure 12.4 (pg. 448) reflects the level 0 DFD for our purchasing process. Take some time to study the figure. To focus our discussion, we have assumed that the purchasing process performs three major processes, represented by the three bubbles in the DFD. The next three sections describe each of those bubbles.

FIGURE 12.3 Purchasing Process—Context Diagram

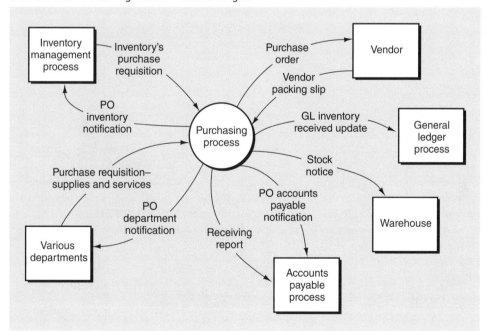

---

[7]As we have in several earlier chapters, we remind you once again that the data stores in the logical DFDs might well be the purchasing process view of an *enterprise database*.

Determine Requirements

The purchasing process begins with each department identifying its need for goods and services. These needs are depicted by one of two data flows entering bubble 1.0: *inventory's purchase requisition* or *purchase requisition—supplies and services.*

Figure 12.5 is an example screen for a **purchase requisition**, which is an internal request to acquire goods and services. Requisitions such as this are received from authorized personnel within an organization and are for inventory replenishment. Similar requisitions are received from automated inventory replenishment systems, such as SCM processes. Take some time to examine the figure, observing the various items included in the requisition such as the material and quantity requested, required delivery date, and location (plant) to which the items are to be shipped. Should the requestor have a suggested or preferred vendor, that would be indicated in the section at the bottom of the screen. The requisition is usually routed by *workflow* for approval by the requisitioning department supervisor.

FIGURE 12.4 Purchasing Process—Level 0 Diagram

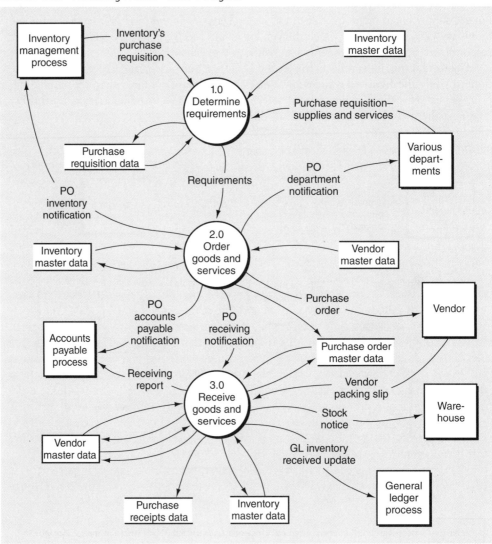

FIGURE 12.5 Sample Purchase Requisition Screen (SAP)

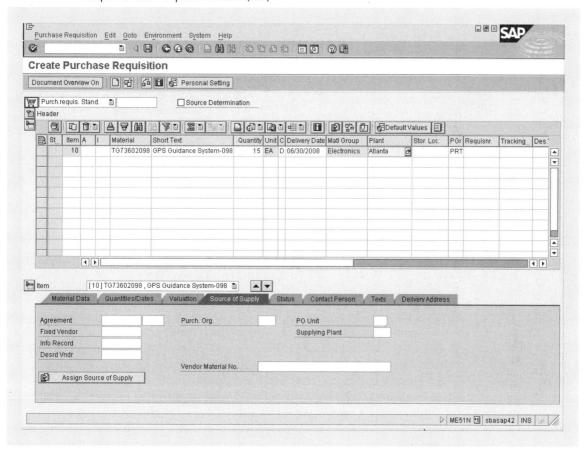

Figure 12.6 (pg. 450) is a lower-level view of bubble 1.0 in Figure 12.4. At first glance, the processes involved in determining an organization's requirements for goods and services may appear to be quite simple and straightforward. However, the earlier section about SCM should make it clear that the techniques and methods involved in determining *what* inventory to order, *when* to order it, and *how much* to order are considerably more intricate and complex than we might first imagine. Many of these determinations are out of our view because they occur in the inventory-management process. In the discussions that follow we describe a *push*-based supply chain, where goods and services are ordered in anticipation of demand based on sales and demand forecasts. A *pull*-based supply chain, on the other hand, uses data from vendors and customers to make purchasing decisions on the basis of actual demand.[8] Some organizations, especially manufacturers, use a combination of push and pull. For example, raw materials and components are ordered on the basis of forecasted requirements (i.e., push) while final assembly waits for specific customer orders (i.e., pull). Dell, Inc. is known to use this combination of pull and push.

The processes associated with reordering inventory involve several important concepts and techniques, such as reorder point (ROP) analysis, economic order quantity

---

[8]In Chapter 15 we discuss the comparable, production-related concepts of *pull manufacturing* and *push manufacturing*.

FIGURE 12.6 Purchasing Process—Diagram 1

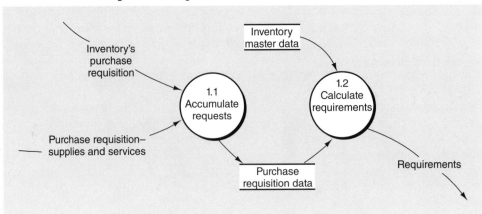

(EOQ) analysis, and ABC analysis. We discuss each of these methods briefly before going on:

- **Reorder point (ROP) analysis** recognizes that each item of inventory is unique with respect to the rate at which it is sold. Based on each inventory item's sales rate, a reorder point is determined. Thus, when the on-hand level for an item falls to its specified reorder point, the item is reordered. The flow "inventory's purchase requisition" might originate from such an analysis in the inventory-management process. Alternatively, the on-hand level for items might be sent to a vendor managing the inventory (i.e., VMI), and the vendor might respond by shipping inventory without a request being made.

- **Economic order quantity (EOQ)** is a technique of analyzing all incremental costs associated with acquiring and carrying particular items of inventory. *Inventory carrying costs* are composed of five cost elements: (1) opportunity cost of investment funds, (2) insurance costs, (3) property taxes, (4) storage costs, and (5) cost of obsolescence and deterioration. In addition to carrying costs, there are costs associated with preparing and sending each PO. As purchasing departments reduce the number of POs—each PO, therefore, being for larger quantities—the total cost of acquiring inventory decreases, while carrying costs increase. Also, as noted below, vendors often provide discounts for larger orders. The EOQ might be used in bubble 1.2 in Figure 12.6 to adjust the quantities received from the inventory-management process to determine how much inventory to order.

- **ABC analysis** is a technique for ranking items in a group based on the value, activity, sales, or other relevant metric for the items. ABC analysis can be used to categorize inventory items according to their importance. A given organization, for example, may have a situation where 15 percent of its inventory items accounts for 70 percent of its sales. Let's call this portion group A. Furthermore, an organization may find that an additional 10 percent of its inventory items accounts for an additional 20 percent of its sales. Let's call this portion group B. From this assessment, we can now deduce that the remaining 75 percent of the organization's inventory items constitutes only 10 percent of its sales. With this information, the supervisor of inventory control can decide which items of inventory are relatively more important to an organization and, consequently, require more attention and control. For instance, category C items might be ordered only when there is a specific request from a customer (i.e., pull system, no stock is kept on hand), whereas categories A and B might be ordered using *reorder point analysis*.

Now let's describe the process depicted in Figure 12.6. Bubble 1.1 receives and stores the requests received from the inventory-management process (inventory's purchase requisition) and various departments (purchase requisition—goods and services). In this way, an organization can consolidate requests, submit larger orders to vendors, and presumably receive concessions in price and payment terms for these larger purchases. Obviously, this benefit must be traded off with the costs associated with delaying a purchase and suffering the consequences of not having inventory available when needed.

At predetermined intervals, bubble 1.2 accesses the accumulated requests held in the purchase requisition data; sorts the requests, perhaps by vendor or product type; and combines that data with the inventory master data to determine what purchases need to be made. For example, data about sales forecasts and scheduled promotions stored in the inventory master data might give bubble 1.2 the latitude to adjust requested amounts that have come from the inventory-management process or the various departments.

Order Goods and Services

Figure 12.7, a lower-level view of bubble 2.0 in Figure 12.4 (pg. 448), provides a look at the logical functions involved in ordering goods and services. The first process involves vendor selection (bubble 2.1). A buyer generally consults the vendor master data to identify potential suppliers that have been approved for use by the organization and then evaluates each prospective vendor for a particular purchase. The requestor may have indicated a preferred vendor, and the buyer needs to determine the appropriateness of this choice. Finally, there may not be a preferred or approved vendor for this purchase, in which case the buyer needs to conduct research to find one. Perhaps an *intelligent agent* will be employed to scan the Web for vendors. *Web Services* and *B2B marketplaces* may be used.

E-Business

Buyers often attempt to combine as many orders as possible with the same vendor by using *blanket orders* or *annual agreements* (SAP calls these "outline agreements"). In such cases, the vendor has been chosen in advance of a particular purchase, and the only determination is the quantity to order at this time. If large expenditures for new or specially made parts are involved, the buyer may need to obtain *competitive bids* by sending a *request for quotation (RFQ)* to prospective vendors. Finally, an organization's merchandising function may have determined that certain brands, such as printers from Hewlett-Packard and Brother®, or computers from Apple® and Lenovo™, would be carried in the stores. In this case, as with annual agreements, the only determination to be

FIGURE 12.7 Purchasing Process—Diagram 2

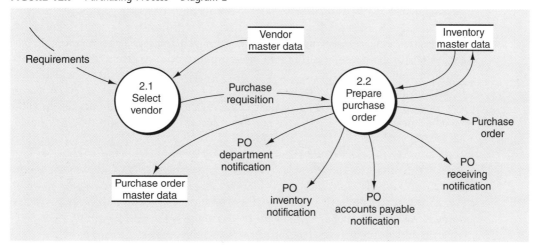

made is the quantity of each model to be purchased at this time and to which distribution center(s) or store(s) the ordered items are to be shipped.

Vendor selection can have a significant impact on the success of an organization's inventory control and manufacturing functions. In Chapter 15, we describe manufacturing processes and just-in-time (JIT) inventory management. With JIT inventory management, parts arrive when needed, thus saving the interest costs associated with storing "excess" inventory and reducing the possibility of inventory becoming obsolete. To use JIT systems effectively, organizations must find and retain reliable vendors.

After the vendor has been selected, the buyer prepares a **purchase order (PO)**, which is a request for the purchase of goods or services from a vendor. Typically, a PO contains data regarding the needed quantities, expected unit prices, required delivery date, terms, and other conditions. **Figure 12.8** displays a PO for the purchase requisition in Figure 12.5 (pg. 449). Notice that the vendor and price have been added.

Process bubble 2.2 of Figure 12.7 (pg. 451) depicts the process of preparing a PO. The "purchase order" data flowing out of process 2.2 is sent to the vendor. At the same time, the inventory master data is updated to reflect the goods on order. A record of the purchase is stored on the PO master data, and PO information is distributed to several departments and processes, as shown by the four other data flows out of process 2.2. All of these flows and updates could be via paper documents, electronic notifications, or by viewing the purchase order and inventory data in the enterprise database.

Enterprise Systems

FIGURE 12.8   Sample Purchase Order Screen (SAP)

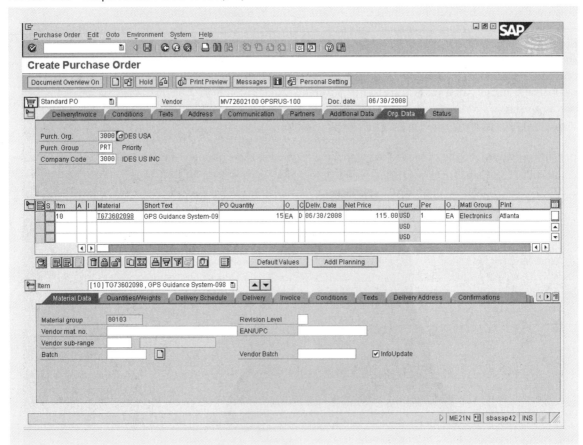

It is not uncommon for the PO copy, or PO data in the enterprise database, available for the receiving department to be a **blind copy**, meaning that certain data is blanked out (i.e., blinded). For instance, the quantities ordered might be blanked out so that the receiving personnel will not be influenced by this information when counting the goods. Price data may also be blinded because receiving personnel have no need to know that information.

Controls

Receive Goods and Services

E-Business

Figure 12.9 (pg. 454) is the lower-level diagram for process 3.0 in Figure 12.4 (pg. 448). In the case of inventory, the **vendor packing slip**, which accompanies the purchased inventory from the vendor and identifies the shipment, triggers the receiving process. As indicated by bubble 3.1 of the figure, goods arriving at the receiving department are inspected and counted, and these data are matched against the vendor packing slip and the "PO receiving notification" (i.e., the blind copy of the PO).[9] Nonconforming goods are denoted by the *reject* stub out of process 3.1. Notation of rejected goods is added to the vendor service record in the vendor master data. After the count and condition of the goods has been obtained, process 3.1 completes the receiving report by noting the quantity received. Once annotated with the quantity received, the PO receiving notification becomes a **receiving report**, which is the document used to record merchandise receipts.

Process 3.2 compares the receiving report data to the information stored in the PO master data—a process that often is automatically completed by the information system. Bubble 3.2 also reflects the following activities:

- Data about vendor compliance with the order terms (product quality, meeting promised delivery dates, etc., data found on the PO master data) are added to the vendor service record on the vendor master data.
- The receiving report data is stored as a copy of the receiving report document or electronically (see the data store "Purchase receipts data").
- Receiving report data is sent to the accounts payable process (i.e., "Receiving report"). Alternatively, the accounts payable process could access the purchase receipts data or the updated PO master data to obtain information about the receipt.
- A copy of the receiving report is sent to the warehouse (i.e., "Stock notice") with the goods.
- The inventory master data is updated to reflect the additional inventory on hand.
- The cost of the inventory received is relayed to the general ledger process (see the data flow "GL inventory received update"). To balance the debit that is made to the general ledger account for inventory, a credit is made to a clearing account. A debit will be made to this clearing account, and the account "cleared," when the invoice is recorded. We will discuss that entry in Chapter 13.[10]
- Finally, the PO master data is updated to reflect the receipt of the goods.

As in the case of the receipt of goods, services received also should be documented properly. Some organizations use an **acceptance report** (SAP calls this a "Service entry sheet") to acknowledge formally the satisfactory completion of a service contract. The

---

[9]Comparison to an open PO might wait until the next step in the process, during which the quantity of goods actually received (the "Receiving report") is compared to data in the PO master data.

[10]As noted earlier in the chapter, the timing of the recording in the general ledger of this receipt transaction (i.e., increase inventory) and the related invoice transaction (i.e., increase accounts payable) may depend on how close together these two activities occur and the specific software employed. If the invoice and goods are received at the same time and place, there may not be a need for the clearing account, and the debit to inventory may be matched with a credit to accounts payable.

FIGURE 12.9 Purchasing Process—Diagram 3

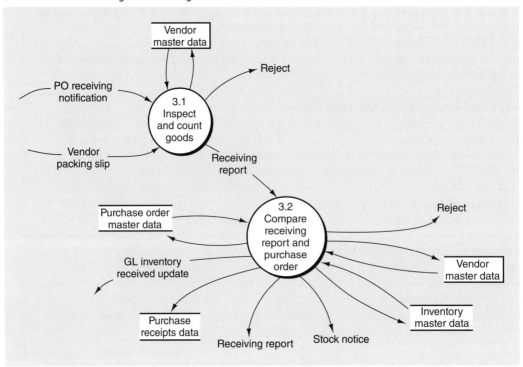

acceptance report data supports the payment due to the vendor in the same way as the receiving report.[11]

Logical Data Descriptions

The purchasing process entails several data stores, as shown earlier in Figure 12.4 (pg. 448). The *inventory master data* was introduced in Chapter 10. The **vendor master data** contains a record of each vendor that is approved for use by the organization. In addition to storing identification data, such as name, address, telephone numbers, e-mail addresses, bank information, and payment terms and methods, the vendor data is used by management to evaluate vendor performance and to make various ordering decisions.

As noted earlier, *purchase requisitions* are internal requests for goods and services. These are compiled in the **purchase requisitions data** store. The **purchase order master data** is a compilation of open POs and includes the status of each item on order. Finally, the **purchase receipts data** is an event data store with each record reflecting a receipt of goods and services.

Logical Database Design

The entity-relationship diagram applicable to the purchasing process is shown in **Figure 12.10**. The INVENTORY, VENDORS, PURCHASE_REQUISITIONS, PURCHASE_ORDERS, and PURCHASE_RECEIPTS entities were described in the previous section. The EMPLOYEES entity contains specific information about each

---

[11]For simplicity in drawing the DFDs, we intend that the single data flow labeled *receiving report* represents either a receiving report (goods) or acceptance report (services).

employee, including authorization levels regarding generating and approving purchase requisitions, preparing and approving POs, receiving goods, and so on. The EMPLOYEES entity will be discussed more fully in Chapter 14.

The PURCHASING_RELATIONS relationship accumulates a record of purchasing-related events—PURCHASE_REQUISITIONS, PURCHASE_ORDERS, and PURCHASE_RECEIPTS—as they progress. The box around this relationship indicates that we will have a relation in our database for this relationship, whereas the other relationships will not have a corresponding relation.

FIGURE 12.10   Entity-Relationship (E-R) Diagram (Partial) for the Purchasing Process

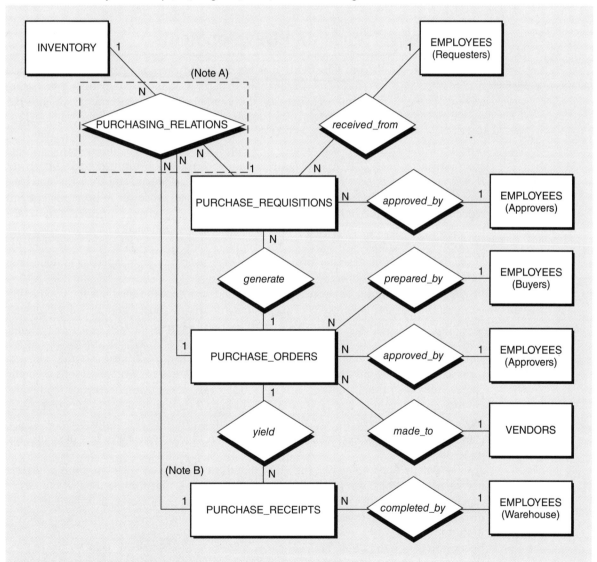

NOTES, for simplicity, we assume that:
A—See (pg. 456) for an explanation of the box around PURCHASING_RELATIONS and why the model is not fully normalized.
B—There are no partial receipts of any line item on a PO.

As with Figure 10.9 (pg. 363) and Figure 11.9 (pg. 408), Figure 12.10 is not fully normalized yet. We include the "extra" relationships and redundant attributes to help you see the logical sequence of events. Also, note B in Figure 12.10 indicates that this is a simplified model. Certainly, realistic models must deal with partial receipts.

The relational tables for the purchasing process are shown in **Figure 12.11**. Notice that each table includes a primary key. In some tables, such as INVENTORY, a single primary key is included. One table, PURCHASE_RELATIONS, has a primary key from the PURCHASE_REQUISITIONS and INVENTORY tables to form a composite (multiple) key. Each relation (row) in this table records the details of each requested item from requisition (the first three columns), to PO (the fourth and fifth columns), to receipt (the last two columns).

Technology Trends and Developments

Enterprise Systems

Controls

You may also recall from Chapter 3 that we discussed the emergence of Internet auction markets and Internet market exchanges that create a more competitive purchasing market. These markets and exchanges are key elements of **e-procurement**, which is the use of information technology to automate significant portions of the procurement process. E-procurement can improve SCM by lowering administrative costs associated with procurement by reducing the number of people and amount of time required for the procurement process. For example, a purchasing organization can use *intelligent agents*, *Web Services*, and *B2B exchanges* to locate vendors and products, and then the purchase process is completed electronically. By reducing manual processes, e-procurement can reduce errors. The use of marketplaces should increase the sources for items and reduce their costs. Electronic purchasing data can be shared among functions and organizations to optimize inventory levels across the supply chain and provide real-time data for SCM. Next, we will describe two elements of e-procurement: paperless systems and B2B marketplaces.

Enterprise Systems

Paperless systems eliminate documents and forms as the medium for conducting business. In a truly paperless system, printed reports disappear and are replaced with computer screen displays. With the increasing use of *Web Services*, *RFID*, *EDI*, *electronic funds transfer (EFT)*, *digital image processing*, *e-mail*, *workflow software*, *enterprise systems*, and similar technologies, is the "paperless office" at hand? We are certainly close in many contemporary environments. In fact, a growing number of organizations arguably operate the bulk of their business processes using *paperless systems*. The major roadblocks are more organizational and behavioral/psychological than technological in nature. Over time, these cultural barriers to the paperless office continue to disintegrate as a new generation of managers—who have grown up with the computer as a fact of their daily lives—emerges.

Technology Application 12.2 (pg. 458) describes some Web spending tools and **B2B marketplaces**, which are particular Web sites or portals that may be used as sources of supply in the procurement process. Recall from Chapter 3, however, that many risks are involved in the move toward electronic marketplaces, and these may limit their success in the short term.

Another technology development that has had a significant effect on SCM and the purchasing process is the radio-frequency identification (RFID) technology described in **Technology Summary 12.4** (pg. 459). **Technology Application 12.3** (pg. 460) describes some early RFID uses.

FIGURE 12.11 Selected Relational Tables (Partial) for the Purchasing Process

Shaded_Attribute(s) = Primary Key

INVENTORY

Item_No	Item_Name	Price	Location	Qty_on_Hand	Reorder_Pt
936	Machine Plates	39.50	Macomb	1,500	950
1001	Gaskets	9.50	Macomb	10,002	3,500
1010	Crank Shafts	115.00	Tampa	952	500
1025	Manifolds	45.00	Tampa	402	400

EMPLOYEES

Emp_No	Emp_First_Name	Emp_Last_Name	Soc_Sec_No	Emp_Dept
B432	Carl	Mast	125-87-8090	492-01
A491	Janet	Kopp	127-93-3453	639-04
A632	Greg	Bazie	350-97-9030	538-22
B011	Christy	Kinman	123-78-0097	298-12

VENDORS

Vend_No	Vend_Name	Vend_Street	Vend_City	Vend_State	Vend_ZIP	Vend_Tel	Vend_Contact	Credit_Terms	FOB_Terms
539	Ace Widget Co.	190 Shore Dr.	Charleston	SC	29915	803-995-3764	S. Emerson	2/10,n/30	Ship Pt
540	Babcock Supply Co.	22 Ribaut Rd.	Beaufort	SC	29902	803-552-4788	Frank Roy	n/60	Destin
541	Webster Steel Corp.	49 Abercorn St.	Savannah	GA	30901	912-433-1750	Wilbur Cox	2/10,n/30	Ship Pt

PURCHASE_REQUISITIONS

PR_No	PR_Date	Emp_No (PR_Requestor)[a]	Emp_No (PR_Approver)[b]	PO_No
53948	20071215	A491	E745	4346
53949	20071215	C457	A632	4350
53950	20071216	9999	540-32	4347
53951	20071216	F494	D548	4352

PURCHASE_ORDERS

PO_No	PO_Date	Vend_No	Ship_Via	Emp_No (Buyer)	Emp_No (PO_Approver)	PO_Status
4345	20071218	539	Best Way	F395	F349	Open
4346	20071220	541	FedEx	C932	F349	Sent
4347	20071222	562	UPS	E049	D932	Acknowledged

PURCHASE_RECEIPTS

Rec_No	Rec_Date	Emp_No (Receiving)	PO_No	Invoice_No
42944	20071216	B260	4322	7-945
42945	20071216	B260	4339	9542-4
42946	20071216	B260	4345	535

PURCHASE_RELATIONS

PR_No	Item_No	Qty_Requested	PO_No	Qty_Ordered	Rec_No	Qty_Received
53947	1005	200	4345	200	42946	200
53947	1006	50	4345	50	42946	50
53947	1015	25	4345	25	42946	25

[a] If automatic purchase requisition, then 9999; if employee, then employee number.
[b] If automatic purchase requisition, then contract number of trading partner; if employee, then employee number.

Technology Application 12.2

BUSINESS-TO-BUSINESS (B2B) MARKETPLACES AND WEB SPENDING TOOLS FOR THE PURCHASING PROCESS

Case 1

The mission of Aeroxchange (www.aeroxchange.com), an airline industry exchange, "is to create supply chain efficiencies that leverage the Internet to provide a global infrastructure for aviation supply chain collaboration." Customers include FedEx, UPS, American Airlines, Cathay Pacific, and Embraer. Aeroxchange services include its "AeroBuy" solution, a catalog-based procurement system with electronic connections to both EDI and non-EDI trading partners. Its "AeroAOG" e-commerce application connects airlines to parts providers via the Internet to facilitate parts searches for aircraft repairs ("AOG" means aircraft on ground). Finally, using Aeroxchange's "Sourcing Services," airlines can procure a variety of commodities and services.

Case 2

Tejari (www.tejari.com) is a B2B marketplace in the Middle East used by companies in the region to buy and sell goods in a secure Internet environment. In addition to finding, comparing, and procuring products and services, buyers can conduct reverse auctions in which sellers bid to supply products and services. Sellers can also list their products and services and sell them through catalogs and auctions. As of April 16, 2010, Tejari was reporting more than 199,000 companies listing products, more than 40,000 products, and 490 active auctions.

Case 3

Web spending tools from vendors such as Ariba Inc. and Rearden Commerce are used to manage the procurement process. For example, PPG Industries, Inc. used a Web Service from Ariba to analyze its spending on materials and services and was able to reduce its suppliers from 307 to 6 and achieve 15 percent savings in costs. GlaxoSmithKline PLC used Reardon Commerce's online software to coordinate and reduce costs in business services such as flights, hotels, rental cars, and package shipping.

Source: www.aeroxchange.com, accessed April 16, 2010; www.tejari.com, accessed April 16, 2010; Mylene Mangalindan, "Web Spending Tools Help in Tight Times; Services Let Firms Track Internal Habits, Select Outside Contractors," *The Wall Street Journal*, June 3, 2008, p. B10.

Physical Process Description

The physical model of the purchasing process presented in this section employs much of the technology mentioned previously. Although the process is not completely *paperless*, hard copy documents are held to a minimum.

Discussion and Illustration

Figure 12.12 (pp. 461–462) presents a systems flowchart of the purchasing process. We assume for this illustration that data for one or more approved vendors is stored on the vendor database and used for purchases. At several points in the flowchart, you will see notations that *exception routines* are not flowcharted. They are also omitted from the discussion in the following paragraphs.

Requisition and Order Merchandise

Enterprise Systems

As shown in the first column, the purchasing process begins when a cost center employee establishes a need. The *enterprise system* displays a screen similar to the one depicted in Figure 12.5 (pg. 449), and the requesting individual keys in the material number and quantity of the items desired, as well as information about the required delivery date and location (plant) to which the items are to be delivered.

Controls

The completed requisition is recorded and then routed via the *workflow* routine to a cost center supervisor for approval. Depending on the amount and nature of the requisition, several approvals may be required. Approval is granted in the system by

RADIO-FREQUENCY IDENTIFICATION TECHNOLOGY (RFID)

Radio-frequency identification (RFID) is a system for sending and receiving data, using wireless technology, between an RFID tag and an RFID transceiver. RFID tags are computer chips containing information about the object to which the tag is attached and an antenna that sends and receives data. *Active* RFID tags store information using a power source within the tag, and *passive* tags obtain their power from a transceiver. Transceivers transmit, receive, and decode data from RFID tags.

RFID tags can be attached to objects much like *bar codes* have been attached to groceries, FedEx and UPS parcels, and clothing, to name just a few. However, unlike bar codes, RFID tags identify an instance of an item, not just an item type (e.g., *this* box of Huggies, not *any* box of Huggies). Unlike bar codes, RFID tags can't be mistakenly read twice because each is unique. RFID tags can be attached to groups of items, such as pallets of groceries, or to individual items, such as boxes of diapers, shaving razors, or pieces of clothing. To read RFID tags, transceivers do not require line-of-sight or proximity to a tag (a requirement for scanning a bar code) to send and receive data from the tag. A reader can obtain data from tags attached to items packed within boxes.

RFID's most useful application to date is to track items through the supply chain. For example, Daisy Brand, Inc. attaches an RFID tag to every pallet of sour cream leaving its warehouse destined for Wal-Mart. RFID readers at the Daisy shipping dock record the movement of the sour cream and send data to Daisy's *enterprise system* to record the shipment. At Wal-Mart's stores, an RFID reader records the receipt of the pallets of sour cream. When RFID tags are attached to individual items—rather than pallets— RFID readers throughout warehouses and stores can keep track of the location of these items as they move from warehouse to shipping to receiving to shelf to checkout. When individually tagged items are sold, RFID readers read data on the tag and record the retail sale, in a manner similar to that used for many years with *scanners*, UPC codes, and POS systems. In fact, an electronic product code (EPC) has been developed for use with RFID technology, much as the UPC is used with bar codes.

Systems similar to the Daisy Brand example are tracking Texas Instruments, Inc. and Kimberly-Clark products at Wal-Mart. RFID technology at Wal-Mart has cut the incidence of out-of-stock products by 30 percent, while improving the efficiency of product movements at stores by 60 percent.

RFID can also be used to track in-process inventory (raw materials through finished products), identify animals (embedded in pets so they can be returned to their owners if lost), operate automobile key-and-lock antitheft systems, track books from libraries and book stores, control building access, track airline baggage, pay highway tolls, identify shipping containers that have been inspected and cleared at a port of entry, and track assets and inventory. Daisy Brand implemented an entire inventory management system based on pallet tags to track goods moving through its facilities. Kimberly-Clark uses RFID tags to locate its trailers more quickly. This latter application may be combined with global positioning system (GPS) coordinates of current location.

Because RFID does not require a line-of-sight between the tag and the reader, and the reading step is passive (e.g., the reader will locate every tag that passes by), this technology can help to reduce theft. Shoe retailer Reno GmbH integrates RFID tags into its shoes to reduce theft of shoes at its stores. At the same time, this feature has caused some privacy concerns because the tags are not necessarily turned off when the item is sold. Left activated, the tag can track the location of the person carrying the item.

Data on the tags can record the manufacturing date, color, and size of an item. Expiration dates, if any, can be stored and relayed to monitoring systems to move product into sales, price reduction, or disposal, as appropriate. RFID has been used to track tainted foods, counterfeit drugs, and medical equipment. At a cost of 10 cents each for passive tags, it is presently more feasible to tag groups of items. Prices probably need to reach 1 to 2 cents each before the technology can be widely adopted and applied to individual items rather than shipping containers, boxes, and pallets.

Advantages, then, of the RFID technology include increased data accuracy, reduced product theft, quicker retail checkout (or self-service checkout), reduced stock-outs, more timely deliveries, and better customer service. Kimberly-Clark, for example, used RFID tags to improve the timely execution of promotional displays from 55 percent to over 75 percent.

Sources: Sharon Gaudin, "Some Suppliers Gain from Failed Wal-Mart RFID Edict," *Computerworld*, April 28, 2008, pp. 12–13; Thomas Wailgum, "Kimberley-Clark's Secrets to RFID Success," *CIO*, July 30, 2007; John Blau, "European Retailer to Put RFID Chips in Shoes," *CIO Tech Informer*, March 2, 2007; Matt Hamblen, "Privacy Concerns Dog IT Efforts to Implement RFID," *Computerworld*, October 15, 2007, p. 26; Marc L. Songini, "Wal-Mart Shifts RFID Plans," *Computerworld*, February 26, 2007, p. 14; S. Srinivasan, "Security and Privacy Trade-offs in RFID Use," *ISACA Journal*, December 1, 2009, pp. 42–46.

Technology Application 12.3

USES OF RADIO-FREQUENCY IDENTIFICATION (RFID) FOR THE PURCHASING PROCESS

Case 1

Dow Chemical attaches *active* RFID tags to the fasteners that hold shipping containers closed. The tags read data from a sensor and clock inside the container to track environmental conditions such as temperature and moisture. The tag is also used for inventory management to locate and redirect containers in transit.

Case 2

The Friedrich Schiller University Hospital in Jena, Germany, uses RFID tags on patients' ID bracelets, nurses' ID badges, and drugs and drug containers. Before administering a drug, the nurse scans his or her badge, the patient badge, and the drug. A computer checks the patient and drug IDs against pharmacy instructions to reduce medication errors.

Case 3

American Apparel, Inc. attaches a tag to each piece of clothing manufactured at its Los Angeles facility. These tags are scanned by readers installed in store stockrooms and sales floors. When an item leaves the sales floor, its departure is disclosed on storeroom workstations so workers can restock it. During a pilot of this application, the pilot store's shelves remained 99 percent stocked, compared to 85 percent at other stores. American Apparel expects that the higher in-stock rate should increase sales by 15 percent to 25 percent.

Case 4

Many of you may be using RFID and not know it. RFID is the technology behind ExxonMobil's Speedpass used for gas purchases and E-ZPass used for paying highway tolls. In each case, the consumer carries the RFID tag (in the Speedpass key tag or in the windshield-mounted E-ZPass) that is read at the gas pump or at the toll booth. The individual (and car or truck) is then charged for the gas or toll.

Source: Galen Gruman, "Your RFID Battle Plan" *CIO*, August 7, 2007; Sharon Gaudin, "Retailer Looks to RFID to Boost Sales," *Computerworld*, April 28, 2008, p. 12.

---

forwarding the requisition to the next person on the list; approval codes are attached to the record and are displayed in the appropriate boxes on the requisition form. When all approvals have been obtained, the requisition is updated to indicate final approval and is routed to the purchasing department.

Enterprise Systems

Periodically (or immediately, depending on priority), the *enterprise system* displays requisitions—including those from various departments, orders from inventory control, and requests based on forecast data—on the screen of the appropriate buyer. The system also displays a list of approved vendors who can provide the required items (see "requisition screen with vendor candidates"). The buyer compares vendors for quality, price, terms, delivery date, and so on, and then selects a vendor. Final vendor selection and price determination may require contact with the potential vendor. When the vendor choice is settled, the buyer converts the requisition to a PO and adds any necessary details, such as vendor, price, and terms.

Next, the system routes the PO via *workflow* to the purchasing manager, and perhaps others, for approval. Depending on the amount and nature of the purchase, several approvals may be required. Approval is granted in the system by forwarding the PO to the next person on the list; approval codes are attached to the record and are displayed in the appropriate boxes on the PO form. When all approvals have been obtained, the PO is updated to indicate final approval. The inventory master data is updated to reflect the quantity on order, and the order is confirmed to the requesting individual. The purchasing process then releases the PO to the EDI translator, where it is converted to the appropriate EDI format. The translation software also *encrypts* the EDI message and appends a *digital signature* to it.

Receive Merchandise

Enterprise Systems

On the second page of the flowchart, we see that the receiving department personnel receive the merchandise sent by the vendor. They enter the PO number into the system, and an RFID reader reads the item numbers and quantities from the RFID tags attached

FIGURE 12.12 Purchasing Process—Systems Flowchart

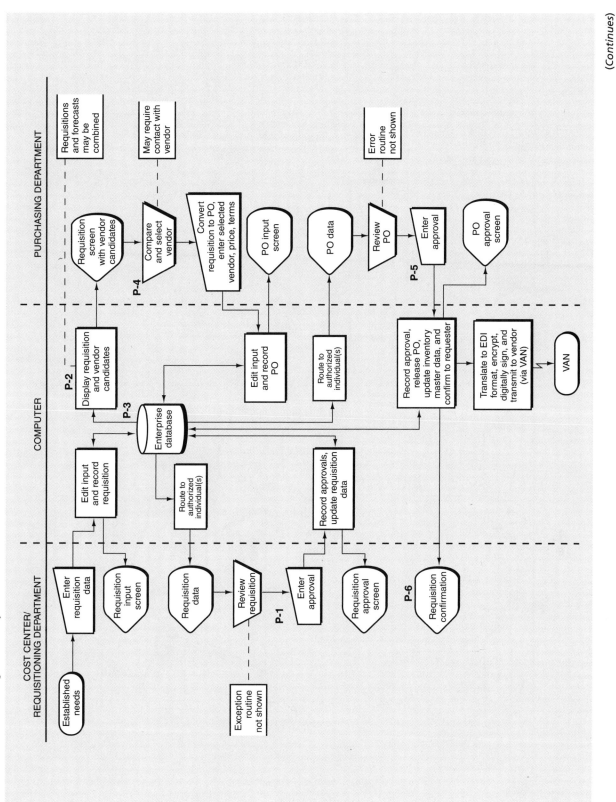

(Continues)

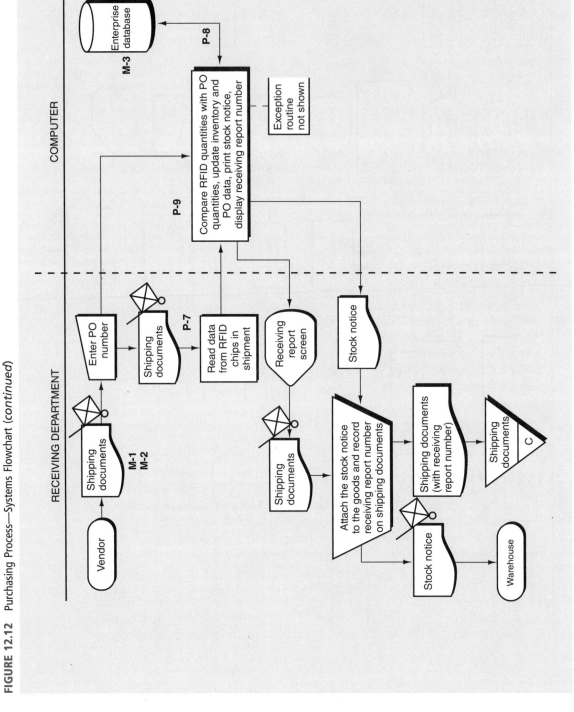

FIGURE 12.12 Purchasing Process—Systems Flowchart (*continued*)

to each item in the shipment. The enterprise system compares the items and quantities received to those on the open PO master data.[12] If the shipment is correct, the system accepts the shipment, creates a record in the purchase receipts data, updates the status field in the PO data to indicate that the items have been received, updates the quantity received in the inventory master data, updates the general ledger to reflect the receipt, prints a stock notice, and displays the receiving report number. (Vendor performance data, such as timeliness and accuracy of the receipt, could also be recorded at this time.) The receiving clerk attaches the stock notice to the goods and sends them to the warehouse. The clerk also records the receiving report number on the shipping documents and files them in chronological sequence to provide an audit trail of receipts. Alternatively, a *digital image* of the shipping documents might be stored on the computer.

The Fraud Connection

Because the *purchase-to-pay process* begins with the purchasing process and culminates with the payment of cash—a firm's most liquid asset—it should not surprise you that this process is rife with potential for exposing an organization to fraud and embezzlement. Indeed, many of the most serious cases of abuse have involved the manipulation of the purchasing process. In this section, we present some of the ways in which the process has been manipulated.

Fraud and the Purchasing Function

The typical cases included in this category of process exploitation are instances in which the following scenarios occur:

- An employee (e.g., a buyer, purchasing manager, or other person) places POs with a particular vendor(s) in exchange for a kickback, secret commission, or other form of inducement from the vendor(s).
- An employee has a *conflict of interest* between his responsibilities to his employer and his financial interest—direct or indirect—in a company with which the employer does business.

As we mentioned in Chapter 7, these kinds of quasi-legal/ethical scenarios are often addressed by an organization as part of a *code of conduct*, which all employees are asked to acknowledge periodically by attesting that they have not engaged in activities that violate the code.

Cases of bribery, kickbacks, and the like present an interesting dilemma. It is accepted business practice for a salesperson to treat a buyer to lunch, to send the buyer promotional "gifts" (e.g., a sleeve of golf balls imprinted with the selling company's logo), or to extend other small favors to make sales. When do such actions stop being "acceptable" and cross the line into being improper, either in substance or appearance? We can't answer that ethical question here except to offer one case example that was clearly fraud. This case involved a company (customer) that made purchases from foreign suppliers. The company's president made it clear to the suppliers that if they wanted to do business with the company, they must agree to pay 2 percent of any business they transacted to the president's personal bank account. In turn, the suppliers inflated their invoices to the company by the amount of the secret commission they

---

[12]The database controls prevent receiving personnel from accessing quantity and price data in the PO master data. In this way, the process implements the *blind copy* concept explained earlier.

paid. To ensure that the higher cost would not be detected by anyone in the purchasing department, the president approved all such invoices for payment.

In purchasing activities, conflicts of interest often arise in situations where an employee with the authority to make (or approve) purchases for an organization has some kind of financial stake in a company that sells to the organization. For instance, the employee might be an owner or principal of the vendor company, either directly or through a relative, and therefore stands to benefit by placing business with that vendor. This condition presents one of the knottier control problems confronting business today.

Here is a brief example of a *conflict of interest* fraud:

> Over an 8-year period, Frick (a fictitious name), a director of buying for toys and related products at a major retailer (Wombat, Inc.), placed some $3 million of business with 12 companies operated by Frack. Although Frick signed annual conflict of interest statements, he did not disclose his significant ownership interest in those 12 companies. When other toy suppliers reported to one of Wombat's directors that they had trouble obtaining sales to Wombat, an investigation ensued. It was discovered that Frick had received more than $500,000 in cash and benefits from the 12 companies.

Application of the Control Framework to Purchasing

In this section, we apply the control framework from Chapter 7 to the purchasing process. **Figure 12.13** (pp. 466–467) presents a completed *control matrix* for the annotated systems flowchart in Figure 12.12 (pp. 461–462). Figure 12.12 is annotated to show the location of the control plans keyed to the control matrix.

Control Goals

The control goals listed across the top of the matrix are similar to those presented in Chapters 7 and 9 through 11, except that they have been tailored to the specifics of the purchasing process.

The *operations process control goals* that are typical of the purchasing process are the following:

- *Effectiveness of operations:* Goals A and B in Figure 12.13 identify *effectiveness goals* that are typical of the purchasing (goal A) and receiving (goal B) processes. In goal C, we include one for complying with the organization's code of conduct concerning conflicts of interest, accepting illegal or improper payments, and like matters. Recall from Chapter 7 that one of the three categories of control objectives recommended by the COSO report on internal control is compliance with applicable laws, regulations, and contractual agreements. For each process to which it applies, we have elected to include COSO's "compliance" objective under our *effectiveness goals*. As you saw in Chapter 7 and earlier in this chapter in the "Fraud Connection" section, many organizations are addressing some of the thorny ethical issues that they face by adopting a corporate code of conduct, giving that code wide publicity throughout the organization, and having employees subscribe to that code by periodically attesting that they have abided by its provisions. In that sense, then, the code of conduct becomes a type of contractual agreement between the company and its employees.
- *Efficient employment of resources:* As noted in Chapter 9 and reinforced in Chapters 10 and 11, people and computers are the resources found in most business processes.
- *Resource security:* As mentioned in Chapter 9, the resource security column should identify assets that are at risk. The resources of interest here are inventory and the vendor and PO master data. Controls should protect the inventory as it is received

and sent to the warehouse. Controls should also prevent the unauthorized accessing, copying, changing, selling, or destroying the vendor and purchasing master data.

The *information process control goals* comprise the second category of control goals in Figure 12.13 (pp. 466–467). To focus our discussion, we have not included other process inputs, such as purchase requisition and PO approvals. The information process control goals are the following:

- *Input validity (IV) of PO inputs (i.e., purchase requisitions):* This begins with a requisition that is approved by the appropriate cost center authorities and results in POs that are themselves approved and issued to an authorized vendor. To be added to the vendor master data, a vendor should be investigated for the quality of its processes and products. By adding a vendor to the vendor master data, management has provided *authorization* to do business with that vendor.
- *Input validity (IV) of vendor packing slip inputs:* This is supported by an approved PO and an actual receipt of goods. Vendor packing slips not supported by an approved PO may result in overstocking inventory and, if the inventory cannot be used, an overstatement of the inventory asset. Vendor packing slips that do not correspond to an actual receipt of goods will cause inaccurate inventory records and an overstatement of inventory and liabilities.
- *Input completeness (IC) of purchase requisitions:* Failure to achieve this goal may result in lost customer sales or suspension of production operations due to lack of inventory. Processing purchase requisitions more than once may lead to excess inventory or other unnecessary purchases.
- *Input completeness (IC) of vendor packing slips:* Failure to achieve this goal may result in the loss of accountability for the inventory and an understatement of inventory and liabilities. Processing vendor packing slips more than once will cause inaccurate inventory records and an overstatement of inventory and liabilities.
- *Input accuracy (IA) of purchase requisitions:* Inaccurate purchase requisition processing may cause the wrong goods or wrong quantities to be purchased (or ordered for the wrong plant, etc.). As with invalid or incomplete inputs, this may cause overstocking or disruption of the sales or manufacturing operations.
- *Input accuracy (IA) of vendor packing slips:* Inaccurate vendor packing slip inputs may cause a lack of accountability and a misstatement of inventory. Also, if we overstate the receipt and rely on the inventory data for replenishment decisions, we may not be aware when reordering is needed.
- *Update completeness (UC) and update accuracy (UA) of the PO and inventory master data:*[13] The PO and inventory master data are updated to reflect that a purchase has been made and then that the goods have been received (and that the PO has been filled). Failure to update correctly when the PO has been issued may result in duplicate orders and an inability to follow up on open orders. Failure to update when the goods are received may result in unauthorized receipts and inaccurate inventory records.

Recommended Control Plans

Recall that application control plans include both those that are characteristic of a particular AIS business process and those that relate to the technology used to

---

[13]These update goals will not apply in this analysis because the updates are simultaneous with the inputs, and the input controls will address any update completeness and update accuracy issues.

FIGURE 12.13 Control Matrix for the Purchasing Process

	Control Goals of the Purchasing Business Process														
	Control Goals of the Operations Process					Control Goals of the Information Process									
Recommended control plans	Ensure effectiveness of operations:			Ensure efficient employment of resources (people, computers)	Ensure security of resources (inventory, and vendor and purchase order master data)	For purchase order inputs (i.e., requisitions), ensure:			For purchase order and inventory master data, ensure:		For vendor packing slip inputs, ensure:			For purchase order and inventory master data, ensure:	
	A	B	C			IV	IC	IA	UC	UA	IV	IC	IA	UC	UA
Present Controls															
P-1: Approve purchase requisition						P-1									
P-2: Use authorized vendor data	P-2		P-2	P-2		P-2									
P-3: Independent vendor master data maintenance	P-3		P-3		P-3	P-3									
P-4: Compare vendors for favorable price, terms, quality, and product availability	P-4														
P-5: Approve purchase order	P-5		P-5			P-5									
P-6: Confirm purchase order to requesting department							P-6								
P-7: Automated data entry				P-7	P-7						P-7		P-7		

(Continues)

FIGURE 12.13 Control Matrix for the Purchasing Process (*continued*)

Recommended control plans	Control Goals of the Purchasing Business Process															
	Control Goals of the Operations Process					Control Goals of the Information Process									
	Ensure effectiveness of operations:			Ensure efficient employment of resources (people, computers)	Ensure security of resources (inventory, and vendor and purchase order master data)	For purchase order inputs (i.e., requisitions), ensure:			For purchase order and inventory master data, ensure:		For vendor packing slip inputs, ensure:			For purchase order and inventory master data, ensure:	
	A	B	C			IV	IC	IA	UC	UA	IV	IC	IA	UC	UA
P-8: Independent authorization to record receipt											P-8				
P-9: Compare input receipt data to PO data		P-9											P-9		
Missing Controls															
M-1: Count goods and compare to vendor packing slip (one-for-one checking)				M-1	M-1								M-1		
M-2: Inspect goods	M-2				M-2						M-2		M-2		
M-3: Monitor open purchase orders (tickler file)			M-3									M-3			

Possible effectiveness goals include the following:

A—Select a vendor who will provide the best quality at the lowest price by the required delivery date

B—Ensure that the right goods in the correct amount are received in acceptable condition in a timely manner

C—Comply with the corporate code of conduct

See Exhibit 12.1 for a complete explanation of control plans and cell entries.

IV = input validity
IC = input completeness
IA = input accuracy
UC = update completeness
UA = update accuracy

implement the application. We introduce you here to those new plans that are particular to the purchasing business process. We first define and explain these controls and then summarize, in **Exhibit 12.1**, each cell entry in Figure 12.13 (pp. 466–467), the control matrix:

- **Approve purchase requisition** (Exhibit 12.1 and Figure 12.13, P-1): An authorized individual, or several individuals, such as cost center or department management, should approve purchase requisitions to ensure that the purchase is within an applicable budget and that the purchase is desirable.
- **Use authorized vendor data** (Exhibit 12.1 and Figure 12.13, P-2): Vendors should be vetted to determine their suitability to provide the organization with goods and services. The screening process might include vendor financial viability and performance record. The vendor data includes payment terms, address, and bank account.
- **Independent vendor master data maintenance** (Exhibit 12.1 and Figure 12.13, P-3):[14] Requires that there is a separation of duties between the personnel who create vendor records (to authorize purchases and payments) and those that create and approve POs, record accounts payable, and approve payments. Without this separation, a buyer could execute a purchase with a vendor with which there is some arrangement (e.g., kickback) or conflict of interest (e.g., ownership). Also, without this separation, accounts payable personnel could create a vendor account to facilitate the creation of an invalid/fraudulent invoice that would subsequently be paid, perhaps to an address or bank account that they created on the vendor record. One-time accounts might be created by accounts payable for one-time payments.
- **Compare vendors for favorable prices, terms, quality, and product availability** (Exhibit 12.1 and Figure 12.13, P-4): Before executing a purchase, prospective vendors should be compared to determine that they are the optimal choice for the purchase.
- **Approve purchase order** (Exhibit 12.1 and Figure 12.13, P-5): Before being issued, the appropriate personnel should approve POs to ensure that an appropriate supplier has been selected and that the correct goods and services, for the correct amounts, are being purchased. Failure of this control will lead to financial loss if the goods are not needed and cannot be returned.
- **Confirm purchase order to requesting department** (Exhibit 12.1 and Figure 12.13, P-6): To prevent duplicate purchase requests and to allow the requesting department to ensure that a PO is created, the requesting department should be informed when a PO has been issued in response to a purchase requisition.
- **Independent authorization to record receipt** (Exhibit 12.1 and Figure 12.13, P-8): Before a receipt can be accepted and recorded, the receipt data should be compared with the PO master data to determine that an approved PO, prepared by someone other than receiving personnel, is on file. Receipts that are not authorized may be paid for and not be needed.
- **Compare input receipt data to PO data** (Exhibit 12.1 and Figure 12.13, P-9): Before a receipt can be accepted and recorded, the receipt data should be compared with the PO master data to determine that the correct goods have been received.
- **Inspect goods** (Exhibit 12.1 and Figure 12.13, M-2): To ensure that the correct goods are received in acceptable condition.

---

[14]While not explicitly mentioned in the physical process description, we are assuming that this control is in place.

EXHIBIT 12.1   Explanation of Cell Entries for the Control Matrix in Figure 12.13

P-1: *Approve purchase requisition.*

- *Purchase requisition input validity:* By obtaining approvals for all purchase requisitions, we reduce the possibility that invalid (unauthorized) requisitions will be input.

P-2: *Use authorized vendor data.*

- *Effectiveness goal A:* Buyers in the purchasing department are presented with a list of vendor candidates that have been approved by management. The screening of vendors that preceded their being added to the authorized data should help ensure the *selection of a vendor that will provide the best quality at the lowest price by the promised delivery date.*
- *Effectiveness goal C:* Screening of vendors helps to ensure that company employees do not have financial interests in a vendor that would jeopardize their ability to be impartial in selecting a vendor with whom to place an order.
- *Efficient employment of resources:* People resources (buyers' time) are used efficiently because time is not wasted in searching for vendors that might not even supply the required goods or services.
- *Purchase requisition input validity:* The *blanket* approval accorded to vendors who are placed on the authorized vendor data also helps ensure the validity of the POs issued.

P-3: *Independent vendor master data maintenance.*

- *Effectiveness goals A and C, security of resources:* By having someone other than the buyers add vendors to the vendor master data, we can obtain independent support for the quality of their products and processes (goal A), ensure that there will be no conflict of interest for the buyer (goal C), and ensure the integrity of the vendor master data (security of resources).
- *Purchase requisition input validity:* Valid purchase requisitions are those that result in POs to vendors that have received prior *authorization.*

P-4: *Compare vendors for favorable prices, terms, quality, and product availability.*

- *Effectiveness goal A:* The comparison of vendors should help ensure the selection of a vendor who will provide the best quality at the lowest price by the promised delivery date.

P-5: *Approve purchase order.*

- *Effectiveness goal A:* After the PO is checked against the requisition details, it is approved by the purchasing manager and other authorized individuals—by adding an approval code to the PO record. The manager's approval includes the vendor chosen by the buyer and the items and quantities purchased.
- *Effectiveness goal C:* This control plan could flag situations in which certain vendors appear to be favored in the vendor-selection process.
- *Purchase requisition input validity:* Approval by the purchasing manager helps to ensure validity of the PO.

P-6: *Confirm purchase order to requesting department.*

- *Purchase requisition input completeness:* After the PO has been released by the purchasing manager, a confirmation of the requisition is sent to the requesting department. Should the confirmation not be received in a timely manner, the requestor will follow up to see that the request is processed.

P-7: *Automated data entry.*

- *Efficient employment of resources:* By reducing the amount of data that must be keyed into the system, we improve the speed and productivity of the receiving personnel.
- *Security of resources:* The accurate and valid recording of the receipt data ensures accountability for the goods, reducing the possibility that they will be lost or stolen.
- *Vendor packing slip input validity* and *input accuracy:* By reading RFID tags to record the receipt, we ensure that the goods are actually there (validity), and we reduce the possibility of input errors that might occur from key-entering the items and quantities received.

P-8: *Independent authorization to record receipt.*

- *Vendor packing slip input validity:* We ensure the validity of the receipt by comparing the data on the RFID tags to an existing PO that was approved and recorded by someone outside of the receiving function.

P-9: *Compare input receipt data to PO data.*

- *Effectiveness goal B:* By comparing the open PO to the data on the RFID tags, we can ensure that we have received the goods that were ordered.

(Continues)

EXHIBIT 12.1   Explanation of Cell Entries for Control Matrix in Figure 12.13 (*continued*)

- *Vendor packing slip input accuracy:* The comparison identifies erroneous or suspect data and reduces input errors.

M-1: *Count goods and compare to vendor packing slip (one-for-one checking).*

- *Effectiveness goal B, security of resources, packing slip input accuracy:* By comparing the goods received to the packing slip that indicates what the vendor shipped, we ensure that we have received the correct goods, that there will be accountability for the goods, and that the packing slip will be input correctly.
- *Efficient employment of resources:* By detecting early in the process that the count of the goods received does not agree with the goods shipped by the vendor, we can correct errors more easily, and in less time, than would be possible later in the process (e.g., in the warehouse).

M-2: *Inspect goods.*

- *Effectiveness goal B:* By inspecting the goods received, we ensure that we have received the correct goods in acceptable condition.
- *Security of resources, packing slip input validity, packing slip input accuracy:* The inspection ensures that what was actually received will be recorded (validity), that there will be accountability for the actual goods received (security), and that the packing slip will be input correctly (accuracy).

M-3: *Monitor open purchase orders (tickler file).*

- *Effectiveness goal B, packing slip input completeness:* By regularly reviewing open POs, an organization could ensure that goods are received and packing slips input in a timely manner.

Each of the recommended control plans listed in the matrix in Figure 12.13 (pp. 466–467) is discussed in Exhibit 12.1. We have intentionally limited the number of plans to avoid redundancy. For example, we do not include several plans from Chapter 9 such as *preformatted screens, online prompting, programmed edits* (e.g., a reasonableness test on the purchase quantity), *procedures for rejected inputs, confirm input acceptance, digital signature,* and *populate inputs with master data.* We could also include *enter receipts data in receiving.* Study the explanations of the cell entries appearing in the control matrix in Exhibit 12.1. As you know from your studies in prior chapters, understanding how the recommended control plans relate to specific control goals is the most important aspect of applying the control framework.

Summary

This chapter covered the purchasing process, which is the backbone of the *purchase-to-pay process* introduced in Chapter 2. Like the OE/S process in the *order-to-cash process,* the purchasing component of the purchase-to-pay process fills a central coordinating role as it supports the supplies and inventory components of an organization's operations.

The physical process implementation presented in this chapter illustrates many attributes of the paperless office of the not-too-distant future. Are these visions of a paperless society that far-fetched? Hardly. The technology exists today, and many companies have availed themselves of some, if not all, of that technology.

SOX   As we did at the end of Chapters 10 and 11, we include here, in **Technology Summary 12.5**, a review of the entity-level controls (i.e., control environment, pervasive controls, and general/IT general controls) that may have an impact on the effectiveness of the purchasing business process controls.

Technology Summary 12.5

CONSIDERING THE EFFECT OF ENTITY-LEVEL CONTROLS ON PURCHASING BUSINESS PROCESS CONTROLS

The effectiveness of purchasing process controls can depend on the operation of several controls described in Chapter 8. In this summary, we examine some of those relationships.

Segregation of Duties

Several functions in the purchasing process must be segregated for the business process controls to be effective, including the following:

- Authorization to create vendor records, as well as payment terms, should be assigned to someone other than those completing the purchasing and accounts payable processes. For example, vendor records might be maintained by a separate function within the purchasing or accounts payable departments.
- The receiving process assumes that there has been an authorized PO. This presumes the segregation between purchasing and receiving functions.
- A warehouse function, separate from receiving, can count the goods sent to the warehouse, compare that count to the stock notice, and thus ensure that receipts are valid and accurate.

Additional Manual Controls

Several manual, pervasive, and general controls can affect the performance of the business process controls:

- The inspection and counting of goods upon receipt are important controls that must be performed well.

- Perhaps, for example, the count of two receiving clerks might be compared before that count is input.
- We might consider *rotation of duties* for buyers (e.g., change the types of products that they buy) to reduce the possibility that they are in collusion with assigned vendors.
- As noted in Technology Summary 9.1 (pg. 318), the performance of these manual controls depends on the quality of the people performing the control activities. Therefore, we expect controls such as *selection and hiring*, *training and education*, *job descriptions*, and *supervision* to be in place.

Automated Controls

All of the purchasing controls performed by the computer depend on the general controls (also known as IT general controls or ITGCs) in Chapter 8. Those controls include *approve purchase requisitions*, *use authorized vendor data*, *approve purchase orders*, *independent authorization to record receipt*, and *compare input receipt data to PO data*. We need to know that the programs will perform the controls as designed (e.g., *program change controls*). Also, we need to know that the stored data used by the computer when executing these controls is valid and accurate (e.g., *physical and logical access controls*). For the purchasing process, we are particularly concerned, for example, with controlled access to the following:

- Vendor master records so that one cannot be added without authorization.
- PO master data so that bogus POs cannot be created to record an unauthorized receipt.

Key Terms

purchasing process, 438

supply chain, 441

supply chain management (SCM), 441

SCM software, 442

bullwhip effect, 445

purchase requisition, 448

reorder point (ROP) analysis, 450

economic order quantity (EOQ), 450

ABC analysis, 450

purchase order (PO), 452

blind copy, 453

vendor packing slip, 453

receiving report, 453

acceptance report, 453

vendor master data, 454

purchase requisitions data, 454

purchase order master data, 454

purchase receipts data, 454

e-procurement, 456

paperless systems, 456

B2B marketplaces, 456

radio-frequency identification (RFID), 459

approve purchase requisition, 468

use authorized vendor data, 468

independent vendor master data maintenance, 468

compare vendors for favorable prices, terms, quality, and product availability, 468

approve purchase order, 468

confirm purchase order to requesting department, 468

independent authorization to record receipt, 468

compare input receipt data to PO data, 468

inspect goods, 468

Review Questions

RQ 12-1   What is the purchasing process?

RQ 12-2   What primary functions does the purchasing process perform? Explain each function.

RQ 12-3   With what internal and external entities does the purchasing process interact?

RQ 12-4   What are the fundamental responsibilities of each position: purchasing manager, buyer, and receiving supervisor?

RQ 12-5   Describe supply chain management (SCM).

RQ 12-6   Describe the five basic components of the Supply Chain Operations Reference (SCOR) model.

RQ 12-7   How does SCM software support SCM?

RQ 12-8   Describe Vendor Managed Inventory (VMI), Co-Managed Inventory, Collaborative Forecasting and Replenishment (CFAR), and Collaborative Planning Forecasting and Replenishment (CPFR).

RQ 12-9   What is the bullwhip effect?

RQ 12-10   What three major *logical* processes does the purchasing process perform? Describe each process.

RQ 12-11   Describe how radio-frequency identification (RFID) works.

RQ 12-12   What types of frauds are typically found in the purchasing process?

RQ 12-13   What are the typical effectiveness goals of the purchasing process? Provide an example illustrating each goal.

RQ 12-14   What characterizes a valid PO input? What characterizes a valid vendor packing slip input?

RQ 12-15   What are the key control plans associated with the purchasing process? Describe how each works and what it accomplishes.

RQ 12-16   Describe the impact that entity-level controls (i.e., control environment, pervasive controls, and general/IT general controls) can have on the effectiveness of purchasing business process controls.

Discussion Questions

DQ 12-1   Refer to the operations process (effectiveness) goals shown in the control matrix, Figure 12.13 (pp. 466–467). Referring to goals A (purchasing) and B (receiving), describe an operations goal other than the one discussed in the chapter.

DQ 12-2   Explain why ambiguities and conflicts exist among operations process goals, and discuss potential ambiguities and conflicts relative to the effectiveness goals you described in DQ 12-1.

DQ 12-3   In designing vendor records, what specific data elements would you include to help you select the best vendor for a particular purchase? Be specific as to the nature of the data to be stored, where it would come from, and how it would be used in the selection process.

DQ 12-4   Without redrawing the figures, discuss how Figures 12.3 (pg. 447), 12.4 (pg. 448), 12.6 (pg. 450), 12.7 (pg. 451), and 12.9 (pg. 454) would change as a result of purchasing a technical product that could not be inspected in the receiving department but had to undergo quality control testing before being accepted.

DQ 12-5   Figure 12.9 (the DFD depicting the receipt of goods and services) shows an update to the vendor master data from bubble 3.1 and another update to that same data from bubble 3.2. Discuss the *difference(s)* between these two updates. Be specific as to the nature of the data being updated in each case. How would your answer to this question be affected by your assumption about whether the PO receiving notification entering bubble 3.1 was "blind" as to quantities? Explain.

DQ 12-6   In terms of effectiveness and efficiency of operations, as well as of meeting the generic information system control goals of validity, completeness, and accuracy, what are the arguments for and against each of the following?

a.   Sending a copy of the PO from the purchasing department to the receiving department.

b.   Having the quantity ordered field "blinded" on the receiving department copy of the PO.

DQ 12-7   "Auditors will never allow an organization to adopt a paperless system, so why do we waste our time bothering to study them?" Discuss fully.

Short Problems

SP 12-1   Compare bar codes and radio frequency identification (RFID) tags by placing a check mark in the appropriate box to indicate which technology is better for each of the criteria listed below.

Criteria	Bar Code	RFID Tag
Need to be a geek to understand.		
Need to see to read.		
Least expensive.		
Oldest.		
Necessary for logistics at UPS and FedEx.		
Reading of data affected by laws of physics.		
Can require significant data storage.		
Can be read at highway speeds.		
Dominates supply chain.		
Useful for tracking medicines.		
Protects privacy better.		
Tracks hospital patients and equipment.		

SP 12-2   Using the following table as a guide, describe for each function (Figure 12.1, pg. 439):

a. A risk (an event or action that will cause the organization to fail to meet its goals/objectives).

b. A control/process or use of technology that will address the risk.

Function	Risks	Controls and Technology
Logistics		
Purchasing		
Receiving Inventory (Debit) ??? (Credit)		

SP 12-3   The following are five process failures that indicate weaknesses in control.

Process Failures

1. A purchasing agent ordered unneeded inventory items from a supplier company of which he is one of the officers.
2. The vendor shipped goods that were never ordered. These receipts are recorded as received and put in stock.
3. Goods were stolen by storeroom personnel. When the shortage was discovered, the storeroom personnel claimed that the goods had never been delivered to them from the receiving department.
4. An organization seems to regularly run out of inventory for some of its most popular items.
5. The materials going into production do not meet quality standards.

For each of the five process failures described, provide a two- to three-sentence description of the control plan that you believe would *best* address that deficiency. Obviously, there could be more than one plan that is germane to a particular situation. However, select *only one* plan for each of the five process failures, and include in your description a justification of why you believe it is *best*. When in doubt, opt for the plan that is *preventive* in nature, as opposed to plans that are *detective* or *corrective*.

SP 12-4   The following is a list of six control plans from this chapter or from Chapters 9, 10, and 11.

Control Plans

A. One-for-one checking of goods received to open PO and vendor packing slip
B. Computer agreement of batch totals
C. Compare input receipt data with PO
D. Employ automated data entry (e.g., RFID, bar codes)
E. Provide receiving with blind copy of PO
F. Monitor open POs

The following five statements describe either the achievement of a control goal (i.e., a system success) or a system deficiency (i.e., a system failure).

Control Goals or System Deficiencies

1. The process in receiving for counting and recording goods is time consuming and error prone.
2. In a periodic/batch environment, helps to ensure the information system control goal of input completeness of the receiving reports.
3. Quantity recorded as received does not correspond to the quantity actually received.
4. Goods recorded as received do not match what was ordered and sent by the vendor.
5. Goods are not being received in a timely manner.

Match the five control goals or systems deficiencies with a control plan that would *best* achieve the desired goal or prevent the system deficiency. A letter may be used only once, with one letter left over.

Problems

Note: As mentioned in Chapters 10 and 11, the first few problems in the business process chapters are based on the processes of specific companies. Therefore, the problem material starts with case narratives of those processes.

CASE STUDIES

CASE A: Bondstreet Company (Purchasing and receiving processes)

The Bondstreet Company sells medical supplies to hospitals, clinics, and doctor's offices. Bondstreet uses an ERP system for all of its business processes. These supplies are maintained on a real-time basis in an inventory database in an enterprise system. The inventory records include reorder points for all regularly used items and one or two preferred vendors for each item. Vendors are researched and approved by the purchasing manager before being added to the vendor database by a clerk designated to maintain the database. Bondstreet employs the following procedures for purchasing and receiving.

Throughout the day, the supplies clerk receives from the enterprise system an online report listing those items that have reached their reorder point. The clerk reviews the report and creates a purchase requisition by filling out a requisition form in the company's enterprise system. Each requisition has a unique identifier, and after creation, the purchase requisition data and inventory master data are updated to reflect the purchase requisition. Inventory manager approval is required for purchases over $1,000 and not covered by a blanket order. The inventory manager can log on to the enterprise system any time to look at open purchase requisitions that require approval and to approve those requisitions by checking the acceptance box. The computer records these approvals on the purchase requisition data.

Throughout the day, buyers in the purchasing department receive from the enterprise system online approved requisitions with a list of appropriate vendors. They select a vendor and enter PO data. After the PO is saved, the purchase requisition data and inventory master data are updated. The completed, prenumbered PO is then printed in the purchasing department and mailed to the vendor.

The receiving department inspects and counts the goods when they are received, compares the count to the packing slip, pulls up the PO in the enterprise system, and enters the quantity received. The PO and inventory master data are updated after the receiving record is saved. The general ledger master data is also updated to reflect the increase in the inventory balance.

CASE B: Internet Payment Platform (Purchasing and receiving processes)

The following describes the purchasing and receiving processes at the United States Department of the Treasury's Bureau of Engraving and Printing (BEP) during a pilot of the Internet Payment Platform (IPP). Components of the IPP include a server with an "appreciating database" located at Xign, Inc. and an Intel server at BEP called the "Enterprise Adapter." BEP's mainframe, legacy enterprise system is called BEPMIS, which has an IDMS network database.

Contracting officers (CO) in BEP's Office of Procurement enter purchase orders (POs) into the BEPMIS purchasing module, where they are stored on the IDMS database. Because the IPP does not accommodate a digitally signed PO and does not include sufficient text to comply with the Federal Acquisition Regulation (FAR), POs are printed by the BEPMIS system, signed by the CO, and mailed to the supplier. A routine on the BEPMIS system, written for the IPP pilot, is manually initiated each evening to extract and format POs for suppliers participating in the pilot. The core PO data (vendor, items, amounts, quantities, etc., but not including additional descriptive and contractual text) are extracted by this routine, as a batch, directly from the IDMS (BEPMIS) database and sent to the enterprise adapter, which converts the PO data from IDMS format into XML, encrypts the batch, and sends it to the IPP server at Xign, where it is stored on the IPP appreciating database. Now a PO record exists on both the IDMS (BEPMIS) database and the IPP appreciating database. After a PO is posted to the IPP database, IPP notifies suppliers via e-mail.

Having been notified that a PO has been issued, an employee at a BEP supplier logs on to IPP and reads the POs onscreen. Depending on the nature of the PO and a supplier's policies, its employees might be required to wait for the paper PO before beginning the process of providing the goods, or they might be permitted to act on the electronic PO. The supplier sends the goods with a packing slip to BEP, where receiving personnel record the receipt into BEPMIS (no record of the receipt was recorded on the IPP appreciating database). BEPMIS prints a stock notice and it and the goods are sent to the warehouse.

P12-1   For the company assigned by your instructor, complete the following requirements:

a.   Prepare a table of entities and activities.

b.   Draw a context diagram.

c.   Draw a physical data flow diagram (DFD).

d.   Prepare an annotated table of entities and activities. Indicate on this table the groupings, bubble numbers, and bubble titles to be used in preparing a level 0 logical DFD.

e.   Draw a level 0 logical DFD.

P12-2   For the company assigned by your instructor, complete the following requirements:

a.   Draw a systems flowchart.

b.   Prepare a control matrix, including explanations of how each recommended existing control plan helps to accomplish—or would accomplish in the case of missing plans—each related control goal. Your choice of recommended control plans could come from this chapter plus any controls from Chapters 9 through 11 that are germane to your company's process.

c. Annotate the flowchart prepared in part (a) to indicate the points where the control plans are being applied (codes P-1, … , P-*n*) or the points where they could be applied but are not (codes M-1, … , M-*n*).

P12-3 The following describes a purchasing process at Ludlow Winter Sports, Inc., a manufacturer of skis, snowshoes, and other winter recreational gear. The description here is limited to the process for ordering *and* receiving parts for repairing and maintaining manufacturing equipment. Please read the narrative and answer the questions that follow.

A small inventory of parts is located in the plant maintenance office. When that inventory needs to be replenished, the maintenance manager fills out a purchase requisition and brings it to the purchasing department. A similar process is used when parts are not available in inventory and are needed immediately to repair or service a machine.

Once received in purchasing, the buyer responsible for plant maintenance purchase requisitions looks up any approved supplier in the corporate book of approved vendors. If an appropriate vendor is not found, the buyer looks in a card file of local suppliers. When a vendor is chosen, the buyer enters the requisition into the purchasing computer system and prints the PO. The purchasing manager at Ludlow must sign all POs, about 75 each day. This is a tedious process. There is no review, just a signature. The PO is a two-part carbon, so each PO must be signed by hand. Several POs to the same vendor may be prepared each day. The purchasing manager gives the POs to a secretary, who mails the original to the vendor and files the copy in a paper file by vendor number.

When goods are received from the vendor, a receiving clerk calls up the PO on the computer screen, does a quick visual inspection and count, and labels the shipment "on hold." The clerk notifies the Quality Control (QC) department of the shipment. QC performs the required quality tests and, if appropriate, changes the "on hold" label to "released." At that point, the goods are moved to the warehouse, and the receipt is entered into the computer to clear the PO and update the inventory balance.

a. Comment on the efficiency and effectiveness of the purchasing process at Ludlow.

b. Draw a systems flowchart of a revised process that would solve the problems identified in part (a).

P12-4 The following is a list of 12 control plans from this chapter or from Chapters 8, 9, 10, and 11.

Control Plans

A. Compare input receipt data with PO data
B. Code of conduct
C. Compare vendors for price, terms, quality, availability
D. Monitor open POs

E. Independent authorization to record receipt
F. Count goods and compare to vendor packing slip
G. Independent vendor master data maintenance
H. Personnel management controls (supervision)
I. Perimeter and building controls
J. Segregate warehouse and receiving
K. Digital signature
L. Logical and physical access controls

The following are 10 system failures that have control implications.

System Failures

1. Sarah, a buyer at Sanford Company, ordered unneeded inventory items from a vendor of which she is an owner.
2. Fred worked in the receiving department at Altos, Inc. One day, goods were received from Adams Company for which no open PO could be found. To get the items received, Fred figured out a way to create a PO. As it turns out, the goods had never been ordered.
3. Bob, a buyer at Medford, Inc., was in a hurry to buy a part needed to get the Medford factory back in operation. He found Merrick Company, a local vendor that could supply the part that day but for a premium price. Because it was an emergency, he created a vendor record for Merrick and issued the PO. Subsequently, other buyers began to use Merrick for other purchases.
4. Doug, who works in the warehouse at Brookline, Inc., has gotten into some financial difficulties and has figured out a way to make some extra cash by working with the folks at Melville Company. He creates orders for purchases from Melville and records a receipt, but no goods are ever received. Subsequently Melville sends a bill to Brookline, which gets paid, and Doug gets paid 20 percent of the take.
5. At Ridgewood, Inc., there are often discrepancies between what is ordered and what is recorded as received. Discrepancies include wrong items and wrong quantities.
6. Woodbury Company is often running out of inventory of certain key items. When research is conducted to find out the reason for the stock-outs, they find that a PO had been issued, but the goods had not yet been received. Typically, these delayed deliveries are consistently from the same vendors whose poor performance has been noted in the past.
7. Warehouse managers at Sarasota, Inc. have been discovering inventory shortages. When they investigate the paperwork transferring the goods from receiving to the warehouse, the evidence indicates that the goods had arrived in the warehouse.
8. The accounts payable clerks at Fairfield Company have difficulty reconciling the quantities recorded as received and the quantities on vendor invoices. Usually, the vendors claim that they are billing for the amounts that they had shipped.

9. Delray Company uses the Internet to send POs to its vendors. The vendors for Delray have been receiving POs that seem to be from Delray but are actually bogus.

10. The internal audits at Morriston Company have found several discrepancies in the inventory data; the inventory is on the shelf, but the records do not reflect those balances. When they investigate further, they find that the goods were received but never recorded.

Match the 10 system failures with a control plan that would *best* prevent the system failure from occurring. Also, give a brief (one- to two-sentence) explanation of your choice. A letter should be used only once, with two letters left over.

P12-5   As we noted when presenting the recommended control plans in the matrix in Figure 12.13 (pp. 466–467) that are discussed in Exhibit 12.1 (pp. 469-470), we intentionally limited the number of plans to avoid redundancy. For example, we did not include several plans from Chapter 9 such as *preformatted screens*, *online prompting*, *programmed edit checks* (e.g., a reasonableness test on the purchase quantity), *procedures for rejected inputs*, *confirm input acceptance*, *digital signature*, and *populate input screens with master data*. We could also include *enter receipts data in receiving*. Prepare a control matrix for just these controls. Include explanations of how each recommended existing control plan helps to accomplish—or would accomplish in the case of missing plans—each related control goal.

Annotate the flowchart in Figure 12.12 (pp. 461–462) to indicate the points where the control plans are being applied (codes P-1, … , P-*n*) or the points where they could be applied but are not (codes M-1, … , M-*n*).

P12-6   *Note:* If you were assigned DQ 12-4, consult your solution to it. Modify the DFDs in Figures 12.3 (pg. 447), 12.4 (pg. 448), 12.6 (pg. 450), 12.7 (pg. 451), and 12.9 (pg. 454), as appropriate, to reflect the purchase of a technical product that could not be inspected in the receiving department but had to undergo quality control testing before being accepted.

P12-7   Modify the DFDs in Figures 12.3, 12.4, 12.6, 12.7, and 12.9, as appropriate, to reflect that the purchase from our vendor was "drop-shipped" to one of our customers instead of being shipped to us.

P12-8   Use the DFDs in Figures 12.4, 12.6, 12.7, and 12.9, to solve this problem.

Prepare a four-column table that summarizes the purchasing processes, inputs, and outputs. In the first column, list the three processes shown in the level 0 diagram (Figure 12.4). In the second column, list the subsidiary functions shown in the three lower-level diagrams (Figures 12.6, 12.7, and 12.9). For each subsidiary process listed in column 2, list the data flow names or the data stores that are inputs to that process (column 3) or outputs of that process (column 4). (See *Note*.) The following table has been started for you to indicate the format for your solution.

Note: To simplify the solution, do not show any reject stubs in column 4.

Solution Format Summary of the Purchasing Processes, Inputs, Outputs, and Data Stores

Process	Subsidiary Functions	Inputs	Outputs
1.0 Determine requirements	1.1 Accumulate requests	Inventory's purchase requisition Purchase requisition—supplies and services	Purchase requisition data
	1.2 Calculate requirements	Purchase requisition data Inventory master data	... Continue solution ...

ACCESS **P12-9** This problem should be completed with database software, such as Microsoft Access. As directed by your instructor, submit the completed database file and the printouts noted below.

1. Using the E-R diagram in Figure 12.10 (pg. 455), select any three or four related entities and implement them as tables using Microsoft Access (or any other database software acceptable to your instructor). Link the tables using the cardinalities shown in the figure. For the tables, you may use attributes shown in Figure 12.11 (pg. 457) or create different attributes.

2. Create forms for each table from part 1 of this problem and use the forms to populate the tables with representative data. Forms should be in good order, readable, and properly formatted. Create at least three records in each table. Print out the populated tables and one instance of each form.

3. Design three queries using the tables from part 1 of this problem. Print out the output of each query and attach an explanation as to why someone would be interested in the output of each query.

4. Using the report function in Access, design a report for each query from part 3 of this problem. Reports should be in good order, readable, and properly formatted. Print out each report.

CHAPTER 13

The Accounts Payable/Cash Disbursements (AP/CD) Process

Learning Objectives

After reading this chapter, you should be able to:

- Describe the relationship between the AP/CD process and its business environment.
- Summarize how various technologies, including e-invoicing and e-payments, can improve the effectiveness of the AP/CD process.
- Depict the logical and physical characteristics of a typical AP/CD process.
- Prepare a control matrix for a typical AP/CD process, including an explanation of how business process control plans can accomplish operations and information process control goals.

KeySpan Corporation, an energy utility located in Brooklyn, NY, provides natural gas and electricity in the Northeastern United States. KeySpan was using a manual process to handle more than 22,000 vendor invoices each month. The process was time consuming and costly. Processing backlogs were causing a high number of vendor inquires and loss of valuable discounts. Ken Daly, KeySpan's vice president of Financial and Employee-Related Services, decided it was time to streamline the accounts payable operations by implementing new processes and technology. KeySpan chose an outsourced, Web-based, order-to-pay solution hosted by J.P. Morgan.[1]

Now, 750 of KeySpan's suppliers, representing $450 million in annual invoices, use the J.P. Morgan Business Settlement Network (BSN) to receive purchase orders (POs), send invoices, execute online inquiries regarding outstanding invoices, and receive electronic payments. As a result of this implementation, KeySpan's on-time payments reached 98 percent, processing efficiency improved by 30 percent, and invoice backlog was reduced from five days to one. Daly stated that accounts payable operating costs were reduced by $500,000 and vendor discounts taken increased by $1 million. Finally, Daly reported that KeySpan earned a 36 percent annualized cash return on early payment discounts and

---

[1] J.P. Morgan's Order-to-Pay process is an example of an electronic invoice presentment and payment (EIPP) system in the B2B environment. In Chapter 11, there is a description of electronic bill presentment and payment (EBPP) systems in the B2C environment. (The J.P. Morgan Order-to-Pay process was formerly known as JP Morgan Xign.)

expanded its days payable outstanding (DPO)[2] by eight days. The J.P. Morgan Order-to-Pay process is described in Technology Summary 13.1 on page 497.[3]

Synopsis

This chapter presents our fourth business process, the accounts payable/cash disbursements (AP/CD) process. The AP/CD process includes the last two steps, invoice verification and payment processing, in the purchase-to-pay process (Figure 2.10, pg. 56). After we introduce the players involved in the AP/CD process, we describe the logic and data typically employed in the process. In addition, we call your attention to the "Physical Process Description" and the "Application of the Control Framework" sections, which cover state-of-the-art material on current and evolving technology.

Introduction

As previously noted, the AP/CD process comprises the last two steps in the purchase-to-pay process (Figure 2.10). Let's now take a closer look at the AP/CD process.

Process Definition and Functions

The **payable/cash disbursements (AP/CD) process** is an interacting structure of people, equipment, activities, and controls designed to create information flows and records that accomplish the following:

- Handle the repetitive work routines of the accounts payable department and the cashier.[4]
- Support the decision needs of those who manage the accounts payable department and cashier.
- Assist in the preparation of internal and external reports.

First, the AP/CD process handles the repetitive work routines of the accounts payable department and cashier by capturing and recording data related to their day-to-day operations such as recording vendor invoices and paying those invoices. The recorded data then may be used to generate source documents (such as disbursement vouchers and vendor payments) and to produce internal and external reports.

The AP/CD process prepares a number of reports that personnel at various levels of management use. For example, the cashier might use an accounts payable aging report to plan cash availability. The cash disbursements manager might use a cash requirements forecast to help decide which invoice(s) to pay next.

---

[2]Days payable outstanding (DPO) is a key performance measure for an accounts payable department. DPO is accounts payable divided by cost of goods sold multiplied by 365 days.

[3]"KeySpan Energizes Working Capital Performance with JPMorgan Xign," available at www.jpmorgan.com/ordertopay, accessed April 28, 2010.

[4]To focus our discussion, we have assumed that these two departments are the primary operating units related to the AP/CD process. For a given organization, however, the departments associated with the process may differ.

Finally, the AP/CD process assists in the preparation of external financial statements. The process supplies the general ledger with data concerning various events related to the procurement activities of an organization. This data is related to accounts payable, the related expenses incurred or assets acquired, and the cash that is disbursed.

Organizational Setting

The AP/CD process is closely linked to functions and processes inside and outside the organization. Let's take a look at those links and the impact that they have on the operation of the AP/CD process.

A Horizontal Perspective

Figure 13.1 and **Table 13.1** (pg. 484) present a horizontal view of the relationship between the AP/CD process and its organizational environment. They show the various information flows generated or captured by the process. Take some time now to study the figure and get acquainted with the number of entities with which the process interacts. The data flows in Table 13.1 indicate the nature of these interactions.

FIGURE 13.1   A Horizontal Perspective of the AP/CD Process

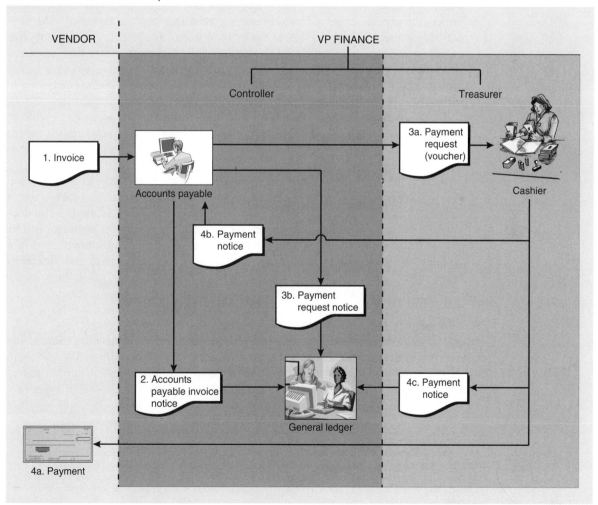

TABLE 13.1 Description of Information Flows

Flow No.	Description
1	Invoice received from vendor
2	Accounts payable invoice notice sent to general ledger
3	Approved voucher (payment request) sent to cashier (3a) and to general ledger (3b)
4	Payment (e.g., check) sent to vendor by cashier (4a), paid voucher (payment notice) returned to the accounts payable department (4b), payment notice sent to the general ledger (4c)

Figure 13.1 (pg. 483) and Table 13.1 reveal four information flows that function as vital communication links among the various departments, business processes, and external entities. We briefly explain each flow here to give you a quick introduction to the AP/CD process. Although Figure 13.1 depicts the flows using the document symbol, most of them can be implemented using electronic communications (e.g., *workflow*) and data stored in the enterprise database.

- Flow 1 is the invoice from a vendor. This could be a mailed paper invoice or an "electronic bill/invoice presentment."
- With flow 2, the accounts payable department notifies (via document or electronic notice) the general ledger that an invoice has been received and recorded. The general ledger uses this data to update the general ledger account for accounts payable to reflect an increase in payables. This is the other half of the entry that was made when the goods were received. This entry is a credit to accounts payable, whereas the entry in Chapter 12 was a debit to inventory. A clearing account entry may be necessary to balance these entries between the times that each is made.[5]
- Flow 3a is a request (via document or electronic notice) from accounts payable to the cashier for a payment to be made, and flow 3b notifies (via document, electronic notice, or record in the enterprise database) the general ledger that a payment is pending (this data will be matched with actual payments).
- Flow 4a is the cashier's payment (via paper check or electronic payment) to the vendor. Flow 4b notifies (via document or electronic notice) accounts payable that a payment has been made so that the invoice can be closed. Flow 4c notifies (via document or electronic notice) the general ledger that a payment has been made. The general ledger matches this against the notice of pending payments (3b) and updates the general ledger accounts for cash, accounts payable, and discounts taken, if any.

A Vertical Perspective

Figure 13.2 presents a representative organization chart that combines the purchasing process of Chapter 12 and the AP/CD process described in this chapter. We put them together here so that we can discuss the interactions of these processes and the players involved. In Chapter 12, we introduced the functions reporting to the VP of logistics.

---

[5] As noted in Chapter 12, the timing of the recording in the general ledger of the receipt transaction (i.e., increase inventory) and this invoice transaction (i.e., increase accounts payable) may depend on how close together these two activities occur and the specific software employed. A clearing account entry will be required when it is not possible to record the increase in inventory and increase in accounts payable simultaneously.

FIGURE 13.2   A Vertical Perspective of the Purchasing and AP/CD Processes

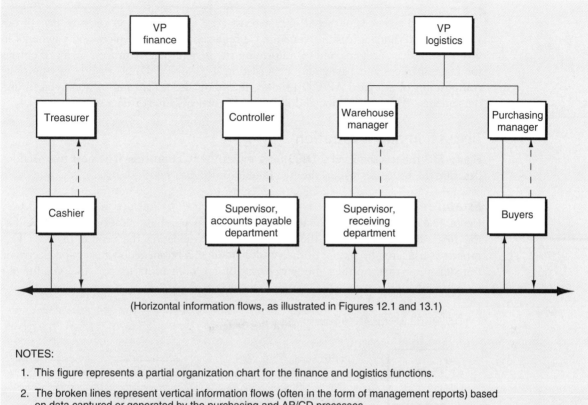

(Horizontal information flows, as illustrated in Figures 12.1 and 13.1)

NOTES:

1. This figure represents a partial organization chart for the finance and logistics functions.

2. The broken lines represent vertical information flows (often in the form of management reports) based on data captured or generated by the purchasing and AP/CD processes.

The new players here include the accounts payable department, which is responsible for processing invoices received from vendors, preparing payment vouchers for the subsequent disbursement of cash for goods or services received, and *recording* purchase and disbursement events. The cashier has *custody* of the organization's cash and *executes* the payments *authorized* by the accounts payable department.

The relationship between these groups, logistics and finance, is very similar to the relationships among the marketing, logistics, and finance functions described in Chapters 10 and 11. For example, we see subprocesses such as order entry and shipping that begin a larger process—order-to-cash—working in conjunction with subprocesses such as billing and cash receipts, which complete the larger process. In Figure 13.2, we represent the functions that start the purchase-to-pay process, purchasing and receiving, and the functions that complete the process, accounts payable and the cashier.

In addition to cooperating in completing these larger processes, these functions and the subprocesses for which they are responsible share data with which the processes operate on a day-to-day basis and make important management decisions. For example, the warehouse manager uses purchasing data to schedule personnel to handle incoming shipments and provide storage space for the goods to be received. The controller uses the purchasing and receiving data to validate incoming vendor invoices. The treasurer uses purchasing data to ensure that funds will be available to meet future obligations. Finally, data also is used "upstream" (i.e., left to right in Figure 13.2). For example, purchasing supervisors may use data about available funds to schedule purchases.

Logical Process Description

The principal activities of the AP/CD process are: (1) processing invoices received from vendors; (2) disbursing cash to vendors; (3) recording vendor invoices and payments in vendor subsidiary ledgers; and (4) informing the general ledger process to make entries for these invoices and payments. This section uses logical DFDs to present the basic composition of a typical AP/CD process, including the processing of noninvoiced disbursements. We also describe and illustrate the process's major data stores.[6]

Discussion and Illustration

Figure 13.3 reflects the level 0 DFD for a typical AP/CD process. The next two sections describe the processes within the two bubbles in Figure 13.3.

Establish Payable

Figure 13.4 presents a DFD for establishing accounts payable.[7] As shown by bubble 1.1, the first step in establishing the payable involves validating the vendor invoice. This process is triggered by receipt of the **vendor invoice**, a business document—or electronic transmission—that notifies the purchaser of an obligation to pay the vendor for

FIGURE 13.3 The AP/CD Process—Level 0 Diagram

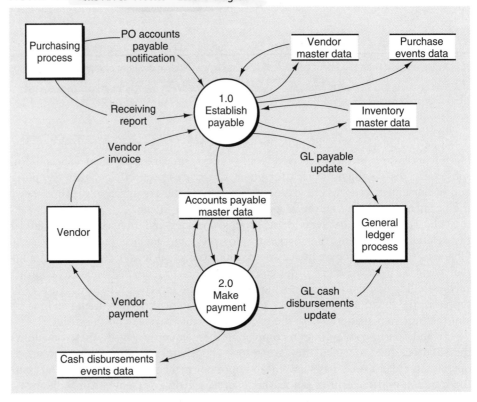

FIGURE 13.4 AP/CD Process—Diagram 1 *Hawei Invoice*

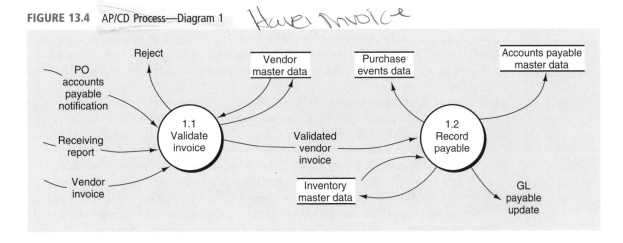

goods (or services) that were ordered by and shipped (or provided) to the purchaser. Figure 11.5 (pg. 403) depicts a typical invoice screen. Process 1.1 comprises a number of steps. First, the vendor invoice is matched against vendor master data to determine that the invoice is from an authorized vendor. Next, the vendor invoice is compared against the PO data (see the flow "PO accounts payable notification") to make sure that there is a PO (i.e., there is an *authorized* purchase) and that the invoiced items, quantities, and prices conform to the PO. Then the invoice is matched against the receiving report data to determine that the items and quantities have been received.[8] These line-by-line comparisons among the vendor invoice, PO (PO accounts payable notification), and receiving report are known as a three-way match, an important control in the AP process by which data from the purchasing process is used to *authorize* the recording of the invoice. Finally, the invoice is further validated by checking for accuracy of terms, computed discounts, extensions, and total amount due. Note that the vendor master data is updated at this point to reflect purchase history data.

If the data items do not agree (e.g., there is no PO, or items and quantities ordered and received do not agree, or prices are wrong), the invoice is rejected and follow-up procedures are initiated (see the reject stub emanating from bubble 1.1). If the data items agree, the invoice is approved, and the validated invoice is sent on to the next step to be used to record the payable.

Controls

Figure 13.5 (pg. 488) depicts the PO and related data that can be displayed in the SAP system. At the top of this display is the PO data. We can drill down here to find the related purchase requisition. At the bottom of the screen, you can see the PO history, including the goods receipt and the invoice receipt. As noted earlier, these are "attached" to the PO. Before the invoice was accepted, a match was performed (i.e., invoice verification) to determine that the PO, goods receipt, and invoice matched (within tolerances chosen by the user).

Enterprise Systems

Bubble 1.2 in Figure 13.4 depicts the process of recording the payable in the purchase events data and accounts payable master data. A payable is recognized and recorded by:

- Creating a record in the *purchase events data* store. This record includes details on the general ledger accounts to be updated, including accounts payable, freight, and

---

[8]Rather than flows from the purchasing process, the PO accounts payable notification data and receiving data are probably obtained from the PO master data and the purchase receipts data that were updated as POs were created and goods received. See Figure 13.5 (pg. 488) for an example of how the receipts data is "attached" to the PO.

sales tax, unless these latter two items are to be added to the cost of the acquired asset. If the vendor invoice is for other than the purchase of inventory, these general ledger accounts could also include assets, such as fixed assets, and expenses.

- Creating a record in the *accounts payable master data* to reflect an open invoice—a payment due to a vendor.
- Updating the *inventory master data* for the cost of the items received. The update to inventory when the goods were received might have been a standard cost or the cost from the PO. Differences among the PO, standard, and actual costs would be accounted for as standard cost variances.
- Notifying the general ledger of the amount of the payable that was recorded (see the data flow "GL payable update"). If the update to the general ledger is periodic, the data for this update would come from a summary of the purchase events data store rather than from the recording of each vendor invoice. To balance these credits to accounts payable for the purchase of inventory, a debit is made to the clearing account that was credited at the time the inventory was received. Balances in this clearing account reflect invoices or receipts that have not been recorded.

Make Payment

Figure 13.6 presents a DFD of the cash disbursements process. The payment process described here is *triggered* by payment due date information residing on the accounts

FIGURE 13.5 Sample SAP Purchase Order Data Screen

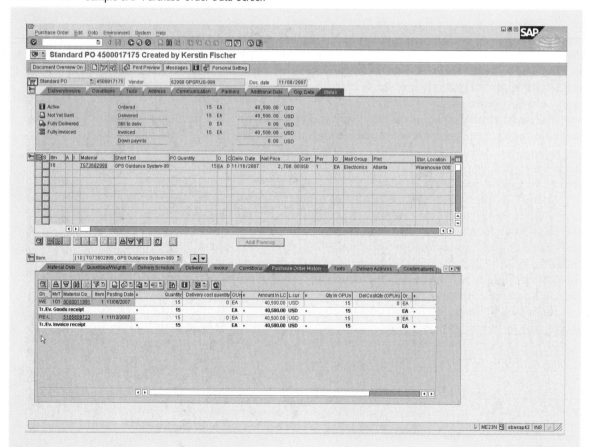

FIGURE 13.6 AP/CD Process—Diagram 2

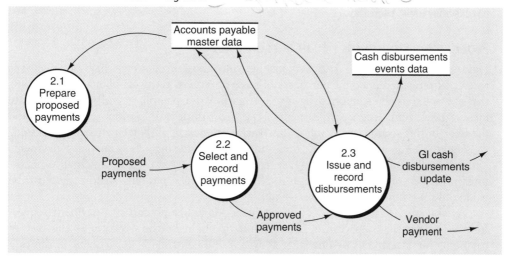

payable master data. This payment date may not be based on the vendor's invoice date but may be the date of the receipt of the goods or the receipt of the vendor invoice, whichever is later.

As you can see, the payment process begins with the periodic[9] preparation of a list of payments that might be made at this time (bubble 2.1). In addition to payment due dates, the selection of items for this list is also based on terms that may indicate a discount can be taken if a payment is made at this time. The proposed list is reviewed and amended (bubble 2.2) to add additional invoices that are not due for payment yet but that can be consolidated with other payments being made to a vendor. Proposed payments may be removed from the list if there are insufficient funds or if payments to a vendor are on hold.

Bubble 2.3 in Figure 13.6 depicts the process of preparing the disbursement, which is equal to the amount of the invoice less any discount taken. The payment is recorded by:

- Marking the invoice as paid on the accounts payable master data.
- Making an entry in the cash disbursements event data store.
- Sending payment data to the general ledger, where an entry is made to reflect the payment (cash, accounts payable, discount taken, etc.). If the update to the general ledger is periodic, the data for this update comes from a summary of the *cash disbursements events data* store rather than from the recording of each vendor payment.

The payment schedule adopted depends on the availability of any favorable discounts for prompt payment and on the organization's current cash position. Some companies pay multiple invoices with one check to minimize the cost of processing invoices. Most cash managers attempt to optimize cash balances to help achieve another operations process (effectiveness) goal: *to ensure that the amount of cash maintained in demand deposit accounts is sufficient (but not excessive) to satisfy expected cash disbursements.* To accomplish this goal, many banks offer their commercial customers a cash-management service by which the bank transfers from the customer's money market or other

`Controls`

---

[9]We say periodic because many organizations have a set schedule, such as twice weekly, for performing the case disbursements process.

investment account into its checking account the exact amount needed to cover the checks that clear each day.

Processing Noninvoiced Disbursements

Figure 13.4 (pg. 487) and 13.6 demonstrate only those events for which an invoice is received from the vendor for purchases of *goods* or *services*. But what about disbursements that are not typically supported by invoices, such as for payroll, payroll taxes, corporate income taxes, rent, security investments, repayment of debt obligations and interest, and the like? In this section, we examine how such noninvoiced disbursements are processed.

Figure 13.7 is a logical DFD that shows the processing of noninvoiced payments under two different assumptions: (1) a true *voucher process* is used in which all expenditures must be vouchered—that is, formally recorded as a payable—before they can be paid, and (2) a nonvoucher process is employed.

As you can see in Figure 13.7, the trigger for either process is a payment request from an originating department. The originator might be the treasurer in the case of payments for investment or financing activities, the controller's department in the case of tax payments, or even an accounts payable software module for recurring monthly payments such as rent. Upon receipt of the payment request, process bubble 1.0 in the voucher process shown in part 1 of the figure, prepares a voucher for all payments without regard to the purpose and no matter how small (even petty cash reimbursements) and adds the account distribution to the disbursement voucher. All vouchered items are then recorded as payables (see process bubble 2.0) before they are paid. This means that from an accounting standpoint, the distribution of charges to asset, expense, or other accounts is reported to the general ledger by process 2.0 (immediately or periodically via a summary of the *purchase events data* store); in process 3.0, the general ledger is notified to eliminate the payable and reduce the cash account (immediately or periodically via a summary of the *cash disbursements event data*).

Controls

In the nonvoucher process depicted in part 2 of Figure 13.7, the payment request also is approved in process bubble 1.0, and the account distribution is added to the request. However, the approval process is less formal than in the voucher process— that is, no disbursement voucher is prepared. Physically, the approved payment request that is passed to process bubble 2.0 usually comprises the same document that entered process 1.0 but with authorized signatures and account distribution now appended. In this process, the payment is issued and recorded in the *cash disbursements event data*, and the general ledger is notified (immediately or periodically via a summary of the *cash disbursements event data*) to reduce the cash account and record the distribution of accounting charges (e.g., expenses).

Logical Data Descriptions

The AP/CD process entails several data stores. The *inventory master data, vendor master data, purchase requisitions master data, purchase order master data*, and *purchase receipts data* were described in Chapter 12. The following are three additional data stores:

- **Purchasing events data** contains, in chronological sequence, the details of each invoice that is recorded. Each record shows the date recorded; vendor invoice number; account distributions, such as assets, expenses, freight, sales tax (or the clearing account for inventory receipts); and gross invoice amount.
- **Accounts payable master data** is a repository of all unpaid vendor invoices. The data includes vendor number, vendor invoice number and date, terms, date due, line item details (items, quantities, cost), and invoice total.

- **Cash disbursements events data** contains, in chronological sequence, the details of each cash payment made. Accordingly, each record in this data store shows the payment date, vendor identification, disbursement voucher number (if a voucher process is used), vendor invoice number(s) and gross invoice amount(s), cash discount(s) taken

FIGURE 13.7   Processing Noninvoiced Disbursements

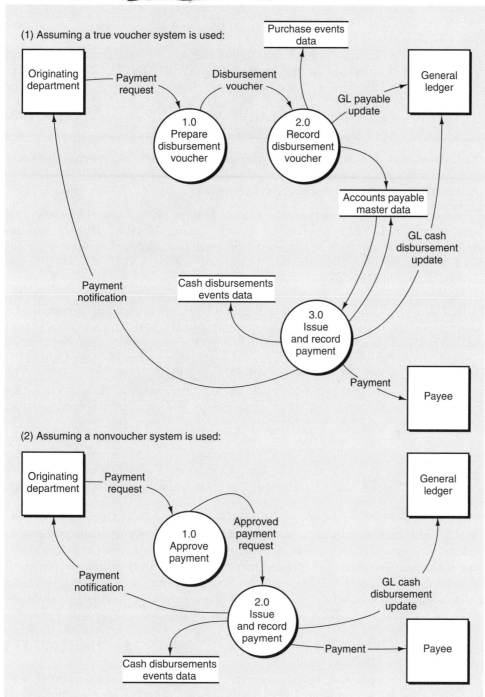

on each invoice, net invoice amount(s), check amount, and check number (or other payment identification such as those used for electronic payments).

Logical Database Design

As in the prior three chapters, this section focuses on a *centralized database approach* to data management. In the bottom portion of **Figure 13.8** we portray the data model for the AP/CD process in an *entity-relationship (E-R) diagram*. We also show (shaded) the entities and relationships from Chapter 12 because these two chapters are interrelated from a database design perspective.

In examining the figure, you'll notice that the *events* of validating invoices and disbursing cash are depicted by two entity boxes (VALID_INVOICES and CASH_DISBURSEMENTS). The E-R diagram reflects how these events relate to prior events (PURCHASE_REQUISITIONS, PURCHASE_ORDERS, and PURCHASE_RECEIPTS), agents (EMPLOYEES and VENDORS), and *resources* (INVENTORY and BANKS). To simplify the figure, we have done the following:

- Assumed that all POs are for merchandise inventory items (i.e., purchases of other goods and services are ignored)
- Assumed that a nonvoucher process is employed

As in its counterpart in Chapter 11 (Figure 11.9, pg. 408), Figure 13.8 shows that there is no need for a separate entity for accounts payable. Rather, accounts payable balances at any point in time—or their counterpart, deferred charges—are computed as the difference between the continuous events, VALID_INVOICES and CASH_DISBURSEMENTS.

Also carried over from Figure 12.10 (pg. 455) in Chapter 12 is the relationship PURCHASING_RELATIONS. As in Figure 12.10, this relationship accumulates a record of events as they occur. In this case, we add the VALID_INVOICES event (i.e., receipt and recording of the vendor invoice) to this relationship. Recall from Figure 12.10 that this relationship already has accumulated a record of the PURCHASE_REQUISITIONS, PURCHASE_ORDERS, and PURCHASE_RECEIPTS. The box around this relationship indicates that we will have a relation in our database for this relationship, whereas the other relationships will not have a corresponding relation.

As with Figures 10.9 (pg. 363), 11.9, and 12.10, the model in Figure 13.8 is not fully normalized yet. We include the "extra" relationships and redundant attributes to help you see the logical sequence of events. Also, the notes on Figure 13.8 indicate that this is a simplified model. Certainly, realistic models must deal with partial receipts, invoices, and payments.

From Figure 13.8, we developed the relational tables shown in **Figure 13.9** (pg. 494–495). As with the E-R diagram, many of the relational tables are the same as shown in Chapter 12 (Figure 12.11, pg. 457) because these two chapters are tightly integrated from a database perspective. We repeat here from Figure 12.11 all but the last three relations shown in Figure 13.9 to emphasize the connections (linkages) among relations and to remind you that before making a cash disbursement, we have requisitioned the goods (or services), sent a PO to a vendor, received the goods, and received the vendor invoice. Also note that the relations in Figure 13.9 are not dissimilar to those shown in Figure 10.9 (e.g., VENDORS is similar to CUSTOMERS, PURCHASE_ORDERS resembles SALES_ORDERS, and so forth).

Finally, we should note that the primary key of the relationship PAYMENT_RELATIONS is a composite key comprised of the invoice number (from

FIGURE 13.8   Entity-Relationship (E-R) Diagram (Partial) for the AP/CD Process

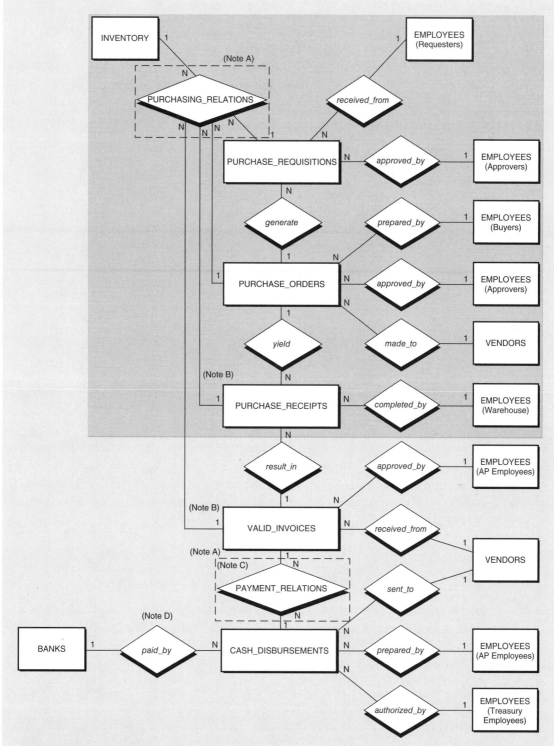

NOTES, for simplicity, we assume that:
A—See pages 492 and 496 for an explanation of the box around PAYMENT_RELATIONS and why the model is not fully normalized.
B—There are no partial receipts of any line item on a PO or partial invoicing of any line item on a receipt.
C—The difference between VALID_INVOICES and CASH_DISBURSEMENTS represents accounts payable and/or deferred charges.
D—A nonvoucher system is used and a single cash disbursement could pay for several vendor invoices, but there are no partial payments
    (each line item and each invoice are paid in full).

FIGURE 13.9 Selected Relational Tables (Partial) for the AP/CD Process

Shaded_Attribute(s) = Primary Key

INVENTORY

Item_No	Item_Name	Price	Location	Qty_on_Hand	Reorder_Pt
936	Machine Plates	39.50	Macomb	1,500	950
1001	Gaskets	9.50	Macomb	10,002	3,500
1010	Crank Shafts	115.00	Tampa	952	500
1025	Manifolds	45.00	Tampa	402	400

EMPLOYEES

Emp_No	Emp_First_Name	Emp_Last_Name	Soc_Sec_No	Emp_Dept
B432	Carl	Mast	125-87-8090	492-01
A491	Janet	Kopp	127-93-3453	639-04
A632	Greg	Bazie	350-97-9030	538-22
B011	Christy	Kinman	123-78-0097	298-12

VENDORS

Vend_No	Vend_Name	Vend_Street	Vend_City	Vend_State	Vend_ZIP	Vend_Tel	Vend_Contact	Credit_Terms	FOB_Terms
539	Ace Widget Co.	190 Shore Dr.	Charleston	SC	29915	803-995-3764	S. Emerson	2/10,n/30	Ship Pt
540	Babcock Supply Co.	22 Ribaut Rd.	Beaufort	SC	29902	803-552-4788	Frank Roy	n/60	Destin
541	Webster Steel Corp.	49 Abercorn St.	Savannah	GA	30901	912-433-1750	Wilbur Cox	2/10,n/30	Ship Pt

PURCHASE_REQUISITIONS

PR_No	PR_Date	Emp_No (PR_Requestor)[a]	Emp_No (PR_Approver)[b]	PO_No
53948	20071215	A491	E745	4346
53949	20071215	C457	A632	4350
53950	20071216	9999	540-32	4347
53951	20071216	F494	D548	4352

PURCHASE_ORDERS

PO_No	PO_Date	Vend_No	Ship_Via	Emp_No (Buyer)	Emp_No (PO_Approver)	PO_Status
4345	20071218	539	Best Way	F395	F349	Open
4346	20071220	541	FedEx	C932	F349	Sent
4347	20071222	562	UPS	E049	D932	Acknowledged

PURCHASE_RECEIPTS

Rec_No	Rec_Date	Emp_No (Receiving)	PO_No	Invoice_No
42944	20071216	B260	4322	7-945
42945	20071216	B260	4339	9542-4
42946	20071216	B260	4345	535

FIGURE 13.9   Selected Relational Tables (Partial) for the AP/CD Process (*continued*)

VALID_INVOICES

Invoice_No	Invoice_Date	Vend_No	Emp_No (AP)
4388	20071224	524	G232
92360	20071223	572	G232
535	20071224	539	D923

PURCHASE_RELATIONS

PR_No	Item_No	Qty_Requested	PO_No	Qty_Ordered	Rec_No	Qty_Received	Inv_No	Qty_Invoiced	Amt_Invoiced
53947	1005	200	4345	200	42946	200	535	200	1200.00
53947	1006	50	4345	50	42946	50	535	50	212.50
53947	1015	25	4345	25	42946	25	535	25	418.75

CASH_DISBURSEMENTS

CD_No	CD_Date	Emp_No (AP)	Emp_No (Treasury)	Amount	Vend_No	Bank
9561	20080102	H263	M0513	1782.10	524	2239
9562	20080102	H263	M513	432.50	572	2240
9563	20080102	H263	E219	1831.25	539	2239

BANKS

Bank_No	Bank_Name
2239	Acme
2240	Benton

PAYMENT_RELATIONS

Invoice_No	CD_No	Amount
4388	9561	1782.10
92360	9562	432.50
535	9563	1831.25

[a]If automatic purchase requisition, then 9999; if employee, then employee number.
[b]If automatic purchase requisition, then contract number of trading partner; if employee, then employee number.

VALID_INVOICES) and the cash disbursement number (from CASH_DISBUR-SEMENTS). This relationship matches the invoices with the disbursements and allows us to easily obtain the total amount of each disbursement. The box around this relationship indicates that we will have a relation in our database for this relationship, whereas the other relationships will not have a corresponding relation.

Technology Trends and Developments

Information technology has fueled significant increases in productivity in accounts payable departments. IOMA's *Report on Managing Accounts Payable* estimates that the cost to process an invoice can be reduced by 40 percent when increasing from a low to a high level of automation. IOMA's *AP Automation 2010 Report*, a survey of AP managers, states that implementing or increasing electronic invoicing and payments and adding Web portals for vendors (e.g., J.P. Morgan's Order-to-Pay process) were AP process automation goals.[10] In this section, we explore e-invoicing, the processing of invoices in electronic form, and e-payments, the electronic submission of payments. These two technology categories have spurred the AP/CD productivity gains.

E-invoicing is accomplished in one of three ways. First, an accounts payable office *scans* paper invoices (companies typically receive 80 percent of their invoices in paper format) upon receipt from the vendors. The *digital images* of the invoices can then be routed for processing and approval using *workflow* processes. To create a payable on the system, however, the *data* from these scanned invoices must either be typed into the accounts payable system or read using *OCR*. Nonstandard formats on the invoices can lead to errors in the input data. This is not unlike the problem experienced in recording *remittance advices* (RA) in the cash receipts process (unless, of course, the RA is a *turnaround document* that would have a standard format). Second, an organization can use purchasing cards, or p-cards, to make purchases for items such as office supplies and less expensive items. In this way, several small purchases that would otherwise lead to individual invoices are consolidated onto one credit card bill. This reduces the number of invoices by as much as 50 percent, along with the costs associated with entering and approving those invoices for payment. Third, vendors can submit invoices electronically in either *EDI* or *XML* formats. These invoices may be submitted using VANs or a Web portal (e.g., J.P. Morgan's Order-to-Pay). Upon receipt, they are fed directly into the accounts payable system (i.e., no manual entry is required).

To recognize the savings that can accrue from reducing the number of invoices, some organizations have eliminated invoices altogether. **Evaluated receipt settlement (ERS)** is a process by which an organization pays for a purchase on the basis of the goods receipt. Upon receipt of the goods, the AP/CD system compares the received quantity to the open purchase quantity and, if appropriate, makes a payment based on the price and terms on the PO. ERS arrangements are only made with vendors who have proven records for quality and reliability. When established, ERS can reduce the costs associated with entering invoices, matching the invoice with the PO and receiving report, and resolving discrepancies between the invoice and the PO and goods receipt.

---

[10]*IOMA's Report on Managing Accounts Payable*, April 2010, p. 1; "Increasing Efficiency and Cut Costs Through Automation," *The Controller's Report*, May 2010, p. 1.

Technology Summary 13.1

USES OF ELECTRONIC DATA INTERCHANGE FOR THE AP/CD PROCESS

EDI can be adopted in most any business process, but it is prevalent in the AP/CD processes, where cost savings can be significant, and buyers can dictate its use with their vendors. Although often considered a dying technology, EDI continues to increase in use among a number of organizations. NACHA, for example, reported that the EDI payments they cleared increased by over 9 percent from 2008 to 2009.[a]

Briefly, with EDI, the AP/CD process works as follows. An organization's purchasing system prepares a PO and sends it to a vendor via EDI. At the vendor organization, the PO is automatically recorded in its OE/S system. As the order is being processed, the vendor may send an advanced shipping notice (ASN) notifying the customer that the goods are, or soon will be, in transit. After

the goods have been shipped, the vendor's billing system creates an invoice and sends it to the customer via EDI. At the customer organization, the invoice is automatically recorded in its accounts payable system. When it is time to pay the invoice, the customer/paying organization prepares an EDI payment directing the bank to pay the vendor. At the same time, the customer/paying organization sends remittance information to the vendor via EDI. All of the translation and formatting required for these automated connections is performed by the EDI systems at each organization (or by VANs).

Both organizations benefit from the improved accuracy and reduced costs associated with the automatic entry of data. Delays and lost documents are reduced or eliminated for all business events, including the purchase, shipment, invoice, and payment.

[a]"NACHA Reports 18.76 Billion ACH Payments in 2009," NACHA Press Release, April 7, 2010, accessed at www.nacha.org on April 29, 2010.

E-payments technologies work toward eliminating the paper checks that still account for 70 percent of all business payments in the United States.[11] E-payments can reduce the cost of paying an invoice by as much as 90 percent, depending on the old and new methods used for payment. EDI- and XML-based technologies are typically employed to make business payments. These payments are settled through the *ACH network*, by wire transfer, or by debit or credit card. **Technology Summary 13.1** describes the use of EDI in the AP/CD processes, and **Technology Summary 13.2** (pg. 498) describes electronic invoice presentment and payment (EIPP), a technology applied in B2B environments that is comparable to *EBPP*, which is applied in B2C environments.

As noted in the story at the start of this chapter, J.P. Morgan offers an EIPP-type system that is used by many organizations to automate their purchasing, accounts payable, and cash disbursements processes. **Technology Application 13.1** (pg. 499) explains the J.P. Morgan Order-to-Pay system and the control techniques that it incorporates.

Controls

E-Business

Physical Process Description

The physical model of the AP/CD process presented in this section employs an *enterprise system* and *e-payments*. As with the purchasing process, this process is not completely *paperless*, but hard copy documents are held to a minimum.

Enterprise Systems

E-Business

---

[11]Steve Bills, "Clearing House to Spur Electronic-Pay Transition," *American Banker*, December 3, 2009, p. 1. However, as noted in Technology Summary 11.3 (pg. 397), paper checks account for only one-third of all payments but exceed electronic payments in value by a 55 to 45 percent margin.

ELECTRONIC INVOICE PRESENTMENT AND PAYMENT (EIPP) SYSTEMS

Electronic invoice presentment and payment (EIPP) systems are B2B systems that combine e-invoicing and e-payment processes to send invoices to customers via a Web portal or secure network using a third-party service provider and to receive electronic payments that are initiated by the payer, processed by the third party, and settled by the ACH network, wire transfer, or debit or credit card company. EIPP is applied in B2B environments where the payer/buyer can typically dictate the invoicing and payment methods to be used. To implement an EIPP system, business partners usually need to change their internal business processes (e.g., approval processes for invoices and payments) and integrate their legacy accounts payable and cash disbursement systems with the systems of the third-party provider.

For accounts payable departments, cost savings come in the form of reduced staff, paper, and postage. The staff cost savings include elimination of data entry and reduced time spent negotiating billing disputes and handling vendor queries regarding invoice approvals and payment schedules. For example, vendors can examine the central repository of invoice and payment data, maintained at the Web portal by the third-party service provider, to receive answers to most of their questions. Also, electronic invoices can be recorded with fewer errors, reconciled with POs and receipts automatically, and routed for approval more efficiently. A disadvantage to the payer is the elimination of *float*. Thus, buying organizations are motivated to adopt e-invoicing but not necessarily e-payments.

Discussion and Illustration

Figure 13.10 (pg. 500) presents a systems flowchart of the process. The following paragraphs describe the flowcharted processes as well as some of the exception routines noted on the flowchart.

Record Accounts Payable

E-Business

Our organization's system picks up batches of the vendor's invoices at the VAN and routes them to the EDI translator. The EDI translator converts the invoices to the appropriate format and records them in the incoming invoice data. Triggered by the receipt of this batch, the accounts payable application accesses the PO and receiving report data and compares the items, quantities, prices, and terms on the incoming invoices to comparable data from the PO and receiving report data. If the data correspond (within tolerances for quantities, costs, dates, etc.), a payable is created, and the general ledger is updated (accounts payable and clearing account[12] or other account distributions such as assets and expenses).

Controls

An AP clerk reviews data that do not correspond and takes appropriate corrective actions. Discrepancies in price, quantity, terms, and so forth are often resolved with discussions with purchasing and the vendor. Mismatches may also include a missing receiving report, indicating that the goods have not yet been received. Investigations would be undertaken with purchasing, receiving, and the vendor to determine the status of the missing receipt. Mismatches could include a missing PO. In this case, the vendor may have mistakenly sent a second, duplicate invoice. If so, the following sequence of events is likely. When the first invoice arrived and was processed, the PO and receiving report were "marked" as closed. When the second invoice arrived and was input, there would no longer be an open PO or receiving report against which to match the invoice. Finally, as more purchasing and payment types, such as p-cards and debit and credit cards, have become popular, the opportunity for duplicate invoices has increased. For example, an organization might pay for something with a p-card and the vendor might still issue an invoice. All of these situations must be resolved by the AP clerk.

---

[12] Assuming that the inventory and clearing accounts were updated upon receipt of the goods.

Make Payments

As shown in Figure 13.10, our organization uses EDI to make the payment. Such payments may be processed through a VAN, such as shown in Figure 13.10, or via the Internet, to be settled by the *ACH Network*.

E-Business

Technology Application 13.1

J.P. MORGAN'S ORDER-TO-PAY PROCESS

Many companies, including KeySpan Corporation, Memorial Sloan-Kettering Cancer Center, Verizon Wireless, Bristol-Myers Squibb, Payless Shoesource, and Armstrong® World Industries, use the Order-to-Pay process hosted by J.P. Morgan for their purchasing, accounts payable, and cash disbursements process. Companies using the J.P. Morgan system report operational savings of millions of dollars each year, in addition to savings that come from capturing early payment discounts.

The J.P. Morgan Order-to-Pay system operates on a Web portal called the Business Settlement Network (BSN). The BSN operates as follows. The buying organization creates POs as it normally would and sends them electronically to a J.P. Morgan "enterprise adapter," where they are translated into the BSN format. The electronic POs are then sent over the Internet to the BSN server. The POs are recorded on the BSN server, and an e-mail is sent to notify the selling organization (i.e., the vendor) that a PO has been issued. The vendor logs on to the BSN server using a standard Web browser and reads and acts on the PO (each vendor can only see POs intended for that specific vendor). A selling organization can contract with J.P. Morgan to have this PO data automatically imported into its OE/S system via electronic file uploads called *e-files*. The vendor can acknowledge the PO and transmit advanced shipping notices.

When it comes time to bill the buyer, the vendor sends an invoice to the buyer in one of three ways. First, the vendor can log on to the BSN server and convert the PO into an invoice. As the vendor converts (or "flips") a PO into an invoice, it makes changes as needed, such as adding charges not included on the PO. Second, the vendor can use an e-file to directly link its billing system with the BSN system. Third, the vendor can use a Web template to create an invoice.

After the invoice has been recorded on the BSN server, the BSN system applies buyer-specified rules to validate the invoice and sends the invoice through an enterprise adapter (for translation from BSN format) to the buyer, where it is posted automatically to the buyer's accounts payable system. BSN's electronic workflow may be used to route the invoice within the buyer organization for approval prior to posting. During this process, the vendor can query the BSN system to determine the status of the invoice.

The buyer acts on the invoice as it normally would and makes a payment through the BSN system (i.e., through the enterprise adapter to the BSN server). The BSN system processes a digitally signed and encrypted electronic payment over a secure network through the banking system, using the payment method (e.g., ACH, wire transfer, debit or credit card) selected by the vendor. Detailed remittance information is sent to the vendor in an e-file for automatic posting to its cash receipts system. The complete history of the purchase is stored on the BSN server to facilitate research required to authorize the payment. This data is also useful to vendors wanting to determine the status of payments due to them. This data includes an audit trail of all payments, including who authorized each payment.

Savings from using the J.P. Morgan Order-to-Pay process come from reduced manual processing, increased efficiency in routing and approval of vendor invoices, and reduced vendor calls inquiring about the status of payments. The information on the BSN server facilitates cash planning for disbursements and cash receipts. Early payment discounts are more easily obtained because data is more accurate (e.g., the PO flip leads to accurate invoices), and payments are approved more quickly and easily. J.P. Morgan estimates actual savings to be 50 percent of accounts payable cost (savings between $5 and $7 to process an invoice and issue a paper check).

J.P. Morgan assists its customers in signing up their vendors for use of the J.P. Morgan system. J.P. Morgan helps these vendors create their accounts on the BSN server and prepare e-file translation routines to automatically connect their order entry and billing systems to the BSN server. Vendors are responsible for maintaining their own data, which relieves the paying organizations of having to keep vendor data current (e.g., addresses, bank account numbers, payment methods). J.P. Morgan charges payers about $1.50 to $2 per invoice and 75¢ to $1 per payment. Vendors use the service free of charge.

Sources: J.P. Morgan press releases, the J.P. Morgan Order-to-Pay Web site (www.jpmorgan.com/ordertopay, accessed on April 28, 2010), and interviews with J.P. Morgan officers and users of the J.P. Morgan system.

FIGURE 13.10 AP/CD Process—Systems Flowchart

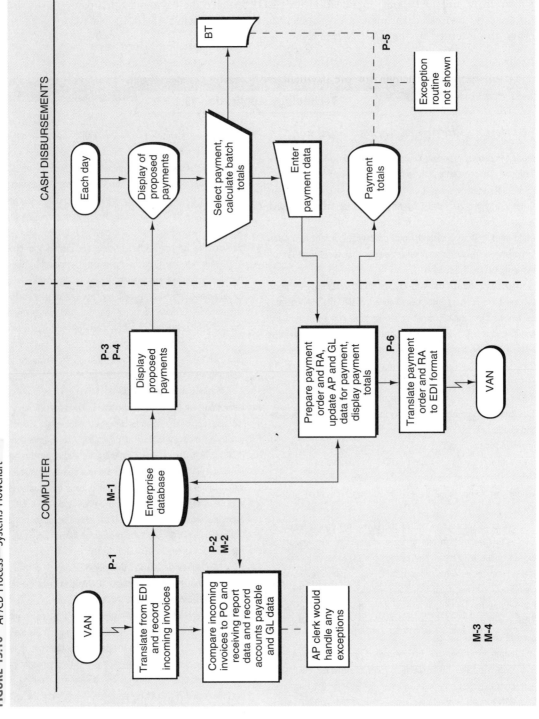

As shown in Figure 13.10, the accounts payable master data is searched periodically (e.g., daily, twice each week) for approved vendor invoices due to be paid. The cash disbursements clerk selects invoices for payment, perhaps eliminating some and adding others, and prepares batch totals. The totals include total accounts payable being paid, discounts taken, and total dollars disbursed.[13] The cash disbursements application prepares the payment order and remittance advice (RA), updates the accounts payable master data and the general ledger for the payment, displays the payment totals (i.e., AP, discounts, cash disbursed), and sends the data to the EDI translator. The translator converts the data to the appropriate format, encrypts the message, adds a digital signature, and sends the EDI payment order and RA to the VAN for pickup by the bank. The dotted line between the batch totals and the display of the payment totals indicates that the disbursement clerk manually reconciles the totals prior to releasing the payments.

What happens next is not depicted on the flowchart. The VAN sends the payment data to our organization's bank, where the bank debits our organization's (the paying organization's) account for the amount of the payments and then sends the payment data to the ACH Network for processing. The ACH Network transfers data between the paying organization's bank and the banks for all the vendors in the batch, and then sends the data to each vendor's bank. The vendor's bank credits (reduces) the vendor's bank account and transmits the RA and payment data to the vendor. If the electronic RA does not accompany the payment order through the banking system, it is forwarded directly (via VAN) to the supplier.[14]

Exception Routines

In the DFDs (Figures 12.9, pg. 454 and 13.4, pg. 487) and the systems flowcharts in Figures 12.12 (pp. 461–462) and 13.10, you see a number of reject data flows or annotations depicting the locations where exceptions may occur; these rejects and exceptions occur for a number of reasons. First, **purchase returns and allowances** frequently arise with respect to purchases. This *exception* usually occurs at the point of inspecting and counting the goods (bubble 3.1 of Figure 12.9 and the computer in Figure 12.12) [15] or at the point of *validating* vendor invoices (bubble 1.1 of Figure 13 and in the computer column in Figure 13.10).

To initiate an adjustment for returned goods or for a price allowance in the case of otherwise nonconforming goods, someone usually prepares a *debit memorandum* and transmits it to the vendor; the vendor commonly acknowledges it by returning a *credit memorandum*. The debit memo data also is transmitted to the accounts payable department. In the case of a return, data also is made accessible to the storeroom and shipping department. The merchandise to be returned then is released from the storeroom and sent to the shipping department. There, the items to be returned are counted, recorded on the debit memorandum, and shipped. The shipping department's recording of the debit memo data also is made available to the accounts payable department.

---

[13]Payments could be routed, using *workflow*, for approval to the controller, vice presidents, or the president, depending on the amount of a payment.

[14]Using EFT to wire funds and employing EDI to transmit remittance data do *not* necessarily go hand in hand. For instance, a company could use EFT to make payments but still rely on separate paper or electronic RAs to notify the vendor of the details of what is being paid.

[15]If the counting (M1) and inspection (M2) controls were not missing in Figure 12.12, there would be an exception routine annotation in the receiving department.

Three other exception routines should be noted. In Figure 13.10, we see that an AP clerk handles any exceptions discovered during the matching of incoming invoices with POs and receiving reports. As a result of a mismatch, the clerk might initiate a purchase allowance (a return [vs. allowance] is initiated at the time of the receipt of the goods). The clerk might also have some latitude to accept nonconforming invoices, should the mismatch be within acceptable tolerances (e.g., the invoice varies by less than 1 percent). Another exception routine is noted where the cash disbursements clerk reconciles batch totals for the payments selected and the payments made. If these totals are not the same, the clerk must determine whether some payments were not made; some extra, unauthorized payments were made; or payments were not correct. A third exception is not noted on the flowchart. Should the payments be routed for approval, some payments might be denied and would need to be removed from the batch of selected payments before the payments were completed.

The Fraud Connection

As noted in Chapter 12, the AP/CD process is part of the *purchase-to-pay process* that culminates with the payment of cash and has a high potential for exposing an organization to fraud and embezzlement. In this section, we continue the Chapter 12 discussion of these abuses by presenting some of the ways the AP/CD process has been manipulated.

Fraud and the Accounts Payable Function

Abuses in this part of the AP/CD process usually entail creating phony vendors in the vendor master data or submitting fictitious invoices. Some examples taken from actual incidents follow:

- Stanley opened a business account at his local bank in the name of SRJ Enterprises. He deposited $100 and told the bank that the company was located at the home address of his girlfriend, Phoebe, a disgruntled colleague from his employer's accounting department. Using his home computer, Stanley printed bogus invoices in the name of SRJ Enterprises. Phoebe created a vendor record for SRJ Enterprises on the company's computer and put the bogus invoice in a stack of much larger invoices for payment and approval. This scheme continued for a year and netted more than $700,000 for Stanley and Phoebe. Stanley's wife became suspicious and called the organization's internal auditor, who tracked down the fraud. As first-time offenders, Phoebe and Stanley only got probation. But both Phoebe and Stanley's wife left him! A typical control to address this type of fraud is to carefully manage the process for creating vendor records. The authority to add vendors should not reside with someone such as Phoebe who can submit invoices for payment. Also, when vendor records are created, a comparison should be made between the vendor's phone number, address, and so on and employee data.[16]
- Veronica, an accounting clerk at a dental supply wholesaler, was responsible for processing invoices for payment. One vendor, a dental appliance manufacturer, printed its invoices in black ink on plain paper. Veronica would make a copy of the invoice and process them both for payment, one a few days after the other.

---

[16]Joseph T. Wells, "Billing Schemes, Part 1: Shell Companies That Don't Deliver," *Journal of Accountancy*, July 2002, pp. 76–79.

When the vendor recognized the duplicate payment, it sent a refund check that was sent to Veronica! She simply deposited the check in her own bank account. The scheme was discovered by a colleague who saw Veronica pocket some checks and turned her in to the organization's internal auditor. Segregation of duties between the controller (accounts payable) and the cashier (who should receive the refund checks), should prevent this type of fraud.[17]

Fraud and the Cash Disbursements Function

Frauds in this category are more direct and less subtle than in the purchasing and accounts payable functions. Usually, the theft of cash entails check forgery or fraudulent wire transfers. Before the advent of computers, fraud committed via bogus corporate checks first required that the thief steal a supply of blank checks. Now, however, those checks can be counterfeited using a laser scanner, a personal computer, and a color printer. For an investment of less than $1,000, the counterfeiter can set up shop.

The risk from computer-generated forgeries has escalated significantly in the past few years. Cheap color ink jet printers can now generate such perfect replicas that even counterfeiting currency has become a desktop computer operation. This is a primary reason for the U.S. Treasury's recent currency redesign, using sophisticated images and papers.

What about checks that are legitimate, made out correctly, and sent to your vendor? Will they be routed to your vendor and result in resolution of your payable? Not always. When the check gets to your vendor, an unscrupulous clerk can simply deposit the check to his or her account,, use it to pay a credit card bill, or whatever. We discussed some of these frauds, such as *lapping*, in Chapter 11.

While the use of checks *should* be rare, as noted earlier, they still account for 70 percent of business payments in the United States. So how do you prevent these frauds? First, we might employ digitally signed electronic payments. These are either sent to the bank directly and cannot be diverted by the clerk, or if sent directly to the vendor, they cannot be altered without alerting the bank to the clerk's fraudulent change when the clerk attempts to deposit the altered check. To reduce frauds with paper checks, we can suggest segregating duties so that no one person can authorize a disbursement (e.g., prepare the check) and execute the payment (e.g., sign and send the check). Finally, as we will discuss later in this chapter, we should segregate the duties of those who make disbursements from those who perform a bank reconciliation.

In the fall of 2009, the U.S. Federal Bureau of Investigation (FBI) reported a significant increase in frauds involving the use of online banking credentials. The FBI estimated that, during a short period of time in 2009, $100 million had already been fraudulently transferred out of the bank accounts of small- to medium-sized businesses, court systems, school districts, and other public institutions across the United States. Common among these targeted institutions is that they employed online banking with local community banks and credit unions, some of which used third-party service providers to process ACH transactions. Typically, these financial institutions and third-party

---

[17]Joseph T. Wells, "Billing Schemes, Part 3: Pay-and-Return Invoicing," *Journal of Accountancy*, September 2002, pp. 96–98.

providers did not have proper *firewalls* or anti-virus software on their servers and desk-tops. These frauds typically unfold as follows:[18]

- A "spear phishing"[19] e-mail is sent to individuals within the target company who can initiate funds transfers, such as wire transfers and ACH transactions.
- Upon opening the e-mail, malware is installed—directly or when the recipient navigates to a bogus Web site—on the recipient's computer.
- The malware contains a key logger that steals the user's online banking credentials (e.g., logon ID and password).
- Using these credentials, the fraudster initiates a funds transfer out of the target organization's bank account.

The fraudulent transfers have ranged from thousands to millions of dollars, often in increments of less than $10,000 to avoid currency transaction reporting. In addition to the obvious controls of adding firewalls and anti-virus software to servers and computers, treasury personnel should be cautioned about the dangers of phishing e-mails. Finally, organizations should consider performing all wire transfers from computers that are not used for any other purpose, such as e-mail and day-to-day Internet usage to reduce the possibility of malware installations.

Nonfraudulent Losses

In Chapter 7, we cautioned you that although the subject of fraud and embezzlement is seductively interesting, resource losses due to unintentional mistakes and inadvertent errors are as costly as—or more costly than—those caused by intentional acts of malfeasance. One major source of loss is the overpayment of accounts payable that are usually caused by simple human errors, such as the following:

- *Situation 1:* Assume that we receive a freight bill (i.e., a bill for which we have no underlying PO against which to verify charges), and a decimal point is inadvertently "slid" one place to the right on that bill. As a result, we are billed for $4,101.30 instead of for the correct amount of $410.13. Without any PO to compare this bill to, we may make a payment for the incorrect, larger amount.
- *Situation 2:* Assume that we confuse a vendor's name, perhaps 3M Co. and Minnesota Mining & Manufacturing Company. We might pay the same invoice twice, not realizing that 3M is the name of the company that once was known as Minnesota Mining & Manufacturing.

Although the latter mistake should be called to our attention by an honest vendor, the first error would have been made by the freight company and would not be caught by us. Even when the overpayment is refunded to us, we have incurred the clerical cost of processing the payment, sending it to the vendor, and correcting the error after the fact.

Application of the Control Framework

In this section, we apply the control framework from Chapter 7 to the AP/CD process. **Figure 13.11** presents a completed *control matrix* for the annotated systems flowchart shown in Figure 13.10 (pg. 500).

---

[18]"Compromise of User's Online Banking Credentials Targets Commercial Bank Accounts," Intelligence Note Prepared by the Internet Crime Complaint Center (IC3), November 3, 2009, accessed May 12, 2010 at www.ic3.gov.

[19]Spear phishing is a type of phishing attack that is directed at select groups of people with something in common, in this case treasury personnel. The e-mail appears to be coming from an individual or organization that the recipient recognizes and from whom they normally receive e-mails.

FIGURE 13.11 Control Matrix for the AP/CD Process

Control Goals of the AP/CD Business Process

Recommended Control Plans	Control Goals of the Operations Process				Control Goals of the Information Process									
	Ensure effectiveness of operations		Ensure efficient employment of resources (people, computers)	Ensure security of resources (cash, accounts payable master data)	For vendor invoice inputs, ensure:			For accounts payable master data, ensure:		For payment inputs, ensure:			For accounts payable master data, ensure:	
	A	B			IV	IC	IA	UC	UA	IV	IC	IA	UC	UA
Present Controls														
P-1: Independent validation of vendor invoices					P-1									
P-2: Match invoice, purchase order, and receiving report	P-2				P-2		P-2							
P-3: Tickler file of payments due			P-3								P-3			
P-4: Independent authorization to make payment				P-4						P-4				
P-5: Agreement of run-to-run totals (reconcile input-output batch totals)				P-5						P-5	P-5	P-5		
P-6: Digital signatures				P-6						P-6	P-6	P-6		
Missing Controls														
M-1 Tickler file of open purchase orders and receiving reports		M-1				M-1								
M-2: Agreement of run-to-run totals (reconcile input-output batch totals)				M-2		M-2	M-2							
M-3: Cash planning report	M-3													
M-4: Reconcile bank account				M-4						M-4	M-4	M-4		

Possible effectiveness goals include the following:

A—Optimize cash discounts

B—Ensure that the amount of cash maintained in demand deposit accounts is sufficient (but not excessive) to satisfy expected cash disbursements

See Exhibit 13.1 for a complete explanation of control plans and cell entries.

IV = input validity
IC = input completeness
IA = input accuracy
UC = update completeness
UA = update accuracy

Control Goals

The control goals listed across the top of the matrix are similar to those presented in Chapters 7 and 9 through 12, except that they have been tailored to the specifics of the purchasing process.

The *operations process control goals* that are typical of the AP/CD process include the following:

- *Effectiveness of operations:* Goals A and B identify *effectiveness goals* that are typical of the AP/CD process. Several processes must be in place to achieve goal A, *optimize cash discounts*, including processes to see that invoices are received in a timely manner, recorded promptly upon receipt, and paid within the discount period, should receiving the discount be financially feasible and advantageous. Goal B, *ensure that the amount maintained in demand deposit accounts is sufficient (but not excessive) to satisfy cash discounts*, requires that sufficient data regarding purchases and upcoming payments is available and used to plan the availability of cash resources. For example, vendor invoices must be recorded with amounts due, dates, and terms so that the treasurer can plan for payments.
- *Efficient employment of resources:* As noted in Chapter 9 and reinforced in Chapters 10 through 12, people and computers are the resources found in most business processes.
- *Resource security:* As mentioned in Chapter 9, the resource security column should identify assets that are at risk. The resources of interest here are the cash and the accounts payable master data. Controls should protect the cash from unauthorized disbursement, fraud, and other losses. Controls should also prevent the unauthorized accessing, copying, changing, selling, or destruction of the accounts payable master data.

The *information process control goals* comprise the second category of control goals in Figure 13.11. Information process control goals include the following:

- *Input validity (IV)* of vendor invoices: Achieved when recorded vendor invoices are for goods actually ordered and actually received (i.e., the invoices are supported by proper POs and receiving reports).
- *Input validity (IV)* of payment inputs: Achieved when there is a documented *valid, unpaid* vendor invoice for each payment.
- *Input completeness (IC)* of vendor invoices: Failure to achieve this goal may result in lost discounts and negative relations with vendors due to late payments, and the unrecorded invoices cause liabilities to be understated. In addition, invoices should be recorded only once to preclude paying an invoice more than once.
- *Input completeness (IC)* of payment inputs: Failure to achieve this goal may also result in lost discounts, late payments, or in making duplicate payments.
- *Input accuracy (IA)* of vendor invoices: Failure to achieve this goal results in a misstatement of liabilities. Incorrect dates and terms can lead to early or late payments.
- *Input accuracy (IA)* of payment inputs: Failure to achieve this goal may result in incorrect payments, payments to the wrong vendor, and so on.
- *Update completeness (UC) and update accuracy (UA)* of the accounts payable master data:[20] The accounts payable data must be updated properly for the vendor invoice

---

[20]These update goals do not apply to this analysis because the updates are simultaneous with the inputs, and the input controls will address any update completeness and update accuracy issues.

to reflect that there is a payment due, when it is due, and the amount and terms of the payment. The data must be updated properly when a payment is made to ensure that invoices are closed to prevent duplicate payments.

Recommended Control Plans

Recall that application control plans include both those that are characteristic of a particular AIS business process and those that relate to the technology used to implement the application. We introduce you here to those new plans that are particular to the accounts payable and cash disbursements business process. We first define and explain these controls and then summarize, in **Exhibit 13.1** (pp. 508–509), each cell entry in Figure 13.11, the control matrix:

- **Independent validation of vendor invoices** (Exhibit 13.1 and Figure 13.11, P-1): To preclude unauthorized and invalid accounts payable records, authority to record a vendor invoice should come from the PO and receiving report data created by entities other than the entity that records the vendor invoice. Typically, this requires a *segregation of duties* among purchasing, receiving, and accounts payable.
- **Match invoice, purchase order, and receiving report** (Exhibit 13.1 and Figure 13.11, P-2): The invoice should be matched to the PO and receiving report data to ensure that items on the invoice were ordered and received (validity) and that the invoice is accurately recorded.
- **Independent authorization to make payment** (Exhibit 13.1 and Figure 13.11, P-4): To ensure that only authorized payments are made, the accounts payable records on which the payment is based should be created by an entity other than the entity that executes the payment. Typically, this requires *segregation of duties* between accounts payable (a controller function) and the cashier (a treasurer function) or between functional areas within accounts payable.
- **Reconcile bank account** (Exhibit 13.1 and Figure 13.11, M-4): Records of cash disbursements should be matched to the bank's records to ensure that all disbursements actually made by the bank were authorized and accurate. This reconciliation attempts to determine that an organization's accounts payable records and general ledger records for cash and accounts payable are in agreement with the bank's records. Discrepancies may be due to inaccurate, incomplete, or invalid recording of disbursements. An entity other than accounts payable and cash disbursements should perform this reconciliation.

Each of the recommended control plans listed in the matrix in Figure 13.11 (pg. 505) is discussed in Exhibit 13.1. We have intentionally limited the number of plans to avoid redundancy. For example, we do not include several plans from Chapter 9 such as *preformatted screens, online prompting, programmed edits* (e.g., a reasonableness test on the invoice amount and quantities), *procedures for rejected inputs, confirm input acceptance,* and *populate input screens with master data.* We could also include *enter receipts data in receiving.*

Some plans are *not* listed in the control matrix nor discussed in Exhibit 13.1 because they aren't appropriate to the procedures used in the process that we are reviewing. However, you might encounter them in practice. The following are a few examples:

- Where paper documents are the basis for making disbursements, paid invoices (and the supporting POs and receiving reports) are often marked "void" or "paid" to prevent their being paid a second time. In paperless systems, the computerized payable records are "flagged" with a code to indicate that they have been paid. This should prevent duplicate or unauthorized payments.

EXHIBIT 13.1 Explanation of Cell Entries for the Control Matrix in Figure 13.11

P-1: *Independent validation of vendor invoices.*

- *Vendor invoice input validity:* The computerized accounts payable application, which is separate from the departments that authorized the purchase and recorded the receipt of the goods or services, actually performs the validation of the vendor invoice. Therefore, validity of the invoice should be ensured.

P-2: *Match invoice, purchase order, and receiving report.*

- *Effectiveness goal A, vendor invoice input validity, and vendor invoice input accuracy:* The accounts payable program matches the invoice to the PO and receiving report data to ensure that the goods were ordered and received (validity) and that the items, quantities, prices, and terms are comparable to data on the PO and receiving report to ensure that the invoice is accurate. By recording terms accurately, we can ensure that appropriate discounts can be obtained (i.e., optimize cash discounts).

P-3: *Tickler file of payments due.* The computer automatically generates a list of proposed payments.

- *Effectiveness goal A:* Action on this list should ensure that payments are made in a timely manner, not too early and not too late (i.e., to optimize cash discounts).
- *Efficient employment of resources:* The computer-generated list is more efficient than a manual scanning of open invoices.
- *Payment input completeness:* Action on this list should ensure that all payments are input.

P-4: *Independent authorization to make payment.*

- *Security of resources:* Because cash cannot be expended in the absence of a valid, open vendor invoice, security over the cash asset is enhanced.
- *Payment input validity:* Records in the accounts payable master data were created by the accounts payable process. Therefore, the data gives independent authorization to the cash disbursements process to approve vendor invoices for payment. The validity of payments is thereby ensured.

P-5: *Agreement of run-to-run totals (reconcile input–output batch totals).*

- *Security of resources and payment input validity:* Determining that payments input and payments made reflect only those authorized by the cash disbursements clerk ensures that cash is not disbursed inappropriately (security of resources) and that all inputs are *valid*.
- *Payment input validity, payment input completeness, and payment input accuracy:* By comparing totals prepared before the input to those produced after the update, we ensure that all selected payments were authorized (input validity), were input once and only once (input completeness), and were input correctly (input accuracy).

P-6: *Digital signatures.*

- *Security of resources, payment input validity, payment input completeness, and payment input accuracy:* When the digital signatures are authenticated at the VAN, the VAN knows that the sender of the message has authority to send it and thus prevents the unauthorized diversion of resources (security of resources). This also determines that the message itself is genuine (validity), whether the payment message has been altered in transit, and thus the message is *incomplete* (i.e., some payments are missing from or added to the payment message/file) or *inaccurate* and does not agree with the inputs and updates that took place prior to sending the payment file.

M-1: *Tickler files of open POs and receiving reports.*

- *Effectiveness goal B and vendor invoice input completeness:* Following up on open POs and receiving reports ensures that all vendor invoices are received and input (i.e., input completeness) in a timely manner (i.e., to ensure that cash discounts can be taken).

M-2: *Agreement of run-to-run totals (reconcile input–output batch totals).* The totals received from the VAN (or prepared before the input) should be compared to those produced after the invoices are recorded.

- *Security of resources, vendor invoice input validity:* Determining that recorded invoices reflect only those received from an authorized vendor ensures the cash will not subsequently be disbursed inappropriately (security of resources) and ensures the *validity* of the vendor invoice inputs.
- *Vendor invoice input validity, vendor invoice input completeness, and vendor invoice input accuracy:* By comparing the totals before and after recording the invoices we can ensure that only valid invoices were input, that all vendor

(Continues)

EXHIBIT 13.1   Explanation of Cell Entries for the Control Matrix in Figure 13.11 (*continued*)

invoices were input once and only once (input completeness), and that all invoices were input correctly (input accuracy).

M-3: *Cash planning report.*

- *Effectiveness goal B:* An aging of open vouchers/accounts payable records must be produced and reviewed on a regular basis to ensure that there is an adequate cash reserve to make required payments. Excess cash on hand should be invested.

M-4: *Reconcile bank account.*

- *Security of resources, payment input validity, payment input completeness, and payment input accuracy:* Comparison of the bank's record of disbursements to those retained in the organization can detect disbursements that should not have been made (security of resources, input validity), were not recorded or were recorded more than once (input completeness), or were made incorrectly (input accuracy).

- Where payments are by check, appropriate physical controls should exist over supplies of blank checks or watermarked paper on which checks are printed, and signature plates that are used for check signing.
- It is not uncommon to have more than one authorized signature required on large-dollar checks.
- Most companies have standing instructions with their banks not to honor checks that have been outstanding longer than a certain number of months (e.g., three months or six months).
- To prevent the alteration of (or misreading of) check amounts, many businesses use check-protection machines to imprint the check amount in a distinctive color (generally a blue and red combination).
- Vendor statements should be reviewed and compared to the accounts payable master data to ensure that invoices and payments have been accurately and completely recorded.

Turn to Exhibit 13.1, and study the explanations of the cell entries appearing in the control matrix. As you know from your studies in prior chapters, understanding how the recommended control plans relate to specific control goals is the most important aspect of applying the control framework.

Summary

This chapter covered the AP/CD process, the fourth and fifth steps in the *purchase-to-pay process*—invoice verification and payment processing—introduced in Chapter 2. Like the process in Chapter 12, the physical process implementation presented in this chapter evidences many attributes of the paperless office of the future. In addition, technologies being employed to improve the efficiency and effectiveness of the accounts payable and cash disbursements processes were introduced. Some questions in the end-of-chapter materials ask you to consider how these technologies also can help reduce the errors and frauds often found in these processes.

As we did at the end of Chapters 10 through 12, we include here, in **Technology Summary 13.3** (pg. 510), a review of the entity-level controls (i.e., control environment, pervasive controls, and general/IT general controls) that may have an impact on the effectiveness of the accounts payable and cash disbursements business process controls.

SOX

Technology Summary 13.3

CONSIDERING THE EFFECT OF ENTITY-LEVEL CONTROLS ON ACCOUNTS PAYABLE AND BUSINESS PROCESS CONTROLS

The effectiveness of AP/CD business process controls depends on the operation of several controls described in Chapter 8. In this summary, we examine some of those relationships.

Segregation of Duties

Several functions in the AP/CD process must be segregated for the business process controls to be effective, including the following:

- Authorization to create vendor records and assign payment terms should be duties that are segregated from those completing the accounts payable and cash disbursements processes. For example, vendor records might be maintained by a separate function within the purchasing department.
- The accounts payable process assumes that there has been an authorized PO and a valid receipt. This presumes the segregation among purchasing, receiving, and accounts payable functions.
- A treasurer/cashier function separate from the controller/accounts payable function must execute payments.

Additional Manual Controls

Several manual, pervasive, and general controls can affect the performance of the business process controls, including the following:

- One-time vendor records created to facilitate one-time payments may not receive the same level of scrutiny as records for other vendors. Management must review these records to determine that there is no abuse of this process.
- Two functions in the AP/CD process must be performed carefully by authorized, qualified personnel. These are at the point where the AP clerk handles exceptions to the three-way match and approves—or rejects—the recording of a vendor invoice and when the cash disbursements clerk selects invoices for payment while adding some and putting others on hold.
- As noted in Technology Summary 9.1 (pg. 318), the performance of manual controls depends on the quality of the people performing the control activities. Therefore, we expect controls such as *selection and hiring*, *training and education*, *job descriptions*, and *supervision* to be in place.

Automated Controls

All of the AP/CD controls performed by the computer depend on the general controls (also known as IT general controls or ITGCs) in Chapter 8. Those controls include *independent validation of vendor invoice* (e.g., check for authorized vendor and valid PO); *match PO, invoice, and receipting report*; and *independent authorization to make payment* (e.g., check for authorized vendor and valid, unpaid invoice). We need to know that the programs will perform the controls as designed (e.g., *program change controls*). Also, we need to know that the stored data used by the computer when executing these controls is valid and accurate (e.g., *physical and logical access controls*). For the AP/CD process, we are particularly concerned, for example, with controlled access to the following:

- Vendor master records so that one cannot be added or modified without authorization
- PO master data and receiving report data so that bogus POs and receipts cannot be created so as to record an unauthorized invoice
- Accounts payable master data so that bogus invoice data cannot be created so as to execute unauthorized payments

---

Key Terms

accounts payable/cash disbursements (AP/CD) process, 482

vendor invoice, 486

purchasing events data, 490

accounts payable master data, 490

cash disbursements events data, 491

evaluated receipt settlement (ERS), 496

electronic invoice presentment and payment (EIPP), 498

purchase returns and allowances, 501

independent validation of vendor invoices, 507

match invoice, purchase order, and receiving report, 507

independent authorization to make payment, 507

reconcile bank account, 507

Review Questions

RQ 13-1 What is the AP/CD process?

RQ 13-2 What primary functions does the AP/CD process perform? Explain each function.

RQ 13-3 With what internal and external entities does the AP/CD process interact?

RQ 13-4 What are the fundamental responsibilities of the accounts payable department and the cashier?

RQ 13-5 What major *logical* processes does the AP/CD process perform? Explain each.

RQ 13-6 Describe how the processing of noninvoiced disbursements is handled in (a) a "true" voucher system and (b) a nonvoucher system.

RQ 13-7 What data is contained in the purchasing events data, the accounts payable master data, and the cash disbursements event data?

RQ 13-8 What are e-invoices and e-payments?

RQ 13-9 How does EDI improve the effectiveness and efficiency of the AP/CD process?

RQ 13-10 What is EIPP? How does it improve the efficiency and effectiveness of the AP/CD process?

RQ 13-11 What are two operations process (effectiveness) goals of the AP/CD process? Provide an example illustrating each goal.

RQ 13-12 What characterizes a valid vendor invoice input? What characterizes a valid payment input?

RQ 13-13 What are the key control plans associated with the AP/CD process? Describe how each works and what it accomplishes.

RQ 13-14 Describe the impact that entity-level controls (i.e., control environment, pervasive controls, and general/IT general controls) can have on the effectiveness of AP/CD business process controls.

Discussion Questions

DQ 13-1 Refer to effectiveness goals A and B shown in the control matrix in Figure 13.11 (pg. 505). For each activity (accounts payable and cash disbursements), describe goals other than the one discussed in the chapter.

DQ 13-2 Explain why ambiguities and conflicts exist among operations process (effectiveness) goals, and discuss potential ambiguities and conflicts relative to the goals you described in DQ 13-1.

DQ 13-3 Without redrawing the figures, discuss how Figures 13.3 (pg. 486), 13.4 (pg. 487), and 13.6 (pg. 489) would change as a result of the following independent situations (be specific in describing the changes):

   a. Employing a voucher system that involved, among other things, establishing vouchers payable that covered several vendor invoices.

   b. Making payments twice per month, on the fifth and 25th of the month, and taking advantage of all cash discounts offered.

DQ 13-4   In terms of effectiveness and efficiency of operations, as well as of meeting the generic information system control goals of validity, completeness, and accuracy, what are the arguments for and against each of the following?

a.   Sending a copy of the vendor invoice to the purchasing department for approval of payment.

b.   Sending a copy of the vendor invoice to the requisitioning department for approval of payment.

DQ 13-5   An electronic data interchange (EDI) system may present an organization with opportunities and risks.

a.   What opportunities might an EDI system present? Discuss your answer.

b.   What risks might an EDI system present? What controls and other responses might an organization choose to address these risks?

DQ 13-6   In the physical implementation depicted in Figure 13.10 (pg. 500), the payment order and the RA were sent together through the banking system. We also described an option of sending the RA directly to the vendor. Which is better? Discuss fully.

DQ 13-7   In the "Fraud and the Accounts Payable Function" section, we described a fraud committed by Stanley and Phoebe and another by Veronica. For each fraud, describe controls and technology that could be used to reduce the risk of those frauds occurring.

Short Problems

SP 13-1   In the physical implementation depicted in Figure 13.10, the computer updated the accounts payable data upon receipt of a vendor invoice (a clerk handled any exceptions). Describe the procedures that you believe should control that process.

SP 13-2   With an EDI system, a customer's order may be entered directly into the OE/S system without human intervention. Discuss your control concerns under these circumstances.

SP 13-3   The following is a list of six control plans from this chapter or from Chapters 8 through 12.

Control Plans

A. Reconcile bank account
B. Match invoice, PO, and receipt
C. Tickler file of open POs and receiving reports
D. Batch sequence check
E. Procedures for rejected inputs
F. Independent authorization to make payment

The following are 10 system failures that have control implications.

System Failures

1.   Pownal Company was sent an invoice for goods that were never received. The invoice was paid in full.

2. Dewey, Inc. has several vendors who do not send invoices in a timely manner. Terms for payment are based on dates that goods are received, and discounts are being lost due to the late receipt, entry, and payment of these invoices.

3. Washington Company processes invoices in batches. The accounts payable program performs a three-way match of the invoice with the PO and receiving report. Those that match are recorded on the accounts payable master data. Those that do not match are printed on an exception and summary report. Some of these invoices are legitimate but are never recorded.

4. Betty Saunders, the cashier at Southwick Company, has been writing small checks to herself for many months. No one has noticed.

5. On a weekly basis, Pete, the cash disbursements clerk at Dalton Company, prepares a batch of payments, including some to himself, and sends the batch to the treasurer for approval. Pete has worked out a deal with Sue, who works in the treasurer's office, to approve these batches, and they split these fraudulent payments.

Match the five system failures with a control plan that would *best* prevent the system failure from occurring. Also, give a brief (one or two sentences) explanation of your choice. A letter should be used only once, with one letter left over.

SP 13-4   The following is a list of six control plans from this chapter or from Chapters 8 through 12.

Control Plans

A. Access control software
B. Batch control plans
C. Compare input data with master data (e.g., vendor master data)
D. Match invoice, PO, and receipt
E. Program change controls
F. Independent validation of vendor invoices

The following are five system failures that have control implications.

System Failures

1. Invoices are received at Becket Company via an EDI feed over the Internet. Some of these are fraudulent invoices from bogus vendors.

2. Vendor invoices are sent to clerks in the AP department at Rochester, Inc., where they are entered once each day to create a file of invoice data that is then processed by the accounts payable program each evening. Several errors have been found in the invoice data.

3. The accounts payable program at Dallas Company compares incoming invoices to open POs and receiving reports. The reject rate is very high, so Jane, the AP clerk, went into the program and changed the tolerance limits so that more invoices would pass the matching process and she would have fewer rejects to correct.

4. Webster Company ordered 15 widgets from Rosen, Inc. Only 12 widgets were received; the other three were on back order at Rosen. An

invoice for 15 widgets was received at Webster, recorded, and eventually paid.

5. Bob Daniels, a clerk in accounts payable at Amherst Company, has a cousin who owns a small office supplies company. Bob's cousin periodically sends invoices to Bob for office supplies that Amherst never ordered or received. Bob creates a one-time vendor record and records the invoice. Once recorded as a payable, the invoice gets paid.

Match the five system failures with a control plan that would *best* prevent the system failure from occurring. Also, give a brief (one or two sentences) explanation of your choice. A letter should be used only once, with one letter left over.

SP 13-5   Using the following table as a guide, describe for each function (Figure 13.1, pg. 483):

a. A risk (an event or action that will cause the organization to fail to meet its goals/objectives)

b. A control/process or use of technology that will address the risk

Function	Risks	Controls and Technology
Finance		

Accounts payable
    ??? (debit)
        Accounts payable (credit)		

Cash disbursements
    Accounts payable (debit)
        Cash (credit)
        Discounts taken (credit)		

Problems

Note: As mentioned in Chapters 10 through 12, the first few problems in the business process chapters are based on the processes of specific companies. Therefore, the problem material starts with case narratives of those processes. (The purchasing and receiving portions of these two cases are in Chapter 12.)

CASE STUDIES

CASE A: Bondstreet Company (Accounts payable and cash disbursements processes)

The Bondstreet Company sells medical supplies to hospitals, clinics, and doctors' offices. Bondstreet uses an ERP system for all of its business processes. Bondstreet employs the following procedures for accounts payable and cash disbursements.

The accounts payable (AP) department receives invoices from vendors. An AP clerk enters the PO number from the invoice into the computer, and the computer displays the PO. The clerk then keys the invoice data. The computer matches the invoice data with data on the PO (purchase and receipt data). If there are price or quantity variances of more than 5 percent, the invoice is routed, via workflow, to a purchasing agent for approval. Once validated (by the computer and, if necessary, purchasing), the computer records the invoice (i.e., accounts payable) and updates the PO and general ledger master data.

Every morning, the accounts payable department reviews open invoices (i.e., accounts payable) to determine if they should be paid. An AP clerk selects those invoices that are to be paid, and the computer prints a check in the accounts payable department and updates the accounts payable and general ledger master data. Accounts payable mails the check to the vendor.

CASE B: Internet Payment Platform (Accounts payable and cash disbursements processes)

The following describes the accounts payable and cash disbursements processes at the U.S. Department of the Treasury's Bureau of Engraving and Printing (BEP) during a pilot of the Internet Payment Platform (IPP). Components of the IPP include a server with an "appreciating database" located at Xign, Inc.[21] and an Intel® server at BEP called the enterprise adapter. BEP's mainframe, legacy enterprise system, called BEPMIS, has an IDMS network database.

After goods or services are provided, a supplier employee logs on to IPP for the PO "flip" (to create and record an invoice that is posted to the IPP appreciating database). IPP then encrypts the invoice data and sends it to the enterprise adapter at BEP, where the invoice data are translated from XML into IDMS format for posting to the BEP-MIS accounts payable database.

After invoices are posted, BEPMIS performs a three-way match of the invoice, PO, and receipt. BEP and the supplier can view these records on the IPP database and resolve disputes (e.g., disagreements regarding price or quantity listed on the invoice) as required. As the status of invoices changes, BEPMIS extracts and formats the change data, and transmits these changes to the enterprise adapter for translation from IDMS format into XML. These changes are then encrypted and sent to the IPP server for posting to the IPP appreciating database. The supplier can review the status of an invoice on IPP as it moves through the payment-generation process. BEP and the supplier can each drill down on IPP from the invoice to the PO.

After invoices are posted to the BEPMIS accounts payable database and payments are due, an accounts payable accountant triggers the payment process for all invoices and selects those invoices that are to be paid. BEPMIS then extracts and formats payments for participating suppliers, generates a payment instruction file (PIF), and transmits this file to the enterprise adapter for translation from IDMS format into XML. The translated file is then digitally signed (using a VeriSign certificate) and sent to the IPP server, where it is posted to the IPP appreciating database. At the same time, a BEP accounts payable accountant manually issues an e-mail notification detailing the number of payments and total dollar amount of payments in the PIF. This notification goes to the BEP contracting officer (CO), the Financial Management Service (FMS) disbursing officer (DO) at the Regional Finance Center (RFC) in Kansas City, and the Boston Fed. The CO and DO log on to IPP to approve payment files. Optionally, an auditor in Kansas City might also be required to approve the payment file. COs and DOs used smartcards with a thumbprint reader (a form of biometric identification) to execute these approvals, via any PC that is equipped with a Web browser and smartcard reader.

Following approvals, IPP generates an ACH-formatted file from the PIF, encrypts the file, and sends it to the Boston Fed. At the same time, IPP automatically sends an e-mail detailing the number of payments and total dollar amount of payments in the

---

[21]Subsequent to the pilot, Xign was acquired by J.P. Morgan and became "JP Morgan Xign" and is presently called "J.P. Morgan Order-to-Pay."

ACH file to the BEP accounts payable accountant, CO at BEP, DO at the RFC, and the Boston Fed. Also, IPP notifies the supplier via e-mail that a payment is coming. The ACH-formatted file is transferred to the Federal Reserve Automated Clearing House (FedACH) system, where the payment is settled by debiting the U.S. Treasury account at the Fed, crediting the accounts of the supplier's bank at the Fed, and notifying the supplier's bank of these credits. FedACH sends a bulk data acknowledgement to the BEP accounts payable accountant, the CO at BEP, the DO at the RFC, and the Boston Fed detailing the number of payments and total dollar amount of those payments. The supplier's bank then credits the supplier's account.

P13-1 For the company assigned by your instructor, complete the following requirements:

   a. Prepare a table of entities and activities.

   b. Draw a context diagram.

   c. Draw a *physical* data flow diagram (DFD).

   d. Prepare an annotated table of entities and activities. Indicate on this table the groupings, bubble numbers, and bubble titles to be used in preparing a level 0 logical DFD.

   e. Draw a level 0 *logical* DFD.

P13-2 For the company assigned by your instructor, complete the following requirements:

   a. Draw a systems flowchart.

   b. Prepare a control matrix, including explanations of how each recommended existing control plan helps to accomplish—or would accomplish in the case of missing plans—each related control goal. Your choice of recommended control plans could come from this chapter plus any controls from Chapters 9 through 12 that are germane to your company's process.

   c. Annotate the flowchart prepared in part (a) to indicate the points where the control plans are being applied (codes P-1, . . . , P-*n*) or the points where they could be applied but are not (codes M-1, . . . , M-*n*).

P13-3 *Note:* If you were assigned DQ 13-3, consult your solution to it. Modify the DFDs in Figures 13.3 (pg. 486), 13.4 (pg. 487), and 13.6 (pg. 489), as appropriate, to reflect the following *independent* assumptions:

   a. Employing a voucher system that involved, among other things, establishing vouchers payable that covered several vendor invoices

   b. Making payments twice per month, on the fifth and 25th of the month, and taking advantage of all cash discounts offered

   Note: Because the two assumptions are independent, your instructor may assign only one of them.

P13-4 The following are 10 process failures that indicate weaknesses in control.

Process Failures

1. A vendor invoice was posted to the wrong vendor record in the accounts payable master data because the data entry clerk transposed digits in the vendor identification number.

2. Several scanned invoice documents were lost and did not get recorded.
3. The amount of a cash disbursement was what the cash disbursements clerk had authorized prior to running the disbursement program.
4. The AP clerk prepares a list of proposed payments that is based on due dates and vendor payment terms. Many of these payments are not approved by the cash disbursements clerk due to lack of funds.
5. The vendor invoiced for goods that were never delivered. The invoice was paid in its full amount.
6. The unit prices the vendor charged were in excess of those that had been negotiated. The invoice tendered by the vendor was paid.
7. A vendor submitted an invoice in duplicate. The invoice got paid twice.
8. Because of several miscellaneous errors occurring over a number of years, the total of the outstanding vendor payable balances shows a large discrepancy from the balance reflected in the general ledger.
9. Several electronic invoices were misrouted to an organization. The invoices were received, input, and paid, but the organization had never purchased anything from the vendors that were paid.
10. Goods receipts from a certain vendor are always on time. However, the invoices from this vendor are often late or never received. As a result, the organization has lost significant amounts of money by failing to obtain cash discounts for prompt payment.

For each of the process failures described, provide a two- to three-sentence description of the control plan that you believe would *best* address that deficiency. Obviously, more than one plan could exist that is germane to a particular situation. However, select *only one* plan for each of the process failures and include in your description a justification of why you believe it is *best*. When in doubt, opt for the plan that is *preventive* in nature, as opposed to plans that are *detective* or *corrective*.

P13-5   Figure 12.4 (pg. 448) and Figure 13.3 (pg. 486) show three data flows running to the general ledger (GL) for the purpose of updating the general ledger master data.

For each of the following three data flows, show the journal entry (in debit/credit journal entry format with no dollar amounts) that would result under all of the five situations below that would apply. Make and state any assumptions you think are necessary.

Data Flows:

A. GL inventory received update (show both debit and credit entries, even if they originate in a process other than AP/CD)
B. GL payable update
C. GL cash disbursements update

Situations:

1. Merchandise is purchased, and a *periodic* inventory process is used.
2. Merchandise is purchased, and a *perpetual* inventory process is used.
3. Office supplies are purchased.
4. Plant assets are purchased.
5. Legal *services* are purchased.

P13-6   Use the DFDs in Figures 13.3 (pg. 486), 13.4 (pg. 487), and 13.6 (pg. 489) to solve this problem.

Prepare a four-column table that summarizes the AP/CD processes, inputs, and outputs. In the first column, list the two processes shown in the level 0 diagram (Figure 13.3). In the second column, list the subsidiary functions shown in the four lower-level diagrams (Figures 13.4 and 13.6). For each subsidiary process listed in column 2, list the data flow names or the data stores that are inputs to that process (column 3) or outputs of that process (column 4). (See *Note*.) The following table has been started for you to indicate the format for your solution.

Note: To simplify the solution, do not show any reject stubs in column 4.

Solution Format Summary of the AP/CD Processes, Inputs, Outputs, and Data Stores

Process	Subsidiary Functions	Inputs	Outputs
1.0 Establish payable	1.1 Validate invoice	PO accounts payable notification Receiving report Vendor invoice Vendor master data	Validated vendor invoice Vendor master data
	1.2 Record payable	Validated vendor invoice Inventory master data	...Continue solution...

P13-7   The following is a list of 12 control plans from this chapter or from Chapters 8 through 12.

Control Plans

A. Digital signature
B. Tickler file of open POs and receiving reports
C. Procedures for rejected inputs
D. Compare input data with master data (e.g., vendor master data)
E. Segregate duties among purchasing, receiving, and accounts payable
F. Program change controls
G. Reconcile bank account
H. Reconcile run-to-run totals
I. Cash planning report
J. Match invoice, PO, and receiving report
K. Access control software
L. Segregate duties between accounts payable and cashier

The following are 10 system failures that have control implications.

System Failures

1. Washington Company receives batches of vendor invoices once each day via an EDI feed from a VAN. Some of these invoices are from vendors that do not do business with Washington.

2. Colchester Corp. often loses discounts on payments to vendors because of cash flow problems.

3. Fred, the AP clerk at Dalton Company, has grown tired of resolving discrepancies among vendor invoices, POs, and receiving reports. To make his life easier and to reduce rejects, he changed the AP invoice program to allow large variances.

4. Twice each week, Sally, the AP clerk at Mystic Company, selects a batch of vendor invoices and sends them to Gary, the clerk in cash disbursements. Occasionally, after Gary makes the electronic payments, it is discovered that not all the payments were made or were made incorrectly.

5. Conway, Inc. receives electronic invoices through a Web portal hosted by a third party. Some of these invoices are not correct. After investigation, it is discovered that the invoices were altered in transit from the vendor.

6. Vendor payments are made on a weekly basis at Westfield Company. Gary, the cashier, looks over the invoices that he has received and makes payments as needed. Some of those payments are to bogus vendors who have not provided any goods or services to Westfield.

7. Ludlow Inc. ordered 30 circuit breakers from Burlington Electric. Only 25 breakers were received; the other five were on back order at Burlington. An invoice for 30 breakers was received at Ludlow, recorded, and eventually paid.

8. Granby Company often does not receive invoices in a timely manner and cannot record them in time to take advantage of payment discounts.

9. Norma, the cashier at Scarsdale Company, has been writing checks to herself. This fraud has gone undetected for years.

10. At Farmington Company, all incoming invoices are matched against open POs and receiving reports. When Janet, the purchasing manager, is performing this match, she sometimes can't find a PO and so she prepares a PO to cover the invoice.

Match the 10 system failures with a control plan that would *best* prevent the system failure from occurring. Because there are 12 control plans, you should have two letters left over.

P13-8   This problem should be completed with database software, such as Microsoft Access. As directed by your instructor, submit the completed database file and the printouts noted below.

1. Using the E-R diagram in Figure 13.8 (pg. 493), select any three or four related entities and implement them as tables using Microsoft Access (or any other database software acceptable to your instructor). Link the tables using the cardinalities shown in the figure. For the tables, you may use attributes shown in Figure 13.9 (pp. 494–495) or create different attributes.

2. Create forms for each table from part 1 of this problem and use the forms to populate the tables with representative data. Forms should be in good order, readable, and properly formatted. Create at least three records in each table. Print out the populated tables and one instance of each form.

3. Design three queries using the tables from part 1 of this problem. Print out the output of each query and attach an explanation as to why someone would be interested in the output of each query.

4. Using the report function in Access, design a report for each query from part 3 of this problem. Reports should be in good order, readable, and properly formatted. Print out each report.

CHAPTER 14

The Human Resources (HR) Management and Payroll Processes

Learning Objectives

After reading this chapter, you should be able to:

- Define and understand the basic functions of the HR management and payroll processes.

- Describe the relationship between the HR management and payroll processes and their environment.

- Comprehend the relationship between the HR management and payroll processes and management decision making.

- Depict the logical and physical elements of the HR management and payroll processes.

- Describe some of the technology used to implement the HR management and payroll processes.

- Prepare a control matrix for a typical payroll process, including an explanation of how business process control plans can accomplish payroll operations and information control goals.

Even after a fully functional ERP system has been installed in a company, there are often opportunities for further improvements, particularly as technology changes. This was especially true for ABB AG, the German-based subsidiary of ABB Ltd., one of the world's leading providers of power and automation technologies.[1] ABB AG had an existing SAP ERP system but found that its HR function still suffered from too many paper-based procedures. These procedures were costly in terms of the amount of time required for HR personnel to process the paper forms and for employees to fill them out. Also, because the forms required subsequent manual entry into the IT system, the employee information was too frequently entered into the system with errors. Further, these paper-based aspects of the system caused information flow problems for HR. Employees did not get changes in HR policies in a timely manner because they were disseminated using printed materials, and collecting forms from the employees and answering their questions were dreadfully slow.

---

[1] This vignette is based on "ABB—SAP® Employee Self-Service Helps Streamline HR Processes" (2008), SAP Customer Success Story, www.sap.com/solutions/business-suite/erp/hcm/customers/index.epx, accessed April 19, 2010.

Using SAP's service-oriented architecture (SOA) NetWeaver, self-service kiosk terminals, and remote software installation, ABB AG was able to radically automate its HR procedures and drastically reduce HR costs. Numerous easy-to-use kiosk terminals were placed throughout the company. This was especially important since a sizable percentage of employees did not have their own computers, e-mail accounts, or Internet connections. By using ABB AG's kiosks, employees were able to access HR policies online without delay and to complete the forms without using cumbersome paper documents. This process enabled the forms to be immediately accepted into the system upon submission, without additional manual entry. Also, SAP's employee interaction center (EIC) functionality allowed HR questions from employees to be tagged electronically so that they could be quickly routed to the appropriate HR recipients. EIC also categorized the questions by subject so that HR could identify common problems and misunderstandings with HR policies.

As a result of this new HR system, ABB AG realized significant cost savings through efficiency gains in terms of the work load on HR staff, and by eliminating paper printing, distribution, and handling. Employee morale also improved due to better information flow between HR and employees, and because employee information was being entered into the HR system with fewer errors. Because of the easy-to-use self-service kiosks, employees could now answer most HR questions without directly contacting HR personnel. And any remaining questions sent to HR personnel were answered more rapidly. HR staff was now freed up to focus on strategic tasks.

Synopsis

Human capital management (HCM), the process of managing how people are hired, trained, assigned, motivated, and retained, presumes that employees reflect a strategic investment, rather than an administrative cost. Some estimates place the value of human capital between $500,000 and $5 million per person. At the same time, the costs of such capital, including compensation, benefits, and HR, represent 43 percent of the average organization's total operating expense. For organizations in the service sector, the percentage is much higher.

The automation of the HR function (sometimes dubbed "e-HR") is positioned to transform HR from a lowly cost center to a highly valued, strategic, mission-critical part of the business. Automating HR can improve employee recruitment, training, and scheduling. In addition, it should affect evaluation and compensation programs to reflect the changing work patterns, including the graying workforce, virtual teams, tele-commuters, consultants, contractors, part-timers, and temporary employees.

In this chapter, we explore three themes. First, we briefly examine the importance of people to the success of any organization. Next, we describe how the HR management and payroll processes assist management in leveraging its human capital. Finally, we introduce some of the technology used to implement modern HR management and payroll processes.

Introduction

This chapter describes the basic roles played by an organization's HR and payroll functions. The organizational structure of the HR function sets the stage for a discussion of the types of decisions HR managers face. We also look at a physical implementation of the HR management process. Next, we move to the payroll process. The organizational placement of the payroll process is followed by a detailed description of its logical and physical characteristics. Finally, control plans for the payroll process are summarized in a control matrix.

Process Definition and Functions

Any organization wanting to improve itself must start by improving its people. Recognizing people as the common denominator of progress has resulted in many organizations paying closer attention to their HR policies and practices. In the previous "Synopsis" section, we introduced the concept of *human capital management (HCM)* and the emphasis that this process places on the value of human capital. HCM follows historically from the concept of "personnel management" and then "human resource management." Classic personnel management began with the handling of payroll and personnel administration, and evolved by adding functions to handle recruiting, employee relations, and so on. Subsequently, human resource management recognized the importance of personnel in achieving organization objectives but, like personnel management, viewed personnel as something that could be controlled.

To manage human capital, you must understand what it includes. Ultimately, it includes an individual's value to an organization, based on knowledge, skills, and attitude. These individuals include all employees—even those considered part-time, temporary, independent contractors, and the employees of business partners, such as those in an organization's supply chain.

Properly managing human capital requires emphasizing personnel development in order to maximize the benefits that each individual can provide to the organization, as well as retention of employees to ensure that important skills are not lost. It turns out that, similar to customers, retaining an employee is far less expensive than replacing one. It has been estimated that it costs up to 2.5 times an employee's annual salary, plus benefits, to replace an employee. Thus, an effective HCM process is central to the achievement of an organization's objectives.

Although the terms and concepts associated with HCM represent contemporary thinking about the HR function within an organization, most organizations still refer to their personnel-related function as human resources (HR). Therefore, in this chapter, we will use HR to refer to the process whose function is to support the HCM concepts and to provide the organization with information with which to manage its personnel (i.e., its human capital).

Definition of the HR Management Process

The **human resources (HR) management process** is an interacting structure of people, equipment, activities, and controls. The primary function of the HR management process is to create information flows that support the following:

* Repetitive work routines of the HR department
* Decision needs of those who manage the HR department

The HR management process supports the work routines of the HR department and provides information for management decisions by doing the following:

- Capturing, recording, and storing data concerning HR activities
- Generating HR forms and documents
- Preparing management reports
- Preparing governmental reports

The first portion of this chapter is devoted to exploring these functions in detail.

Definition of the Payroll Process

The **payroll process** is an interacting structure of people, equipment, activities, and controls that creates information flows to support the repetitive work routines of the payroll department. To that end, the payroll process maintains records containing data for payroll taxes and fringe benefits, attendance reporting, timekeeping, and paying employees for work performed. We look at these functions in the second portion of this chapter.

Payroll represents an events-oriented process that has traditionally been considered separate from the HR management process. However, because of the close relationship between the two processes, we start by discussing why many companies merge the HR management and payroll processes into a single entity. Then we separate the processes so that we can analyze the distinct features of each. In the course of this analysis, you will notice that the HR management process, more than any other information process, captures, records, and stores data that fall outside the normal accounting-oriented transaction stream. For example, data concerning an employee's health or the level of an employee's skills certainly do not fit the transaction model established by GAAP. However, from a holistic business perspective, it is important for accountants to realize the immense value of human capital and how it affects the long-term financial health of the organization.

Integration of the HR Management and Payroll Processes

Enterprise Systems

Because of its heavy reliance on complex calculations, labor intensiveness, and repetitiveness, the payroll function was one of the first systems within many organizations to be automated. In fact, payroll software was among the first to be commercially developed and marketed. However, the current generation of HR software has far outgrown its payroll roots. These new packages include such applications as cafeteria benefits administration, applicant tracking and processing, skills inventories, and compliance reporting. The menu for the HR module of the Microsoft Dynamics® GP system is depicted in **Figure 14.1**. Examine the menu options, and notice the variety of functions supported by the HR module.

Because the HR management and payroll processes share so much employee data, the integration of these functions into an *enterprise system* is extremely advantageous, if not absolutely necessary. As you can see in Figure 14.1, the HR module includes many options for managing employees. Including HR data within the enterprise system allows sharing of common data providing benefits, including:

Enterprise Systems

- Creating a single source for obtaining HR information
- Providing for faster data access
- Minimizing data redundancy
- Ensuring data integrity and consistency
- Facilitating data maintenance
- Improving data accuracy

Although there is much overlap between the HR management and payroll processes, we will discuss the HR management and payroll processes individually. We do so because the analysis is facilitated by differentiating between the broad HR management process and the narrower accounting event–based payroll process. You will see how the two processes are integrated through the shared data contained in the employee/payroll master data and through certain common forms and documents used by both processes.

The HR Management Process

In this section, we look at the imprint of the HR function on the organization and illustrate some of the decisions HR managers confront. Our examination will reveal that the HR and payroll functions are profoundly different in terms of their organizational significance. In some organizations, for example, the HR function is large enough to support a separate organizational unit, headed by a vice president of HR.[2] On the other

FIGURE 14.1   Human Resources Menu Options in Microsoft Dynamics® GP

---

[2]In smaller companies, a director of HR is often housed within an organizational unit headed by a vice president of administration.

FIGURE 14.2 Organization Chart of the HR Function

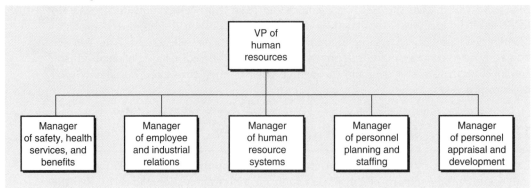

hand, the payroll function is typically housed within the controller's area and is placed at the same organizational level as the billing and accounts receivable functions.

Organizational Setting and Managerial Decision Making

Figure 14.2 identifies the key players in the HR function. For each manager shown in Figure 14.2, **Table 14.1** describes the manager's key functions, types of decisions made, and some of the information needed to make those decisions. Today, the broadening scope of HR management requires decision making that directly affects an organization's internal policies and strategic plans. Table 14.1 should help you understand the various informational needs of HR managers. Obviously, we can only introduce the topic here.

TABLE 14.1 Key Functions, Decisions, and Information Needs of HR Managers

HR Manager	Key Functions[a]	Types of Decisions Made[a]	Information Needs[a]
Manager of safety, health services, and benefits	Ensures workers' health and safety. Promotes a work environment that supports an acceptable "quality" of work life. Develops new programs for improving existing work conditions. Monitors and administers employee benefits plans.	Assesses the adequacy of employee benefits packages. Addresses the problem of rising insurance costs. Determines ways to improve the physical work environment (e.g., should new overhead lights be installed?). Investigates ways to improve the quality of work life (e.g., should factory workers have more input into the design of new products?).	Status of existing work conditions Employee attitudes and morale Governmental regulations concerning worker safety, health, and benefits Emerging trends in employee benefits packages—features, costs, and the like Industry and specific competitors' innovations
Manager of employee and industrial relations	Handles employee complaints. Negotiates with organizations, such as unions, that represent employees.	Defines the nature and extent of employee influence in management's decision-making process (e.g., what role should seniority and other criteria play in deciding which employees to terminate, transfer, or promote?). Settles employee complaints and grievances (e.g., allegations of job discrimination, sexual harassment).	Current economic statistics Outcome of grievance proceedings Governmental laws and regulations on handling grievances

(continued)

TABLE 14.1   Key Functions, Decisions, and Information Needs of HR Managers (*continued*)

HR Manager	Key Functions[a]	Types of Decisions Made[a]	Information Needs[a]
Manager of HR systems	Ensures that the information needs of HR managers and staff workers are satisfied. Serves as liaison between the IT department and the HR department.	Discovers how IT can assist HR managers in performing their day-to-day activities (e.g., helping managers to choose software packages). Ascertains the nature and timing of training needed for HR management users.	New and evolving HR management process technology developments Information needs of personnel managers and staff workers User feedback on their experience(s) in working with the HR management process
Manager of personnel planning and staffing	Plans and forecasts an organization's short- and long-term HR needs. Analyzes jobs to determine the skills necessary to perform them. Assists in recruiting job applicants, screening candidates, and helping new hires adjust to their work environment.	Projects an organization's future personnel needs and anticipates how to meet those needs. Decides the ways positions will be filled (i.e., outside hiring or internal promotion). Selects the means for recruiting and screening job applicants.	Labor force staffing forecasts Job descriptions Skills possessed by current employees Sources of potential job candidates (e.g., college placement departments, search firms) Government laws and regulations concerning equal employment opportunity, affirmative action, and the like
Manager of personnel appraisal and development	Assists line managers in assessing how well employees are performing. Cooperates with line managers in setting rewards for good performance. Helps line managers provide training or take disciplinary action in cases of substandard performance. Reduces employee turnover by helping workers achieve their career goals.	Chooses the means of training and developing employees. Determines the methods for charting employees' careers.	Data on employee performance Employee job experience, training, and salary histories Economic statistics on general employment conditions, supply and demand of job candidates, salary levels, and so forth

[a]Examples only. A complete listing is beyond the scope of this chapter.

In addition to supporting the HR managers shown in Figure 14.2, the HR management process supports the various departmental managers (other than HR and payroll) who have direct managerial responsibility over employees assigned to them. These responsibilities may include assigning tasks, coordinating departmental activities, and monitoring and evaluating employee performance. Although departmental managers rely on observation and personal experience for much of their information, the HR management process supplies them with certain types of useful information. For example, the rate of absenteeism, quality of work performed, and level of skills an employee possesses represent information provided by a typical HR management process.

Technology Trends and Developments

As noted in the story about ABB AG at the start of this chapter, IT has greatly improved the efficiency and effectiveness of HR management processes. **Technology**   E-Business

Summary 14.1 describes one such technology innovation, self-service systems, which, as you will recall, was an important part of ABB AG's new HR system. These systems are often part of an HR portal that allows employees to access personal as well as business-related information and functions.

Technology Summary 14.1

HUMAN RESOURCES SELF-SERVICES SYSTEMS

It was not that long ago that it was pretty difficult for employees to make changes to their HR records. An employee might need to update emergency contact information, change the number of payroll exemptions, or change the beneficiaries for insurance policies. The employee would need to submit a form—a handwritten form, no doubt—to the HR department to make such changes. And it would take days, or even weeks, for those changes to take place. Performing job-related functions also was difficult. Authorizing pay raises for employees or recording performance reviews also was challenging and inefficient.

Fast-forward to today, and you will find that many employees can make such changes from their offices or from the comfort of their homes. HR self-service systems, using convenient, easy-to-use Web browser interfaces, can be used to view and change HR records. These systems automate manually intensive processes and can reduce the cost of some HR processes by as much as 85 percent (see the following table).

Typically, employees can open a Web browser and point it to their organization's HR Web site (or computer kiosk on the factory floor, as in the ABB AG example above). After inputting their user name and password, employees can then view their records and make changes. A typical self-service system might have the following features:

- HR manuals, policies, and procedures that might include employee handbooks, codes of conduct, explanation of benefits programs, harassment policies, and procedures for travel reimbursement

- Helpful information such as how to get a social security number for a new member of the family
- Calculators for retirement income based on retirement age and investment choices
- Personal profile containing job, payroll (e.g., check stubs), and benefits data
- Forms for enrolling in health, retirement, and other programs
- Places to make changes to existing programs—for example, to change payroll deductions, elections for pretax withholding of supplement retirement, and health care choices
- Links to other important Web sites, such as the administrator of the 401(k) program

Some of the changes that an employee might make will require a written signature. In those cases, the employee might fill out the form online and follow up through interoffice mail with a signed form. Often, however, electronic signature techniques are now legally acceptable substitutes for written ones.

Both the employee and the employer benefit from HR self-service systems. The employee gains ready access to records and can easily make changes to them. Employees typically view such systems as substantive and responsive. The employer gets to provide a higher level of service and increase the validity and accuracy of HR records, while reducing its own operating costs. The following table summarizes some of these cost savings.

The Lower Cost of Self-Service[a]

Application/Business Process	Manual Cost	Self-Service Application Costs	Percent Savings
Enroll in benefits	$30.06	$4.59	85%
Enroll in training	$9.58	$2.31	76%
Change home address	$1.58	$0.36	78%
Apply for a job	$11.55	$6.09	47%
Request salary change	$4.20	$1.53	64%
Approve promotion	$3.38	$0.87	74%
Create job requisition	$29.89	$9.36	69%

[a]www.cedarcrestone.com/whitepapers/CedarCrestone_Value_of_HR_Tech.pdf (accessed April 30, 2010).
Source: CedarCrestone 2002–2006 ROI Studies.

In addition to employee self-service systems, organizations might outsource other E-Business functions to support HR management processes. Examples of outsourcing include hiring companies such as Automatic Data Processing, Inc. (ADP®) or Paychex,® Inc. to administer payroll and benefits.

In addition to the best of breed and outsourced services previously described, *enterprise systems* play a major role in implementing required HR and payroll functionality. For example, systems from vendors such as SAP and Microsoft (see Figure 14.1 on pg. 525 for the HR-related menu of reports options within Microsoft Dynamics® GP) include employee master data to support both HR management and payroll processes. They contain employee self-services for employees to maintain their own data and for managers to maintain and monitor data related to subordinate employees. **Figure 14.3** depicts a menu from the Microsoft Dynamics® GP system that is used to access employee data so that the information can then be maintained. Notice that options exist to access education data, position history, reviews, skills and training, and so on.

When an organization implements its HR management process with an enterprise system, the organization can realize the benefits of integration of the HR management process with other enterprise systems modules such as financial accounting, logistics, and sales and distribution. In addition, the organizational assignment data in the HR

Enterprise Systems

Controls

FIGURE 14.3   Options for Maintaining Employee Master Data in the Microsoft Dynamics® GP

module can join with the workflow module of the enterprise system to facilitate the routing and proper authorization of daily work. For example, this joined functionality can ensure the proper authorization of purchase requisitions, purchase orders, and payroll.

Implementing the HR Management Process

Enterprise Systems

E-Business

Controls

This section offers a physical view of the HR management process. Using a systems flowchart as the framework for discussion, we will examine the inputs, processes, and outputs. The presentation also describes several of the operational and control aspects of a typical HR management process. The section concludes with an examination of what key data the process uses and how those data support decision making by HR managers.

Figure 14.4 presents a systems flowchart of a typical HR management process. This physical implementation employs important HR-related technology such as employee self-service systems, employee access to these systems via Web browsers or kiosks, and *enterprise systems* with workflow modules. Let's start by looking at the type of processing depicted. It generally is considered essential to record HR actions as soon as they are approved. A number of reasons exist for immediately recording changes affecting employees, including the need to ensure that each employee's paycheck reflects the employee's current status. For example, paychecks that fail to reflect recent pay hikes can have a demoralizing effect on a workforce. To achieve this type of immediacy, many HR management processes use some form of *immediate mode* of processing, implemented with *online* technology. The process depicted in Figure 14.4 entails immediate recording of data, immediate updating of master data, and immediate generation of output. Let's take some time to walk through the flowchart, keeping an eye open for operational, technological, and control features.

Processing Inputs

As shown in the "Various Departments" column of the flowchart, actions taken by departmental managers or supervisors are captured in a variety of online forms (i.e., enterprise system screens); these forms are discussed in the following paragraphs. In general, the HR forms in the figure capture information about three HR-related events: (1) selecting employees, (2) evaluating employees, and (3) terminating employees.

Selecting Employees. *Selecting* employees may be initiated in one of two ways. First, departmental supervisors and managers (outside the HR department) may initiate the process to satisfy their immediate hiring needs. The needs request screen indicated in the flowchart illustrates this type of initiation. Second, the selection process may be started automatically by the system. For example, the system may be programmed to predict an organization's employment needs. In projecting this need, the program might correlate labor-force requirements (stored in the labor-force planning data) with such factors as expanding sales or production statistics.

The actual selection and hiring of employees can be accomplished by several means. First, candidates for an open or new position could be selected from the population of workers currently employed by the company. These candidates might be identified from (1) recommendations set forth in the needs request form, (2) recommendations based on the results of scanning the employee/payroll master data, or (3) recommendations based on the results of scanning the skills inventory data. Second, applications could be received from candidates outside the organization; the employment request entry and

FIGURE 14.4 Human Resources Management Process—Systems Flowchart

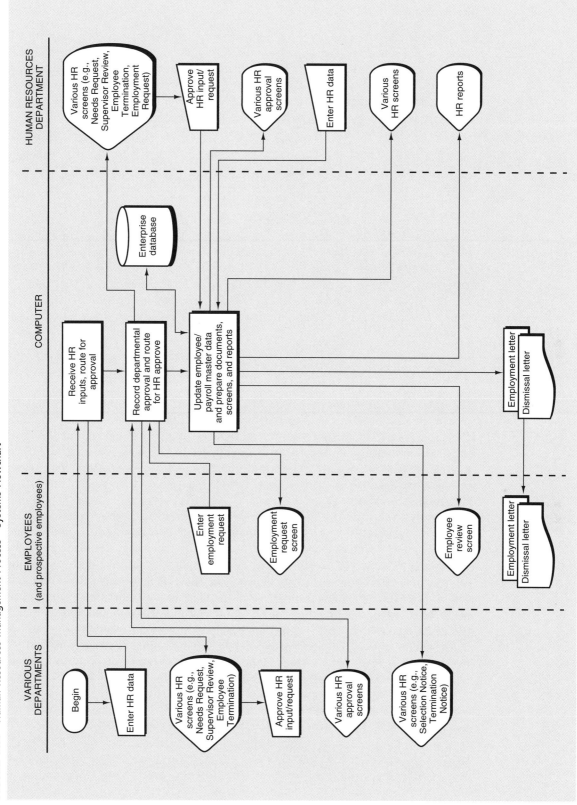

screen in the "Employees (and prospective employees)" column of the flowchart illustrates this interface.

Evaluating Employees. *Evaluating* employees involves numerous activities. Departmental managers and supervisors (again, outside the HR function) usually initiate actions affecting employees via the supervisor review screen shown in the flowchart. Then the manager of personnel appraisal and development (in HR) typically approves the review and implements such changes.

Terminating Employees. *Terminating* employees closes the employment process loop. Periodically, departmental managers and supervisors (in conjunction with HR managers) must make difficult decisions about the retention of employees. If a termination seems to be in order, the employee change screen is used to initiate the process of changing an employee's status from current employee to terminated employee.

The decision to terminate an employee is usually based on both qualitative and quantitative data. The HR management process assists the decision process by keeping track of certain kinds of quantitative data. For example, data concerning the number of absences during a given period, the number of times tardy, or the number of poor performance reviews an employee has received may be maintained in the employee/payroll master data. Additionally, data supplied by the labor force planning table may indicate a need to reduce the size of the workforce. Besides termination, any other changes in the employee's status, such as changes in salary or skill levels, also are transmitted through the employee change form.

Processing Logic and Process Outputs

Let's take some time now to follow the processing logic and review the process' outputs. HR requests initiated outside of the HR department must be approved within that department and then be routed to HR for approval. Some data may be entered within HR (e.g., inputs from unions, government agencies) and may or may not need approval within HR (no such approval is shown in Figure 14.4). Once approved in HR, the employee/payroll master data, skills inventory data, and labor force planning data within the enterprise database are updated, and various reports are made available to HR and other interested parties.

As you can see from the flowchart in Figure 14.4 (pg. 531), several outputs are also produced. In the case of a new hire, an employment letter is sent to the employee, and a selection notice is sent to the department manager or supervisor. Feedback to employees concerning their job performance is provided through an employee review form (paper, online, or both), which may be just a copy of the supervisor review form with some additional comments and notes added by the manager of personnel appraisal and development. Also, employees are notified of a dismissal action through a dismissal letter, with a termination notice being sent to the operating department manager.

In addition to the outputs shown on the flowchart, an HR management process must prepare reports for a variety of government and nongovernment entities. For example, the payroll process must send reports concerning employee federal, state, and local taxes. These payroll reports are discussed later in the chapter. HR-type reports might include those provided to the following:

- Unions
- Equal Employment Opportunity (EEO)
- Occupational Safety and Health Administration (OSHA)
- Department of Labor

Also not shown in the flowchart are the numerous communications to employees of HR-related information. This information might take the form of job opening announcements, training information, phone books, benefits literature, policy and procedure manuals, and the like. Many companies have found that such materials can be disseminated effectively and efficiently through an HR portal, which serves as a central data source for such information.

E-Business

Key Data Tables

Several tables of data are used by the HR and payroll processes. In an enterprise system, these tables are included within the enterprise database. Although these tables don't appear as separate data stores in Figure 14.4, we will discuss each next.

Controls

The *employee/payroll master data* will be defined and illustrated when we cover the payroll process. For now, let's consider how that data facilitates the HR function. Employee/payroll master data can help management determine the total cost of its workforce. It also aids in setting hiring policies in the context of providing information for compliance with affirmative action measures. Projected hiring needs may be influenced by seniority profiles. In addition, management may be given some sense of how well it is retaining employees; whether sick leave and vacation leave patterns are shifting; and, in conjunction with sales and productivity reports, how well performance matches workforce experience levels.

Enterprise Systems

The **labor-force planning data** maintains data concerning an organization's short-term and long-term staffing requirements. It includes data about various job specifications, with the specifications delineating the training and experience necessary to perform each job. The data also may contain statistical information regarding employee attrition by department, overall employee turnover, and so forth.

The **skills inventory data** catalogs each employee's set of relative skills. As employees gain new experience through on-the-job training or formal educational channels, the skills data is updated. When a job opening becomes available, HR managers often consult the skills inventory data in search of qualified internal candidates. Management also may refer to this data in assigning employees to specific job tasks.

Although not discussed here, several other data stores are commonly found in an HR management process. Coverage of these data stores is beyond the scope of the chapter, but an end-of-chapter discussion question will ask you to speculate on what these data stores might be.

The Payroll Process

In this section, we first look at the imprint of the payroll function on the organization, and then we describe the logic and data of the payroll process. We follow that with a description of a typical physical implementation of the payroll process and an analysis of the internal controls in that process.

Organizational Setting

Let's look briefly at the organizational structure of the payroll function. The discussion here is limited to an examination of *structure* only; we do not discuss the role of the controller or the other positions related to the payroll function. The organizational significance of the controller's area (where payroll resides) has been covered in earlier chapters.

The payroll function generally falls under the authority of the controller's office. Although the controller's office usually has line responsibility over the payroll function,

FIGURE 14.5 Organization Chart Illustrating the Payroll Function

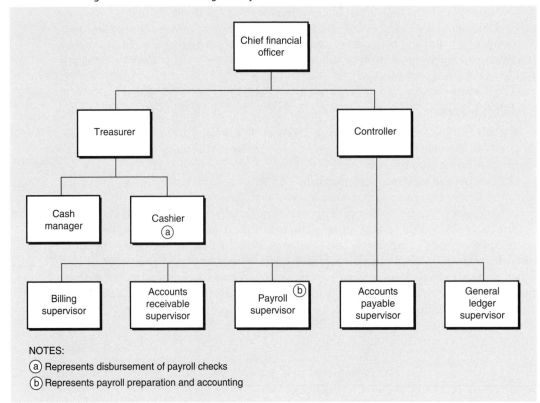

NOTES:
ⓐ Represents disbursement of payroll checks
ⓑ Represents payroll preparation and accounting

it is important to note that certain activities, such as distributing paychecks, are influenced by the treasury function. **Figure 14.5** is an organization chart illustrating the location of the payroll function.

Logical Description of the Payroll Process

This section describes and illustrates the logical characteristics of a typical payroll process. Once again, we use data flow diagrams (DFDs) to explain the process logic. In addition, the section includes a discussion of the employee/payroll master data as they relate to the payroll process. We conclude this section by presenting the accounting transactions that are generated by the payroll process.

Figure 14.6 is a context diagram of the payroll process. Study the diagram now to gain a broad overview of the major inputs, outputs, and interfaces in the process. **Figure 14.7** (pg. 536) presents a level 0 DFD of the payroll process. This figure shows seven major activities carried out by the process; they are discussed and illustrated next.

To begin, process 1.0 (Perform data maintenance) periodically updates the *tax rates data* to ensure that current tax rates (federal, state, county, and city) are being used in preparing employee paychecks. Using a separate tax rates table (data store) rather than storing the rates in the employee/payroll master data allows for easier data maintenance whenever tax rates change.

Two data flows enter the payroll process from departmental managers and supervisors: attendance time records and job time records. **Attendance time records** show the time periods that employees are in attendance at the job site and available for work.

These records are used to calculate the gross amount of each employee's pay. **Job time records**, on the other hand, reflect the start and stop times on specific jobs. Their purpose is to allow the distribution of payroll costs to jobs in process (or to other accounts).[3] Attendance time records are maintained near the entrance of the workplace and often take the physical form of time cards that are punched as employees come and go. Increasingly, however, employees "punch" in and out of work by swiping an employee identification card through or by a magnetic card reader. Job time records are prepared at the worksite by employees entering the time each job is started and stopped.

FIGURE 14.6   Payroll Process—Context Diagram

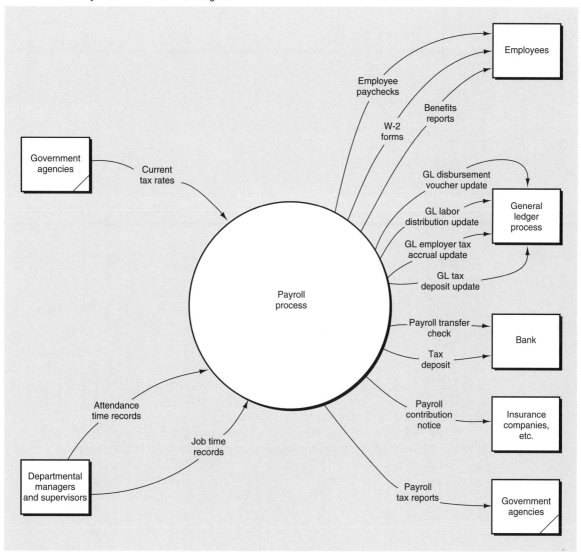

FIGURE 14.7   Payroll Process—Level 0 Diagram

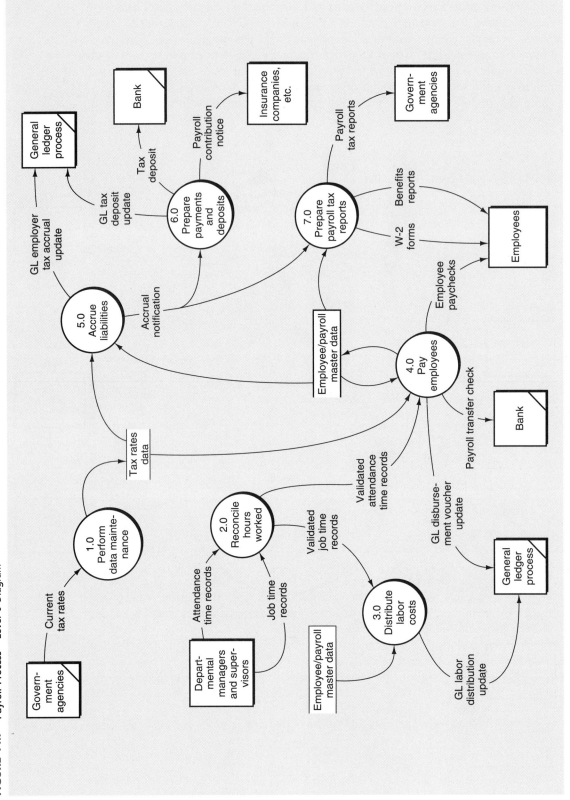

FIGURE 14.8   Payroll Process—Diagram 4

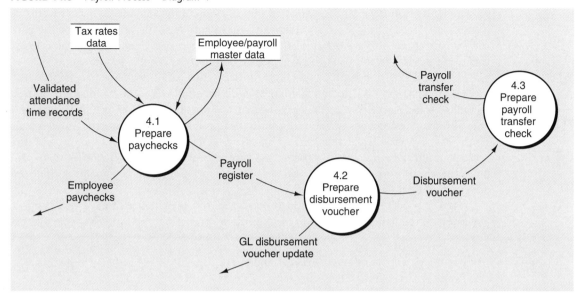

Process 2.0 (Reconcile hours worked) compares the total hours of each worker as shown by the attendance record with the hours reflected on the job time records for that employee. The hours should agree. This reconciliation is one of the payroll process *control plans*, which are discussed in a subsequent section. Validated job time records are sent to process 3.0, which distributes labor costs to individual jobs, projects, or departments. Process 3.0 (Distribute labor costs) interfaces with the general ledger process to provide necessary journal entries for the distribution of labor charges.

Validated attendance time records initiate the payment to workers in process 4.0 (Pay employees). **Figure 14.8** explores process 4.0 down to its next lower level. Let's discuss it next.

In calculating employees' gross and net pay, process 4.1 (Prepare paychecks) retrieves data from both the employee/payroll master data and the tax rates data. Data retrieved from the employee/payroll master data include the employee identification code; employee status (active, inactive, etc.); employee name and address; employee tax status (single or married, number of exemptions, etc.); employee payment code (wage, salary, or commission employee); employee wage, salary, or commission rate; employee overtime rate; employee vacation accrual rate; and employee sick leave accrual rate. In addition, various kinds of payroll deductions, such as IRA or 401(k) deductions, union dues, and life insurance, are retrieved from the employee/payroll master data when an employee's gross and net pay are calculated.

Additions, deletions, and adjustments of various kinds to the employee/payroll master data represent another class of data necessary for processing an organization's payroll. This category of adjustments includes changes in salary or wage rates, address, department, tax exemptions, deduction authorizations, and so forth. For *control* reasons, personnel in the *HR function* enter these data items in the data table.

Process 4.1 accumulates current, quarter-to-date, and year-to-date totals for each employee and reports this information via the data flow "Payroll register." This information also is used to update the employee/payroll master data. Finally, process 4.1 prints and distributes paychecks to employees, as reflected in the "Employee paychecks" data flow.

Controls

Controls

The data flow "Payroll register" triggers process 4.2 (Prepare disbursement voucher). As we discussed in Chapter 13, many organizations use a disbursement voucher as documentation to recognize their payroll liability and to authorize the preparation of the payroll transfer check. Process 4.3 (Prepare payroll transfer check) then prepares the transfer check and sends it to the bank to cover the organization's periodic net payroll.

Having walked through the details of process 4.0, let's now return to Figure 14.7 (pg. 536). Process 5.0 (Accrue liabilities) accrues employer and withheld liabilities, including social security tax (Federal Insurance Contributions Act [FICA]), state and federal unemployment insurance taxes, insurance premiums, and pension plan contributions. These accruals are reported to the general ledger process. On receipt of the accrual notification data flow, process 6.0 (Prepare payments and deposits) then prepares the tax and other deposits (such as insurance premium payments) and notifies the general ledger process of the deposit.

Finally, process 7.0 (Prepare payroll tax reports) provides assistance in satisfying government regulations regarding employees by preparing the following payroll tax reports:

- Form 941 (report of wages taxable under FICA)
- Form W-2 (wage and tax statement)
- Form 1099-R (annuities, pensions, or retired pay)
- Employee Retirement Income Security Act (ERISA) reports

The Employee/Payroll Master Data

Enterprise Systems

Controls

The **employee/payroll master data** is the central repository for data about people who work for an organization. This data table combines data that originate in two functional areas: HR and payroll. Each record contains employee identification data (e.g., personal data) as well as data used for the computation of employee paychecks (i.e., payroll data). The periodic preparation of the company payroll is greatly simplified by having both personal and payroll data available on each employee record. However, this situation has the potential of raising some *control* problems because staff in two departments have the capability of making changes to the data. Furthermore, having both departments participate in the review of exception reports may result in duplication of effort and, in the case of accepting responsibility for errors, can lead to interdepartmental conflict. The solution to these problems is to restrict online access for purposes of making data updates and reviewing errors so that each department can alter only those data fields over which it has predetermined authority. Such features are easily implemented with *enterprise systems* through organizational assignments in the employee/payroll master data.

Employee payroll records are keyed by an employee identification code, such as a social security number or other identifier. The employee code can be designed to reflect certain employee attributes, such as department, factory, and position. Such code numbers can be used to provide management with labor-cost distributions.

Payroll data usually are recorded currently as well as on a quarterly and year-to-date basis. This technique greatly reduces the effort necessary to meet periodic government reporting requirements and to produce ad hoc summary information for internal use. In addition, accumulating totals facilitates filing reports of amounts withheld for state and federal income taxes, unemployment insurance taxes, and social security taxes. At year-end, W-2 statements can be produced easily.

Accounting Entries Related to the Payroll Process

Exhibit 14.1 illustrates the four primary accounting entries recorded by the payroll process. The exhibit shows the source of each entry by cross-referencing the entry to the

EXHIBIT 14.1   Accounting Entries Related to the Payroll Process

1.   PAY EMPLOYEES

    A.   ESTABLISH VARIOUS PAYROLL LIABILITIES[a]
       (from process 4.2 in Figure 14.8 on pg. 537):

Payroll clearing	XXXXX	
FIT withholdings payable		XXXXX
SIT withholdings payable		XXXXX
FICA tax withholdings payable		XXXXX
Accrued payroll		XXXXX

    B.   RECORD THE DISBURSEMENT OF CASH
       (from process 4.3 in Figure 14.8):

Accrued payroll	XXXXX	
Cash		XXXXX

2.   DISTRIBUTE PAYROLL TO VARIOUS ACCOUNTS
    (from process 3.0 in Figure 14.7 on pg. 536):

Work in process (direct labor)	XXXXX	
Manufacturing overhead (indirect labor)	XXXXX	
General and administrative expense	XXXXX	
Selling expense	XXXXX	
Payroll clearing		XXXXX

3.   ACCRUE EMPLOYER PAYROLL TAXES[a]
    (from process 5.0 in Figure 14.7):

Manufacturing overhead (tax on factory workers)	XXXXX	
General and administrative expense	XXXXX	
Selling expense	XXXXX	
FICA taxes payable		XXXXX
SUT taxes payable		XXXXX
FUTA taxes payable		XXXXX

4.   RECORD TAX DEPOSITS[a]
    (from process 6.0 in Figure 14.7):

FIT withholdings payable	XXXXX	
SIT withholdings payable	XXXXX	
FICA tax withholdings payable	XXXXX	
FICA taxes payable	XXXXX	
SUT taxes payable	XXXXX	
FUTA taxes payable	XXXXX	
Cash		XXXXX

[a]Entries 1A, 3, and 4 would typically include deductions or accruals for nontax items, such as health insurance premiums, pension plan contributions, and union dues.

corresponding logical process in either Figure 14.7 (pg. 536) or Figure 14.8. (pg. 537) Take some time to study Exhibit 14.1. We assume you are already familiar with the entries from other accounting courses. In the "Application of the Control Framework" section, we'll have more to say about the use of the "Payroll clearing" account in entries 1 and 2 of the exhibit.

Implementing the Payroll Process

Enterprise Systems

E-Business

Controls

This section provides a physical view of the *payroll process*. Again, we use a systems flowchart as the basis for discussion. The presentation also describes various operational and control aspects of a typical payroll process. Selected process outputs will be discussed as well.

Figure 14.9 shows a systems flowchart for a typical payroll process. Unlike its counterpart, Figure 14.4 (pg. 531), in which HR activities were processed in the *immediate mode*, Figure 14.9 shows payroll events being entered in real time but processed in batches. In most organizations, payroll processing is generally done on a periodic basis. The process shown in Figure 14.9 reflects periodic recording of data, periodic updating of master data, and immediate generation of output.

This physical implementation employs much of the technology described earlier in this chapter, including employee self-service systems, employee access to these systems via Web browsers or kiosks, and *enterprise systems* with workflow modules. In addition, employee inputs to record attendance and work on specific jobs are made into an **electronic time management system**, a computer-based system that captures, stores, and reports time. Inputs to such systems are via the reading of magnetic strips on employee identification badges, *bar code* readers, and key entry. Payments to employees are made through a **payroll direct deposit system** whereby employee net pay is sent electronically through the banking system, typically using the *ACH Network*, and deposited directly to the employees' bank accounts. One technology that is not used here is a **payroll service bureau**, a company that specializes in rendering payroll services to client companies for a fee. By using a service bureau, an organization can *outsource* much of the process depicted in Figure 14.9, including payroll calculation, paycheck preparation and direct deposit, payroll tax reporting and payments, and payments to insurance and retirement programs.[4]

Let's take some time now to follow the process logic. For now, please ignore the control annotations (P-1, P-2, etc.); we'll return to them in the "Application of the Control Framework" section. The process begins with factory workers recording attendance and job time in an *electronic time management system*.[5]

Periodically (e.g., weekly, bi-weekly), time data and batch totals are downloaded from the *electronic time management system* and sent to the payroll system, where the batch totals are reconciled to ensure the integrity of the data transfer. The data are then sent to the appropriate supervisory personnel for approval. Once approved, the total hours worked for a pay period are reconciled (attendance time hours and job time hours). The payroll system then does the following:

- Distributes the labor costs and updates the employee/payroll master data
- Prepares the *employee paychecks* (i.e., electronic payments) and sends the payments to the bank for deposit into employee accounts

---

[4]Organizations typically employ payroll service bureaus. We depict our payroll system without one so that you can more easily see all of the steps in the payroll process.

[5]Remember that the procedures shown in Figure 14.9 relate to factory workers only. However, many of the steps illustrated could apply to payroll processing for other employee categories. Generally, all employees are required to record their attendance and job time via some online time sheet.

FIGURE 14.9 The Payroll Process—Systems Flowchart

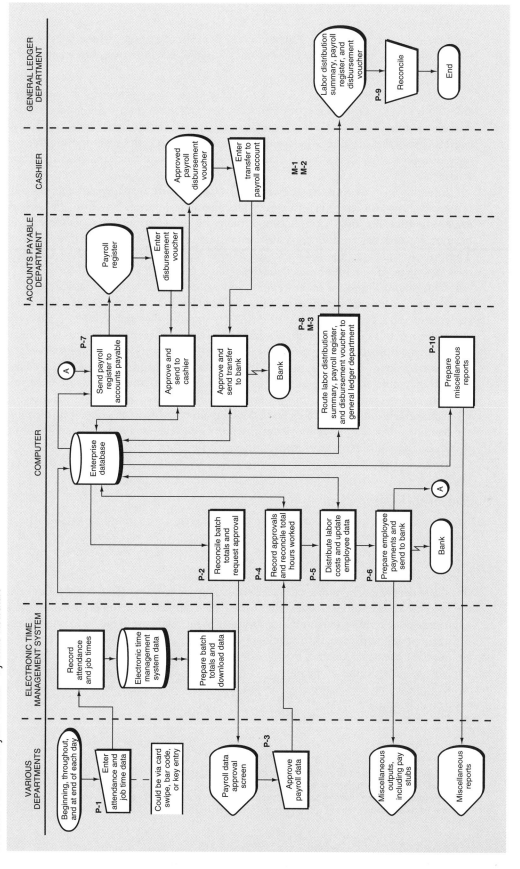

- Prepares various outputs, including the employee *pay stubs* that are posted to the HR portal
- Sends the *payroll register* to the accounts payable department, where a disbursement voucher is prepared for the amount of the payroll, including employee payments for taxes, insurance, and so on

The disbursement voucher is sent to the cashier, where a transfer is made for the amount of the payroll from the general checking account to the imprest payroll account. Finally, several items are sent to the general ledger department so that they can reconcile the amount to be paid (the *payroll register*), the job time incurred (the *labor distribution summary*), and the amount disbursed from the bank (the *disbursement voucher*).[6]

Controls

Enterprise
Systems

In addition to the outputs previously discussed, many management reports can be produced for online viewing (paper outputs also may be available) from the *enterprise database* to manage and *control* the operations of the enterprise. They become more meaningful and powerful if the data can be aggregated across the entire enterprise. These reports include the *deduction and benefits register*, the *state and local tax register*, the employees' *W-2 withholdings statements*, and a variety of reports and forms for government agencies. Several other reports and analyses may be generated from payroll processing. These could include reports of absenteeism and tardiness by employee and analyses of indirect labor by type of cost—supervision, materials handling, inspection, and so on. Also valuable in staff planning are certain aggregate statistics accumulated during payroll processing, such as total number of employees, total hours worked, total labor costs, average wage rate, rate of absenteeism, rate of turnover, and average cost of total fringe benefits. These statistics are most meaningful when trends in their values are analyzed and correlated with one another and with other factors. For example, useful management information may be obtained from correlating the rate of turnover with average hours worked per employee or the rate of absenteeism with the number of units that fail to pass quality control inspection.

The Fraud Connection

Payroll, similar to cash disbursements, is an area ripe with fraud potential. After all, large organizations will make thousands of payments to employees for payroll and expense account reimbursements every payroll period (e.g., weekly, bi-weekly). Here are some of the types of payroll frauds that are committed:

- *Ghost employees:* Employees who do not currently work for the company but receive paychecks. These can be ex-employees, or completely fictitious. Over time, the losses associated with ghost employees can be relatively large because the entire amount of the payment is fraudulent.
- *Falsified hours and salary:* Employees record more time than actually worked or are able to increase the salary in their employee data. These losses are usually less than for ghost employees because the amount above the actual amount worked is the fraudulent amount.

---

[6]The procedures performed by accounts payable, the cashier, and the general ledger department could be automated. We show them here as manual procedures so that you can see the entire process more clearly. To simplify the flowchart, we have not shown the *exception routines* that would be needed wherever there is an approval or reconciliation.

- *Commission schemes:* Employees overstate the sales on which commissions are based or increase the commission rate in their employee data.
- *False workers' compensation claims:* Employees pretend to have injuries to collect disability payments. The employer's workers' compensation insurance usually increases based on claims against the policy; the fraud impacts the insurance company and the employer.

Some of the procedures that can be used to prevent or detect these schemes include the following:

Controls

- *Segregate duties* among personnel data creation and modification (HR), payroll preparation (payroll), and disbursement (AP and cashier).
- *Direct deposit* payroll to eliminate alteration, forgery, and theft of paper check. (Diversion of deposits into unauthorized accounts is not affected.)
- Check for *duplicate names*, *addresses*, and *social security* numbers in the employee data.
- Compare actual to budgeted payroll.

Other than compensation for work performed, as depicted in Figure 14.9, employees are reimbursed for expenses incurred while conducting business for their employer. Employees may record such expenses online, in a manner similar to that used to record attendance and job times. Documentation of the expenses must then be sent to the accounts payable department so that they can verify the legitimacy of the expenses. Employee reimbursement may then take place much as it would for regular payroll.

These reimbursements, often termed *expense accounts*, are often an area of fraud and abuse. Employee fraud schemes include the following:[7]

- Using legitimate documentation from personal expenses for a business expense
- Overstating expenses by altering receipts
- Submitting fictitious expenses by producing fake receipts
- Obtaining multiple reimbursements for one expense by submitting multiple copies of invoices

Such abuses can be minimized by formulating reasonable policies that compensate employees for their out-of-pocket expenses. Copies of invoices should only be accepted in extreme circumstances. Finally, expense account activities should be monitored on a regular basis to detect unusual patterns. In the next section, we describe *controls* to prevent these abuses, as well as other typical payroll controls.

Controls

Application of the Control Framework

In this section, we apply the control framework from Chapter 7 to the payroll process. **Figure 14.10** on page 544–545 presents a completed *control matrix* for the annotated systems flowchart shown in Figure 14.9 (pg. 541).

Control Goals

The control goals listed across the top of the matrix are similar to those presented in Chapters 7 and 9 through 13, except they have been tailored to the specifics of the payroll process.

---

[7] Joseph T. Wells, "The Padding That Hurts," *Journal of Accountancy*, February 2003, pp. 67–69.

FIGURE 14.10 The Payroll Process—Control Matrix

	Control Goals of the Payroll Business Process								
	Control goals of the operations process					Control goals of the information process			
Recommended control plans	Ensure effectiveness of operations			Ensure efficient employment of resources (people and computers)	Ensure security of resources (cash, employee/ payroll master data)	For time data inputs, ensure:			For employee/ payroll master data, ensure:	
	A	B	C			IV	IC	IA	UC	UA
Present Controls										
P-1: Enter time data close to the data's originating source	P-1			P-1			P-1	P-1		
P-2: Computer agreement of batch totals									P-2	P-2
P-3: Approve attendance time data and job time data						P-3		P-3		
P-4: Reconcile attendance time data and job time data	P-4			P-4		P-4	P-4	P-4		
P-5: Distribute labor costs						P-5	P-5	P-5		
P-6: Independent paycheck distribution					P-6	P-6				
P-7: Approve payroll transfer check					P-7					
P-8: Accumulate payroll data for reconciliation of the payroll clearing account						P-8	P-8	P-8	P-8	P-8
P-9: Use a payroll clearing account						P-9	P-9	P-9	P-9	P-9
P-10: Prepare miscellaneous reports		P-10	P-10							
Missing Controls										
M-1: Independent reconciliation of payroll bank account					M-1					

FIGURE 14.10 The Payroll Process—Control Matrix (*Continued*)

	Control Goals of the Payroll Business Process							
	Control goals of the operations process			Control goals of the information process				
Recommended control plans	Ensure effectiveness of operations	Ensure Efficient employment of resources (people and computers)	Ensure security of resources (cash, employee/ payroll master data)	For time data inputs, ensure:			For employee/ payroll master data, ensure:	
M-2: Use an imprest payroll bank account		M-2	M-2			M-2		M-2
M-3: Computer agreement of batch totals (agree run-to-run totals)			M-3	M-3	M-3	M-3	M-3	M-3

Possible effectiveness goals include the following:	
A — Provide employees with timely paychecks.	IV = Input validity
B — Provide timely filing of tax returns and other reports to government agencies.	IC = Input completeness
	IA = Input accuracy
C — Comply with requirements of payroll and tax laws and regulations.	UC = Update completeness
See Exhibit 14.2 for a complete explanation of control plans and cell entries.	UA = Update accuracy

The *operations process control goals* that are typical of the payroll process include:

- *Effectiveness of operations:* Three *representative effectiveness* goals are listed within this goal: A, *Provide employees with timely paychecks*; B, *Provide timely filing of tax returns and other reports to government agencies*;[8] and C, *Comply with the requirements of payroll tax laws and regulations*.[9]
- *Efficient employment of resources:* As noted in Chapter 9 and reinforced in Chapters 10 through 13, people and computers are the resources found in most business processes.
- *Resource security:* The resources of interest include cash and the information resources residing in the employee/payroll master data. Control plans should be in place to prevent unauthorized accessing, copying, changing, selling, or destroying of the employee/payroll master data. Equally, plans should be in place to prevent theft or any unauthorized use of cash.

---

[8]Both effectiveness goals B and C are "compliance" goals as called for by the COSO report on internal control, which was discussed in Chapter 7. Whereas goal B speaks to ensuring the timeliness of complying with such laws and regulations, goal C covers all other aspects of compliance, such as who must report, what wages are subject to payroll taxation, and so on.

[9]In the interest of simplicity, we have not included goal columns in the matrix to show compliance with other laws and regulations related to the payroll process, such as compliance with Equal Employment Opportunity (EEO), Occupational Safety and Health Administration (OSHA), and Employee Retirement Income Security Act (ERISA) provisions. Many of these provisions apply more to the *HR* function than to the *payroll* function.

The *information process* control goals, as adapted to the payroll process, are the following:

- Input validity (IV)[10] from the viewpoint of the payroll process; valid time data include those that reflect services performed by real employees.
- Input completeness (IC) and input accuracy (IA) for the time data.
- Update completeness (UC) and update accuracy (UA) for the employees/payroll master data.

Recommended Control Plans

Recall that application control plans include both those that are characteristic of a particular AIS business process and those that relate to the technology used to implement the application. Here, you are introduced to some of the new plans that are particular to the payroll business process. We first define and explain these controls and then summarize, in **Exhibit 14.2**, each cell entry in Figure 14.10 (pg. 544–545), the control matrix:

- *Enter time data close to the data's originating source* (Exhibit 14.2 and Figure 14.10, P-1): Capture data automatically, if possible, when an event occurs. As time passes, it is more difficult to capture accurate, complete data.
- *Approve attendance time data and job time data* (Figure 14.2 and Figure 14.10, P-3): Even when time data entry is automatic, there should be a review and approval of the time worked by a department supervisor.
- *Reconcile attendance time data and job time data* (Exhibit 14.2 and Figure 14.10, P-4): An automatic reconciliation of attendance data with job time data makes sure that time is recorded in both segments of the system, ensuring that time worked (attendance) is available for billing (job time), and time available for billing is included as time worked for an employee.
- *Independent paycheck distribution* (Exhibit 14.2 and Figure 14.10, P-6): Periodically, paychecks should be distributed by someone other than the supervisor of an employee to ensure that everyone being paid is actually a working employee.
- *Use a payroll clearing account* (Exhibit 14.2 and Figure 14.1, P-9): A **payroll clearing account** is a bank account used solely for payroll purposes and is separate from a company's other, more general purpose bank accounts. Funds are transferred into the account prior to the generation of payroll checks and for the total amount of all checks to be issued. Accordingly, the net of the transfer to the clearing account and payroll disbursements should zero out each pay period, assuming all checks are cashed. Also note that as a control plan (P-9, Figure 14.10), the payroll clearing account effectively reconciles the dollars that are calculated from two different input sources (i.e., from time data and job data; Exhibit 14.1, journal entries 1 and 2).
- *Use an imprest payroll bank account* (Exhibit 14.2 and Figure 14.10, M-2): In an **imprest payroll bank account**, the fund (account) is reimbursed for the *exact amount* of the disbursements made from the fund, rather than being supplemented for expected amounts in advance, as with the payroll clearing account above. In other words, an imprest account is reimbursed for the actual payroll checks cashed rather than the payroll checks distributed (as with the clearing account). Of course, in most cases, the amounts of the checks distributed and cashed will be the same. Similar to a petty cash fund, an imprest account maintains a cash balance considered sufficient for upcoming payroll requirements. The imprest account is then

---

[10]To focus our discussion, we have limited our coverage of process inputs to time data. Tax rates and job time data inputs have been ignored in the control matrix to simplify the illustration. Furthermore, neither of those two inputs is used to update the employee/payroll master data.

reimbursed after the payroll checks are cashed to bring it back up to this normal account balance. As can be seen from the title of the account, the cash is kept in a bank account for security reasons.

Each of the recommended control plans listed in the matrix in Figure 14.10 is discussed in Exhibit 14.2. We have intentionally limited the number of plans to avoid redundancy with presentations in previous chapters. Study Exhibit 14.2's explanations of the cell entries appearing in the control matrix. As you know from your studies in prior chapters, understanding how the recommended control plans relate to specific control goals is the most important aspect of applying the control framework.

EXHIBIT 14.2   Explanation of Cell Entries for the Control Matrix in Figure 14.10

P-1: *Enter time data close to the data's originating source.*

- *Effectiveness goal A:* By having time information captured automatically and eliminating the keying in of data, the timeliness of paycheck preparation is improved.
- *Efficient employment of resources:* Entering time data directly into the computer system as that time is worked eliminates several payroll processing steps and the associated costs, making for a more efficient employment of resources.
- *Time data input completeness:* Eliminating hard copy time sheets and job time tickets removes the possibility that these documents could be lost or misplaced. As a result, real-time data capture should help to ensure that all inputs are processed once and only once (completeness).
- *Time data input accuracy:* Because input errors can be corrected immediately, input accuracy should be improved. Additionally, automation of input entry reduces the opportunity for input errors to enter the process.

P-2: *Computer agreement of batch totals.*

- *Employee/payroll master data update completeness and accuracy:* The attendance time data and batch totals—let's assume hash totals are used—are received from the *electronic time management system*. The computer calculates comparable hash totals for all attendance time data that were successfully updated to the employee/payroll master data. The computer-calculated totals are then compared to the input totals and discrepancies are reconciled (the reconciliation process is not shown). Assuming that differences are promptly investigated and corrected, the control plan addresses both the goals of update completeness and update accuracy (UC and UA).

P-3: *Approve attendance time data and job time data.*

- *Time data input validity:* Before they are forwarded to the payroll department for processing, time sheets and job time tickets are approved by operating department supervisors. These written approvals help to ensure input validity by assuring that time sheets are submitted only by bona fide employees and that these employees actually worked the time for which they will be paid.
- *Time sheet input accuracy:* Because we assume that the supervisors also check that the hours reflected by the time sheets are correct, a cell entry is made in the input accuracy column.

P-4: *Reconcile attendance time data and job time data.*

- *Effectiveness goal A:* By performing the reconciliation prior to undertaking further processing steps, we prevent errors from entering the process, thereby helping ensure that employee paychecks are prepared on a timely basis.
- *Efficient employment of resources:* By performing the reconciliation, we preclude the wasted effort (inefficiency) that could result from detecting and correcting errors after the fact.
- *Time data input validity, completeness, and accuracy:* If this control plan were not in place, discrepancies between the two data sets could result in employees being paid for work not performed. For example, if the number of hours captured on an employee's time record exceeds the total number of hours the employee has charged to various jobs throughout the week, then the company might pay this employee for services that the employee did not perform. This plan also addresses input completeness because we should have a valid attendance time record for every employee who has submitted job time tickets (and vice versa), thereby helping to ensure that time data are input once and only once.

P-5: *Distribute labor costs.*

- *Time data input validity, completeness, and accuracy:* See accounting entry 2 in Exhibit 14.1 (pg. 545). This process distributes all of the labor costs to the appropriate expense categories. When this entry balances, as it should, we will detect and correct any discrepancies between the attendance time and job time.

(continued)

EXHIBIT 14.2 Explanation of Cell Entries for the Control Matrix in Figure 14.10 (*continued*)

Therefore, in a manner similar to control P-4, this process ensures that no extra time data will be input to the payroll process (validity), that all time data inputs will be processed in payroll once and only once (completeness), and that all such inputs will be processed correctly (accuracy).

P-6: *Independent paycheck distribution.*

- *Security of resources:* This plan entails having paychecks distributed to employees by an entity not otherwise involved in payroll processing (i.e., by an independent party such as a paymaster, a bursar, or via direct deposit to an employee's bank account). Of course, as part of this control plan, a paycheck would be released only if the employee presented proper identification. By *preventing* fraudulent payments, this plan protects the cash resource.
- *Time data input validity:* The plan ensures that cash is expended only to employees who actually exist. In other words, this plan *detects* invalid inputs.

P-7: *Approve payroll transfer check.*

- *Security of resources:* To transfer funds from the company's general account to its payroll bank account, the payroll register is sent to the accounts payable department, a disbursement voucher is prepared and *approved* in accounts payable and by the cashier, and the transfer is sent to the bank electronically. P-7 in Figure 14.9 (pg. 541) corresponds to these steps. Approval of the payroll bank transfer helps to ensure that the cash asset is disbursed only for authorized expenditures.

P-8: *Accumulate payroll data for reconciliation of the payroll clearing account.*

- *Time data input validity, completeness, and accuracy:* This plan accumulates the data from the enterprise database and presents it for reconciliation. Therefore, as described for plan P-9, matrix entries are appropriate in the input validity (IV), input completeness (IC), and input accuracy (IA).
- *Payroll master data update completeness and accuracy:* Because plan P-9 is exercised *after* updates to the employee/payroll master data have occurred, the plan also meets the goals of update completeness (UC) and update accuracy (UA).

P-9: *Use a payroll clearing account.*

- *Time data input validity, completeness, and accuracy:* Because this plan reconciles the amounts that were calculated from two different input sources, entries are appropriate in the input validity (IV), input completeness (IC), and input accuracy (IA) columns. That is, control plan P-9 helps ensure that no extra time data were input to the payroll process (validity), that all time data inputs are processed in payroll once and only once (completeness), and that all such inputs will be processed correctly (accuracy).

- *Payroll master data update completeness and update accuracy:* Because plan P-9 is exercised *after* updates to the employee/payroll master data have occurred, the plan also meets the goals of update completeness (UC) and update accuracy (UA).

P-10: *Prepare miscellaneous reports.*

- *Effectiveness goals B and C:* Various reports can be prepared, electronically or on paper, to comply in a timely manner with tax and other government regulations. These reports can be prepared and sent automatically or by request of appropriate individuals.

M-1: *Independent reconciliation of payroll bank account.*

- *Security of resources:* Implementation of this control plan helps ensure the safety of resources (cash) by identifying missing or unusual items entered into the account.

M-2: *Use an imprest payroll bank account.*

- *Efficient employment of resources:* The plan helps ensure efficiency of resource use because reconciling the payroll bank account is simpler when it is operated on an imprest basis.
- *Security of resources:* Safety of the cash asset is ensured because fraudulent checks drawn on the payroll account should be readily detected. Losses due to fraudulent events are limited to the amount of funds transferred to the account.
- *Time data input accuracy and employee/payroll master data update accuracy:* Using an imprest payroll bank account helps check the accuracy of payroll processing (input accuracy and update accuracy) because the bank transfer prepared from the disbursement voucher must agree with the total net pay reflected by the payroll register.

M-3: *Computer agreement of batch totals (agree run-to-run totals).*

- *Security of resources, input validity:* By determining that updates to the employee/payroll master data reflect actual hours worked (attendance and jobs), we reduce the possibility of recording an invalid payroll event and dispensing cash for work that was not performed.
- *Input completeness, input accuracy, update completeness, update accuracy:* By comparing totals prepared before the input to those produced after the update, we ensure that all events were input once and only once (input completeness), all events were input correctly (input accuracy), all events were updated to the master data once and only once (update completeness), and all events were updated correctly to the master data (update accuracy).

Summary

Although not described as such in Chapters 10 through 13, the HR management and payroll processes are an integral part of all the order-to-cash and the purchase-to-pay processes. As a part of the *purchase-to-pay process* in a merchandising organization, the HR management and payroll processes focus on business events and reports data related to employee expenses. As a part of the *order-to-cash process* in a service organization, the HR management and payroll processes assist in managing a service firm's major resource—people. In addition, the HR management and payroll processes capture employee work-related activities and use that data to bill customers for services rendered and to analyze service-related activities. As a part of the *purchase-to-pay process* in a manufacturing organization, the HR management and payroll processes capture and analyze data related to a major component of a manufactured product—employee labor.

Let us leave you with a final thought about the HR management and payroll processes. We have emphasized the importance of these processes to the success of an organization and the significant resources dedicated to their operation. Here are six guidelines that can help an organization optimize the operation of these processes. At the same time, these guidelines provide some criteria to assess the *efficiency* and *effectiveness* of the operation of these processes:

1. Integrate payroll with other related processes such as HR management, electronic time and attendance recording, tax reporting, retirement, and general ledger, and then use the Web (i.e., HR portal) to connect these processes.
2. Customize pay delivery to meet the organization goals. Typical options include paper checks, direct deposit, payroll debit cards (pay is loaded on the card), and cash. Recognize that when cash payments are made, compensating controls must be in place to reduce misappropriation risks.
3. Understand each organization's culture and develop strategies to increase the adoption of secure payroll options, such as direct deposit.
4. Consolidate related processes such as payroll, HR, and expense reimbursement, and minimize pay cycles. For example, moving from bi-weekly to monthly payroll can reduce costs by 30 to 50 percent.
5. Because payroll and HR management are not key competencies, it typically makes sense to outsource these processes.
6. Build effective reporting and analytics. Analysis of labor costs can provide a powerful tool to improve the efficiency and effectiveness of operations.

Key Terms

human capital management (HCM), 522

human resources (HR) management process, 523

payroll process, 524

labor-force planning data, 533

skills inventory data, 533

attendance time records, 534

job time records, 535

employee/payroll master data, 538

electronic time management system, 540

payroll direct deposit system, 540

payroll service bureau, 540

payroll clearing account, 546

imprest payroll bank account, 546

Review Questions

RQ 14-1   What is human capital management (HCM)?

RQ 14-2   What does "human capital" include?

RQ 14-3   What is the human resources management process? What functions and activities does the process perform?

RQ 14-4   What is the payroll process? What functions and activities does the process perform?

RQ 14-5   What is the relationship between the HR process and the payroll process?

RQ 14-6   What role does each HR manager listed in Figure 14.2 (pg. 526) play?

RQ 14-7   What key decisions do the HR managers shown in Figure 14.2 make?

RQ 14-8   Describe an employee self-service system.

RQ 14-9   What are the principal inputs and outputs of the HR management process as reflected in the systems flowchart in Figure 14.4 (pg. 531)?

RQ 14-10   What data does the HR management process use? Describe the purpose of each.

RQ 14-11   How are the tax rates data and the employee/payroll master data used by the payroll process?

RQ 14-12   What are an attendance time record and a job time record? How is each used by the payroll process?

RQ 14-13   What are the major logical functions the payroll process performs? Be sure to consult the logical DFDs presented in the chapter.

RQ 14-14   What classes of general ledger journal entries are generated by the payroll process?

RQ 14-15   What are four major types of payroll fraud schemes?

RQ 14-16   What are four procedures that can be used to prevent or detect payroll fraud schemes?

RQ 14-17   What is the purpose of each control plan listed in the control matrix (Figure 14.10, on pp. 544–545).

Discussion Questions

DQ 14-1   Discuss the significance of having a separate organizational unit for the HR function (reporting to the vice president of HR), as opposed to having the HR function housed within an administrative organizational unit (reporting to a manager of HR).

DQ 14-2   Examine the placement of the manager of HR systems in the organization chart of Figure 14.2 (pg. 526) and review the typical functional responsibilities of this manager, decisions made, and information needs as shown in Table 14.1 (pg. 526–527). Describe possible alternatives for the placement of this function in the formal organization chart, and discuss the relative advantages for each placement. Consider the variables of centralized versus decentralized organizational structures.

DQ 14-3   Discuss the role unions and government agencies play in the design of procedures for the HR management process.

DQ 14-4   A number of organizations have recently instituted a position called "manager of human resource systems." Speculate about why this position may become strategically important to organizations in the future.

DQ 14-5   Discuss the significance of the employee/payroll master data in relation to the HR function and the payroll function.

DQ 14-6   Tax rates data are depicted in both the logical DFDs and the physical implementation systems flowchart for the payroll process in this chapter. Discuss the advantages of maintaining a separate data store versus incorporating such data into "master" data, such as the employee master data. Support your argument by constructing an analogy between the tax rates data and pay rates data (i.e., one containing hourly pay rates) for employees who are compensated for the hours actually worked.

DQ 14-7   Consult the systems flowcharts in Figures 14.4 (pg. 531) and 14.9 (pg. 541). Discuss how these processes implement the concept of segregation of duties discussed in Chapter 8. Be specific as to which entity (or entities) performs each of the four functions depicted in Table 8.2 (pp. 267–268). Limit your discussion to the process of preparing employee paychecks.

Short Problems

SP 14-1   In this chapter, we stated that many organizations view their human capital as an important variable in the formula for economic success. Discuss the role the HR management process plays in optimizing an organization's human capital.

SP 14-2   Without redrawing the figures, discuss *how*, if at all, the DFDs shown in Figures 14.6 (pg. 535), 14.7 (pg. 536), and 14.8 (pg. 537) would change as a result of the following *independent* situations (be specific in describing the changes):

   a.   Paying a worker for vacation or sick pay, as opposed to paying for hours actually worked

   b.   Paying some workers on a piecework basis

   c.   Paying some workers a commission based on sales

   d.   Preparing and distributing a paycheck "early" (i.e., in advance of the customary pay date)

   e.   Having a work environment where all employees are salaried (i.e., none are paid hourly)

SP 14-3   Following is a list of six control plans from this chapter (or from earlier chapters and tailored to the HR management and payroll processes of this chapter):

Control Plans
   A. Personnel termination procedures
   B. Computer matching of employee ID numbers
   C. Independent reconciliation of payroll bank account

D. One-for-one checking of hours per attendance time data and hours shown on pay stubs

E. Reconciling total hours per attendance time data with total hours per job time data

F. Computer agreement of batch totals

Required

Listed next are four process failures that have control implications. Write the numbers 1 through 4 on your solution sheet. Next to each number, insert *one* letter from the preceding list indicating the control plan that would *best* prevent the process failure from occurring. Also, give a brief, one- to two-sentence explanation of your choice. A letter should be used only once, with two letters left over.

Process Failures

1. A computer operator was fired for incompetence. During the two-week notice period, the operator "fired a parting shot" by destroying several computer files.

2. A novice data entry clerk had an error rate ranging from 10 to 20 percent during the first few weeks on the job. These errors resulted in several overpayments and underpayments to employees.

3. A payroll clearing account in the general ledger is debited for the gross pay amount paid to employees and is credited for the gross pay amount distributed to jobs in process or to expense categories. In theory, the clearing account should reflect a zero balance, but it consistently shows either a debit or credit balance.

4. The supervisor of an operating department prepared a fictitious attendance time record for a nonexistent employee and then deposited the bogus paycheck to her personal bank account.

SP 14-4 Following is a list of five control plans from this chapter (or from earlier chapters and tailored to the HR management and payroll processes of this chapter):

Control Plans

A. Specific approval of HR/payroll changes

B. One-for-one checking of hours per attendance time data and hours shown on pay stubs

C. Imprest payroll bank account

D. Hash totals of employee ID numbers

E. Electronic time management system

Required

Listed next are four process failures that have control implications. Write the numbers 1 through 4 on your solution sheet. Next to each number, insert *one* letter from the preceding list indicating the control plan that would *best* prevent the process failure from occurring. Also, give a brief, one- to two-sentence explanation of your choice. A letter should be used only once, with one letter left over.

Process Failures

1. An employee in the HR department prepared a bogus change of pay form to increase his salary by $25 per week. The form was submitted for processing and was entered into the system without being challenged.
2. Attendance time data is often not entered, not entered in a timely manner, or not accurate.
3. Each weekly pay period, a check is drawn on the general cash account and deposited to the payroll bank account in an amount "estimated" to be sufficient to cover the actual total of payroll checks issued that week. As a result, the payroll account runs a balance of several thousand dollars (non–interest-bearing), a situation that the newly hired treasurer has questioned.
4. In entering attendance time data, the data entry clerk misread all 7s as 9s. Although some time data were rejected, other data were processed against wrong employees, who happened to have a 9 instead of a 7 in the comparable position in their employee ID number.

SP 14-5   Following is a list of 10 control plans from this chapter (or from earlier chapters and tailored to the HR management and payroll processes of this chapter).

Control Plans

A. Online data entry of HR/payroll data
B. Automatic preparation of attendance time sheets for the next pay period (i.e., turnaround documents)
C. Review of all HR changes for compliance with union and government regulations
D. Use of a skills inventory data
E. Programmed edits—reasonableness checks
F. Preformatted screens
G. Computer calculations of gross pay, deductions, and so on
H. Fidelity bonding
I. Periodic performance reviews
J. Preformatted HR/payroll screens

Required

Listed next are eight statements describing either the achievement of a control goal (i.e., a process success) or a process deficiency (i.e., a process failure). Write the numbers 1 through 8 on your solution sheet. Next to each item insert *one* letter from the preceding list indicating the *best* control to achieve the desired goal or to address the process deficiency described. A letter should be used only once, with two letters left over.

Control Goals or Process Deficiencies

1. Should have prevented a data entry error of keying all hours worked with an extra digit (40 hours entered as 400, 45 hours as 450, etc.)
2. Helps to achieve efficiency of resource use (i.e., by reducing time needed for data entry) and accuracy of data entry

3. Should have prevented the organization's being sanctioned for failure to abide by Equal Employment Opportunity (EEO) guidelines

4. Should have prevented a data entry error of keying all zeroes as the letter *o* (40 entered as 4o, ID# 3062 entered as 3o62, etc.)

5. Would not have prevented employee dishonesty but would have helped the organization "recover" from such dishonesty

6. Helps in assigning employees to particular jobs

7. Precludes time card input errors by having certain data preprinted on the attendance time sheet

8. Helps ensure employee job satisfaction by providing employees with appropriate feedback

SP 14-6   a. List several *effectiveness* goals for the HR management process.

b. List some of the additional data stores that a typical HR management process might have.

c. Discuss the significance of the data stores in part (b) in relation to achieving the effectiveness goals of the HR management process (part [a]).

Problems

Note: As with the other business process chapters, the first few problems are based on the processes of specific companies. Therefore, the problem material starts with case narratives of those processes.

CASE STUDIES

CASE A: College Products

College Products is a division of a large manufacturing company. College makes a variety of collegiate branded products, sold on campuses worldwide. Most employees are paid on an hourly basis. Employees receive yearly reviews to evaluate performance and to determine an appropriate pay increase. College's payroll is processed by the corporate payroll department from input documents prepared by College. The following *HR and payroll* procedures are related to the hourly payroll employees at College.

Department supervisors initiate requests for additional employees by filling out a three-part employee requisition form. After a requisition is completed, the department supervisor signs it, files a copy by date, and gives the remaining two copies to the production supervisor. The production supervisor reviews and signs the copies and gives them to the HR manager. The HR manager reviews the request with the division controller. They both sign the requisition. The pay rate for the job also is determined at that time and included on the requisition. If the requisition is approved, the HR manager initiates hiring procedures by placing advertisements in local papers and announcing the opening internally. The HR manager and the supervisor interview the applicants together. They then evaluate the applicants and make a selection. The HR manager and the employee fill out the two-part wage and deduction form. The HR manager files a copy of the wage and deduction form and the personnel requisition by employee name. The remaining copies of each form are given to the division accountant.

The HR manager selects and reviews the records from the personnel file for employees who are due for their annual review. The HR manager puts some basic employee information on a three-part review form and gives it to the appropriate supervisor for evaluation. The supervisor completes and signs the form, files a copy, and gives the remaining copies to the production supervisor, who reviews and signs the evaluation. The production supervisor returns it to the HR manager. The HR manager reviews it with the controller. They assign a new rate and sign the review form, which is given to the division accountant.

The division accountant uses the new employee information and the employee review form to prepare payroll action notices. The accountant signs the payroll action notices and files them with the other related forms by date. Each week, a clerk in the corporate payroll department retrieves the payroll forms from the division accountant, checks the signature on all payroll action notices, and processes the payroll. The forms, checks, and reports are sent back to the division accountant. The division accountant refiles the forms and gives the checks to the production supervisor, who in turn distributes them to the employees.

CASE B: Compu-Fix, Inc.

Compu-Fix, Inc. is an independent contractor that provides technical support services under contract to government and nongovernment entities. The following process is used by Compu-Fix to process weekly payroll for hourly support and service personnel. Compu-Fix has a legacy computer system to which payroll personnel have online access from PCs located on their desks.

Each week, the computer prints time sheets using the employee/payroll master data. After receiving the time sheets from IT, the payroll department distributes them to the various department supervisors, who give them to employees. The employees fill in the time sheets each day and give them to their supervisors at the end of each week. Department supervisors review and sign the time sheets and return them to the payroll department. Payroll clerks key the time sheets into the current week's payroll activity data and then file them alphabetically by department.

At the start of the weekly payroll process, the computer creates the current week's pay data using the employee/payroll master and the current week's activity data. The following items are then printed from the pay data: checks with attached stubs, stubs for directly deposited checks, bank deposit slips for directly deposited checks (one deposit slip for each bank, which lists all the accounts to be credited), a single check for each bank receiving direct deposits, a check register, and various payroll reports. The computer operator gets the check-signing machine from the cashier and signs the checks. The checks, stubs, direct deposit slips, and check register are given to the cashier. The payroll reports are given to the payroll department.

The cashier checks the total and the number of checks against the payroll register and then sends the checks with attached stubs and the stubs for direct deposits to the department supervisors, who give them to the employees. The cashier then mails the direct deposit slips and checks to the banks.

P14-1   For the company assigned by your instructor, complete the following requirements:

   a.   Prepare a table of entities and activities.

   b.   Draw a context diagram.

   c.   Draw a *physical* data flow diagram (DFD).

d. Prepare an annotated table of entities and activities. Indicate on this table the groupings, bubble numbers, and bubble titles to be used in preparing a level 0 logical DFD.

e. Draw a level 0 logical DFD.

P14-2 For the company assigned by your instructor, complete the following requirements:

a. Draw a systems flowchart.

b. Prepare a control matrix, including explanations of how each recommended existing control plan helps to accomplish—or would accomplish in the case of missing plans—each related control goal.

c. Annotate the flowchart prepared in part (a) to indicate the points where the control plans are being applied (codes P-1, ... , P-*n*) or the points where they could be applied but are not (codes M-1, ... , M-*n*).

P14-3 For the company assigned by your instructor, redraw the systems flowchart assuming that the company uses an enterprise system.

P14-4 King Manufacturing has several large divisions. The flowchart shown in **Figure 14.11** describes the termination and exit interview procedures used by each division.

Required

(Make and state any assumptions that you think are necessary.) For the King Manufacturing process:

a. Prepare a table of entities and activities.

b. Draw a context diagram.

c. Draw a physical DFD.

d. Prepare an annotated table of entities and activities. Indicate on this table the groupings, bubble numbers, and bubble titles to be used in preparing a level 0 logical DFD.

e. Draw a level 0 logical DFD.

f. Identify the principal weaknesses in the process from the standpoint of both operational effectiveness/efficiency and the generic information process control goals of validity, completeness, and accuracy.

P14-5 Bubble 4.1 in Figure 14.8 (pg. 537) is called "Prepare paychecks."

Required

a. Explode that bubble down to the next level (i.e., prepare diagram 4.1.1) to show the detailed steps involved in this process. *Hint:* Recognize that each employee paycheck also includes a pay stub. Also note, in Figure 14.8, that the data flows out of bubble 4.1 include a payroll register.

b. In your solution to part (a), you should have some data flows out of data stores to process bubbles and other data flows from bubbles to data stores. For each data flow to or from data stores, *specify* the nature of the data that is being accessed or stored.

FIGURE 14.11 Ace Manufacturing: Divisional Employee Termination/Exit Interview Procedures for Problem 14-4

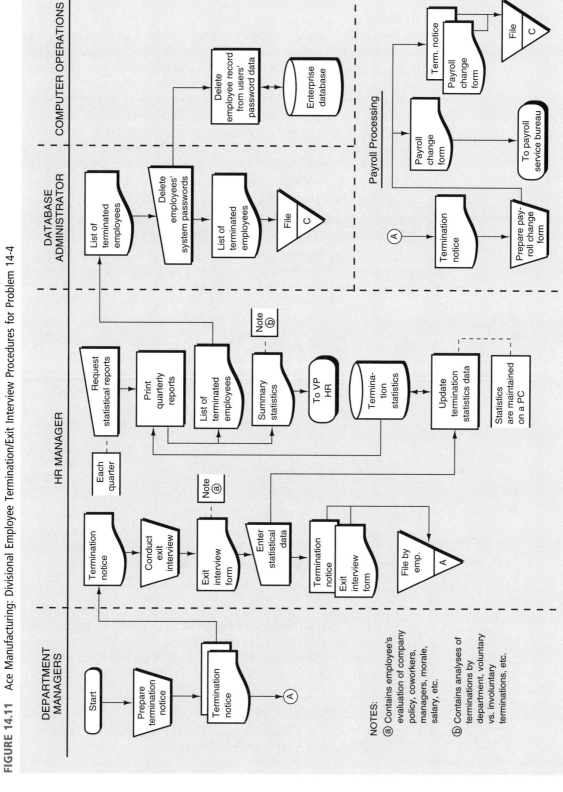

P14-6 Use the DFDs in Figures 14.7 (pg. 536) and 14.8 (pg. 537) to solve this problem.

Required

Prepare a four-column table that summarizes the payroll processes, inputs, and outputs. In the first column, list the seven processes shown in the level 0 diagram (Figure 14.7). In the second column, for bubble 4.0 only, list the subsidiary functions shown in the lower-level diagram (Figure 14.8). For bubbles other than 4.0, there will be no subsidiary functions shown in column 2. For each process shown in column 1 (or subsidiary process listed in column 2), list the data flow names or the data stores that are inputs to that process (column 3) or outputs of that process (column 4). The following table has been started for you to indicate the format for your solution.

Solution Format Summary of the Payroll Processes, Inputs, and Outputs

Process	Subsidiary Functions	Inputs	Outputs
1.0 Perform data maintenance	None diagrammed in this chapter	Current tax rates	Tax rates data
2.0 Reconcile hours worked	None diagrammed in this chapter	Attendance time records	. . . Continue solution . . .

P14-7 The chapter mentions that companies frequently outsource the payroll function. Using the Internet, locate at least one company that provides payroll services and a software package (or module of an enterprise system) that may be used for in-house payroll processing. Write a paper on the positive and negative aspects of in-house versus outsourced payroll processing. (The length of the paper is at the discretion of your instructor.)

P14-8 Interview an HR manager (either by phone or in person). You should ask about the interviewee's job functions, types of decisions that are made, and information needs. Write a paper describing what you find out, and how it compares to the information from Table 14.1 (pp. 526–527).

P14-9 Find and describe an instance of payroll fraud (you may use the Internet, newspapers, or other news sources). How was the fraud committed? How was it detected? What was the control weakness that allowed the fraud to happen? What were the monetary losses associated with the fraud?

ACCESS P14-10 This problem should be completed with database software, such as Microsoft Access.

1. Using the E-R diagram in **Figure 14.12**, implement the four related entities as tables using Microsoft Access (or any other database software acceptable to your instructor). Link the tables using the cardinalities shown in the figure. For the tables, use the following attributes:

   a. Skill Sets table: Skill ID (as primary key), description, pay rate, and any required foreign keys

   b. Training Courses table: Course ID (as primary key), course date, location, and any required foreign keys

FIGURE 14.12

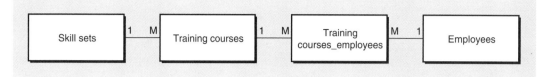

c. Training Course_Employees relationship table: since this is a relationship table, you need to determine the composite primary key, and course grade

d. Employees table: Employee ID (as primary key), last name, first name, date hired, pay rate, and any foreign keys

2. Create forms for each table from part 1 of this problem and use the forms to populate the tables with representative data. Forms should be in good order, readable, and properly formatted. Create at least three records in each table. Print out the populated tables and one instance of each form.

3. Design three queries using the tables from part 1 of this problem. Print out the output of each query and attach an explanation as to why someone would be interested in the output of each query.

4. Using the report function in Access, design a report for each query from part 3 of this problem. Reports should be in good order, readable, and properly formatted. Print out each report.

Required

As directed by your instructor, submit the completed database file and the printouts noted above.

CHAPTER 15

Integrated Production Processes (IPP)

Learning Objectives

After reading this chapter, you should be able to:

- Appreciate the forces that exist in the contemporary production environment and the trends that have emerged.
- Understand the role of enterprise systems (ES) in the integration of the total manufacturing environment.
- Understand the key inputs, outputs, data, processes, and terminology included in modern integrated production processes (IPP).
- Understand the relationship between integrated production processes (IPP) and other key business processes within a manufacturing organization, including HR management, purchasing, order entry/sales (OE/S), and inventory management.
- Understand the role of inventory management systems and their relationship to integrated production processes (IPP).

In 2008, Avid, a leading producer of digital audio and video technologies, hired Omnify Software to implement its Empower Product Lifecycle Management (PLM) software. A primary reason for this decision was Avid's desire to improve collaboration and integration among its manufacturing, engineering, logistics, and purchasing departments, as well as with its customers and suppliers. In particular, Avid wanted to streamline its design and production processes, to improve communication and cooperation between its engineering and manufacturing departments, and to create a unified environment for its global product development teams to easily find and share product information in real time. To achieve these goals, Omnify installed a wide range of software applications that, for example, allow engineers instantaneous access to global information about device components and provide manufacturing personnel state-of-the-art visualization of engineering designs. Omnify also replaced Avid's multiple separate databases with a centralized database built around Avid's SAP ERP system and tied their Empower PLM software to the SAP system. These changes dramatically improved interdepartmental communication, allowing engineering change orders (ECOs), bills of materials (BOMs), and various other documents and forms to be immediately available to authorized users. Among the many significant benefits Avid has gained from installing Omnify's Empower PLM are radically shortened design-to-production cycles, new products built to the latest revisions from customers, and automatic receipt of parts from its global suppliers by allowing them real-time—although restricted—access to Avid's database. Other improvements include eliminating manual data entry, seamless bidirectional data sharing between SAP and Empower, and—probably best of all—increased bottom-line profitability.[1]

Because integrated production systems can help companies achieve greater success, this chapter explores issues surrounding production scheduling and inventory management. We also look at the role of the accountant and business advisor in improving the efficiency and effectiveness of integrated production processes, and ultimately the profitability of the firm.

Synopsis

We begin by examining the state of competition in the international manufacturing environment and the pressures that continue to increase for organizations to reduce costs, increase the global reach of their operations across the value chain, and promptly design and deliver innovative products to meet customers' ever-increasing demands. In this context, we discuss how product and process innovation, supply chain management (SCM), and management accounting systems combine with IPP to manage global complexity. Then we provide an overview of the steps in IPP, emphasizing the role of enterprise systems and management accounting information in managing this process. We also describe inventory management and its important role in IPP.

Our approach in this chapter is to provide a broad overview of IPP, focusing on how they integrate with other processes we discussed in earlier chapters and their importance to achieving the strategic objectives of manufacturing businesses. Entire books have been devoted to some individual topics in this chapter, so each process described may encompass many individual activities. Our aim is to provide you with an idea of the key goals of the processes, a basic understanding of how they work, and exposure to some of the key terminology involved.[2]

Competing in a Global Manufacturing Environment

If one area in particular has been most impacted by global competition, it is clearly the manufacturing sector. Manufacturing is generally the quickest route for developing countries to increase their wealth and increase the wages of their citizens. Further, business as a whole and manufacturing in particular know no national boundaries in the rapidly growing global marketplace.

---

[1]This vignette is based on "Integration of Omnify PLM and SAP Helps Avid Eliminate Duplicate Data Entry and Improve Communication between Design and Manufacturing," (2009), Omnify Success Stories, www.omnifysoft.com/customers/Stories/Omnify-Avid-PLM-Success-Story.pdf, accessed June 3, 2010; and "Omnify Software Streamlines Design and Manufacturing Processes for Avid," Marketwire, December 7, 2009, www.marketwire.com/press-release/Omnify-Software-Streamlines-Design-and-Manufacturing-Processes-for-Avid-1086510.htm, accessed June 3, 2010.

[2]We do not present a system flowchart or control matrix for IPP. Although controls are very important in IPP, especially for assuring a high level of operational effectiveness, the level of detail necessary to make these documents meaningful is beyond the scope of our coverage.

For instance, several Asian countries have become major players in the automobile industry, competing heavily in the United States, Australia/New Zealand, and European markets. Automakers (as well as manufacturers in a host of other industries) have been forced to become lean, automated, customer-focused, and efficient organizations in order to survive. Recent studies have reflected such efforts with observations of marked improvements in productivity.

Successful manufacturers must deal with the complexity caused by exploding globalization. In a 2003 survey of more than 392 manufacturing executives across North America and Europe, Deloitte® Touche Tohmatsu identified three key drivers of complexity in manufacturing operations in the new millennium:[3]

- *Pressure to reduce costs throughout the value chain:* Because of global competition and the enormous buying power of "mega-retailers" such as Wal-Mart, many companies have been forced to move operations across their value chains throughout the globe to reduce costs. Companies surveyed expect growth in sourcing of operations, from engineering to raw materials to manufacturing, in other countries such as China and India, with little growth in these domestic operations.

- *Pursuit of new lucrative markets and channels:* Given the cost of developing and manufacturing products, companies continually seek to enter new markets around the globe to pursue growth and economies of scale and scope. The pursuit of new, growing markets such as China also explains why these same manufacturers are sourcing more and more of their value chain operations in these countries, to better and more efficiently serve these customers.

- *The quickening pace of product innovation:* Executives surveyed reported new product innovation as the number one driver of revenue growth. Additionally, with competition and globalization come greater and greater efforts to customize products to meet local needs. Joining this need for customization with reductions in the life cycle for new products leads to a need to introduce more successful products more quickly than ever.

Another Deloitte & Touche report describes the key characteristics of those companies that are successful at managing the pressures resulting from global complexity.[4]

Enterprise Systems

- *Improved internal business processes in the areas of customers, products, and supply chains:* These efforts include increased activities related to marketing, sales, and customer service; better innovation, engineering, and research and development for products; and improved sourcing, manufacturing, and distribution for supply chains.

- *Better use of technology to increase integration within and among these three areas (customers, products, and supply chains):* Benefits from improved operations in these three areas are further leveraged by using *enterprise systems* technologies such as *customer relationship management (CRM)*, as discussed in Chapter 10, to link marketing sales and service and provide information measures such as customer service and retention; *product life-cycle management (PLM)* (introduced in Chapter 2 and discussed

---

[3]*The Challenge of Complexity in Global Manufacturing: Critical Trends in Supply Chain Management* (London: Deloitte & Touche, 2003).

[4]*Mastering Complexity in Global Manufacturing: Driving Profits and Growth through Value Chain Synchronization* (London: Deloitte & Touche, 2003).

later in this chapter) to tie together the steps of product development and better manage profitability; and warehouse and transportation optimization systems to tie together suppliers, distribution, and manufacturing, and develop end-to-end SCM strategies, as discussed in Chapter 12.

- *Better general capabilities in the areas of collaboration, flexibility, visibility, and technology:* These capabilities, both within the company and extending out to customers and suppliers, help the best companies integrate their efforts across customer, product, and supply chain activities to focus on overall profitability. They ensure that *engineers consider the flexibility of products they design*, that supply chain designers consider the future need for rapid change in supply chain processes, and that customer communication lines lead to products that meet or exceed customer expectations.

Technology Application 15.1 (pg. 564) presents three case studies illustrating how companies have demonstrated these characteristics to increase overall profitability.

Deloitte's research shows that globalization and efforts to manage it pay off. The 7 percent of survey respondents with both high *value chain* capabilities and high global dispersion of sourcing, manufacturing, engineering, and marketing/sales operations across their value chains were 73 percent more profitable than their counterparts with low value chain capabilities and global dispersion.

In the following sections, we further explore several of the trends in global manufacturing companies that help them achieve the level of integration described previously. In particular, we examine the following four key components of effective, integrated production processes in more depth:

1. Product innovation
2. Production process innovation
3. Supply chain management
4. Management accounting systems

Product Innovation

Designing innovative products and getting them to market quickly is critical for being competitive in today's complex global manufacturing environment. To accomplish rapid product innovation, cooperation among engineering, manufacturing, and marketing is vital. Production conventionally has been organized along functional lines. Under the functional approach to developing a product, the process is undertaken as a series of discrete, independent steps, such as design, engineering, purchasing, manufacturing, and so forth. The schism that results between the "me think" design component and the "you do" manufacturing element has been extremely inefficient both in terms of getting products to market on time and in controlling production costs.

Enterprise systems facilitate the integration of all aspects of the product design, manufacturing, and marketing processes. Dramatic productivity gains have been achieved by companies that adopt a *value chain* approach that views production as a continuum, beginning with product design and running all the way through materials acquisition, manufacturing, distribution, marketing, and servicing of the product in the field. For example, with a value chain approach and effective use of enterprise systems, when changes are made to product design (engineering change orders), the change is automatically messaged to the production facilities, and the change is incorporated in real time. Japanese manufacturers have been particularly successful in improving product quality by fostering close cooperation between the functions of design and

Enterprise
Systems

manufacturing. Design engineers and manufacturing engineers coordinate their efforts to design a defect-free product (also known as a *zero defect* product—described later in Exhibit 15.1, pg. 579). The result has been a streamlined manufacturing process that eliminates (or drastically reduces) the need to inspect the product.

More recently, companies have worked to implement *product life-cycle management (PLM)* systems, which are *ERP* modules or *enterprise systems* add-ons that organize data by product, including designs, manufacturing specifications, quality, and warranty performance. These systems allow collaborative access to this data across the organization by key suppliers and customers, and increase innovation in product design, reduce design time, and improve product performance. See the story about Avid and Omnify at the beginning of this chapter for a recent example of how PLM can benefit a company.

Technology Application 15.1

MANAGING GLOBAL MANUFACTURING COMPLEXITY

Case 1: Fiorucci Foods—Old World Quality Supported by High-Tech Systems

Since the mid 1800s, Fiorucci Foods has manufactured and distributed Italian deli meats. As the company grew, management decided that although its traditional products were a key to success, the company's traditional systems were a hindrance. In addition to internal needs to track products through the production process (sometimes, nearly a year for products such as prosciutto), there are also government regulations that must be considered. After replacing fragmented information systems with a state-of-the-art ERP system that included integrated production capabilities, Fiorucci has improved order accuracy and customer satisfaction; at the same time, product cost has declined through improved inventory control and usage. In addition to the positive impact on the company's bottom line, the capability of the system to track and trace products through the manufacturing process of the company helps protect Fiorucci's reputation as a supplier of quality products throughout the world.

Case 2: GlaxoSmithKline Synchronizes Manufacturing Plants to Optimize Supply Chain Management

GlaxoSmithKline, a U.K. pharmaceutical company with a history going back to the 1700s, tackled complexity through global, rather than local, optimization of its supply chain. Prior to reengineering, plants produced goods for the countries or continents where they were located. The changes resulted in a drastic reduction in the number of plants, which now serve regions of the world. Plants are focused on one of three areas—flexible plants that can ramp up quickly to make new products; plants procuring large quantities of established drugs, whose volumes are more predictable; and plants dedicated to established pharmaceuticals, especially those for small markets. This strategy, which results in single plants serving larger regions around the world, helps the company optimize supply chain activities for each type of product and overcome local supply constraints that might get in the way of quickly delivering new products. The result was savings of $500 million a year.

Case 3: Samsung Electronics Gets in Touch with Customers and Markets

Samsung, a South Korean consumer electronics company, is the number one maker of TVs in the world. Although many management decisions have supported the company's growth to capture 13.6 percent of the global TV market, Lee Chun Jae, the operating chief of Samsung's SCM system, gives that system much of the credit. Lee compares his job to the conductor of an orchestra and says "SCM allows all units to operate in harmony." That harmony is especially sweet sounding because Samsung's 20 TV and monitor factories span 11 countries. Having a reliable SCM system is key when gathering information and making decisions in the fast-changing electronics business. The system also helps Samsung when local shortages occur. Because many internal components of their products have been standardized, the system can easily recommend production shifts to alternate facilities. The bottom line—leveraging the supply chain, and the corresponding SCM system, helped Samsung's TV revenues grow from $3.3 billion in 2004 to 18.6 billion in 2007!

Sources: K. Hoffman, "New Technology Helps Assure Old World Quality," *Supply Chain Manufacturing & Logistics,* September 26, 2005; www.fioruccifood.it, accessed May 28, 2010; *Mastering Complexity in Global Manufacturing: Driving Profits and Growth through Value Chain Synchronization* (London: Deloitte & Touche, 2003); "What Makes Samsung Tops in TVs," *BusinessWeek,* March 13, 2008.

Production Process Innovation

A major contribution of Japanese manufacturers has been their managing of *through-put* time. **Throughput time** is the time it takes from when authorization is made for goods to be produced to when the goods are completed. Japanese companies have accomplished much in this area, mainly by switching from *push* to *pull* manufacturing. With **push manufacturing**, the sales forecast drives the production plan, and goods are produced in large batches. Each machine performs its operation on the batch, and then the entire job waits until the operation can be started on the next machine in the sequence.

Conversely, with **pull manufacturing**, production is initiated as individual sales orders are received. Theoretically, each job consists of a "batch" of one unit. In pacing production, an idle machine pulls the next part from the previous machine as soon as that part is available, thus pulling goods through the factory only when needed to satisfy demand. As soon as machine A completes its operation on unit 1, machine B starts work on that unit, and machine A begins on unit 2.

Adopting the pull approach has several natural concomitants:

- *Short production runs:* Rather than producing for stock, production runs reflect the size of orders received.
- *Continuous flow operations:* To approach the "ideal" batch size of one unit, plant layouts are reorganized so that goods can proceed in a continuous flow from one operation to the next.
- *Cellular manufacturing:* The modified plant layouts have led to a "cellular" arrangement of machines. In the traditional factory layout, machines are organized by departments, each containing similar types of machines. With **cellular manufacturing**, on the other hand, machines are organized in clusters or "cells" that contain all of the needed resources (machines, tools, labor) to produce a family of products. A natural extension of the cellular physical layout is a management orientation that takes a global view of overall work cell throughput rather than a narrower focus related to the productivity of individual machines. In fact, it is not uncommon for a single worker to run several machines in a cell or for workers to be at least trained to operate multiple machines.
- *Reduced work-in-process and finished goods inventories:* By reducing production runs, fewer resources are in process at any point in time, reducing work-in-process inventory. In a pure pull environment, finished goods inventory includes only items that await shipment, thereby reducing inventory storage costs.
- *Reduced floor space:* This economy is a result of improved plant layout and elimination of space needed for inventory storage.

Supply Chain Management (SCM)

Chapter 12 defines *supply chain management (SCM)* as the combination of processes and procedures used to ensure the delivery of goods and services to customers at the lowest cost while providing the highest value to customers. Figure 12.2 in Chapter 12 (pg. 442) provided an overview of the many internal and external linkages that make up a modern supply chain and described these in the context of a merchandising organization. As evidenced by the prominence of SCM in our earlier discussion of the challenges facing manufacturers in an age of global complexity, the challenges of SCM discussed in Chapter 12 are further magnified in a manufacturing setting. Rather than being concerned with forecasting demand, lead times, and reorder points for finished goods, a manufacturer must forecast demand, determine lead times, monitor inventory levels for

Enterprise
Systems

numerous raw materials, *and* plan for the manufacture of finished goods. Additionally, the time and resources necessary to manufacture key subassemblies, separately manufactured components used in the final product, must be considered. These subassemblies may be manufactured in the same plant as the final product, or they may be manufactured in a separate plant across the globe.

E-Business

E-business plays an increasingly important role in this process. Ever more often, suppliers are gaining access to the organization's production planning schedules to set their own production schedules and to ensure the capability to fulfill orders. Similarly, the organization is opening its systems to the customer to allow the customer to view inventory and production levels before placing orders. To accomplish this in a cost-effective manner, Internet technologies are being linked to organizations' *ERP* and *SCM software* to provide *portals* to external organizations for safe and secure access to critical business information. In short, the simplicity of the Internet is enabling the continual growth in complexity of business processes and the underlying organizational information systems.

Of particular interest is the enhanced capability that SCM software provides for *available to promise* and *capable to promise* planning. **Available to promise planning** is the accumulation of the data on current inventories, sales commitments, and planned production to determine whether the production of finished goods will be sufficient to commit to additional sales orders. **Capable to promise planning** is the accumulation of the data on current inventories, sales commitments, planned production and excess production capacity, or other planned production capacity that could be quickly converted to production of the desired finished goods necessary to fulfill a sales order request. The former addresses the planned production capacity that can be used to fulfill *additional* customer orders. The latter addresses the capability to divert production capacity from other production facilities that have not been previously planned for use in producing the product needed for an incoming customer order.

Management Accounting Systems

E-Business

In this section, we will introduce you to some changes that have already occurred (or are evolving) in cost management and cost accounting. Many of these changes have their origins in the developments that have transpired in the production arena and that were discussed or alluded to in the preceding sections. In addition, many of these changes are a result of the capability of *enterprise systems* to capture sales, product design, and production data in real time and to share this data across the *value chain*. **Table 15.1** summarizes several key accounting changes as related to parallel changes in production processes.

Take some time to study Table 15.1. As do certain other parts of this chapter, the table assumes that you have a background in managerial/cost accounting. Probably the most important theme in Table 15.1 is the importance of increasing the accuracy and timeliness of cost information and the use of this information for the strategic management of products and processes throughout the value chain from design to manufacturing to marketing and post-sales servicing.

Activity-based costing is prevalent in companies seeking to increase cost accuracy and usefulness. **Activity-based costing (ABC)** is a costing approach in which detailed costs to perform activities throughout the value chain are computed and can be managed or assigned to cost objects, including products. ABC recognizes that *cost drivers* (measures of the amount of activity performed) other than production volume or direct labor explain many activity costs. Cost per unit of the cost driver is computed for each activity. Costs are then assigned to products based on the amount of the cost driver used.

TABLE 15.1 Summary of Trends in Cost Management/Cost Accounting

Development in the Production Process Environment	Related[a] Trend in Cost Management/Accounting
Shorter product life cycles that require cost recovery over a shorter period	Emphasis on product life-cycle costing
	Shift from after-the-fact cost control reporting to reporting designed to assist strategic planning and decision making
	Increased emphasis on managing costs versus merely accounting for costs
	Attack waste as opposed to merely reporting variances
Flexible manufacturing systems	Flexible cost systems that are also responsive to change
Factory automation	Shift in cost structure from variable costs to fixed costs
	Reduction in the direct labor cost component and in the use of direct labor for applying overhead[b]
	Increase in the overhead component of total cost[c]
	Use of a fourth cost category, direct technology, in addition to the traditional direct materials, direct labor, and overhead categories
	Use of activity-based costing (ABC) systems
Automating the information system	Real-time data capture on the factory floor
	Shift away from standard cost systems back to actual cost systems
	Reduction in the administrative costs of gathering data
	Automated inventory orders via EDI without human interaction
	Collecting statistical data in addition to financial data
Cellular organization of the factory	Elimination of *detail* reporting by shop order and by operation; instead, use of accounting for cell throughput time
	Use of cell throughput time instead of direct labor to apply overhead
	Trend toward process cost systems and away from job order cost systems
Reduced work-in-process and finished goods inventories	For internal purposes at least, abandonment of full-absorption costing, which loses its significance in the absence of inventories
	Accumulation of costs for decision making instead of for valuing inventories

[a]For simplicity, each cost trend has been listed only once. You should recognize that the items in the right column might relate to more than one development in the left column.
[b]For instance, in some high-tech companies, direct labor could account for as little as 5 percent of total cost.
[c]For some companies, manufacturing overhead may be as much as 70 percent of total cost.

An example of an activity that might be performed for a production facility is purchasing materials; and the cost driver might be the number of purchase orders prepared.

By using a variety of cost drivers, activity-based costs can be computed for all activities across the value chain, not just manufacturing activities. Detailed activity cost information and increasingly accurate and comprehensive product costs can be used to aid strategic decision making throughout the value chain. Information about cost drivers and activity costs can be used to improve product designs and production processes, to determine the best mix of marketing campaigns, or to assess the cost of poor quality. Using ABC information, product managers can more effectively manage **life-cycle costs** (the sum of the costs to design, produce, market, deliver, and support a product throughout the product's life cycle from initial conception to final discontinuance) and more precisely predict product profitability.

Many of the other changes identified in Table 15.1 are also aimed at more accurate identification of costs in a timely manner so that this information can be used more strategically. Many of the changes also stem from the importance of technology in the production process. For example, the use of a new cost category—direct technology—allows these costs, which are becoming a larger component of manufacturing costs, to be directly estimated and more effectively managed. A separate cost category for these items is possible because of *cellular manufacturing*, which devotes machines exclusively to single product lines.

Integrated Production Processes (IPP)

Within the framework of the globally complex manufacturing organization, our primary purposes in this section are to (1) acquaint you with the principal components of a modern integrated production process (IPP) and the interactions that can exist among those components and (2) provide you with basic definitions of manufacturing terms that you may encounter in your professional careers.

Enterprise
Systems

Figure 15.1 provides a level 0 DFD of an IPP. Consistent with the goal of integration across functional areas, the process actually begins at the start of the *value chain* with the design of the product and production processes (step 1.0). With information about expected or actual sales orders from the OE/S process and inventory levels from the inventory management process, a master production schedule is developed (step 2.0), followed by a detailed definition of needs for materials (step 3.0) and detailed production instructions (step 4.0). These steps initiate activities in the purchasing and HR management processes to put materials and labor resources in place to complete production. Throughout these steps, and especially as resources are used to manufacture the goods, information about the process is continuously captured (step 5.0) so that valuable managerial information can be generated. As you can see from the number of integration points with other business processes in Figure 15.1, *enterprise systems* will play a vital part in managing the IPP. Each of these steps will be discussed in more detail in the following sections.

In practice, one key to understanding the information processes described in Figure 15.1 is to understand the underlying terminology and recognizing the acronyms used to describe the processes by engineers, manufacturing managers, and software developers. **Table 15.2** (pg. 570) lists each of the steps in the process and provides a summary of the common manufacturing terminology used at each step, which also will be discussed in the following sections.

Design Product and Production Processes

(Figure 15.1, bubble 1.0) Consistent with the value chain concept, the IPP begins with the design of the product and production processes. With approximately 80 percent of the future cost of producing the product locked in with decisions made during design, this step is vital to determining the profitability of new product lines. *Activity-based costing (ABC)*, which provides information about the cost of production activities for existing products, can be used to develop estimates of the future cost of producing new products as well as potential cost changes from product and production process design changes.

The entire design process can be automated through the use of **computer-aided design (CAD)** and **computer-aided engineering (CAE)**. Because of their close relationships to each other, it is not uncommon to talk about CAD/CAE as a single element. CAD/CAE is an application of computer technology that automates the product

FIGURE 15.1   Level 0 DFD of the IPP

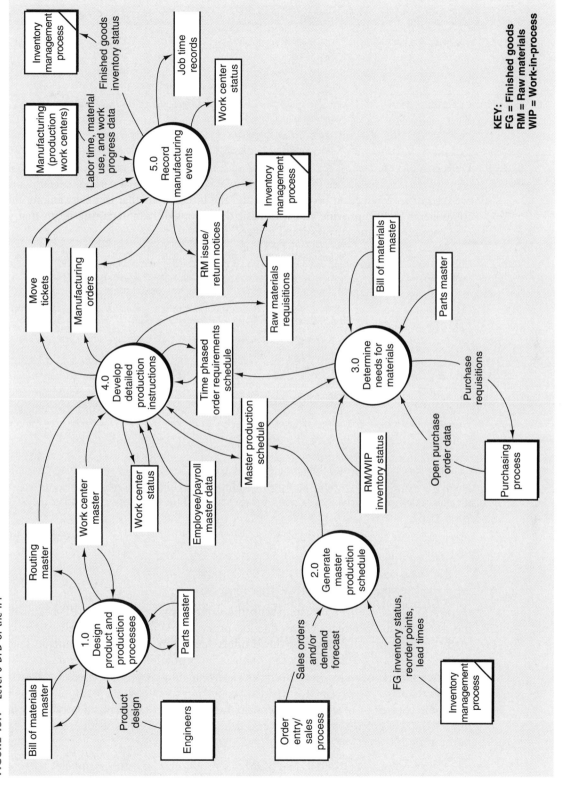

KEY:
FG = Finished goods
RM = Raw materials
WIP = Work-in-process

TABLE 15.2   Key Manufacturing Terminology in the IPP Steps

IPP Step	Related Manufacturing Terminology
Step 1.0: Design product and production processes	*Computer-aided design/computer-aided engineering* (CAD/CAE) is used to automate product design. *Computer-aided process planning (CAPP)* is used to generate manufacturing instructions and routings based on product requirements.
Step 2.0: Generate master production schedule	*Global inventory management* ensures that production schedules consider inventory availability across the global enterprise. *Production, planning, and control* is the process of generating a schedule, determining detailed material needs, developing detailed production instructions, and tracking data during production.
Step 3.0: Determine needs for materials	*Materials requirements planning (little mrp)* is used to develop a time-phased requirements schedule for materials and subassemblies.
Step 4.0: Develop detailed production instructions	*Capacity requirements planning (CRP)* is used to develop detailed machine- and labor-use schedules that consider available capacity. *Manufacturing resource planning (MRP)* incorporates mrp, CRP, and planning for labor and financial capital.
External entity: Manufacturing (production work centers)	*Flexible manufacturing systems (FMS)* are automated systems used to control production that can quickly incorporate automated engineering design changes. *Computer-aided manufacturing (CAM)* is used to link machines, monitor production, and provide automatic feedback to control operations. *Automated storage and retrieval systems (AS/RS)* store and retrieve parts and tools. *Automated guided vehicle systems (AGVS)* deliver parts and tools among multiple work centers.
Step 5.0: Record manufacturing events	*Shop floor control (SFC)* is used to monitor and record the status of manufacturing orders and work centers during the manufacturing process.

design process, including but not limited to the functions of geometric modeling, materials stress and strain analysis, drafting, storing product specifications, and mechanically simulating a product's performance. The main objectives of CAD/CAE are to:

- Improve design productivity
- Reduce design lead time
- Enhance design quality
- Facilitate access to and storage of product designs
- Make the design of multiple products more efficient by eliminating redundant design effort
- Execute design changes almost immediately through the use of electronic messaging to notify the shop floor

Enterprise
Systems

With the use of *enterprise systems*, the electronic designs produced using CAD/CAE become the basis for developing detailed production schedules (step 2.0) as well as the electronic control of production machines. In addition to the detailed product design, the CAD/CAE process results in several data stores of information that are used later in the IPP:

- **Bill of materials (BOM):** The BOM is a listing of all the subassemblies, parts, and raw materials that go into a parent assembly showing the quantity of each that is required to make an assembly. Often, engineers will work to design several products with common subassemblies. This way, manufacturing processes are more standardized, quality can be improved, and costs are reduced. The BOM provides the basis for later orders of raw materials (bubble 3.0) when a finished good is to be produced.

- **Parts master:** The parts master or raw material (RM) inventory master lists the detailed specifications for each raw materials item. An engineer must specify the information for a new record in the parts master when a new part is used in a product design. Often, existing parts will be used in new products to reduce needed ordering and carrying costs for the inventory.

- **Routing master:** The routing master specifies the operations necessary to complete a subassembly or finished good and the sequence of these operations. The routing master also includes the machining tolerances; the tools, jigs, and fixtures required; and the time allowance for each operation. The routing master is vital when developing detailed production instructions (step 4.0). **Computer-aided process planning (CAPP)** is often used in developing the routing master for new products. CAPP is an automated decision support system that generates manufacturing operations instructions and routings based on information about machining requirements and machine capabilities.

- **Work center master:** The work center master describes each *work center* available for producing products, including information such as the machine available at the station, its capacity, its maintenance requirements, labor needs to operate it, and so on. A **workstation** is the assigned location where a worker performs his or her job; it could be a machine or a workbench. A group of similar workstations constitutes a **work center**. When new products require new machines or production activities, a new record in the work center master must be created.

Generate Master Production Schedule

(*Figure 15.1, pg. 569, bubble 2.0*) With products and production processes in place, the next step in the IPP is generating a *master production schedule (MPS)* to drive the production process. The **master production schedule (MPS)** is a statement of *specific* production goals developed from forecasts of demand, actual sales orders, or inventory information. It describes the specific items to be manufactured, the quantities to be produced, and the production timetable. Depending on the company's approach, the schedule may be based on information about finished goods' inventory levels and reorder points, sales forecasts, or actual sales orders coupled with inventory levels. Based on the master production schedule, more detailed schedules for ordering raw materials and scheduling work center operations are developed in steps 3.0 and 4.0. **Figure 15.2** (pg. 572) depicts a forecast of manufacturing orders (master production schedule), including the specific items to be manufactured, the quantities to be produced, and the production timetable. This schedule, developed without regard to actual sales orders, shows zero actual demand.

Given the increased emphasis on cost reduction for successful global competition in manufacturing, companies cannot afford to generate too much of the wrong products and absorb their costs. Instead, extensive use of *enterprise systems* to gather and analyze data from past and future (i.e., forecast) sales and inventory levels is used to develop a more accurate production plan. The result minimizes unnecessary inventory investment and maximizes the likelihood that the right products will be in place at the right time.

Enterprise Systems

The master production schedule is based on information from multiple sources. A primary source is actual orders from customers. Ideally, a manufacturer can cut *throughput time* to the point that it can produce goods only as customer orders are received. In this way, the manufacturer minimizes the risk of goods not selling and maximizes the likelihood that it will produce exactly the product desired by the customer.

Enterprise
Systems

Often, however, the time necessary to produce goods and distribute them to locations around the globe necessitates producing goods in anticipation of sales orders. In this case, a variety of techniques may be used to develop sophisticated demand forecasting models that help manufacturers estimate the need for goods. These techniques can

FIGURE 15.2   Forecasted Manufacturing Orders (Microsoft Dynamics GP)

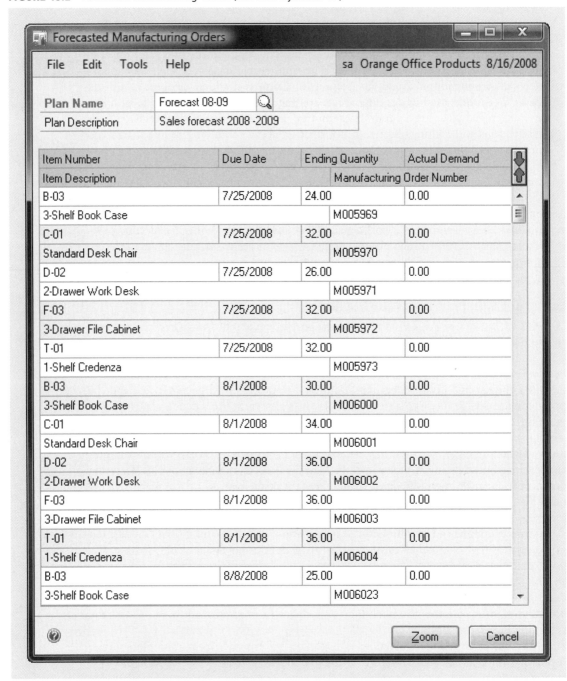

use the full complement of customer data available in the *enterprise system* about past sales levels and buying patterns to improve forecast accuracy. These models frequently take advantage of information from the *CRM* system as discussed in Chapter 10 and likely use some of the *data mining* techniques also described in Chapter 10 to identify important patterns and relationships in the level of demand.

Finally, the inventory management system also provides vital inputs to developing a better master production schedule. The inventory management system provides data about levels of finished goods (FG) inventory currently on hand and also gathers data about goods scheduled to be produced. Additionally, inventory data tracked over time by the company's *enterprise system*, such as lead times, optimal inventory levels, frequency of stock-outs, and expected quality levels, all help develop better production schedules.

One trend in inventory management facilitated by *enterprise systems* has been particularly useful in reducing inventory levels and better satisfying customer demand. This trend is *global inventory management*. In the **global inventory management** approach, inventory needs and production capabilities are matched across the entire global enterprise, not just at a regional level. Less sophisticated inventory management systems associate specific inventory locations and manufacturing plants with specific sales regions. For example, the South American sales region of a large electronics manufacturer might look primarily at manufacturing plants and warehouses within its own geographic region when examining the availability of inventory or production capacity to fill a large order. If insufficient capacity was available in this region, the order might be rejected, or a delivery date too far in the future might be quoted, resulting in losing the business to a competitor.

With *global inventory management*, the South American sales region can examine inventory and production capacity across the entire company's global organization when determining its capability to fill an order. Of course, if the product was to be produced in a factory across the globe in Germany, for example, the South American sales division would need to consider additional lead time to transport the goods to the customer and also the associated distribution costs, but these pieces of information would be readily available from the *enterprise database*.

Armed with information from the *enterprise system* about the sales forecast, actual sales orders, and inventory data, the *master production schedule* can be developed, as depicted in Figure 15.1 (pg. 569), bubble 2.0. Developing the MPS, along with the remaining steps in the IPP, is often referred to as the production, planning, and control process. *Production, planning, and control* involves the *logistics*, or "physical" aspects of converting raw materials into finished goods. As such, the **production, planning, and control** process manages the orderly and timely movement of goods through the production process. It includes activities such as planning material, people, and machine requirements; scheduling; routing; and monitoring the progress of goods through the factory.

Determine Needs for Materials

(*Figure 15.1, bubble 3.0*) After the master production schedule is determined, an important step in completing production in a timely manner is identifying, ordering, and receiving materials. At the heart of this task is the *materials requirements planning (little mrp)* process. **Materials requirements planning (mrp)** is a process that uses BOMs, raw material and work-in-process (RM/WIP) inventory status data, open order data, and the master production schedule to calculate a **time-phased order requirements schedule** for materials and subassemblies. The schedule shows the time period when a *manufacturing order* or purchase order should be released so that the subassemblies and raw materials will be available when needed. The process involves working backward from the date production is to begin to determine the timing for manufacturing subassemblies and then moving back further to determine the date that orders for materials must be issued into the purchasing process. In an *enterprise system*, this process is performed automatically using a variety of data from the enterprise database, including the following:

- *Bills of materials (BOMs)* showing the items and quantities required as developed by engineering
- *Parts master* data, which contains information about part number, description, unit of measure, where used, order policy, lead time, and safety stock
- *Raw materials (RM)* and *work-in-process inventory status* data showing the current quantities on hand and quantities already reserved for production for the materials and subassemblies
- *Open purchase order (PO)* data showing the existing orders for materials

The process begins by **exploding the BOM** (shown in **Figure 15.3**), which involves extending a BOM to determine the total of each component required to manufacture a given quantity of an upper-level assembly or subassembly, such as the 3-Shelf Book Case, specified in the MPS. Based on lead-time data for producing and ordering, materials and subassembly requirements are output in a *time-phased order requirements schedule*, which is illustrated in **Figure 15.4** for the 3-Shelf Book Case.

FIGURE 15.3 Bill of Materials (Microsoft Dynamics GP)

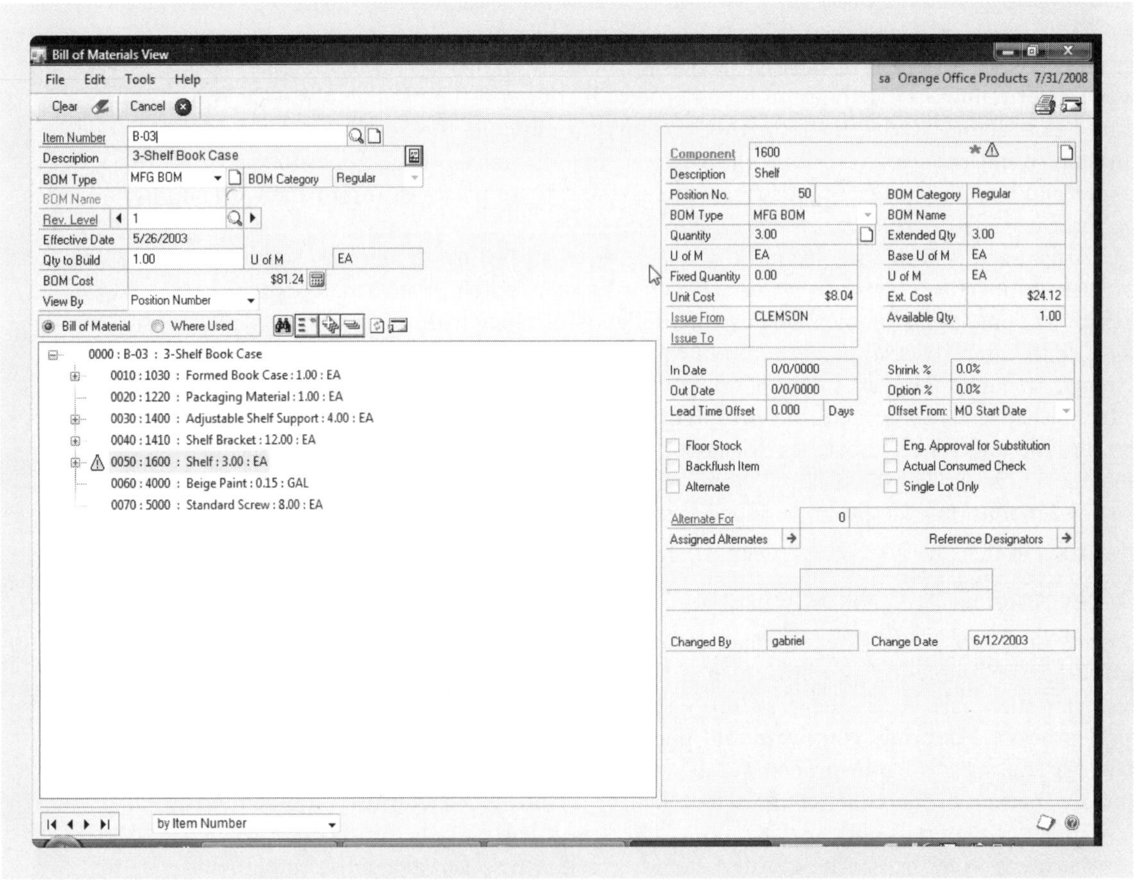

FIGURE 15.4   MRP Workbench, Including Order Requirements (Microsoft Dynamics GP)

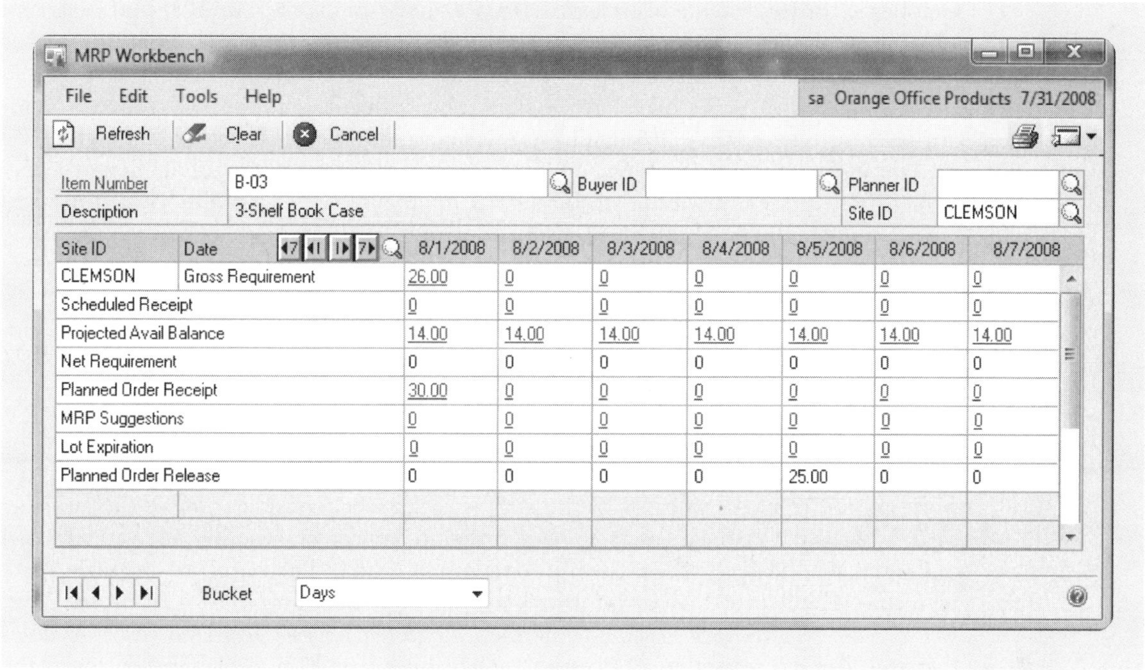

Based on this schedule and open PO data, purchase requisitions are generated and sent to purchasing.

To illustrate the "explosion" of a BOM, suppose that the BOM for one mousetrap reflects the following:

Part No.	Description	Quantity
100	Wood base (36 in.)	1
101	Coil spring	2
102	Wood screw (5/8 in.)	2
103	U-shaped wire rod (24 in.)	1
104	Cheese holder and hook	1

Assume that the MPS calls for making 500 mousetraps in the week ended October 4, 20XX. Exploding the BOM results in the following materials requirements:

Part No.	Quantity	Calculation (End Units Times Quantity Per)
100	500	(500×1)
101	1,000	(500×2)
102	1,000	(500×2)
103	500	(500×1)
104	500	(500×1)

Allowing for the lead time needed to have the parts available during the week of October 4, orders would be released for 500 units of parts 100, 103, and 104, and 1,000 units of parts 101 and 102, assuming open orders were not already in process for these materials.

E-business and SCM may have a significant influence on the *mrp* process. With greater integration between manufacturer and vendor systems, actual orders for raw materials may be triggered by vendor systems that monitor master production schedule information and automatically ship orders at the appropriate time (i.e., *vendor-managed inventory, VMI*). Even if this ideal level of integration is not quite achieved, electronic transmission of orders may greatly reduce the necessary lead time for placing orders for raw materials.

Develop Detailed Production Instructions

(Figure 15.1, pg. 569, bubble 4.0) Materials are not the only resources necessary for beginning production. Detailed instructions showing exactly when the goods will be processed through each necessary work center and the labor necessary to complete the work are the result of step 4.0 of the IPP. In particular, consideration of the available capacity of these resources may have a profound impact on whether the organization can ultimately achieve the master production schedule. The **capacity requirements planning (CRP)** process uses information from the *master production schedule* and *time-phased order requirements schedule* to develop *detailed* machine- and labor-use schedules that consider the feasibility of production schedules based on available capacity in the work center status records. Ultimately, this process may lead to modifications to the *master production schedule* or *time-phased inventory requirements schedule* if sufficient capacity does not exist to complete these schedules as planned. After these adjustments are completed, CRP assigns targeted start/completion dates to operations (*workstations*) or groups of operations (*work centers*) and releases manufacturing orders and move tickets to the factory.

Manufacturing orders (MOs) convey authority for the manufacture of a specified product or subassembly in a specified quantity and describe the material, labor, and machine requirements for the job. The MO is the official trigger to begin manufacturing operations. When MOs are released, they are generally accompanied by **move tickets** (typically in the form of bar code tags) that authorize and record movement of a job from one work center to another. The move ticket contains various information for tracing work completion, such as the shop work authorization number representing the job being completed; the department, machine, operator, and time of completion; and check boxes for completion of current task and inspection of prior tasks' completion. Generally, these data are captured by scanning the bar code to expedite data entry and improve accuracy.

Additionally, *raw materials requisitions* are sent to the inventory process. A **raw materials (RM) requisition** is an authorization that identifies the type and quantity of materials to be withdrawn from the storeroom and tracks the manufacturing order being produced and the work center needing the raw materials.

Triggered by the *time-phased order requirements*, CRP uses the following additional inputs from the *enterprise system* to accomplish its functions:

- The *routing master* shows the necessary steps and time to complete each operation to produce the product. Whereas the *BOM* shows the raw material inputs required for a single unit of finished goods output, the *routing master*, illustrated in **Figure 15.5**, performs a similar function in respect to labor and machine requirements. The *routing* *master* typically shows the sequence of operations to manufacture an end item and the standard time allowance (labor time and machine time) for each operation. Based on the production orders, the total standard (required) labor and machine hours can be predicted by reference to the routing master. The calculations are similar to those used to explode a BOM. Another parallel between the BOM and *routing master* is internal date tracking. The BOM contains the effective date of the components, whereas the *routing master* contains the date the routing was created or changed. Both of these dates provide information that may help prevent erroneous decision making in the manufacturing process.

- Resource capacity information (i.e., hours available each day/week by work center) from the *work center master data*.
- Data about the current status of work center loads from the *work center status data* (also known as *loading data*). These data can include MOs now at each work center, anticipated MOs, backlogs, and actual hours ahead or behind schedule. This data is supplemented by information from the *employee/payroll master data* that shows available labor capacities.

FIGURE 15.5   View of the Production Routing Master (Microsoft Dynamics GP)

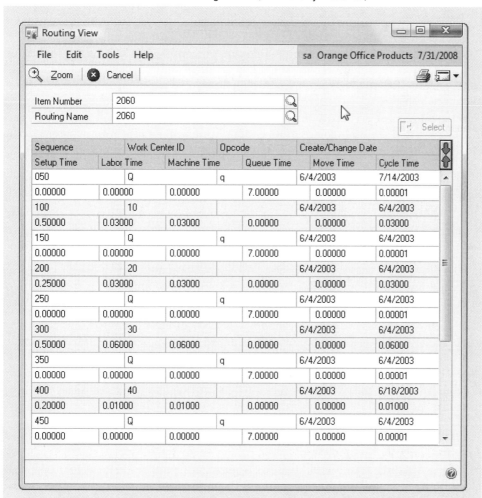

Together, mrp, CRP, and the process of planning cash flows to accommodate needs generated by the production schedule are referred to as **manufacturing resource planning (MRP)**. MRP is an integrated decision support system for planning, executing, and controlling manufacturing operations. It includes facilities for planning all manufacturing resources, including material, machines, labor, and financial capital.

Manufacturing (Production Work Centers)

The next information process shown in the DFD (Figure 15.1, pg. 569) is recording information about the manufacture of goods (step 5.0). However, before discussing the recording process and to help you understand the process, it is important to understand how the IPP accomplishes the manufacturing steps from which the data are recorded. First, we describe automating the production process, followed by a discussion of the just-in-time aspects of manufacturing.

Manufacturing Automation

Flexible manufacturing systems (FMS) are used to control the actual production of the goods. *FMS* are automated manufacturing operations systems that can react quickly to product and design changes because centralized computer controls provide real-time routing, load balancing, and production scheduling logic. Regardless of its components, any FMS has as its goal making the plant more flexible—that is, achieving the capability to quickly produce wide varieties of products using the same equipment.

Enterprise Systems

A component of FMS, **computer-aided manufacturing (CAM)**, is the application of computer and communications technology to improve productivity by linking computer numerical control (CNC) machines, monitoring production, and providing automatic feedback to control operations. CAM is intended to improve manufacturing control and reporting, coordinate material flow between machines, and facilitate rerouting. CAM systems take advantage of integration within *enterprise systems* to automatically incorporate design changes made by engineering into production processes on a nearly real-time basis, thereby decreasing the time to integrate new innovations.

Central to the *actual work performed* in an FMS environment is the use of machines that use *computer numerical control (CNC)*. These machines might be industrial robots or automated materials handling systems in the form of **automated storage and retrieval systems (AS/RS)**, which are computer-controlled machines that store and retrieve parts and tools, or **automated guided vehicle systems (AGVS)**, which are computer-based carts that are capable of delivering parts and tools among multiple work centers. Regardless of the type, numerically controlled machines, in general, represent one of the earliest efforts at factory automation; they were developed in an attempt to improve worker productivity, enhance product quality and precision, and avoid the risk posed to humans by hazardous working conditions. Differences among numerically controlled machines lie mainly in the degree of process knowledge (i.e., how to perform an action) that is transferred from the laborer to the machine (i.e., by being programmed into the machine). In some settings, a worker is still needed to load, unload, and set up the machine. Robotics and industrial parts inspection done by digital image processing machines virtually eliminate the worker and achieve productivity that is technology-paced only.

Just-in-Time Manufacturing

Enterprise Systems

Many manufacturers have simplified their manufacturing operations and reduced inventories through the use of a **just-in-time (JIT)** approach to controlling activities on the shop floor. JIT is a *pull* manufacturing philosophy or business strategy for designing

EXHIBIT 15.1   Just-in-Time (JIT) Objectives

- *Zero defects:* Products are designed to be defect-free and to eliminate the need to inspect the product after production is completed. In fact, the total quality control (TQC) approach to manufacturing, a subset of JIT, places responsibility for quality in the hands of the builder rather than in those of the inspector.
- *Zero setup times:* For instance, one world-class automobile manufacturer can change from one car model to another in 2.5 minutes, including complete retooling.

- *Small lot sizes:* Continuous flow operations are designed so that material does not sit idle and machine utilization is maximized (95 percent utilization is not uncommon).
- *Zero lead times:* As mentioned earlier, the goal is to eliminate the non–value-added (i.e., wasted in moving, waiting, and inspecting activities) portion of the total lead time.
- *Zero inventories:* In successful JIT installations, a goal is to maintain only enough inventory to satisfy demand for a few hours or days.

production processes that are more responsive to precisely timed customer delivery requirements. Several inherent JIT objectives and the means of attaining them are summarized in **Exhibits 15.1** and **15.2**, respectively. JIT success stories are impressive, but you should realize that not everyone agrees that JIT is the panacea for all ills. Before proceeding, take some time to study these exhibits. Although JIT goes beyond production, planning, and control, it frequently has a profound impact on the production, planning, and control process. Especially in repetitive manufacturing operations where inventories of raw materials are maintained, the use of a pull approach can greatly reduce the need for CRP and detailed mrp.

Record Manufacturing Events

(*Figure 15.1, pg. 569, bubble 5.0*) As previously indicated, the process of recording information about the manufacturing activities (step 5.0) is highly automated. The process used to collect this data is often called *shop floor control*. The **shop floor control (SFC) process** is devoted to monitoring and recording the status of manufacturing orders as they proceed through the factory. The SFC process also maintains work center status information showing the time ahead of or behind schedule and use levels. As each operation is finished, this fact is reported to SFC through a *completed move ticket*, and updates are made to the *open MO data* and the *work center status data*. When the final operation in the manufacturing sequence is finished, the MO is removed from the open MO data, and the inventory process is advised to add the quantities (and costs) to its finished goods records.

EXHIBIT 15.2   Just-in-Time (JIT) Implementation Features

- Arranging the factory in U-shaped work cells to optimize material flow.
- Assigning one worker to multiple machines.
- Giving production workers the responsibility and authority to stop the production line if they are running behind schedule or if they discover defective parts.
- Requiring that the daily schedule for each part or assembly remain nearly the same each day.
- Developing close working relationships with vendors to ensure that they deliver quality raw materials on the promised delivery

dates. In effect, vendors serve as extended storage facilities of the company. We alluded to these relationships when we discussed choosing a vendor and deciding when and how much to purchase in Chapter 12.
- Simplifying the process for tracking the movement of goods through the factory. JIT is often called a *kanban* process, a name taken from the Japanese words for "visual" and "card." As such, the simple kanban or *move ticket* replaces the *manufacturing order* and *route sheet* of the traditional process.

Through automation, the SFC process is able to collect valuable real-time data that can be used for immediate feedback and control. Automated data collection might involve obtaining information by scanning a *bar code* label attached to the product, coupled with entering quality and quantity information through workstations located on the factory floor. Frequently, the time needed to key-enter information about the operator is greatly shortened by reading those data from an employee badge inserted in the workstation.

Information also is collected about the time worked by laborers on each production task. Although old-fashioned paper time tickets may be used to enter data into the time records, more likely this process also will be automated through scanning employee badges and touching a few places on a computer touch screen to indicate the completion of manufacturing tasks. This same information becomes the necessary input for the payroll process. Finally, as additional raw materials are needed or unused raw materials are returned to the storeroom, raw materials issue and return notices will be recorded.

Generate Managerial Information

Enterprise Systems

The data provided by the IPP system is vital to management of the global enterprise. **Figure 15.6** shows how data collected through SFC, coupled with financial data available through other systems, help populate the enterprise database, providing key information both for managing the IPP and also for driving other processes.

Because automation is used to collect data, it is generally available in real time. For example, information about actual machine time used at a work center, collected after the move ticket is scanned following the operation, can be compared with standards from the routing master to give real-time information about variances from standard for that work center before the product is even completed. In this way, managers can take corrective action *before* they receive formal variance reports.

Key manufacturing decision-making outputs from the enterprise database include the following:

- Throughput time information derived by identifying start and completion times for manufacturing orders
- Productivity information related to labor, machines, and materials derived by comparing the standard allowance for actual production outputs to the actual levels of labor machine time and materials used
- Quality information showing actual product quality levels achieved as well as machine and process performance
- ABC information showing the costs to perform activities at each work center as well as actual cumulative costs of producing subassemblies and final products
- Information about raw materials, including quality and on-time delivery
- Other cost accounting information such as variances discussed in the next section

This information provides vital feedback for improving the IPP as follows:[5]

- Information about productivity, product quality, and activity costs can all feed back to the product and process design process to help engineers design more cost-effective products and production processes (step 1.0).
- Better information about production times can be used to develop more effective production schedules and detailed production plans (steps 2.0 and 4.0).

---

[5]The "steps" in this list refer to the process bubbles in the level 0 DFD of the IPP in Figure 15.1, pg. 569.

FIGURE 15.6 The IPP Role in Generating Managerial Information

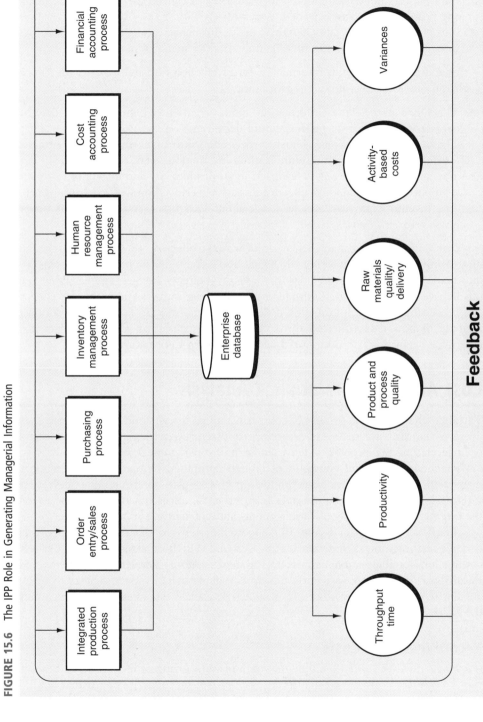

- Information about raw materials quality and delivery can help improve timing of RM orders (step 3.0).
- Information about machine and labor use levels can be used to identify, manage, and possibly eliminate unneeded capacity (step 4.0).
- Information linking quality and machine performance can be used to develop better strategies for operating machines and developing machine maintenance plans.

In addition to using this information for production decision making, the data also is used in other business processes as follows:

- The OE/S process uses information about actual throughput times to determine necessary lead times for quoting future deliveries.
- The human resources management process uses information about labor productivity and usage to determine future staffing levels and specific labor needs.
- The purchasing process uses feedback about productivity and quality of raw materials inputs to assess supplier effectiveness at delivering promised levels of quality.
- The inventory process uses feedback about lead times and throughput times to revise reorder points.

One component of management information collected about the IPP is variance information used in monitoring efficiency and adherence to production plans. This information also can help organizations identify better strategies for managing trade-offs between cost of inputs and productive use of these inputs. The process of collecting and processing variance information is described in more detail in the next section as an example of how data collected throughout IPP is combined with other data in the enterprise database to produce useful decision-making information.

Cost Accounting: Variance Analysis

Enterprise
Systems

Controls

Variance analysis is the process of comparing actual information about input costs and usage to standards for costs and usage for manufacturing inputs. Although criticism has been leveled at the process, when used in its proper context, variance analysis is an important and beneficial control tool. When computed in real time, variances help manufacturing managers monitor production processes to determine that they are performing as expected. Taking a longer-term view, variances can be monitored to assess the interplay between costs of various inputs and efficient use of these inputs.

The level 0 DFD in **Figure 15.7** shows the steps in the process of performing *variance analysis* using a standard costing system. We chose standard instead of actual costing for our illustration because this system is more prevalent in *current* practice. Recall from Table 15.1 (pg. 567), however, that with ERP systems, some companies are abandoning standard costing and returning to actual cost systems. Let's now examine the DFD, bubble by bubble.

Record Standard Costs

(*Figure 15.7, bubble 1.0*) At the time that each manufacturing order is released to the factory, a record is normally created in the *work-in-process inventory data*. At that point, the record contains identification data (job number, end product description, quantity to be produced, start date, etc.). You might think of the work-in-process inventory data as a *subsidiary ledger* in support of the work-in-process inventory *control account* in the general ledger.

FIGURE 15.7   Level 0 DFD—Cost Accounting: Variance Analysis

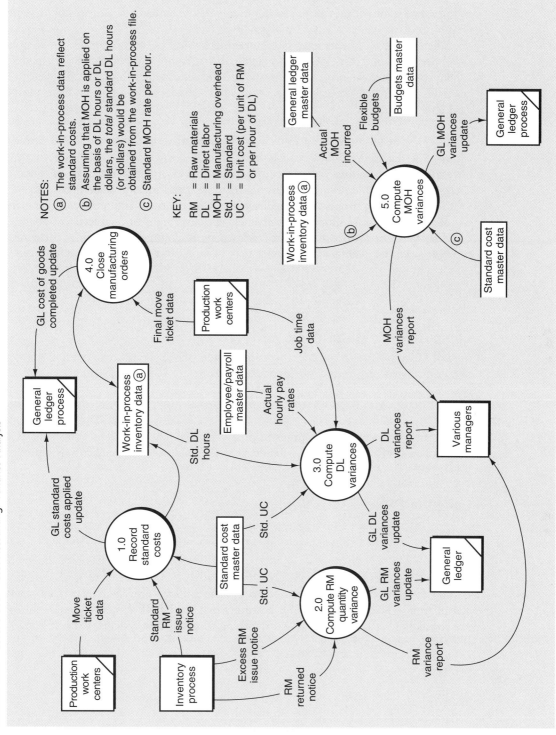

The standard cost master data contains quantity standards (RM quantity, DL hour, and machine hour allowances per FG unit) and price standards (standard purchase price per unit of RM, standard labor rates per hour, etc.).

The data flow "Move ticket data" entering bubble 1.0 occurs at the completion of *each* operation until the job is completed. Each completed move ticket triggers an update to the work-in-process inventory data for the standard cost of labor and overhead allowed for that particular operation. These standards are obtained from the standard cost master data.

When CRP released the MO, it sent a raw materials requisition to the inventory process. The requisition authorized the storeroom to issue the *standard* RM quantities allowed for the MO. After the RMs have actually been issued by the storeroom, the inventory process notifies cost accounting that this has occurred (through the data flow "Standard RM issue notice"). This notification prompts an update to the work-in-process inventory data for the standard cost of the materials (i.e., standard quantities × standard prices).

Although this process may be transparent in an automated system, in a traditional paper process, the issue materials notice may be a physical copy of the materials requisition, dated and signed by the storeroom clerk to signify that the goods were issued. Through the data flow "GL standard costs applied update," process 1.0 notifies the general ledger to make the appropriate entry to apply standard costs to WIP.[6]

Compute Raw Material Quantity Variance

(*Figure 15.7, pg. 583, bubble 2.0*) In the discussion of bubble 1.0, you learned that RMs were first issued to production in *standard* quantities. If additional materials are later issued to complete the MO (unfavorable condition) or unused materials are returned to stock (favorable usage variance), these events are reported through the data flows "Excess RM issue notice" and "RM returned notice," respectively. The usage variance[7] is calculated by multiplying the quantities by standard unit costs from the standard cost master data. This variance is then reported to the general ledger and to the appropriate managers.[8]

Compute Direct Labor Variances

(*Figure 15.7, bubble 3.0*) The inputs to bubble 3.0 are available through electronic capture or from data stores (electronic or paper) existing within the system. The actual hours an employee works on a job is the job time data. This information can largely be captured with an employee card swipe and a bar code scan of the job order. Employee pay rates are obtained from the *employee/payroll master data* (see Chapter 14). For each operation required to complete the job, the standard hours for the operation are retrieved from the work-in-process data; the standard cost master data provides the standard labor rates per hour. As in the case of raw materials, the direct labor variances are computed and reported to the general ledger and the various managers.

---

[6]A discussion of general ledger standard costing entries is beyond the scope of this chapter. Your managerial/ cost accounting courses will probably cover this topic.

[7]We assume that the RM *price* variance is isolated when the materials are *purchased*. Therefore, computing the purchase price variance is a function of the inventory process.

[8]Reporting variances to the general ledger and to various managers is shown happening three times in Figure 15.7 (pg. 583) (i.e., from bubbles 2.0, 3.0, and 5.0). Obviously, the three might be combined into a single update notice to the general ledger and one variance report to each manager.

Close Manufacturing Orders

(*Figure 15.7, bubble 4.0*) As discussed in an earlier section, the *final move ticket data* marks the end of the conversion process and the movement of goods to the FG warehouse. Information processing activities that result from the final move ticket are the following:

- Close the cost record maintained in the work-in-process inventory data and compute the standard cost of the goods completed.
- Through the data flow "GL cost of goods completed update," notify the general ledger to make the appropriate entries.

Compute Manufacturing Overhead Variances

(*Figure 15.7, bubble 5.0*) Process 5.0 is triggered by a temporal event and is performed at the end of an accounting period (e.g., each month) rather than being triggered by a specific data flow from an external entity. To compute the manufacturing overhead variances, process 5.0 would do the following:

- Obtain the *flexible budget* from the budgets master data; the budget amount is based on the standard hours allowed to complete the actual finished goods output for the period.
- Retrieve the figures for actual MOH incurred from the general ledger master data.
- Access the work-in-process data to determine the standard hours charged to *all* jobs during the period; these hours would be multiplied by the standard MOH rate per hour from the standard cost master data.

Once again, the variances are reported to the general ledger and the appropriate managers.

Inventory Management

In addition to the management of human resources, inventory management is another major area of concern for manufacturers—particularly those operating in JIT environments. Manufacturers must estimate needed levels of inventory to meet customer demands, often at a moment's notice. As illustrated through our description of IPP, a major challenge for the inventory manager is determining appropriate levels of raw materials, subassemblies, and finished goods inventory to ensure that production can be maintained and finished goods delivered in a timely manner. Information about finished goods is an important input to the production scheduling process, whereas raw materials and subassemblies inventory variables play an important role in mrp.

Balancing inventory levels to satisfy customer demands in this type of environment, where customer demands are uncertain and production processes are complex and fast-paced, can be challenging. For example, if you are a manufacturer of specialized parts for a large automaker, such as General Motors, and you cannot consistently fill orders in the desired time frame, you probably will not be a partner company for long! Similarly, companies such as HP and Lenovo may require suppliers to ship orders for products such as CD-ROMs within hours after orders are placed.

The purpose of this section is to give you a better understanding of how the inventory management process supports the information needs of those responsible for managing it. The section provides a sample of the kinds of decisions made by the warehouse manager and the supervisor of the inventory control department. We also briefly discuss some of

Controls

the risks associated with inventory control. We conclude this section with an exploration of the control processes for both safeguarding and efficiently using inventory.

Decision Makers and Types of Decisions

Table 15.3 presents a *sample* of the types of decisions the warehouse manager and the supervisor of the inventory control department confront. Concentrating on the decisions presented in the table allows you to see both the opportunities and the challenges that typically face those managers. We'll discuss one of those decisions next.

Making the first decision listed in Table 15.3, *the proper balance of inventory to achieve optimal customer service and optimal investment in inventory*, requires information from a number of sources, including customer sales and services (Chapter 10), the master production schedule (MPS), materials requirements planning (mrp), and the warehouse manager. Recall from Chapter 10 that the OE/S process often captures data regarding customer needs, customer satisfaction, and so forth. This information may impact production and capacity planning schedules.

From the standpoint of the production manager, inventory availability is a vital element in the ability to maintain production requirements for meeting customer demands. Consequently, this manager's inclination may be to inflate the inventory investment. However, an unwarranted increase in an organization's inventory investment can result in lowering its return on investment and decreasing its space use. Thus, data emanating from several functional areas must be gathered and analyzed before an organization can achieve an optimal inventory balance. An optimal inventory balance often translates to a level of inventory availability that is commensurate with some predetermined level of production capacity and upper bounds on expectations of customer orders.

Part of the responsibility of the inventory control manager is to help manage the composition of an organization's inventory investment. This responsibility may include adjusting the inventory balance so that it better fulfills flexible manufacturing needs or so that it turns over more quickly. Unfortunately, the inventory processes of many organizations may not provide the inventory control manager with the information needed to determine whether the inventory investment is out of balance. Take some time now to examine the remainder of Table 15.3.

The Fraud Connection

Controls

Before we discuss internal control as it relates to the inventory process, let's first consider the topic of inventory fraud. Inventory is a primary area in which *management*

TABLE 15.3 Sample of Decision Making Relative to Inventory

Organizational Decision Makers	Decisions
Supervisor of inventory control department	The proper balance of inventory to achieve optimal customer service and optimal investment in inventory The proper models for measuring inventory performance The particular inventory items that require reordering How much inventory to reorder When to reorder inventory From whom to order inventory
Warehouse manager	Best techniques for maintaining physical control over inventory as it is received, while it is stored, and as it is shipped Schedules for taking physical inventory counts How and where inventory should be stored

fraud occurs. Although numerous cases of inventory theft could also be presented here, we will confine our discussion to management fraud connected with inventory. In particular, we will revisit a topic introduced in Chapter 7—namely, "cooking the books" by fraudulently misstating inventory in the financial statements.

The problem of inventory manipulation—both its frequency and the materiality of the financial statement misstatements—is massive. One authority states that inventory fraud has grown fourfold in five years and is one of the biggest single reasons for the proliferation of accounting scandals and their associated lawsuits. One such case is Del Global Technologies. Del Global kept obsolete inventory on its books at full value, rather than writing it down to market. At the same time, the company capitalized operating expenses, reducing expenses and overstating income a total of $3.7 million to $7.9 million per year for the years 1997–2000. To keep the fraud hidden, the company used two sets of books—one for internal use and one for their auditors.[9]

Although this chapter focuses on manufacturing and production processes, it should be noted that inventory control issues are similar for merchandising firms. Unfortunately, merchandising organizations are perhaps even more susceptible to inventory fraud. One illustrative case of merchandising inventory fraud dates back to the 1920s. McKesson & Robbins, among other things, falsified documents to support inventory that was reported in their financial statements. In late 1938, the SEC opened an investigation into the company; in mid-1939, the American Institute of Accountants (now the AICPA) appointed its first committee on auditing procedures. This committee adopted the requirement that auditors must observe inventory during the annual audit to obtain evidence that reported inventory actually exists.[10] You can see that many things that influence your life as an accountant have deep roots in inventory fraud!

In 1994, the AICPA issued *Practice Alert No. 94-2: Auditing Inventories—Physical Observations*. This *Practice Alert* includes the following examples of inventory fraud, among others:

- Including items in physical inventory counts that are not what they are claimed to be, or including nonexistent inventory. Examples are counting empty boxes, mislabeling boxes that contain only scrap or obsolete goods, and diluting inventory so that it appears to be of greater quantity than it actually is (e.g., adding water to liquid inventories).
- Counting obsolete inventory as salable or usable.
- Counting merchandise to which the company does not have title, such as consigned goods and "billed and held" inventory.[11]
- Increasing physical inventory counts for those items that the auditors did not test count.
- Double-counting inventory that is in transit between locations, or moving inventory and counting it at two locations.
- Arranging for false confirmations of merchandise purportedly held by others, such as inventory in public warehouses or out on consignment.
- Including inventory for which the corresponding payable has not been recorded.

---

[9]"Financial Statement Fraud in the Katrina Aftermath: A Whirlwind of Opportunities," *Fraud Magazine*, January/February 2006, www.acfe.com, accessed June 4, 2010.

[10]Paul M. Clikeman. "The Greatest Frauds of the (Last) Century," *New Accountant*, www.newaccountantusa.com, accessed June 4, 2010.

[11]Billed and held inventory is common in certain industries, such as the textile industry. Under the bill and hold arrangement, the seller invoices the buyer for purchased goods—thereby passing title to the buyer at the time of billing—but then holds the inventory at the seller's location until such time as the buyer issues shipping instructions.

- Manipulating the reconciliations of inventory that was counted at other than the financial statement date. It is not uncommon to perform physical inventory taking on a "cycle" basis. That is, items are counted at staggered times throughout the year. When counts are done after the financial statement date, the counted quantities then must be reconciled to year-end quantities by adding purchases and subtracting sales made between the count date and year-end. Attempts to manipulate these reconciliations entail either overstating purchased quantities or understating sold quantities to make it appear that there is a greater on-hand balance at year-end than actually exists.
- Programming the computer to produce false tabulations of physical inventory quantities or priced summaries.[12]

Inventory Process Controls

Controls

The criticalness of maintaining adequate inventory levels should be apparent at this point. Keep in mind, however, that we must balance the desire for high inventory levels with the need to avoid both excessive inventory carrying costs and leftover supplies of materials that are no longer required in revamped production processes. As such, inventory process controls are primarily oriented toward operational (i.e., effectiveness and efficiency) and security objectives. We focus here on three categories of control goals:

1. *Effectiveness of operations:* This is relative to the following goals (note that these goals address the concepts discussed earlier in the chapter, namely *optimizing* the inventory investment):

   a. To maintain a sufficient level of inventory to prevent stock-outs

   b. To maintain a sufficient level of inventory to minimize operational inefficiencies

   c. To minimize the cost of carrying inventory

   Sample controls in the area categorized as effectiveness of operations might include the following:

   a. *Perpetual inventory records:* Maintenance of a continuous record of the physical quantities maintained in each warehouse facilitates inventory management. The receipt or shipment of each item is recorded in the inventory master data to facilitate monitoring of inventory levels and to minimize stock-out risks and production interruptions. *Radio frequency identification (RFID)* tags can be attached to inventory items to track their movement throughout the warehouse and even through the entire supply chain. A perpetual inventory process helps to achieve the goals by providing an up-to-date record of the status of the firm's overall inventory investment, including an account of the activity rate of each inventory item. Thus, fast-moving inventory can be identified to help prevent stock-outs. Additionally, monitoring of slow-moving or excessive inventory can help minimize the cost of carrying inventory.

   b. *Just-in-time materials acquisition:* JIT acquisition essentially eliminates the risk of overstocks while also minimizing inventory carrying costs. Suppliers should be careful in selecting supplier partners, however, to ensure they can deliver on a timely basis when demands for raw materials arise.

---

[12]Division for CPA Firms—Professional Issues Task Force, *Practice Alert No. 94-2: Auditing Inventories—Physical Observations* (New York: American Institute of Certified Public Accountants, July 1994).

c. *Internal transfer procedures:* Often, materials and finished goods inventory will be stored in multiple warehouse or plant locations. As described earlier, with *global inventory management*, needs for raw materials or finished goods orders would initially be satisfied with excess inventory available through transfers from other locations. Only when inventory needs cannot be fulfilled through internal transfers should procedures be initiated for requisitioning materials from suppliers or initiating increased production scheduling. Coordination between warehouses and plants helps maintain more optimal inventory levels and helps avoid inventory outages.

E-Business

2. *Efficient employment of resources:* Sample controls in the area categorized as efficiency might include the following:

a. *Just-in-time materials acquisition:* JIT inventory acquisition, when automated through *EDI* or other related approaches, can improve the efficiency of the inventory process by reducing the amount of manual labor necessary to determine when to reorder materials inventory. *Vendor-managed inventory (VMI)* can shift the burden of the reordering decisions to the suppliers.

b. *Warehouse bin location:* This plan calculates the approximate amount of space to devote to each inventory item. It also analyzes the total warehouse space available to determine *where* to locate each item to increase requisition picking efficiency.

3. *Resource security:* The resources of interest here are the raw materials, work-in-process, and finished goods inventory assets, and the information resources stored in the inventory master data. Control plans should be in place to prevent unauthorized accessing, copying, changing, selling, or destruction of the inventory master data. Of equal importance, plans should be in place to prevent theft or unauthorized sale of merchandise inventory. Sample controls in the area categorized as resource security might include the following:

a. *Periodic physical inventory counts:* Used in conjunction with a perpetual inventory process, this control plan assists in protecting materials, work-in-process, and finished goods inventory by providing the warehouse manager or the inventory control supervisor with a record of the actual (on-hand) balance of each item of inventory. This record can be compared to the corresponding perpetual records to detect any differences between the two balances. Differences between the balances may suggest the possibility of pilferage, which, in turn, exposes an organization to the risk of not achieving the control goal of resource security over its inventory. *RFID* tags can make the inventory count process more efficient and accurate.

b. *Locked storerooms:* Locked storerooms contribute to the achievement of the operations system control goal of securing inventory. Over the years, a number of organizations have experienced a high rate of theft by employees because of inadequately secured rooms where materials and finished goods inventory are stored. In addition to theft prevention, when inventory is secured, a company can make sure the use of items is properly recorded, yielding available inventory when needed and ensuring operations efficiency. As a control plan, locked storerooms limit access to an organization's inventory to authorized employees only.

One final note before leaving the area of inventory control is the parallel between the processes we have discussed in this section for integrated production processes and those used in merchandising environments. Inventory acquisition and product sales have been discussed previously in Chapters 10 through 13. However, we did not focus on inventory control in those chapters, in part because the procedures would be redundant with the discussion presented in this section. The same concerns over operational (i.e., effectiveness and efficiency) and security risks also exist in merchandising environments, and controls similar to those discussed in this section should be implemented to control the receipt, storage, and distribution of merchandise as it is stored in or moved between various stores and warehouses.

Summary

Enterprise Systems

Clearly, IPP represents an excellent example of the power of *enterprise systems*. The process integrates tightly with nearly every other process described so far, especially OE/S, purchasing, HR management, payroll, and inventory management. With costs generated in production representing a significant portion of operating costs for manufacturing businesses and with huge pressures related to controlling product life-cycle costs, increasing innovation, and decreasing time to market, the importance of enterprise systems for managing the process is paramount. Potential costs from poor information include lost sales due to stock-outs; excess finished goods inventories; delays due to poor planning for labor, material, and production resources; excess raw materials due to poor forecasting; and poor reputation resulting from poor quality.

Accounting systems designers face significant challenges in meeting financial accounting needs while taking advantage of the vast array of information production capability in enterprise systems to generate more useful managerial information. In particular, they will be expected to take a life-cycle costing approach and provide valuable information in all stages of the value chain:

- Take an active role in the early stages of product development. This role should emphasize cost-reduction activities.
- Provide more advice, not only during development, but also throughout the entire manufacturing process. Some people have even suggested that cost accountants should spend most of their time on the factory floor performing value analysis to prevent variances from occurring in the first place.
- Develop nontraditional measurements that can help in managing the business, and share that information with the workers on a timely basis. Measures might include such factors as employee morale, product quality (perhaps in the form of warranty data), disaggregated production and scrap data by machine or by work center, schedule and delivery attainment, throughput time, and space devoted to value-added activities versus non–value-added activities.
- Develop new standard cost systems that will focus on quality and production as well as price and efficiency. These updated cost systems would employ input/output analysis rather than focus only on inputs as the conventional standard cost system does.
- Design new ways to evaluate investments. Traditional tools such as *return on investment (ROI)* and *net present value* analyses have proved inadequate for making decisions about major commitments of resources to enterprise systems technology, especially the important cross-functional systems such as CRM, SRM, and PLM so critical for managing globally diverse manufacturing operations. The traditional cost justification methods must be supplemented with an analysis of intangible benefits, including items such as improved shop floor flexibility, reduced manufacturing lead time, faster delivery of product to market, improved product quality, improved product design, better customer service, and similar factors.

One final thought about how the accountant can take a leadership role in manufacturing companies concerns that of designing *simplified* processes. Part of simplification involves making the data we capture in the information system easier to access. Another part requires that we be constantly alert to opportunities to reduce paperwork. The trend toward *paperless processes* must accelerate to keep pace with other technological changes occurring in production processes.

Key Terms

throughput time, 565

push manufacturing, 565

pull manufacturing, 565

cellular manufacturing, 565

available to promise planning, 566

capable to promise planning, 566

activity-based costing (ABC), 566

life-cycle costs, 567

computer-aided design (CAD), 568

computer-aided engineering (CAE), 568

bill of materials (BOM), 570

parts master, 571

routing master, 571

computer-aided process planning (CAPP), 571

work center master, 571

workstation, 571

work center, 571

master production schedule (MPS), 571

global inventory management, 573

production, planning, and control, 573

Materials requirements planning (mrp), 573

time-phased order requirements schedule, 573

exploding the BOM, 574

capacity requirements planning (CRP), 576

Manufacturing orders (MOs), 576

move tickets, 576

raw materials (RM) requisition, 576

manufacturing resource planning (MRP), 578

flexible manufacturing systems (FMS), 578

computer-aided manufacturing (CAM), 578

automated storage and retrieval systems (AS/RS), 578

automated guided vehicle systems (AGVS), 578

just-in-time (JIT), 578

total quality control (TQC), 585

shop floor control (SFC) process, 579

variance analysis, 582

Review Questions

RQ 15-1   How has global competition impacted the domestic manufacturing environment? How can technology help domestic companies compete?

RQ 15-2   Explain the three key drivers of complexity in manufacturing operations in the new millennium.

RQ 15-3   Describe the three key characteristics of companies that successfully manage global complexity.

RQ 15-4   What is the role of product innovation and product life-cycle management (PLM) in helping manufacturing companies compete in the global arena?

RQ 15-5   What are the differences between push manufacturing and pull manufacturing?

RQ 15-6   How does supply chain management (SCM) help organizations improve their competitiveness, especially in a manufacturing organization?

RQ 15-7   What important trends have occurred during the past few decades in cost management and cost accounting?

RQ 15-8   What are the roles of the order entry/sales (OE/S) and inventory management processes in the IPP?

RQ 15-9   What are the steps in the IPP, and what happens at each step?

RQ 15-10   Describe the importance of both activity-based costing (ABC) and product life-cycle costing for managing IPP.

RQ 15-11   From the inventory perspective, what is the advantage of producing goods as customer orders are received?

RQ 15-12   What is global inventory management, and how can it be used to increase the capability of a company to deliver goods on a timely basis and manage inventories?

RQ 15-13   a.   How are a bill of materials (BOM) and a routing master similar? How are they different?

                b.   What does "exploding a BOM" mean?

RQ 15-14   What are some of the components of flexible manufacturing systems (FMS), and how do they work?

RQ 15-15   What are some of the characteristics and advantages of a JIT system?

RQ 15-16   How are materials requirements planning (mrp), detailed capacity requirements planning (CRP), and shop floor control (SFC) similar? How are they different?

RQ 15-17   How is information generated about the IPP used for managing the IPP as well as other business processes?

RQ 15-18   What are the key processes, data, and data flows in the cost accounting system for variance analysis of a manufacturer that uses a standard cost system?

RQ 15-19   Why is inventory management and control important to the manufacturing and production processes?

RQ 15-20   How would a company gain (short term) from a fraudulent overstatement of inventories?

Discussion Questions

DQ 15-1   This chapter discusses the complexities of competing in a highly competitive global manufacturing environment. Discuss how enterprise systems can help an organization streamline its processes and become more competitive.

DQ 15-2   What industry do you believe is a leader in enterprise systems implementations? Discuss what you think are the major contributing reasons for that leadership.

DQ 15-3   Table 15.1 (pg. 567) presents a summary of trends in cost management and cost accounting that have occurred during the past two decades.

a. Which trends do you consider most significant? Explain your answer.

b. The first footnote to Table 15.1 indicates that additional cause-and-effect relationships could be shown between the items in the right column and those in the left column. Give several examples (with explanations) of those other relationships.

DQ 15-4   "A company cannot implement a just-in-time (JIT) process without making a heavy investment in computer resources." Do you agree? Discuss fully.

DQ 15-5   "A company cannot implement manufacturing resource planning (MRP) without making a heavy investment in computer resources." Do you agree? Discuss fully.

DQ 15-6   "A company cannot implement a flexible manufacturing system (FMS) without making a heavy investment in computer resources." Do you agree? Discuss fully.

DQ 15-7   A main goal of JIT is zero inventories.

a. Assume your company does not aspire to JIT and has $1,000,000 in raw materials in stock. Identify costs that may be incurred to maintain the inventory level.

b. Now assume that you implement JIT, and your raw materials in stock drop to zero. Explain how you expect this change to impact your income statement and balance sheet.

DQ 15-8   Without redrawing the figure, discuss the changes that would occur in Figure 15.7 (pg. 583) if the company used an actual costing system instead of a standard cost system.

DQ 15-9   Discuss how the inventory process supports the production planning process and the risks to the production process if inventory process control goals are not achieved. Do not limit your discussion to losses from fraud.

DQ 15-10   With the convergence of U.S. GAAP and IFRS standards moving forward, there is the possibility of the elimination of the LIFO inventory valuation method. If this happens, what will be the impact on manufacturing operations?

Short Problems

SP 15-1   Refer to the level 0 DFD in Figure 15.1 (pg. 569). Study the portion of the figure and accompanying narrative that deals with the product and production process design process *only*. Prepare a level 1 DFD for the product and production process design process (bubble 1.0) *only*.

SP 15-2   Refer to the level 0 DFD in Figure 15.1. Study the portion of the figure and accompanying narrative that deals with the mrp process *only*. Prepare a level 1 DFD for the mrp process (bubble 3.0) *only*.

SP 15-3   Refer to the level 0 DFD in Figure 15.1. Study the portion of the figure and accompanying narrative that deal with the capacity requirements planning (CRP) process *only*. Prepare a level 1 DFD for the CRP process (bubble 4.0) *only*.

SP 15-4   Consider all of the data stores shown in Figure 15.1. Draw an E-R diagram showing the database for the IPP based on the data stores shown in the figure. You do not need to include cardinalities.

SP15-5   Refer to the level 0 DFD in Figure 15.1 (pg. 569). Study the portion of the figure and accompanying narrative that deal with the shop floor control (SFC) process *only*. Prepare a level 1 DFD for the SFC process (bubble 5.0) *only*.

Problems

P15-1   Refer to the DFD in Figure 15.7 (pg. 583). Study the portions of the figures and the accompanying narrative that deal with the cost accounting–variance analysis system *only*. Prepare a detailed systems flowchart for the cost accounting–variance analysis system *only*.

P15-2   Study Figure 15.7, showing the level 0 DFD of the cost accounting system. Note that the raw materials and finished goods inventory processes are *outside* the context of the system shown (i.e., the DFD covers work-in-process inventory only).

   a.   Draw a *context diagram* for the system as it *currently* exists.

   b.   Assume that both the raw materials and finished goods inventories are *within* the system context. Prepare a *context diagram* for the revised system, and redraw Figure 15.7 to reflect the revised system. Ignore the ordering of raw materials from vendors; start the raw materials process with the receipt of goods. Also ignore the issue of finished goods. Keep the assumption that the company uses standard costing for all inventories.

P15-3   Study Figure 15.7, the level 0 DFD of the cost accounting system for a company using standard costing. Redraw Figure 15.7, assuming that the company uses an actual cost instead of a standard cost system.

P15-4   Figure 15.7 shows several data flows running to the general ledger (GL) for the purpose of updating the general ledger master data.

   a.   For each of the following data flows in Figure 15.7, show the journal entry (in debit/credit journal entry format, with no dollar amounts) that would result (make and state any assumptions you think are necessary):

   • GL standard costs applied update
   • GL RM variances update
   • GL DL variances update
   • GL MOH variances update
   • GL cost of goods completed update

   b.   What other standard cost accounting entries are not included in your answer to requirement a? Show those journal entries; describe *when* they would be made and *what* event they are recording.

P15-5   Based on the inventory process control goals discussed in the chapter, explain the impact of using a periodic inventory process instead of a perpetual process. Be sure to also discuss how you would design the process to attempt to meet the same control objectives using this periodic process.

P15-6   In many popular publications, the terms "lean accounting" and "lean manufacturing" are used periodically.

a. Research "lean manufacturing" and find out what concepts are conveyed by the term. How does lean manufacturing overlap with, and how is it different from, IPP?

b. Research "lean accounting" and find out what concepts are conveyed by the term. Compare and contrast what you find in Table 15.1 (Summary of Trends in Cost Management/Cost Accounting, pg. 567).

P15-7 This chapter begins by discussing the global competition faced by manufacturing firms. Identify two companies in your local area—one that has thrived in a global market and one that has failed. Compare and contrast the companies. Based on your understanding of manufacturing and the failed company, identify strategies that might have helped the company be successful.

P15-8 This chapter discusses fraud from an inventory perspective. Research inventory fraud cases, and write a paper on a case you find interesting (your instructor will provide guidance regarding the paper's length). At a minimum, you should include the following items:

- A description of the organization
- The perpetrator(s) of the fraud
- A description of the method used to defraud
- An analysis of the missing control(s) that would have prevented the fraud
- The length of time the organization was deceived
- The impact over time (including monetary and other losses)
- The penalty received by the perpetrator(s)

P15-9 This problem should be completed with database software, such as Microsoft Access.

1. Using the E-R diagram from SP 15-4, select any three or four related entities and implement them as tables using Microsoft Access (or any other database software acceptable to your instructor). To link the tables you will need to determine the cardinalities. For the tables, create representative attributes as needed, including primary keys and foreign keys.

2. Create forms for each table from part 1 of this problem and use the forms to populate the tables with representative data. Forms should be in good order, readable, and properly formatted. Create at least three records in each table. Print out the populated tables and one instance of each form.

3. Design three queries using the tables from part 1 of this problem. Print out the output of each query and attach an explanation as to why someone would be interested in the output of each query.

4. Using the report function in Access, design a report for each query from part 3 of this problem. Reports should be in good order, readable, and properly formatted. Print out each report.

Requirements: As directed by your instructor, submit the completed database file and the printouts noted above.

Reporting

CHAPTER 16

The General Ledger and Business Reporting (GL/BR) Process

Learning Objectives

After reading this chapter, you should be able to:

- Describe how the business processes discussed in Chapters 10 through 15 provide data required for general ledger (GL) updates.
- Understand how the GL and business reporting (BR) capabilities support an organization's external and internal reporting functions.
- Understand the limitations of the traditional GL approach in contemporary systems.
- Analyze control issues and control plans associated with the GL and related business reporting extensions.
- Describe the technological trends and advances in financial reporting.

Finance executives are generally proud of their strong data analysis and decision support capabilities, so does it make sense that they are spending only one-third of their day using those strengths? Business complexity, globalization, and nonstandard systems throughout their organizations contribute to the problem. Acknowledging the problem, almost all of these executives (97 percent in one survey) indicate they need to spend less time on transaction processing to be able to focus on analysis. Most of them say they have spent money—and will likely spend more money—to improve efficiency, but they are not getting the results they want.[1]

Can an organization's accounting system help? Definitely! With financial transactions captured accurately at the point of the business event and then flowing to a flexible general ledger system that is consistent throughout the enterprise (a true enterprise system), there should be less time required for reconciliations and journal entries. Today's (and tomorrow's) business reporting software can create opportunities for a significant reduction in a finance department's manual processes—leaving more time for the fun part of the job!

In this chapter, we will explore the databases and information processes that must be in place to capture and store accounting and other business-related data, and the production of internal and external business reports, including International Financial

---

[1]The source for this vignette is Kate O'Sullivan, "Stuck in a Rut," *CFO Magazine*, November 1, 2007, available at www.cfo.com.

Reporting Standards (IFRS)[2] and Generally Accepted Accounting Principles (GAAP)[3]–based financial reports. These reports can be used by internal and external decision makers to make and support quality decisions.

Synopsis

Before you began your study of AIS, you might have defined the term *accounting information system* by describing the general ledger (GL) component. After all, the GL is probably familiar to you from your earlier accounting courses. Now that you have journeyed through some or all of the business processes in Chapters 10 through 15, you should appreciate that the GL is the storage area where it all comes together. During your studies of these earlier chapters you may have realized that organizations need more than just GL/accounting-based reports. The general area of business reporting that supports an organization's decision-making needs requires the ability to blend business information on operational and strategic performance obtained from a multitude of sources.

Topically, this chapter's organization is the same as that of the business process chapters. We start by defining the boundaries of the GL, explaining its functions, and examining its organizational context. We then proceed to a discussion of the *logical* system features. Sections on extended business reporting processes, technology, and controls follow.

System Definition and Functions

Similar to the business processes covered in Chapters 10 through 15, the **general ledger and business reporting (GL/BR) process** is an interacting structure of people, equipment, activities, and controls that is designed to accomplish both operations and information system functions. Unlike the other business processes, the GL/BR process has fewer *operational* functions; it focuses mainly on *information* functions. Whereas the other processes perform important functions related to their "work" of providing goods and services to customers, the *work* of the GL/BR process is the processing and communicating of information.

What are the important information services functions of the GL/BR process? This chapter emphasizes two categories: general ledger activities and other business reporting.

The **general ledger (GL) process** comprises the following:

- Accumulating data, *classifying* data by general ledger *accounts*, and recording data in those accounts.
- Fueling the *financial reporting*, *business reporting*, and other reporting subsystems by providing the information needed to prepare external and internal reports. In

---

[2]We do not directly address international (IFRS) standards. Software will deal with the differences in the accumulating and reporting of financial data as worldwide accounting rules converge toward IFRS standards.

[3]It should also be noted that effective, January 1, 2011, the U.S. CPA Exam Content Standards include not only U.S. GAAP, but also IFRS. For the current content standards, see www.aicpa.org/BecomeACPA/CPAExam/ExaminationContent/ContentAndSkills/, accessed June 14, 2010.

servicing the information needs of *managerial* reporting, the GL interacts with the *budgeting* modules, as we will see in the next section.

The **business reporting process** encompasses the following:

- Preparing *general purpose, external* financial statements (e.g., the "conventional four" that you have studied in other accounting courses: balance sheet, income statement, statement of owners' equity, and statement of cash flows).
- Ensuring that the external financial statements conform to GAAP; therefore, among other things, the statements must contain appropriate *footnote disclosures.*
- Generating Web-based forms of key financial statement and related business reporting information for dissemination via the Internet.
- Supporting the generation of both ad hoc business reports and predetermined business reports that support operational and strategic decision making.

Organizational Setting

E-Business In this section, we examine the placement of the GL/BR process in the organization and the interactions with its relevant environment. We will describe the roles of the new "players" who are involved most directly with the GL/BR process and will review the horizontal and vertical information flows within an organization. While beyond the scope of this text, it is important to realize that these information flows may cross international boundaries, requiring you to consider issues such as differences in language, currency, and accounting requirements.

Before we begin, we should define a term that is used throughout the chapter. A **feeder process** is any business process that accumulates *business event* data that are then communicated to and processed within the GL. Accordingly, the feeder processes include all those discussed in the earlier business process chapters. In addition, we show the treasurer as a feeder because the treasurer furnishes the GL with updates for *investing activities* and *financing activities*.

Horizontal Perspective of the General Ledger and Business Reporting Process

Like their counterparts in earlier chapters, **Figure 16.1** and **Table 16.1** (pg. 602) show the placement of the general ledger and business reporting functions in the organization and the horizontal information flows between the GL/BR process and other entities. Take some time now to review them before we highlight the key points.

Let's begin by examining some of the horizontal flows appearing in the figure. You should first note that flow 1 consolidates several different updates from the *feeder processes* studied in other business process chapters. However, the individual updates will be shown as separate data flows in the logical data flow diagrams (DFDs) appearing in the next section.

As we mentioned, another feeder appearing in Figure 16.1 is the treasurer. Whereas updates for *operating activities* are depicted by flow 1, the *investing* and *financing* activity updates are shown by flow 2. Moving to flow 3, we have *assumed* that all adjusting entry updates come from the controller. Obviously, such notifications could come from other sources instead. For instance, the financial reporting officer might provide the adjustments mandated by GAAP. Another example is depreciation adjustments, which in some companies come from a separate fixed asset system, but in many contemporary systems, they are simply generated automatically by the system supporting the GL. The descriptions in Table 16.1 of the remaining flows in Figure 16.1 should be fairly self-explanatory.

At this point, we also should consider how these information flows are affected by integrated *enterprise systems* such as ERP systems. First, for flow 1, which is the entry of data from the *feeder processes*, the ERP system *automatically* updates the centralized database to reflect the journal entries for the GL and to capture the information needed for other business reporting by using embedded update rules within the system. In other words, the business reporting department does not have to enter the data—it is already entered directly as business events are recorded in the business processes. Those flows to the GL are often labeled "GL update." Similarly, for flow 2, the ERP system sends the entries to the GL when personnel in the treasurer's office record investing or financing activities in the treasury module of the ERP system. The output side from the ERP systems operates in much the same manner. Flows 6 and 7 are information

Enterprise Systems

FIGURE 16.1 Horizontal Perspective of the General Ledger and Business Reporting Process

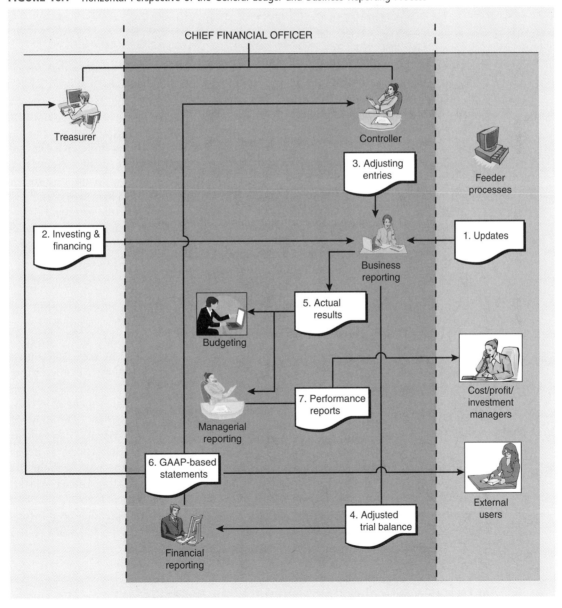

TABLE 16.1 Description of Information Flows

Flow No.	Description
1	Business processes (feeder processes) send updates to the business reporting department.
2	The treasurer notifies the business reporting department of investing and financing transaction activities.
3	The controller notifies the business reporting department of various adjusting entries.
4	Adjusted trial balance figures are sent from the business reporting department to the financial reporting officer.
5	Actual results are sent from the business reporting department to the budgeting and managerial reporting managers; the actual results will be one of the inputs used in formulating next period's budgets.
6	The financial reporting officer sends GAAP-based financial statements to the treasurer, controller, and various external constituencies (e.g., owners, potential investors, banks, potential lenders).
7	The managerial reporting officer sends performance reports to various cost centers, profit centers, or investment centers.

that can be extracted by the respective departments or constituencies using either preestablished reporting forms or through queries of the enterprise database.

Note that flow 3 is the only entry from Figure 16.1 (pg. 601) that needs to be made directly into the GL. The automation of the various activities clearly reduces the number of people needed to handle the mundane accounting entry work in the business reporting department. Rather, the department can focus on the provision of more complex and interesting information that can be used to aid in the improvement of the effectiveness and efficiency of the organization's operations and strategies. We will explore some of the possibilities within this extended business reporting capability later in this chapter.

E-Business As we look to emerging capabilities, we also should consider how the external reporting model is changing. Increasingly, organizations are deciding to make their financial information available on the Internet. Currently, little standardization of this information exists among companies, although the SEC has recently issued regulatory guidance regarding the use of technology to provide information to investors.[4] Flow 6 increasingly includes the release of information to corporate Web sites.

From prior chapters, you should be familiar with the typical division within the finance function between the treasurer and the controller. To emphasize differences in their functional responsibilities, we have shown four managers reporting to the controller. In some organizations, two or more of the four functions might be combined into a single job function. In others, managers might exist who are not shown in the figure, such as the manager of a tax department.

One objective of Figure 16.1 is to portray the organizational alignment of certain key entities within the finance function. However, recalling our earlier definitions of the GL/BR process, you should recognize that only the business reporting department and the financial reporting officer are technically *within* the GL/BR process as it has been defined. Therefore, when we discuss the logical system in the next section, the treasurer, controller, budgeting department, and managerial reporting officer will all be shown as external entities lying *outside* the *context* of the GL/BR process.

Before you leave Figure 16.1, ask yourself, "What are the functions of the four managers reporting to the controller?" We have already described the functions of the

---

[4]"Commission Guidance on the Use of Company Web Sites," Release Nos. 34-58288, IC-28351, August 1, 2008, available at www.sec.gov/rules/interp/2008/34-58288.pdf, accessed June 7, 2010.

business reporting department and the financial reporting officer in the preceding section (see the definitions of *general ledger process* and *business reporting process*, respectively). The budgeting department advises and assists the cost center, profit center, and investment center managers in preparing the budget. The budgeting department should not actually prepare the budget estimates; it should offer technical advice to the *operating line managers* as they develop the budgets for their centers. Good participative management practice argues that the *responsibility* for budget preparation should fall to the operating center managers who later will be held *accountable* for budget variations. One final comment about the budgeting function is in order. Because the "advise and assist" role of the budgeting department cuts across all functions in the organization, it is not uncommon in practice to see the department placed much higher in the organization chart, perhaps on the same horizontal level as the president or CEO.

The **managerial reporting officer** has responsibilities similar to those of the **financial reporting officer**. The latter possesses expertise in the area of financial reporting to external parties, and the former performs a similar role in respect to preparing internal reports to assist management decision making (this distinction may sound familiar from your earlier studies of *financial accounting* versus *managerial accounting*). Many of the reports prepared by the managerial reporting officer are called **performance reports** because they compare actual performance with budgeted expectations. Often, these reports are part of a managerial reporting system known as a **responsibility accounting/reporting system** because it is tied to the hierarchy or chain of responsibility/authority reflected by the firm's organization chart. In such a system, as information is reported upward, the level of detail is filtered, meaning that figures are aggregated (summarized) as they are reported to successive management levels. **Figure 16.2** shows a sample *performance reporting* flow for the production arm of an organization that uses a *responsibility accounting/reporting* model. An example of this flow may

FIGURE 16.2   Responsibility Accounting Performance Reporting

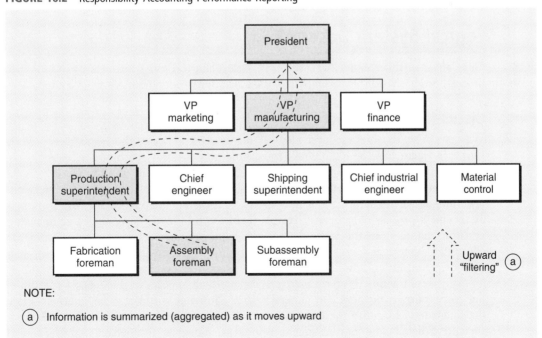

NOTE:

(a) Information is summarized (aggregated) as it moves upward

Source: Adapted with permission from James D. Wilson, "Human Relations and More Effective Reporting," *NAA Bulletin*, May 1961, pp. 13–24.

include a report of the details of today's production output for the assembly foreman, with weekly, monthly, and annual aggregations reported to the production superintendent, VP of manufacturing, and president, respectively. In that example, the detailed reporting of daily production used for decisions at the lowest organization level is not useful for strategic decisions made by the president. Conversely, the annual aggregations provide little useful information for the work the assembly foreman has to do on a daily basis. Thus, the upward filtering of details provides each decision maker the information needed for his or her specific job.

Enterprise Systems

As we will be discussing later in this chapter, the major ERP vendors are providing additional functionality to support much of this additional business reporting demand for performance reporting. The integration of this functionality allows these reports to be easily generated from information captured by the business processes and maintained at the business event level in the enterprise database.

Horizontal and Vertical Information Flows

In Figure 1.9 in Chapter 1 (pg. 25), the distinction between horizontal and vertical information flows was introduced at a conceptual level. Now we will review the concepts shown in Figure 1.9 and enhance that figure based on our study of AIS to date. **Figure 16.3** is intended to do exactly that.

Along the bottom of Figure 16.3, we can trace the horizontal transaction flows as they progress from left to right through the various *operations systems*, culminating in the GL/BR process, and resulting in reporting to external parties. We also see the vertical reporting dimension (in the form of internal performance reports prepared from information supplied by the GL and through budgeting) flowing upward in each of the principal functional columns. This figure demonstrates information development through the reporting process, data accumulation (horizontal flows) as the data flow from the initiating event, and aggregation (vertical flows) as the data flow up through the management levels of each functional area of the organization.

Logical System Description

Once again in this chapter, we use DFDs to explain the *logical* features of the GL/BR process. Study the DFDs carefully to make sure that you understand their contents.

Discussion and Illustration

We start with the highest-level view of the GL/BR process, the *context diagram*, as shown in **Figure 16.4** (pg. 606). Take some time now to study the figure.

Do you agree that there is nothing really new here? Note the *business event* data flows from the business processes discussed in Chapters 10 through 15. If you are uncertain about the nature and timing of any of these updates, go back to the appropriate business process chapter and review them. Note also the investing and financing updates coming from the treasurer and the adjusting entry updates coming from the controller. Note that each system output data flow was shown earlier in the discussion of information flows (flows 5–7, in Figure 16.1).

Enterprise Systems

We should define the term *journal voucher*, which appears in the data flow "Adjusting entry journal vouchers." In general terms, a **journal voucher** is an internal source document used to notify the GL to make an accounting entry. In addition to showing the entry's details, the journal voucher should be signed by the person(s) authorized to initiate the entry. Remember, in the case of an *enterprise system*, this voucher document

FIGURE 16.3   Horizontal and Vertical Information Flows

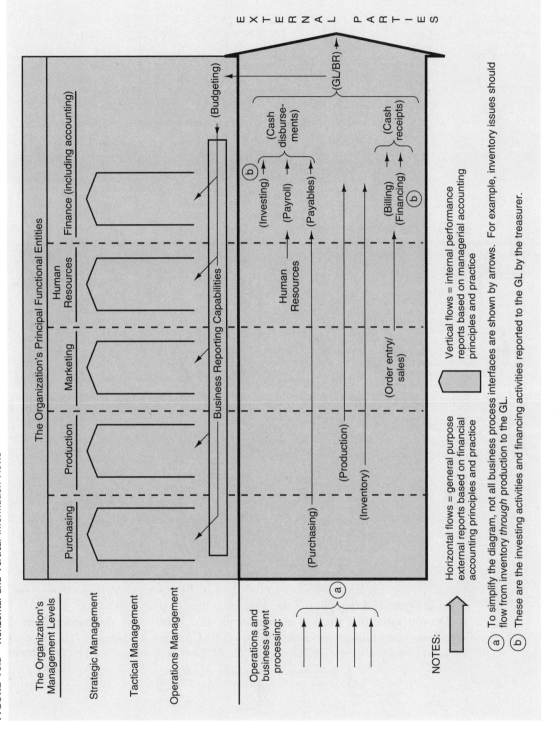

FIGURE 16.4   General Ledger/Business Reporting Process—Context Diagram

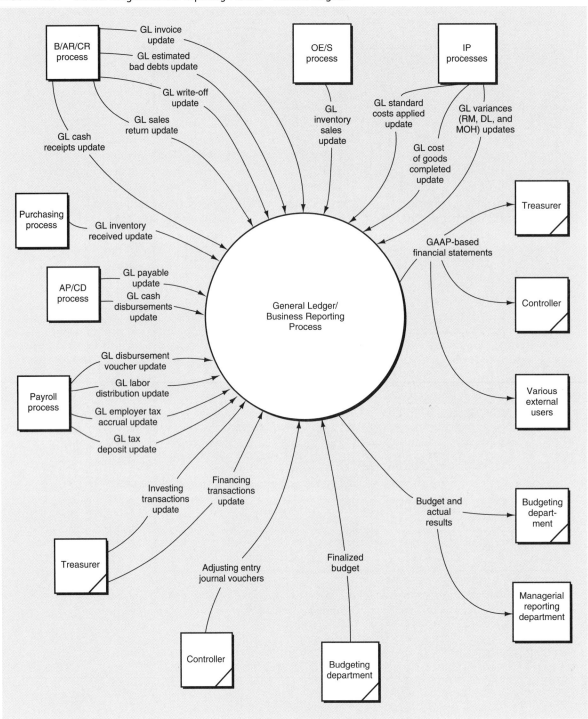

will likely be electronic, the person completing the adjustment will generally enter it directly into the system, and the signature will be represented through a capturing of the electronic identification of the individual making the entry (i.e., *electronic approval using a pin number*). These vouchers might be routed, using the *workflow* features of an ERP, to individuals given the authority to approve the entries. Although the DFDs use the term *journal voucher* only in connection with adjusting entry updates from the controller, you should recognize that any of the business event updates from the feeder processes might also take the *form* of a journal voucher.

Let's pursue that last point. *Logically*, each business event from a feeder process can be posted *directly*, *individually*, and *immediately* to the GL. As a practical matter, *physical* implementations will vary. For example, the flows from the feeder processes could comprise *summaries* of a number of business events posted *periodically* at the end of a day, week, or month. For example, the B/AR/CR process may collect the data related to sales in the *sales event data* store and send the summary of that data to the general ledger. The resulting summarized entry to the general ledger would include postings to the sales and accounts receivable accounts.

In an *enterprise system*, this business event data is recorded separately for each sale within the module designed for that business process (e.g., sales, accounts receivable). In some enterprise systems implementations, this business event data could be batched during sales (or accounts receivable) processing and then used to update the GL database at one point in time. If the GL processing is done through this type of aggregation of the source records (e.g., business events), the impact of many business events will be posted as a batch, and the balances in the GL accounts will be adjusted accordingly. However, the enterprise system will maintain data for each individual business event in the underlying business process database, and a user can view this detail by simply drilling down on the GL balance data. At this point, however, let's continue to concentrate on the logical connections of the individual feeder processes with the GL.

Enterprise Systems

Figure 16.5 (pg. 608) shows the GL/BR process level 0 DFD. Bubble 1.0 is titled "Validate business event updates." What might be involved here? Some examples follow.

- We want to check business event updates to make sure they come from the correct feeder process. Do you agree that this check addresses the information system goal of ensuring event data *input validity*?
- We also want to make sure that no business event updates have been overlooked (recall the discussion of *input completeness* in each business process chapter).
- Finally, we verify the debit and credit equality of "halves" of entries flowing from different systems (e.g., from the receipt of inventory and the vendor invoice). What control goals are we trying to achieve with this kind of verification? If you answered input completeness (IC) and input accuracy (IA), you were right on the money.[5]

Bubbles 2.0 through 4.0, plus 6.0, should be reminiscent of the *bookkeeping/accounting cycle* that you studied in earlier accounting courses. Consider these observations:

Controls

- You should recognize that process 4.0, "Prepare business reports," involves several steps. These steps *might* include activities such as preparing a *worksheet*, drafting financial statement footnotes, formatting the financial statements and footnotes, and compiling the financial statements into an attractive and informative reporting

E-Business

---

[5]Note that this problem is alleviated in many contemporary systems through the use of clearing accounts, such as the account described in Chapters 12 and 13.

package. For general distribution, these financial statements and related information are often posted to the entity's Web site.

- Process 6.0, like some that you encountered in previous chapters, is *triggered* by a temporal event (i.e., the data flow into the process from the GL master data), rather than by a data flow from another process or from an external entity. Specifically, at an appropriate *point in time*, the condition of the GL accounts indicates that the accounts should be closed before repeating the accounting cycle for the next accounting period.

Our final comment about Figure 16.5 concerns process 5.0, "Record budget." Because GAAP-based external reports seldom, if ever, include budget information, we might have excluded process 5.0 and its related data flows. However, we included it to provide one example of how the GL/BR process can "fuel" reporting systems that rely on the information that has been aggregated in the system—in this case, providing information related to both budgeted and actual results.

FIGURE 16.5   General Ledger and Business Reporting Process—Level 0 Data Flow Diagram

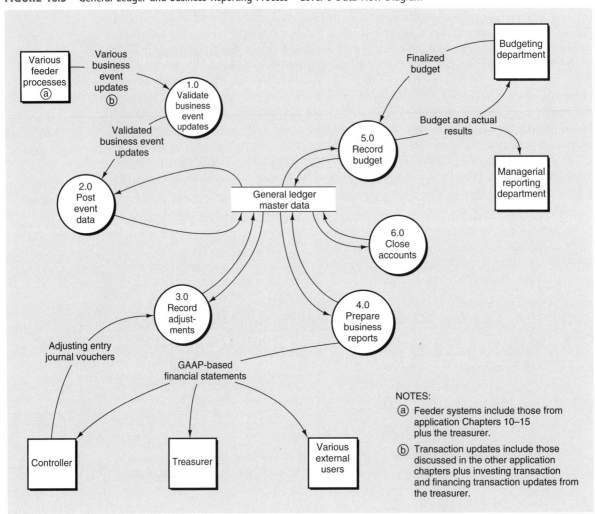

The General Ledger Master Data

The **general ledger master data** contains summarized information of all of an organization's business event data. The main inputs to the GL consist of transactions (in detail or summary), from the business event data captured in the various feeder processes discussed earlier. Adjusting entry journal vouchers, originating with the controller, are the other principal source of entries.

In traditional accounting systems, the GL's utility has depended largely on a well-designed and complete *chart of accounts*. The more sophisticated the *data classification and coding* scheme used for the chart of accounts (a subject discussed in the next section), the broader the range of financial reports that can be produced. For example, the first three digits in an account number might show the account's general classification. Other digits in the account number may indicate the responsibility center, project number, and so on. This way, job or plant financial statements can be generated, in addition to the consolidated statements that are made available to outside users.

The source code field of each GL entry provides a beginning point of reference for developing a proper **audit trail**. The code gives the auditor a means of tracing from the GL entry back to the feeder system, and ultimately to the individual business events that have been aggregated into the GL balances. For instance, using a batch number, an auditor can follow an entry to the appropriate batch file. From there, the batched event data can be identified. The path then leads to the original source document. Journal vouchers can be substantiated by using the source code to locate the specific input form used by the controller (or another employee in the controller's office). In many systems today, you can simply "drill down" through the path until you reach the level of detail needed for the transaction.

Controls

Note that in addition to storing the entries of the current period, beginning-of-period balances are also generally available, allowing you to compute the period-to-date balance for the account at any point in time.

Because the source business event data is usually stored in a centralized database, the user can select a beginning and ending date to accumulate information for any period of time. Thus, if a manager wants to examine sales over a two-week, three-month, or any other period, the information can be aggregated through a query to provide the manager the precise information of interest.

Coding the General Ledger Chart of Accounts

The discussion of *classifying* and *coding* data appeared in Chapter 5. You might want to review that material before proceeding. Do any of the coding systems presented in Chapter 5 seem particularly relevant to the GL chart of accounts? Consider *hierarchical coding*. To illustrate the application of this method to the GL, let's suppose the number 1113 was assigned to the account "cash in bank." Moving from left to right, the hierarchy might be as follows:

$$1XXX = \text{assets}$$
$$X1XX = \text{current assets}$$
$$XX1X = \text{cash accounts}$$
$$XXX3 = \text{cash in bank}$$

Following this structure, you can see how the following account numbers may be used: 1111 for petty cash, 1112 for a change fund, 1121 for trade accounts receivable, 1122 for receivables from officers, and so on.

In designing a coding scheme for a chart of accounts, you should consider the following questions:

• On which financial statements, if any, must an account appear?
• Is there a need for segmental reporting (e.g., division or department)?
• In which category on a financial statement (e.g., current asset or fixed asset) should it appear?
• Is there a specific order in which the accounts should appear (e.g., liquidity or maturity)?
• Which accounts and categories should be aggregated for presentation (e.g., show one cash balance, or total current assets)?
• Which internal reports will be required (e.g., departmental or cost center *performance reports*)?

Limitations of the General Ledger Approach

Recall that Chapter 5 includes a discussion regarding the limitations of traditional file processing approaches and the emerging focus on event-driven systems (you may want to review this material before proceeding). The discussion focused on the limitations that come from disjointed stores of data for financial and nonfinancial information, and the elimination of source data after business event information has been added to account summaries. The traditional GL approach has been a primary suspect as the source of many of these problems.

If you think about the driving force in constructing a chart of accounts, the goal is to add structure to the classification of financial information. This is a good thing, but the problem is that in implementing the chart of accounts, the focus usually becomes one of "How can we classify every piece of business event data as fitting into a specific account?" Also, the formation of the coding scheme (as discussed in the previous section) is based on summary aggregation requirements for creating financial reports. In reality, most GL systems capture the chart of accounts number and the debit or credit entry, and the remainder of the information about a business event is discarded.

Although other business event information may be captured in separate systems operated by other departments, such as marketing, nonfinancial information frequently becomes separated from the financial information. After the end-of-period closings are completed for the GL, the detailed business event-level data are eventually purged from the system—the GL being only interested in maintaining correct current balances for each entry in the chart of accounts. At that point, even if a link exists between the financial and nonfinancial information in the business event data, the relationships are lost. From that point on, information for decision making is limited to only that information captured in the accounts as specified by the chart of accounts. If you decide you want more detailed information than the chart of accounts provides, historical business events generally cannot be reconstructed. The information can be captured in the future only if alterations are made to the chart of accounts and the programs that use those accounts (i.e., the financial report generator).

As an example, let's take the hierarchy discussed in the preceding section and adapt it to sales. The hierarchy might start out as follows:

$$7XXX = \text{revenues}$$
$$X1XX = \text{merchandise sales}$$

After a while, one of the corporate managers decides that the system needs to capture sales by region. We could add *region* as a third digit, but that doesn't fit our hierarchical structure very well. Logically, the second digit needs to be region so that all types of revenues can be grouped by region. We can revise our system, but keep in mind that after we make this change, all the programs using the data will also need to be revised to recognize the new system—no small task. The new system may look as follows:

$$7XXX = \text{revenues}$$
$$X1XX = \text{sales region}$$
$$XX1X = \text{merchandise sales}$$

Just when we think we satisfied the manager's needs, the corporate sales manager decides that merchandise sales should be coded by another digit representing each of six sporting goods categories. Again, we revise our coding scheme and update applicable programs. Our scheme now looks like this:

$$7XXX = \text{revenues}$$
$$X1XX = \text{sales region}$$
$$XX1X = \text{merchandise sales}$$
$$XXX1 = \text{golf merchandise sales}$$

Now the real headaches begin. The sales manager has decided it is imperative that the coding scheme include a digit to represent each unique salesperson. But we don't have any digits left in the coding scheme! If we add a digit, we will have to completely revise our entire chart of accounts to a five-digit system, not just change the revenue accounts.

Changing account numbers and account structure can raise a significant information use problem: *comparability*. If a GL account number is changed, it must be changed not only in the GL but also in every place in the accounting system that it is used, including all subsystems and historical references. If the account number is not changed in historical details, comparative information from prior periods will not be synchronized. It should be noted that in well-controlled systems, changes to historical details are not allowed. To change an existing transaction, you would be required to make a correcting entry that reverses the original entry and updates the balance of the new account. Such a process is likely not practical for a large system. Alternatively, users may need to develop an external mapping (using a spreadsheet, for example, with column A containing the new account numbers, and column B containing the old account numbers) to allow comparison of current revenue accounts (from our previous example) to the corresponding accounts from the periods prior to the account number change. Otherwise, the system's users can potentially lose the richness of comparative financial information for many years.

These are just some of the problems that charts of accounts create in limiting the flexibility of information aggregation and analysis. We already noted the limitations on other nonfinancial information. You will recall that in Chapters 5 and 6, we noted the push toward centralized database–driven systems—and in particular, event-driven systems. This discussion should add to your understanding of why the rapidly expanding information needs of management are creating conflict with traditional GL structures. Later in this chapter, we will focus briefly on using database technology to perform our traditional financial report generation processes without having to limit the capturing of broad event data.

Before going on, we will address one issue more explicitly. When we talk about the advantages of centralized database–driven systems, you should keep in mind that this broader range of systems has similar implications for ERP systems because they are

Enterprise Systems

centralized database driven and enabled. Thus, as we move toward an *enterprise system* environment, the chart of accounts becomes increasingly less important. If it exists at all, it will probably be the concatenation of several fields in a database record that can be changed more easily simply through adding fields to the database to handle necessary information relationships, such as the salesperson number in the previous example.

Technology-Enabled Initiatives and the Reporting Environment

We explore a variety of topics in this section that demonstrate how technology has simplified much of the financial reporting process and enabled a far greater level of business reporting to support management decision making. We begin with three topics related to enterprise systems. The first is simply a brief look at the financial reporting module in an ERP system; the second and third topics relate to contemporary extensions to ERP systems to accommodate contemporary business reporting interests— namely, balanced scorecard and business intelligence. The fourth topic also is related to enterprise systems in that the major vendors are including the functionality for XBRL (eXtensible Business Reporting Language) for business reporting and the standardization of this reporting. The XBRL discussion is also important because of its growing use to comply with reporting requirements of many regulators around the world.

Following the XBRL discussion, you are introduced to two additional compliance issues in the United States: the Sarbanes-Oxley Act of 2002 and the convergence of U.S. GAAP and IFRS. The section ends with a discussion of the impact of today's technology environment on external financial reporting.

ERP Financial Module Capability

Although we discussed earlier in this chapter the integration of business reporting in ERP systems (as well as integration of information from other business process activities), conceptually this integration may still be a bit foggy in your mind. For purposes of clarification, let's take a closer look at integration within the financial module.

Enterprise Systems

Figure 16.6 shows the reports screen for Microsoft Dynamics GP ERP software. We have exploded the menu options for the financial section to show you the wide range of options that are available in the software just for the financial module.

In addition to the Financial option, the first-level menu options for all reports are displayed. These options include links to the information processing capabilities that are related to the business processes we have discussed in this text; for example, the Sales menu item (which could also be described as order-to-cash) will include the processes for the Order Entry/Sales and Billing/Accounts Receivable/Cash Receipts processes. Note also that the financial reports go beyond just the trial balance to include other reports such as budgeting, a variety of financial reports, and a custom report writer (FRx) for when standard reports will not meet your needs.

Enterprise Systems

Controls

This multitude of options should give you some understanding of the complexity and magnitude of ERP systems. You also might have realized during this discussion that all users do not need all these options. For security reasons as well as ease of use, you should limit access to menu items to only those needed by a given user to perform his or her responsibilities. This will mean setting up the security for an individual user to limit the menu options that appear. Most ERP systems have the option to help deal with individual user security by providing for user roles or groups (e.g., accounts

FIGURE 16.6 Financial Reporting Menu for Microsoft Dynamics GP Software

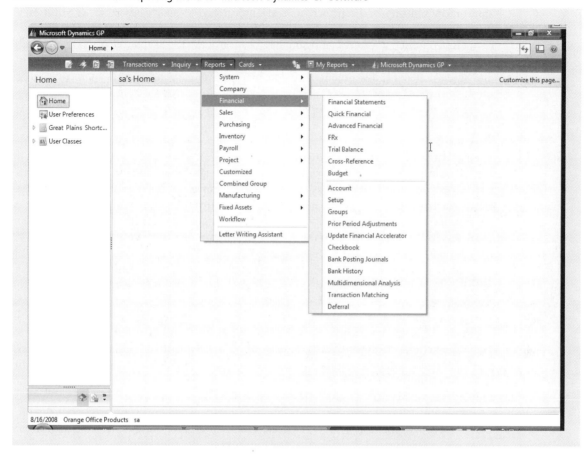

payable clerk) to which a user may be assigned. The security for a given role then becomes the security for the user, making it easier to add additional users who perform the same job responsibilities as existing users. ERP security can become detailed and complex, as you may want to allow a given user (or group of users) to have different privilege levels for different information—that is, view access, write access, entry access, or change access. Sometimes users only need to be able to view information in one area of the system, whereas they may need to be able to enter new event data or be able to change existing records of event data in other areas of the system. All this must be carefully specified in the user's profile to set up the system limitations for that specific user. Normally, this profile is set up with the user's ID to be automatically initiated at logon. This is implemented via *logical access controls* such as those in the *access control software*.

Balanced Scorecard

Balanced scorecard is a methodology for assessing an organization's business performance via four components: (1) financial, (2) internal business processes, (3) customers, and (4) innovation and improvement activities. The financial aspect focuses on more traditional measures of business performance related to how shareholders view the organization's performance. The internal business processes relate to the organization's ability to identify its core competencies and to assess how well it performs in these identified areas of competency. The customer component focuses on identifying how

Enterprise
Systems

customers perceive the organization in terms of the value that it is creating for them. Innovation and improvement activities are monitored to assess how the organization is continuing to improve and how it is creating additional value.

The concept of *balanced scorecard* has been around for several years, but it is only within the past few years that ERP vendors have focused on integrating this functionality and in turn making assessment a reasonable possibility. Fundamental to incorporating effective *balanced scorecard* assessment is the aggregation of varied data in a *data warehouse* (discussed in Chapter 5) that can then be analyzed using powerful analytical tools—that is, *business intelligence* tools, as discussed in the next section. Because an ERP system provides the capability to aggregate the necessary data in its underlying centralized database, linking this data with other data to create the necessary *data warehouse* is a logical and efficient way to provide *balanced scorecard* capabilities. Accordingly, all the major ERP vendors have announced, and many have included, product integration to provide the *balanced scorecard* functionality. Take a few minutes before going on to reflect on how the data captured in the various business processes could be used to support assessment in each of the four areas underlying the *balanced scorecard*.

Business Intelligence

Enterprise Systems

Fundamental to providing *balanced scorecard* functionality is the development of *business intelligence* functionality within accounting and ERP systems. **Business intelligence** is the integration of statistical and analytical tools with decision support technologies to facilitate complex analyses of *data warehouses* by managers and decision makers. A *business intelligence* solution within an accounting and ERP system should provide the tools, including an interface and access to data, for effective business decision making.

A typical ERP *business intelligence* module provides information details in a hierarchical form. At the top level, the user generally receives summary information on selected key performance indicators and can arrange this information into a variety of reports for analysis, performance measurement, or business modeling. From these summary reports (presented in electronic format), the user can subsequently drill down through further levels of detail to determine the key underlying factors driving performance. Although on the surface this does not seem complex, the reality is that the *business intelligence* modules use highly complex analytical techniques to search for relationships in the data that will provide insight for decision making.

eXtensible Business Reporting Language (XBRL)

E-Business

Perhaps the most exciting technology-driven advancement in business reporting is that of *XBRL*. **eXtensible Business Reporting Language (XBRL)** is an *XML*-based language consisting of a set of tags that are used to unify the presentation of business reporting information into a single format, easily read by almost any software package, and easily searched by Web browsers. **Technology Summary 16.1** details the background of XBRL and the impact it has on financial reporting.

Enterprise Systems

As described in Chapter 3, *XML* is a generalized system for the customized tagging of data to enable the definition, transmission, and interpretation of data over the Internet. *XML* uses predefined tags to let information providers create uniform information for users. XBRL provides the framework for uniformity of information for financial statements and other business reporting to simplify the delivery and use of that information. XBRL enhances the searchability of the information, its comparability among periods and organizations, and enables easy transfer of information among a variety of systems including those of regulators. This framework is based on the concept of a **taxonomy**,[6] a group of definitions that together provide meaning to reporting concepts. *Taxonomies* are used to define accounting, financial and nonfinancial reporting terms in a disciplined manner. For example, the US-GAAP-INS taxonomy describes the tags that are used for business reporting by U.S.-based insurance companies. Using the unified formats, most ERP vendors (and other accounting software vendors) have added functionality that allows an organization to automatically generate XBRL-based financial reports as well as any other business report. This makes it easier (less costly and less complex) to deliver business information via the Web. Thus, accessibility of information should increase for external users of business reports, and the information should be easier to interpret, analyze, and use for comparisons. **Technology Application 16.1** (pg. 616) provides an example of XBRL tags, from a trial balance *instance document*.

Technology Summary 16.1

XBRL: TRANSFORMING BUSINESS REPORTING

XBRL is a language for the electronic communication of business and financial data that is revolutionizing business reporting around the world. It provides major benefits in the preparation, analysis, and communication of business information. It offers cost savings, greater efficiency, and improved accuracy and reliability to all those involved in supplying or using financial data.

XBRL is being developed by an international nonprofit consortium of approximately 450 major companies, organizations, and government agencies. It is an open standard, free of license fees. Already being put to practical use in a number of countries, implementations of XBRL are growing rapidly around the world.

The idea behind XBRL is simple. Instead of treating financial information as a block of text—as in a standard Internet page or a printed document—it provides an identifying tag for each individual item of data that is computer readable. For example, company net profit has its own unique tag.

The introduction of XBRL tags enables automated processing of business information by computer software, cutting out laborious and costly processes of manual re-entry and comparison. Computers can treat XBRL data "intelligently": they can recognize the information in a XBRL document, select it, analyze it, store it, exchange it with other computers, and present it automatically in a variety of ways for users. XBRL greatly increases the speed of handling financial data, reduces the chance of error, and permits automatic checking of information.

Companies can use XBRL to reduce costs and streamline their processes for collecting and reporting financial information. Consumers of financial data, including investors, analysts, financial institutions, and regulators, can receive, find, compare, and analyze data much more rapidly and efficiently in XBRL format.

XBRL can handle data in different languages and accounting standards as well. It can be adapted flexibly to meet different requirements and uses. Data can be transformed into XBRL by suitable mapping tools, or it can be generated in XBRL by appropriate software. XBRL offers major benefits at all stages of business reporting and analysis. The benefits are seen in automation; cost savings; faster, more reliable, and more accurate handling of data; improved analysis; and better quality of information and decision making.

XBRL enables producers and consumers of financial data to switch resources away from costly manual processes, typically involving time-consuming comparison, assembly, and re-entry of data. They are able to concentrate effort on analysis, aided by software that can validate and manipulate XBRL information. As just one example, searches for particular information, which might in the past have taken hours, can be completed with XBRL in a fraction of a second.

Those who stand to benefit include all who collect business data, including governments, regulators, economic agencies, stock exchanges, financial information companies, and the like, and those who produce or use business data, including accountants, auditors, company managers, financial analysts, investors, and creditors. Among those who can take advantage of XBRL are accountancy software vendors, the financial services industry, investor relations companies, and the information technology industry.

Sources: www.xbrl.org/whatisxbrl/ and www.xbrl.org/BenefitsAndUses/. Copyright © 2002 XBRL International. All Rights Reserved. www.XBRL.org/legal/. Accessed May 25, 2010.

---

[6]For this information as well as more information on taxonomies, instance documents, and other XBRL-related concepts that are beyond the scope of this text, see "XBRL Specification and Guidance Stack" at www.xbrl.org/technical/SGS-PWD-2005-05-17.htm; accessed June 2, 2010.

Technology Application 16.1

AN EXAMPLE OF XBRL

You have heard much about XBRL, but would you recognize the codes if you saw them?

The following is based on an example of an *instance document* for an XBRL-GL trial balance. The excerpt relates to the presentation of two accounts: Prepaid Expenses and Sales. As you can see, the general structure is similar to other Web-based languages such as HTML or XML. Tags (identifiers) are enclosed in angle

brackets (< and >, e.g., <glc:entryDetail>). The end of a specific tag includes a slash before the identifier (/, e.g., </glc:entryDetail>). Several tags are included for each data element. The excerpt for Prepaid Expenses includes GL account number: 1600; account name: Prepaid Expenses; amount: 500; date: December 31, 2011; as well as the GL category to which the item belongs: currentAssets. Also embedded in the item is the version of XBRL taxonomy that was used to create the data item and the location of that definition.

Instance of Prepaid Expenses:
```
<glc:entryDetail>
  <glc:account>
      <glc:accountMainID nonNumericContext="s1">1600</glc:accountMainID>
      <glc:accountMainDescription nonNumericContext="s1">Prepaid
      Expenses</glc:accountMainDescription>
  </glc:account>
  <glc:amount numericContext="c1">500</glc:amount>
  <glc:postingDate nonNumericContext="s1">2011-12-31</glc:postingDate>
  <glc:xbrlInfo>
      <glc:xbrlTaxonomy nonNumericContext="s1">http://www.xbrl.org/us/gaap/ci/2000-07-31/
      us-gaap-ci-2000-07-31</glc:xbrlTaxonomy>
      <glc:xbrlElement nonNumericContext="s1">currentAssets.prepaidExpenses</glc:xbrlElement>
  </glc:xbrlInfo>
</glc:entryDetail>
```

Instance of Sales:
```
<glc:entryDetail>
    <glc:account>
        <glc:accountMainID nonNumericContext="s1">4000</glc:accountMainID>
        <glc:accountMainDescription nonNumericContext="s1">Sales</glc:accountMainDescription>
</glc:account>
    <glc:amount numericContext="c1">-82000</glc:amount>
    <glc:postingDate nonNumericContext="s1">2011-12-31</glc:postingDate>
    <glc:xbrlInfo>
        <glc:xbrlTaxonomy nonNumericContext="s1">http://www.xbrl.org/us/gaap/ci/2000-07-31/
        us-gaap-ci-2000-07-31</glc:xbrlTaxonomy>
        <glc:xbrlElement nonNumericContext="s1">salesRevenueNet.salesRevenueGross</glc:xbrlElement>
        </glc:xbrlInfo>
</glc:entryDetail>
```

From this example, you can see the richness of information about a "number" (500 in our example) that can be included in an XBRL instance document. Decision makers can use this information when they are trying to make comparisons between companies that support the taxonomy.

An **instance** or **instance document** is an XBRL document that contains all information, at a given point in time, including tags, about the occurrence of an item—for example, a trial balance *instance document* is a document that contains data and tags necessary to produce a trial balance at a specific point in time. After studying Technology Application 16.1, you should have an idea of how XBRL tags identify many characteristics of a data item and how those characteristics flow with the data because they are attached as tags.

For years, numerous regulators around the world have been accepting or requiring filing to be completed in an XBRL format. Recently, in the United States, the Securities and Exchange Commission has updated their filing system and has begun a phased-in requirement that filings be submitted using XBRL. This requirement came after a period of voluntary filings, and is being implemented over several years beginning with large companies (2009); all filers are required to use XBRL for filings related to fiscal periods ending after June 15, 2011.[7] The SEC's move to require XBRL filing is perhaps one of the most significant signs of support for XBRL as a reporting standard. Each of the XBRL-enabled filings will be available to the public for use in a variety of analytical processes, enabling improved analytical efficiency (it is faster to gather data electronically than manually) and effectiveness (companies will tag their own data, reflecting their intent rather than the analyst making certain assumptions). It should be noted that, initially, many companies have outsourced the tagging process and generation of SEC filings, although as the filing processes and ERP systems are refined, many of these companies may choose to bring the filing process back in-house.

The information in Technology Summary 16.1 places XBRL in the context of business reporting and should give you some sense of the scope of XBRL's impact on the reporting, reading, and analysis of financial information.

The Sarbanes-Oxley Act

In Chapter 1, we briefly introduced you to the impact that the Sarbanes-Oxley Act of 2002 (SOX) has had on the accounting profession. In Chapter 7, we described how SOX has affected organizational governance. Exhibit 7.4 (pg. 226) outlines the 11 parts of SOX. In this section, we discuss a few parts of this law that pertain specifically to business and financial reporting. We should note that at the time of this writing, the law only applies to SEC-registered companies, although many smaller companies and not-for-profits are applying similar procedures.

The intent of SOX, as stated in the act, is "To protect investors by improving the accuracy and reliability of corporate disclosures made pursuant to the securities laws, and for other purposes." Practically speaking, it is a new set of rules that applies to many areas, including financial reporting. Section 302 establishes who is responsible for financial reporting. It states that the CEO and CFO of an organization must certify that the statements neither contain material untrue facts nor omit material facts. The CEO and CFO also must certify that they have established and evaluated internal controls for the accounting system that produces the reports. Let's think about what this means. In earlier chapters, we discussed many controls that are necessary to ensure the proper operation of an accounting system. Historically, we made internal auditors, officers, department heads, and management throughout the organization responsible for internal controls. SOX makes top management responsible, with penalties of up to 20 years in prison and $5 million in fines for violations.

SOX

---

[7]For the specific SEC rules on XBRL filing requirements, see www.sec.gov/rules/final/2009/33-9002.pdf; accessed May 25, 2010.

Section 401 of the act covers disclosures in financial reports. Generally accepted accounting principles (GAAP) include circumstances where certain items may or may not be disclosed in financial reports. "Off balance sheet" items are addressed in Section 401, thereby redefining GAAP for these items. The section also calls for transparent reporting of the economic effect of such transactions. This means that the report should clearly reflect, rather than obscure, the economic reality of business events.

As previously discussed, top management is responsible for internal controls. Section 404 mandates that the SEC sets rules defining a report of internal controls that must be included in a company's annual report. The report must include the responsibility of management and an attestation to the control relative to internal control evaluation and reporting.

The last section of SOX we will discuss is Section 409. This section states that companies "shall disclose to the public on a rapid and current basis such additional information concerning material changes in the financial condition or operations of the issuer…." This means that if anything material occurs, the SEC and the public must be notified. With this, Congress is taking us a step toward continuous or real-time reporting. If companies have in place the capability to report business events as they occur, as well as the financial impact of those events, providing key financial information to the public on a much more frequent basis than quarterly reporting is a relatively small step. We believe that this legislation will ultimately have a major effect on financial and business reporting for a multitude of organizations. As we leave this discussion, we ask that you consider the impact that these requirements will have on the GL/BR process.

The Impact of U.S. GAAP and IFRS Convergence

In the United States, there has been much uncertainty recently regarding the direction of accounting standard setting. The United States has a history of developing accounting standards independent of the rest of the world. Currently in the United States, the Financial Accounting Standards Board (FASB) is the body with the mission of establishing and improving financial accounting and reporting standards. This body of standards is typically referred to as U.S. GAAP. A separate entity, the International Accounting Standards Board (IASB), is a standard-setting body located in London, with the objective of developing globally accepted international financial reporting standards (IFRS). Over the past few years, there has been much discussion regarding "convergence" of U.S. GAAP and IFRS. Convergence implies that the standards will blend together, with differences reconciled, and ultimately we will have one set of standards that can be used worldwide.

While the FASB and IASB communicate when working on new standards, and are generally consistent in that arena, the reconciliation of differences from existing standards can be significant and sometimes a political issue. One example of differences between U.S. GAAP and IFRS relates to the use of last-in-first-out (LIFO) for inventory costing. In the United States it is the costing method that many companies adopted during periods of high inflation to best match costs and revenues. A side effect of LIFO is that the balance sheet value of inventories tends to be well below current cost (for cost of sales, companies have been using the newer, higher-cost items, leaving the lower-cost items in inventory). U.S. GAAP allows LIFO costing, while IFRS does not. If LIFO costing is eliminated, many companies will have inflated income in the year of changing from LIFO, as well as significant tax liabilities. Any time there is the potential for significant tax liabilities, there will likely be a political issue.

Depending on the political climate at any point in time, interest in the convergence of GAAP and IFRS changes. Ultimately, as accountants, we should be prepared to deal with international standards. With the existence of many international organizations, it is highly likely that during your career, you will need knowledge of standards beyond U.S. GAAP (or beyond your country's standards). To be prepared, the AICPA has adjusted its guidelines and now includes IFRS as a topic that can be included on the Uniform CPA Examination. From a systems perspective, you should ensure that your system will provide the utmost in flexibility—allowing the preparation of financial and business information in any format that may be required. Some obvious considerations include flexibility in the aggregation of accounts and the order of presentation in financial reports. In Chapter 17, you will consider the process of creating and/or selecting accounting systems; that process should consider the impact of changing accounting standards, including significant changes such as GAAP/ IFRS convergence.

Current Environment for External Financial Reporting

In the past few years, technology has created an environment in which users can demand immediate information. "Overnight delivery," once the fastest way to transfer information between two entities, is frequently too slow and expensive and is replaced by a fax. The fax eliminates the one-day wait for the information. Today, many people opt for e-mail with document attachments, eliminating the need for a walk to the fax machine or the cost of a call. Many who continue to use faxes have them directly routed to their e-mail with other messages. The same trend is occurring with respect to financial reporting. Year-end financial reports contain information that already has been released or, at a minimum, is based on events that occurred months or even more than a year prior to the financial statement release. Investors want more information faster. The government is also pushing for timelier reporting. In addition to the Sarbanes-Oxley Act's requirement of "rapid and current" disclosures, the SEC has marginally shortened the time in which companies are required to file some reports, and roundtables have indicated that real-time reporting is not only feasible but also desirable. To obtain real-time reporting, *enterprise systems* must be in place so that data flows to the GL in a real-time manner. If it is feasible, and investors and regulators want it, real-time reporting is likely just over the horizon.

Enterprise Systems

One of the issues directly related to real-time reporting, or continuous reporting as it is sometimes called, is the assurance that the reports reflect the reality of the firm. **Continuous assurance (continuous auditing)**[8] is the process by which assurance is provided through monitoring of automated controls and business events in real time or near real time. This monitoring may be accomplished through the use of "audit modules" embedded in ERP software or by providing the auditor access through a query tool (such as SQL). Much of the interest in continuous auditing has been driven by internal auditors who see the benefit of detecting problems quickly to prevent them from recurring or getting larger. A complete rethinking of the audit process, continuous assurance is an area that is currently under study by several large accounting firms, internal auditors at large organizations, and many academics.[9]

---

[8]The terms "continuous audit" and "continuous assurance" are frequently used interchangeably. Continuous audit is descriptive of moving the traditional audit product to a continuous form. Continuous assurance includes audit as well as the continuous implementation of nonaudit assurance services.

[9]For more information on continuous auditing, see http://raw.rutgers.edu/wcars/.

Summary

This chapter had much to say about electronic inputs to the GL/BR process. But what about system outputs? We have been somewhat conditioned by our other accounting courses to expect hard-copy documents. Will we ever see the day when business reporting will do away with paper reports and use "electronic reports"? The answer is a resounding yes! The advent of XBRL is one clear indicator that major changes are on the way. Other projects also have existed for several years at the IRS (electronic tax return filing) and at the SEC (electronic filing of annual 10-Ks). Electronic filing at the IRS has mushroomed since its inception. In fact, from 1989 to 2009, the number of electronically filed returns grew from 1.2 million to more than 100 million. Ultimately, the IRS wants 80 percent of all returns to be electronically filed by 2012.[10]

At the heart of the SEC's system is EDGAR (Electronic Data Gathering, Analysis, and Retrieval) and a front-end processing package called FSA—financial statement analyzer. Such a system is imperative when the filings are in a text format. Now, the SEC is committed to the future use of XBRL and moving away from EDGAR to an interactive environment. Although current connection to EDGAR through the Internet provides easy access to the text-based financial statements of public companies for almost anyone, using those statements remains difficult. One company, EDGAR Online, Inc., has developed an online database that interprets the text-based SEC filings and provides them in a database form, complete with XBRL tagging. The service is available for a fee.

Some accounting visionaries predict that in the near future, traditional, *periodic financial reporting*, such as that available through EDGAR, will be displaced by *continuous online financial reporting*.[11] Part of the centralized database reporting scenario runs along the following lines: Interested parties (i.e., all "users" who are interested in an organization's financial statements) could access a company's centralized database *at any time* through the Internet. The database would contain both financial and operating data. Through menu options, users would make different inquiries of the database, depending on their needs; a report-writing facility would allow them to tailor reports to suit those varied needs. Finally, the independent auditor's role would change from that of rendering an opinion on the fairness of periodic financial statements to one of rendering an opinion on the integrity of the database and the reliability of the systems generating the information. Does this sound a lot like the capability that XBRL is promising to provide? It should. Are you prepared to assume the auditor's revised role as information assurer? Changes are coming just about as quickly as graduation.

Key Terms

general ledger and business reporting (GL/BR) process, 599

general ledger (GL) process, 599

business reporting process, 600

feeder process, 600

managerial reporting officer, 603

financial reporting officer, 603

---

[10]www.treas.gov/irsob/press_posting_01272010.shtml, accessed May 25, 2010.

[11]See Robert K. Elliott, "Assurance Services and the Audit Heritage," *Auditing: A Journal of Practice and Theory*, Supplement 1998; and Steve G. Sutton, "The Changing Face of Accounting and the Driving Force of Advanced Information Technologies," *International Journal of Accounting Information Systems*, March 2000.

Review Questions

RQ 16-1   What are the primary functions the GL/BR process performs?

RQ 16-2   What, in your own words, does business reporting entail?

RQ 16-3   What are the fundamental responsibilities of each of the following positions or departments: business reporting department, budgeting department, financial reporting officer, managerial reporting officer?

RQ 16-4   What, in your own words, are a performance report and the responsibility accounting/reporting model?

RQ 16-5   What major *logical* processes does the GL/BR process perform?

RQ 16-6   Why is the *hierarchical coding* system a good fit for the general ledger system?

RQ 16-7   What limitations are faced by contemporary accounting systems applying traditional general ledger account structures?

RQ 16-8   In your own words, how do ERP financial modules facilitate the GL/BR process?

RQ 16-9   In your own words, how do ERP systems facilitate *balanced scorecard* and *business intelligence*?

RQ 16-10 Why is XBRL so important to efficient Web-based business reporting?

RQ 16-11 How does the Sarbanes-Oxley Act of 2002 affect the GL/BR process?

RQ 16-12 What process is used to monitor controls and events to provide assurance in real-time? Why has the internal auditor been the main driver of the process?

RQ 16-13 What two groups of information users are interested in real-time reporting?

Discussion Questions

DQ 16-1   Discuss fully the difference between the "contexts" of Figure 16.1 (pg. 601) and Figure 16.4 (pg. 606).

DQ 16-2   Four managers (or departments) are shown in Figure 16.1 as reporting to the controller. Setting aside your personal career inclinations and aspirations and ignoring any work experience you have, for which position do you think your college academic studies to date have best prepared you? Discuss. Does your answer hold any implications for the curriculum design at your college? Explain.

DQ 16-3 In the real world, what problems might an organization face in performing *interim closings*? For example, the books might be left open after a December 31 closing until auditing adjusting entries are made in March or April. During the same period, interim financial statements for the new year are required. Can you suggest any solutions for those problems? Discuss fully.

DQ 16-4 This chapter assumed that the controller was the source of all *adjusting entry* journal vouchers. Mention at least one alternative source for each of the following adjustments (and explain your answers):

    a. Estimated bad debts

    b. Interest accruals

    c. Lower of cost or market adjustments for inventories

    d. Lower of cost or market adjustments for investments

    e. Depreciation adjustments

    f. Differences between physical inventory counts and perpetual inventories

DQ 16-5 "Defining the codes for a chart of accounts is no big deal—nothing is permanent—I can change it at any time in the future." Why do you agree (or disagree) with this statement?

DQ 16-6 Read Section 409 from the Sarbanes-Oxley Act of 2002. Do you agree that this supports real-time financial reporting? Research both sides of the issue, and provide a conclusion based on your findings.

DQ 16-7 What is the overall significance of the Sarbanes-Oxley Act of 2002 to financial reporting?

DQ 16-8 Discuss why internal auditors may be more open to *continuous assurance* than external auditors.

Short Problems

SP 16-1 Design a chart of accounts for an international distribution company's income statement. Include flexibility to allow reports by country, division, and type of sale (wholesale and retail). You do not need to provide a complete chart, but include at a minimum sales and cost of sales. Identify each digit or segment of the account numbers.

SP 16-2 Many business events are recorded in the general ledger from feeder processes. The first list below identifies eight business events. The second list specifies five feeder processes. Match the events with the processes. Each process may have one or more event specified. Some events may not be used.

Business Events

    A. Purchase order is issued to a vendor

    B. Inventory is received from a vendor

    C. Inventory is returned from a customer

    D. Cash is disbursed for inventory purchased

    E. Bad debts are written off

F. Employer taxes are accrued

G. Cash is received from a sale

H. Employer taxes are deposited

I. Inventory is sold to a customer

Feeder Processes

____ 1. B/AR/CR process

____ 2. Purchasing process

____ 3. OE/S process

____ 4. AP/CD process

____ 5. Payroll process

Problems

P16-1   The context diagram in Figure 16.4 (pg. 606) shows the data flows running to the general ledger from the feeder processes studied in Chapters 10 through Chapters 15.

    a.   For each data flow in Figure 16.4, show the journal entry (in debit/credit journal entry format, with no dollar amounts) that would result (make and state any assumptions that you think are necessary).

    b.   Name at least two other entries that would normally come from the feeder processes that are not shown in Figure 16.4.

    c.   In journal form, show one *representative* entry (including an entry explanation) that the treasurer would furnish for (1) investing transaction activities and (2) financing transaction activities.

P16-2   Refer to the level 0 DFD shown in Figure 16.5 (pg. 608).

Draw a lower-level DFD for each of the following processes shown in Figure 16.5. Make sure that each lower-level DFD is *balanced* with its parent.

    a.   Process 3.0—Record adjustments

    b.   Process 4.0—Prepare business reports

P16-3   In this chapter, we acknowledged the inconsistency between the "context" assumed in Figure 16.1 (pg. 601) and that in Figures 16.4 and Figure 16.5.

Redraw the DFDs in Figures 16.4 and Figure 16.5 to make them consistent with Figure 16.1. *Hint:* Figure 16.1 includes the treasurer, controller, and certain others *within* the system.

P16-4   Examine the *responsibility accounting performance reporting* illustration shown in Figure 16.2 (pg. 603).

    a.   Design a data-coding scheme that will facilitate the aggregation of data as the data "filter" upward. Use the specific facts that appear in Figure 16.2. Make and state any assumptions you think are necessary.

    b.   In no more than two paragraphs, explain how your coding scheme works. Include a discussion of positions in the organization other than those in the production function.

      c. In no more than three paragraphs, explain how your scheme might be handled in a centralized database environment without the codes.

P16-5   Find two sets of financial statements from companies within one industry.

List any problems you have in doing a comparison of the balance sheets. Describe how using XBRL could help alleviate these problems.

P16-6   For this problem, use an enterprise system with which you are familiar, or identify a system by searching vendor sites on the Internet.

      a. How does the package's "feeder" systems compare to those presented in Figure 16.4 (pg. 606)?

      b. What financial reports are included in the standard suite of reports? Is a custom report-writer module available? Discuss the significance of report-writer modules.

P16-7   Using the Internet, find an article that describes an area where an author believes continuous assurance will be (or would have been) of great value to solve a problem, or prevent a problem in the future.

Write a short paper, two pages maximum (unless your instructor directs otherwise) describing the author's position, and present an opposing point of view (you can use other articles to support your opposing view). It is likely that the author also describes weaknesses in the position. Be sure to include references.

P16-8   There are many alternatives to help companies prepare XBRL-tagged financial information for regulatory filings. XBRL.org provides a listing of many of the organizations that provide these alternatives (http://xbrl.org/frontend.aspx?clk=SLK&val=96). Identify two service providers, one that provides outsourcing services for the tagging/filing process and another that helps complete the process internal to the company. What do each of the vendors purport to be their strengths? (For example, the outsource vendor will likely provide reasons why outsourcing is the preferred method, while the internal software provider will likely claim the converse.) What are weaknesses of each alternative?

P16-9   Describe how the GL/BR process focuses more on information functions than operational functions. Contrast the GL/BR with another business process (payroll, AP/ CD, B/AR/CR, etc.) to highlight the different focuses inherent in the processes.

P16-10   Discuss how emerging technologies, such as the Internet, affect the GL/BR process. In what ways will organizations have to adapt their business processes to reflect the changes in these external factors?

ACCESS   P16-11   This problem illustrates how business event data from feeder processes can be transformed into GL/accounting information. It should be completed with database software, such as Microsoft Access.

      1. Using the E-R diagram in Figure 11.9 (pg. 408), select the CUSTOMERS, SALES_INVOICES, and CASH_RECEIPTS entities and implement them as tables using Microsoft Access (or any other database software acceptable to your instructor). Link the tables using the cardinalities shown in the figure. For the tables, you may use attributes shown in Figure 11.10 (pg. 410) or create different attributes.

2. Create forms for each table from part 1 of this problem and use the forms to populate the tables with representative data. Forms should be in good order, readable, and properly formatted. Create at least three records in each table. Print out the populated tables and one instance of each form.

3. Design a query using the tables from part 1 of this problem to determine outstanding accounts receivables for each customer (i.e., the difference between how much each customer has been invoiced and how much each customer has paid toward the invoice). Print out the output of the query and attach an explanation as to why someone would be interested in the query output.

4. Using the report function in Access, design a report for the query from part 3 of this problem. Reports should be in good order, readable, and properly formatted. Print out the report.

Requirements: As directed by your instructor, submit the completed database file and the printouts noted above.

Acquiring an AIS

CHAPTER 17

Acquiring and Implementing Accounting Information Systems

Learning Objectives

After reading this chapter, you should be able to:

* Describe the systems acquisition/development process and its major phases and steps.
* Understand the differences in the development process for acquiring a system versus developing it in-house.
* Understand the nature and importance of the accountant's involvement in the systems acquisition/development process.

Political power struggles. Jockeying for position. Personal ambition. Multijurisdictional conflict. Is this a story of conflict between nations—or the plot of an international thriller? Well, in reality, these are things you must consider when acquiring and installing a new or revised accounting information system (AIS). There is much more to an AIS than debits and credits—or even software and hardware. Managing the process and the people involved requires a considerable effort for the successful implementation of the new or revised system.

If we measure the success of a systems implementation as meeting user requirements, delivering the system on time, and completing the implementation within the budget, we are successful in fewer than one of every three instances.[1] In one recent year, the cost of such project failures in the European Union was €142 billion (over $200 billion). Now, look into the future—as a professional accountant, at some time in your career, you will likely be asked to participate in, or manage, a project to implement a new or revised AIS. The cost of that project may be from a few thousand to hundreds of millions of dollars (or euros). How can you make sure your project is successful? One way is to equip yourself with the knowledge of the factors that make projects fail or succeed. That knowledge includes the business processes presented in earlier chapters, and the processes presented in this chapter.

Many systems development projects are canceled when the new system fails to work with the organization's business processes, the project lacks leadership, benefits are overstated, and the project managers do not use adequate change management

---

[1]The Standish Group's "CHAOS Summary 2009" reports that only 32 percent of all projects are successful; http://standishgroup.com/newsroom/chaos_2009.php, accessed June 15, 2010.

procedures. Many of these factors are also involved in projects that were completed but considered unsuccessful. Additionally, causes of failure have included poor communication with stakeholders, poorly defined software requirements, bad technical design, and inadequate test planning for the new system.

Based on the likelihood of failure, do you think that maybe you ought to leave the "systems stuff" to others? That probably will not be an option. The International Federation of Accountants (IFAC), in its International Education Guideline No. 11, states that in addition to being a systems user, as a professional accountant, you should expect to serve as a designer, evaluator, and/or manager of information systems. As you study this chapter, try to imagine yourself in each of these roles. As a designer, you will need to know what systems development tasks need to be completed—and when and how—for an IT project to be successful. For example, you will need to work with users to obtain systems specifications and to receive help in testing the system before implementation. As an evaluator and/or manager, you will need to determine if the system's outputs are correct and if the system consumes resources efficiently. Knowing how the system was developed and installed will help you zero in on problem areas. From each perspective, knowledge of the system's development process can help ensure that your IT project falls within that one of every three attempted that is successful. Otherwise, you may be trying to explain why your project is in the other 68 percent.[2]

Synopsis

Driven by a host of sometimes complementary but often conflicting demands, the selection of AIS and other information systems for use throughout organizations requires considerable planning and forethought. There are constraints, trade-offs, and tough decisions at every turn in the road. For instance, users are demanding more robust services from their information systems, customers are insisting on quicker response times and more flexible interfaces, organizations are becoming more internally interconnected, trading partners are moving toward fully integrated supply chains, competitive business pressures are bearing down on today's organizations, and new opportunities provided by advanced information technologies are cropping up everywhere. As a result, a modern organization must adapt its information systems quickly and continuously. And because the tentacles of AIS reach deep into information systems throughout the organization, AIS must also continuously adjust to rapidly changing conditions.

To be successful in the acquisition and implementation of AIS and other IS, organizations typically follow procedures that are considered best practices. These procedures, called **systems development**, comprise the steps undertaken to create, modify, or maintain an organization's information system. The systems development process is made up of four primary phases: systems analysis, design, implementation, and

---

[2]The source of the information included in this vignette is John McManus and Trevor Wood Harper, "Understanding the Sources of Information Systems Project Failure," *Management Services* 51(3), Autumn 2007, pp. 38–43.

operation. The *systems development life cycle (SDLC)* is the term often used to describe the progression through the phases of the systems development process, from birth through implementation to ongoing use.

During the analysis phase, an organization decides whether it will develop the IT system in-house (i.e., make) or acquire the system from a third party (i.e., buy). In either case, the organization must perform a structured systems analysis, or needs analysis, to determine the features that the new system must have. Without a well-understood and documented target (i.e., user requirements), there is no chance of achieving a successful development process.

The second phase, systems design, takes the needs determined during the analysis process and defines the details of the system—to be developed in-house or acquired—that will meet those needs. The hardware and infrastructure to support the system are also selected in this phase.

After the design is complete, the next step is the implementation of the new system. With a purchased system, the implementation includes configuring the software, as well as converting data, training users, and performing other practical tasks. The implementation process for a system developed in-house additionally includes the programming and testing of code.

The final phase of the SDLC is the systems operation. This phase includes the post-implementation review, in which the project is evaluated. This phase is important because successes and failures in the current project can provide valuable lessons for future projects.

At different points in your professional career, you will probably have many roles within the systems development process. You will be a system user or business process owner articulating your needs, or you will be a member of the development team that must determine and document such needs. You may be in a position to decide what system to buy. You may manage an implementation or find problems that must be resolved in a new system. As an auditor, you might provide assurance that a system meets user needs, has adequate controls, and has been developed in accordance with prescribed procedures. This chapter exposes you to the systems development process to give you an understanding of that process. That understanding should help ensure the success of your projects and audits.

Introduction

The acquisition or in-house development of an information system is a major event in the life of an organization, and both require many of the same techniques of analysis, design, implementation, and systems operations. The major difference is how the system is implemented: with a prepackaged solution, an internally developed system, or some combination of the two. On the surface, it seems intuitively appealing to build your own IS that is specifically tailored to your organization's needs. But in reality, this is a time-consuming and complex undertaking. However, in some circumstances, in-house development is the only reasonable solution. In such cases, organizations should take precautionary measures aimed at reducing the risk of failure to an acceptably low level by following a structured approach to managing the project at every step of the process.

In this chapter, you will study a structured approach to developing information systems called the **systems development life cycle (SDLC) methodology**, which is a formalized, standardized, documented set of activities used to manage a systems development project.

Acquiring an AIS from External Parties

Organizations not wanting to or unable to develop software in-house may purchase, rent, or lease a commercially available software package. Such software can be acquired from computer manufacturers, software vendors, mail-order houses and retail stores (for PC software), turnkey system suppliers, service bureaus, systems integrators, outsourcing firms, application service providers (ASP), and software as a service (SaaS) providers. ASPs are currently an important segment of the outsourcing market. SaaS is a growing segment of the software market. **Technology Summary 17.1** describes ASPs and SaaSs.

An organization should consider the financial implications of the decision to develop (make) versus buy software. Because software vendors can allocate development costs across many products and across multiple copies of each product, the prices they charge to recover these costs are usually substantially less than the organization would pay to develop the package in-house. Generally, software developed in-house can cost up to ten times more than purchased software. Additionally, the annual maintenance of in-house software is typically 50 percent of the development cost, whereas

---

Technology Summary 17.1

APPLICATION SERVICE PROVIDER (ASP)

An application service provider (ASP) offers a traditional outsourcing mechanism whereby it hosts, manages, and provides access to application software and hardware over the Internet to multiple customers. The fee is really a rental based on usage. Some ASPs provide service for free, obtaining revenue from advertising and the sale of other services. ASPs relieve the organization of the burden of developing or buying and installing software and hardware. Because ASPs are accessed over the Internet, a user needs only a Web browser and a basic PC or other method of accessing the Internet (such as a browser-enabled mobile phone) to obtain the ASP service.

When using an ASP, a user obtains constantly updated software. The user does not need the technical resources to install or support the application. ASPs are a good choice for applications where the user does not want to purchase and maintain the application or simply wants access from any Internet access point. QuickBooks Online Edition and TurboTax, both from Intuit, Inc., are two consumer products that traditionally have been sold as "purchase and install" but are now available as an ASP service.

SOFTWARE AS A SERVICE (SaaS)

Software as a service (SaaS) is a Web-based model of software distribution where multiple users may simultaneously use the software. SaaS provides results similar to an ASP, with some underlying differences. ASPs are generally traditional applications with Web interfaces, whereas SaaSs are typically created for the Web environment and are frequently implemented in a cloud computing setting. With an ASP, the hosting site may have application knowledge as well as hardware configured to optimize the software, whereas SaaS applications may be hosted by third parties unrelated to the software provider or developer. One of the more widely adopted examples of SaaS is Google Apps.[a] Google Apps' offerings include on-demand, net-based document creation and management (Docs), e-mail (Gmail), video hosting and streaming (Video), and sharing capabilities (Sites).

[a]See www.google.com/a for more information.

the annual maintenance for purchased software normally costs only 25 percent of the purchase price.

To increase the potential market for a software package, vendors develop packages for a wide audience. This strategy leads to products that seldom possess characteristics exactly matching any particular organization's requirements. Organizations not satisfied with these generic packages can contract with a vendor to modify one of the vendor's existing software packages or develop a custom-tailored software package written specifically to meet the organization's unique requirements.

The bottom line is that when a *suitable* standard package exists, buy it rather than try to reinvent it in-house. Notice the emphasis on *suitable*. By using a standard package, you are gaining the benefit of a system that incorporates the best practices of other organizations—potentially providing you a way to improve your operations. However, an organization's ability to distinguish itself and gain competitive advantage may be limited when it uses the same systems as competitors. Other considerations when choosing to develop a system in-house include the organization's internal resources (personnel, capital) and available vendor support.

Managing the Systems Development Process

The systems development objectives are the following:

- To ensure the information system satisfies an organization's informational and operational needs (product-oriented objective)
- To develop/acquire an information system in an efficient and effective manner (process-oriented objective)

Controls

The key to achieving the first objective is to control the process. We can understand the complexity of controlling the systems development process by comparing it to a construction project. Assume you are in charge of the construction of an industrial park. What problems and questions might you encounter? For instance, you might want to know the following: "How much of the project is whose responsibility?" "Who should handle legal and financial matters?" "Who obtains the building permits?" "Who is responsible for contacting the tenants/buyers to determine special needs?"

The project's size and duration cause another set of problems. How will you coordinate the work of the carpenters, masons, electricians, and plumbers? How will you see that a tenant's special needs are incorporated into the specifications and then into the actual construction?

Information systems developers encounter similar problems. Given such problems, they have concluded that systems development must be carefully controlled and managed by following reliable project management principles and the organization's quality assurance framework, including its SDLC methodology. To help manage a development process, general tools, such as project management software, may be used. Additionally, some vendors have developed product-specific tools to aid with the time-consuming and complex tasks of selecting and implementing an ERP system. Microsoft has developed a project planning solution called Sure Step to help in this process for its Dynamics line of programs. Sure Step is a methodology providing a set of tools and templates that guides a project team throughout the life cycle of a project. The tools help with project diagnostics, analysis, design, deployment, operations, and upgrades of Microsoft Dynamics products.[3] Sure Step provides guidelines for project management processes and the roles involved in an implementation project. By defining the consultant and customer roles, as well as the responsibilities for the processes and deliverables associated with each segment of the project, the likelihood of the success of the project increases. Sure Step's tools and techniques are based on concepts and standards developed by the Project Management Institute (www.pmi.org). The concepts discussed in this chapter are easily adaptable to methodologies such as Sure Step.

Systems Development Methodology

To effectively manage a systems development project, a standardized methodology, such as the *SDLC*, should be used. The *SDLC methodology* is appropriate when information systems are developed, acquired, or maintained. **Exhibit 17.1** describes characteristics of a systems development methodology. Following such a methodology should ensure that development efforts are efficient and consistently lead to information systems that meet organizational needs. These guidelines should be followed whether an organization is going to acquire an AIS or develop it in-house.

Figure 17.1 (pg. 634) presents the SDLC. The right side of the figure depicts the four development phases: systems analysis, systems design, systems implementation, and systems operation. The bubbles in Figure 17.1 identify the seven development steps undertaken to complete the four phases of development. Arrows flowing into each bubble represent the inputs needed to perform that step, whereas outward-flowing arrows represent the product of a step. A development process may not necessarily proceed

EXHIBIT 17.1   Characteristics of a Systems Development Methodology

- The project is divided into a number of identifiable processes, each having a starting and ending point. Each process comprises several activities, one or more *deliverables*, and several *management control points*. The division of the project into these small, manageable steps facilitates both project planning and project control.

- Specific reports and other documentation, called deliverables, must be produced periodically during systems development to make development personnel accountable for faithful execution of systems development tasks. An organization monitors the development process by reviewing the deliverables that are prepared at the end of each key step. Many organizations rely on this documentation for training new employees; it also provides users with a reference while they are operating the system.

- Users, managers, and auditors are required to participate in the project. These people generally provide approvals, often called *signoffs*, at preestablished management control points. Signoffs signify approval of the development process and the system being developed.

- The system must be tested thoroughly prior to implementation to ensure that it meets users' needs.

- A training plan is developed for those who will operate and use the new system.

- Formal program change controls (see Chapter 8) are established to preclude unauthorized changes to computer programs.

- A post-implementation review of all developed systems must be performed to assess the effectiveness and efficiency of the new system and of the development process.

---

[3]http://technet.microsoft.com/en-us/library/dd979122.aspx, accessed June 10, 2010; www.albaspectrum.com/V2.0/ Services/SureStep_Methodology.pdf, accessed June 10, 2010.

FIGURE 17.1 Systems Development Life Cycle

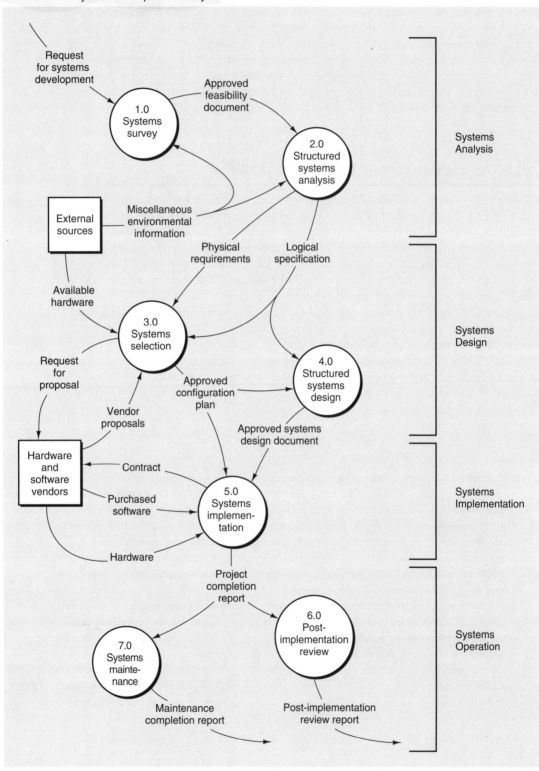

TABLE 17.1   Information Systems Development Phases, Purposes, and Tasks[a]

Phase	Purpose	Tasks
Analysis (bubbles 1.0 and 2.0)	Develop specifications for a new or revised system.	Study the problem and the problem's environment. Propose alternative problem solutions.
Design (bubbles 3.0 and 4.0)	Develop an appropriate system manifestation.	Convert the logical solution into a physical design. Choose software and hardware. Write the detailed design specifications. Devise implementation plans, system tests, and training programs.
Implementation (bubble 5.0)	Begin using the new system.	Write, test, and debug the computer programs. Convert to new or revised system.
Operation (bubbles 6.0 and 7.0)	Use the new system.	Conduct post-implementation review. Perform systems maintenance.

[a]Refers to Figure 17.1.

sequentially through these steps. Rather, steps may be performed iteratively, out of sequence, or not at all. **Table 17.1** lists the key purposes and tasks associated with the seven development steps (bubbles) shown in Figure 17.1. You should take some time now to review both the table and the figure. First, we will focus on the initial phase of the SDLC—systems analysis.

Systems Survey

The **systems survey**, often called a **feasibility study** or **preliminary feasibility study**, is a set of procedures conducted to determine the practicability of a potential systems development project and to prepare a systems development plan for projects considered feasible. Refer to Figure 17.1 to see the systems survey's place in the SDLC (bubble 1.0), its inputs (request for systems development and miscellaneous environmental information), and its output (approved feasibility document). An organization conducts a systems survey to determine, as quickly and as inexpensively as possible, whether it is worthwhile to proceed with subsequent development steps.

So that we can understand the systems survey process, we will compare systems development to building an industrial park. The architect's role for the industrial park is analogous to the analyst's role for systems development. In the preliminary stages of the industrial park project, the architect learns the general purpose of the industrial park (light manufacturing, warehousing, etc.). The architect also learns the approximate number of buildings and the size of each. From that information, the architect "sketches" a proposed park. From that sketch and the accompanying general specifications, estimated costs, and estimated schedule, the developer decides whether or not to proceed with the proposed project. This process is similar to that followed in the systems survey, with the systems analyst assuming the architect's role, and the organization's management (or the IT steering committee) replacing the developer.

The tasks required to complete the systems survey are as follows:

- *Determine the nature and the extent of each reported problem:* For instance, if a sales department reports a problem of late deliveries, we want to know whether deliveries really are late or if sales personnel are promising unrealistic delivery dates, or if there are delays within the organization or after goods leave the organization.
- *Determine the scope of the problem:* For example, is a reported purchasing problem confined to the purchasing process, or is there a broader problem requiring more extensive analysis?
- *Propose a course of action that might solve the problem:* For example, propose a modification of the purchasing process to correct a purchasing problem.
- *Determine the feasibility of any proposed development:* Is there a technically, operationally, legally, and economically feasible solution to the problem? For example, does computer technology exist to solve the problem (technical feasibility), is the organization ready to accept the new solution (operational feasibility), is the new solution in compliance with laws and regulations (legal feasibility), and are the payback and internal rate of return estimates sufficient to allow the development project to proceed (economic feasibility)?
- *Devise a detailed plan for conducting the analysis step:* Determine who will conduct the analysis, who will head the project team, what tasks are required, and the development timetable.
- *Develop a summary plan for the entire development project:* This should include, for example, when the system will be implemented, what divisions will participate, and so forth.

The systems survey tasks are important to help us determine the problem, the feasibility of solutions, and a plan for the project, but it is a *preliminary* analysis. After it is complete, we move to the *detailed* study of the proposed solution, the structured systems analysis.

Structured Systems Analysis

To help understand systems analysis, we will continue our industrial park analogy. If the developer approves the continuation of the project, the architect must conduct a *detailed* study to determine each building's specific use, required room sizes, electrical and plumbing requirements, floor load weights, private versus public areas, number of people that will occupy the completed buildings, technical requirements, and so on. During this detailed study, the architect develops a *functional* model of the proposed project. The detailed study by the architect is similar to systems analysis, and the logical specification (one of the outputs of the analysis step) is the model for the new system.

Systems Analysis Definition and Tasks

Structured systems analysis reflects a set of procedures conducted to generate the *specifications* for a new (or modified) information system or subsystem. Systems analysis is often called *structured systems analysis* when certain "structured" tools and techniques, such as *data flow diagrams (DFDs)*, are used in conducting the analysis. To simplify our discussions, we will refer to structured systems analysis as simply systems analysis.

The tasks required to complete the *systems analysis* are as follows:

- *Define the problem precisely:* In the systems survey, we verified that there was a problem and determined the problem's sources. In systems analysis, we want to know and understand the problem in enough detail to solve it.
- *Devise alternative designs (solutions):* There is always more than one way to solve a problem or to design a system, and we want to develop several solutions from which to choose.
- *Choose and justify one of these alternative design solutions:* One solution must be chosen, and the choice should be justified using cost/effectiveness analysis or some other criterion, such as political or legal considerations (e.g., government reporting requirements).
- *Develop logical specifications for the selected design:* These detailed specifications are used to design the new system.
- *Develop the physical requirements for the selected design:* For example, we want to define requirements such as the amount of data to be stored, functional layouts for computer inquiry screens and reports, and processing response times, which lead to equipment requirements. There can be several alternative physical designs for each logical requirement.
- *Develop the budget for the next two systems development phases, systems design and systems implementation*: These budgets are critical in determining development costs and controlling later development activities.

The logical specifications and physical requirements become the criteria by which the user will accept the new or modified system. The better we perform systems analysis, the more likely that the system will meet user requirements and become accepted, implemented, and used effectively.

Determination of user requirements in the analysis step can be more difficult in an e-business implementation. In such an implementation, we must determine user requirements inside *and outside* the organization. We must consider the functional needs of customers and business partners, as well any requirements for infrastructure to connect our internal systems to the outside users (e.g., customers, business partners).

`E-Business`

The Analysis Deliverable: The Approved Systems Analysis Document

Systems analysis has three outputs: the logical specification and physical requirements, the budget, and the schedule. All three outputs are generally part of a single **approved systems analysis document**—the final output of systems analysis. **Exhibit 17.2** (pg. 638) outlines the contents of this document. The logical specification consists of all items except those designated as the budget and schedule (part 7) and the physical requirements (part 8). Study Exhibit 17.2 before proceeding. An understanding of the information collected and included in the approved systems analysis document will help you understand the steps that an analyst must perform *during* the systems analysis.

The main objective of the systems analysis phase is to define a future logical system and a future physical system. Completing the following steps will lead to the most successful development efforts:

1. Study the current physical system.
2. Document the current logical system.
3. Define the future logical system.
4. Design the future physical system.

The first step the analysis team performs is to *study and document the current physical system*.[4] The team should read and interpret existing documentation, such as DFDs and systems flowcharts, and may correct that documentation or prepare new documentation as required. The team wants to build on the information available in the *approved feasibility document* and understand completely the current system operations. Given the system's goals, what should the system be doing? Should the order entry system be supporting customer inquiries? For what reason is the system operating as it is? Why are there errors?

To document the current logical system, the analyst removes all the physical elements from the *current physical DFD* and produces a *current logical DFD*, which reflects a description of the current logical system.

The next task, to *define user requirements for the new/modified system*, is one of the most important and most problematic tasks in systems analysis. In the event that resources or other constraints make it impossible to satisfy all user requirements, they are placed in three categories. The first includes critical features without which the system would be unusable. The second category includes those features that make the system easier to use but are not critical in nature. The third category includes those features that are considered "nice to have" but do not materially add to the usefulness of the system.

EXHIBIT 17.2 Typical Contents of an Approved Systems Analysis Document

1. **Executive summary**
   a. Project summary
   b. Summary of proposed system
   c. Summary of impact of new system
   d. Summary of cost/effectiveness and recommendations

2. **Systems analysis summary**
   a. Summary of the facts gathered and analysis performed

3. **User requirements for the new system**
   a. Operating requirements
   b. Information requirements
   c. Control requirements

4. **Logical specifications for the new system**
   a. DFDs and narrative describing the new logical system
   b. Summary of improvements brought about by new logical design (effectiveness)

5. **Description of future physical system**
   a. DFDs, flowcharts, and narrative describing the new physical system
   b. Summary of cost/benefit improvements brought about by the new physical system

6. **New system constraints**
   a. Hardware and software constraints
   b. Interface constraints
   c. Contractual and legal requirements

7. **Design phase budget and schedule**
   a. Design phase personnel and computer requirements
   b. Development schedule

8. **Physical requirements**
   a. Workload and volume
   b. Response times
   c. Functional layouts of computer inquiry screens and reports
   d. System growth

9. **Recommendations**
   a. Project leader's recommendations

10. **Approvals**

11. **Attachments**
    a. Approved feasibility document
    b. Analysis memos, summaries, tables, graphs, charts
    c. Cost/effectiveness schedules

---

[4]Many development projects have proceeded without documenting the current physical environment. Either there was *no existing* system, or the analysts considered documenting the current physical system too costly.

After defining the requirements for the new system, the current logical DFD should be modified to reflect the components of the future system. The development team may propose logical design alternatives for the future logical system that may involve derivatives of the following:

- Activities
- Data stores
- Control activities

Having described the logical system, we are now at the point of describing how the new system will operate. Working with a future logical system, an analysis team could devise several physical alternatives. An example of the alternatives that must be considered is the decision concerning which processes will be manual and which will be automated. These physical requirements are the core of the new system. Any new system selected will be based on the outcome of this process.

Cost/Effectiveness Study

To facilitate selecting a future physical system, the systems analysis team conducts a **cost/effectiveness study**, which provides quantitative and certain qualitative information concerning each of the alternatives. This information is used to decide which alternative best meets a user's needs. In making this determination, the team asks two questions: (1) Which alternative accomplishes the user's goals for the least cost (or greatest benefit)? and (2) Which alternative best accomplishes the user's goals for the system being developed?

Perform the Cost/Benefit Analysis

The **cost/benefit analysis** or study is performed first because the data are *relatively* easy to obtain and are more objective than the data on effectiveness. Also, for many decision makers and for many decisions, the cost/benefit criterion is the most important.

In conducting the cost/benefit study, the analyst *estimates* the costs and the benefits of the new system. **Direct costs (benefits)** are those directly attributable to the system or the system change. Examples of direct costs include equipment purchased, personnel salaries, site preparation, and materials and supplies. Direct benefits attributable to the system include items such as reduced personnel and hardware costs, and improved data reliability. **Indirect costs (benefits)** are not *directly* attributable to the system or the system change. Costs that we would normally associate with overhead expenses, such as personnel fringe benefits and utilities, are indirect costs. Indirect benefits are perhaps the most difficult to quantify. An example of an indirect benefit is increased revenue resulting from improved customer support; such benefits are extremely difficult to measure.

Tangible costs (benefits) *can* be *reasonably* quantified. Examples of costs include software purchases and insurance, whereas reduced equipment costs and increased revenue are examples of benefits. An **intangible cost (benefit)** is one that *cannot* be *reasonably* quantified. A productivity loss caused by low employee morale is an example of such a cost, whereas intangible benefits may accrue from improved information.

We incur **nonrecurring costs**, such as those for systems development, only once to get the system operational. **Recurring costs**, such as those for equipment rental, occur throughout all or most of the system's life.

Early in the development process, it may be difficult to estimate all costs. For example, hardware costs depend on decisions made in the next development phase, systems selection. The amount of intangible costs may never be known. What is important is to *identify* all costs. Costs such as those incurred by users participating in the development process should be, but seldom are, charged to the development project.

Intangible benefits take on increased importance as organizations develop a larger percentage of systems aimed at solving management and decision-making problems. Determining the benefits for the traditional operational systems, such as payroll and accounts receivable, is relatively easy. The benefits for such systems usually include items such as reduced clerical costs. However, determining the benefits for strategic systems, such as a market analysis system, presents problems. For such systems, the benefits may include "increased sales if we provide management with better information" or "improved morale with a modern user interface"—these benefits are difficult to quantify. In the cost/benefit analysis, we do our best to estimate costs and benefits. In the effectiveness analysis, we handle costs and benefits for which estimates were not possible.

Perform the Effectiveness Analysis

After conducting the cost/benefit analysis, the analysis team should determine each alternative's effectiveness. The ranking of each alternative on its relative capability to satisfy the user's requirements (goals) for the system either verifies the team's cost/benefit results or produces conflicting results. The effectiveness analysis might proceed as follows: The analysts and the users list all relevant criteria, including costs and benefits used in the cost/benefit analysis. At this time, we include intangible items for which monetary costs and benefits could not be estimated during the cost/benefit study. The users and the analysts jointly assign subjective rankings to each criterion for each alternative. The team then ranks the alternatives by summarizing the ratings.

The final step in selecting the alternative physical system is to recommend an alternative to the user, to management, and to the *IT steering committee*. Normally, making the recommendation is a straightforward process because the team recommends the highest-ranking alternative. However, there may be conflicting information, such as when one alternative ranks best in the cost/benefit analysis but another ranks best in the effectiveness analysis. In cases where one alternative is not clearly superior, the users and analysts must reach a consensus on the alternative to be proposed to the IT steering committee. Usually, information about all alternatives, along with the development team's recommendation, is presented to the committee.

Complete and Package the Approved Systems Analysis Document

To complete the systems analysis phase, the project team must collect the products of the analysis and organize these products into the *approved systems analysis document* (Exhibit 17.2, pg. 638).

The first analysis deliverable is the logical specification. This is used in *systems selection* to choose the appropriate software to be acquired from external sources. Alternatively, if the software is developed in-house, it is used in *structured systems design* to design the software and to develop manual procedures, training programs, and so on.

The second analysis deliverable is the *physical requirements*. These requirements are used in *systems selection* to acquire computer equipment for the new system. In addition to the physical requirements related to hardware, the physical requirements should include *functional* layouts of inquiry screens and reports. These are important for at least two reasons. First, users are as much concerned with how they will interface with the system as they are with the system's logic. Their information needs must be clearly and completely identified at this point in the development. Second, it is virtually impossible to perform a high-quality software study unless we can compare the outputs of proposed vendor systems to our specific requirements. At this point, the sample reports and screens are called *functional* layouts because they show the information elements that are needed without getting into all the *details* of the screen or report design, a topic that is beyond the scope of this chapter.

Another deliverable, implicit at the conclusion of each systems development step, is the *budget and schedule*, which contains two major parts:

- The *budget*, obtained during the cost/benefit analysis, specifies the expected costs to complete the systems development.
- *Schedules* control systems development efforts by setting limits on the time to be spent on development activities and by coordinating those activities.

The final step in completing and packaging the approved systems analysis document is to obtain approvals. As discussed earlier, *signoffs* may be obtained from users, information services, management, and internal auditors. In addition, the controller may sign off to indicate that the cost/benefit analysis is reasonable. When the signoff step is complete, we are ready to move to the selection and design phases of the new system.

Systems Selection

The outcome of the system selection process will support either the purchase or the development of an AIS. While many of the concepts are the same regardless of the source of the system, in this section, we discuss the process and identify the concepts that are different for purchased or developed systems. As you can see in Figure 17.1 (pg. 634), systems selection lies between structured systems analysis (bubble 2.0) and structured systems design (bubble 4.0). **Systems selection** is a set of procedures performed to choose the software specifications and hardware resources for an information system. Systems selection uses the new system's functional requirements (the logical specification) and physical requirements that were developed in the analysis phase to decide what software design and hardware resources will be used to implement the new system. Only after preliminary software design elements and hardware resources are chosen does the detailed design begin.

The systems selection tasks are as follows:

- Determine what computer software design will implement the logical specification   Controls
developed in structured systems analysis. When developing an information system, careful attention must be paid to integrating sound internal controls into the software rather than treating controls as a bolt-on afterthought.
- Determine what computer hardware will satisfy the physical requirements established in structured systems analysis (e.g., wireless versus wired access for warehouse picking operations, local versus off-site for file storage, and so on).[5] In making our choice, we should also be cognizant of the implications for the security and control of our information systems. Additionally, to fully understand the cost implications, consideration should be given to environmental controls (i.e., temperature, electrical, etc.).
- Choose acquisition financing methods that are in the best interest of the organization. We must decide whether it is better to purchase, rent, or lease the computer equipment. In addition, we must decide if our data center will be completely within

---

[5]An organization's existing hardware might be used to implement a new information system. In this case, the hardware phase of the study would verify that the existing hardware is adequate, given the physical requirements.

our control, or if we will use a service bureau, *application service provider*, or other outsourcing option.
- Determine appropriate acquisition ancillaries. We must establish contract terms, software site-licensing arrangements, computer maintenance terms, and software revision procedures and responsibilities.

The Systems Selection Deliverable: The Approved Configuration Plan

The **approved configuration plan**, the final output of systems selection (Figure 17.1, pg. 634), summarizes the choices made in the study. The information in the configuration plan is used in the next phase of systems development and acquisition, structured systems design, to build the software (for a system to be developed), acquire the hardware, acquire the software (for a system to be purchased), and develop the implementation plan. The approved configuration plan usually specifies the following items:

- Chosen software configuration and expected performance specifications
- Chosen hardware type, manufacturer, and model, including expected performance specifications
- Items to be included in the hardware contracts, such as proposed computer maintenance procedures and proposed procedures by which vendors will provide hardware revisions
- Results of testing alternative software design and hardware resources
- Assessment of financing and outsourcing alternatives

As indicated earlier, a company can decide to purchase an AIS solution from an external vendor, rather than developing an in-house solution. If acquisition is chosen over development, the configuration plan includes an analysis of the purchase alternatives and the recommended system based on the system selection process. Similarly, there are alternative ways to acquire needed computer hardware, as discussed next. The hardware issues raised next apply to situations in which an AIS is acquired from an external vendor or developed internally.

Hardware Acquisition Alternatives

Before we proceed to the intermediate steps in systems selection, let's spend time examining the various hardware procurement options that an organization must consider. Hardware can be acquired (rented, leased, or purchased) by an organization and managed by the organization's personnel. Alternatively, the hardware can be owned and managed by external entities. **Table 17.2** compares these external and internal sources for computer hardware. A review of the table should lead you to conclude that external sources usually provide more capacity and affect the organization's resources less, whereas internal sources can be matched more easily with the organization's needs.

Under the internal acquisition option, computer hardware can be purchased, rented, or leased from the manufacturer (vendor) or from a leasing company. In such cases, the hardware is acquired, installed in the organization's facilities, and operated by the organization's personnel. As noted in Table 17.2, possession and management by the organization (internal hardware source) is less flexible (e.g., because of fixed cost and limited capacity) than is the use of external sources, but it does permit the organization to control and tailor the system.

TABLE 17.2   Internal versus External Hardware Sources

Internal	External
Can determine level of control, security, and privacy.	Level of control may vary and be difficult to attain, especially if many companies use the same hardware.
Management and staff must be in-house.	Management and staff are provided.
Capacity limited.	Additional capacity may be available.
Costs are mostly fixed.	Costs are mostly variable.
Tailored to our needs.	Tailoring varies.

External acquisition is suited for an organization preferring not to own or manage its own computer facilities. The organization can use **outsourcing**, the assignment of an internal function to an outside vendor, through the use of a service bureau, *ASP*, or *SaaS*—to fulfill its hardware needs. A **service bureau**, a firm providing information processing services, including hardware and software for a fee, can provide the services less expensively and in a timelier manner than would be possible with an in-house computer. Generally, service bureau contracts include company involvement with the system.

Outsourcing has come to encompass many of the external hardware acquisition alternatives that have been available for years. The new twist to these alternatives is the ownership by the outsourcing firm of the user organization's computer facility. Organizations can retain management of their IT while obtaining some application functionality through ASPs or SaaS in a more flexible and less costly way than through a service bureau.

The main advantage of using a service bureau, an ASP, or SaaS is that the user organization does not have to operate and maintain the computing resource. The downside to any of these external acquisition methods is that the organization must be willing to sacrifice its independence and may compromise scheduling and data security. Outsourcing is a decision that should not be made lightly. Once outsourced, it is often very difficult to bring a function back in-house.

The Intermediate Steps in Systems Selection

There are two primary steps in the systems selections phase of the SDLC:

1. Prepare requests for proposal.
2. Evaluate vendor proposals.

Prepare Requests for Proposal

A **request for proposal (RFP)** is a document sent to vendors that invites submission of plans for providing hardware, software (for a purchased system), and related services. Before preparing any requests for proposal, a firm must decide what approach will be taken for soliciting the proposals. An organization can ask one vendor for a proposal, or it can ask many. An organization satisfied with its present vendor might send an RFP to only that vendor. An organization might choose to stay with its present vendor to minimize program conversion costs, to obtain attractive contract clauses (such as discounts or future benefits), and to reduce retraining costs. Also, if an organization has a specialized need that can be met by only one vendor, the organization might send an RFP to only that vendor. Unless an organization has a particular reason for limiting its RFPs to a single vendor, submission to multiple vendors is preferred because it provides an organization with a variety of possibilities from which to choose. In addition, vendor concessions and discounts may be available if an organization retains a bargaining position by dealing with multiple vendors.

The organization can request bids on specific computer *configurations* (e.g., request a bid for Model "XYZ") or to meet general performance *objectives* (e.g., request a bid for a computer system capable of handling the entry of 5,000 business events, such as customer orders, each hour). The former approach leads to a simple evaluation of proposals, but it assumes that the systems analyst preparing the RFP knows what equipment will meet the organization's requirements. The latter approach allows vendors to propose solutions to an organization's requirements; the organization may not have anticipated some of these solutions. Choices made from solutions generated entirely within the organization may be suboptimal.

After deciding how to prepare the requests (i.e., the approach to be used), the organization must then decide to which specific vendors the RFPs will be sent. Vendors from which the organization has previously done business are candidates for receiving proposals. The analysts assigned to conduct systems selection also might research vendor evaluations published in the computer press or in other computer-based or paper-based services. This research is described in **Technology Summary 17.2**.

Using the information contained in the logical specification or in the physical requirements, the analysts prepare the RFPs and send them to the chosen vendors. **Exhibit 17.3** lists the typical contents of an RFP.[6]

Technology Summary 17.2

SOURCES OF VENDOR INFORMATION

Analysts can use a variety of paper-based, computer-based, and online services to identify and evaluate computer hardware, software, and vendors. The information contained in these services, especially that resulting from independent expert analysis of a vendor and its products or from user surveys, can provide valuable insight into the vendor's quality, financial condition, number of installed systems, and similar information. Some are reports such as those available from Gartner Group, Inc. (www.gartner.com). Gartner's services include Dataquest, with research and advice in a number of areas, including market insights related to market share, forecasts, industry norms, and a variety of other metrics. Gartner also publishes reports in a variety of technology areas to provide insight to IT managers when making decisions.

Magazines—both printed and online—also provide independent reviews of vendors, hardware, and software. For example, ZDNet (www.zdnet.com) publishes reviews in their online magazine *eWEEK* and in magazines that are both printed and published online, such as *PC Magazine* (www.pcmag.com) and *Computer Shopper* (computershopper.com).

In addition to these independent sources of information about software, hardware, and vendors, the Internet provides a wealth of information directly from the vendors. For example, in a quick tour of the Web (June 2010), sites were found for Symantec (network security, virus protection, etc.—www.symantec.com), IBM (www.ibm.com), Microsoft (www.microsoft.com), SAP (www.sap.com), Dell (www.dell.com), and Gateway (www.gateway.com). Through these sites, news was obtained about upcoming products, lists of existing products, customer support, technical support, software purchases, and software fixes and upgrades.

Finally, in addition to traditional software vendors, many open-source vendors exist. These vendors may be able to meet your software needs in less time and for less money than can be done through other means. They build applications using existing open-source components rather than developing them from scratch or by using commercial software. Once developed, however, the application is made available to others via the open-source software network. Consequently, knowing that the improvements made while creating your open-source system may be used by others (including your competitors) should be considered when using open-source vendors for business-critical systems or those that provide a competitive advantage.

---

[6]For current, actual examples of RFPs, see www.fbo.gov (accessed June 10, 2010), the site that the U.S. government uses to post RFPs for items it is acquiring.

EXHIBIT 17.3   Typical Contents of a Request for Proposal

1. A description of the scope of the request, including a brief description of the hardware, software, and services for which a proposal is requested
2. A description of the AIS, including, if applicable, the *logical specification* and *physical requirements*, which in turn include specifications for the following:
   - Inputs
   - Outputs
   - Data storage
   - Processes
   - Controls
3. Procedures for submitting proposals, including a timetable for proposal submission, evaluation of proposals, and final decision date
4. Price and budget constraints
5. Vendor information required, including the following:
   - Contract terms
   - Warranty
   - General company information
6. Hardware performance objectives, such as the following:
   - Data storage capacities and access requirements
   - Input/output speeds and volumes

- Data communication requirements
- Computational demands

7. Software performance objectives, such as the following:
   - Inputs
   - Required outputs
   - Data table sizes and access requirements
   - Operating system requirements
   - Utilities
   - Language compilers
8. Projected growth requirements, including expected changes in input/output volumes
9. Criteria to be used in evaluating vendor proposals, such as the following:
   - Ability to meet performance objectives
   - Benchmarks
   - Reliability
   - Documentation
   - Training
   - Backup
   - Maintenance assistance

Note that Exhibit 17.3 assumes that the RFP asks for a bid for performance objectives, rather than for a particular computer configuration or product. The section on projected growth requirements is important relative to the RFP. The better an organization accurately projects the long-term requirements for a new system and obtains hardware that can satisfy that long-term demand, the longer it will be before the system needs to be revised and new hardware obtained.

Evaluate Vendor Proposals

The second task in the system selection phase is to evaluate vendor proposals. Using the vendor responses to the RFP and the physical requirements, the analysts must decide which, if any, proposal best meets the organization's needs. The process of evaluating the vendor proposals includes three steps:

1. Validate vendor proposals.
2. Consider other data and criteria.
3. Suggest resources.

Many organizations assign a team to evaluate the proposals. The team could consist of personnel with IT technical expertise, business process owners, system users, external consultants, lawyers, and accountants. The evaluation team completes these three steps to suggest the hardware and services that best meet the organization's requirements.

The first evaluation step is to validate the vendor proposal to assess whether the system hardware does what the organization requires. To determine whether a system meets the requirements of the RFP, the evaluation team can study a proposed system's specifications and performance.

Specifications are straightforward descriptions of the hardware. For example, a server's storage space or a printer's speed can be examined to determine whether or not the hardware meets performance requirements. Other specifications include items such as compatibility with other current or future technologies, as well as potential for future expandability and upgrades.

Performance features can be determined only through testing, measurement, or evaluation and often include items such as effective vendor support, documentation quality, system reliability, and scalability. One commonly used method for measuring system performance involves measuring the system's throughput, which reflects the quantity of work performed in a period of time. For instance, the number of invoices that a system can process in one hour is a measure of throughput. Other performance measures, such as ease of use, are more subjective and may be more difficult to evaluate.

Notice that during validation, we are not comparing vendor proposals; we are determining which proposals can meet our requirements. Only the proposals that can meet our requirements are compared when we "suggest resources."

RFPs often distinguish mandatory and desirable system characteristics. As a first step in the validation process, many proposals can be rejected because they fail to meet mandatory effectiveness requirements. At this point in our analysis, we have not yet tested the system and can evaluate the system only on the basis of the system's parameters, not the system's performance. Still, even these specifications might not hold up in a test. For example, hardware compatibility may be specified but not work in certain configurations.

After completing the first-level effectiveness analysis, the evaluation team tests[7] the remaining systems (i.e., those that satisfy mandatory requirements) to determine the accuracy of the vendors' specifications and how well the equipment will work for the organization. One way to compare systems is to use benchmark data. A **benchmark** is a representative workload, processed on each vendor's proposed system configuration, to obtain comparative throughput measures. In the first step in our analysis, we determined what a system is; in testing, we determine what that system can do.

After validating vendor proposals, we might consider other data and criteria. For large systems, vendor presentations are often made at the site of an existing user. This approach gives the evaluation team an opportunity to see the system in a working environment. External interviews—interviews conducted with personnel outside the organization—can provide valuable insights into vendor performance.

Finally, the team must summarize its findings by recommending one vendor proposal. To recommend one vendor, the evaluation team must compare the proposals that have not been eliminated. To support the recommendation, the evaluation team should list the relevant criteria and indicate the performance of each vendor on each criterion. **Table 17.3** is a simple depiction of such an analysis. The criteria—we have presented only a sample here—are those indicated in the logical specification and physical requirements as well as any others the evaluation team considers important. The evaluation team uses the performance measures gathered during system testing and when other data and criteria were considered.

---

[7]Often, vendors will propose a system that does not actually exist *yet*. In such cases, we cannot test an actual system; our only option is to *simulate* the proposed system, as discussed later in this section.

TABLE 17.3   Detailed Vendor Comparison

Criteria	Vendors		
	A	**B**	**C**
Documentation quality	good	good	poor
Cost of typical configuration	$53,630	$29,900	$59,300
Monthly maintenance of typical configuration	$422	$515	$448
Maximum number of workstations	8	32	32
Benchmark results:			
Number of invoices/minute	2	4	6
Query response time (seconds)	1	1.5	2.0

An analysis such as that in Table 17.3 might not clearly indicate a superior vendor. It is normally advisable and necessary to perform a detailed analysis that assigns scores to each vendor on each relevant criterion. In addition to scoring, the evaluation team ranks the importance of each criterion by assigning it a weight. Of course, the comparison is only as valid as the weights and scoring values used. Also, if the results of this analysis agree with the previous evaluations and the intuition of the evaluation team, then the team receives a certain amount of comfort from this analysis. Finally, using this type of weighted scoring system facilitates communication of the team's recommendations to the IT steering committee and the user, and thus helps gain support for that recommendation. Although you see the concept in this example, how would you go about a multi-system comparison, when there are hundreds or even thousands of criteria? Using technology, obviously! There are software tools to help you make the comparison. Examples include The Accounting Library (www.accountinglibrary.com) for a wide range of software, or CTSGuide's Accounting Software Selection Kit (www.ctsguides.com) if you are interested in accounting software comparisons for a small or mid-sized company.

Structured Systems Design

In structured systems design, for systems under development, the software specifications are refined for new or revised business process applications, and implementation plans are prepared. If the AIS is being purchased, an organization will focus on the implementation process.

Recall from earlier discussions that certain systems development tasks are comparable to tasks undertaken in the construction of an industrial park. Systems selection, in which the software design and hardware resources are chosen, is similar to drafting blueprints and choosing contractors for a construction project. Structured systems design, in which the software is designed and the implementation is planned, is similar to finalizing blueprints and other construction-related plans.

Studies have shown that systems developed using structured systems design techniques are less costly over the life of the system because maintenance of the system is less expensive. Also, structured systems design avoids design errors that further increase the cost of the system. Implementation planning, conducted during structured systems design and introduced in this section, increases the probability of a smooth transition to the new information system.

Definition and Goals

Structured systems design is a set of procedures performed to convert the logical specification into a design that can be implemented on the organization's computer system. Concurrent with specification of the system's design, plans are developed for testing and implementing the new system and for training personnel. Portions of the user manual are also developed at this time.

Figure 17.1 (pg. 634) shows that structured systems design is the fourth major step in the development of an information system (bubble 4.0). Examine this figure again to see the position that structured systems design holds in the SDLC.

Let's return to our earlier analogy between systems development and the construction of an industrial park. Converting the information system's logical specification into detailed design specifications is similar to finalizing the construction blueprints. The models developed earlier in the construction project are not detailed enough to allow the actual construction to begin; final blueprints provide that detail. Also, planning must be undertaken to determine the construction schedule for the buildings. Preconstruction planning is analogous to the computer system implementation planning done at this juncture in the SDLC. For example, the development team must plan how much of the system to implement and when.

The structured systems design tasks are as follows:

* *Convert the structured specification into a reliable, maintainable design:* This is similar to the process of converting the building model into a final blueprint.
* *Develop a plan and budget that will ensure an orderly and controlled implementation of the new system:* Procedures must be devised to get the hardware in place, the programming completed, the training conducted, and the new system operating.
* *Develop an implementation test plan that ensures the system is reliable, complete, and accurate:* A plan must be developed to test the system to ensure that it does what the user wants it to do.
* *Develop a user manual that facilitates efficient and effective use of the new system by operations and management personnel:* These personnel must know how to use the new system effectively, and the information processing staff must know how to operate the system.

The Systems Design Deliverable: The Approved Systems Design Document

The approved systems design document, the final deliverable of structured systems design (Figure 17.1), documents the system design and summarizes the implementation, training, and test plans. The design document is used by the following:

* *Programmers:* To write the computer programs and program interfaces.
* *Personnel department:* To develop and conduct training and education programs.
* *Information systems personnel:* To test and implement the system.

The design project leader must assemble the components of the systems design document and obtain the required user approvals (to ensure the adequacy of the design and plans) and management approvals (to signify concurrence with the design, training, and implementation process). In addition, for systems to be developed, IT management furnishes a supervisory/technical approval of the adequacy of the software specifications, and auditors ensure adequacy of the controls and the design process (including implementation planning).

Systems Implementation

Systems implementation reflects a set of procedures performed to complete the design contained in the approved systems design document and to test, install, and begin to use the new or revised information system. Figure 17.1 (pg. 634) depicts systems implementation as the fifth major step in the development of an information system. Examine this figure to see the position that systems implementation holds in the SDLC. You can see that systems implementation follows structured systems design and has two major inputs, the approved configuration plan (developed during the systems selection step) and the approved systems design document (produced in the structured systems design step of systems development).

In the implementation stage of the SDLC, the most significant difference between in-house development of a system and the purchase of a system is the application programming. For purchased systems, the software manufacturer completes the programming step. However, even purchased systems frequently require programming tasks, such as writing interfaces between the new system and existing software.

Recall our earlier analogy that certain systems development tasks are comparable to those undertaken in the planning and construction of an industrial park. Systems implementation (in which the computer programs are written, and the system is put into operation) is analogous to the process of actually constructing the industrial park. When developed internally, the construction analogy corresponds to the actual construction phase of the buildings, while purchased systems correspond to the purchase of prefabricated buildings that are installed on the site.

During systems implementation, the organization acquires the specified computer resources, prepares the site to receive them, and installs the new software and hardware. The approved systems design document is used to complete the design, write the computer programs, conduct the training, test the system, and install the new or revised system.

The systems implementation tasks are as follows:

- Complete, as necessary, the design contained in the approved systems design document. New information may have become available since the design was approved. It is easier to address such issues before the programs are written. This applies to in-house systems only.
- Write, test, and document the programs and procedures required by the approved systems design document. This applies to in-house systems only.
- Ensure, by completing the preparation of user manuals and other documentation and by educating and training personnel, that the organization's personnel can operate the new system.
- Determine, by thoroughly testing the system with users, that the system satisfies the users' requirements.
- Ensure a correct conversion by planning, controlling, and conducting an orderly installation of the new system.

The Systems Implementation Deliverable: The Project Completion Report

To understand the implementation process, you need to see where you are going. Systems implementation ends with the operation of the newly acquired or revised system and with the submission of a project completion report. The project completion report summarizes the implementation activities and provides documentation for operating the new system and for conducting the post-implementation review and systems maintenance. The project completion report usually includes the following items:

- Summary of requirements satisfied by the new system
- Estimated and actual duration of each development stage
- Estimated and actual systems performance (e.g., response time, costs, benefits)
- System documentation, which provides an overview of the new system
- Program documentation, which includes source code and other related items
- User manual, which describes operating procedures for both manual and automated procedures
- Operations run manual, which contains operating instructions for computer operations
- System test report
- User training programs and manuals
- Operator training programs and manuals

Approaches to Implementation

There are alternative implementation approaches that can be taken to install whatever segment of the system that has been developed. Selecting an appropriate approach can greatly facilitate conversion to the new system. Depending on the approach and circumstances, greater control and user satisfaction can be ensured. **Figure 17.2** depicts the three most common implementation approaches.

Controls

Figure 17.2(a), the parallel approach, provides the most control of the three. Under the parallel approach, both the old and new systems operate together for a time. During this period, time x to time y (which is usually one operating cycle, such as one month or one quarter), the outputs of the two systems are compared to determine whether the new system is operating comparably to the old. At time y, management makes a decision, based on the comparison of the two systems' outputs, concerning whether to terminate the operation of the old system. The parallel approach provides a high level of control because the old system is not abandoned until users are satisfied that the new system adequately replaces the old. However, greater control comes at a cost—meaning, it is expensive to keep two systems running simultaneously. For instance, running two systems side-by-side can require duplicate or excess computer processing capacity, data storage space, and human labor.

Enterprise Systems

Controls

Figure 17.2(b), the direct approach, is the riskiest of the three approaches because at time x, the old system is stopped and the new system is begun. This implementation method is also referred to as the "big bang" or "cold turkey" approach. There can be no validation that the new system operates comparably to the old because the lights are "turned off" with the old system and simultaneously "turned on" with the new system. Direct implementations can lead to disaster if not carefully tested, planned, and executed. So why take this approach? Certainly, some level of comfort or control is lost with the direct approach. But this implementation method can be less costly than the parallel approach—if all goes well. With very large implementations, such as enterprise systems, it is often capacity- or cost-prohibitive to take the parallel approach. On the bright side, the direct approach forces users to learn the new system because they do not have the old system to fall back on. Although this might have immediate negative effects on satisfaction because users do not want to let go of the old system, or they fear the new system, the new system can get up and running very quickly. And, if the implementation is properly planned, and the users are thoroughly trained, direct implementations can ultimately lead to increased user satisfaction as compared to the old system.

Figure 17.2(c), the modular approach, can be combined with the parallel or the direct approaches to tailor the implementation to the circumstances. With the modular approach, the new system is either implemented one subsystem or module at a time or is introduced one organizational unit at a time. The modular approach is also referred to as the phased approach. For example, a new order entry/sales (OE/S) system could be implemented by first changing the sales order preparation and customer inquiry portions, followed by implementing the link to the billing system, followed by the link to the inventory system. Figure 17.2(c) depicts the gradual implementation of a new system into three organizational units. A new payroll system is installed for the employees of plant 1 at time x, followed by plant 2 at time y, and finally by plant 3 at time z. Implementation at any plant could be direct or parallel. Modular implementation

Controls

FIGURE 17.2 Implementation Approaches

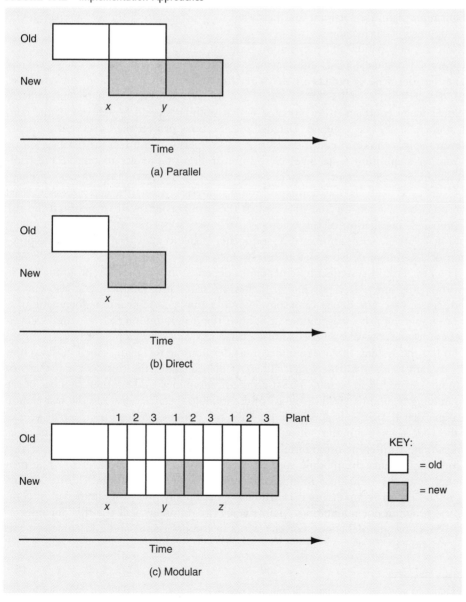

permits pilot testing of a system or system component and elimination of any problems discovered before full implementation. If properly planned and executed, modular implementations can combine the safety and control of a parallel implementation with the cost/time savings of a direct approach.

The Intermediate Steps in Systems Implementation

The first step of the implementation process is to complete or update the design of input and output reports, documents, computer screens, the database, manual processes, and certain computer processes. This completion is required to reflect changes because the design document was approved. No matter the scope of a project and the diligence of the design team, there are always changes! By adjusting the design at this point, you will minimize the cost and impact on the overall system.

At any time after the computer resources are chosen and indicated in the approved configuration plan, the software and hardware may be acquired, the site prepared, and the computer system installed.

Contract negotiation and preparation is an important part of the computer acquisition process. Computer, legal, and financial expertise must be combined to negotiate and execute the contracts. Contracts are necessary for computer hardware and software lease, rental, or purchase, as well as for hardware and software service. One important point to remember when contracts are negotiated is that nothing should be left out of the contract; nothing should be assumed. Detailed specifications protect the buyer and the seller and keep them both out of court, unless one fails to perform contract provisions.

Another acquisition issue involves the preparation of the site to receive the computer equipment. Sufficient electrical power and power protection, air conditioning, and security, as well as the computer room's physical structure and access to that room, must be planned for and provided. If the contracts are well written and the site well prepared, installation of the computer hardware, software, and related equipment should be relatively straightforward. Contingency plans to allow for delays in site preparation or equipment delivery should be considered.

The next task in systems implementation depends on whether the programs are to be custom programmed or purchased. If they are to be programmed, you also have to include time to test and debug the programs, and complete the program documentation. The programming process is important because the programming task in systems development consumes more resources and time than any other development task.

To test the system, the programmer must develop the test plan, which outlines how each program module will be tested. The test plan includes the test data that the program unit is expected to handle. The user, the programmer, and another member of the programming team do a "walkthrough" of the module specifications and the test plan to determine that the latter is adequate; then the programmer codes the program or creates the code using computer software (a code generator) that "writes" program code. After coding, a different programmer[8] does a "walkthrough" of the code to see that the code implements the module specifications faithfully and without error. The programmer tests the individual module and removes any errors found during testing. This removal of program errors is called *debugging*. Finally, the programmer must complete the program documentation. Maintenance programmers will use this documentation to make program changes, correct errors in the programs, and add enhancements to the programs.

---

[8]This is done by a different programmer because it is easier for someone who did not do the coding to find errors.

If a software package has been purchased, much of the programming step is replaced with procedures to configure the system for this application. During the implementation of an enterprise system, this process can be quite extensive as we configure the system to select, for example, the steps to be completed for each business process; the design of the screens to be displayed at each step of the process; and the data to be captured, stored, and output during the processes. Even if software is purchased, frequently there will be programming required to link the new system with existing applications.

Enterprise Systems

The organization must choose the personnel who will operate the new system and must train them to perform their system-related duties. The system's users must be educated about the new system's purpose, function, and capabilities. Training may be received through a combination of courses provided by software vendors, hardware vendors, third parties, and programs conducted by the organization itself. Computer-assisted learning, such as interactive tutorials, is frequently used.

An organization must choose the training delivery system that matches its specific needs. The two variables to be considered in choosing a delivery method are the person being trained and the training objective. For example, formal classroom presentations, delivered to any audience, are appropriate for general overviews of a computer system. On-the-job training can be an effective component of a plan that includes instruction, follow-up, and ongoing assistance. Tutorials introduce relatively computer-literate users to software and hardware use.

Resident experts may also be a cost-effective way to deliver knowledge of a system to a large audience. In such situations, the experts are trained first, and then they instruct the other users. Online Help and Explanation facilities, along with well-designed screens and reports, can reduce the amount of upfront training necessary and provide ongoing guidance to system users.

Test the System

Beyond testing program modules, the entire system is tested to determine that it meets the requirements established by the business process owners and users and that it can be used and operated to the satisfaction of both users and system operators. Testing is carried out by the systems developers, by the developers and the users together, and finally by the users. The more closely the test can simulate a production environment (e.g., people, machines, data, and inputs), the more representative the test will be and the more conclusive the results will be. Each test consists of the following steps:

1. Specify the test conditions.
2. Review the test conditions (i.e., walkthrough).
3. Create test data.
4. Execute the tests.
5. Evaluate the results.

Several types or levels of tests are usually completed before a system can be implemented. From the users' point of view, three of these tests are the most important. The *system test* verifies the new system against the original specifications. This test is conducted first by the development team and then by the users with the assistance of the team. The *acceptance test* is a user-directed test of the complete system in a test environment. The purpose is to determine, from the user's perspective, whether all components of the new system are satisfactory. The user tests the adequacy of the system (both manual and automated components), of the manuals and other documentation, and of the training the users received. Finally, the *operations test* or environmental test runs a subset of the system in the actual production environment. This final test determines whether new equipment and other factors in the environment—such as data entry areas, document and report deliveries, telephones, and electricity—are satisfactory. After this final test, it is time for the conversion.

Conduct Conversion

Controls After all the previous implementation steps have been completed and signed off, the organization must carefully convert to the new system. Conversion includes converting the data and the processes (i.e., the programs). Controls must be in place to ensure the accurate, complete, and authorized conversion of the data and programs.

As the existing data are mapped into the new system, exception-reporting situations must be devised to ensure that the data are converted accurately. The user must suggest control totals that can be used to test the completeness and accuracy of the data conversion. For example, the total number of inventory items, the total on-hand quantity for all inventory items, or a hash total of inventory item numbers might be used as totals.

Both manual-based processes and computer-based processes must be converted. Conversion to new computer programs must be undertaken using program change controls to ensure that only authorized, tested, and approved versions of the programs are promoted to production status.

After the conversion is completed, the systems development project team writes the project completion report, the final step in the implementation process.

Post-Implementation Review

The **post-implementation review** involves an examination of a working information system, conducted soon after that system's implementation, to determine whether the user's requirements have been satisfied and whether the development effort was efficient and conducted in accordance with the organization's systems development standards. The review should be brief and inexpensive. Examinations conducted in response to a specific deficiency, systems maintenance, are discussed in the next section.

The post-implementation review tasks are as follows:

* Determine if the user is satisfied with the new system.
* Identify how well the system's achieved performance corresponds to the performance requirements, recommending improvements if necessary.
* Evaluate the quality of the new system's documentation, training programs, and data conversions.
* Ascertain that the organization's project management framework and SDLC were followed during development.
* Recommend improvements to the systems development/acquisition standards manual if necessary.
* Improve the cost/effectiveness analysis process by reviewing cost projections and benefit estimations and determining the degree to which these were achieved.
* Improve project-planning procedures by examining total project costs and the project team's ability to adhere to project cost estimates and schedules.
* Make any other recommendations that might improve the operation of the system or the development of other information systems.

Controls Internal auditors, IT auditors, or systems analysts (other than those who developed the system) may conduct the post-implementation review. If the organization has insufficient personnel with the required expertise who are independent of the system's development, consultants may be hired to conduct the review. The independence of the review is important because the review provides feedback (i.e., a control) on the development process.

The post-implementation review is performed as soon as the system is operating at full capacity, which could be one month to one year after implementation. The review should examine a fully functioning system so as not to draw erroneous conclusions about system performance. The review should be conducted soon enough after implementation to take advantage of any improvements that can be made to the system or to the systems development methods used.

The following parties sign off on the post-implementation review report:

- Business process owners/users sign off to indicate that the system was performing as described in the report and to indicate concurrence with the report's conclusions and recommendations.
- Internal auditors participating in the review sign off to indicate that appropriate procedures were followed in performing the review and to concur with the report's conclusions and recommendations.

Systems Maintenance

Systems maintenance is the modification (e.g., repair, correction, or enhancement) of existing applications. Systems maintenance expenditures can account for 50 to 80 percent of the total cost of a system over its total life cycle. These costs should be reason enough to reduce the need for maintenance and to carefully monitor maintenance that cannot be avoided.

You should realize that not all maintenance expense is necessarily bad. After all, applications must be adapted to a changing environment and improved over time. There are three types of maintenance activities:

- *Corrective* maintenance must be performed to fix errors.
- *Perfective* maintenance is conducted to improve the performance of an application.
- *Adaptive* maintenance adjusts applications to reflect changing business needs and environmental challenges.

The competitiveness of many industries and the need for organizations to remain flexible in such environments increase the importance of adaptive maintenance.

The following systems maintenance tasks are based on the systems maintenance costs and concerns cited, as well as other issues to be discussed in this section:

- Accomplish system changes (and reconfigurations) quickly and efficiently.
- Prevent system changes from causing other system problems.
- Make system changes that are in the organization's overall best interest.
- Perfect systems development and systems maintenance procedures by collecting and using information about system changes.
- Replace systems maintenance with the systems survey process, if requested changes are significant or if they would destroy the system.
- Minimize control exposure and organizational disruption that can be caused by systems maintenance.

To accomplish the systems maintenance tasks, organizations often adopt the following procedures and controls for their systems maintenance process: `Controls`

- Because systems maintenance is like a miniature (or sometimes large!) systems development project, it should include analysis, cost/benefit study, design, implementation, and approvals for each development step. In systems maintenance, certain *SDLC* procedures deserve more attention than others. For example, changes must be tested prior to implementation to determine that a change corrects the problem and does not cause other problems. Participants and signoffs should be the same as those required for systems development. For example, the user should review system changes.

- By charging user departments for maintenance costs, an organization can reduce the submission of frivolous maintenance requests.

Controls

- By adopting a formal procedure for submitting change requests, batching these requests together for each application, and then prioritizing the batches, management can gain control of systems maintenance and reduce the expense and disruptions caused by the maintenance process.

- During systems maintenance, information should be gathered that provides feedback to improve the operation of the system and to improve the systems development process. For instance, poor-quality application documentation and inadequate user training can cause numerous systems maintenance requests. Correcting these deficiencies can preclude the need for similar maintenance requests in the future. Likewise, improvements in the systems development process can prevent deficiencies from occurring in other systems when they are being developed.

Controls

- Management should see that *program change controls* are used to ensure that all modifications to computer programs are authorized, tested, and properly implemented.

- High-quality documentation must be created and maintained. Without current, accurate documentation, maintenance programmers cannot understand, and therefore cannot effectively or efficiently modify, existing programs.

Accountant Involvement in AIS Acquisition/Development and Implementation

As an accountant, you are uniquely qualified to participate, and even lead, the acquisition/development and implementation process. As an information management and business measurement professional, you will bring to the table important knowledge and skills, including knowledge of the business processes and the business context for the new AIS, expertise in internal controls that will be extremely important during the development process and for the new system, and skills with metrics that will be needed to make important decisions and to monitor the acquisition process. Consider some of the specific roles you will eventually play in the process:

- *User:* Whether you are a staff accountant, controller, or CFO, you will be using an AIS on a regular basis. In any of these roles, you might be a business process owner as well, which means that you will be responsible for (or own) certain data sets (such as payroll, general ledger, or customer billing data). As such, you very well could be the person who initiates the AIS acquisition cycle because you will be in prime position to recognize deficiencies and incompatibilities related to the existing AIS.

- *Analyst:* Because you will be intimately familiar with functionality and controllability aspects of accounting systems, you could be asked to participate on a systems analysis team to conduct a preliminary survey used to determine what is needed in a new AIS. Even when the accountant is not familiar with a particular business process, he or she can contribute skills in acquiring and documenting descriptions of processes.

- *Purchaser:* You could also become a member of the AIS selection team. In this capacity, you will have to match the organization's requirements with the capability of various commercially available accounting systems, evaluate a set of potential AIS solutions, and help to make the final purchase selection.

- *Implementer:* After the AIS is purchased, it is time to switch the old with the new, which is much easier said than done. You could become involved with this vitally important phase of the acquisition cycle. If so, you will have to be equally adept at dealing with people, accounting, and technology. In particular, your intimate knowledge of accounting and information technology will help you be successful in this role.

- *Consultant:* Although the Sarbanes-Oxley Act prohibits CPA firms who audit a public company to also serve as systems consultants for the same company,[9] AIS consulting is nevertheless alive and well. Even though most CPA firms have spun off their consulting divisions into separate entities, these new consulting companies continue to need accountants. There are also many opportunities for traditional management consulting firms. Furthermore, CPA firms still consult (they often call themselves "business advisors"), just not for their audit clients. As a consultant, you can become involved with any or all of the AIS acquisition phases.   `SOX`

- *Internal auditor:* Because internal auditors are knowledgeable about AIS function and control requirements, they often serve as advisors or consultants during the acquisition cycle. Also, as agents of management and the board of directors, internal auditors ensure that the acquisition team has followed the organization's standard procedures for systems acquisition and that the process has been efficient and effective.   `Controls`

- *External auditor:* As an external auditor, you will conduct an internal control assessment. During your assessment, you will have to determine how changes in the AIS might have affected overall audit risk. As discussed in Chapter 7 of this textbook, professional guidance in this regard is found in the Statement on Auditing Standards (SAS) 94, entitled "The Effect of Information Technology on the Auditor's Consideration of Internal Control in a Financial Statement Audit." Thus, external auditors will review the acquisition cycle and assess if and how internal controls have been impacted.   `Controls`

You can clearly see how accountants can play many valuable roles in the AIS acquisition and development cycle. Most likely, you will eventually find yourself in one or more of these roles. Even if you do not think you enjoy technology, you cannot escape the natural marriage of accounting and information technology because the lines between the two have been forever blurred.

Summary

In the past, it often took years for a new system to move through the initial steps in the SDLC (i.e., bubbles 1 through 5 in Figure 17.1, pg. 634). Now we move at "Internet speed," and expectations are that systems development must occur in a time frame that seems almost instantaneous. If we do not, we may be put out of business or absorbed by those organizations that say they can. Oftentimes, new systems development projects involve changes in the way a company operates. Such changes, coupled with the "need for speed," raise the stakes regarding the odds of successfully accomplishing the systems development objectives.

---

[9]The rationale for this change was to prevent auditors from assessing the quality (i.e., auditing) of the work performed by members of their own firm. To do so would violate their independence in appearance or in fact.

In Chapter 8, you were introduced to COBIT, a framework addressing controls and governance over the IT functions of an organization. COBIT can provide significant guidance through the process of acquisition and implementation of accounting information systems.

In this chapter, you were introduced to the SDLC methodology, a tool that can help ensure successful system development projects. It can help address and deal with many of the problems cited at the start of this chapter. With successful projects, an organization can compete effectively in today's fast-paced environment. Knowledge of tools such as COBIT and the SDLC can help you succeed in your job and bring technological success to your organization.

Key Terms

systems development, 629

systems development life cycle (SDLC) methodology, 631

application service provider (ASP), 631

software as a service (SaaS), 631

deliverables, 633

signoffs, 633

systems survey, 635

feasibility study, 635

preliminary feasibility study, 635

structured systems analysis, 636

approved systems analysis document, 637

cost/effectiveness study, 639

cost/benefit analysis, 639

direct costs (benefits), 639

indirect costs (benefits), 639

tangible costs (benefits), 639

intangible cost (benefit), 639

nonrecurring costs, 639

recurring costs, 639

systems selection, 641

approved configuration plan, 642

outsourcing, 643

service bureau, 643

request for proposal (RFP), 643

benchmark, 646

structured systems design, 648

systems implementation, 649

post-implementation review, 654

systems maintenance, 655

Review Questions

RQ 17-1   What is systems development?

RQ 17-2   What is the systems development life cycle (SDLC)?

RQ 17-3   What is the systems development life cycle (SDLC) methodology?

RQ 17-4   What are the systems development objectives?

RQ 17-5   What are the tasks required to complete the systems survey?

RQ 17-6   What is structured systems analysis?

RQ 17-7   What are the tasks required to complete a structured systems analysis?

RQ 17-8   Why do we study and document the current physical environment?

RQ 17-9   Compare and contrast tangible and intangible benefits.

RQ 17-10   What is the purpose of conducting an effectiveness analysis?

RQ 17-11   What is systems selection?

RQ 17-12   What does the approved configuration plan specify?

RQ 17-13   What are the reasons for using external versus internal sources of hardware?

RQ 17-14   What is a request for proposal (RFP)?

RQ 17-15   What are the approaches to obtaining an RFP?

RQ 17-16   Why might a company issue an RFP for general performance objectives?

RQ 17-17   What is the difference between a specification and a performance measure?

RQ 17-18   Describe the process used to evaluate vendor proposals.

RQ 17-19   What is structured systems design?

RQ 17-20   What is systems implementation?

RQ 17-21   What are the three major approaches to implementing an information system?

RQ 17-22   What is the riskiest approach to systems implementation?

RQ 17-23   What two variables should be considered when choosing a method to train employees to operate a new system?

RQ 17-24   What is the purpose of testing the entire system as opposed to testing part of the system?

RQ 17-25   Describe the major steps in a post-implementation review.

RQ 17-26   What are the three types of maintenance activities?

RQ 17-27   What skills do accountants have to contribute to the development/acquisition process?

RQ 17-28   What roles can an accountant play in the development or acquisition of an AIS?

Discussion Questions

DQ 17-1   Discuss several factors affecting (negatively or positively) the achievement of systems development objectives.

DQ 17-2   How might the absence of an organization's strategic plan for the information system affect the conduct of a preliminary survey? *Hint:* Discuss the potential difficulties of making preliminary survey decisions in the absence of each of the strategic plan components.

DQ 17-3   In doing a preliminary survey for the proposed automation of the payroll system of Kay Company, the analyst in charge reached the tentative conclusion that Adam Clay, the popular cashier with more than 30 years of company service, will be displaced and perhaps asked to consider early retirement. Discuss how this scenario relates to the concept of "operational feasibility" presented in this chapter. Discuss the potential impact on the success of the new disbursements system.

DQ 17-4   "Choosing among renting, leasing, and purchasing an AIS is strictly a financial decision and should be done by the finance staff." Do you agree? Discuss fully.

DQ 17-5   "A vendor would never propose a system that would not meet an organization's needs. Therefore, external validation of vendor proposals is not really needed." Do you agree? Discuss fully.

DQ 17-6 "As long as we plan a systems development project and carry out the project in an orderly manner, we don't need a formal, documented systems development methodology." Do you agree? Discuss fully.

DQ 17-7 One of the tasks of systems analysis is to choose and justify one of the alternative design solutions. Would it not be more effective, efficient, and practical for the systems analyst to pass along *all* alternative design solutions to top management (perhaps to the IT steering committee), together with arguments for and against each alternative, and let top management choose one of them? After all, top management has a broad perspective that the systems analyst does not possess. Discuss fully.

DQ 17-8 Discuss the decisions that must be made prior to initiating structured systems analysis. Indicate how the systems survey contributed to the decisions.

DQ 17-9 Indicate who you would include on a systems analysis project team in each of the following situations, and discuss fully the reasons why you would include each member you suggest.

    a.   A college's system for tracking students from "cradle to grave" (i.e., from the time that prospective students apply for admission until the time that alumni die and are listed in the "In Memoriam" section of the alumni magazine).

    b.   A bank's system for *integrating* the various, previously separate affiliations that it has with its customers.

    c.   A *materials requirements planning (mrp)* system, as discussed in Chapter 15. (*Note:* Discuss only if you have studied Chapter 15.)

DQ 17-10 "If the results of the cost/benefit analysis do not agree with those of the effectiveness analysis, there is probably no difference among the alternatives." Discuss fully.

DQ 17-11 Discuss why the knowledge of documentation procedures (such as DFDs and systems flowcharts) is important to the acquisition/development process.

DQ 17-12 The Eureka Company requests bids from hardware vendors for specific configurations rather than bids for general performance objectives because it "knows what it needs." Discuss fully.

DQ 17-13 "An organization puts itself at a disadvantage by asking only one vendor (versus asking several vendors) for a proposal for software or hardware." Do you agree? Discuss fully.

DQ 17-14 Compare and contrast the efficiency and effectiveness of an in-house data center, an arrangement with an *outsourcing* vendor to own and operate a data center for you, a *service bureau*, an *application service provider (ASP)*, and *software as a service (SaaS)*.

DQ 17-15 Assume that you are the manager of an accounts receivable department. How might you be involved in system testing? Discuss fully.

DQ 17-16 a.   Which, if any, category of application systems *maintenance—corrective, perfective,* or *adaptive*—presents the greatest risk from a *control* standpoint? Explain.

    b.   Which, if any, pervasive control plans from Chapter 8 might be effective in controlling systems maintenance activities? What control plans other than those in Chapter 8 might be used? Discuss fully.

DQ 17-17   Refer to the typical contents of a project completion report. Which parts of the report would be useful in performing a *post-implementation review*? Discuss fully.

DQ 17-18   Periodically, students comment that they are studying to be an accountant, not an IS worker. Discuss the flaw in such reasoning.

Short Problems

SP 17-1   Table 17.3 (pg. 647) provides a vendor comparison for a system that is under consideration for purchase. Based on the data provided, which system should be selected under each of the following scenarios?

a.   Lowest total system cost for ten years of operations.

b.   Lowest cost of monthly maintenance per workstation at the maximum number of workstations.

c.   Most invoices processed per hour per data entry clerk. (Assume maximum number of workstations required to produce the provided number of invoices per minute.)

SP 17-2   Propose ways that the following intangible and/or indirect costs and benefits *might* be measured. Justify why they are indirect and/or intangible.

a.   Decreased worker productivity.

b.   Increased customer support in the form of improved product service and maintenance.

c.   Increased customer support in the form of more timely and accurate responses to customer inquiries.

d.   Deteriorated vendor relations, as evidenced by more stringent credit terms offered by vendors.

e.   Deteriorated vendor relations, as evidenced by longer lead times, poorer quality goods, and more frequent backorder situations.

f.   Improved management decision making.

g.   Improved competitive advantage.

SP 17-3   Give examples, other than those used in this chapter, of situations in which each of the three implementation approaches is most appropriate. Explain why that implementation approach is most appropriate.

Problems

P17-1   Conduct research of current literature and databases to find reports of systems development project failures. Prepare a report or presentation (subject to your instructor's instructions) describing the failure. Include in your report the elements of feasibility and project risk that may have been miscalculated or mismanaged and that led to the project failure.

P17-2   Conduct research of current literature and databases to find two *software as a service (SaaS)* providers that might be of interest to accountants. Prepare a report or presentation (subject to your instructor's guidelines) that discusses the positives and negatives of each program. If you were the decision maker in a large, multinational manufacturing company, would you use either of these programs? Why or why not?

P17-3   ABC Office Supplies, Inc. is a wholesale distributor of office supplies. It sells pencils and pens, paper goods (including computer paper and forms), staplers, calendars, and other items, excluding furniture and other major items such as copy machines that you would expect to find in an office. Sales have been growing at 5 percent per year during the past several years. Mr. Armoire, the president of ABC Office Supplies, recently attended a national office supplies convention. In conversations during that convention, he discovered that sales for ABC Office Supplies' competitors have been growing at 15 percent per year. Arriving back home, he did a quick investigation and discovered the following:

- ABC Office Supplies' customer turnover is significantly higher than the industry average.
- ABC Office Supplies' vendor turnover is significantly lower than the industry average.
- The new market analysis system was supposed to be ready two years ago but has been delayed for more than one year in systems development.
- A staff position, reporting to the president, for a person to prepare and analyze cash budgets was created two years ago but has never been filled.

Mr. Armoire has called on you to conduct a systems survey of this situation. You are to assume that a request for systems development has been prepared and approved. The information system at ABC Office Supplies is much like that depicted in Chapters 10 through 16.

Make and describe all assumptions that you believe are necessary to solve any of the following:

a.   What are the specific tasks of *this* systems survey?

b.   Indicate specific *quantifiable* benefits and costs that should be examined in assessing the economic feasibility of any solutions that might be proposed. Explain how you would go about quantifying each benefit or cost.

c.   Propose and explain three different scopes for the systems analysis. Use a context diagram to describe each scope alternative. *Hint:* What subsystems *might* be involved in an analysis?

P17-4   For each problem described, list and explain the documentation you would recommend for gathering and analyzing related facts. *Note:* It is *not* necessary to simulate the documentation. Confine your answer to a listing and brief explanation (one to two sentences) for each type of documentation that you recommend.

a.   The college admissions office is experiencing a decline in applications.

b.   The college admissions office is experiencing a decline in the percentage of students coming to the college after being accepted by the college.

c. A company is experiencing an increase in the size of receivables.

d. A faculty member has noticed that fewer students are signing up for her classes.

P17-5   Stanley Insurance Agency (SIA) is negotiating for the acquisition of computer equipment from Harmonic Industries effective 1/1/XXXX. SIA has asked for your assistance in evaluating the available financing alternatives. One alternative is to purchase the equipment outright for a unit purchase price (UPP) of $120,000 plus 5 percent sales tax, plus destination, unpacking, and installation charges estimated at $2,000. The estimated useful life of the equipment is five years, at the end of which the salvage value is estimated at $8,000. If SIA purchases the equipment, it will use straight-line depreciation over a five-year life for tax purposes (instead of the MACRS method). Its marginal income tax rate is 40 percent. For simplicity, assume that the UPP and other out-of-pocket costs will come from existing working capital.

Leasing the equipment through the financing subsidiary of Harmonic Industries is another possibility. The key provisions of the lease arrangements include those shown in **Exhibit 17.4**.

Required:

Use spreadsheet software to prepare a comparative analysis of the following financing alternatives, using an approach based on discounted cash flows.

EXHIBIT 17.4   Lease Arrangements for Problem 17-5

Initial lease term:	
Duration[a]	3 years
Monthly lease payment	$4,000
Payable	In arrears at end of each month
Renewal option terms (one-year renewal periods at election of lessee):	
Annual renewal rate as a percent of unit purchase price (UPP):	
Year 4	5 percent
Year 5	3.5 percent
Payable	Annually in advance
Option to purchase—at end of any lease anniversary date, starting with the second anniversary. Purchase option price is a sliding scale, based on UPP, as follows:	
Second lease anniversary	46 percent of UPP
Third anniversary	10 percent of UPP
Fourth and fifth anniversaries	Excluded from consideration[b]
Other charges borne by lessee:	
Destination, unpacking, and installation	$2,000 (estimated)

[a] The lease is written as a "net" lease, whereby the lessee pays for maintenance and casualty insurance. Because these annual expenses would also apply to the purchase alternative, they have been ignored.

[b] Although purchase options beyond the third-year anniversary are available, SIA has excluded them from consideration.

Show the *details of each* alternative in two columns: one column for nominal dollars and one for discounted amounts. Use a before-tax discount factor of 12 percent.

- Outright purchase
- Lease, with exercise of option to purchase at the end of year 2
- Lease, with exercise of option to purchase at the end of year 3
- Lease, with renewal at the end of year 3 and another renewal at the end of year 4

Whenever income tax calculations are required, assume that the cash savings from income taxes occurs at the *end of the year* in which the tax deduction occurs.

Personal property taxes are paid at the end of each year by the title holder. The tax rate is $50 per $1,000 of "value." For alternatives b and c, as in the case of the purchase alternative, assume that the option purchase price will come from existing working capital. Also, for cost and personal property tax purposes, consider that the option purchase price is subject to a 5 percent sales tax. Obtain hard-copy printouts of both the results of the calculations and the spreadsheet formulas.

P17-6   Using the Web sites listed in Technology Summary 17.2 (pg. 644) as a starting point, resolve the following issues:

   a. Select sites (or parts of sites) that describe two similar software or hardware products. Write a summary that compares and contrasts the information provided about those products.

   b. Select two sites that provide demos of a system. Write a report that compares and contrasts those demos in terms of the functionality and what you are able to learn about the system from the demo.

   c. Select two sites that provide tests of a system. Write a report that compares and contrasts those tests in terms of the functionality and what you are able to learn about the system from the test.

P17-7   Assume that you are working with a payroll application that produces weekly paychecks, including pay stubs. Listed on page 645 are 20 data elements that appear on the paycheck/pay stub. For each numbered item, indicate the immediate (versus ultimate) source of the item. For instance, the immediate source of the number of exemptions for an employee would be the employee master data, as opposed to the ultimate source, which is the W-4 form filed by the employee. Some items may have more than one source, as in the case of item 1. You have the following choices:

- E = employee master data
- T = time records (these are in machine-readable form and show, for each employee for each day, the time punched *in* in the morning, *out* at lunch, *in* after lunch, and *out* in the evening)
- H = table of hourly wage rates (i.e., wage rate "class" and hourly rate for each class)
- W = table of state and federal income tax withholding amounts plus FICA tax rate and annual "cutoff" amount for FICA wages
- CG = computer generated (such as a date or time of day supplied by the system)

- CC = computer calculated
- CO = console operator (such as batch totals or a date to be used)

Arrange your answer as follows:

Item No.	Source
1	E
2	?
etc	

The items to be considered are as follows:

Number	Description
1	Social security number
2	Employee name
3	Employee address
4	Employee identification number
5	Pay rate classification
6	Regular hours worked
7	Overtime hours worked
8	Hourly pay rate
9	Regular earnings
10	Overtime earnings
11	Total earnings
12	Deduction for state income tax
13	Deduction for FICA tax
14	Deduction for federal income tax
15	Union dues withheld (flat amount based on length of service)
16	Net pay
17	Check number (same number is also preprinted on each check form)
18	Year-to-date amounts for items 11 through 14
19	Pay period end date
20	Date of check (employees are paid on Wednesday for the week ended the previous Friday)

P17-8   Select an AIS system segment (such as purchasing, sales, or payroll), investigate, and write a report on the tangible and intangible costs and benefits associated with your selection.

P17-9   The chapter discusses the role of accountants in the acquisition/development process. Select a role that you expect to play in the process by the time you are at mid-career. Determine the skills you currently have and those you need to play that role. Develop a plan to attain the missing skills. (In addition to the text, you should use the IFAC #11 document, as well as other resources.)

P17-10   Select an accounting, auditing, or information systems RFP from the site www.fbo.gov. In one page or less (unless otherwise instructed by your professor), summarize what is being procured, how you would approach answering the RFP (vendor perspective), and how long you believe it would take to respond to the RFP. Include your reasoning for the approach and response time.

GLOSSARY

accounting information system (AIS) A specialized subsystem of the IS that collects, processes, and reports information related to the financial aspects of business events.

ABC analysis A technique for ranking items in a group based on the value, activity, sales, or other relevant metric for the items.

acceptance report A report that formally acknowledges the satisfactory completion of an agreed upon service.

access control software In an online environment, it ensures that (1) only authorized users gain access to a system through a process of identification (e.g., a unique account number for each user) and authentication (e.g., a password to verify that users are who they say they are), (2) restricts authorized users to specific data they require and sets the action privileges for that data (e.g., read, copy, write data), and (3) monitors access attempts and violations.

accounts payable master data A repository of all unpaid vendor invoices

accounts receivable (AR) adjustments events data Created as sales returns, bad debt write-offs, estimated doubtful accounts, or similar adjustments are processed.

accounts receivable master data Repository of all unpaid invoices issued by an organization and awaiting final disposition.

accuracy The correspondence or agreement between the information and the actual events or objects that the information represents.

activity Any action being performed by an internal or external entity.

activity-based costing (ABC) A costing approach where detailed costs to perform activities throughout the value chain are computed and can be managed or assigned to cost objects including products.

agents People or organizations that participate in events.

agree run-to-run totals (reconcile input and output batch totals) Reconciling totals prepared before a computer process has begun to totals prepared at the completion of the computer process.

anomalies Errors that otherwise might occur when adding, changing, or deleting data stored in the database.

application controls Automated business process controls contained within IT application systems (i.e., computer programs).

application program interface (API) A means for connecting to a system or application provided by the developer of that system or application.

application service provider (ASP) Offers an outsourcing mechanism whereby it hosts, manages, and provides access to application software and hardware over the Internet to multiple customers.

applications approach to business event processing Under this approach, each application collects and manages its own data, generally in dedicated, separate, physically distinguishable files for each application.

approve purchase orders Before being issued, the appropriate personnel should approve POs to ensure that an appropriate supplier has been selected and that the correct goods and services, for the correct amounts, are being purchased.

approve purchase requisition An authorized individual, or several individuals, such as cost center or department management, should approve purchase requisitions to ensure that the purchase is within an applicable budget and that the purchase is desirable.

approved configuration plan The final output of systems selection, which summarizes the choices made in the study.

approved systems analysis document The final output of the systems analysis process.

artificial intelligence Decision support systems can imitate human decision making when confronting situations that are complex and ambiguous. This ability in computers is often referred to as artificial intelligence.

attendance time records These records show the time periods that employees are in attendance at the job site and available for work. These records are used to calculate the gross amount of each employee's pay.

attribute An item of data that characterizes an entity or relationship.

audit trail A means of tracing back to the individual business events that have been aggregated into the general ledger balances.

automated clearing house (ACH) network A batch processing system for the interbank clearing of electronic payments.

automated data entry A strategy for the capture and entry of event-related data using technology such as OCR, bar codes, RFID, and EDI.

automated guided vehicle systems (AGVS) Computer-based carts that are capable of delivering parts and tools to multiple work centers.

automated storage and retrieval systems (AS/RS) Computer-controlled machines that store and retrieve parts and tools.

availability Relates to information being available when required by the business process now and in the future. It also concerns the safeguarding of necessary resources and associated capabilities.

available to promise planning An accumulation of the data on current inventories, sales commitments, and planned production to determine whether the production of finished goods will be sufficient to commit to additional sales orders.

B2B marketplaces Particular Web sites or portals that may be used as sources of supply in the procurement process.

backup To have data, programs, and documentation ready to continue operations, we must periodically make a copy called a backup.

balance-forward system Accounts receivable records consist of a customer's balance, categorized as current and past-due, and current account activity includes items such as current charges, finance charges for past-due balances, and payments.

balanced When two DFDs have equivalent external data flows, we say that the DFDs are balanced.

balanced scorecard A methodology for assessing an organization's business performance via four components: (1) financial, (2) internal business processes, (3) customers, and (4) innovation and improvement activities.

bar code readers Devices that use light reflection to read differences in bar code patterns to identify a labeled item.

batch control plans Control plans used to regulate information processing by calculating control totals at various points in a processing run and subsequently comparing these totals.

batch processing The aggregation of several business events over some period of time with the subsequent processing of these data as a group by the information system.

batch sequence check A process to check event data within a batch including the following steps: (1) the range of serial numbers constituting the documents in the batch is entered; (2) each individual, serially prenumbered document is entered; (3) the computer program sorts the input documents into numerical order, checks the documents against the sequence number range, and reports missing, duplicate, and out-of-range data.

benchmark A representative workload, processed on each vendor's proposed system configuration, to obtain comparative throughput measures.

best-of-breed approach The best-of-breed approach combines modules from various vendors to create an information system that better meets an organization's needs than a standard ERP system.

bill of lading A contract between the shipper and the carrier in which the carrier agrees to transport the goods to the shipper's customer.

bill of materials (BOM) A listing of all the subassemblies, parts, and raw materials that go into a parent assembly showing the quantity of each required to make an assembly.

billing/accounts receivable/cash receipts (B/AR/CR) process An interacting structure of people, equipment, activities, and controls designed to create information flows and records that support repetitive work routines of the credit department, cashier, and accounts receivable department, support the problem-solving processes of financial managers, and assist in the preparation of internal and external reports.

biometric identification systems Identify authorized personnel through unique physical traits such as fingers, hands, voice, eyes, face, writing dynamics, and the like.

blind copy A copy of a document on which certain data is blanked out (i.e., blinded) so that persons receiving that copy will not have access to those data.

block coding Groups of numbers are dedicated to particular characteristics of the objects being identified.

brainstorming A method for freely and creatively generating as many ideas as possible without udue regard for their practically or realism.

bubble symbol A DFD related symbol that depicts an entity or a process within which incoming data flows are transformed into outgoing data flows.

bullwhip effect Wild demand and supply fluctuations caused by the multiplication of orders up the supply chain.

business continuity planning A process that identifies events that may threaten an organization and provides a framework to ensure that the organization will continue to operate when the threatened event occurs or will resume operations with a minimum of disruption. Also known as disaster recovery planning, business interruption planning or contingency planning.

business event A meaningful change in the state of the enterprise such as creating a new employee record, submitting a purchase order to a vendor, receiving a payment from a customer, picking goods from the warehouse and delivering them to the shipping department, and revaluing inventory.

business event data store A book of original entry used for recording business events; also known as a transaction file.

business intelligence The integration of statistical and analytical tools with decision support technologies to facilitate complex analyses of data warehouses by managers and decision makers.

business intelligence (BI) Uses state-of-the-art information technologies for storing and analyzing data to help managers make the best possible decisions for their companies.

business interruption planning A process that identifies events that may threaten an organization and provides a framework to ensure that the organization will continue to operate when the threatened event occurs or will resume operations with a minimum of disruption. Also known as disaster recovery planning, business continuity planning or contingency planning.

business process control plans Plans that relate those particular controls specific to a business process, such as billing or cash receipts.

business process management (BPM) Modeling, automating, managing, and optimizing business processes; often used interchangeably with business process management systems.

business process management (BPM) systems Systems for modeling, automating, managing, and optimizing business processes; often used interchangeably with business process management (BPM).

business reporting process This process is concerned with preparing general purpose, external financial statements; ensuring that the external financial statements conform to GAAP; generating Web-based forms of key financial statement and related business reporting information for dissemination via the Internet; and supporting the generation of both ad hoc and predetermined business reports that support operational and strategic decision making.

capable to promise planning The accumulation of the data on current inventories, sales commitments, planned production and excess production capacity, or other planned production capacity that could be quickly converted to production of the desired finished goods necessary to fulfill a sales order request.

capacity requirements planning (CRP) This process uses the information from the master production schedule and time-phased order requirements schedule to develop detailed machine and labor-utilization schedules that consider the feasibility of production schedules based on available capacity in the work center status records.

cardinality A characteristic in each relationship that shows the degree to which each entity participates in the relationship.

cash disbursements events data Contains, in chronological sequence, the details of each cash payment made. Accordingly, each record in this data store shows the payment date, vendor identification, disbursement voucher number (if a voucher process is used), vendor

invoice number(s) and gross invoice amount(s), cash discount(s) taken on each invoice, net invoice amount(s), check amount, and check number (or other payment identification such as those used for electronic payments).

cash receipts event data The data created when customer payments are recorded, which contains the details of each payment as reflected on the RA accompanying a payment.

cellular manufacturing Machines are organized in clusters or "cells" that contain all of the needed resources (machines, tools, labor) to produce a family of products.

centralized database approach to business event processing In this approach, facts about events are stored in relational database tables instead of separate files, which solves many of the problems caused by data redundancy.

check digit A type of programmed edit in which an extra digit—a check digit—is included in the identification number of entities such as customers and vendors. Through mathematical formulae, the computer uses the check digit to verify that the identification number is input correctly.

check for authorized prices, terms, freight and discounts Prices, terms, freight, and discounts are calculated during the billing process using authorized data in the enterprise database.

child records Records that are included in a record one level above in hierarchical DBMS records. Child records are included in parent records.

classifying The process of grouping or categorizing data according to common attributes.

client/server technology The physical and logical division between user-oriented application programs that are run at the client level (i.e., user level) and the shared data that must be available through the server (i.e., a separate computer that handles centrally shared activities—such as databases and printing queues—between multiple users).

Cloud Computing Use of the Internet to provide scalable services, such as software, and resources, such as data storage to users.

COBIT Control Objectives for Information and Related Technology. Framework that has been widely adopted for IT governance and IT controls.

coding The creation of substitute values, or codes.

cold site Less costly and less responsive data center. Facility usually comprised of air-conditioned space with a raised floor, telephone connections, and computer ports into which a subscriber can move equipment.

comparability The information quality that enables users to identify similarities and differences in two pieces of information.

compare input data with master data A process to determine the accuracy and validity of the input data. Such comparisons may be done manually or by the computer.

compare input receipt data to PO data Before a receipt can be accepted and recorded, the receipt data should be compared with the PO master data to determine that the correct goods have been received.

compare shipment to sales order and picking ticket An example of one-for-one checking that ensures that the shipment will be authorized and accurate. Any discrepancy among these items might indicate an unauthorized or duplicate shipment (no open sales order) or an inaccurate shipment (quantities to be shipped do not agree with the picking ticket or open sales order).

compare ticket to picked goods An example of one-for-one checking that ensures that the correct goods are picked from the shelf and that any errors are detected and corrected in a timely manner (e.g., before the goods get to the shipping department).

compare vendors for favorable prices, terms, quality, and product availability Before executing a purchase, prospective vendors should be compared to determine that they are the optimal choice for the purchase.

completeness The degree to which information necessary to make a decision includes data about every relevant object or event and includes that information only once.

compliance Deals with complying with the laws, regulations, and contractual arrangements to which the business process is subject, that is, externally imposed business criteria, as well as internal policies.

composite attributes Attributes that consist of multiple subattributes.

composite primary key The primary key formed by combining two or more columns in a table.

computer agreement of batch totals A control plan that works in the following manner: (1) batch totals are established manually; (2) the manually prepared total is entered into the computer and is written to the computer batch control totals data; (3) as individual source documents are entered, a computer program accumulates independent batch totals and compares these totals to the manually prepared totals; (4) the computer prepares a report, which usually contains batch details and whether the totals agreed or disagreed.

computer-aided design (CAD) An application of computer technology that automates the product design process, including but not limited to the functions of geometric modeling, materials stress and strain analysis, drafting, storing product specifications, and mechanical simulation of a product's performance. Also called computer-aided engineering (CAE).

computer crime Crime in which the computer is the target of the crime or the means used to commit the crime.

computer hacking and cracking Reflects the intentional, unauthorized access to an organization's computer system, accomplished by bypassing the system's access security controls.

computer virus Program code that can attach itself to other programs (including macros within word processing documents), thereby "infecting" those programs and macros.

computer-aided engineering (CAE) An application of computer technology that automates the product design process, including but not limited to the functions of geometric modeling, materials stress and strain analysis, drafting, storing product specifications, and mechanical simulation of a product's performance. Also called computer-aided design (CAD).

computer-aided manufacturing (CAM) The use of computer and communications technologies to improve productivity by linking computer numerical control (CNC) machines, monitoring production, and providing automatic feedback for control of operations.

computer-aided process planning (CAPP) An automated decision support system that generates manufacturing operations instructions and routings based on information about machining requirements and machine capabilities.

confidentiality Concerns the protection of sensitive information from unauthorized disclosure.

confirm customer accounts regularly The customer can be used as a means of controlling the billing process. By sending regular customer statements, we use the customer to check that invoices were valid and accurate.

confirm input acceptance This control causes the data entry program to inform the user that input has been accepted for processing.

confirm purchase order to requesting department To prevent duplicate purchase requests and to allow the requesting department to ensure that a PO is created, the requesting department should be informed when a PO has been issued in response to a purchase requisition.

consistent Information that is the same, when compared from the same object or event collected at two points in time.

context diagram A top-level, or least detailed, data flow diagram of an information system that depicts the system and all of its activities as a single bubble and shows the data flows into and out of the system and into and out of the external entities.

contingency planning Process that identifies events that may threaten an organization and provides a framework to ensure that the organization will continue to operate when the threatened event occurs or will resume operations with a minimum of disruption. Also known as disaster recovery planning, business continuity planning or business interruption planning.

continuous assurance/continuous auditing Process by which assurance is provided through monitoring of automated controls and business events in real-time or near real time.

Continuous Data Protection (CDP) A data replication strategy whereby all data changes are data stamped and saved to secondary systems as the changes are happening.

control environment A state of control consciousness that reflects the organization's (primarily the board of directors' and management's) general awareness of and commitment to the importance of control throughout the organization.

control goals Business process objectives that an internal control system is designed to achieve

control matrix A tool designed to assist in evaluating the potential effectiveness of controls in a business process by matching control goals with relevant control plans.

control plans Reflect information processing policies and procedures that assist in accomplishing control goals.

corrective control plans A control plan that is designed to rectify problems that have occurred.

cost/benefit analysis The feasibility evaluation of estimates of the costs and benefits of a new system (or system modification).

cost/effectiveness study Provides quantitative and certain qualitative information concerning each alternative solution to an information processing problem. This information is used to decide which alternative best meets a user's needs.

cracker Someone who simply gets a kick out of breaking into a computer system with the motive of crime theft or destruction.

credit card A method of payment whereby a third party (such as a bank), for a fee, removes from the collector the risk of noncollection of the account receivable; also known as a charge card.

cumulative sequence check Provides input control when the serial numbers are assigned within the organization (e.g., sales order numbers issued by the sales order department) but later are not entered in perfect serial number sequence (i.e., picking tickets do not necessarily arrive at the shipping department in sequence).

customer acknowledgement Sent to the customer to provide notification of an order's acceptance and expected shipment date.

customer credit check A control process performed to ensure that an organization does not extend more credit to a customer than is prudent. Usually performed before accepting a customer's order.

customer master data Contains a record of every customer with whom a company is authorized to regularly do business.

customer relationship management (CRM) software A software application used to build and maintain an organization's customer-related database.

customer self-service (CSS) software Software that allows an organization's customers to complete an inquiry, perform a task (including sales), or troubleshoot problems without the aid of an organization's employees; often an extension of CRM software.

data Facts or figures in raw form. Data represent the measurements or observations of objects and events.

database management system (DBMS) A set of integrated programs designed to simplify the tasks of creating, accessing, and managing data.

data encryption A process that employs mathematical algorithms and keys to encode data making it unintelligible to the human eye and useless to those who should not have access to it.

data flow diagram (DFD) A DFD depicts a system's components; the data flows among the components; and the sources, destinations, and storage of data.

data flow symbol A DFD related symbol that represents a pathway for data.

data independence Decoupling of data from the system applications (making the data independent of the application). A major difference between the database approach and the applications approach.

data maintenance A process that includes activities related to adding, deleting, or replacing the standing data portions of master data.

Data Manipulation language (DML) A language much like ordinary language used to access a database and to produce inquiry reports. DML allows nontechnical users to bypass the programmer and to access the database directly. Also known as query language.

data mining The exploration, aggregation, and analysis of large quantities of varied data from across the organization. Used to better understand business processes, trends, and opportunities to improve efficiency and effectiveness, as well as to discover anomalies.

data model A model that depicts user requirements for data stored in a database.

data redundancy Data stored in multiple locations within a system.

data store symbol A DFD related symbol that represents a place where data are stored.

data warehousing The use of information systems facilities to focus on the collection, organization, integration, and long-term storage of entity-wide data. Data warehousing provides users with easy access to large quantities of varied data from across an organization to improve decision-making capabilities.

debit card A form of payment that authorizes the collector to transfer funds electronically from the payer's bank account to the collector's bank account.

decision aid Information tools that can help decision makers to make better decisions.

decision making The process of making choices; the central activity of management.

decision support systems(DSS) Computer-based systems that support collaborative intellectual work such as idea generation, elaboration, analysis, synthesis, information sharing, and decision making. GSS/GDSS use technology to solve the time and space dimension problems associated with group work.

deliverables Specific reports and other documentation that are produced and provided as accountability points for a systems development project.

denial-of-service attack A Web site is overwhelmed by an intentional onslaught of thousands of simultaneous messages, making it impossible for the attacked site to engage in its normal activities.

destination A DFD related concept, portrayed by an external entity symbol, of data outside the system.

detective control plans These plans are used to discover that problems have occurred.

digital image processing systems Computer based systems for capture, storage, retrieval, and presentation of images of objects such as pictures and documents.

digital signature This technology validates the identity of the sender and the integrity of an electronic message to reduce the risk that a communication was sent by an unauthorized system or user or was intercepted/modified in transit.

direct costs (benefits) Those costs directly attributable to the system or the system change. Examples of direct costs include equipment purchased, personnel salaries, site preparation, and materials and supplies.

disaster recovery planning A process that identifies events that may threaten an organization and provides a framework to ensure that the organization will continue to operate when the threatened event occurs or will resume operations with a minimum of disruption. Also known as business continuity planning, business interruption planning or contingency planning.

distributed denial-of service attack Uses many computers that unwittingly cooperate in a denial-of-service by sending messages to the target Web sites.

document design A control plan in which a source document is designed to make it easier to prepare the document initially and later to input data from the document.

document/record counts Simple counts of the number of documents entered (e.g., 25 documents in a batch). This procedure represents the minimum level required to control input completeness.

document/record hash totals These totals reflect a summarization of any numeric data field within the input document or record, such as item numbers or quantities on a customer order.

dollar totals A summation of the dollar value of items in the batch, such as the total dollar value of all remittance advices in a batch.

e-procurement The use of information technology and networks (such as the Internet) to automate significant portions of the procurement process.

economic order quantity (EOQ) A technique that calculates the optimum quantity of an item to order, analyzing all incremental costs associated with acquiring and carrying the particular item in inventory.

effectiveness (a quality of information) Deals with information being relevant and pertinent to the business process as well as being delivered in a timely, correct, consistent, and usable manner.

effectiveness (a control goal) A measure of success in meeting one or more goals for the operations process.

efficiency (a quality of information) Concerns the provision of information through the optimal (most productive and economical) use of resources.

efficiency (a control goal) A measure of the productivity of the resources applied to achieve a set of goals.

electronic approvals Using a computer system's workflow facility to route business events to persons authorized to approve the event online.

electronic bill presentment and payment (EBPP) B2C systems that use a Web site to post customer bills and to receive their electronic payments.

electronic business (e-business) The application of electronic networks (including the Internet) to undertake business processes between individuals and organizations.

electronic data interchange (EDI) The computer to- computer exchange of business data (i.e., documents) in structured formats that allow direct processing of those electronic documents by the receiving computer system.

electronic document management (EDM) The capturing, storage, management, and control of electronic document images for the purpose of supporting management decision making and facilitating business event data processing.

electronic funds transfer (EFT) A variety of procedures for transmitting cash funds between entities via electronic transmission instead of using paper checks.

electronic invoice presentment and payment (EIPP) B2B systems that combine e-invoicing and e-payment processes to (1) send invoices to customers via a Web portal or secure network using a third-party service provider and to (2) receive electronic payments that are initiated by the payer, processed by the third party, and settled by the ACH network, wire transfer, or debit or credit card company.

electronic mail (e-mail) The electronic transmission of nonstandardized messages between two individuals who are linked via a communications network (usually an intranet or the Internet).

Electronic storefronts Internet-located resources for displaying goods and services for sale and for conducting related sales events.

electronic time management system A computer based system that captures, stores, and reports time. Inputs to such systems are via the reading of magnetic strips on employee identification badges, bar code readers, and key entry.

electronic vaulting Service whereby data changes are automatically transmitted over the Internet on a continuous basis to an off-site server maintained by a third party.

employee/payroll master data The central repository of data about people who work for an organization.

enter data close to the originating source A strategy for the capture and entry of event-related data close to the place (and probably time) that an event occurs, reducing the likelihood that events will be lost and not entered into the system and that errors will be introduced into the system.

enterprise application integration (EAI) Combines processes, software, standards, and hardware to link together two or more systems and allow them to operate as one.

enterprise database The central repository for all the data related to an organization's business activities and resources.

enterprise information systems Integrate the business process and information from all of an organization's functional areas, such as marketing and sales, cash receipts, purchasing, cash disbursements, human resources, production and logistics, and business reporting (including financial reporting). Also called enterprise systems or enterprise systems.

enterprise resource planning (ERP) systems Software packages used for the core systems necessary to support enterprise systems.

Enterprise Risk Management (ERM) A process, effected by an entity's board of directors, management, and other personnel, applied in strategy setting and across the enterprise, designed to identify potential events that may effect the entity, and manage risk to be within its risk appetite, to provide reasonable assurance regarding the achievement of entity objectives.

enterprise services bus (ESB) Uses standardized protocols to let event-driven applications communicate less expensively than can the tightly coupled, synchronous EAI platforms.

enterprise-wide information systems Integrate the business process and information from all of an organization's functional areas, such as marketing and sales, cash receipts, purchasing, cash disbursements, human resources, production and logistics, and business reporting (including financial reporting). Also called enterprise systems or enterprise information systems.

entities Any object, event, or agent about which data are collected.

entity-relationship diagram (E-R diagram) Reflects the system's key entities and the relationships among those entities.

entity-relationship model A diagram of the relational model that includes entities and relationships.

entity-relationship modeling Reflects the system's key entities and the relationships among those entities.

error routines These processes handle the required actions when processing can't proceed as planned; also called error routines. Also called exception routines.

evaluated receipt settlement (ERS) A process by which an organization pays for a purchase on the basis of the goods receipt.

event-driven architecture (EDA) An approach to designing and building enterprise systems in which business events trigger messages to be sent by middleware between independent software modules that are completely unaware of each other.

events Occurrences related to resources that are of interest to the business.

exception and summary report This report reflects the events—either in detail, summary, or both—that were accepted or rejected by the system.

exception routines These processes handle the required actions when processing can't proceed as planned; also called error routines.

executive information systems (EIS) A subset of DSS, these systems combine information from the organization and the environment, organize and analyze the information, and present the information to the manager in a form that assists in decision making; also called executive support systems or ESS.

executive support systems (ESS) A subset of DSS, these systems combine information from the organization and the environment, organize and analyze the information, and present the information to the manager in a form that assists in decision making; also called executive information systems or EIS.

expert systems (ES) Rule-based systems that emulate the problem-solving techniques of human experts. Appropriate when decisions are extremely complex, consistency of decision making is desirable, and the decision maker wants to minimize time spent making the decision while maximizing the quality of the decision.

exploding the BOM A process that involves extending a bill of materials to determine the total of each component required to manufacture a given quantity of an upper-level assembly or subassembly specified in the MPS.

eXtensible Business Reporting Language (XBRL) An XML-based language consisting of a set of tags that are used to unify the presentation of business reporting information into a single format, easily produced and read by almost any financial software package, and easily searched by Web browsers.

external entities Entities (i.e., persons, places, or things) outside the system that send data to, or receive data from, the system.

external entity symbol A DFD related symbol that portrays a source or destination of data outside the system.

extranet A type of internal network (intranet) that has been extended to limited external access to members of an organization's value system.

feasibility study A set of procedures conducted to determine the practicability of a potential systems development project.

feedback value Improves a decision maker's capacity to predict, confirm, or correct earlier expectations.

feeder process Any business process that accumulates business event data that are then communicated to and processed within the general ledger.

fidelity bond Indemnifies a company in case it suffers losses from defalcations committed by its employees.

financial reporting officer A manager with responsibilities for reporting financial information to external parties.

firewall A technique to protect one network from another "untrusted" network. May be used to protect a system from intrusions from the Internet by blocking certain kinds of traffic from flowing into or out of the organization.

first normal form (1NF) A relation is in 1NF if its tables do not contain repeating groups.

flexible manufacturing systems (FMS) An automated manufacturing operations system that can react quickly to product and design changes because centralized computer control provides real-time routing, load balancing, and production scheduling logic.

float When applied to cash receipts, the time between the customer tendering payment and the availability of good funds.

forced vacations A policy that requires an employee to take leave from the job and substitutes another employee in his or her place.

foreign key These primary key attributes when inserted into other tables to establish links.

forms Onscreen presentations of data in tables and queries.

fraud A deliberate act or untruth intended to obtain unfair or unlawful gain.

freedom from bias The quality of being not biased. Bias is the tendency of information to fall more often on one side than on the other of the object or event that it represents. Also called neutrality.

functionally dependent An attribute is functionally dependent on another attribute (or a collection of other attributes) if a value for the first attribute determines a single value for the second attribute at any time.

general controls Controls applied to all IT service activities. Also called IT general controls.

general ledger (GL) process This process involves accumulating data, classifying data by general ledger accounts, and recording data in those accounts; and fueling the financial reporting, business reporting, and other reporting subsystems by providing the information needed to prepare external and internal reports.

general ledger and business reporting (GL/BR) process An interacting structure of people, equipment, activities, and controls that is designed to accomplish both operations and information system functions, including maintenance of the general ledger and preparation of internal and external business reports.

general ledger master data A data repository that contains summarized information about all of an organization's business event data.

global inventory management An inventory management approach where inventory needs and inventory and production capabilities are matched across the entire global enterprise, not just at a local or regional level.

good funds Funds on deposit and available for use.

group decision support systems (GDSS) Computer-based systems that support collaborative intellectual work such as idea generation, elaboration, analysis, synthesis, information sharing, and decision making. GSS/GDSS use technology to solve the time and space dimension problems associated with group work. Also called group support systems (GSS).

group support systems (GSS) Computer-based systems that support collaborative intellectual work such as idea generation, elaboration, analysis, synthesis, information sharing, and decision making. GSS/GDSS use technology to solve the time and space dimension problems associated with group work. Also called group decision support systems (GDSS).

hacker Someone who simply gets a kick out of breaking into a computer system but does NOT hold malicious intentions to destroy or steal.

hash totals A summation of any numeric data existing for all documents in the batch, such as a total of customer numbers or invoice numbers in the case of remittance advices; used for control purposes only.

help desk Assistance to overcome problems encountered in using those resources.

hierarchical coding Hierarchical codes attach specific meaning to particular character positions. Hierarchical coding orders items in descending order, where each successive rank order is a subset of the rank above it.

hierarchical database model A logical database model where records are organized in a pyramid structure, and no child record may have more than one parent record. All relationships are 1:N.

hot site A fully equipped data center, often housed in bunker-like facilities, that can accommodate many businesses and that is made available to client companies for a monthly subscriber fee.

human capital management (HCM) The process of managing how people are hired, developed, assigned, motivated, and retained.

human resources (HR) management process An interacting structure of people, equipment, activities, and controls used to create information flows that support repetitive work routines of the human resources department and decision needs of those who manage the human resources department.

immediate mode The data processing mode in which little or no delay occurs between any two data processing steps.

immediately endorse incoming checks The checks are restrictively endorsed as soon as possible after receipt in the billing organization to protect them from being fraudulently appropriated. The endorsement should indicate that the check is for deposit only, the name of the organization depositing the check, and the account number and bank to which the check is being deposited.

immediately separate checks and remittances advices When checks are received in the billing organization, the RAs should be immediately separated from the checks. This will accelerate the deposit and the recording of the RAs because the customer payment can be recorded at the same time that the deposit is being prepared. The faster the checks are deposited, the less chance that the cash can be diverted. Also, if the person posting the RA does not have the check, lapping can be prevented.

imprest payroll bank account This fund (account) is reimbursed for the *exact amount* of the payroll disbursements made from the fund, rather than being supplemented for expected amounts in advance, as with the payroll clearing account. Similar to a petty cash fund, an imprest account maintains a cash balance considered sufficient for upcoming payroll requirements. The imprest account is then reimbursed after the payroll checks are cashed to bring it back up to this normal account balance.

independent authorization to make payment A control to ensure that only authorized payments are made by enforcing segregation of duties between the accounts payable record keeping and payment execution.

independent authorization to record receipt Before a receipt can be accepted and recorded, the receipt data should be compared with the PO master data to determine that an approved PO, prepared by someone other than receiving personnel, is on file.

independent billing authorization Comparison of sales orders, entered by a sales representative, with shipping notifications entered by shipping, verifies that each shipment is supported by a valid sales order.

independent customer master data maintenance This assumes that there is a segregation of duties between the personnel who create the customer record (to authorize sales to the customer) and the personnel who create the sales order (execute the sale).

independent pricing data This assumes that a segregation of duties exists between those who approve unit prices and those involved in the selling function, such as customer sales representatives and billing clerks. Typically, selling prices will be obtained from inventory master data, a source for those prices that *is independent* of those in the selling functions.

independent shipping authorization This establishes, for the shipping personnel, that someone other than the warehouse personnel authorized the shipment. Typically this would be accomplished by sending a copy of the sales order from customer service directly to the shipping department or by giving the shipping personnel access to open sales order records on the sales order master data. Without this control, warehouse personnel could cause a shipment by simply sending goods to the shipping department. This control assumes a segregation of duties among sales, the warehouse, and shipping.

independent validation of vendor invoices A control to ensure that recorded vendor invoices come from purchase order and receiving data created by entities other than the entity that records the vendor invoices; used to preclude unauthorized and invalid accounts payable records.

independent vendor master data maintenance Requires that there is a separation of duties between the personnel who create vendor records (to authorize purchases and payments) and those that create and approve POs, record accounts payable, and approve payments.

indirect costs (benefits) These costs are not directly attributable to the system or the system change. Indirect costs are normally associated with overhead expenses, such as personnel fringe benefits and utilities.

information Data presented in a form that is useful in a decision-making activity.

information processing Data-processing functions related to economic events such as accounting events, internal operations such as manufacturing, and financial statement preparation such as adjusting entries.

information processing activities Data-processing functions related to economic events such as accounting events, internal operations such as manufacturing, and financial statement preparation such as adjusting entries.

information system (IS) A man-made system that generally consists of an integrated set of computer based components and manual components established to collect, store, and manage data and to provide output information to users.

input accuracy All valid events must be correctly captured and entered into a system.

input completeness All valid events or objects are captured and entered into a system once and only once.

input validity Input data are appropriately approved and represent actual economic events and objects.

inspect goods Upon receipt of goods they should be inspected by qualified personnel to ensure that the correct goods are received in acceptable condition.

instance (in relation to XBRL) An XBRL document that contains all information, including tags, about the occurrence of an item. Also called instance document.

instance (in relation to REA modeling) One specific thing of the type defined by the entity.

instance document An XBRL document that contains all information, including tags, about the occurrence of an item. Also just called instance.

intangible costs (benefits) These costs and benefits cannot be reasonably quantified. A productivity loss caused by low employee morale is an example of such a cost; whereas intangible benefits may accrue from improved information availability.

integrity Relates to the accuracy and completeness of information as well as to its validity in accordance with business values and expectations.

intelligent agent A software program that may be integrated into a DSS or other software tool (such as word processing, spreadsheet, or database packages) that provides automated assistance, advice, and/or information for decision making.

internal control A process—effected by an entity's board of directors, management, and other personnel—designed to provide reasonable assurance regarding the achievement of objectives in effectiveness and efficiency of operations, reliability of reporting, and compliance with applicable laws and regulations.

internal entity An entity (i.e., person, place, or thing) within the system that transforms data. Internal entities include persons (for example, accounting clerks), places (for example, departments), and things (for example, computers).

Internet assurance A service provided for a fee to vendors to provide limited assurance to users of the vendor's Web site that the site is in fact reliable, and event data security is reasonable.

Internet auction markets Provide an Internet base for companies to place products up for bid or for buyers to put proposed purchases up for bid.

Internet commerce The computer-to-computer exchange of business event data in structured or semi-structured formats via Internet communication that allows the initiation and consummation of business events.

Internet market exchanges These exchanges bring together a variety of suppliers in a given industry with one or more buyers in the same industry to provide Internet commerce through organized markets.

Internet A massive interconnection of computer networks worldwide that enables communication between dissimilar technology platforms.

intranet Mini-internal equivalents to the Internet that link an organization's internal documents and databases into a system that is accessible only to members of the organization, through Web browsers or, increasingly, through internally developed software designed to maximize the benefits from utilization of organizational information resources.

intrusion detection systems (IDS) Log and monitor who is on or trying to access a network. Accumulate profiles, flag and report exceptional activity.

intrusion prevention systems (IPS) Actively block unauthorized traffic using rules specified by the organization.

inventory master data A file or table of data that contains a record of each item stocked in the warehouse or regularly ordered from a vendor.

invoice A business document used to notify the customer of an obligation to pay the seller for the merchandise (or service) ordered and shipped (or provided, if a service).

IT general controls Controls applied to all IT service activities. Also called general controls.

IT governance A process that ensures that the enterprise's IT sustains and extends the organization's strategies and objectives.

IT steering committee Coordinates the organizational and IT strategic planning processes and reviews and approves the strategic IT plan.

item counts Counts of the number of items or lines of data entered, such as a count of the number of invoices being paid by all the customer remittances. Also known as line counts.

job time records Records that reflect the start and stop times on specific jobs. Their purpose is to allow the distribution of payroll costs to jobs in process (or to other accounts).

journal voucher An internal source document used to notify the general ledger to make an accounting entry.

journalize The process of recording a business event (i.e., accounting transaction) in a book of original entry (i.e., a special or general journal).

just-in-time (JIT) A pull manufacturing philosophy or business strategy for designing production processes to be more responsive to precisely timed customer delivery requirements.

key attribute The attribute whose value is unique (i.e., different) for every entity that will ever appear in the database and is the most meaningful way of identifying each entity.

key verification A control plan in which documents are keyed by one individual and then rekeyed by a second individual. The data entry software compares the second keystrokes to the strokes keyed by the first individual. If there are differences, it is assumed that one person misread or miskeyed the data.

knowledge Information that has been formatted and distributed in accordance with an organization's standards.

knowledge management The process of capturing, storing, retrieving, and distributing the knowledge of the individuals in an organization for use by others in the organization to improve the quality and efficiency of decision making across the firm.

labor-force planning data A repository of data concerning an organization's short-term and long-term staffing requirements. It may include data about various job specifications, with the specifications delineating the training and experience necessary to perform each job.

lapping A fraud by which funds being received by one customer are stolen, and the theft is covered up by applying funds received from another customer to the first customer's account.

legacy systems Systems that have existed in an organization over a long period of time and developed using an organization's previous computer hardware and software platforms.

library controls Restrict access to data, programs, and documentation.

life-cycle costs The sum of the costs to design, produce, market, deliver, and support a product throughout the product's lifecycle from conception to ultimate discontinuance.

limit checks A type of programmed edit check that tests whether the contents (e.g., values) of the entered data fall within predetermined limits; also called reasonableness checks.

line counts Counts of the number of items or lines of data entered, such as a count of the number of invoices being paid by all the customer remittances. Also known as item counts.

local area networks (LANs) Communication networks that link several different local user machines with printers, databases, and other shared devices.

lockbox A postal address, maintained by the firm's bank, which is used solely for the purpose of collecting checks. The bank processes the receipts, providing a quick update to the firm's bank balance, and provides the collecting company with the remittance advice (RA) data to update customer accounts.

logical data flow diagram A graphical representation of a system showing the system's processes (as bubbles), data stores, and the flows of data into and out of the processes and data stores.

malware Software designed specifically to damage or disrupt a computer system.

management information system (MIS) A man-made system that generally consists of an integrated set of computer-based components and manual components established to collect, store, and manage data and to provide output information to users. See also information systems (IS).

management process A man-made system consisting of the people, authority, organization, policies, and procedures whose objective is to plan and control the operations of the organization.

managerial reporting officer A manager with responsibilities and expertise for preparing internal reports to assist management decision making.

manual reconciliation of batch totals A control plan that works in the following manner: (1) batch totals are established manually; (2) as individual source documents are entered, a computer program accumulates independent batch totals; (3) the computer prepares a report that includes the relevant totals that must be manually reconciled with the totals established prior to the particular process; (4) the person who reconciles the batch totals must determine why the totals do not agree and make corrections as necessary to ensure integrity of the input data.

manufacturing orders (MOs) Orders that convey authority for the manufacture of a specified product or subassembly in a specified quantity and describe the material, labor, and machine requirements for the job.

manufacturing resource planning (MRP) An integrated decision support system for planning, executing, and controlling manufacturing operations. It includes facilities for planning all manufacturing resources, including material, machines, labor, and financial capital.

master data Repositories of relatively permanent data maintained over an extended period of time.

master production schedule (MPS) A statement of specific production goals developed from forecasts of demand, actual sales orders, and/or inventory information.

match invoice with purchase order and receiving report A control plan where an invoice should be matched to the corresponding purchase order and receiving report data to ensure that items on the invoice were ordered and received and that the invoice is accurately recorded.

materials requirements planning (mrp) This process uses bills of material, raw material and work-in process (RM/WIP) inventory status data, open order data, and the master production schedule to calculate a time-phased order requirements schedule for materials and subassemblies.

mathematical accuracy checks These edit checks compare calculations performed manually to those performed by the computer to determine whether a document has been entered correctly.

matrix A tool designed to help analyze a situation and relate processes to desired results.

maximum cardinality A measure of the highest level of participation that one entity can have in another entity.

middleware A software product that connects two or more separate applications or software modules.

mirror site Site that maintains copies of the primary site's programs and data.

mnemonic coding Coding in which some or all of the identifying characters are letters of the alphabet.

model Simplified representation of a complex entity or phenomenon.

monitor open accounts receivable An organization should regularly review accounts receivable aging reports to ensure that cash is received in a timely manner. Follow-up procedures should be undertaken for payments that are overdue, and those that are deemed uncollectible should be written off to ensure that accounts receivable balances are not overstated. Errors in accounts receivable discovered during this follow-up should be corrected immediately.

monitoring In an internal control system means assessment by management to determine whether the control plans in place are continuing to function appropriately over time.

move tickets Authorize and record movement of a job from one work center to another.

network database model A logical database model that handles complex data structures, such as a child record that has more than one parent record.

network providers Companies that provide a link to the Internet by making their directly connected networks available for access by fee-paying customers.

neural networks (NN) Computer hardware and software systems that mimic the human brain's capability to recognize patterns or predict outcomes using less-than-complete information.

neutrality The quality of being not biased. Bias is the tendency of information to fall more often on one side than on the other of the object or event that it represents. Also called freedom from bias.

non-key attribute An attribute that is not part of the primary key.

nonrecurring costs Costs that occur only once to get a system operational.

normal forms Rules based on set theory, the branch of mathematics on which relational database models are based. These rules include specifications that must be met by relational database tables.

null A missing value in a relational database.

object-oriented database model A model that allows the storage of both simple and complex objects (including items such as video, audio, and pictures). Characteristics also include inheritance and encapsulation.

object-relational databases A relational DBMS framework with the capability to store complex data types.

offline A device that is not directly connected to a central computer or network.

one-for-one checking An business process control that uses a detailed comparison of individual elements of two or more data sources to determine that they agree.

online A computer configuration in which certain equipment is directly connected to the computer.

online prompting A control plan that requests user input or asks questions that the user must answer.

online real-time (OLRT) systems These systems gather business event data at the time of occurrence, update the master data almost instantaneously, and provide the results arising from the business event within a very short amount of time—that is, in real-time.

online transaction entry (OLTE) The use of data entry devices allows business event data to be entered directly into the information system at the time and place that the business event occurs.

open-item system A complex accounts receivable system appropriate in situations where invoices are prepared and sent for each sale (i.e., each shipment), and the customer typically makes payments for specific invoices when those invoices are due.

operations process A man-made system consisting of the people, equipment, organization, policies, and procedures whose objective is to accomplish the work of the organization.

optical character recognition Data entry into a system using light reflection for pattern recognition of handwritten or printed characters.

order entry/sales (OE/S) process An interacting structure of people, equipment, activities, and controls that is designed to create information flows that support the repetitive work routines of the sales order department, credit department, and shipping department and the decision needs of those who manage various sales and marketing functions.

order-to-cash process A process that includes the events surrounding the sale of goods to a customer, the recognition of the revenue, and the collection of the customer payment.

organizational governance A process by which organizations select objectives, establish processes to achieve objectives, and monitor performance.

outsourcing The assignment of an internal function to an outside vendor.

packing slip A shipping document that is included with a package and identifies the customer and the contents of the package.

paperless systems A system that eliminates documents and forms as the medium for conducting business.

parent records Records that include the lower level child records within a hierarchical DBMS.

partial dependency A problem that arises because an attribute is dependent on a portion of the primary key and not on the entire key.

participation constraint A specification of both the minimum and maximum degree of participation of one entity in the relationship with another entity.

parts master A list of the detailed specifications for each raw material item contained in a product.

payable/cash disbursements (AP/CD) process An interacting structure of people, equipment, activities, and controls that is designed to handle the repetitive work routines of the accounts payable department and the cashier, to support the decision needs of those who manage the accounts payable department and cashier, and to assist in the preparation of internal and external reports.

payroll clearing account A bank account used solely for payroll purposes and is separate from a company's other, more general purpose bank accounts. Funds are transferred into the account prior to the generation of payroll checks and for the total amount of all checks to be issued. Accordingly, the net of the transfer to the clearing account and payroll disbursements should zero out each pay period, assuming all checks are cashed.

payroll direct deposit system A system where employees' net pay is sent electronically through the banking system and deposited directly to the employees' bank accounts.

payroll process An interacting structure of people, equipment, activities, and controls that creates information flows to support the repetitive work routines of the payroll department. The payroll process maintains records containing data for payroll taxes and fringe benefits, attendance reporting, timekeeping, and paying employees for work performed.

payroll service bureau A company that specializes in rendering payroll services to client companies for a fee.

performance reports A managerial accounting report that compares actual performance with budgeted expectations.

periodic mode The processing mode in which a delay exists between any two data processing steps.

pervasive control plans Control plans that relate to a multitude of goals and processes. Like the control environment, they provide a climate or set of surrounding conditions in which the various business processes operate.

physical data flow diagram Graphical representation of a system showing the system's internal and external entities and the flows of data into and out of these entities.

picking ticket A data flow—often a sales order copy—that authorizes the warehouse to "pick" the goods from the shelf and send them to shipping.

policy A policy is a plan or process put in place to guide actions and thus achieve goals.

populate input screens with master data A control plan that operates when a clerk enters the identification code for an entity, such as a customer, and the system retrieves data about that entity from the master data, to eliminate the need for re-entry of those data.

post-billing system A billing system in which invoices are prepared after goods have been shipped and the sales order notification (sales order) has been matched to shipping's billing notification (shipping notice).

post-implementation review An examination of a working information system, conducted soon after that system's implementation to determine whether the user's requirements have been satisfied and whether the development effort was efficient and conducted in accordance with the organization's systems development standards.

post Moving business event from a journal to a subsidiary ledger.

pre-billing system A billing system in which invoices are prepared immediately on acceptance of a customer order—that is, after inventory and credit checks have been accomplished but before the goods have been shipped.

predictive value An information quality that improves a decision maker's capacity to predict, confirm, or correct earlier expectations.

preformatted screens A computer screen designed to control the entry of data by defining the acceptable format of each data field, automatically moving to the next field, requiring that certain fields are completed, and/or by automatically populating fields.

preliminary feasibility study A set of procedures conducted to determine the practicability of a potential systems development project.

preventive control plans A control plan that is designed to stop problems from occurring.

preventive maintenance Periodic cleaning, testing and adjusting of computer equipment to ensure equipment's continued efficient and correct operation.

primary key The unique identifier for each row of a table (or record within a file) that serves as an address for the row.

procedures for rejected inputs A control plan designed to ensure that erroneous data (i.e., not accepted for processing) are corrected and resubmitted for processing.

process A series of actions or operations leading to a particular and usually desirable result.

product lifecycle management (PLM) software Software that manages product data during a product's life, beginning with the design of the product, continuing through manufacture, and culminating in the disposal of the product at the end of its life.

production, planning, and control A production subsystem concerned with managing the orderly and timely movement of goods through the production process.

program change controls Provide assurance that all modifications to programs are authorized and that the changes are completed, tested and properly implemented.

programmed edit checks An edit that is automatically performed by data entry programs upon entry of the input data.

public-key cryptography Helps to keep the problem of keeping encryption keys secret by employing a pair of matched keys for each system user, one private and one public.

pull manufacturing An approach to manufacturing where production is initiated as individual sales orders are received. Theoretically, each job consists of a "batch" of one unit. In pacing production, an idle machine pulls the next part from the previous machine as soon as that part is available thus pulling goods through the factory only when needed to satisfy demand.

purchase order (PO) A request for the purchase of goods or services from a vendor.

purchase order master data A compilation of open purchase orders that includes the status of each item on order.

purchase receipts data An event data store with each record reflecting a receipt of goods and services.

purchase requisition An internal request to acquire goods and services..

purchase requisitions data A file or table where purchase requisitions are compiled.

purchase returns and allowances Events that include the reduction of accounts payable due to returning items purchased or for a price allowance or other agreement with the vendor.

purchase-to-pay process A process that includes the events surrounding the purchase of goods from a vendor, the recognition of the cost of those goods, and the payment to the vendor

purchasing events data Contains, in chronological sequence, the details of each invoice that is recorded. Each record shows the date recorded; vendor invoice number; account distributions, such as assets, expenses, freight, sales tax (or the clearing account for inventory receipts); and gross invoice amount.

purchasing process An interacting structure of people, equipment, activities, and controls to handle the repetitive work routines of the purchasing department and receiving department, support the decision needs of those who manage the purchasing and receiving departments, and assist in the preparation of internal and external reports.

push manufacturing An approach to manufacturing management in which sales forecasts drive the production plan, and goods are produced in large batches. Each machine performs its operation on the batch, and then the entire job waits until the operation can be started on the next machine in the sequence.

queries An element of a DBMS that allows users and programmers to access the data stored in various tables.

query language A language much like ordinary language used to access a database and to produce inquiry reports. Query language allows nontechnical users to bypass the programmer and to access the database directly. Also known as Data Manipulation language (DML).

Radio-Frequency Identification (RFID) A system for sending and receiving data, using wireless technology, between an RFID tag (a chip with an antenna) and an RFID transceiver.

raw materials (RM) requisition An authorization that identifies the type and quantity of materials to be withdrawn from the storeroom.

reasonableness checks A type of programmed edit check that tests whether the contents (e.g., values) of the entered data fall within predetermined limits; also called limit checks.

receiving report Document used to record merchandise receipts.

reconcile bank account Records of cash disbursements and receipts are matched to the bank's records to ensure that all disbursements and receipts recorded by the bank were authorized and accurate. An entity other than accounts payable and cash disbursements should perform this reconciliation.

reconcile bank accounts regularly A bank statement will reflect actual cash deposits and the correct amount of those deposits. These should be reconciled to the cash receipts event data to ensure that all valid deposits were recorded correctly. Ideally, a person who is independent of those who handle and record cash receipts and disbursements should perform the reconciliation.

recovery The process whereby we restore the lost data and resume operations.

recurring costs Costs that occur throughout all or most of the system's life.

recursive relationship A relationship between two different instances of the same entity type.

referential integrity A specification that for every attribute value in one relation that has been specified to allow reference to another relation, the tuple being referenced must remain intact.

reject stub A data flow assigned the label "Reject" that leaves a bubble but does not go to any other bubble or data store and indicates processing that is performed in other-than-normal situations.

relation A collection of data representing multiple occurrences of a resource, event, or agent.

relational database model A logical model for a database in which data are logically organized in two-dimensional tables. Each individual type of information or event is stored in its own table.

relationships In entity relationships modeling, the designer identifies how the things are related to each other.

relevance A quality indicating if information is capable of making a difference in a decision-making situation by reducing uncertainty or increasing knowledge for that particular decision.

reliability Relates to the provision of appropriate information for management to operate the entity and exercise its fiduciary and governance responsibilities.

remittance advice (RA) A business document used by the payer to notify the payee of the items being paid.

reorder point (ROP) analysis A technique for determining when to reorder an item based on the item's unique sales rate.

reports An element that makes up DBMSs, that provides printed lists and summaries of data stored in tables or collected by queries from one or more tables.

request for proposal (RFP) A document sent to vendors that invites submission of plans for providing hardware, software (for a purchased system), and related services.

resources Assets (tangible or intangible) that an organization owns.

responsibility accounting/reporting system A managerial reporting system that is tied to the hierarchy or chain of responsibility/authority reflected by a firm's organization chart, and as information is reported upward, the level of detail is filtered, meaning that figures are aggregated (summarized) as they are reported to successive management levels.

Review file of open sales orders (tickler file) By reviewing a file of open sales orders, i.e., shipments that should have taken place, we can ensure that all shipments are made in a timely manner

risk An event that would have a negative impact on organization objectives.

rotation of duties A policy that requires an employee to alternate jobs periodically.

routing master A data store that specifies the operations necessary to complete a subassembly or finished good and the sequence of these operations.

sales event data A file comprised of invoice or sales order records created as the sales process captures sales events, through the preparing and sending of an invoice.

sales force automation (SFA) software Software that automates sales tasks such as order processing, contact management, inventory monitoring, order tracking, and employee performance evaluation.

sales order master data Records in the sales order master data are created on completion of a sales order.

scanners Input devices that capture printed images or documents and convert them into electronic digital signals (i.e., into binary representations of the printed image or document) that can be stored on computer media.

schema A complete description of the configuration of record types, data items and the relationships among them. Defines the overall organizational view of the data.

SCM software Software that helps plan and execute the steps in an organization's supply chain, including demand planning; acquiring inventory; and manufacturing, distributing, and selling the product.

second normal form (2NF) A table (relation) is in 2NF if it is in first normal form and has no partial dependencies; that is, no nonkey attribute is dependent on only a portion of the primary key.

security of resources Protecting an organization's resources from loss, destruction, disclosure, copying, sale, or other misuse.

security officer Safeguards the IT organization and does so by establishing employee passwords and access to data and making sure the IT organization is secure from physical threats.

segregation of duties Consists of separating the four basic functions of event processing: authorizing events, executing events, recording events, safeguarding resources resulting from consummating events.

sequence check A type of control in a batch processing system where documents that are numbered sequentially are used to determine that all documents have been processed (completeness) and that no extra documents have been processed (completeness, if a duplicated document, or validity, if a bogus document).

sequential coding Assigns numbers to objects in chronological sequence; also known as serial coding. Also called serial coding.

serial coding Assigns numbers to objects in chronological sequence; also known as serial coding. Also called sequential coding.

service bureau A firm providing information processing services, including hardware and software for a fee; frequently providing the services less expensively and in a timelier manner than would be possible with an in-house computer.

service-oriented architecture (SOA) Well-defined, independent functions (or applications) that can be distributed over a network via Web Services.

shop floor control (SFC) process Monitors and records the status of manufacturing orders as they proceed through the factory or production sequence.

significant digit coding Assigns specific digits a meaning of their own, allowing selective inquiries of a database.

signoffs At predefined control points, these signify approval of the development process and deliverables of the system being developed.

skills inventory data A repository of data that catalogs each employee's set of relative skills, experience, education, and training.

software as a service (SaaS) A Web-based model of software distribution where multiple users may simultaneously use the software. SaaS provides results similar to an ASP, with some underlying differences. ASPs are generally traditional applications with Web interfaces, whereas SaaSs are typically created for the Web environment and are frequently implemented in a cloud computing setting.

source A DFD related concept, portrayed by an external entity symbol, of data outside the system.

standing data Relatively permanent portions of master data, such as the credit limit on customer master data and the selling price and warehouse location on inventory master data.

structured decisions Decisions for which all three decision phases (intelligence, design, and choice) are relatively routine or repetitive.

structured systems analysis A set of procedures conducted to generate the specifications for a new (or modified) information system or subsystem.

structured systems design A set of procedures performed to convert the logical specification into a design that can be implemented on the organization's computer system.

subschema A description of a portion of a schema. Defines a particular user's view of the data.

subsystem A part of a system; these parts are interrelated or integrated as a single system.

summarize Prepare a trial balance to show the total impact on each general ledger account of a set of business events.

supplier relationship management (SRM) software Software that manages the interactions with the organizations that supply the goods and services to an enterprise just as CRM software streamlines the processes between the enterprise and its customers.

supply chain Comprises the connections from the suppliers of merchandise and raw materials through to an organization's customers. These connections include the flow of information, materials, and services.

supply chain management (SCM) software The combination of processes and procedures used to ensure the delivery of goods and services to customers at the lowest cost while providing the highest value to the customers.

supply chain management (SCM) The combination of processes and procedures used to ensure the delivery of goods and services to customers at the lowest cost while providing the highest value to the customers.

system A set of interdependent elements that together accomplish specific objectives.

systems development Comprises the steps undertaken to create, modify, or maintain an organization's information system. The systems development process is made up of four primary phases: systems analysis, design, implementation, and operation.

systems development life cycle (SDLC) methodology This structured approach to developing information systems is a formalized, standardized, documented set of activities used to manage a systems development project.

systems development life cycle (SDLC) The progression through the phases of the systems development process, from birth through implementation to ongoing use.

systems flowchart A graphical representation of a business process, including information processes (inputs, data processing, data storage, and outputs), as well as the related operations processes (people, equipment, organization, and work activities).

systems implementation A set of procedures performed to complete the design contained in the approved systems design document and to test, install, and begin to use the new or revised information system.

systems maintenance The modification (e.g., repair, correction, or enhancement) of existing applications.

systems selection Set of procedures performed to choose the software specifications and hardware resources for an information system.

systems survey A set of procedures conducted to determine the practicability of a potential systems development project and to prepare a systems development plan for projects considered feasible.

tables An element that makes up DBMSs. A place to store data.

tangible costs (benefits) These costs and benefits can be reasonably quantified Software, equipment, and insurance costs are examples of such a cost; whereas reduced equipment cost and increased revenue are examples of benefits.

taxonomy A group of definitions that together provide meaning to reporting concepts.

third normal form (3NF) A relation is in 3NF if it is in second normal form with no transitive dependencies.

three-tier architecture A decoupled approach consisting three tiers being the user or presentation tier, the application or business logic tier (also called "middleware"), and the data or database tier.

throughput time The time it takes from when authorization is made for goods to be produced to when the goods are completed.

tickler file A manual file of documents, or a computer file, reviewed on a regular basis, that contains business event data that is pending further action.

time-phased order requirements schedule A schedule that shows the time period when a manufacturing order or purchase order should be released so that the subassemblies and raw materials will be available when needed.

timeliness Information available to a decision maker before it loses its capacity to influence a decision.

top-down partitioning The successive subdividing, or "exploding," of logical DFDs that, when performed, leads to a set of balanced DFDs.

total quality control (TQC) A manufacturing philosophy or business strategy that places responsibility for quality in the hands of the builder or producer of an item rather than in those of the inspector of the item. Generally considered a subset of JIT.

transitive dependency Exists in a table when a nonkey attribute is functionally dependent on another nonkey attribute.

tuple A set of data that describes a single instance of the entity represented by a relation (for example, one employee is an instance of the EMPLOYEE relation); frequently a row within a table.

turnaround documents Documents such as remittance advices that are used to capture and input a subsequent event.

understandability The information quality that enables users to perceive the information's significance.

unnormalized table Contains repeating attributes (or fields) within each row (or record).

unstructured decision A decision for which none of the decision phases (intelligence, design, or choice) are routine or repetitive.

update accuracy Data entered into a system must be reflected correctly in the respective master data.

update anomalies Errors created when modifying data within a system. One of many problems caused by functional dependencies.

update completeness All events entered into a system must be reflected in the respective master data once and only once.

use authorized vendor data Vendors should be vetted to determine their suitability to provide the organization with goods and services. The screening process might include vendor financial viability and performance record. The vendor data includes payment terms, address, and bank account

validity An information quality concerning the inclusion of actual authorized events and actual objects.

value chain A chain of activities performed by the organization to transform inputs into outputs valued by the customer.

value-added network (VAN) A service that acts as the EDI "post office." An organization can connect to the VAN when it wants, leave its outgoing messages, and, at the same time, pick up incoming messages from its "mailbox."

variance analysis Process of comparing actual information about input costs and usage to standards for inputs costs and usage. Used primarily in manufacturing.

vendor invoice A business document that notifies the purchaser of an obligation to pay the vendor for goods (or services) that were ordered by and shipped to the purchaser.

vendor master data Contains a record of each vendor that is approved for use by the organization.

vendor packing slip A list that accompanies the purchased inventory from the vendor and identifies the contents of a shipment and triggers the receiving process.

verifiability If there is a high degree of consensus about the information among independent measurers using the same measurement methods, the information has verifiability.

Web 2.0 A set of tools that allow people to build social and business connections, share information, and collaborate on projects online. Tools include blogs, wikis, social-networking and other online communities, and virtual worlds.

Web browsers Software programs designed specifically to allow users to easily view various documents and data sources available on the Internet.

Web Services A software application that supports direct interactions with software objects over an intranet or the Internet.

wide area networks (WANs) Communication networks that link distributed users and local networks into an integrated communications network.

work center A group of similar workstations.

work center master Describes each work center available for producing products, including information such as the machine available at the station, its capacity, its maintenance needs, labor needs to operate it, and so on.

workstation The assigned location where a worker performs his or her job; it could be a machine or a workbench.

written approvals A signature or initials on a document to indicate that an event has been authorized.

INDEX

Note: Pages followed by an e indicate exhibits; illustrations are indicated by *illus.*; followed by a t indicate tables.